The Handbook of Bible Application

The Handbook of Bible Application

Second Edition

NEIL S. WILSON, Editor

Senior Editorial Team for the original
Life Application notes:

DR. BRUCE B. BARTON
RONALD A. BEERS
DR. JAMES C. CALVIN
LINDA CHAFFEE TAYLOR
REV. DAVID R. VEERMAN

Tyndale House Publishers, Inc.
CAROL STREAM, ILLINOIS

Visit Tyndale's exciting Web site at www.tyndale.com

TYNDALE and Tyndale's quill logo are registered trademarks of Tyndale House Publishers, Inc.

Life Application is a registered trademark of Tyndale House Publishers, Inc.

The Handbook of Bible Application

Tyndale House Publishers gratefully acknowledges the role of Youth for Christ/USA in preparing the Life Application notes.

Library of Congress Cataloging-in-Publication Data

The Handbook of Bible application / Neil S. Wilson, editor; senior editorial team for the
　　original Life application notes, Bruce B. Barton . . . [et al.].
　　　　p.　cm.
　　Notes from the Life application Bible, keyed to Bible verses excerpted from the
　　Living Bible and New International versions.
　　ISBN-13: 978-0-8423-1044-4
　　ISBN-10: 0-8423-1044-4
　　1. Bible—Reading. 2. Bible—Commentaries. I. Wilson, Neil S., date.
　　II. Barton, Bruce B. III. Bible. English. Living Bible. Selections. 1992.
　　IV. Bible. English. New International. Selections. 1992.
　　BS432.H28 1992
　　220.3—dc20　92-3125

Printed in the United States of America

10　09　08　07　06
12　11　10　9　8　7　6

CONTENTS

INTRODUCTION

Any study of the Bible should accomplish two goals. First, it should develop in us a sense of humility. God does not hesitate to point out one of our major shortcomings: "'My thoughts are completely different from yours,' says the LORD. 'And my ways are far beyond anything you could imagine.'" (Isaiah 55:8).

Second, consistent exposure to God's Word should create a desire within us to fill our mind with God's thinking. As our confidence in God's way of thinking grows, our confidence in God himself also grows.

The change in perspective can be startling:

> For just as the heavens are higher than the earth, so are my ways higher than your ways and my thoughts higher than your thoughts. The rain and snow come down from the heavens and stay on the ground to water the earth. They cause the grain to grow, producing seed for the farmer and bread for the hungry. It is the same with my word. I send it out, and it always produces fruit. It will accomplish all I want it to, and it will prosper everywhere I send it. (Isaiah 55:9-11)

A topical approach to Bible study is an effective way to renew our thinking:

> And so, dear brothers and sisters, I plead with you to give your bodies to God. Let them be a living and holy sacrifice—the kind he will accept. When you think of what he has done for you, is this too much to ask? Don't copy the behavior and customs of this world, but let God transform you into a new person by changing the way you think. Then you will know what God wants you to do, and you will know how good and pleasing and perfect his will really is. (Romans 12:1-2)

When we study and think about God's Word, God molds our thoughts. May *The Handbook of Bible Application* be a useful guide in leading you to think about life as God does.

How to use *The Handbook of Bible Application*

This book is for anyone interested in a topical study of the Bible. If there is a life-related topic to which the Bible speaks, chances are you will find it here.

The topics are arranged alphabetically and cross-referenced with other related topics, key Bible verses, and longer Bible readings. Each entry is designed to address life's everyday struggles and questions. And each topic leads you directly to the Bible passages that speak to those struggles and questions.

The purpose of this book is not to supplement the Bible's answers to life's questions, but to lead you to them. Under each topic you will find:

- Key questions often asked about the topic
- Suggested Bible readings related to the topic
- Key Bible verses (printed in a version which best highlights the meaning)
- Answers to the key questions
- Notes adapted from the *Life Application Bible*
- Related topics found elsewhere in *The Handbook of Bible Application*

All you need to know to use this book is what topic you want to study. Once you've chosen a topic, just find the entry and select the information you need!

If you are a small group leader or Sunday school teacher

You can use *The Handbook of Bible Application* to help in planning lessons, supplementing other curriculum, or building lessons from scratch. As you sit down to prepare, the *Handbook* will help you answer several important questions:

- What life issues should we focus our discussion on?
- What are the Bible's answers to the questions people have about this topic?
- What are the key Bible passages we should study together?
- What Bible verses would serve well for memorization or summary?
- What other topics might lead us to more answers?

Use the information that's most helpful to you.

If you are using *The Handbook of Bible Application* for your own personal study

You can use the *Handbook* in several ways to structure your devotional time around topics. Rather than wondering what passage of Scripture to study on any given day, choose the topic you are interested in and use the suggested Bible reading to guide each day's devotions. The *Life Application* notes will serve as your devotional reading for the day. Using the *Handbook* in this way will take over a year. Another approach is to use the *Handbook* for one quarter, selecting only the topics of interest to you.

You can also use the *Handbook* to help you select memory verses. If you are memorizing verses related to your small group's study topic, your pastor's sermons, or some other source, the topics will help you find appropriate Scripture passages.

ABANDON (*Leave, Desert, Betray*)

▶ **ABANDONING GOD**
How can people, once they are aware of God, even consider abandoning him?

BIBLE READING: 2 Chronicles 12:1-16
KEY BIBLE VERSE: *But when Rehoboam was firmly established and strong, he abandoned the law of the LORD, and all Israel followed him in this sin.* (2 Chronicles 12:1)

Reasons why we abandon God. At the height of his popularity and power, the king abandoned the Lord. What happened? Often it is more difficult to be a believer in good times than in bad. Tough times push us toward God; but easy times can make us feel self-sufficient and self-satisfied. When everything is going right, guard your faith.

Personal consequences when we abandon God. Popularity and power, the two benefits that Rehoboam chose above God, were the first two things he lost when the Egyptians invaded the land. Through Rehoboam we discover the real price to be paid for rejecting God. Even though Rehoboam later confessed his sin, the damage had already been done. He was not destroyed, but much of what was precious to him was lost. His reign could have been as glorious as the golden shields in Solomon's temple, which the Egyptians took. Instead, he had to settle for bronze replacements and an insignificant reign.

Consequences for others when we abandon God. We don't have to be a king, like Rehoboam, before our actions deeply affect the lives of others. Rehoboam's abandonment of God led to the humiliation of his people. How does the quality of your relationship with God affect those around you?

▶ **FEELING ABANDONED BY GOD**
What about when our awareness of God is weak or he seems distant and removed?

BIBLE READING: Exodus 2:11-22
KEY BIBLE VERSE: *In time, Reuel gave Moses one of his daughters, Zipporah, to be his wife. Later they had a baby boy, and Moses named him Gershom, for he said, "I have been a stranger in a foreign land."* (Exodus 2:21-22)

We should not give up. To escape punishment for killing an Egyptian, Moses ran away to the land of Midian. He became a stranger in a foreign land, separated from his home and family. Many years went by before Moses was once again ready to serve God. But he trusted God instead of fearing the king (Hebrews

11:27). We often feel abandoned or isolated because of things we have done. But when we are fearful or feeling separated, we should not give up. Moses didn't. He trusted God to deliver him in spite of his dark past and his seemingly bleak future.

BIBLE READING: Job 2:1-13

KEY BIBLE VERSE: *So Satan left the LORD's presence, and he struck Job with a terrible case of boils from head to foot.* (Job 2:7)

Suffering does not mean God has abandoned you. At times believers may actually suffer more than unbelievers because those who follow God sometimes become Satan's special targets. Believers, therefore, may have to endure hardship, persecution, or testing. This was the case with Job. We must be prepared for Satan's attacks. When we suffer, we must not conclude that God has abandoned us. He did not abandon Job. Consistent faith is the way to defeat Satan.

Related Topics: DESPAIR, FAITHFULNESS, TRUST

ABILITIES (*Skills, Talents, Gifts*)

▶ ABILITIES: THEIR SOURCE
How are our abilities an indication of God's care for us?

BIBLE READING: Exodus 28:1-14

KEY BIBLE VERSE: *Instruct all those who have special skills as tailors to make the garments that will set Aaron apart from everyone else, so he may serve me as a priest.* (Exodus 28:3)

God has given everyone special abilities. Tailors used their special skills to help with the work on God's tabernacle. Each one of us has special abilities. God wants us to use them for his glory. Think about your special talents and abilities and the ways you could use them for God's work in the world. A talent must be used and polished or it will tarnish.

▶ ABILITIES: THEIR PURPOSE
What does God want us to do with the abilities he gives?

BIBLE READING: Luke 12:35-48

KEY BIBLE VERSE: *People who are not aware that they are doing wrong will be punished only lightly. Much is required from those to whom much is given, and much more is required from those to whom much more is given.* (Luke 12:48)

Have a proper attitude toward your abilities. Jesus told us how to live until he comes. We must watch for him and work diligently to obey his commands. Such attitudes are especially important for leaders. Watchful and faithful leaders will be given increased opportunities and responsibilities. The more resources, talent, and understanding we have, the more responsible we must be to use them effectively. We must not serve grudgingly, but willingly, lovingly, and with joy.

BIBLE READING: Exodus 35:4-35

KEY BIBLE VERSE: *Come, all of you who are gifted craftsmen. Construct everything that the LORD has commanded.* (Exodus 35:10)

Develop your abilities. Moses asked people with various abilities to help with the tabernacle. God has gifted each believer with special abilities. We are responsible to develop these abilities—even the ones not considered "religious"—and to use them for God's glory. We can become skilled through study, by watching others, and through practice. Take note of the skills and abilities you have that could be used to help others in your church, workplace, or community.

▶ DETERMINING YOUR GOD-GIVEN ABILITIES
What if you don't think God has given you any special abilities?

BIBLE READING: Luke 19:11-26
KEY BIBLE VERSE: *To those who use well what they are given, even more will be given. But from those who are unfaithful, even what little they have will be taken away.* (Luke 19:26)

Everyone has special abilities. Why was the king so hard on this man who had not gained more money? He punished the man because (1) he didn't share his master's interest in the kingdom; (2) he didn't trust his master's intentions; and (3) his only loyalty was to himself. Like the king in this story, God has given you gifts to use for the benefit of his kingdom. Do you want the kingdom to grow? Do you trust God to govern it fairly? Are you as concerned for the welfare of others as for your own? If you can answer yes to these questions, you are faithfully using what he has entrusted to you.

BIBLE READING: Deuteronomy 32:48–33:29
KEY BIBLE VERSE: *This is the blessing that Moses, the man of God, gave to the people of Israel before his death.* (Deuteronomy 33:1)

Each person's abilities can make a contribution. Note the different blessings God gave each tribe. To one he gave the best land, to another strength, to another safety. Too often we see someone with a particular gift and think that God must love that person more than others. Remember that God draws upon the unique talents of all his people. All these gifts are needed to complete his plan. Don't be envious of the gifts others have. Instead, look for the gifts God has given you, and resolve to do the tasks he has uniquely qualified you to do.

BIBLE READING: Acts 6:1-7
KEY BIBLE VERSE: *Now look around among yourselves, brothers, and select seven men who are well respected and are full of the Holy Spirit and wisdom. We will put them in charge of this business.* (Acts 6:3)

The needs you see are opportunities to use your abilities. As the early church increased in size, so did their needs. The apostles focused on preaching and chose others to organize the distribution of food to the poor. Each person has a necessary part to play in the life of the church (see 1 Corinthians 12). Often, the needs you notice are the very ones you can have a part in meeting. If you are in a position of leadership and find yourself overwhelmed by responsibilities, determine *your* God-given abilities and priorities and then find others to help. If you are not in leadership, you have gifts that can be used by God in various areas of the church's ministry. Offer these gifts in service to him.

Related Topics: CRAFTSMANSHIP, RESPONSIBILITY, SERVING

ABORTION *(Killing, Life, Murder)*
What does God say about life in the womb?

BIBLE READING: Jeremiah 1:1-5

KEY BIBLE VERSE: *I knew you before I formed you in your mother's womb. Before you were born I set you apart and appointed you as my spokesman to the world.* (Jeremiah 1:5)

Persons have worth even before they are born. God knew you, as he knew Jeremiah, long before you were born or even conceived. He knew you, thought about you, and planned for you. When you feel discouraged or inadequate, remember that God has always thought of you as valuable and has had a purpose in mind for you.

BIBLE READING: Psalm 139:1-24

KEY BIBLE VERSE: *You made all the delicate, inner parts of my body and knit me together in my mother's womb. Thank you for making me so wonderfully complex! Your workmanship is marvelous—and how well I know it.* (Psalm 139:13-14)

God is at work in a person's life even while in the womb. God's character goes into the creation of every person. When you feel worthless or even begin to hate yourself, remember that God's Spirit is ready and willing to work within you. God thinks of you constantly (Psalm 139:1-4). We should have as much respect for ourselves as our Maker has for us.

What is behind the practice of abortion today?

BIBLE READING: 2 Chronicles 28:1-8

KEY BIBLE VERSE: *Ahaz was twenty years old when he became king, and he reigned in Jerusalem sixteen years. He did not do what was pleasing in the sight of the LORD, as his ancestor David had done.* (2 Chronicles 28:1)

Abortion is a sin against God. Imagine the monstrous evil of a religion that offers young children as sacrifices. God allowed Judah to suffer heavy casualties in response to Ahaz's evil practices. Even today the practice hasn't abated. The sacrifice of children to the harsh gods of convenience, economy, and whim continues in sterile medical facilities in numbers that would astound even the wicked Ahaz. If we are to allow children to come to Christ (Matthew 19:14), we must first allow them to come into the world.

Related Topics: CHILDREN, LIFE, MURDER

ABUNDANCE (Wealth, Materialism, Blessing)

▶ **ABUNDANCE: ITS SOURCE**
Why does God give us so much?

BIBLE READING: Deuteronomy 8:10-20

KEY BIBLE VERSE: *Always remember that it is the LORD your God who gives you power to become rich, and he does it to fulfill the covenant he made with your ancestors.* (Deuteronomy 8:18)

Material blessings are one expression of God's care. In times of plenty, it is easy to take credit for your prosperity and begin to feel that your own hard work and cleverness have made you rich. It is easy to get so busy collecting and managing your wealth that God is pushed right out of your life. But it is God who blesses us with abundance, and it is God who asks us to manage it for him. Don't forget God in your abundance, or he will remove his blessing from you. Remember that the most valuable thing in life—your relationship with God—is free.

▶ ABUNDANCE: ITS DANGER
How can wealth get in the way of our relationship with God?

BIBLE READING: Mark 10:17-31
KEY BIBLE VERSE: *Jesus looked around and said to his disciples, "How hard it is for rich people to get into the Kingdom of God!"* (Mark 10:23)

Wealth can tempt us to declare independence from God. Jesus said it was very difficult for the rich to get into the kingdom of God because the rich, with most of their basic physical needs met, often become self-reliant. When they feel empty, they can buy something new to dull the pain that was meant to drive them toward God. Their abundance becomes their deficiency. The person who has everything on earth can still lack what is most important—eternal life.

BIBLE READING: Luke 12:13-21
KEY BIBLE VERSE: *Then he said, "Beware! Don't be greedy for what you don't have. Real life is not measured by how much we own."* (Luke 12:15)

Wealth can give us wrong attitudes about material things. Problems like this were often brought before the rabbis to be settled. Jesus doesn't respond to the immediate situation at hand. Instead, he points to a higher issue—a correct attitude toward the accumulation of wealth. Life is more than material goods; far more important is our relationship with God. Jesus put his finger on this questioner's heart. When we bring problems to God in prayer, he often does the same thing—showing us how we need to change and grow in our attitude toward the problem. This answer is often not the one we were looking for, but it is more effective.

▶ ABUNDANCE: HAVING THE BEST!
What is God's greatest gift?

BIBLE READING: John 10:1-21
KEY BIBLE VERSE: *The thief's purpose is to steal and kill and destroy. My purpose is to give life in all its fullness.* (John 10:10)

Jesus gives life. In contrast to the thief who takes, Jesus gives. The life he gives now is rich and full. It is eternal, yet it begins immediately. Life in him is lived on a higher plane because of his abundant forgiveness, love, and guidance.

Related Topics: CONTENTMENT, GREED, WEALTH

ACCEPT/ACCEPTANCE *(Affirmation, Encouragement, Support)*

▶ GOD ACCEPTS US
What is God's acceptance of us based upon?

BIBLE READING: Romans 5:1-11
KEY BIBLE VERSE: *Therefore, since we have been made right in God's sight by faith, we have peace with God because of what Jesus Christ our Lord has done for us. Because of our faith, Christ has brought us into this place of highest privilege where we now stand, and we confidently and joyfully look forward to sharing God's glory.* (Romans 5:1-2)

Our acceptance is based on Christ. These verses introduce a section that contains some difficult concepts. To understand the next four chapters, it helps to keep in mind the two-sided reality of the Christian life. On the one hand, we are complete in Christ (our acceptance with him is secure); on the other hand, we are growing in Christ (we are becoming more and more like him). At the same time we have the status of kings and the duties of slaves. We feel both the presence of Christ and the pressure of sin. We enjoy the peace that comes from being made right with God, but we still face daily problems that help us grow. If we remember these two sides of the Christian life, we will not grow discouraged as we face temptations and problems. Instead, we will learn to depend on the power available to us from Christ, who lives in us by the Holy Spirit.

Can I depend on God's acceptance?

BIBLE READING: Hebrews 6:13-20

KEY BIBLE VERSE: *God also bound himself with an oath, so that those who received the promise could be perfectly sure that he would never change his mind. So God has given us both his promise and his oath. These two things are unchangeable because it is impossible for God to lie. Therefore, we who have fled to him for refuge can take new courage, for we can hold on to his promise with confidence.* (Hebrews 6:17-18)

We are accepted by a God who does not change. God's two "unchangeable things" are his nature and his promise. God embodies all truth, and he therefore cannot lie. Because God is truth, you can be secure in his promises; you don't need to wonder if he will change his plans. To the true seeker who comes to God in belief, God gives an unconditional promise of acceptance. When you ask God with openness, honesty, and sincerity to save you from your sins, *he will do it.* This assurance should give you courage and hope.

What would be an example of God demonstrating his acceptance of us?

BIBLE READING: Luke 2:8-20

KEY BIBLE VERSE: *That night some shepherds were in the fields outside the village, guarding their flocks of sheep. Suddenly, an angel of the Lord appeared among them, and the radiance of the Lord's glory surrounded them.* (Luke 2:8-9)

He has singled out the humble for his acceptance. The greatest event in history had just happened! The Messiah was born! For ages the Jews had waited for this, and when it finally occurred, the announcement came to humble shepherds. The good news about Jesus is that he comes to all, including the plain and the ordinary. He comes to anyone with a heart humble enough to accept him. Whoever you are, whatever you do, you can have Jesus in your life. Don't think you need extraordinary qualifications—he accepts you as you are.

▶ OUR ACCEPTANCE OF GOD

How did people accept God when he came to his world in the flesh?

BIBLE READING: John 1:1-18

KEY BIBLE VERSE: *Although the world was made through him, the world didn't recognize him when he came. Even in his own land and among his own people, he was not accepted.* (John 1:10-11)

Jesus experienced widespread rejection. Although Christ created the world, the people he created didn't recognize him (1:10). Even the people chosen by God to prepare the rest of the world for the Messiah rejected him (1:11), though the entire Old Testament pointed to his coming. But all who welcome or accept

Jesus Christ as Lord of their life are reborn spiritually, receiving new life from God. Through faith in Christ, this new birth changes us from the inside out—rearranging our attitudes, desires, and motives. Being born makes you physically alive and places you in your parents' family (1:13). Being reborn makes you spiritually alive and puts you in God's family (1:12). Have you asked Christ to make you a new person? This fresh start in life is available to all who believe in Christ.

BIBLE READING: Luke 4:16-30

KEY BIBLE VERSE: *But the truth is, no prophet is accepted in his own hometown.* (Luke 4:24)

Those closest to Jesus had the most difficulty accepting him. Even Jesus himself was not accepted as a prophet in his hometown. Many people have a similar attitude—an expert is anyone who carries a briefcase and comes from more than two hundred miles away. Don't be surprised when your Christian life and faith are not easily understood or accepted by those who know you well.

BIBLE READING: Luke 9:1-9

KEY BIBLE VERSE: *When reports of Jesus' miracles reached Herod Antipas, he was worried and puzzled because some were saying, "This is John the Baptist come back to life again." Others were saying, "It is Elijah or some other ancient prophet risen from the dead."* (Luke 9:7-8)

Some tried to accept Jesus as someone other than who he was. It was so difficult for the people to accept Jesus as the Son of God that they tried to come up with other solutions—most of which sound quite unbelievable to our ears. Many thought he must be someone come back to life, perhaps John the Baptist or another prophet. Some suggested he was Elias (Elijah), the great prophet who did not die but was taken to heaven in a chariot of fire (2 Kings 2:1-12). Very few found the correct answer, as Peter did (Luke 9:20). For many people today, it is still not easy to accept Jesus as the fully human yet fully divine Son of God. People are still trying to find alternate explanations—a great prophet, a radical political leader, a self-deceived rabble-rouser. None of these explanations can account for Jesus' miracles or, especially, his glorious resurrection—so these too have to be explained away. In the end, the attempts to explain Jesus away are far more difficult to believe than the truth.

BIBLE READING: Mark 8:27-38

KEY BIBLE VERSE: *Then Jesus asked, "Who do you say I am?" Peter replied, "You are the Messiah."* (Mark 8:29)

Acceptance of Jesus must be personal. Jesus asked the disciples who others thought he was; then he asked them the same question. It is not enough to know what others say about Jesus: you must know, understand, and accept for yourself that he is the Messiah. You must move from curiosity to commitment, from admiration to adoration.

▶ ACCEPTING EACH OTHER
How important is it to accept other people?

BIBLE READING: Romans 15:1-13

KEY BIBLE VERSE: *So accept each other just as Christ has accepted you; then God will be glorified.* (Romans 15:7)

Accepting others grows out of obedience to Christ. To accept Jesus' lordship in all areas of life means to share his values and his perspective. Just as we accept

Jesus' views on the authority of Scripture, the nature of heaven, and the Resurrection, so we are to have his attitude of love toward other Christians. As we grow in faith and come to know Jesus better, we become more capable of maintaining this attitude throughout each day. Christ's attitude is explained in more detail in Philippians 2.

BIBLE READING: Judges 11:1-11

KEY BIBLE VERSE: *So Jephthah fled from his brothers and lived in the land of Tob. Soon he had a large band of rebels following him.* (Judges 11:3)

When we don't accept others we miss out on their contribution. Circumstances beyond his control forced Jephthah away from his people and into life as an outcast. Today, both believers and nonbelievers may drive away those who do not fit the norms dictated by our society, neighborhoods, or churches. Often, as in Jephthah's case, great potential is wasted because of prejudice— a refusal to look beyond ill-conceived stereotypes. Look around you to see if there are potential Jephthahs being kept out due to factors beyond their control. As a Christian you know that everyone can have a place in God's family. Can you do anything to help these people gain acceptance for their character and abilities?

When does acceptance become dangerous?

BIBLE READING: Exodus 34:1-17

KEY BIBLE VERSE: *Be very careful never to make treaties with the people in the land where you are going. If you do, you soon will be following their evil ways.* (Exodus 34:12)

Acceptance becomes dangerous when we condone sinful behavior. God told the Israelites not to join in religious rites with the sinful people around them, but to give their absolute loyalty and exclusive devotion to him. Heathen worship simply cannot be mixed with the worship of the holy God. As Jesus pointed out, "No one can serve two masters. . . . You cannot serve both God and money" (Luke 16:13). The love of money is the god of this age, and many Christians attempt to "make a covenant" with this enslaving god. Are you trying to worship two gods at once? Where is your first allegiance? Do you need to break down any "altars" or cut down any "poles"?

Related Topics: FORGIVENESS, GRACE, OPENNESS

ACCESS *(Acceptance, Availability, Welcome)*

How can we gain access to God?

BIBLE READING: Hebrews 10:19-25

KEY BIBLE VERSE: *And so, dear brothers and sisters, we can boldly enter heaven's Most Holy Place because of the blood of Jesus. This is the new, life-giving way that Christ has opened up for us through the sacred curtain, by means of his death for us. And since we have a great High Priest who rules over God's people, let us go right into the presence of God, with true hearts fully trusting him. For our evil consciences have been sprinkled with Christ's blood to make us clean, and our bodies have been washed with pure water.* (Hebrews 10:19-22)

We gain immediate access to God through Christ. We have significant privileges
with our new life in Christ: (1) we have personal access to God through
Christ and can approach him without an elaborate system (10:22); (2) we
may grow in faith, overcome doubts and questions, and deepen our relationship with God (10:23); (3) we may enjoy encouragement from one another
(10:24); (4) we may worship together (10:25).

How did Jesus give us access to God?

BIBLE READING: Leviticus 16:1-10
KEY BIBLE VERSE: *The LORD said to Moses, "Warn your brother Aaron not to enter
the Most Holy Place behind the inner curtain whenever he chooses; the penalty
for intrusion is death. For the Ark's cover—the place of atonement—is there,
and I myself am present in the cloud over the atonement cover." (Leviticus
16:2)*

Jesus replaced the complicated ceremonies and rituals of the past. Aaron had to
spend hours preparing himself to meet God. But we can approach God anytime
(Hebrews 4:16). What a privilege! We are offered easier access to God than the
high priests of Old Testament times! Still, we must never forget that God is holy
nor let this privilege cause us to approach God carelessly. The way to God has
been opened to us by Christ. But easy access to God does not eliminate our
need to prepare our hearts as we draw near in prayer.

BIBLE READING: Hebrews 10:1-18
KEY BIBLE VERSE: *Christ said, "You did not want animal sacrifices or grain offerings
or animals burned on the altar or other offerings for sin, nor were you pleased
with them" (though they are required by the law of Moses). Then he added,
"Look, I have come to do your will." He cancels the first covenant in order to
establish the second. (Hebrews 10:8-9)*

Old sacrifices were temporary; Christ's sacrifice was permanent. When people
gathered for sacrifice on the Day of Atonement, they were reminded of their
sins and felt guilty all over again. Animal sacrifices could not take away sin; they
provided only a temporary way to deal with sin. What they needed was forgiveness—the permanent, powerful, sin-destroying forgiveness we have from
Christ. Once we have confessed a sin to him, we need never think of it again.
He has forgiven it, and it no longer exists.

How, then, were people forgiven in Old Testament times? Old Testament
believers were following God's command, and he graciously forgave them
when, by faith, they made their sacrifices. But that practice looked forward to
Christ's perfect sacrifice. Canceling the first system in favor of a far better one
meant doing away with the system of sacrifices contained in the ceremonial
law. It didn't mean eliminating God's *moral* law (the Ten Commandments).
The ceremonial law prepared people for Christ's coming. With Christ's death
and resurrection it was no longer needed. Through Christ we can fulfill the
moral law as we let him live in us.

Christ's way was superior to the Old Testament way because the old way
only pointed to what he would do. The priests' work was never finished so they
always had to stand and make sacrifices; Christ's sacrifice (dying in our place)
is finished, so he is seated. The priests repeated the sacrifices often; Christ sacrificed once for all. The sacrifice system couldn't completely remove sin; Christ's
sacrifice effectively cleansed us.

Related Topics: FAITH, PRAYER, SACRIFICE

ACCOMPLISHMENTS (*Achievements, Efforts, Success*)

▶ **GOD'S ACCOMPLISHMENTS**
How does God view his own accomplishments?

 BIBLE READING: Genesis 1:1-31
KEY BIBLE VERSE: *God made all sorts of wild animals, livestock, and small animals, each able to reproduce more of its own kind. And God saw that it was good.* (Genesis 1:25)

God enjoys his work. God saw that his work was good, and he was pleased. People sometimes feel guilty for having a good time or for feeling good about an accomplishment. This need not be so. Just as God was pleased with his work, we can be pleased with ours. However, we cannot be pleased with our work if God is not pleased with it. What are you doing that pleases both you and God?

▶ **PEOPLE'S ACCOMPLISHMENTS**
Why do life's accomplishments seem at times so meaningless?

BIBLE READING: Ecclesiastes 1:1-11
KEY BIBLE VERSE: *"Everything is meaningless," says the Teacher, "utterly meaningless!"* (Ecclesiastes 1:2)

Sometimes people expect too much from their accomplishments. Solomon had a purpose in writing skeptically and pessimistically. Near the end of his life he looked back over everything he had done, and most of it seemed futile. A common belief was that only good people prospered and that only the wicked suffered, but that hadn't proven true in his experience. Solomon wrote this book after he had tried everything and achieved much, only to find that nothing apart from God made him happy. Solomon wanted the people to see that success and prosperity can disappear like a vapor of breath on a cold day (Psalm 103:14-16; Isaiah 40:6-8; James 4:14). All human accomplishments will one day disappear, and we must keep this in mind in order to live wisely. If we don't, we can become either proud and self-sufficient when we succeed or sorely disappointed when we fail. Solomon shows us that pursuing earthly possessions and accomplishments is ultimately futile. Only the pursuit of God brings real satisfaction. We should honor him in all we say, think, and do.

If accomplishments are not a good basis for security, what is?

BIBLE READING: Luke 10:1-24
KEY BIBLE VERSE: *But don't rejoice just because evil spirits obey you; rejoice because your names are registered as citizens of heaven.* (Luke 10:20)

God's acceptance is more important than any accomplishment. The disciples had seen tremendous results as they ministered in Jesus' name and with his authority. They were elated by the victories they had witnessed, and Jesus shared their enthusiasm. He brought them down to earth, however, by reminding them of their most important victory—that their names were registered in heaven. This honor was more important than any of their accomplishments. As we see God's wonders at work in us and through us, we should not lose sight of the greatest wonder of all—our heavenly citizenship.

BIBLE READING: 1 Peter 2:1-12
KEY BIBLE VERSE: *But you are not like that, for you are a chosen people. You are a kingdom of priests, God's holy nation, his very own possession. This is so you can*

show others the goodness of God, for he called you out of the darkness into his wonderful light. "Once you were not a people; now you are the people of God. Once you received none of God's mercy; now you have received his mercy." (1 Peter 2:9-10)

Ultimate value comes from God's acceptance, not accomplishments. People often base their self-concept on their accomplishments, but our relationship with Christ is far more important than our job, our success, our wealth, or our knowledge. We have been chosen by God as his very own, and we have been called to represent him to others. Remember that your value comes from being one of God's children, not from what you can achieve. You have worth because of what God does, not because of what you do.

BIBLE READING: Philippians 3:1-16

KEY BIBLE VERSE: *For we who worship God in the Spirit are the only ones who are truly circumcised. We put no confidence in human effort. Instead, we boast about what Christ Jesus has done for us. Yet I could have confidence in myself if anyone could. If others have reason for confidence in their own efforts, I have even more!* (Philippians 3:3-4)

Even great accomplishments cannot match what Christ has done for us. At first glance, it seems that Paul is boasting about his achievements. But he is actually doing the opposite, showing that human achievements, no matter how impressive, cannot earn a person salvation and eternal life with God. Paul had impressive credentials. He had the upbringing, nationality, family background, inheritance, orthodoxy, involvements, and morality to qualify him for great respect in the Jewish community (see 2 Corinthians 11; Galatians 1:13-24, for more of his credentials). But when he was converted to faith in Christ (Acts 9), it wasn't based upon his credentials but upon the grace of Christ. Paul did not depend on his credentials to please God because even the most impressive credentials fall short of God's holy standards. Are you depending on Christian parents, church affiliation, or just being good to make you right with God? Credentials, accomplishments, or reputation cannot earn salvation. You must realize that salvation comes only through faith in Christ.

Related Topics: ACHIEVEMENTS, EFFORT, SUCCESS

ACCOUNTABILITY *(Consistency, Integrity, Responsibility)*

▶ **INDIVIDUAL ACCOUNTABILITY**
Will there be any excuses when we stand before God?

BIBLE READING: Romans 14:1-23

KEY BIBLE VERSE: *Yes, each of us will have to give a personal account to God.* (Romans 14:12)

We will appear alone before God. Each person is accountable to Christ, not to others. While the church must be uncompromising in its stand against activities expressly forbidden by Scripture (adultery, homosexuality, murder, theft), it should not create additional rules and regulations and give them equal standing with God's law. Many times Christians base their moral judgments on opinion, personal dislikes, or cultural bias rather than on the Word of God. When they do this, they show that their own faith is weak. They do not think God is powerful enough to guide his children. When we stand before God's court of justice (see 2 Corinthians 5:10), we won't be worried about what our Christian neighbor has done.

▶ GROUP ACCOUNTABILITY
How do individual choices affect a group of people?

BIBLE READING: Joshua 7:1-15
KEY BIBLE VERSE: *Israel has sinned and broken my covenant! They have stolen the things that I commanded to be set apart for me. And they have not only stolen them; they have also lied about it and hidden the things among their belongings.* (Joshua 7:11)

Our actions often affect others. Why did Achan's sin bring judgment on the entire nation? Although it was one man's failure, God saw it as national disobedience to a national law. God needed the entire nation to be committed to the job they had agreed to do—conquer the land. Thus, when one person failed, everyone failed. Achan's sin was not merely the act of keeping some of the booty (which was allowed in some cases), but disobedience to God's explicit command to destroy everything connected with *this* city. His sin was indifference to the evil and idolatry of the city, not just a desire for money and clothes. God would not protect Israel's army again until the sin was removed and the army returned to obeying him without reservation. If Achan's sin went unpunished, unlimited looting could break out. The nation as a whole had to take responsibility for preventing this. God is not content with our doing what is right some of the time. He wants us to do what is right all the time. We are under his orders to rid our lives of anything that hinders our devotion to him.

BIBLE READING: Judges 6:1-16
KEY BIBLE VERSE: *"Sir," Gideon replied, "if the LORD is with us, why has all this happened to us? And where are all the miracles our ancestors told us about? Didn't they say, 'The LORD brought us up out of Egypt'? But now the LORD has abandoned us and handed us over to the Midianites."* (Judges 6:13)

Accountability means taking personal responsibility for national sin. Gideon questioned God about the problems he and his nation faced and about God's apparent lack of help. What he didn't acknowledge was the fact that the people had brought calamity upon themselves when they decided to disobey and neglect God. How easy it is to overlook personal accountability and blame our problems on God and others. Unfortunately this does not solve our problems. It brings us no closer to God, and it brings us to the very edge of rebellion and backsliding.

When problems come, the first place to look is within. Our first action should be confession to God for sins that may have created our problems.

Related Topics: JUDGMENT, OBEDIENCE, RESPONSIBILITY

ACCURACY (*see* TRUTH)

ACCUSATION (*Criticism, Gossip, Judgment*)

How does a person respond to false accusations?

BIBLE READING: Daniel 6:1-28

KEY BIBLE VERSE: *So they concluded, "Our only chance of finding grounds for accusing Daniel will be in connection with the requirements of his religion."* (Daniel 6:5)

Silence is often an effective response to false accusations. At this time, Daniel was over eighty years old and one of Darius's top three administrators. He was working with those who did not believe in his God, but he worked more efficiently and capably than all the rest. Thus, he attracted the attention of the pagan king and earned a place of respect. He also attracted the envy of coworkers. These jealous officials couldn't find anything about Daniel's life to criticize, so they attacked his religion. If you face jealous critics because of your faith, be glad they're criticizing that part of your life—perhaps they had to focus on your faith as a last resort! Respond by continuing to believe and live as you should. Then remember that God is in control, fighting this battle for you.

BIBLE READING: Psalm 35:1-28

KEY BIBLE VERSE: *Malicious witnesses testify against me. They accuse me of things I don't even know about.* (Psalm 35:11)

Prayer is an effective response to accusations. This is one of the "imprecatory" (cursing) psalms that call upon God to deal with enemies. These psalms sound extremely harsh, but we must remember: (1) David was fleeing from men who were unjustly seeking to kill him. As God's anointed king over a nation called to annihilate the evil people of the land, David found it difficult to understand. (2) David's call for justice was sincere; it was not a cover for vengeance. He truly wanted to seek God's perfect ideal for his nation. (3) David did not say *he* would take vengeance, but gave the matter over to God. These are merely his suggestions. (4) These psalms use hyperbole (or overstatement). They were meant to motivate others to take a strong stand against sin and evil.

Cruelty is far removed from the experience of many, but it is a daily reality for others. God promises to help the persecuted and bring judgment on unrepentant sinners. David cried out to God to defend him when he was unjustly accused. When we pray for justice to be done, we are praying as David did. If you are unjustly accused, your natural reaction may be to lash out in revenge or to give a detailed defense of your every move. Ask God to fight the battle for you. He will clear your name in the eyes of those who really matter. When Christ returns, the wicked will be punished.

BIBLE READING: Matthew 5:1-16

KEY BIBLE VERSE: *God blesses you when you are mocked and persecuted and lied about because you are my followers.* (Matthew 5:11)

Joy is an effective response to accusations. Jesus said to rejoice when we're persecuted. Persecution can be good because (1) it takes our eyes off earthly rewards, (2) it strips away superficial believers, (3) it strengthens the faith of those who endure, and (4) it serves as an example for others to follow. We can take comfort in knowing that many of God's greatest prophets were persecuted (Elijah, Jeremiah, Daniel). Our persecution means we have shown ourselves faithful. In the future God will reward the faithful by letting them enter his eternal kingdom where there is no more persecution.

Related Topics: CRITICISM, GOSSIP, INJUSTICE

ACHIEVEMENTS *(Accomplishments, Goals, Success)*

How can achievements be an expression of rebellion?

BIBLE READING: Genesis 11:1-9

KEY BIBLE VERSE: *Let's build a great city with a tower that reaches to the skies— a monument to our greatness! This will bring us together and keep us from scattering all over the world.* (Genesis 11:4)

Our achievements often indicate the central focus of our lives. The tower of Babel was a great human achievement, a wonder of the world. But it was a monument to the people themselves rather than to God. We often build monuments to ourselves (expensive clothes, big houses, fancy cars, important jobs) to call attention to our achievements. These may not be wrong in themselves, but when we use them to give us identity and self-worth, they take God's place in our lives. We are free to develop in many areas, but we are not free to think we have replaced God. What "towers" are in your life?

How complete and lasting are people's achievements?

BIBLE READING: Judges 15:1-20

KEY BIBLE VERSE: *Now Samson was very thirsty, and he cried out to the LORD, "You have accomplished this great victory by the strength of your servant. Must I now die of thirst and fall into the hands of these pagan people?"* (Judges 15:18)

Personal achievements do not diminish our dependence on God. Samson was physically and emotionally exhausted. After a great personal victory, his attitude declined quickly into self-pity—"Must I now die of thirst?" Emotionally, we are most vulnerable after a great effort or when faced with real physical needs. Severe depression often follows great achievements, so don't be surprised if you feel drained after a personal victory.

Even our achievements should remind us to be thankful to God. During times of vulnerability, avoid the temptation of thinking that God owes you for your efforts. It was his strength that gave you victory. Concentrate on keeping your attitudes, actions, and words focused on God instead of yourself.

How does God describe real achievement?

BIBLE READING: Mark 10:35-45

KEY BIBLE VERSE: *But among you it should be quite different. Whoever wants to be a leader among you must be your servant, and whoever wants to be first must be the slave of all.* (Mark 10:43-44)

Achievements do not change our position with God. James and John wanted the highest positions in Jesus' kingdom. But Jesus told them that true greatness comes in serving others. Peter, one of the disciples who heard this message, expands the thought in 1 Peter 5:1-4.

Most businesses, organizations, and institutions measure greatness by high personal achievement. In Christ's kingdom, however, service is the way to get ahead. The desire to be on top will hinder, not help. Rather than seeking to have your needs met, look for ways you can minister to the needs of others.

What difference do our good achievements make with God?

BIBLE READING: Romans 3:21-31

KEY BIBLE VERSE: *Can we boast, then, that we have done anything to be accepted by God? No, because our acquittal is not based on our good deeds. It is based on our faith. So we are made right with God through faith and not by obeying the law.* (Romans 3:27-28)

Our best achievements are efforts at thanking God for what he has done. Most religions prescribe specific duties that must be performed to make a person acceptable to God. Christianity is unique in teaching that the good works we do will not make us right with God. No amount of human achievement or progress in personal development will close the gap between God's moral perfection and our imperfect daily performance. Good deeds are important, but they will not earn us eternal life. We are saved only by trusting in what God has done for us (see Ephesians 2:8-10).

Related Topics: ACCOMPLISHMENTS, ACTIONS, FAITH

ACKNOWLEDGMENT (*Appreciation, Recognition, Value*)

What kind of acknowledgment does God require from us?

BIBLE READING: Daniel 4:1-37
KEY BIBLE VERSE: *His rule is everlasting, and his kingdom is eternal.* (Daniel 4:34)

Sooner or later we must acknowledge that God is sovereign. Nebuchadnezzar's pilgrimage with God is one of the themes of Daniel. In 2:47, he acknowledged that God revealed dreams to Daniel. In 3:28-29 he praised the God who delivered the three Hebrews. Despite Nebuchadnezzar's recognition that God exists and works great miracles, in 4:30 we see that he still did not acknowledge God as his Lord. We may recognize that God exists and does wonderful miracles, but God is not going to shape our life until we acknowledge him as Lord.

BIBLE READING: Matthew 9:9-17
KEY BIBLE VERSE: *Now go and learn the meaning of this Scripture: "I want you to be merciful; I don't want your sacrifices." For I have come to call sinners, not those who think they are already good enough.* (Matthew 9:13)

We must also acknowledge our own sinfulness. Those who are sure they are righteous can't be saved because the first step in following Jesus is acknowledging our need and admitting that we don't have all the answers.

Related Topics: CONFESSION, FAITH, HUMILITY

ACTIONS (*Doing, Efforts, Work*)

How do actions and faith fit together?

BIBLE READING: Genesis 15:1-6
KEY BIBLE VERSE: *And Abram believed the LORD, and the LORD declared him righteous because of his faith.* (Genesis 15:6)

Actions mean little without underlying faith. Although Abram had been demonstrating his faith through his actions, it was believing in the Lord, not his actions, that made Abram right with God (Romans 4:1-5). God credited righteousness to Abram because of his faith. We too can have a right relationship with God by trusting him with our life. Our outward actions—church attendance, prayer, good deeds—will not by themselves make us right with God.

A right relationship is based on faith—the heartfelt inner confidence that God is who he says he is and does what he says he will do. Right actions follow naturally as by-products.

BIBLE READING: Luke 3:1-18

KEY BIBLE VERSE: *Prove by the way you live that you have really turned from your sins and turned to God. Don't just say, "We're safe—we're the descendants of Abraham." That proves nothing. God can change these stones here into children of Abraham.* (Luke 3:8)

Faith naturally leads to action. Confession and a changed life are inseparable. Faith without works is lifeless (James 2:14-26). Jesus' harshest words were to the respectable religious leaders who lacked the desire for real change. They wanted to be known as religious authorities, but they didn't want to change their hearts and minds. Thus, their lives were unproductive. Repentance must be tied to action, or it isn't real. Following Jesus means more than saying the words; it means acting on what he says.

BIBLE READING: Matthew 5:13-20

KEY BIBLE VERSE: *But I warn you—unless you obey God better than the teachers of religious law and the Pharisees do, you can't enter the Kingdom of Heaven at all!* (Matthew 5:20)

There must be genuine faith behind actions. The Pharisees were exacting and scrupulous in their attempts to follow their laws. So how could Jesus reasonably call us to a greater righteousness than theirs? The Pharisees' weakness was that they were content to obey the laws outwardly without allowing God to change their hearts (or attitudes). Jesus was saying, therefore, that the *quality* of our goodness should be greater than that of the Pharisees. They looked pious, but they were far from the kingdom of God. God judges our heart as well as our deeds, for the heart determines our real allegiance. Be just as concerned about your attitudes, which people don't see, as your actions, which are seen by all.

BIBLE READING: Esther 4:1-17

KEY BIBLE VERSE: *If you keep quiet at a time like this, deliverance for the Jews will arise from some other place, but you and your relatives will die. What's more, who can say but that you have been elevated to the palace for just such a time as this?* (Esther 4:14)

God uses the actions of faithful people. After the decree to kill the Jews was given, Mordecai and Esther could have despaired, decided to save only themselves, or just waited for God's intervention. Instead, they saw that God had placed them in their positions for a purpose, so they seized the moment and acted. When it is within our power to save others, we must do so. In a life-threatening situation, don't withdraw, behave selfishly, wallow in despair, or wait for God to fix everything. Instead, ask God for his direction, and *act!* God may have placed you where you are "for just such a time as this."

BIBLE READING: James 1:19-27

KEY BIBLE VERSE: *And remember, it is a message to obey, not just to listen to. If you don't obey, you are only fooling yourself.* (James 1:22)

Believing God's Word will lead to obeying God's Word. It is important to know what God's Word says, but it is much more important to obey it. We can measure the effectiveness of our Bible study time by the effect it has on our behavior and attitudes.

When is more required than prayer?

 BIBLE READING: Exodus 14:5-18
KEY BIBLE VERSE: *Then the LORD said to Moses, "Why are you crying out to me? Tell the people to get moving!"* (Exodus 14:15)

Prayer should not be used to avoid action. The Lord told Moses to stop praying and get moving! Prayer must have a vital place in our life, but there is also a place for action. Sometimes we know what to do, but we pray for more guidance as an excuse to postpone doing it. If we know what we should do, then it is time to get moving.

BIBLE READING: 1 Samuel 7:1-17
KEY BIBLE VERSE: *Then Samuel said to all the people of Israel, "If you are really serious about wanting to return to the LORD, get rid of your foreign gods and your images of Ashtoreth. Determine to obey only the LORD; then he will rescue you from the Philistines."* (1 Samuel 7:3)

Obedience overcomes a sense of God's absence. Sorrow gripped Israel for twenty years. The ark was put away like an unwanted box in an attic, and it seemed as if the Lord had abandoned his people. Samuel, now a grown man, roused the people to action by saying that if they were truly sorry, they should do something about it. How easy it is for us to complain about our problems, even to God, while we refuse to act, to change, and to do what he requires. We don't even take the advice he has already given us. Do you ever feel as if God has abandoned you? Check to see if there is anything he has already told you to do. You may not be able to receive new guidance until you have acted on his previous directions.

Related Topics: ACCOMPLISHMENTS, ACHIEVEMENTS, FAITH

ADEQUACY (*Ability, Competence, Completeness*)

Can we ever feel adequate in serving Christ?

BIBLE READING: 2 Corinthians 2:14-17
KEY BIBLE VERSE: *Our lives are a fragrance presented by Christ to God. But this fragrance is perceived differently by those being saved and by those perishing.* (2 Corinthians 2:15)

We must depend on Christ for our sense of adequacy. Paul asks who is worthy for the task of representing Christ. Our adequacy is always from God (1 Corinthians 15:10; 2 Corinthians 3:5). He has already commissioned and sent us (see Matthew 28:18-20). He has given us the Holy Spirit to speak with Christ's power. He keeps his eye upon us, protecting us as we work for him. Thus, if we realize that it is God who makes us competent and useful, we can overcome our feelings of inadequacy. Serving him, therefore, requires that we focus on what he can do through us, not on what we can't do by ourselves.

Related Topics: ABILITIES, EFFECTIVENESS, SELF-ESTEEM

ADMINISTRATION (*Leadership, Organization, Structure*)

How do I handle being in charge?

BIBLE READING: Exodus 18:13-26

KEY BIBLE VERSE: *Now let me give you a word of advice, and may God be with you. You should continue to be the people's representative before God, bringing him their questions to be decided. You should tell them God's decisions, teach them God's laws and instructions, and show them how to conduct their lives.* (Exodus 18:19-20)

Even Moses needed help. Moses was spending so much time and energy hearing complaints by the Hebrews that he could not get to other important work. Jethro suggested that Moses delegate most of this work to others and focus his efforts on jobs only he could do. People in positions of responsibility sometimes feel they are the only ones who can do necessary tasks; but others are capable of handling part of the load. Delegation relieved Moses' stress and improved the quality of the government of the people. It helped prepare them for the system of government set up in Canaan. Proper delegation can multiply your effectiveness while giving others a chance to grow.

BIBLE READING: Acts 6:1-4

KEY BIBLE VERSE: *Now look around among yourselves, brothers, and select seven men who are well respected and are full of the Holy Spirit and wisdom. We will put them in charge of this business.* (Acts 6:3)

Responsibility should be the mark of every worker's efforts. If you are in a position of leadership and find yourself overwhelmed by responsibilities, determine *your* God-given abilities and priorities and then find others to help. Notice the requirements for the men who were to handle the feeding program: (1) good, with reputations for being honest; (2) full of the Holy Spirit; and (3) wise. We too must look for honest, spiritually mature, and wise men and women to lead our churches. If you are not in leadership, you have gifts that can be used by God in various areas of the church's ministry. Offer these gifts in service to him.

Related Topics: GOVERNMENT, LEADERSHIP, RESPONSIBILITY

ADMIRATION (*see* LOVE)

ADMIT (*see* CONFESSION)

ADMONISH (*see* CORRECTION)

ADOPTION (*Accept, Inclusion, Welcome*)

In what way is a Christian part of God's family?

BIBLE READING: Romans 8:1-17

KEY BIBLE VERSE: *For his Holy Spirit speaks to us deep in our hearts and tells us that we are God's children.* (Romans 8:16)

God adopts us into his family through Christ. Paul uses the image of adoption to illustrate the believer's new relationship with God. In Roman culture, the adopted person lost all rights in his old family and gained all the rights of a legitimate child in his new family. He became a full heir to his new father's estate. Likewise, when a person becomes a Christian, he gains all the privileges

and responsibilities of a child in God's family. One of these outstanding privileges is being led by the Spirit (see Galatians 4:1-7). We may not always feel
like we belong to God, but the Holy Spirit is our witness. His inward presence
reminds us of who we are and encourages us with his love (Romans 5:5).

BIBLE READING: Ephesians 1:1-10

KEY BIBLE VERSE: *His unchanging plan has always been to adopt us into his own
family by bringing us to himself through Jesus Christ. And this gave him great
pleasure.* (Ephesians 1:5)

Adoption was his plan all along. *Predestined* means marked out beforehand. This
is another way of saying salvation is God's work and not our own doing. God
has adopted us as his own children. Through Jesus' sacrifice, he has brought us
into his family and made us heirs along with Jesus (Romans 8:17). In Roman
law, adopted children had the same rights and privileges as natural children.
Paul uses this term to show how strong our relationship to God is. For more on
the meaning of adoption, see Galatians 4:1-7.

Related Topics: CHURCH, GRACE, SALVATION

ADULTERY *(Betrayal, Sexual Immorality, Unfaithfulness)*

What did Jesus have to say about adultery?

BIBLE READING: Matthew 5:27-32

KEY BIBLE VERSE: *You have heard that the law of Moses says, "Do not commit
adultery."* (Matthew 5:27)

Lust is a form of adultery. The Old Testament law said that it is wrong for a person to have sex with someone other than his or her spouse (Exodus 20:14). But
Jesus said that the *desire* to have sex with someone other than your spouse is
mental adultery and thus sin—if the *act* is wrong, then so is the *intention*. To be
faithful to your spouse with your body but not your mind is to break the trust
so vital to a strong marriage. Jesus is not condemning natural interest in the
opposite sex or even healthy sexual desire, but the deliberate and repeated filling of one's mind with fantasies that would be evil if acted out.

Acting out sinful desires draws others into sin. Some think, if lustful thoughts
are sin, why shouldn't a person go ahead and act upon their thoughts? Acting
out sinful desires is harmful in several ways: (1) it causes people to excuse sin
rather than eliminate it; (2) it destroys marriages; (3) it is deliberate rebellion
against God's Word; and (4) it always hurts others besides those immediately
involved. Sinful desire is not as dangerous as sinful action, and that is why
it should not be acted out. Nevertheless, sinful desire is just as damaging to
righteousness. Left unchecked, wrong desires result in wrong actions and turn
people away from God.

BIBLE READING: Luke 16:16-18

KEY BIBLE VERSE: *Anyone who divorces his wife and marries someone else commits
adultery, and anyone who marries a divorced woman commits adultery.* (Luke
16:18)

Even legal adultery is sin. Most religious leaders of Jesus' day permitted a man
to divorce his wife for nearly any reason. Jesus' teaching about divorce went
beyond Moses' (Deuteronomy 24:1-4). Stricter than any of the then-current

schools of thought, it shocked his hearers (see Matthew 19:10) just as it shakes today's readers. Jesus says in unmistakable terms that marriage is a lifetime commitment. To leave your spouse for another person may be legal, but it is adultery in God's eyes. As you think about marriage, remember that God intends it to be a permanent commitment.

How did Jesus treat an adulterous person?

BIBLE READING: John 8:1-11

KEY BIBLE VERSE: *Then Jesus stood up again and said to her, "Where are your accusers? Didn't even one of them condemn you?" "No, Lord," she said. And Jesus said, "Neither do I. Go and sin no more."* (John 8:10-11)

Jesus accepted the adulterer without condemning or condoning. Jesus didn't condemn the woman accused of adultery, but neither did he ignore or condone her sin. He told her to go and sin no more. Jesus stands ready to forgive any sin in your life, but confession and repentance mean a change of heart. With God's help we can accept Christ's forgiveness and stop our wrongdoing.

What is spiritual adultery?

BIBLE READING: Isaiah 1:1-31

KEY BIBLE VERSE: *See how Jerusalem, once so faithful, has become a prostitute. Once the home of justice and righteousness, she is now filled with murderers.* (Isaiah 1:21)

God compares his relationship with his people to marriage. The people had turned from the worship of the true God to worshiping idols. Their faith was defective, impure, and diluted. Idolatry, outward or inward, is spiritual adultery, breaking our commitment to God in order to love something else. Jesus described the people of his day as adulterous, even though they were religiously strict. The church is the "bride" of Christ (Revelation 19:7), and by faith we can be clothed in his righteousness. Are we his impure or faithful bride?

BIBLE READING: Hosea 1:1-11

KEY BIBLE VERSE: *When the LORD first began speaking to Israel through Hosea, he said to him, "Go and marry a prostitute, so some of her children will be born to you from other men. This will illustrate the way my people have been untrue to me, openly committing adultery against the LORD by worshiping other gods."* (Hosea 1:2)

Spiritual unfaithfulness is as serious as adultery. Just as Hosea's wife, Gomer, was eventually unfaithful to him, so the nation of Israel had been unfaithful to God. Israel's idolatry was like adultery. They sought "illicit" political relationships with other nations, and they mixed Baal worship with the worship of God. Like Gomer, we can chase after other loves—power, pleasure, money, or recognition. The temptations in this world can be very seductive. Are we loyal to God, remaining completely faithful, or have other loves taken his rightful place?

Related Topics: HEALING, IDOLATRY, MARRIAGE

ADVANTAGE *(Injustice, Cheating, Unfairness)*

Why is it wrong to take advantage of others?

BIBLE READING: 1 Samuel 2:12-26

KEY BIBLE VERSE: *The man offering the sacrifice might reply, "Take as much as you want, but the fat must first be burned." Then the servant would demand, "No, give it to me now, or I'll take it by force." So the sin of these young men was very serious in the LORD's sight, for they treated the LORD's offerings with contempt.* (1 Samuel 2:16-17)

Taking advantage of others is sinful arrogance. It was stipulated in the Law that the needs of all the Levites were to be met through the people's tithes (Numbers 18:20-24; Joshua 13:14, 33). Since Eli's sons were priests, they were to be taken care of in this way. But Eli's sons took advantage of their position of trust to satisfy their lust for power, possessions, and control. Their contempt and arrogance toward the people and the worship of God endangered the integrity of the whole priesthood.

Eli knew his sons were evil, but he did little to correct or stop them, even when the integrity of God's sanctuary was threatened. As the high priest, Eli should have executed his sons (Numbers 16:16-38). No wonder Eli chose not to confront the situation. But by choosing to ignore their selfish actions, Eli let his sons ruin their own lives and the lives of many others. There are times when serious problems must be confronted, even if the consequences might be painful.

BIBLE READING: Matthew 21:12-17

KEY BIBLE VERSE: *Jesus entered the Temple and began to drive out the merchants and their customers. He knocked over the tables of the money changers and the stalls of those selling doves.* (Matthew 21:12)

Taking advantage of people is disrespectful to God. This is the second time Jesus cleared the temple (see John 2:13-17). Merchants and money changers set up their booths in the Court of the Gentiles in the temple, crowding out the Gentiles who had come from all over the civilized world to worship God. The merchants sold sacrificial animals at high prices, taking advantage of those who had come long distances. The money changers exchanged all international currency for the special temple coins—the only money the merchants would accept. They often deceived foreigners who didn't know the exchange rates. Their commercialism in God's house frustrated people's attempts at worship. This, of course, greatly angered Jesus. Any practice that interferes with worshiping God should be stopped.

How can we keep from taking advantage of others?

BIBLE READING: Deuteronomy 24:10-22

KEY BIBLE VERSE: *If you lend anything to your neighbor, do not enter your neighbor's house to claim the security.* (Deuteronomy 24:10)

Realize that God will hold us accountable for our treatment of others. God told his people to treat the poor with justice. The powerless and poverty-stricken are often looked upon as incompetent or lazy when, in fact, they may be victims of oppression and circumstance. God says we must do all we can to help these needy ones. His justice did not permit the Israelites to insist on profits or quick payment from those who were less fortunate. Instead, his laws gave the poor every opportunity to better their situation, while providing humane options for those who couldn't. We are called to treat the poor fairly and to see their needs met.

BIBLE READING: Matthew 18:1-9

KEY BIBLE VERSE: *About that time the disciples came to Jesus and asked, "Which of us is greatest in the Kingdom of Heaven?"* (Matthew 18:1)

Realize that seeking advantage is a form of insecurity. The disciples had become so preoccupied with the organization of Jesus' earthly kingdom, they lost sight of its divine purpose. Instead of seeking a place of service, they sought positions of advantage. How easy it is to lose our eternal perspective and compete for promotions or status in the church. How hard it is to identify with the "little children"—weak and dependent people with no status or influence.

Related Topics: AMBITION, HUMILITY, POWER

ADVERSITY (*see* PAIN)

ADVICE (*Counsel, Direction, Help*)

▶ **ADVICE THAT HURTS**
How can someone tell when they are getting bad advice?

 BIBLE READING: 1 Kings 12:1-15
KEY BIBLE VERSE: *But Rehoboam rejected the advice of the elders and instead asked the opinion of the young men who had grown up with him and who were now his advisers.* (1 Kings 12:8)

Both the advice and the advisers should be evaluated. Rehoboam asked for advice, but he didn't carefully evaluate that advice. If he had, he would have realized that the advice offered by the older men was wiser than that of his peers. To evaluate advice, ask if it is realistic, workable, and consistent with biblical principles. Determine if the results of following the advice will be fair, make improvements, and give a positive solution or direction. Seek counsel from those more experienced and wiser. Advice is helpful only if we evaluate it with God's standards in mind.

 BIBLE READING: Job 18:1–19:6
KEY BIBLE VERSE: *How long will you torture me? How long will you try to break me with your words?* (Job 19:2)

Evaluate advice in the light of God's Word. Bildad's second speech was really no different from his first except that it was more harsh, as was Eliphaz's. Job's friends accused him of sin to make him feel guilty, not to encourage or correct him. When we face difficulties, pain, and suffering, we can expect well-meaning Bildads to come along, quoting proverbs and giving advice and not really listening to us or identifying with our pain. Rather than seeking to understand, they give unhelpful, trite answers. When receiving this useless advice, listen politely. Then, in order to sort out the helpful advice from the empty words, talk to God about what was said. When giving advice, avoid empty words. It is more important to convey care and support than to speak the right words.

▶ **ADVICE THAT HELPS**
How important are the sources of our advice?

 BIBLE READING: Proverbs 6:20-24
KEY BIBLE VERSE: *My son, obey your father's commands, and don't neglect your mother's teaching.* (Proverbs 6:20)

Those who have been trustworthy in the past ought to be considered in the future. It is natural and good for children, as they grow toward adulthood, to strive to become independent of their parents. Young adults, however, should take care not to turn a deaf ear to their parents—to reject their advice just when they may need it most. If you are struggling with a decision or looking for insight, check with your parents or other older adults who know you well. Their extra years of experience may have given them the wisdom you seek.

BIBLE READING: Mark 10:17-31

KEY BIBLE VERSE: *Jesus felt genuine love for this man as he looked at him. "You lack only one thing," he told him. "Go and sell all you have and give the money to the poor, and you will have treasure in heaven. Then come, follow me."* (Mark 10:21)

Good advice comes from those who genuinely love others. Jesus showed genuine love for this man, even though he knew he might not follow him. Those who love are able to give tough advice that doesn't hedge around the truth. Christ loved us enough to die for us, and he also loves us enough to talk straight to us. If his love were superficial, he would give us only approval; but because his love is complete, he gives us life-changing challenges.

▶ EVALUATING ADVICE
How can we know when advice is worth trusting?

BIBLE READING: Numbers 13:1–14:19

KEY BIBLE VERSE: *But Caleb tried to encourage the people as they stood before Moses. "Let's go at once to take the land," he said. "We can certainly conquer it!"* (Numbers 13:30)

Is the advice based on facts? Two wise men, Joshua and Caleb, encouraged the people to act on God's promise and move ahead into the land. Imagine standing before a crowd and loudly voicing an unpopular opinion! Caleb was willing to take the unpopular stand to do as God had commanded. To be effective when you go against the crowd, you must (1) have the facts (Caleb had seen the land himself); (2) have the right attitude (Caleb trusted God's promise to give Israel the land); and (3) state clearly what you believe (Caleb said, "We can certainly conquer it!").

The people rejected the advice and even talked of killing Joshua and Caleb. Don't be too quick to reject advice you don't like. Evaluate it carefully and weigh it against the teaching in God's Word. Those who offer the advice may be conveying God's message.

BIBLE READING: Job 5:8-27

KEY BIBLE VERSE: *But consider the joy of those corrected by God! Do not despise the chastening of the Almighty when you sin.* (Job 5:17)

Does the advice fit the situation? Eliphaz was correct—it is a blessing to be disciplined by God when we do wrong. His advice, however, did not apply to Job. As we know from the beginning of the book, Job's suffering was not a result of some great sin. We sometimes give people excellent advice only to learn that it does not apply to them and is therefore not very helpful. All who offer counsel from God's Word should take care to thoroughly understand a person's situation *before* giving advice.

BIBLE READING: Proverbs 10:1-21

KEY BIBLE VERSE: *The words of the godly are like sterling silver; the heart of a fool is worthless.* (Proverbs 10:20)

Is the adviser trustworthy? A lot of poor advice is worth less than a little good advice. It is easy to get opinions from people who will tell us only what they think will please us, but such advice is not helpful. Instead we should look for those who will speak the truth, even when it hurts. Think about the people to whom you go for advice. What do you expect to hear from them?

▶ **RESPONDING TO ADVICE**
How should good advice be handled?

BIBLE READING: Proverbs 1:1-9
KEY BIBLE VERSE: *Fear of the LORD is the beginning of knowledge. Only fools despise wisdom and discipline.* (Proverbs 1:7)

Good advice should be given with humility and accepted with thanks. One of the most annoying types of people is a know-it-all, a person who has a dogmatic opinion about everything and who is closed to anything new. Solomon calls this kind of person a fool. Don't be a know-it-all. Instead, be open to the advice of others, especially those who know you well and can give valuable insight and counsel. Learn how to learn from others. Remember, only God knows it all.

Related Topics: LISTENING, UNDERSTANDING, WISDOM

ADVISERS *(see* ADVICE*)*

ADVOCATE *(see* MEDIATOR*)*

AFFECTIONS *(Likes, Loves, Priorities)*

How do affections impact our lives?

BIBLE READING: Proverbs 4:23-27
KEY BIBLE VERSE: *Above all else, guard your heart, for it affects everything you do.* (Proverbs 4:23)

Actions tend to follow affections. Our heart—our feelings of love and desire—dictates to a great extent how we live, because we always find time to do what we enjoy. Solomon tells us to keep our heart with all diligence, making sure we concentrate on those desires that will keep us on the right path. Make sure your affections push you in the right direction. Put boundaries on your desires: don't go after everything you see. Look straight ahead, keep your eyes fixed on your goal, and don't get sidetracked on detours that lead to temptation.

Related Topics: EMOTIONS, FRIENDSHIP, LOVE

AFFIRMATION *(Encouragement, Strength, Support)*

What kind of affirmation do people really need?

BIBLE READING: Luke 14:7-14
KEY BIBLE VERSE: *The proud will be humbled, but the humble will be honored.* (Luke 14:11)

Honest affirmation is important. How can we humble ourselves? Some people try to give the appearance of humility in order to manipulate others. Others think that humility means putting themselves down. Truly humble people compare themselves only with Christ, realize their own sinfulness, and understand their limitations. On the other hand, they also recognize their gifts and strengths and are willing to use them as Christ directs. Humility is not self-degradation; it is realistic assessment and commitment to serve.

BIBLE READING: 1 Corinthians 1:4-9
KEY BIBLE VERSE: *I can never stop thanking God for all the generous gifts he has given you, now that you belong to Christ Jesus.* (1 Corinthians 1:4)

Helpful affirmation is important. Paul wrote some strong words to the Corinthians in this letter, but he began on a positive note. He affirmed their privilege of being in God's family, the power God gave them to speak out for him and understand his truth, and the presence of their spiritual gifts. Regardless of his letters' contents, Paul's style was always affirming. He began most of them by stating what he most appreciated about his readers and the joy he felt because of their faith in God. When we must correct others, it helps to begin by affirming what God has already accomplished in them.

Related Topics: ENCOURAGEMENT, HUMILITY, STRENGTH

AFFLICTION (*see* SUFFERING)

AFRAID (*see* FEAR)

AGE (*Life, Maturity, Years*)

▶ **AGE AND HONOR**
How should age affect the way we treat each other?

BIBLE READING: Leviticus 19:32
KEY BIBLE VERSE: *Show your fear of God by standing up in the presence of elderly people and showing respect for the aged. I am the LORD.* (Leviticus 19:32)

Our elders deserve our respect. People often find it easy to dismiss the opinions of the elderly and avoid taking time to visit with them. But the fact that God commanded the Israelites to honor the elderly shows how seriously we should take the responsibility of respecting those older than we. Their wisdom gained from experience can keep us from many pitfalls.

BIBLE READING: 1 Timothy 4:1-16
KEY BIBLE VERSE: *Don't let anyone think less of you because you are young. Be an example to all believers in what you teach, in the way you live, in your love, your faith, and your purity.* (1 Timothy 4:12)

Each age group should be worthy of respect. Timothy was a young pastor. It would be easy for older Christians to look down on him because of his youth. He had to earn the respect of his elders by setting an example in his teaching, living, love, faith, and purity. Regardless of your age, God can use you. Whether you are young or old, don't think of your age as a handicap. Live so others can see Christ in you.

▶ **AGE AND GOD'S PURPOSE**
Does our age affect God's work in us and through us?

BIBLE READING: 1 Samuel 2:12-26
KEY BIBLE VERSE: *Now Samuel, though only a boy, was the LORD's helper. He wore a linen tunic just like that of a priest.* (1 Samuel 2:18)

God can use people of any age. Samuel was a young child, and yet he "was the Lord's helper." Children can often serve God just as effectively as adults. God will use anyone who is willing to learn from him and serve him. He has no age limits. Don't discount the faith of a child or let your age keep you from serving God.

BIBLE READING: 2 Kings 22:1-20
KEY BIBLE VERSE: *He did what was pleasing in the LORD's sight and followed the example of his ancestor David. He did not turn aside from doing what was right.* (2 Kings 22:2)

Even the young can play a significant role. In reading the biblical lists of kings, it is rare to find one who obeyed God completely. Josiah was such a person, and he was only eight years old when he began to reign. For eighteen years he reigned obediently; then, when he was twenty-six, he began the reforms based on God's laws. Children are the future leaders of our churches and our world. A person's major work for God may have to wait until he is an adult, but no one is ever too young to take God seriously and obey him. Josiah's early years laid the base for his later task of reforming Judah.

BIBLE READING: Luke 1:5-25
KEY BIBLE VERSE: *Zechariah said to the angel, "How can I know this will happen? I'm an old man now, and my wife is also well along in years."* (Luke 1:18)

Even the very old can play a significant role. When Zechariah was told he would have a son, he doubted the angel's word. From his human perspective, his doubts were understandable—but with God, anything is possible. Although Zechariah and Elizabeth were past the age of childbearing, God gave them a child. It is easy to doubt or misunderstand what God wants to do in our life. Even God's people sometimes make the mistake of trusting their reason or experience rather than God. When tempted to think that one of God's promises is impossible, remember God's work throughout history. His power is not confined by narrow perspectives nor bound by human limitations.

BIBLE READING: Ecclesiastes 11:7–12:8
KEY BIBLE VERSE: *Don't let the excitement of youth cause you to forget your Creator. Honor him in your youth before you grow old and no longer enjoy living.* (Ecclesiastes 12:1)

There's no time like the present to serve God. A life without God can produce a bitter, lonely, and hopeless old age. A life centered around God is fulfilling; it makes the days of old age—when disabilities, sickness, and handicaps can become barriers to enjoying life—satisfying because of the hope of eternal life. Being young is exciting. But the excitement of youth can become a barrier to closeness with God if it makes young people focus on passing pleasures instead of eternal values. Make your strength available to God when it is still yours— during your youthful years. Don't waste it on evil or meaningless activities that become bad habits and make you callous. Seek God now.

Related Topics: SERVING, WISDOM, YOUTH

AGGRESSIVE (*see* AMBITION)

AGNOSTICISM (*see* DOUBT)

AGREEMENTS (*see* COVENANT)

ALCOHOL (*see* DRINKING)

ALLEGIANCE (*see* LOYALTY)

ALLIANCES (*see* COVENANT)

ALONE (*Privacy, Quietness, Solitude*)

How important are personal times of solitude?

BIBLE READING: Matthew 14:22-36
KEY BIBLE VERSE: *Afterward [Jesus] went up into the hills by himself to pray. Night fell while he was there alone.* (Matthew 14:23)

Jesus took time out for quiet. Seeking solitude was an important priority for Jesus (see also Matthew 14:13). He made room in his busy schedule to be alone with the Father. Spending time with God in prayer nurtures a vital relationship and equips us to meet life's challenges and struggles. Develop the discipline of spending time alone with God—it will help you grow spiritually and become more and more like Christ.

BIBLE READING: Luke 5:12-16
KEY BIBLE VERSE: *Jesus often withdrew to the wilderness for prayer.* (Luke 5:16)

Solitude was a habit even for Jesus. People were clamoring to hear Jesus preach and to have their diseases healed, but Jesus made sure he often withdrew to quiet, solitary places to pray. Many things clamor for our attention, and we often run ourselves ragged attending to them. Like Jesus, however, we should take time to withdraw to a quiet place to pray. Strength comes from God, and we can get it only by spending time with him.

Related Topics: DEVOTION, PRAYER, SILENCE

AMBASSADORS (*Representatives, Messengers, Missionaries*)

In what way might Christians be called God's ambassadors?

BIBLE READING: 2 Corinthians 5:11-21
KEY BIBLE VERSE: *We are Christ's ambassadors, and God is using us to speak to you. We urge you, as though Christ himself were here pleading with you, "Be reconciled to God!"* (2 Corinthians 5:20)

Christians represent the kingdom of God. An ambassador is an official representative from one country to another. As believers, we are Christ's ambassadors, sent with his message of reconciliation to the world. An ambassador of reconciliation has an important responsibility. We dare not take this responsibility lightly. How well are you fulfilling your commission as Christ's ambassador?

BIBLE READING: Exodus 7:1-14

KEY BIBLE VERSE: *Then the LORD said to Moses, "Pay close attention to this. I will make you seem like God to Pharaoh. Your brother, Aaron, will be your prophet; he will speak for you."* (Exodus 7:1)

Christians represent God. God called Moses his ambassador. An ambassador represents another country, another type of people, and often another point of view. We are each God's ambassadors—representing to the world that Christians are a different kind of people with a different lifestyle. Much of the world knows nothing about God except what it sees in the lives of God's people. What kind of God would they think you represent? Taking note of how you come across to others gives you a good indication of how well you are representing God.

Related Topics: LIFESTYLE, MINISTRY, REPRESENTATIVES

AMBITION (*Desire, Motivation, Schemes*)

How can ambition become destructive?

BIBLE READING: Numbers 16:1-40

KEY BIBLE VERSE: *They went to Moses and Aaron and said, "You have gone too far! Everyone in Israel has been set apart by the LORD, and he is with all of us. What right do you have to act as though you are greater than anyone else among all these people of the LORD?"* (Numbers 16:3)

Ambition can destroy present achievements. Korah and his associates had seen the advantages of the priesthood in Egypt. Egyptian priests had great wealth and political influence, something Korah desired for himself. Korah might have assumed that the Israelite priesthood would be the same kind of political machine. He did not understand that Moses' main ambition was to serve God rather than control others.

Ambition can destroy everything. Moses saw through their charge to their true motivation—some of the Levites wanted the power of the priesthood. Like Korah, we often desire the special qualities God has given others. Korah had significant, worthwhile abilities and responsibilities of his own. In the end, however, his ambition for more caused him to lose everything. Inappropriate ambition is greed in disguise. Concentrate on seeking from God the special purpose he has for you.

BIBLE READING: Judges 9:1-20

KEY BIBLE VERSE: *So Abimelech's uncles spoke to all the people of Shechem on his behalf. And after listening to their proposal, they decided in favor of Abimelech because he was their relative.* (Judges 9:3)

Ambition puts our plans ahead of God's. The Lord was to be Israel's king, not a mere man. But Abimelech wanted to usurp the position reserved for God alone. In his selfish quest, he killed all but one of his seventy half brothers. People with selfish desires often seek to fulfill them in ruthless ways. Examine your ambitions to see if they are self-centered or God-centered. Be sure you always seek to meet your desires in a way God would approve.

BIBLE READING: Mark 9:33-37

KEY BIBLE VERSE: *After they arrived at Capernaum, Jesus and his disciples settled in the house where they would be staying. Jesus asked them, "What were you* discussing out on the road?" But they didn't answer, because they had been arguing about which of them was the greatest. (Mark 9:33-34)

Ambition reveals wrong priorities. The disciples, caught up in their constant struggle for personal success, were embarrassed to answer Jesus' question. It is always painful to compare our motives with Christ's. It is not wrong for believers to be industrious or ambitious, but when ambition pushes obedience and service to one side, it becomes sin. Pride or insecurity can cause us to overvalue position and prestige. In God's kingdom, such motives are destructive. The only safe ambition is for Christ's kingdom, not our own advancement.

How can ambition be controlled?

BIBLE READING: 2 Samuel 5:6-12

KEY BIBLE VERSE: *David realized that the LORD had made him king over Israel and had made his kingdom great for the sake of his people Israel.* (2 Samuel 5:12)

Our ambitions must be regularly compared with God's purposes. Although the heathen kingdoms based their greatness on conquest, power, armies, and wealth, David knew that his greatness came only from God. To be great means keeping a close relationship with God personally and nationally. To do this, David had to keep his ambition under control. Although he was famous, successful, and well liked, he gave God first place in his life and served the people according to God's purposes. Do you seek greatness from God or from people? In the drive for success, remember to keep your ambition under God's control.

Related Topics: DESIRES, MOTIVES, PLANS

ANGELS (*Messenger, Protector, Spirit*)

What are angels?

BIBLE READING: Matthew 1:18-25

KEY BIBLE VERSE: *As he considered this, he fell asleep, and an angel of the Lord appeared to him in a dream. "Joseph, son of David," the angel said, "do not be afraid to go ahead with your marriage to Mary. For the child within her has been conceived by the Holy Spirit."* (Matthew 1:20)

Angels are beings created for God's purposes. The conception and birth of Jesus Christ are supernatural events beyond human logic or reasoning. Because of this, God sent angels to help certain people understand the significance of what was happening (see Matthew 2:13, 19; Luke 1:11, 26; 2:9).

Angels are spiritual beings created by God who help carry out his work on earth. They bring God's messages to people (Luke 1:26), protect God's people (Daniel 6:22), offer encouragement (Genesis 16:7ff.), give guidance (Exodus 14:19), carry out punishment (2 Samuel 24:15-17), patrol the earth (Zechariah 1:9-14), and fight the forces of evil (2 Kings 6:16-18; Revelation 20:1-2). There are both good and bad angels (Revelation 12:7), but because bad angels are allied with the devil, or Satan, they have considerably less power and authority than good angels. Eventually the main role of angels will be to offer continuous praise to God (Revelation 7:11-12).

BIBLE READING: Luke 1:5-20
KEY BIBLE VERSE: *Then the angel said, "I am Gabriel! I stand in the very presence of God. It was he who sent me to bring you this good news!"* (Luke 1:19)

Angels serve as God's messengers. Angels are spirit beings who live in God's presence and do his will. Only two angels are mentioned by name in Scripture—Michael and Gabriel—but there are many who act as God's messengers. Here, Gabriel delivered a special message to Zechariah (1:19). This was not a dream or a vision. The angel appeared in visible form and spoke audible words to the priest.

BIBLE READING: Matthew 18:10-14
KEY BIBLE VERSE: *Beware that you don't despise a single one of these little ones. For I tell you that in heaven their angels are always in the presence of my heavenly Father.* (Matthew 18:10)

Angels are special guardians. Our concern for children must match God's treatment of them. Certain angels are assigned to watch over children, and they have direct access to God. These words ring out sharply in cultures where children are taken lightly, ignored, or aborted. If their angels have constant access to God, the least we can do is to allow children to approach us easily in spite of our far too busy schedules.

BIBLE READING: Hebrews 1:1-14
KEY BIBLE VERSE: *But angels are only servants. They are spirits sent from God to care for those who will receive salvation.* (Hebrews 1:14)

Angels have several functions. Angels are spiritual beings created by God and under his authority (Colossians 1:16). They have several functions: serving believers (Hebrews 1:14), protecting the helpless (Matthew 18:10), proclaiming God's messages (Revelation 14:6-12), and executing God's judgment (Acts 12:1-23; Revelation 20:1-3).

Related Topics: DEMONS, HEAVEN, SATAN

ANGER *(Fury, Hostility, Rage)*

▶ **UNCONTROLLED ANGER**
When does anger become sin?

BIBLE READING: Genesis 4:1-16
KEY BIBLE VERSE: *"Why are you so angry?" the* LORD *asked him. "Why do you look so dejected?"* (Genesis 4:6)

Uncontrolled anger will lead to sin. The Bible does not say why God rejected Cain's offering. Perhaps Cain's attitude was improper, or perhaps his offering was not up to God's standards. God evaluates both our motives and the quality of what we offer him. When we give to God and others, we should have a joyful heart because of what we are able to give.

How do you react when someone suggests you have done something wrong? Do you move to correct the mistake or deny that you need to correct it? After Cain's offering was rejected, God gave him the chance to right his wrong and try again. God even encouraged him to do this! But Cain refused, and the rest of his life is a startling example of what happens to those who refuse to admit their mistakes. The next time someone suggests you are wrong, take an honest look at yourself and choose God's way instead of Cain's.

BIBLE READING: Genesis 27:1-41

KEY BIBLE VERSE: *Esau hated Jacob because he had stolen his blessing, and he said to himself, "My father will soon be dead and gone. Then I will kill Jacob."* (Genesis 27:41)

Anger is often the result of bad decisions. Esau was so angry at Jacob that he failed to see his own wrong in giving away his birthright in the first place. Jealous anger keeps us from seeing the benefits we have and makes us dwell on what we don't have.

When Esau lost the valuable family blessing, his future suddenly changed. Reacting in anger, he decided to kill Jacob. When you lose something of great value, or if others conspire against you and succeed, anger is the first and most natural reaction. But you can control your feelings by (1) recognizing your reaction for what it is; (2) praying for strength; and (3) asking God for help to see the opportunities that even your bad situation may provide.

BIBLE READING: James 3:1-12

KEY BIBLE VERSE: *The tongue is a flame of fire. It is full of wickedness that can ruin your whole life. It can turn the entire course of your life into a blazing flame of destruction, for it is set on fire by hell itself.* (James 3:6)

Anger's choice tool is the tongue. James compares the damage the tongue can do to a raging fire—the tongue's wickedness has its source in hell itself. The uncontrolled tongue can do terrible damage. Satan uses the tongue to divide people and pit them against one another. Idle words are damaging because they spread destruction quickly, and no one can stop the results once they are spoken. We dare not be careless with our words, thinking we can apologize later, for even if we do, the scars remain. A few words spoken in anger can destroy a relationship that took years to build. Before you speak, remember that words are like fire—you can neither control nor reverse the damage they can do.

▶ CONTROLLED ANGER
How can we be angry without sinning?

BIBLE READING: Mark 3:5

KEY BIBLE VERSE: *He looked around at them angrily, because he was deeply disturbed by their hard hearts. Then he said to the man, "Reach out your hand." The man reached out his hand, and it became normal again!* (Mark 3:5)

Anger can be a holy response to sin. Jesus was angry about the Pharisees' uncaring attitudes. Anger itself is not wrong. It depends on what makes us angry and what we do with our anger. Too often we express our anger in selfish and harmful ways. By contrast, Jesus expressed his anger by correcting a problem—healing the man's hand. Use your anger to find constructive solutions rather than tear people down.

BIBLE READING: Mark 11:15-19

KEY BIBLE VERSE: *He taught them, "The Scriptures declare, 'My Temple will be called a place of prayer for all nations,' but you have turned it into a den of thieves."* (Mark 11:17)

Anger does not have to lead to sin. Jesus became angry, but he did not sin. There is a place for righteous indignation. Christians are right to be upset about sin and injustice and should take a stand against them. Unfortunately, believers are often passive about these important issues and instead get angry over personal insults and petty irritations. Make sure your anger is directed toward the right issues.

BIBLE READING: Matthew 5:21-26

KEY BIBLE VERSE: *But I say, if you are angry with someone, you are subject to judgment! If you call someone an idiot, you are in danger of being brought before the high council. And if you curse someone, you are in danger of the fires of hell.* (Matthew 5:22)

Anger is a danger signal. When Jesus said, "But I say," he was not doing away with the law or adding to it his own beliefs. Rather, he was giving a fuller understanding of why God made that law in the first place. For example, when Moses said, "Do not murder" (Exodus 20:13), Jesus taught, "Don't even become angry enough to murder, for then you have already committed murder in your heart." The Pharisees read this law and, not having murdered, felt righteous. Yet they were angry enough with Jesus that they would soon plot his murder, though they would not do the dirty work themselves. We miss the intent of God's Word when we read his rules for living without trying to understand why he made them. When do you keep God's rules but close your eyes to his intent?

Killing is a terrible sin, but *anger* is a great sin too because it also violates God's command to love. Anger in this case refers to a seething, brooding bitterness against someone. It is a dangerous emotion that always threatens to leap out of control, leading to violence, emotional hurt, increased mental stress, and spiritual damage. Anger keeps us from developing a spirit pleasing to God. Have you ever been proud that you didn't strike out and say what was really on your mind? Self-control is good, but Christ wants us to practice thought-control as well. Jesus said we will be held accountable even for our attitudes.

How does God express his anger?

BIBLE READING: Romans 1:18-32

KEY BIBLE VERSE: *But God shows his anger from heaven against all sinful, wicked people who push the truth away from themselves.* (Romans 1:18)

God's anger is directed at sin. Why is God angry at sinful people? Because they have substituted the truth about him with a fantasy of their own imagination (Romans 1:25). They have stifled the truth God naturally reveals to all people in order to believe anything that supports their own self-centered lifestyles. God cannot tolerate sin because his nature is morally perfect. He cannot ignore or condone such willful rebellion. He wants to remove the sin and restore the sinner—if the sinner does not distort or reject the truth. But his anger erupts against those who persist in sinning.

Related Topics: EMOTIONS, FORGIVENESS, HATRED

ANGUISH (*see* SUFFERING)

ANOINTING (*see* BLESSING)

ANSWERS *(Comfort, Guidance, Responses)*

What kind of answers should we expect from God?

BIBLE READING: Daniel 2:1-49

KEY BIBLE VERSE: *He urged them to ask the God of heaven to show them his mercy by telling them the secret, so they would not be executed along with the other wise men of Babylon.* (Daniel 2:18)

Expect positive answers. Daniel was at a crisis point. Imagine going to see a powerful, temperamental king who had just angrily ordered your death! Daniel did not shrink back in fear, however, but confidently believed God would tell him all the king wanted to know. When the king gave Daniel time to find the answer, Daniel found his three friends and they prayed. After Daniel asked God to reveal Nebuchadnezzar's dream to him, he saw a vision of the dream. His prayer was answered. Before rushing to Arioch with the news, Daniel took time to give God credit for all wisdom and power, thanking him for answering his request.

When you find yourself in a tight spot, share your needs with trusted friends who also believe in God's power. Prayer is more effective than panic. Panic confirms your hopelessness; prayer confirms your hope in God. Daniel's trust in God saved himself, his three friends, and all the other wise men.

How do you feel when your prayers are answered? Excited, surprised, relieved? There are times when we seek God in prayer and, after receiving an answer, dash off in our excitement, forgetting to give God thanks. Match your persistence in prayer with gratitude when your requests are answered.

BIBLE READING: 1 Corinthians 13:1-13

KEY BIBLE VERSE: *Now we see things imperfectly as in a poor mirror, but then we will see everything with perfect clarity. All that I know now is partial and incomplete, but then I will know everything completely, just as God knows me now.* (1 Corinthians 13:12)

We shouldn't expect all the answers. Paul offered a glimpse into the future to give us hope that one day we will be complete when we see God face to face. This truth should strengthen our faith—we don't have all the answers now, but then we will. Someday we will see Christ in person and be able to see with God's perspective.

BIBLE READING: James 1:1-8

KEY BIBLE VERSE: *If you need wisdom—if you want to know what God wants you to do—ask him, and he will gladly tell you. He will not resent your asking.* (James 1:5)

God has promised to give us wisdom. By *wisdom,* James is talking not only about knowledge but the ability to make wise decisions in difficult circumstances. If we need wisdom, we can pray to God, and he will supply what we need. Christians never need to grope around in the dark, hoping to stumble upon answers. We can ask for God's wisdom to guide our choices.

Related Topics: PERSISTENCE, PRAYER, TRUST

ANXIETY (*see* WORRY)

APATHY (*see* DESPAIR)

APPEARANCE *(Exterior, Image, Impression)*

How can we avoid judging only by appearance?

BIBLE READING: 1 Samuel 16:1-13

KEY BIBLE VERSE: *But the LORD said to Samuel, "Don't judge by his appearance or height, for I have rejected him. The LORD doesn't make decisions the way you do! People judge by outward appearance, but the LORD looks at a person's thoughts and intentions."* (1 Samuel 16:7)

Remember that God looks beyond appearance. Saul was tall and handsome; he was an impressive looking man. Samuel may have been trying to find someone who looked like Saul to be Israel's next king, but God warned him against judging by appearance alone. When people judge by outward appearance, they may overlook individuals who lack the particular physical qualities society currently admires. But appearance doesn't reveal what people are really like or their true value.

Fortunately, God judges by faith and character, not appearances. And because only God can see on the inside, only he can accurately judge people. Most people spend hours each week maintaining their outward appearance; they should do even more to develop their inner character. While everyone can see your face, only you and God know what your heart really looks like. Which is the more attractive part of you?

BIBLE READING: Matthew 9:9-12

KEY BIBLE VERSE: *When he heard this, Jesus replied, "Healthy people don't need a doctor—sick people do."* (Matthew 9:12)

Try to see the world from God's point of view. The Pharisees constantly tried to trap Jesus, and they thought his association with these "lowlifes" was the perfect opportunity. They were more concerned with their own appearance of holiness than with helping people, with criticism than encouragement, with outward respectability than practical help. But God is concerned for all people, including the sinful and hurting ones. The Christian life is not a popularity contest! Following Jesus' example, we should share the gospel with the poor, immoral, lonely, and outcast, not just the rich, moral, popular, and powerful.

BIBLE READING: Matthew 15:1-20

KEY BIBLE VERSE: *These people honor me with their lips, but their hearts are far away.* (Matthew 15:8)

Try to see ourselves from God's point of view. We work hard to keep our outward appearance attractive, but what is in our hearts is even more important. The way we are deep down (where others can't see) matters much to God. What are you like inside? When people become Christians, God makes them different on the inside. He will continue the change process inside them if they only ask. God wants us to have healthy thoughts and motives, not just healthy food and good exercise.

BIBLE READING: 2 Corinthians 11:1-15

KEY BIBLE VERSE: *These people are false apostles. They have fooled you by disguising themselves as apostles of Christ.* (2 Corinthians 11:13)

Beware of appearances. Satan and his servants can deceive us by appearing attractive, good, and moral. Many unsuspecting people follow smooth-talking, Bible-quoting leaders into cults that alienate them from their families and practice immorality and deceit. Don't be fooled by external appearances. Our impressions alone are not an accurate indicator of who is or isn't a true follower of Christ; so it helps to ask these questions: (1) Do their teachings confirm Scripture (Acts 17:11)? (2) Do the teachers affirm and proclaim that Jesus Christ is God who came into the world as a man to save people from their sins (1 John 4:1-3)? (3) Are their lifestyles consistent with biblical morality (Matthew 12:33-37)?

Related Topics: BEAUTY, HYPOCRISY, SELF-ESTEEM

APPLICATION *(Lesson, Understanding, Usefulness)*

How important is learning how to apply the Bible's teaching?

BIBLE READING: Numbers 9:1-14

KEY BIBLE VERSE: *If foreigners living among you want to celebrate the Passover to the LORD, they must follow these same laws and regulations. The same laws apply both to you and to the foreigners living among you.* (Numbers 9:14)

God's standards apply to everyone. Sometimes we are tempted to excuse non-Christians from following God's guidelines for living. Christmas and Easter, for example, often have other meanings for them. We would not expect them to understand Lent. Yet foreigners at this time were expected to follow the same laws and ordinances as the Israelites. God did not have a separate set of standards for unbelievers and he still does not today. The phrase "The same laws apply both to you and to the foreigners living among you" emphasizes that non-Israelites were also subject to God's commands and promises. God singled out Israel for a special purpose—to be an example of how one nation could, and should, follow him. His aim, however, was to have all people obey and worship him.

BIBLE READING: 2 Chronicles 17:1-9

KEY BIBLE VERSE: *They took copies of the Book of the Law of the LORD and traveled around through all the towns of Judah, teaching the people.* (2 Chronicles 17:9)

God's Word must be known in order to be correctly applied. The people of Judah were biblically illiterate. They had never taken time to listen to and discuss God's Word and understand how it could change them. Jehoshaphat realized that knowing God's Word was the first step to getting people to live as they should, so he initiated a nationwide religious education program. He reversed the religious decline that had occurred at the end of Asa's reign by putting God first in the people's minds and instilling in them a sense of commitment and mission. Because of this, the nation began to follow God. Churches and Christian schools today need solid Christian education programs. Exposure to good Bible teaching through Sunday school, church, Bible study, and personal and family devotions is essential for living as God intended.

BIBLE READING: Nehemiah 8:1-12

KEY BIBLE VERSE: *So the people went away to eat and drink at a festive meal, to share gifts of food, and to celebrate with great joy because they had heard God's words and understood them.* (Nehemiah 8:12)

Applying the Bible actually leads to freedom! The people paid close attention to Ezra as he read God's Word, and their lives were changed. Because we hear the Bible so often, we can become dulled to its words and immune to its teachings. Instead, we should *listen carefully* to every verse and ask the Holy Spirit to help us answer the question, How does this apply to *my* life? We must *do* something about what we have learned if it is to have real significance for our lives.

BIBLE READING: Isaiah 42:18-25
KEY BIBLE VERSE: *Will not even one of you apply these lessons from the past and see the ruin that awaits you?* (Isaiah 42:23)

Sometimes we fail to learn from the mistakes of others. How could Israel and Judah be God's servants and yet be so blind? How could they be so close to God and see so little? Jesus condemned the religious leaders of his day for the same disregard of God (John 9:39-41). Yet do we not fail in the same way? Sometimes partial blindness—seeing but not understanding, or knowing what is right but not doing it—can be worse than not seeing at all.

We may condemn our predecessors for their failures, but we are twice as guilty if we repeat the same mistakes that we recognize as failures. Often we are so ready to direct God's message at others that we can't see how it applies to our own life. Make sure you are willing to take your own advice as you teach or lead.

BIBLE READING: 2 Timothy 3:10-16
KEY BIBLE VERSE: *All Scripture is inspired by God and is useful to teach us what is true and to make us realize what is wrong in our lives. It straightens us out and teaches us to do what is right.* (2 Timothy 3:16)

God's Word applies to all areas of life. The whole Bible is God's inspired Word. Because it is inspired and trustworthy, we should *read* it and *apply* it to our life. The Bible is our standard for testing everything else that claims to be true. It is our safeguard against false teaching and our source of guidance for how we should live. It is our only source of knowledge about how we can be saved. God wants to show you what is true and equip you to live for him. How much time do you spend in God's Word? Read it regularly to discover God's truth and become confident in your life and faith. Develop a plan for reading the whole Bible, not just the same familiar passages.

Related Topics: LEARNING, OBEDIENCE, UNDERSTANDING

APPRECIATION (*Enjoyment, Thankfulness, Value*)

How does our appreciation affect other people?

BIBLE READING: Numbers 10:11-34
KEY BIBLE VERSE: *"Please don't leave us," Moses pleaded. "You know the places in the wilderness where we should camp."* (Numbers 10:31)

Appreciation builds relationships. By complimenting Hobab's wilderness skills, Moses let him know he was needed. People cannot know you appreciate them if you do not tell them they are important to you. Complimenting those who deserve it builds lasting relationships and helps people know they are valued. Think about those who have helped you this month. What can you do to let them know how much you need and appreciate them?

In what ways can we appreciate Christ?

BIBLE READING: John 1:35-51
KEY BIBLE VERSE: *"How do you know about me?" Nathanael asked. And Jesus replied, "I could see you under the fig tree before Philip found you."* (John 1:48)

We should want to know Christ as well as he knows us. These new disciples used several names for Jesus: Lamb of God (1:36), Rabbi (1:38), Messiah (1:41), Son of God (1:49), King of Israel (1:49). As they got to know Jesus, their appreciation for him grew. The more time we spend getting to know Christ, the more we understand and appreciate who he is. We may be drawn to him for his teaching, but we will come to know him as the Son of God. Although these disciples made this verbal shift in a few days, they would not fully understand until three years later (Acts 2). What they so easily professed had to be worked out in experience. We may find that words of faith come easily, but deep appreciation for Christ comes with living by faith.

BIBLE READING: Luke 7:36-50

KEY BIBLE VERSE: *Then he turned to the woman and said to Simon, "Look at this woman kneeling here. When I entered your home, you didn't offer me water to wash the dust from my feet, but she has washed them with her tears and wiped them with her hair." (Luke 7:44)*

Recognizing how much we need Jesus will deepen our appreciation for him. Luke contrasts the Pharisees with sinners—and again the sinners come out ahead. Simon had committed several social errors in neglecting to wash Jesus' feet (a courtesy extended to guests because sandaled feet got very dirty), to anoint his head with oil, and to offer him the kiss of greeting. Did he perhaps feel he was too good to treat Jesus as an equal? The sinful woman, by contrast, lavished tears, expensive perfume, and kisses on her Savior. In this story it is the grateful prostitute, not the stingy religious leader, whose sins are forgiven. Although it is God's grace through faith that saves us, not acts of love or generosity, this woman's act demonstrated her true faith, and Jesus regarded it.

Overflowing love is the natural response to forgiveness and the consequence of faith. But only those who realize the depth of their sin can appreciate the complete forgiveness God offers them. Jesus has rescued all of his followers, whether they were once extremely wicked or conventionally good, from eternal death. Do you appreciate the wideness of his mercy? Are you grateful for his forgiveness?

Related Topics: RELATIONSHIP(S), SACRIFICE, THANKFULNESS

APPROVAL (*Consent, Permission, Respect*)

How do we know we have God's approval?

BIBLE READING: Judges 18:1-31

KEY BIBLE VERSE: *The men replied, "Let's attack! We have seen the land, and it is very good. You should not hesitate to go and take possession of it. When you get there, you will find the people living carefree lives. God has given us a spacious and fertile land, lacking in nothing!" (Judges 18:9-10)*

God's approval comes through God's Word. Just because the Danites successfully defeated Laish doesn't mean their actions were right. Their idolatry showed that God was not guiding them. Today many justify their wrong actions by outward signs of success. They think that wealth, popularity, or lack of suffering is an indication of God's blessing. But many stories in the Bible indicate that evil and earthly success can go hand in hand (see, for example, 2 Kings 14:23-29). Success doesn't indicate God's approval. Don't allow personal success to become a measuring rod of whether or not you are pleasing God.

BIBLE READING: Romans 2:1-16

KEY BIBLE VERSE: *Don't you realize how kind, tolerant, and patient God is with you? Or don't you care? Can't you see how kind he has been in giving you time to turn from your sin?* (Romans 2:4)

God's patience is not the same as his approval. It is easy to mistake God's patience for approval of the wrong way we are living. Self-evaluation is difficult, and it is even more difficult to expose our conduct to God and let him tell us where we need to change. But as Christians we must pray constantly that God will point out our sins, so that he can forgive them. Unfortunately, we are more likely to be amazed at God's patience with others than humbled at his patience with us.

BIBLE READING: Acts 14:8-20

KEY BIBLE VERSE: *Now some Jews arrived from Antioch and Iconium and turned the crowds into a murderous mob. They stoned Paul and dragged him out of the city, apparently dead.* (Acts 14:19)

The approval of other people is not the same as God's approval. Only days after the people in Lystra attempted to offer sacrifices to Paul and Barnabas, thinking they were gods, they stoned Paul and left him for dead. That's human nature. Jesus understood how changeable crowds can be (John 2:24-25). When many people approve of us, we feel good, but that should never cloud our thinking or affect our decisions. We should not live to please the crowd—especially in our spiritual lives. Be like Jesus. Know the nature of the crowd and don't put your trust in it. Put your trust in God alone.

How important is God's approval?

BIBLE READING: John 5:31-47

KEY BIBLE VERSE: *Your approval or disapproval means nothing to me, because I know you don't have God's love within you.* (John 5:41-42)

God's approval should be our highest priority. Whose approval do you seek? The religious leaders enjoyed great prestige in Israel, but their stamp of approval meant nothing to Jesus. He was concerned about God's approval. This is a good principle for us. If even the highest officials in the world approve of our actions and God does not, we should be concerned. But if God approves, even though others don't, we should be content.

Related Topics: ADEQUACY, BLESSING, SECURITY

ARGUMENTS *(Anger, Disputing, Fighting)*

How can arguments be prevented between Christians?

BIBLE READING: Philippians 2:12-18

KEY BIBLE VERSE: *In everything you do, stay away from complaining and arguing.* (Philippians 2:14)

Unity around the person of Jesus Christ should be maintained. Why are complaining and arguing so harmful? If all that people know about a church is that its members constantly argue, complain, and gossip, they get a false impression of Christ's gospel. Belief in Christ should unite those who trust him. If the people in our church are always complaining and arguing, they lack the unifying power of Jesus Christ. Stop arguing with other Christians or complaining about people and conditions within the church and let the world see Christ.

BIBLE READING: Proverbs 15:1-9
KEY BIBLE VERSE: *A gentle answer turns away wrath, but harsh words stir up anger.* (Proverbs 15:1)

Arguments are prevented when people exercise self-control. Have you ever tried to argue in a whisper? It is equally hard to argue with someone who insists on answering softly. On the other hand, a rising voice and harsh words almost always trigger an angry response. To turn away wrath and seek peace, quiet words are your best choice.

BIBLE READING: Titus 3:1-11
KEY BIBLE VERSE: *Do not get involved in foolish discussions about spiritual pedigrees or in quarrels and fights about obedience to Jewish laws. These kinds of things are useless and a waste of time.* (Titus 3:9)

Clear understanding avoids arguments. Paul warned Titus, as he warned Timothy, not to get involved in arguments over unanswerable questions (2 Timothy 2:14). This does not mean we should refuse to study, discuss, and examine different interpretations of difficult Bible passages. Paul is warning against petty quarrels, not honest discussions that lead to wisdom. When foolish arguments develop, it is best to turn the discussion back to a track that is going somewhere or politely excuse yourself.

How should we respond to arguments between others?

BIBLE READING: Proverbs 26:17-28
KEY BIBLE VERSE: *Yanking a dog's ears is as foolish as interfering in someone else's argument.* (Proverbs 26:17)

Avoid interfering with arguments between others. Yanking a dog's ears is a good way to get bitten, and interfering in arguments is a good way to get hurt. Many times both arguers will turn on the person who interferes. It is best simply to keep out of arguments that are none of your business. If you must become involved, try to wait until the arguers have stopped fighting and cooled off a bit. Then maybe you can help them mend their differences and their relationship.

Related Topics: CONFLICTS, DISAGREEMENTS, INSULT(S)

ARMOR *(Defense, Protection, Weapons)*

How can Christians defend themselves spiritually?

BIBLE READING: Ephesians 6:10-18
KEY BIBLE VERSE: *Put on all of God's armor so that you will be able to stand firm against all strategies and tricks of the Devil.* (Ephesians 6:11)

To fight spiritual battles we need God's armor. In the Christian life we battle against "the spiritual forces of evil" (the evil forces of fallen angels headed by Satan who is a vicious fighter, see 1 Peter 5:8). To withstand their attacks, we must depend on God's strength and use every piece of his armor. Paul is not only giving this counsel to the church as a whole, but to each individual within the church. The entire body of Christ needs to be armed. As you do battle against "the powers of this dark world," fight in the strength of the church, whose power comes from the Holy Spirit.

ARROGANCE (*see* PRIDE)

ASHAMED (*see* SHAME)

ASKING (*see* PRAYER)

ASSERTIVENESS (*see* CONFIDENCE)

ASSUMPTIONS (*Attitudes, Guesses, Impressions*)

▶ **DANGEROUS ASSUMPTIONS**
How can we prevent assumptions from becoming dangerous?

BIBLE READING: Genesis 20:1-18
KEY BIBLE VERSE: *"Well," Abraham said, "I figured this to be a godless place. I thought, 'They will want my wife and will kill me to get her.' "* (Genesis 20:11)

Beware of assumptions that lead to disobeying God. Because Abraham mistakenly assumed that Abimelech was a wicked man, he made a quick decision to tell a half-truth. Abraham thought it would be more effective to deceive Abimelech than to trust God to work in the king's life. Don't assume that God will not work in a situation that has potential problems. You may not completely understand the situation, and God may intervene when you least expect it.

BIBLE READING: Joshua 22:9-34
KEY BIBLE VERSE: *Phinehas son of Eleazar, the priest, replied to them, "Today we know the LORD is among us because you have not sinned against the LORD as we thought. Instead, you have rescued Israel from being destroyed by the LORD."* (Joshua 22:31)

Check assumptions before acting on them. When the tribes of Reuben and Gad and the half-tribe of Manasseh built an altar at the Jordan River, the rest of Israel feared that these tribes were starting their own religion and rebelling against God. But before beginning an all-out war, Phinehas led a delegation to learn the truth. He was prepared to negotiate rather than fight an unnecessary battle. When he learned that the altar was for a memorial rather than for heathen sacrifice, war was averted and unity restored.

As nations and as individuals, we would benefit from a similar approach to resolving conflicts. Assuming the worst about the intentions of others only brings trouble. Israel averted the threat of civil war by asking before attacking. Beware of reacting before you hear the whole story.

▶ **DAMAGING ASSUMPTIONS**
How do assumptions hurt people?

BIBLE READING: Job 13:1-12
KEY BIBLE VERSE: *For you are smearing me with lies. As doctors, you are worthless quacks.* (Job 13:4)

Assumptions concerning the lives of others lead to trouble. Job compared his three friends to doctors who did not know what they were doing. They were like eye surgeons trying to perform open-heart surgery. Many of their ideas about God were true, but they did not apply to Job's situation. They were right to say that God is just. They were right to say God punishes sin. But they were wrong to assume that Job's suffering was a just punishment for his sin. They took a true principle and applied it wrongly, ignoring the vast differences in human circumstances. We must be careful and compassionate in how we apply biblical condemnations to the lives of others; we must be slow to judge others.

BIBLE READING: John 3:1-21

KEY BIBLE VERSE: *After dark one evening, a Jewish religious leader named Nicodemus, a Pharisee, came to speak with Jesus.* (John 3:1-2)

Assumptions can make us devalue people. Are there people you disregard, thinking they could never be brought to God—such as a world leader for whom you have never prayed or a successful person to whom you have never witnessed? Don't assume that anyone is beyond the reach of the gospel. God, through his Holy Spirit, can reach anyone, and you should pray diligently for whomever he brings to your mind. Be a witness and example to everyone with whom you have contact. God may touch those you think most unlikely—and he may use you to do it.

BIBLE READING: Acts 9:1-18

KEY BIBLE VERSE: *"But Lord," exclaimed Ananias, "I've heard about the terrible things this man has done to the believers in Jerusalem!"* (Acts 9:13)

Assumptions can make us give up on people. "Not him, Lord, that's impossible. He could never become a Christian!" This was the essence of Ananias's response when God told him of Paul's conversion. After all, Paul had pursued believers to their death. Despite these understandable feelings, Ananias obeyed God and ministered to Paul. We must not limit God. He can do anything. We must obey, following God's leading even to difficult people and places.

Related Topics: ATTITUDE, LOVE, TRUTH

ASSURANCE *(Confidence, Hope, Security)*

▶ **FALSE ASSURANCE**

How do we know when we are basing our security on the wrong things?

BIBLE READING: Luke 18:18-30

KEY BIBLE VERSE: *Jesus watched him go and then said to his disciples, "How hard it is for rich people to get into the Kingdom of God!"* (Luke 18:24)

False assurance leads us away from dependence on God. This man's wealth smoothed his life and gave him power and prestige. When Jesus told him to sell everything he owned, he was touching the man's very basis for security and identity. The man did not understand that he would be even more secure if he followed Jesus than he was with all his wealth. Jesus does not ask all believers to sell everything they have, although this may be his will for some. He does ask us all, however, to get rid of anything that has become more important to us than God. If your basis for security has shifted from God to what you own, it would be better for you to get rid of those possessions.

▶ **FIRM ASSURANCE**

In what ways does God give us assurance?

BIBLE READING: Exodus 4:1-17

KEY BIBLE VERSE: *And be sure to take your shepherd's staff along so you can perform the miraculous signs I have shown you.* (Exodus 4:17)

Firm assurance is dependence on God's promises. Moses clung tightly to the shepherd's staff as he left for Egypt to face the greatest challenge of his life. The staff was his assurance of God's presence and power. When feeling uncertain, some people need something to stabilize and reassure them. For assurance when facing great trials, God has given promises from his Word and examples from great heroes of faith. Any Christian may cling tightly to these.

BIBLE READING: Exodus 13:17-22

KEY BIBLE VERSE: *The LORD guided them by a pillar of cloud during the day and a pillar of fire at night. That way they could travel whether it was day or night.* (Exodus 13:21)

Firm assurance is based on God's Word. God gave the Hebrews a pillar of cloud and a pillar of fire so they would know day and night that God was with them on their journey to the Promised Land. What has he given us so that we can have the same assurance? The Bible—something the Israelites did not have. Look to God's Word for reassurance of his presence. As the Hebrews looked to the pillars of cloud and fire, we can look to God's Word day and night to know he is with us, helping us on our journey.

BIBLE READING: Luke 21:5-19

KEY BIBLE VERSE: *Don't worry about how to answer the charges against you, for I will give you the right words and such wisdom that none of your opponents will be able to reply!* (Luke 21:14-15)

Firm assurance is based on God's care for us. Jesus warned his followers of coming persecutions in which they would be betrayed by their family members and friends. Christians of every age have had to face this possibility. It is reassuring to know that even when we feel completely abandoned, the Holy Spirit stays with us. He will comfort us, protect us, and give us the words we need. This assurance can give us the courage and hope to stand firm for Christ no matter how difficult the situation.

BIBLE READING: Romans 6:1-14

KEY BIBLE VERSE: *And since we died with Christ, we know we will also share his new life.* (Romans 6:8)

Firm assurance is based on Christ's resurrection. Because of Christ's death and resurrection, his followers need never fear death. This frees us to fellowship with him and do his will. This will affect all our activities—work and worship, play and Bible study, quiet times and times of caring for others. When you know you need not fear death, you will experience renewed vigor in life.

Related Topics: HOPE, RESURRECTION, SECURITY

ATONEMENT *(Covering, Payment, Sacrifice)*

What did the Old Testament sacrifices mean?

BIBLE READING: Leviticus 17:10-14

KEY BIBLE VERSE: *The life of any creature is in its blood. I have given you the blood so you can make atonement for your sins. It is the blood, representing life, that brings you atonement.* (Leviticus 17:11)

Blood meant an exchange of one life for another. How does blood make atonement for sin? When offered with the right attitude, the sacrifice and the blood shed from it made forgiveness of sin possible. On the one hand, blood represented the sinner's life, infected by his sin and headed for death. On the other hand, the blood represented the innocent life of the animal that was sacrificed in place of the guilty person making the offering. The death of the animal (of which the blood was proof) fulfilled the penalty of death. God therefore granted forgiveness to the sinner. It is God who forgives based on the faith of the one sacrificing.

How does Jesus' death offer atonement for our sin?

BIBLE READING: Romans 3:21-31
KEY BIBLE VERSE: *God sent Jesus to take the punishment for our sins and to satisfy God's anger against us. We are made right with God when we believe that Jesus shed his blood, sacrificing his life for us. God was being entirely fair and just when he did not punish those who sinned in former times.* (Romans 3:25)

In his death Jesus took upon himself our punishment. After all this bad news about our sinfulness and God's condemnation, Paul now gives the wonderful news. There is a way to be declared not guilty—by trusting Jesus Christ to take away our sins. Trusting means putting our confidence in him to forgive our sins, to make us right with God, and to empower us to live the way he taught us. God's solution is available to all of us regardless of our background or past behavior.

BIBLE READING: Hebrews 7:11-28
KEY BIBLE VERSE: *He does not need to offer sacrifices every day like the other high priests. They did this for their own sins first and then for the sins of the people. But Jesus did this once for all when he sacrificed himself on the cross.* (Hebrews 7:27)

Jesus' death secured forgiveness for us. In Old Testament times when animals were sacrificed, they were cut into pieces, the parts were washed, the fat was burned, the blood was sprinkled, and the meat was boiled. Blood was demanded as atonement for sins, and God accepted animal blood to cover the people's sins (Leviticus 17:11). Because of the sacrificial system, the Israelites were generally aware that sin costs and that they themselves were sinful. Many people take Christ's work on the cross for granted. They don't realize how costly it was for Jesus to secure our forgiveness—it cost him his life (1 Peter 1:18-19).

These verses help explain why Jesus had to die. As we better understand the Jewish sacrificial system, we see that Jesus' death served as the perfect atonement for our sins. His death brings us eternal life. How callous, how cold, how stubborn it would be to refuse God's greatest gift.

Related Topics: FORGIVENESS, SACRIFICE, SIN

ATTITUDE *(Appearance, Feelings, Perspective)*

▶ **NEGATIVE ATTITUDES**
How do negative attitudes affect our relationship with God?

BIBLE READING: Genesis 4:1-16

KEY BIBLE VERSE: *"Why are you so angry?"* the LORD *asked him. "Why do you look so dejected?"* (Genesis 4:6)

Negative attitudes may cause us to turn away from God. The Bible does not say why God rejected Cain's offering. Perhaps Cain's attitude was improper, or perhaps his offering was not up to God's standards. God evaluates both our motives and the quality of what we offer him. When we give to God and others, we should have a joyful heart because of what we are able to give. We should not worry about how much we are giving up, for everything belongs to God in the first place. Instead, we should joyfully give to God our best in time, money, possessions, and talents.

BIBLE READING: 1 Samuel 8:1-22

KEY BIBLE VERSE: *"Look,"* they told him, *"you are now old, and your sons are not like you. Give us a king like all the other nations have."* (1 Samuel 8:5)

Negative attitudes lead to wrong decisions. Israel was called to be a holy nation, separate from and unique among all others (Leviticus 20:26). The Israelites' motive in asking for a king was to be like the nations around them. This was in total opposition to God's original plan. It was not their desire for a king that was wrong but their reasons for wanting a king.

Often we let others' values and actions dictate our attitudes and behavior. Have you ever made a wrong choice because you wanted to be like everyone else? Be careful that the values of your friends or "heroes" don't pull you away from what God says is right. When God's people want to be like unbelievers, they are heading for spiritual disaster.

▶ **POSITIVE ATTITUDES**
What are the benefits of a positive attitude?

BIBLE READING: Genesis 39:1-23

KEY BIBLE VERSE: *After hearing his wife's story, Potiphar was furious! He took Joseph and threw him into the prison where the king's prisoners were held. But the LORD was with Joseph there, too, and he granted Joseph favor with the chief jailer.* (Genesis 39:19-21)

Positive attitudes allow God to work. As a prisoner and slave, Joseph could have seen his situation as hopeless. Instead, he did his best with each small task given him. His diligence and positive attitude were soon noticed by the jail warden, who promoted him to prison administrator. Are you facing a seemingly hopeless predicament? At work, at home, or at school, follow Joseph's example by taking each small task and doing your best. Remember how God turned Joseph's situation around. He will see your efforts and can reverse even overwhelming odds.

BIBLE READING: Exodus 14:1-14

KEY BIBLE VERSE: *But Moses told the people, "Don't be afraid. Just stand where you are and watch the LORD rescue you. The Egyptians that you see today will never be seen again."* (Exodus 14:13)

Positive attitudes can influence others. The people were hostile and despairing, but Moses encouraged them to watch the wonderful way God would rescue them. Moses had a positive attitude! When it looked as if they were trapped, Moses called upon God to intervene. We may not be chased by an army, but we may still feel trapped. Instead of giving in to despair, we should adopt Moses' attitude to "stand firm" and see the deliverance that the Lord will accomplish.

BIBLE READING: Ruth 2:1-13

KEY BIBLE VERSE: *The foreman replied, "She is the young woman from Moab who came back with Naomi. She asked me this morning if she could gather grain behind the harvesters. She has been hard at work ever since, except for a few minutes' rest over there in the shelter."* (Ruth 2:6-7)

Positive attitudes will help overcome difficulties. Ruth's task, though menial, tiring, and perhaps degrading, was done faithfully. What is your attitude when the task you have been given is not up to your true potential? The task at hand may be all you can do, or it may be the work God wants you to do. Or, as in Ruth's case, it may be a test of your character that can open up new doors of opportunity.

Whose attitude should we imitate?

BIBLE READING: Philippians 2:5-11

KEY BIBLE VERSE: *Your attitude should be the same that Christ Jesus had.* (Philippians 2:5)

The best positive attitude is one like Christ's. Often people excuse selfishness, pride, or evil by claiming their "rights." They think, *I can cheat on this test; after all, I deserve to pass this class,* or *I can spend all this money on myself—I worked for it,* or *I can get an abortion; I have a right to control my own body.* But as believers, we should have a different attitude; one that enables us to lay aside our rights in order to serve others. If we say we follow Christ, we must live as he lived. We should develop his attitude of humility as we serve, even when we are not likely to get recognition for our efforts. Are you selfishly clinging to your rights, or are you willing to serve?

Related Topics: EMOTIONS, FEELINGS, PURPOSE

AUTHORITY *(Confidence, Control, Leadership)*

▶ **SELF-CENTERED AUTHORITY**
What happens when people think they know best?

BIBLE READING: Judges 21:13-25

KEY BIBLE VERSE: *In those days Israel had no king, so the people did whatever seemed right in their own eyes.* (Judges 21:25)

Self-centered authority defies God. During the time of the judges, the people of Israel experienced trouble because everyone became his own authority and acted on his own opinions of right and wrong. This produced horrendous results. Our world is similar. Individuals, groups, and societies have made themselves the final authorities without reference to God. It is the ultimate heroic act to submit all our plans, desires, and motives to God. When people selfishly seek to satisfy their personal desires at all costs, everyone pays the price.

▶ **GOD-CENTERED AUTHORITY**
How does God affirm his authority in people?

BIBLE READING: 1 Samuel 3:1-21

KEY BIBLE VERSE: *Now the LORD called a third time, and once more Samuel jumped up and ran to Eli. "Here I am," he said. "What do you need?" Then Eli realized it was the LORD who was calling the boy.* (1 Samuel 3:8)

God doesn't always work in ways we would expect. One would naturally expect an audible message from God to be given to the priest Eli and not to the child Samuel. Eli was older and more experienced, and he held the proper position. But God's chain of command is based on faith. His view of authority is not based on age or position. In finding faithful followers, God may use unexpected channels. Be prepared for the Lord to work at any place, at any time, and through anyone he chooses.

▶ **CHRIST'S AUTHORITY**
What made Jesus more than a great teacher?

BIBLE READING: Matthew 7:21-29
KEY BIBLE VERSE: *After Jesus finished speaking, the crowds were amazed at his teaching, for he taught as one who had real authority—quite unlike the teachers of religious law.* (Matthew 7:28-29)

Jesus spoke with authority. The scribes (religious scholars) often cited traditions and quoted authorities to support their arguments and interpretations. But Jesus spoke with a new authority—his own. He didn't need to quote anyone because he was the original Word (John 1:1).

BIBLE READING: Colossians 1:15-20
KEY BIBLE VERSE: *Christ is the one through whom God created everything in heaven and earth. He made the things we can see and the things we can't see—kings, kingdoms, rulers, and authorities. Everything has been created through him and for him.* (Colossians 1:16)

Jesus is the source of all authority. This is one of the strongest statements about the divine nature of Christ found anywhere in the Bible. Jesus is not only equal to God (Philippians 2:6), he is God (John 10:30, 38; 12:45; 14:1-11). He not only reflects God, but he reveals God to us (John 1:18; 14:9). He came from heaven, not from the dust of the ground (1 Corinthians 15:47), and is Lord of all (Romans 9:5; 10:11-13; Revelation 1:5; 17:14). He is completely holy (Hebrews 7:26-28; 1 Peter 1:19; 2:22; 1 John 3:5), and he has authority to judge the world (Romans 2:16; 2 Corinthians 5:10; 2 Timothy 4:1). Therefore, he is supreme over all creation, including the spirit world. We, like the Colossian believers, must believe that Jesus is God or our Christian faith is hollow and meaningless.

Related Topics: BIBLE, LEADERSHIP, TRUTH

AWE *(Amazement, Wonder, Worship)*

What makes people experience awe?

BIBLE READING: Exodus 3:1-6
KEY BIBLE VERSE: *Then he said, "I am the God of your ancestors—the God of Abraham, the God of Isaac, and the God of Jacob." When Moses heard this, he hid his face in his hands because he was afraid to look at God.* (Exodus 3:6)

Personal contact with God is awe inspiring. Moses saw a burning bush and spoke with God. Many people in the Bible experienced God in visible (not necessarily human) form. Abraham saw the smoking firepot and flaming torch (Genesis 15:17); Jacob wrestled with a man (Genesis 32:22-32). When the slaves were freed from Egypt, God led them by pillars of cloud and fire (Exodus 13:17-22). God made such appearances to encourage his new nation, to guide them, and to prove the reliability of his verbal message.

At God's command, Moses removed his shoes and covered his face. Taking off his shoes was an act of reverence, conveying his own unworthiness before God. God is our friend, but he is also our sovereign Lord. To approach him frivolously shows a lack of respect and sincerity. When you come to God in worship, do you approach him casually, or do you come as though you were an invited guest before a king? If necessary, adjust your attitude so it is suitable for approaching a holy God.

BIBLE READING: Daniel 10:1-12

KEY BIBLE VERSE: *So I was left there all alone to watch this amazing vision. My strength left me, my face grew deathly pale, and I felt very weak.* (Daniel 10:8)

An experience of spiritual power can be awe inspiring. The person seen by Daniel was a heavenly being. This is believed by some commentators to be an appearance of Christ (see Revelation 1:12-18), while others contend it is an angel (because he required Michael's help—10:13). In either case, Daniel caught a glimpse of the battle between good and evil supernatural powers.

Daniel was frightened by this vision, but the messenger's hand calmed his fears; Daniel lost his speech, but the messenger's touch restored it; Daniel felt weak, but the messenger's words strengthened him. God can bring us healing when we are hurt, peace when we are troubled, and strength when we are weak. Ask God to minister to you as he did to Daniel.

BIBLE READING: Ephesians 1:15-23

KEY BIBLE VERSE: *And God has put all things under the authority of Christ, and he gave him this authority for the benefit of the church.* (Ephesians 1:22)

Eventually every person will experience awe before Christ. Having been raised from the dead, Christ is now the supreme head of the church, the ultimate authority over the world. Christ is the Messiah, God's anointed one, the one Israel longed for, the one who would set their broken world right. As Christians we can be confident that God has won the final victory and is in control of everything. We need not fear any dictator, nation, death, or Satan himself. The contract has been signed and sealed; we are waiting just a short while for delivery. Paul says, in Romans 8:37-39, that nothing can separate us from God and his love.

Related Topics: GOD, HOLINESS, WORSHIP

BABIES (*see* CHILDREN)

BACKSLIDE (*Forget, Give Up, Turn Away*)

▶ REASONS FOR BACKSLIDING
What causes people to forget God's faithfulness so quickly?

BIBLE READING: Deuteronomy 8:10-20
KEY BIBLE VERSE: *But that is the time to be careful! Beware that in your plenty you do not forget the LORD your God and disobey his commands, regulations, and laws.* (Deuteronomy 8:11)

Pride leads to backsliding. In times of plenty, we often take credit for our prosperity and become proud that our own hard work and cleverness have made us rich. It is easy to get so busy collecting and managing wealth that we push God right out of our life. But it is God who gives us everything we have, and it is God who asks us to manage it for him.

BIBLE READING: Judges 2:6-19
KEY BIBLE VERSE: *Yet Israel did not listen to the judges but prostituted themselves to other gods, bowing down to them. How quickly they turned away from the path of their ancestors, who had walked in obedience to the LORD's commands.* (Judges 2:17)

Selfishness leads to backsliding. Why would the people of Israel turn so quickly from their faith in God? Simply put, the Canaanite religion appeared more attractive to the sensual nature and offered more short-term benefits (sexual permissiveness and increased fertility in childbearing and farming). One of its most attractive features was that people could remain selfish and yet fulfill their religious requirements. They could do almost anything they wished and still be obeying at least one of the many Canaanite gods. Male and female prostitution were not only allowed but encouraged as forms of worship.

Faith in the one true God, however, does not offer short-term benefits that appeal to our sinful human nature. The essence of sin is selfishness; the essence of God's way of life is selflessness. We must seek Christ's help to live God's way.

BIBLE READING: Mark 4:1-20
KEY BIBLE VERSE: *The thorny ground represents those who hear and accept the Good News, but all too quickly the message is crowded out by the cares of this life, the lure of wealth, and the desire for nice things, so no crop is produced.* (Mark 4:18-19)

Distractions can cause backsliding. Worldly worries, the false sense of security brought on by prosperity, and the desire for things plagued first-century disciples as they do us today. How easy it is for our daily routines to become overcrowded. A life packed with materialistic pursuits deafens us to God's Word. Stay free so you can hear God when he speaks.

▶ PREVENTING BACKSLIDING
How can we keep from forgetting God's faithfulness?

BIBLE READING: Luke 9:57-62
KEY BIBLE VERSE: *Jesus told him, "Anyone who puts a hand to the plow and then looks back is not fit for the Kingdom of God." (Luke 9:62)*

Commitment to Jesus prevents backsliding. What does Jesus want from us? Total dedication, not halfhearted commitment. We can't pick and choose among Jesus' ideas and follow him selectively; we have to accept the cross along with the crown, judgment as well as mercy. We must count the cost and be willing to abandon everything else that has given us security. With our focus on Jesus, we should allow nothing to distract us from the manner of living that he calls good and true.

BIBLE READING: James 5:15-20
KEY BIBLE VERSE: *My dear brothers and sisters, if anyone among you wanders away from the truth and is brought back again, you can be sure that the one who brings that person back will save that sinner from death and bring about the forgiveness of many sins. (James 5:19-20)*

Commitment to other believers prevents backsliding. Clearly this person who has wandered away is a believer who has fallen into sin—one who is no longer living a life consistent with his beliefs. Christians disagree over whether or not it is possible for people to lose their salvation, but all agree that those who move away from their faith are in serious trouble and need to repent. James urges Christians to help backsliders return to God. By taking the initiative, praying for them, and acting in love, we can meet them where they are and bring them back to God and his forgiveness.

Related Topics: ABANDON, DISOBEDIENCE, ENDURANCE

BACKSTABBING (*see* CONVERSATION)

BALANCE (*Consistency, Maturity, Stability*)

▶ THE PERFECT MODEL
Whose life should serve as a pattern for our own?

BIBLE READING: Luke 2:41-52
KEY BIBLE VERSE: *Jesus grew both in height and in wisdom, and he was loved by God and by all who knew him. (Luke 2:52)*

Jesus is our model. The second chapter of Luke shows us that although Jesus was unique, he had a normal childhood and adolescence. In terms of development, he went through the same progression we do. He grew physically and mentally, he related to other people, and he was loved by God. A full human life is not unbalanced. It was important to Jesus—and it should be important to all believers—to develop fully and harmoniously in each of these key areas: physical, mental, social, and spiritual.

▶ BALANCED LIVING
How does balance affect specific areas of life?

BIBLE READING: John 2:1-11

KEY BIBLE VERSE: *The next day Jesus' mother was a guest at a wedding celebration in the village of Cana in Galilee. Jesus and his disciples were also invited to the celebration.* (John 2:1-2)

Balance affects work and pleasure. Jesus was on a mission to save the world, the greatest mission in the history of mankind. Yet he took time to attend a wedding and participate in its festivities. We may be tempted to think we should not take time out from our "important" work for social occasions. But maybe these social occasions are part of our mission. Jesus valued these wedding festivities because they involved people, and Jesus came to be with people. Our mission can often be accomplished in joyous times of celebration with others. Bring balance to your life by bringing Jesus into times of pleasure as well as times of work.

BIBLE READING: 1 Timothy 4:6-16

KEY BIBLE VERSE: *Don't let anyone think less of you because you are young. Be an example to all believers in what you teach, in the way you live, in your love, your faith, and your purity.* (1 Timothy 4:12)

Balance in physical and spiritual areas. Are you in shape both physically and spiritually? In our society, much emphasis is placed on physical fitness, but spiritual health (godliness) is even more important. Our physical bodies are susceptible to disease and injury, but faith can sustain us through these tragedies. To train for godliness, we must develop our faith by using our God-given abilities in the service of the church (see 4:14-16). Are you developing your spiritual muscles?

Balance in how our lives affect others. Timothy was a young pastor. It would be easy for older Christians to look down on him because of his youth. He had to earn the respect of his elders by setting an example in his speech, life, love, faith, and purity. Regardless of your age, God can use you. Whether you are young or old, don't think of your age as a handicap. Live so others can see Christ in you.

Balanced input. The Scripture that Paul mentions is in fact the Old Testament. We must make sure to emphasize reading the entire Bible, both the Old and the New Testaments. There are rich rewards in studying the people, events, prophecies, and principles of the Old Testament.

Balance in choosing good models to follow. Timothy's commission as a church leader was confirmed by prophecy (see also 1 Timothy 1:18) and by the laying on of hands by the elders of the church. He was not a self-appointed leader. If you aspire to church leadership, seek the counsel of mature Christians who know you well and who will hold you accountable.

Balance in pursuing excellence. As a young leader in a church that had a lot of problems, Timothy may have felt intimidated. But the elders and prophets encouraged him and charged him to use his spiritual gift responsibly. Highly skilled and talented athletes lose their abilities if their muscles aren't toned by constant use, and we will lose our spiritual gifts if we don't put them to work.

Our talents are improved by exercise, but failing to use them causes them to waste away from lack of practice and nourishment. What gifts and abilities has God given you? Use them regularly in serving God and others. (See Romans 12:1-8 and 2 Timothy 1:6-8 for more on using the abilities God has given us.)

Balance in self-evaluation. We know the importance of watching our lives closely. We must be on constant guard against falling into sin that can so easily destroy us. Yet we must watch what we believe just as closely. Wrong beliefs can quickly lead us into sin and heresy. We should be on guard against those who would persuade us that how we live is more important than what we believe. We should persevere in both.

Related Topics: DISCIPLINE, GROWTH, MATURITY

BARGAINING *(Arguing, Exchanging, Negotiating)*

▶ **BARGAINING WITH GOD**
In what ways do people bargain with God?

BIBLE READING: 1 Samuel 1:1-20
KEY BIBLE VERSE: *[Hannah] made this vow: "O LORD Almighty, if you will look down upon my sorrow and answer my prayer and give me a son, then I will give him back to you. He will be yours for his entire lifetime, and as a sign that he has been dedicated to the LORD, his hair will never be cut."* (1 Samuel 1:11)

God takes our promises seriously. Be careful what you promise in prayer, because God may take you up on it. Hannah so desperately wanted a child that she was willing to strike a bargain with God. God took her up on her promise, and to Hannah's credit, she did her part, even though it was painful (1:27-28).

Although we are not in a position to barter with God, he may still choose to answer a prayer that has an attached promise. When you pray, ask yourself, "Will I follow through on any promises I make to God if he grants my request?" It is dishonest and dangerous to ignore a promise, especially to God. God keeps his promises, and he expects you to keep yours.

BIBLE READING: Genesis 28:10-22
KEY BIBLE VERSE: *Jacob made this vow: "If God will be with me and protect me on this journey and give me food and clothing, and if he will bring me back safely to my father, then I will make the LORD my God. This memorial pillar will become a place for worshiping God, and I will give God a tenth of everything he gives me."* (Genesis 28:20-22)

Our bargains rarely match God's promises. Was Jacob trying to bargain with God? It is possible that he, in his ignorance of how to worship and serve God, treated God like a servant who would perform a service for a tip. More likely, Jacob was not bargaining but pledging his future to God. He may have been saying, in effect, "Because you have blessed me, I will follow you." Whether Jacob was bargaining or pledging, God blessed him. But God also had some difficult lessons for Jacob to learn.

BIBLE READING: Jonah 2:1-10
KEY BIBLE VERSE: *But I will offer sacrifices to you with songs of praise, and I will fulfill all my vows. For my salvation comes from the LORD alone.* (Jonah 2:9)

Thanking God is often better than bargaining. Obviously Jonah was not in a position to bargain with God. Instead, he simply thanked God for saving his life. Our troubles should cause us to cling tightly to God, not attempt to bargain our way out of the pain. We can thank and praise God for what he has already done for us and for his love and mercy.

▶ GOD'S GREAT BARGAIN
What does God offer us?

 BIBLE READING: Isaiah 55:1-13
KEY BIBLE VERSE: *Seek the* LORD *while you can find him. Call on him now while he is near. Let the people turn from their wicked deeds. Let them banish from their minds the very thought of doing wrong! Let them turn to the* LORD *that he may have mercy on them. Yes, turn to our God, for he will abundantly pardon.* (Isaiah 55:6-7)

God offers his mercy. Food costs money, lasts only a short time, and meets only physical needs. But God offers us *free* nourishment that feeds our soul. How do we get it? We come (55:1), listen (55:2), seek, and call on God (55:6). God's salvation is freely offered, but to nourish our souls, we must eagerly receive it. We will starve spiritually without this food as surely as we will starve physically without our daily bread.

BIBLE READING: John 3:1-21
KEY BIBLE VERSE: *God so loved the world that he gave his only Son, so that everyone who believes in him will not perish but have eternal life.* (John 3:16)

God offers his love. The entire gospel comes to a focus in this verse. God's love is not static or self-centered; it reaches out and draws others in. Here God sets the pattern of true love, the basis for all love relationships: When you love someone dearly, you are willing to pay dearly as an expression of that love. God paid dearly with the life of his Son, the highest price he could pay. Jesus accepted our punishment, paid the price for our sins, and then offered us the new life that he had bought for us. When we share the gospel with others, our love must be like Jesus'. We must be willing to give up our own comfort and security so that others might join us in receiving God's love.

Related Topics: COVENANT, FORGIVENESS, SALVATION

BARRIERS *(Blocks, Challenges, Obstacles)*

▶ HARMFUL BARRIERS
What barriers can keep us from God and others?

BIBLE READING: Matthew 8:5-13
KEY BIBLE VERSE: *When Jesus heard this, he was amazed. Turning to the crowd, he said, "I tell you the truth, I haven't seen faith like this in all the land of Israel!"* (Matthew 8:10)

Life is full of natural and artificial barriers. The centurion could have let many obstacles stand between him and Jesus—pride, doubt, money, language, distance, time, self-sufficiency, power, race. But he didn't. If he did not let these barriers block his approach to Jesus, we don't need to either. What keeps you from Christ?

BIBLE READING: John 4:1-26
KEY BIBLE VERSE: *The woman was surprised, for Jews refuse to have anything to do with Samaritans. She said to Jesus, "You are a Jew, and I am a Samaritan woman. Why are you asking me for a drink?"* (John 4:9)

Social and spiritual barriers are real. This woman (1) was a Samaritan, a member of the hated mixed race, (2) was known to be living in sin, and (3) was in a public place. No respectable Jewish man would talk to a woman under such circumstances. But Jesus did. The gospel is for every person regardless of race, social position, or past sins. We must be prepared to share this gospel at any time and in any place. Jesus crossed all barriers to share the gospel, and we who follow him must do no less.

▶ HELPFUL BARRIERS
How can barriers help us grow?

BIBLE READING: Judges 3:1-6
KEY BIBLE VERSE: *These people were left to test the Israelites—to see whether they would obey the commands the LORD had given to their ancestors through Moses.* (Judges 3:4)

Barriers can be challenges to overcome. We learn from an earlier chapter that these enemy nations were still in the land because the Israelites had failed to obey God and drive them out. Now God would allow the enemies to remain in order to "test" the Israelites; that is, to give them an opportunity to exercise faith and obedience. By now the younger generation that had not fought in the great battles of conquest was coming of age. It was their job to complete the conquest of the land. There were many obstacles yet to be overcome in their new homeland. How they would handle these obstacles would be a test of their faith.

Barriers also remind us to rely on God. Perhaps God has left obstacles in your life—hostile people, difficult situations, baffling problems—to allow you to develop faith and obedience. They can be overcome with his help.

▶ HANDLING BARRIERS
How can barriers be overcome?

BIBLE READING: Deuteronomy 1:19-36
KEY BIBLE VERSE: *Don't be afraid! The LORD your God is going before you. He will fight for you, just as you saw him do in Egypt. And you saw how the LORD your God cared for you again and again here in the wilderness, just as a father cares for his child. Now he has brought you to this place.* (Deuteronomy 1:29-31)

God is greater than any barrier. The spies were not sent into the land to determine *whether* they should enter, but *where* they should enter. Upon returning, however, most of the spies concluded that the land was not worth the obstacles. God would give the Israelites the power to conquer the land, but they were afraid of the risk and decided not to enter. God gives us the power to overcome our obstacles, but like the Israelites who were filled with fear and skepticism, we often let difficulties control our life. Following God regardless of the difficulties is the way to have courageous, overcoming faith.

BIBLE READING: Matthew 27:45-56
KEY BIBLE VERSE: *At that moment the curtain in the Temple was torn in two, from top to bottom. The earth shook, rocks split apart, and tombs opened.* (Matthew 27:51)

God has already destroyed the greatest barrier. The temple had three main parts—the courts, the Holy Place (where only the priests could enter), and the Most Holy Place (where only the high priest could enter, and only once a year, to atone for the sins of the nation—Leviticus 16:1-35). The curtain separating the Holy Place from the Most Holy Place was torn in two at Christ's death, symbolizing that the barrier between God and humanity was removed. Now all people are free to approach God because of Christ's sacrifice for our sins (see Hebrews 9:1-14; 10:19-22).

Related Topics: ENDURANCE, PROBLEMS, SALVATION

BASHFUL (*see* CONFIDENCE)

BASICS OF THE FAITH (*Beginnings, Fundamentals, Essentials*)

▶ **KNOWING THE BASICS**
Why are the basics of the faith important?

BIBLE READING: 1 John 2:18-29
KEY BIBLE VERSE: *You must remain faithful to what you have been taught from the beginning. If you do, you will continue to live in fellowship with the Son and with the Father.* (1 John 2:24)

The basics protect us from error. These Christians had heard the gospel, very likely from John himself. They knew that Christ was God's Son, that he died for their sins and was raised to give them new life, and that he would return and establish his kingdom in its fullness. But they were being infiltrated by teachers who denied these basic doctrines of the Christian faith, and some of the believers were in danger of succumbing to false arguments. John encouraged them to hold on to the truth they heard at the beginning of their walk with Christ. It is important to grow in our knowledge of the Lord, to deepen our understanding through careful study, and to teach these truths to others. But no matter how much we learn, we must never abandon the basic truths about Christ. Jesus will always be God's Son, and his sacrifice for our sins is permanent. No truth will ever contradict these teachings in the Bible.

BIBLE READING: 1 Peter 1:3-16
KEY BIBLE VERSE: *Think clearly and exercise self-control. Look forward to the special blessings that will come to you at the return of Jesus Christ. Obey God because you are his children. Don't slip back into your old ways of doing evil; you didn't know any better then. But now you must be holy in everything you do, just as God—who chose you to be his children—is holy.* (1 Peter 1:13-15)

The basics are never outdated. Outstanding coaches constantly review the basics of the sport with their teams, and good athletes can execute the fundamentals consistently well. We must not neglect the basics of our faith when we go on to study deeper truths. Just as an athlete needs constant practice, we need constant reminders of the fundamentals of our faith and of how we came to believe in the first place. Don't allow yourself to remain bored or impatient with messages on the basics of the Christian life. Instead, take the attitude of an athlete who continues to practice and refine the basics even as he learns more advanced skills.

Related Topics: BELIEF/BELIEVE, FAITH, GROWTH

BATTLES (*see* CONFLICTS)

BEAUTY (*Appearance, Attractiveness, Loveliness*)

▶ **BEAUTY IN THE BIBLE**
What kind of beauty is really worth having?

BIBLE READING: Genesis 24:1-67
KEY BIBLE VERSE: *"Certainly, sir," she said, and she quickly lowered the jug for him to drink. When he had finished, she said, "I'll draw water for your camels, too, until they have had enough!"* (Genesis 24:18-19)

Real beauty is inside the person. Rebekah had physical beauty, but the servant was looking for a sign of inner beauty. Physical appearance is important to us, and we spend time and money improving it. But how much effort do we put into developing our inner beauty? Patience, kindness, and joy are the beauty treatments that help us become truly lovely—on the inside.

BIBLE READING: 1 Peter 3:1-7
KEY BIBLE VERSE: *Don't be concerned about the outward beauty that depends on fancy hairstyles, expensive jewelry, or beautiful clothes. You should be known for the beauty that comes from within, the unfading beauty of a gentle and quiet spirit, which is so precious to God.* (1 Peter 3:3-4)

Real beauty affects others positively. A changed life speaks loudly and clearly, and it is often the most effective way to influence a family member. Peter instructs Christian wives to develop inner beauty rather than being overly concerned about their appearance. Their husbands will be won by their love rather than by their looks. Live your Christian faith quietly and consistently in your home, and your family will see Christ in you.

We should not be obsessed by fashion, but neither should we be so unconcerned that we do not bother to care for ourselves. Hygiene, neatness, and grooming are important, but even more important are a person's attitude and spirit. True beauty begins inside.

BIBLE READING: 1 Timothy 2:1-10
KEY BIBLE VERSE: *I want women to be modest in their appearance. They should wear decent and appropriate clothing and not draw attention to themselves by the way they fix their hair or by wearing gold or pearls or expensive clothes. For women who claim to be devoted to God should make themselves attractive by the good things they do.* (1 Timothy 2:9-10)

Real beauty is not self-centered. Apparently, some Christian women were trying to gain respect by looking beautiful rather than becoming Christlike in character. Some may have thought that they could win unbelieving husbands to Christ through their appearance (see Peter's counsel to such women in 1 Peter 3:1-6). It is not unscriptural for a woman to want to be attractive. Beauty, however, begins inside a person. A gentle, modest, loving character gives a light to the face that cannot be duplicated by the best cosmetics and jewelry in the world. A carefully groomed and well-decorated exterior is artificial and cold unless inner beauty is present.

Related Topics: APPEARANCE, IMAGE, SELF-ESTEEM

BEHAVIOR (*see* ACTIONS)

BELIEF/BELIEVE (*Faith, Hope, Trust*)

What kind of believing does God expect?

BIBLE READING: Romans 10:5-13

KEY BIBLE VERSE: *If you confess with your mouth that Jesus is Lord and believe in your heart that God raised him from the dead, you will be saved.* (Romans 10:9)

Believing is a confession from the heart. Have you ever been asked, "How do I become a Christian?" These verses give you the beautiful answer—salvation is as close as your own mouth and heart. People think it must be a complicated process, but it is not. If we believe in our heart and say with our mouth that Christ is the risen Lord, we will be saved.

BIBLE READING: Deuteronomy 27:1-10

KEY BIBLE VERSE: *Obey the LORD your God by keeping all these commands and laws that I am giving you today.* (Deuteronomy 27:10)

Believing includes action. Moses was reviewing the law with the new generation of people. When we decide to believe in God, we must also decide to follow his ways. What we do shows what we really believe. Can people tell that you are a member of God's family?

BIBLE READING: Genesis 15:1-6

KEY BIBLE VERSE: *And Abram believed the LORD, and the LORD declared him righteous because of his faith.* (Genesis 15:6)

Believing is more than action. Although Abram had been demonstrating his faith through his actions, it was his belief in the Lord, not his actions, that made Abram right with God (Romans 4:1-5). We too can have a right relationship with God by trusting him. Our outward actions—church attendance, prayer, good deeds—will not by themselves make us right with God. A right relationship is based on faith—the heartfelt inner confidence that God is who he says he is and does what he says he will do. Right actions will follow naturally as by-products.

What kind of believing does God reject?

BIBLE READING: James 2:14-24

KEY BIBLE VERSE: *Do you still think it's enough just to believe that there is one God? Well, even the demons believe this, and they tremble in terror!* (James 2:19)

It is not enough to believe God exists. At first glance, these verses seem to contradict Romans 3:28, "We are made right with God through faith and not by obeying the law." Deeper investigation, however, shows that the teachings of James and Paul are not at odds. While it is true that our good deeds can never earn salvation, true faith always results in a changed life *and* good deeds. Paul speaks against those who try to be saved by deeds instead of true faith; James speaks against those who confuse mere intellectual assent with true faith. After all, even demons know who Jesus is, but they don't obey him. True faith involves a commitment of your whole self to God.

Related Topics: BELIEVERS, CHURCH, FAITH

BELIEVERS *(Christians, Disciples, Followers)*

▶ **CHARACTERISTICS**
What should be true about believers?

 BIBLE READING: Colossians 3:1-17
KEY BIBLE VERSE: *Whatever you do or say, let it be as a representative of the Lord Jesus, all the while giving thanks through him to God the Father.* (Colossians 3:17)

Believers are marked by Christlike living. Paul offers a strategy to help us live for God day by day: (1) imitate Christ's merciful, forgiving attitude (3:12-13); (2) let love guide your life (3:14); (3) let the peace of Christ rule in your heart (3:15); (4) always be thankful (3:15); (5) keep God's Word in you at all times (3:16); (6) live as Jesus Christ's representative (3:17).

Doing everything "as a representative of the Lord Jesus" means bringing honor to Christ in every aspect and activity of daily living. As a Christian, you represent Christ at all times—wherever you go and whatever you say. What impression do people have of Christ when they see or talk with you? What changes would you make for your life to honor Christ?

Believers are marked by the way they treat each other. Christians should live in peace. This does not eliminate all differences in opinion, but loving Christians will work together despite their differences. Such love is not a feeling, but a decision to meet others' needs (see 1 Corinthians 13). This commitment to others leads to peace between individuals and among the members of the body of believers. Do problems in your relationships with other Christians cause open conflicts or mutual silence? Consider what you can do to heal those relationships with love.

The word *rule* (3:15) comes from athletics: Paul tells us to let Christ's peace be umpire or referee in our hearts. Our heart is the center of conflict because there our feelings and desires clash—our fears and hopes, distrust and trust, jealousy and love. How can we deal with these constant conflicts and live as God wants? Paul explains that we must decide between conflicting elements by using the rule of peace: Which choice will promote peace in our souls and in our churches? For more on the peace of Christ, see Philippians 4:9.

Believers are marked by the way they treat outsiders. The Christian church should have no barriers of nationality, race, education, social standing, wealth, gender, religion, or power. Christ breaks down all barriers and accepts all people who come to him. Nothing should keep us from telling others about Christ or accepting into our fellowship any and all believers (Ephesians 2:14-15). Christians should be building bridges, not walls.

▶ **CHALLENGES FOR BELIEVERS**
What can believers expect to experience?

BIBLE READING: Job 1:1-12
KEY BIBLE VERSE: *Take away everything he has, and he will surely curse you to your face!* (Job 1:11)

Believers shouldn't expect a safe life. Satan attacked Job's motives, saying that Job was blameless and upright only because he had no reason to turn against God. Ever since he had started following God, everything had gone well for Job. Satan wanted to prove that Job worshiped God not out of love, but because God had given him so much.

Satan accurately analyzed why many people trust God. They are fair-weather believers, following God only when everything is going well or for what they can get. Adversity destroys this superficial faith. But adversity strengthens real faith by causing believers to dig their roots deeper into God in order to withstand the storms. How deep does your faith go? Put the roots of your faith down deep into God so that you can withstand any storm you may face.

BIBLE READING: James 1:2-16

KEY BIBLE VERSE: *Dear brothers and sisters, whenever trouble comes your way, let it be an opportunity for joy.* (James 1:2)

Believers can expect difficulties. James doesn't say *if* the way is rough, but *when* it is rough. He assumes we will have trials and that it is possible to profit from them. The point is not to pretend to be happy when we face pain, but to have a positive outlook ("be happy") because of what difficulties can produce in our life. James tells us to turn our hardships into times of learning. Tough times can teach us perseverance. For other passages dealing with perseverance (also called patience and steadfastness), see Romans 2:7; 5:3-5; 8:24-25; 2 Corinthians 6:3-7; 2 Peter 1:2-9.

▶ REQUIREMENTS FOR BELIEVERS
How can you know when you're a believer?

BIBLE READING: Romans 8:1-17

KEY BIBLE VERSE: *But you are not controlled by your sinful nature. You are controlled by the Spirit if you have the Spirit of God living in you. (And remember that those who do not have the Spirit of Christ living in them are not Christians at all.)* (Romans 8:9)

God helps faith grow. Have you ever worried about whether or not you really are a Christian? A Christian is anyone who has the Spirit of God living in him. If you have sincerely trusted Christ for your salvation and acknowledged him as Lord, then the Holy Spirit has come into your life, and you are a Christian. You won't know that the Holy Spirit has come if you are waiting for a certain feeling; you will know he has come because Jesus promised he would. When the Holy Spirit is working within you, you will believe that Jesus Christ is God's Son and that eternal life comes through him (1 John 5:5); you will begin to act as Christ directs (Romans 8:5; Galatians 5:22-23); you will find help in your daily problems and in your praying (Romans 8:26-27); you will be empowered to serve God and do his will (Acts 1:8; Romans 12:6ff.); and you will become part of God's plan to build up his church (Ephesians 4:12-13).

Related Topics: CHURCH, FAITH, SUFFERING

BENEFITS *(Advantages, Profits, Results)*

▶ MISSING GOD'S BENEFITS
What keeps people from receiving all God has for them?

BIBLE READING: 2 Kings 13:10-25

KEY BIBLE VERSE: *But the man of God was angry with him. "You should have struck the ground five or six times!" he exclaimed. "Then you would have beaten Aram until they were entirely destroyed. Now you will be victorious only three times."* (2 Kings 13:19)

Halfhearted obedience yields partial benefits. When Jehoash was told to strike the ground with the arrows, he did it only halfheartedly. As a result, Elisha told the king that his victory over Aram would not be complete. Receiving the full benefits of God's plan for our life requires us to receive and obey God's commands fully. If we don't follow God's complete instructions, we should not be surprised that his full benefits and blessings are not present.

BIBLE READING: Matthew 19:16-30
KEY BIBLE VERSE: *Then Peter said to him, "We've given up everything to follow you. What will we get out of it?"* (Matthew 19:27)

Most of God's benefits are not experienced in this life. In the Bible, God rewards his people according to his justice. In the Old Testament, obedience often brought reward in this life (Deuteronomy 28), but obedience and immediate reward are not always linked. If they were, good people would always be rich, and suffering would always be a sign of sin. Our true reward, as believers, is God's presence and power through the Holy Spirit. Later, in eternity, we will be rewarded for our faith and service. If material rewards in this life came to us for every faithful deed, we would be tempted to boast about our achievements and act out of wrong motivations.

Jesus assured the disciples that anyone who gives up something valuable for his sake will be repaid many times over in this life, although not necessarily in the same form. For example, a person may be rejected by his or her family for accepting Christ, but he or she will gain the larger family of believers.

BIBLE READING: Acts 3:11-26
KEY BIBLE VERSE: *Now turn from your sins and turn to God, so you can be cleansed of your sins.* (Acts 3:19)

Without repentance we miss God's benefits. John the Baptist prepared the way for Jesus by preaching repentance. The apostles' call to salvation also included repentance—acknowledging personal sin and turning away from it. Many people want the benefits of being identified with Christ without turning from sin and admitting their own disobedience. The key to forgiveness is confessing your sin and turning from it (see Acts 2:38).

When we repent, God promises not only to wipe away our sin, but to bring spiritual refreshment. Repentance may at first seem painful because it is hard to give up certain sins. But God will give you a better way. As Hosea promised, "Oh, that we might know the Lord! Then he will respond to us as surely as the arrival of dawn or the coming of rains in early spring" (Hosea 6:3). Do you feel a need to be refreshed?

▶ **RECEIVING GOD'S BENEFITS**
What does God offer, and how do we receive it?

BIBLE READING: Colossians 1:9-14
KEY BIBLE VERSE: *He has rescued us from the one who rules in the kingdom of darkness, and he has brought us into the Kingdom of his dear Son.* (Colossians 1:13)

God's many benefits come through Christ. Paul lists five benefits God gives all believers through Christ: (1) he made us qualified to share his inheritance (see also 2 Corinthians 5:21); (2) he rescued us from Satan's dominion of darkness and made us his children (see also Colossians 2:15); (3) he brought us into his eternal kingdom (see also Ephesians 1:5-6); (4) he redeemed us—bought our freedom from sin and judgment (see also Hebrews 9:12); and (5) he forgave all our sins (see also Ephesians 1:7). Thank God for what you have received in Christ.

Related Topics: GIFTS, HEAVEN, REWARDS

BETRAYAL (*see* ABANDON)

BIBLE (*God's Word, Gospel, Scripture*)

▶ SOURCE OF THE BIBLE
How did we get the Bible?

BIBLE READING: 2 Peter 1:12-21
KEY BIBLE VERSE: *Above all, you must understand that no prophecy in Scripture ever came from the prophets themselves or because they wanted to prophesy. It was the Holy Spirit who moved the prophets to speak from God.* (2 Peter 1:20-21)

God gave us the Bible through people. "It was the Holy Spirit who moved the prophets to speak from God" means that the Scripture did not come from the creative work of the prophets' own invention or interpretation. God inspired the writers, so their message is authentic and reliable. God used the talents, education, and cultural background of each writer (they were not mindless robots); and God cooperated with the writers in such a way to insure that the message he intended was faithfully communicated in the very words they wrote.

BIBLE READING: 2 Timothy 3:10-17
KEY BIBLE VERSE: *All Scripture is inspired by God and is useful to teach us what is true and to make us realize what is wrong in our lives. It straightens us out and teaches us to do what is right.* (2 Timothy 3:16)

God is the source of the Bible. The Bible is not a collection of stories, fables, myths, or merely human ideas about God. It is not a mere human book. Through the Holy Spirit, God revealed his person and plan to certain believers, who wrote down his message for his people (2 Peter 1:20-21). This process is known as *inspiration.* The writers wrote from their own personal, historical, and cultural contexts. Although they used their own mind, talents, language, and style, they wrote what God wanted them to write. Scripture is completely trustworthy because God was in control of its writing. Its words are entirely authoritative for our faith and lives. The Bible is "God-breathed." Read it, and use it to guide your conduct.

▶ PURPOSE OF THE BIBLE
Why was the Bible given to us?

BIBLE READING: Psalm 119:1-176
KEY BIBLE VERSE: *I am but a foreigner here on earth; I need the guidance of your commands. Don't hide them from me!* (Psalm 119:19)

The Bible is a map to guide us. The psalmist says that he is a "foreigner here on earth," and so he needed guidance. Almost any long trip requires a map or guide. As we travel through life, the Bible should be our road map, pointing out safe routes, obstacles to avoid, and our final destination. We must recognize ourselves as pilgrims, travelers here on earth who need to study God's map to learn the way. If we ignore the map, we will wander aimlessly through life and risk missing our real destination.

KEY BIBLE VERSE: *I have more insight than all my teachers, for I am always thinking of your decrees.* (Psalm 119:99)

The Bible gives us wisdom. God's Word makes us wise—wiser than our enemies and wiser than any teachers who ignore it. True wisdom goes beyond amassing knowledge; it is *applying* knowledge in a life-changing way. Intelligent or experienced people are not necessarily wise. Wisdom comes from allowing what God teaches to guide us.

KEY BIBLE VERSE: *Your word is a lamp to my feet and a light for my path.* (Psalm 119:105)

The Bible is a light for our life. To walk safely in the woods at night we need a light so we don't trip over tree roots or fall into holes. In this life, we walk through a dark forest of evil. But the Bible can be our light to show us the way ahead so we won't stumble as we walk. It reveals the entangling roots of false values and philosophies. Study the Bible, so you will be able to see your way clear enough to stay on the right path.

BIBLE READING: 2 Timothy 3:10-17
KEY BIBLE VERSE: *It is God's way of preparing us in every way, fully equipped for every good thing God wants us to do.* (2 Timothy 3:17)

The Bible is basic equipment. In our zeal for the *truth* of Scripture, we must never forget its *purpose*—to equip us to do good. We should not study God's Word simply to increase our knowledge or to prepare us to win arguments. We should study the Bible so that we will know how to do Christ's work in the world. Our knowledge of God's Word is not useful unless it strengthens our faith and leads us to good works.

▶ MESSAGE OF THE BIBLE
What does the Bible tell us?

BIBLE READING: Matthew 5:17-20
KEY BIBLE VERSE: *I assure you, until heaven and earth disappear, even the smallest detail of God's law will remain until its purpose is achieved.* (Matthew 5:18)

The Bible gives us God's commands. If Jesus did not come to abolish the law, does that mean all the Old Testament laws still apply to us today? In the Old Testament, there were three categories of law: ceremonial, civil, and moral.

(1) The *ceremonial law* related specifically to Israel's worship (see Leviticus 1:2-3, for example). Its primary purpose was to point forward to Jesus Christ; these laws, therefore, were no longer necessary after Jesus' death and resurrection. While we are no longer bound by ceremonial laws, the principles behind them—to worship and love a holy God—still apply. Jesus was often accused by the Pharisees of violating ceremonial law.

(2) The *civil law* applied to daily living in Israel (see Deuteronomy 24:10-11, for example). Because modern society and culture are so radically different from that time and setting, all of these guidelines cannot be followed specifically. But the principles behind the commands are timeless and should guide our conduct. Jesus demonstrated these principles by example.

(3) The *moral law* (such as the Ten Commandments) is the direct command of God, and it requires strict obedience (see Exodus 20:13, for example). The moral law reveals the nature and will of God, and it still applies today. Jesus obeyed the moral law completely.

BIBLE READING: Luke 24:1-12

KEY BIBLE VERSE: *He isn't here! He has risen from the dead! Don't you remember what he told you back in Galilee, that the Son of Man must be betrayed into the hands of sinful men and be crucified, and that he would rise again the third day?* (Luke 24:6-7)

The Bible reveals the living God to us. The two angels (appearing as men "clothed in dazzling robes") asked the women why they were looking in a tomb for someone who was alive. Often we run into people who are looking for God among the dead. They study the Bible as a mere historical document and go to church as if going to a memorial service. But Jesus is not among the dead—he lives! He reigns in the hearts of Christians, and he is the head of his church. Do you look for Jesus among the living? Do you expect him to be active in the world and in the church? Look for signs of his power—they are all around you.

BIBLE READING: Hebrews 1:1-3

KEY BIBLE VERSE: *Long ago God spoke many times and in many ways to our ancestors through the prophets. But now in these final days, he has spoken to us through his Son. God promised everything to the Son as an inheritance, and through the Son he made the universe and everything in it.* (Hebrews 1:1-2)

The Bible introduces us to Jesus Christ. The book of Hebrews describes in detail how Jesus Christ not only fulfills the promises and prophecies of the Old Testament, but Jesus Christ is better than everything in the Jewish system of thought. The Jews believed in the Old Testament, but most of them rejected Jesus as the long-awaited Messiah. The recipients of this letter seem to have been Jewish Christians. They were well-versed in Scripture, and they had professed faith in Christ. Whether through doubt, persecution, or false teaching, however, they may have been in danger of giving up their Christian faith and returning to Judaism.

God used many approaches to send his messages to people in Old Testament times. He spoke to Isaiah in visions (Isaiah 6), to Jacob in a dream (Genesis 28:10-22), and to Abraham and Moses personally (Genesis 18; Exodus 31:18). Jewish people familiar with these stories would not have found it hard to believe that God was still revealing his will, but it was astonishing for them to think that God had revealed *himself* by speaking through his Son, Jesus Christ. Jesus is the fulfillment and culmination of God's revelation through the centuries. When we know him, we have all we need to be saved from our sin and to have a perfect relationship with God.

Related Topics: APPLICATION, INSPIRATION, LAW

BITTERNESS *(Anger, Hatred, Joylessness)*

▶ **DANGERS OF BITTERNESS**
Why is it important to resist bitterness?

BIBLE READING: Hebrews 12:14-17

KEY BIBLE VERSE: *Look after each other so that none of you will miss out on the special favor of God. Watch out that no bitter root of unbelief rises up among you, for whenever it springs up, many are corrupted by its poison.* (Hebrews 12:15)

Bitterness will affect others. Like a small root that grows into a great tree, bitterness springs up in our heart and overshadows even our deepest Christian relationships. A "bitter root" comes when we allow disappointment to grow into resentment, or when we nurse grudges over past hurts. Bitterness brings with it jealousy, dissension, and immorality. When the Holy Spirit fills us, however, he can heal the hurt that causes bitterness.

BIBLE READING: 1 John 3:11-24

KEY BIBLE VERSE: *Anyone who hates another Christian is really a murderer at heart. And you know that murderers don't have eternal life within them.* (1 John 3:15)

Bitterness undermines our relationship with God. John echoes Jesus' words that whoever hates another person is a murderer at heart (Matthew 5:21-22). Christianity is a religion of the heart; outward compliance alone is not enough. Bitterness against someone who has wronged you is an evil cancer within you and will eventually destroy you. Don't let a "bitter root" (Hebrews 12:15) grow in you or your church.

▶ AVOIDING BITTERNESS
How can we keep bitterness from taking root?

BIBLE READING: Genesis 33:1-20

KEY BIBLE VERSE: *Then Esau ran to meet him and embraced him affectionately and kissed him. Both of them were in tears.* (Genesis 33:4)

Bitterness doesn't leave by itself. It is refreshing to see Esau's change of heart when the two brothers meet again. The bitterness over losing his birthright and blessing (25:29-34) seems gone. Instead, Esau was content with what he had. Jacob even exclaimed how great it was to see his brother obviously pleased with him (33:10).

Life can bring us some bad situations. We can feel cheated, as Esau did, but we don't have to remain bitter. We can remove bitterness from our life by honestly expressing our feelings to God, forgiving those who have wronged us, and being content with what we have.

BIBLE READING: Luke 15:11-32

KEY BIBLE VERSE: *We had to celebrate this happy day. For your brother was dead and has come back to life! He was lost, but now he is found!* (Luke 15:32)

Bitterness can be removed by forgiveness. In the story of the lost son, the father's response is contrasted with the older brother's. The father forgave because he was filled with love. The older son refused to forgive because he was bitter about the injustice of it all. His resentment rendered him just as lost to the father's love as his younger brother had been. Don't let anything keep you from forgiving others. If you are refusing to forgive people, you are missing a wonderful opportunity to experience joy and share it with others. Make your joy grow: forgive somebody who has hurt you.

Related Topics: ANGER, HATRED, PEACE

BLAME (*see* EXCUSES)

BLASPHEMY (*Arrogance, Deceit, Lying*)

Why is blasphemy treated so seriously in the Bible?

BIBLE READING: Matthew 9:1-8
KEY BIBLE VERSE: *"Blasphemy! This man talks like he is God!" some of the teachers of religious law said among themselves.* (Matthew 9:3)

Jesus was accused of blasphemy. Blaspheming is claiming to be God and applying his characteristics to yourself. The religious leaders rightly saw that Jesus was claiming to be God. What they did not understand was that he *is* God and thus has the authority to heal and to forgive sins.

It's easy to tell someone his sins are forgiven; it's a lot more difficult to reverse a case of paralysis! Jesus backed up his words by healing the man's legs. Jesus' action showed that his words were true; he had the power to forgive as well as to heal. Talk is cheap; our words lack meaning if our actions do not back them up. We can say we love God or others, but if we are not taking practical steps to demonstrate that love, our words are empty and meaningless. How well do your actions back up what you say?

BIBLE READING: Mark 3:20-30
KEY BIBLE VERSE: *Anyone who blasphemes against the Holy Spirit will never be forgiven. It is an eternal sin.* (Mark 3:29)

Blasphemy is a deadly sin. Christians sometimes wonder if they have committed this sin of blasphemy against the Holy Spirit. Christians need not worry about this sin because this sin is attributing to the devil the work of the Holy Spirit. It reveals a heart attitude of unbelief and unrepentance. Deliberate, ongoing rejection of the work of the Holy Spirit is blasphemy because it is rejecting God himself. The religious leaders accused Jesus of blasphemy, but ironically they were the guilty ones when they looked Jesus in the face and accused him of being possessed by Satan.

Related Topics: CONVERSATION, PRAISE, WORDS

BLESSING (*Benediction, Benefit, Hoped-for Result*)

▶ **SAMPLE BLESSINGS**
What is a blessing?

BIBLE READING: Numbers 6:22-27
KEY BIBLE VERSE: *May the LORD bless you and protect you. May the LORD smile on you and be gracious to you. May the LORD show you his favor and give you his peace.* (Numbers 6:24-26)

A blessing is a hopeful prayer. A blessing was one way of asking for God's divine favor to rest upon others. The ancient blessing in these verses helps us understand what a blessing was supposed to do. Its five parts conveyed hope that God would (1) bless and keep them (bless and protect); (2) make his face shine upon them (smile); (3) be gracious; (4) turn his face toward them (show his favor); (5) give peace. When you ask God to bless others or yourself, you are asking him to do these five things. The blessing you offer will not only help the one receiving it, it will also demonstrate love, encourage others, and provide a model of caring to others.

BIBLE READING: Ephesians 3:14-21
KEY BIBLE VERSE: *I pray that Christ will be more and more at home in your hearts as you trust in him. May your roots go down deep into the soil of God's marvelous love.* (Ephesians 3:17)

Christian growth is a blessing. The family of God includes all who have believed in him in the past, all who believe in the present, and all who will believe in the future. We are all a family because we have the same Father. God is the source of all creation, the rightful owner of everything. He promises his love and power to his family, the church (Ephesians 3:16-21). If we want to receive God's blessings, it is important that we stay in contact with other believers in the body of Christ. Those who isolate themselves from God's family and try to go it alone cut themselves off from God's power. But those who live within the body of Christ discover the blessing of Jesus becoming more and more at home in them.

▶GOD'S BLESSING
In what ways does God bless?

BIBLE READING: Genesis 12:1-7
KEY BIBLE VERSE: *I will bless those who bless you and curse those who curse you. All the families of the earth will be blessed through you.* (Genesis 12:3)

God blesses through his eternal plans. God planned to develop a nation of people he would call his own. He called Abram from the godless, self-centered city of Ur to a fertile region called Canaan, where a God-centered, moral nation could be established. Though small in dimension, the land of Canaan was the focal point for most of the history of Israel as well as for the rise of Christianity. This small land given to one man, Abram, has had a tremendous impact on world history.

God promised to bless Abram and make him great, but there was one condition. Abram had to do what God wanted him to do. This meant leaving his home and friends and traveling to a new land where God promised to build a great nation from Abram's family. Abram obeyed, walking away from his home for God's promise of even greater blessings in the future. God may be trying to lead you to a place of greater service and usefulness for him. Don't let the comfort and security of your present position make you miss God's plan for you.

BIBLE READING: Ephesians 1:3-14
KEY BIBLE VERSE: *How we praise God, the Father of our Lord Jesus Christ, who has blessed us with every spiritual blessing in the heavenly realms because we belong to Christ.* (Ephesians 1:3)

Jesus is God's greatest blessing. "Who has blessed us with every spiritual blessing in the heavenly realms" means that in Christ we have all the benefits of knowing God—chosen for salvation, being adopted as his children, forgiveness, insight, the gifts of the Spirit, power to do God's will, the hope of living forever with Christ. Because we have an intimate relationship with Christ, we can enjoy these blessings now. The *heavenly realms* means that these blessings are eternal, not temporal. They are from Christ's spiritual realm, not the earthly realm of the goddess Artemis. Other references to the heavenly realms in Ephesians include 1:20; 2:6; 3:10. They show Christ in his victorious, exalted role as ruler of all.

▶ **HUMAN BLESSINGS**
In what ways can we bless others?

BIBLE READING: Psalm 103
KEY BIBLE VERSE: *Praise the LORD, I tell myself; with my whole heart, I will praise his holy name.* (Psalm 103:1)

We can bless God. Everything everywhere is to bless the Lord: all angels—mighty ones and heavenly hosts—and all his works! Blessing God means remembering all he has done for us (103:2), fearing him and obeying his commands (103:17-18), and doing his will (103:21). Does your life bless the Lord?

David's praise focused on God's glorious deeds. It is easy to complain about life, but David's list gives us plenty for which to praise God—he forgives our sins, heals our diseases, redeems us from death, crowns us with love and compassion, satisfies our desires, and gives righteousness and justice. We receive all of these without deserving any of them. No matter how difficult your life's journey, you can always count your blessings—past, present, and future. When you feel as though you have nothing for which to praise God, read David's list.

BIBLE READING: Genesis 49:1-28
KEY BIBLE VERSE: *These are the twelve tribes of Israel, and these are the blessings with which Jacob blessed his twelve sons. Each received a blessing that was appropriate to him.* (Genesis 49:28)

We can bless family members. Jacob blessed each of his sons and then made a prediction about each one's future. The way the men had lived played an important part in Jacob's blessing and prophecy. There was a strong tradition at this time of a father passing on special blessings to his children. These blessings were a heartfelt expression of a parent's hopes or vision for his children's future. How often do you share with your children, spouse, or parents the wishes and prayers you make for their future?

BIBLE READING: Luke 2:21-35
KEY BIBLE VERSE: *Then Simeon blessed them, and he said to Mary, "This child will be rejected by many in Israel, and it will be their undoing. But he will be the greatest joy to many others. Thus, the deepest thoughts of many hearts will be revealed. And a sword will pierce your very soul."* (Luke 2:34-35)

We can bless complete strangers. Although Simeon was very old, he had never lost his hope that he would see the Messiah. Led by the Holy Spirit, he was among the first to bear witness to Jesus. In the Jewish culture, elders were respected, so because of Simeon's age, his blessing carried extra weight. Our society, however, values youthfulness over wisdom, and potential contributions by the elderly are often ignored. As Christians, we should reverse those values wherever we can. Encourage older people to share their wisdom and experience. Listen carefully when they speak. Offer them your friendship and help them find ways to continue to serve God. In this way you will bless and be blessed.

BIBLE READING: Luke 6:27-36
KEY BIBLE VERSE: *Pray for the happiness of those who curse you. Pray for those who hurt you.* (Luke 6:28)

We are commanded to bless our enemies. The Jews despised the Romans because they oppressed God's people, but Jesus told the people to love and bless these enemies. Such words turned many away from Christ. But Jesus wasn't talking about having affection for enemies; he was talking about an act of the will. You can't "fall into" this kind of love—it takes conscious effort. Loving our enemies means acting in their best interests. We can bless them by praying for them, and we can think of ways to help them. Jesus loved the whole world, even though the world was in rebellion against God. Jesus asks us to follow his example by loving our enemies. Grant your enemies the same respect and rights that you desire for yourself.

Related Topics: BENEFITS, FAITHFULNESS, GOD'S WILL

BLINDNESS *(Lostness, Rebellion, Sightlessness)*

How is blindness treated in the Bible?

BIBLE READING: John 9:1-41

KEY BIBLE VERSE: *He told them, "The man they call Jesus made mud and smoothed it over my eyes and told me, 'Go to the pool of Siloam and wash off the mud.' I went and washed, and now I can see!"* (John 9:11)

Blindness was a physical disease Jesus healed. A common belief in Jewish culture was that calamity or suffering was the result of some great sin. But Christ used this man's suffering to teach others about faith and to glorify God. We live in a fallen world where good behavior is not always rewarded and bad behavior not always punished. Therefore, innocent people sometimes suffer. If God took suffering away whenever we asked, we would follow him for comfort and convenience, not out of love and devotion. Regardless of the reasons for our suffering, Jesus has the power to help us deal with it. When you suffer from disease, tragedy, or disability, try not to ask, "Why did this happen to me?" or "What did I do wrong?" Instead, ask God to give you strength for the trial and a clearer perspective on what is happening.

BIBLE READING: Psalm 139:13-16

KEY BIBLE VERSE: *Thank you for making me so wonderfully complex! Your workmanship is marvelous—and how well I know it.* (Psalm 139:14)

God is the creator of the human body. As an artist gives value to his or her work, so God gives infinite value to us by being our artist. God's character goes into the creation of every person. When you feel worthless or even begin to hate yourself, remember that God's Spirit is ready and willing to work within you. We should have as much respect for ourselves as our Maker has for us.

BIBLE READING: 1 Corinthians 15:35-58

KEY BIBLE VERSE: *Our earthly bodies, which die and decay, will be different when they are resurrected, for they will never die.* (1 Corinthians 15:42)

We do not die when our physical body dies. In this section Paul launches into a discussion about what our resurrected bodies will be like. If you could select your own body, what kind would you choose—strong, athletic, beautiful? Paul explains that we will be recognized in our resurrected bodies, yet they will be better than we can imagine, for they will be made to live forever. Our present bodies are perishable and liable to decay. Our resurrection bodies will be transformed. We will still have our own personalities and individualities, but these will be perfected through Christ's work. These spiritual bodies will not be limited by the laws of nature. This does not necessarily mean we'll be superhuman, but our bodies will be different and more capable than our present earthly bodies. The Bible does not reveal everything that our resurrected bodies will be able to do, but we know they will be perfect, without sickness or disease (see Philippians 3:21).

BIBLE READING: Romans 12:1-8
KEY BIBLE VERSE: *Dear brothers and sisters, I plead with you to give your bodies to God. Let them be a living and holy sacrifice—the kind he will accept. When you think of what he has done for you, is this too much to ask?* (Romans 12:1)

Our body is to be a living sacrifice. When sacrificing an animal according to God's law, a priest would kill the animal, cut it in pieces, and place it on the altar. Sacrifice was important, but even in the Old Testament God made it clear that obedience from the heart was much more important (see 1 Samuel 15:22; Psalm 40:6; Amos 5:21-24). God wants us to offer ourselves, not animals, as *living* sacrifices—daily laying aside our own desires to follow him, putting all our energy and resources at his disposal and trusting him to guide us. We do this out of gratitude that our sins have been forgiven.

BIBLE READING: 1 Corinthians 6:15-20
KEY BIBLE VERSE: *Don't you know that your body is the temple of the Holy Spirit, who lives in you and was given to you by God? You do not belong to yourself, for God bought you with a high price. So you must honor God with your body.* (1 Corinthians 6:19-20)

God's Spirit lives in the bodies of Christians. What did Paul mean when he said that our body belongs to God? Many people say they have the right to do whatever they want with their own bodies. Although they think that this is freedom, they are really enslaved to their own desires. When we become Christians, the Holy Spirit fills us and lives within us. Therefore, we no longer own our body. "Bought with a high price" refers to slaves purchased at auction. Christ's death freed us from sin but also obligates us to his service. If you live in a building owned by someone else, you try not to violate the building rules. Because your body belongs to God, you must not violate his standards for living.

Related Topics: CHURCH, FELLOWSHIP, RESURRECTION

BOLDNESS (*see* COURAGE)

BOREDOM (*Apathy, Restlessness, Tiredness*)

▶ **BOREDOM: ITS SOURCE**
What brings on boredom?

BIBLE READING: Ecclesiastes 2:1-11
KEY BIBLE VERSE: *As I looked at everything I had worked so hard to accomplish, it was all so meaningless. It was like chasing the wind. There was nothing really worthwhile anywhere.* (Ecclesiastes 2:11)

Boredom comes from a self-centered outlook. Solomon conducted his search for life's meaning as an experiment. He first tried pursuing pleasure. He undertook great projects, bought slaves and herds and flocks, amassed wealth, acquired singers, added many women to his harem, and became the greatest person in Jerusalem. But none of these gave him satisfaction. Some of the pleasures Solomon sought were wrong and some were worthwhile, but even the worthy pursuits were futile when he pursued them as ends in themselves. We must look beyond our activities to the reasons we do them and the purpose they fulfill. Is your goal in life to search for meaning or to search for God who gives meaning?

BIBLE READING: Galatians 3:1-5
KEY BIBLE VERSE: *I ask you again, does God give you the Holy Spirit and work miracles among you because you obey the law of Moses? Of course not! It is because you believe the message you heard about Christ.* (Galatians 3:5)

Boredom may actually be fatigue. The Holy Spirit gives Christians great power to live for God. Some Christians want more than this. They want to live in a state of perpetual excitement. The tedium of everyday living leads them to conclude that something is wrong spiritually. But power-filled living and busyness are different things. Often the Holy Spirit's greatest work is teaching us to persist, to keep on doing what is right even when it no longer seems interesting or exciting. The Galatians quickly turned from Paul's Good News to the teachings of the newest teachers in town; they needed the Holy Spirit's gift of persistence. If the Christian life seems ordinary, you may need the Spirit to stir you up. Every day offers a challenge to live for Christ.

Related Topics: DEPRESSION, ENTHUSIASM, WORK

BORN AGAIN (*see* SALVATION)

BORROWING (*see* MONEY)

BOUNDARIES (*see* AUTHORITY, BARRIERS)

BOWING (*Honoring, Kneeling, Worshiping*)

How is bowing a proper response to God?

BIBLE READING: Ezekiel 1:1-28
KEY BIBLE VERSE: *All around him was a glowing halo, like a rainbow shining through the clouds. This was the way the glory of the LORD appeared to me. When I saw it, I fell face down in the dust, and I heard someone's voice speaking to me.* (Ezekiel 1:28)

God's holiness is completely humbling. The glory of the Lord appeared like fire and brilliant light to Ezekiel. Ezekiel fell facedown, overwhelmed by the contrast between God's holiness and his own sinfulness and insignificance. Eventually every person will fall before God, either out of reverence and awe for his mercy or out of fear of his judgment. Based on the way you are living today, how will you respond to God's holiness?

BIBLE READING: Philippians 2:5-11
KEY BIBLE VERSE: *God raised him up to the heights of heaven and gave him a name that is above every other name, so that at the name of Jesus every knee will bow, in heaven and on earth and under the earth, and every tongue will confess that Jesus Christ is Lord, to the glory of God the Father.* (Philippians 2:9-11)

God's holiness is completely convincing. At the Last Judgment, even those who are condemned will recognize Jesus' authority and right to rule. People can choose to regard Jesus as Lord now as a step of willing and loving commitment, or be forced to acknowledge him as Lord when he returns. We can bow in obedience and accept his loving grace now or bow before his judgment in the future. Christ may return at any moment. Are you prepared to meet him?

Related Topics: HONOR, OBEDIENCE, WORSHIP

▬
BRAGGING *(see* PRIDE*)*

▬
BREVITY *(see* LIFE*)*

▬
BRIBES *(see* DISHONESTY*)*

▬
BUILDINGS *(Churches, Homes, Structures)*

What does the Bible teach about buildings?

BIBLE READING: 1 Kings 8:1-21
KEY BIBLE VERSE: *Blessed be the LORD, the God of Israel, who has kept the promise he made to my father, David. For he told my father, "From the day I brought my people Israel out of Egypt, I have never chosen a city among the tribes of Israel as the place where a temple should be built to honor my name. But now I have chosen David to be king over my people."* (1 Kings 8:15-16)

God is more concerned with people than buildings. For 480 years after Israel's escape from Egypt, God did not ask them to build a temple for him. Instead he emphasized the importance of his presence among them and their need for spiritual leaders. It is easy to think of a building as the focus of God's presence and power, but God chooses and uses *people* to do his work. He can use you more than he can use a building of wood and stone. Building or enlarging our place of worship may be necessary, but it should never take priority over developing spiritual leaders.

BIBLE READING: Acts 7:44-53
KEY BIBLE VERSE: *The Most High doesn't live in temples made by human hands. As the prophet says, "Heaven is my throne, and the earth is my footstool. Could you ever build me a temple as good as that?" asks the Lord. "Could you build a dwelling place for me?"* (Acts 7:48-49)

God is not confined to buildings set aside for him. Stephen had been accused of speaking against the temple (6:13). Although he recognized the importance of the temple, he knew that it was not more important than God. God is not limited; he doesn't live only in a house of worship, but wherever hearts of faith are open to receive him (Isaiah 66:1-2). Solomon knew this when he prayed at the dedication of the temple (2 Chronicles 6:18). God wants to live in us. Is he living in you?

Related Topics: BELIEVERS, CHURCH, WORSHIP

BURDENS (*Concerns, Problems, Worries*)

How can we handle burdens?

 BIBLE READING: Exodus 1:1-14

KEY BIBLE VERSE: *The more the Egyptians oppressed them, the more quickly the Israelites multiplied! The Egyptians soon became alarmed and decided to make their slavery more bitter still.* (Exodus 1:12-13)

Burdens can make us stronger. The Egyptians tried to wear down the Hebrew people by forcing them into slavery and mistreating them. Instead, the Hebrews multiplied and grew stronger. When we are burdened or mistreated, we may feel defeated. But our burdens can make us stronger and develop qualities in us that will prepare us for the future. We cannot be overcomers without troubles to overcome. Be true to God in the hard times because even the worst situations can make us better people.

BIBLE READING: Psalm 145:1-21

KEY BIBLE VERSE: *The LORD helps the fallen and lifts up those bent beneath their loads.* (Psalm 145:14)

God can help us carry burdens. Sometimes our burdens seem more than we can bear, and we wonder how we can go on. David stands at this bleak intersection of life's road and points toward the Lord, the great burden-bearer. God is able to lift us up because (1) his greatness is unfathomable (145:3); (2) he does mighty acts across many generations (145:4); (3) he is full of glorious splendor and majesty (145:5); (4) he does wonderful and awesome works (145:5-6); (5) he is righteous (145:7); (6) he is gracious, compassionate, patient, and loving (145:8-9); (7) he rules over an everlasting kingdom (145:13); (8) he is the source of all our daily needs (145:15-16); (9) he is righteous and loving in all his dealings (145:17); (10) he remains near to those who call on him (145:18); (11) he hears our cries and saves us (145:19-20). If you are bending under a burden and feel that you are about to fall, turn to God for help. He is ready to lift you up and bear your burden.

BIBLE READING: Matthew 11:25-30

KEY BIBLE VERSE: *Then Jesus said, "Come to me, all of you who are weary and carry heavy burdens, and I will give you rest."* (Matthew 11:28)

Jesus frees us from burdens. A yoke is a heavy wooden harness that fits over the shoulders of an ox or oxen. It is attached to a piece of equipment the oxen are to pull. A person may be carrying heavy burdens of (1) sin, (2) excessive demands of religious leaders (Matthew 23:4; Acts 15:10), (3) oppression and persecution, or (4) weariness in the search for God. Jesus frees people from all these burdens. The rest that Jesus promises is love, healing, and peace with God, not the end of all labor. A relationship with God changes meaningless, wearisome toil into spiritual productivity and purpose.

Related Topics: PEACE, PROBLEMS, TRUST

BUSINESS (*see* WORK)

BUSYNESS (*see* ACTIONS)

CALL *(Assignment, Ministry, Vocation)*

▶ GOD'S CALL
How does God call people?

 BIBLE READING: 1 Chronicles 22:2-19
KEY BIBLE VERSE: *Now, my son, may the LORD be with you and give you success as you follow his instructions in building the Temple of the LORD your God.* (1 Chronicles 22:11)

God communicates through our parents. God told David he would not be the one to build the temple. Instead the task would be left to his son Solomon. David graciously accepted this "no" from God. He was not jealous of the fact that his son would have the honor of building God's temple. Instead, he made preparations for Solomon to carry out his task. Similarly, we should take steps now to prepare the way for our children to find and fulfill God's purpose. Sooner or later our children will have to make their own decisions, but we can help by supplying them with the proper tools: showing them how to pray and study God's Word, teaching them the difference between right and wrong, and modeling the importance of church involvement.

BIBLE READING: Matthew 4:18-25
KEY BIBLE VERSE: *Jesus called out to them, "Come, be my disciples, and I will show you how to fish for people!"* (Matthew 4:19)

Being Christ's disciple involves firm commitment. These men already knew Jesus. He had talked to Peter and Andrew previously (John 1:35-42) and had been preaching in the area. When Jesus called them, they knew what kind of man he was and were willing to follow him. They were not in a hypnotic trance when they followed but had been thoroughly convinced that following him would change their lives forever.

James and his brother, John, along with Peter and Andrew, were the first disciples that Jesus called to work with him. Jesus' call motivated these men to get up and leave their jobs—immediately. They didn't make excuses about why it wasn't a good time. They left at once and followed. Jesus calls each of us to follow him. When Jesus asks us to serve him, we must be like the disciples and do it at once.

▶ GOD'S PURPOSE
What does God call people to do?

BIBLE READING: Jeremiah 1:1-10
KEY BIBLE VERSE: *I knew you before I formed you in your mother's womb. Before you were born I set you apart and appointed you as my spokesman to the world.* (Jeremiah 1:5)

God calls people to serve him. Jeremiah was "appointed" by God "as my spokesman to the world." God has a purpose for each Christian, but some people are appointed by God for specific kinds of work. Samson (Judges 13:3-5), David (1 Samuel 16:12, 13), John the Baptist (Luke 1:13-17), and Paul (Galatians 1:15-16) were also called to do particular jobs for God. Whatever work you do should be done for the glory of God (1 Corinthians 10:31). If God gives you a specific task, accept it cheerfully and do it with diligence. If God has not given you a specific call or assignment, then seek to fulfill the mission common to all believers—to love, obey, and serve God—until his guidance becomes more clear.

BIBLE READING: Matthew 10:1-18
KEY BIBLE VERSE: *Jesus called his twelve disciples to him and gave them authority to cast out evil spirits and to heal every kind of disease and illness.* (Matthew 10:1)

God calls people to represent him in the world. Jesus *called* his twelve disciples. He didn't draft them, force them, or ask them to volunteer; he chose them to serve him in a special way. Christ calls us today. He doesn't twist our arms and make us do something we don't want to do. We can choose to join him or remain behind. When Christ calls you to follow him, how do you respond?

The list of Jesus' twelve disciples doesn't give us many details—probably because there weren't many impressive details to tell. Jesus called people from all walks of life—fishermen, political activists, tax collectors. He called common people and uncommon leaders; rich and poor; educated and uneducated. Today, many people think only certain people are fit to follow Christ, but this was not the attitude of the Master himself. God can use anyone, no matter how insignificant he or she appears. When you feel small and useless, remember that God uses ordinary people to do his extraordinary work.

Related Topics: COMMITMENT, OBEDIENCE, SERVING

CAPABILITY (*see* ABILITIES)

CARELESSNESS (*Apathy, Recklessness, Unconcern*)

How can carelessness be a dangerous attitude?

BIBLE READING: Matthew 7:24-29
KEY BIBLE VERSE: *But anyone who hears my teaching and ignores it is foolish, like a person who builds a house on sand.* (Matthew 7:26)

Carelessness can lead to fatal mistakes. Like a house of cards, the fool's life crumbles. Most people do not deliberately seek to build on a false or inferior foundation; instead, they just don't think about their life's purpose. Many people are headed for destruction, not out of stubbornness but out of thoughtlessness. Part of our responsibility as believers is to help others stop and think about where their lives are headed and to point out the consequences of ignoring Christ's message.

BIBLE READING: 2 Chronicles 24:1-16
KEY BIBLE VERSE: *He summoned the priests and Levites and gave them these instructions: "Go at once to all the towns of Judah and collect the required annual offerings, so that we can repair the Temple of your God. Do not delay!" But the Levites did not act right away.* (2 Chronicles 24:5)

Carelessness can be a form of disobedience to God. The Levites took their time carrying out the king's order, even though he told them not to delay. A tax for keeping the temple in order was not just the king's order but God's command (Exodus 30:11-16). The Levites, therefore, were not only disregarding the king but disregarding God. When it comes to following God's commands, a slow response may be little better than disobedience. Obey God willingly and immediately.

BIBLE READING: Leviticus 10:1-7
KEY BIBLE VERSE: *Aaron's sons Nadab and Abihu put coals of fire in their incense burners and sprinkled incense over it. In this way, they disobeyed the LORD by burning before him a different kind of fire than he had commanded.* (Leviticus 10:1)

Carelessness can be a form of disrespect towards God. Aaron's sons were careless about following the laws for sacrifices. In response, God destroyed them with a blast of fire. Performing the sacrifices was an act of obedience. Doing them correctly showed respect for God. It is easy for us to grow careless about obeying God, to live our way instead of God's. But if one way were just as good as another, God would not have commanded us to live his way. He always has good reasons for his commands, and we always place ourselves in danger when we consciously or carelessly disobey them.

Related Topics: ATTITUDE, CONSISTENCY, OBEDIENCE

CARING *(Concern, Kindness, Love)*

▶ **GOD CARES**
Does God really care?

BIBLE READING: 2 Kings 4:8-37
KEY BIBLE VERSE: *Then Elisha summoned Gehazi. "Call the child's mother!" he said. And when she came in, Elisha said, "Here, take your son!"* (2 Kings 4:36)

God cares for hurting people. Elisha's prayer and method of raising the dead boy show God's personal care for hurting people. We must express genuine concern for others as we carry God's message to them. Only then will we faithfully represent our compassionate Father in heaven.

BIBLE READING: John 11:17-44
KEY BIBLE VERSE: *Then Jesus wept.* (John 11:35)

Jesus demonstrated God's care. John stresses that we have a God who cares. This portrait contrasts with the Greek concept of God that was popular in that day—a God with no emotions and no messy involvement with humans. Here we see many of Jesus' emotions—compassion, indignation, sorrow, even frustration. When Jesus saw the weeping and wailing, he too wept openly. Perhaps he empathized with their grief, or perhaps he was troubled at their unbelief. In either case, Jesus showed that he cares enough for us to weep with us in our sorrow. He often expressed deep emotion, and we must never be afraid to reveal our true feelings to him. He understands them, for he experienced them. Be honest, and don't try to hide anything from your Savior. He cares.

BIBLE READING: Luke 14:7-14

KEY BIBLE VERSE: *Invite the poor, the crippled, the lame, and the blind. Then at the resurrection of the godly, God will reward you for inviting those who could not repay you.* (Luke 14:13-14)

Jesus taught the importance of genuine caring. Jesus taught two lessons in this passage. First, he spoke to the guests, telling them not to seek places of honor. Service is more important in God's kingdom than status. Second, he told the host not to be exclusive about whom he invites. Caring is demonstrated when we reach out to those who don't expect our help. Caring focuses on the less fortunate. God opens his kingdom to everyone.

▶ **HUMAN CARING**

What kind of caring does God expect from his people?

BIBLE READING: Romans 1:1-12

KEY BIBLE VERSE: *You are among those who have been called to belong to Jesus Christ, dear friends in Rome. God loves you dearly, and he has called you to be his very own people. May grace and peace be yours from God our Father and the Lord Jesus Christ.* (Romans 1:6-7)

God expects caring that encourages. Paul showed his love for the Roman Christians by expressing God's love for them and his own thanks and prayers for them. To have an effect on people's lives, you first need to love them and believe in them. Paul's passion to teach these people began with his love for them. Thank God for your Christian brothers and sisters, and let them know how deeply you care for them.

BIBLE READING: Galatians 4:8-14

KEY BIBLE VERSE: *But even though my sickness was revolting to you, you did not reject me and turn me away. No, you took me in and cared for me as though I were an angel from God or even Christ Jesus himself.* (Galatians 4:14)

God expects us to care for those in need. Paul's illness was a sickness that he was enduring while he visited the Galatian churches. The world is often callous to people's pain and misery. Paul commended the Galatians for not scorning him, even though his condition was a trial to them (he didn't explain what was wrong with him). Such caring was what Jesus meant when he called us to serve the homeless, hungry, sick, and imprisoned as if they were Jesus himself (Matthew 25:34-40). Do you avoid those in pain or facing difficulty—or are you willing to care for them as if they were Jesus Christ himself?

BIBLE READING: Acts 20:25-38

KEY BIBLE VERSE: *When he had finished speaking, he knelt and prayed with them.* (Acts 20:36)

Real caring is often returned. Paul's relationship with these believers is a beautiful example of Christian fellowship. He had cared for them and loved them, even cried over their needs. They responded with love and care for him and sorrow over his leaving. They prayed together and comforted one another. Like Paul, you can build strong relationships with other Christians by sharing, caring, sorrowing, rejoicing, and praying with them. You will gather others around you only by giving yourself away to them.

Related Topics: COMPASSION, KINDNESS, LOVE

CELEBRATION *(Excitement, Party, Praise)*

How does the Bible make celebration an important part of life?

BIBLE READING: Leviticus 23:1-44

KEY BIBLE VERSE: *The LORD said to Moses, "Give the Israelites instructions regarding the LORD's appointed festivals, the days when all of you will be summoned to worship me." (Leviticus 23:1-2)*

True worship includes celebration. Worship involves both celebration and confession. But in the case of Israel's national holidays, the balance seems heavily tipped in favor of celebration—five joyous occasions to two solemn ones. The God of the Bible encourages joy! For example, the Feast of Tabernacles, also called the Feast of Ingathering, was a special celebration involving the whole family (see Leviticus 23:34; Exodus 23:16; Deuteronomy 16:13). Like Passover, this feast taught family members of all ages about God's nature and what he had done for them and was a time of renewed commitment to God.

God does not intend for religion to be only meditation and introspection. He also wants us to celebrate. Serious reflection and immediate confession of sin is essential, of course. But this should be balanced by celebrating who God is and what he has done for his people. Families also need rituals of celebration to renew their faith and to pass it on to their children. In addition to Christmas and Easter, we should select other special days to commemorate God's goodness.

BIBLE READING: Nehemiah 8:1-18

KEY BIBLE VERSE: *Then Nehemiah the governor, Ezra the priest and scribe, and the Levites who were interpreting for the people said to them, "Don't weep on such a day as this! For today is a sacred day before the LORD your God." All the people had been weeping as they listened to the words of the law. And Nehemiah continued, "Go and celebrate with a feast of choice foods and sweet drinks, and share gifts of food with people who have nothing prepared. This is a sacred day before our Lord. Don't be dejected and sad, for the joy of the LORD is your strength!" (Nehemiah 8:9-10)*

Celebration is a way of giving. The people wept openly when they heard God's laws and realized how far they were from obeying them. But Ezra told them they should be filled with joy because the day was holy. It was time to celebrate and to give gifts to those in need.

Celebration is not to be self-centered. Ezra connected celebration with giving. This gave those in need an opportunity to celebrate as well. Often when we celebrate and give to others (even when we don't feel like it), we are strengthened spiritually and filled with joy. Enter into celebrations that honor God and allow him to fill you with his joy.

BIBLE READING: 2 Kings 23:1-23

KEY BIBLE VERSE: *There had not been a Passover celebration like that since the time when the judges ruled in Israel, throughout all the years of the kings of Israel and Judah. (2 Kings 23:22)*

God encourages heartfelt celebration. When Josiah rediscovered the Passover in the Book of the Covenant, he ordered everyone to observe the ceremonies exactly as prescribed. This Passover celebration was to have been a yearly holiday celebrated in remembrance of the entire nation's deliverance from slavery in Egypt (Exodus 12), but it had not been kept for many years. It is a common misconception that God is against celebration, wanting to take all the fun out of life. In reality, God wants to give us life in its fullness (John 10:10), and those who love him have the most to celebrate.

BIBLE READING: Luke 15:1-10
KEY BIBLE VERSE: *There is joy in the presence of God's angels when even one sinner repents.* (Luke 15:10)

There is celebration in heaven. Palestinian women received ten silver coins as a wedding gift. Besides their monetary value, these coins held sentimental value like that of a wedding ring, and to lose one would be extremely distressing. Just as a woman would rejoice at finding her lost coin or ring, so the angels would rejoice over a repentant sinner. Each individual is precious to God. He grieves over every loss and rejoices whenever one of his children is found and brought into the kingdom. Perhaps we would have more joy in our churches if we shared Jesus' love and concern for the lost.

Related Topics: HEAVEN, PRAISE, WORSHIP

CHALLENGE *(Confront, Dare, Test)*

▶ **CHALLENGES FROM PEOPLE**
How can people challenge one another?

BIBLE READING: Nehemiah 2:11-20
KEY BIBLE VERSE: *I told them about how the gracious hand of God had been on me, and about my conversation with the king. They replied at once, "Good! Let's rebuild the wall!" So they began the good work.* (Nehemiah 2:18)

We can challenge others by sharing our vision. Spiritual renewal often begins with one person's vision. Nehemiah had a vision, and he shared it with enthusiasm, inspiring Jerusalem's leaders to rebuild the walls.

We frequently underestimate people and don't challenge them with our dreams for God's work in the world. When God plants an idea in your mind to accomplish something for him, share it with others and trust the Holy Spirit to impress them with similar thoughts. Don't regard yourself as the only one through whom God is working. Often God uses one person to express the vision and others to turn it into reality. When you encourage and inspire others, you put teamwork into action to accomplish God's goals.

BIBLE READING: 2 Peter 3:1-18
KEY BIBLE VERSE: *Grow in the special favor and knowledge of our Lord and Savior Jesus Christ. To him be all glory and honor, both now and forevermore. Amen.* (2 Peter 3:18)

We can expect the world to challenge our faith. Peter concludes this brief letter as he began, by urging his readers to grow in the grace and knowledge of the Lord and Savior Jesus Christ—to get to know him better and better. This is the most important step in refuting false teachers. No matter where we are in our spiritual journey, no matter how mature we are in our faith, the sinful world always will challenge our faith. We still have much room for growth. If every day we find some way to draw closer to Christ, we will be prepared to stand for truth in all circumstances.

▶ CHALLENGES FROM GOD
In what ways does God challenge us?

BIBLE READING: John 8:31-47
KEY BIBLE VERSE: *Which of you can truthfully accuse me of sin? And since I am telling you the truth, why don't you believe me?* (John 8:46)

We are challenged to "test" Jesus. In a number of places Jesus intentionally challenged his listeners to test him. He welcomed those who wanted to question his claims and character as long as they were willing to follow through on what they discovered. Jesus' challenge clarifies the two most frequent reasons that people miss encountering him: (1) they never accept his challenge to test him, or (2) they test him but are not willing to believe what they discover. Have you made either of those mistakes?

BIBLE READING: Joshua 1:1-9
KEY BIBLE VERSE: *No one will be able to stand their ground against you as long as you live. For I will be with you as I was with Moses. I will not fail you or abandon you.* (Joshua 1:5)

God challenges us to let him help with our challenges. Joshua's new job consisted of leading more than 2 million people into a strange new land and conquering it. What a challenge—even for a man of Joshua's caliber! Every new job is a challenge. Without God it can be frightening. With God it can be a great adventure. Just as God was with Joshua, he is with us as we face our new challenges. We may not conquer nations, but every day we face tough situations, difficult people, and temptations. However, God promises that he will never abandon us or fail to help us. By asking God to direct us we can conquer many of life's challenges.

Related Topics: BARRIERS, ENCOURAGEMENT, TESTING

CHANGE *(Difference, Improvement, Movement)*

Can people change?

BIBLE READING: Genesis 44:1-34
KEY BIBLE VERSE: *Please, my lord, let me stay here as a slave instead of the boy, and let the boy return with his brothers.* (Genesis 44:33)

God can help people change. When Judah was younger, he showed no regard for his brother Joseph or his father, Jacob. First he convinced his brothers to sell Joseph as a slave (Genesis 37:27); then he joined his brothers in lying to his father about Joseph's fate (Genesis 37:32). But what a change had taken place in Judah! The man who sold one favored younger brother into slavery now offered to become a slave himself to save another favored brother. He was so concerned for his father and younger brother that he was willing to die for them. When you are ready to give up hope on yourself or others, remember that God can work a complete change in even the most selfish personality.

BIBLE READING: Joshua 11:16-23

KEY BIBLE VERSE: *Joshua waged war against all these kings for a long time.* (Joshua 11:18, NIV)

Change doesn't usually happen quickly. The conquest of much of the land of Canaan seems to have happened quickly (we can read about it in one sitting), but it actually took seven years. We often expect quick changes in our life and quick victories over sin. But our journey with God is a lifelong process, and the changes and victories may take time. It is easy to grow impatient with God and feel like giving up hope because things are moving too slowly. When we are close to a situation, it is difficult to see progress. But when we look back we can see that God never stopped working.

BIBLE READING: Numbers 10:11-36

KEY BIBLE VERSE: *When the time to move arrived, the LORD gave the order through Moses.* (Numbers 10:13)

God helps us handle change. Those who travel, move, or face new challenges know what it is to be uprooted. Life is full of changes, and few things remain stable. The Israelites were constantly moving through the desert. They were able to handle change only because God's presence in the tabernacle was always with them. The portable tabernacle signified God and his people moving together. For us, stability does not mean lack of change, but moving with God in every circumstance.

BIBLE READING: John 4:27-42

KEY BIBLE VERSE: *Many Samaritans from the village believed in Jesus because the woman had said, "He told me everything I ever did!"* (John 4:39)

God can change the worst in us. The Samaritan woman immediately shared her experience with others. Despite her reputation, many took her invitation and came out to meet Jesus. Perhaps there are sins in our past of which we're ashamed. But Christ changes us. Often, those things for which we are most ashamed become the very changed areas that catch other people's attention. As people see these changes, they become curious. We can use these opportunities to introduce them to Christ.

How do people change?

BIBLE READING: Matthew 15:1-20

KEY BIBLE VERSE: *From the heart come evil thoughts, murder, adultery, all other sexual immorality, theft, lying, and slander.* (Matthew 15:19)

God desires to change people on the inside. We work hard to keep our outward appearance attractive, but what is in our heart is even more important. The way we are deep down (where others can't see) matters much to God. What are you like inside? When people become Christians, God makes them different on the inside. He will continue the process of change inside them if they only ask. God wants us to seek healthy thoughts and motives, not just healthy food and good exercise.

BIBLE READING: 2 Corinthians 5:11-21

KEY BIBLE VERSE: *Those who become Christians become new persons. They are not the same anymore, for the old life is gone. A new life has begun!* (2 Corinthians 5:17)

God's changes are complete. Christians are brand-new people on the *inside.* The Holy Spirit gives them new life, and they are not the same anymore. We are not reformed, rehabilitated, or reeducated—we are re-created (new creations), living in vital union with Christ (Colossians 2:6-7). At conversion we are not merely turning over a new leaf; we are beginning a new life under a new Master.

BIBLE READING: Matthew 3:1-12

KEY BIBLE VERSE: *Prove by the way you live that you have really turned from your sins and turned to God.* (Matthew 3:8)

Inward changes should lead to outward changes. John the Baptist called people to more than a mere assent to words or performance of ritual; he told them to change their behavior. God looks beyond our words and religious activities to see if our conduct backs up what we say, and he judges our words by the actions that accompany them. Do your actions match your words?

Just as a fruit tree is expected to bear fruit, God's people should produce a crop of good deeds. God has no use for people who call themselves Christians but do nothing about it. Like many people in John's day who were God's people in name only, we are of no value if we are Christians in name only. If others can't see our faith in the way we treat them, we may not be God's people at all.

BIBLE READING: Luke 7:18-35

KEY BIBLE VERSE: *Wisdom is shown to be right by the lives of those who follow it.* (Luke 7:35)

People are open to change when they stop rationalizing. Wisdom's children were the followers of Jesus and John. These followers lived changed lives. Their righteous living demonstrated the wisdom that Jesus and John taught.

The Pharisees, on the other hand, were good at rationalizing their inconsistencies. This helped them keep up a good appearance, but it also kept them from changing where change was needed. If we excuse our wrong actions or inconsistent attitudes, we will strengthen them. If we face up to our inconsistencies, then we will grow in wisdom. Jesus was saying that if the Pharisees were really wise, the people would be able to see it by their consistent behavior.

BIBLE READING: John 8:1-11

KEY BIBLE VERSE: *Jesus stood up again and said to her, "Where are your accusers? Didn't even one of them condemn you?" "No, Lord," she said. And Jesus said, "Neither do I. Go and sin no more."* (John 8:10-11)

The starting point for change is repentance. When Jesus said that only someone who had not sinned should throw the first stone, the leaders slipped quietly away, from oldest to youngest. Evidently the older men were more aware of their sins than the younger. Age and experience often temper youthful self-righteousness. But whatever your age, take an honest look at your life. Recognize your sinful nature, and look for ways to help others rather than hurt them.

Jesus didn't condemn the woman accused of adultery, but neither did he ignore or condone her sin. He told her to leave her life of sin. Jesus stands ready to forgive any sin in your life, but confession and repentance mean a change of heart. With God's help we can accept Christ's forgiveness and stop our wrongdoing.

Related Topics: BELIEVERS, FUTURE, POWER

CHARACTER *(Identity, Personality, Quality)*

What kind of character is desirable?

BIBLE READING: Matthew 5:43-48

KEY BIBLE VERSE: *You are to be perfect, even as your Father in heaven is perfect.* (Matthew 5:48)

Christ is the model for perfect character. How can we be perfect? (1) *In character.* In this life we cannot be flawless, but we can aspire to be as much like Christ as possible. (2) *In holiness.* Like the Pharisees, we are to separate ourselves from the world's sinful values. But unlike the Pharisees, we are to be devoted to God's desires, rather than our own, and carry his love and mercy into the world. (3) *In maturity.* We can't achieve Christlike character and holy living all at once, but we must grow toward maturity and wholeness. Just as we expect different behavior from a baby, a child, a teenager, and an adult, so God expects different behavior from us, depending on our stage of spiritual development. (4) *In love.* We can seek to love others as completely as God loves us. We can be "perfect" if our behavior is appropriate for our maturity level—perfect, yet with much room to grow. Our tendency to sin must never deter us from striving to be more like Christ. Christ calls all of his disciples to excel, to rise above mediocrity, and to mature in every area, becoming like him. Those who strive to become perfect will one day be perfect, even as Christ is perfect (1 John 3:2-3).

BIBLE READING: 1 Samuel 16:1-13

KEY BIBLE VERSE: *But the LORD said to Samuel, "Don't judge by his appearance or height, for I have rejected him. The LORD doesn't make decisions the way you do! People judge by outward appearance, but the LORD looks at a person's thoughts and intentions."* (1 Samuel 16:7)

A desirable character is molded by God's standards, not just human ones. Saul was tall and handsome; he was an impressive-looking man. Samuel may have been trying to find someone who looked like Saul to be Israel's next king, but God warned him against judging by appearance alone. When people judge by outward appearance, they may overlook quality individuals who lack the particular physical qualities society currently admires. Appearance doesn't reveal what people are really like or their true value.

Fortunately, God judges by faith and character, not appearances. And because only God can see on the inside, only he can accurately judge people. Most people spend hours each week maintaining their outward appearance; they should do even more to develop their inner character. While everyone can see your face, only you and God know what your heart really looks like. What steps are you taking to improve your heart's attitude?

How is character developed?

BIBLE READING: Genesis 22:1-14

KEY BIBLE VERSE: *Later on God tested Abraham's faith and obedience. "Abraham!" God called. "Yes," he replied. "Here I am."* (Genesis 22:1)

Character is developed through challenges. God tested Abraham, not to trip him and watch him fall, but to deepen his capacity to obey God and thus develop his character. Just as fire refines ore to extract precious metals, God refines us through difficult circumstances. When we are tested, we can complain, or we can try to see how God is stretching us to develop our character.

BIBLE READING: Romans 5:1-11

KEY BIBLE VERSE: *We can rejoice, too, when we run into problems and trials, for we know that they are good for us—they help us learn to endure. And endurance* develops strength of character in us, and character strengthens our confident expectation of salvation. (Romans 5:3-4)

Character is developed through suffering. For first-century Christians, suffering was the rule rather than the exception. Paul tells us that in the future we will *become*, but until then we must *overcome*. This means we will experience difficulties that help us grow. We rejoice in suffering, not because we like pain or deny its tragedy, but because we know God is using life's difficulties and Satan's attacks to build our character. The problems that we run into will develop our perseverance—which in turn will strengthen our character, deepen our trust in God, and give us greater confidence about the future. You probably find your patience tested in some way every day. Thank God for those opportunities to grow, and deal with them in his strength (see also James 1:2-4; 1 Peter 1:6-7).

BIBLE READING: Mark 1:1-13

KEY BIBLE VERSE: *Immediately the Holy Spirit compelled Jesus to go into the wilderness. He was there for forty days, being tempted by Satan. He was out among the wild animals, and angels took care of him.* (Mark 1:12-13)

Character is developed by temptation. Jesus left the crowds and went into the desert where he was tempted by Satan. Temptation is bad for us only when we give in. We should not hate or resent times of inner testing, because through them God can strengthen our character and teach us valuable lessons. When you face Satan and must deal with his temptations and the turmoil he brings, remember Jesus. He used God's Word against Satan and won. You can do the same.

Related Topics: FAULTS, INTEGRITY, SUFFERING

CHEATING (*see* DISHONESTY)

CHERISH (*see* LOVE)

CHILDREN (*Babies, Descendants, Youths*)

▶ **PARENTS AND CHILDREN**
What does God expect from parents as they raise children?

BIBLE READING: Deuteronomy 6:1-25

KEY BIBLE VERSE: *You must commit yourselves wholeheartedly to these commands I am giving you today. Repeat them again and again to your children. Talk about them when you are at home and when you are away on a journey, when you are lying down and when you are getting up again.* (Deuteronomy 6:6-7)

Parents must be godly examples by word and deed. This passage provides the central theme of Deuteronomy. It sets a pattern that helps us relate the Word of God to our daily life. We are to love God, think constantly about his commandments, teach his commandments to our children, and live each day by the guidelines in his Word. God emphasized the importance of parents teaching the Bible to their children. The church and Christian schools cannot be used to escape from this responsibility. The Bible provides so many opportunities for object lessons and practical teaching that it would be a shame to study it only one day a week. Eternal truths are most effectively learned in the loving environment of a God-fearing home.

The Hebrews were extremely successful at making religion an integral part of life. The reason for their success was that religious education was life-oriented, not information-oriented. They used the context of daily life to teach about God. The key to teaching your children to love God is stated simply and clearly in these verses. If you want your children to follow God, you must make God a part of your everyday experiences. You must teach your children diligently to see God in all aspects of life, not just those that are church related.

BIBLE READING: Ephesians 6:1-4

KEY BIBLE VERSE: *And now a word to you fathers. Don't make your children angry by the way you treat them. Rather, bring them up with the discipline and instruction approved by the Lord.* (Ephesians 6:4)

God expects parents to be patient with their children. If our faith in Christ is real, it will usually prove itself at home, in our relationships with those who know us best. Children and parents have a responsibility to each other. Children should honor their parents even if the parents are demanding and unfair. Parents should care gently for their children, even if the children are disobedient and unpleasant. Ideally, of course, Christian parents and children will relate to each other with thoughtfulness and love. This will happen if both parents and children put the others' interests above their own—that is, if they submit to one another.

The purpose of parental discipline is to help children grow, not to exasperate and provoke them to anger or discouragement (see also Colossians 3:21). Parenting is not easy—it takes lots of patience to raise children in a loving, Christ-honoring manner. But frustration and anger should not be causes for discipline. Instead, parents should act in love, treating their children as Jesus treats the people he loves. This is vital to children's development and to their understanding of what Christ is like.

What does God expect from children?

BIBLE READING: Exodus 20:1-12

KEY BIBLE VERSE: *Honor your father and mother. Then you will live a long, full life in the land the LORD your God will give you.* (Exodus 20:12)

Children are to honor their parents. This is the first commandment with a promise attached. To live in peace for generations in the Promised Land, the Israelites would need to respect authority and build strong families. But what does it mean to "honor" parents? Partly, it means speaking well of them and politely to them. It also means acting in a way that shows them courtesy and respect (but not to obey them if this means disobedience to God). It means following their teaching and example of putting God first. Parents have a special place in God's sight. Even those who find it difficult to get along with their parents are still commanded to honor them.

BIBLE READING: 1 Timothy 4:1-16

KEY BIBLE VERSE: *Don't let anyone think less of you because you are young. Be an example to all believers in what you teach, in the way you live, in your love, your faith, and your purity.* (1 Timothy 4:12)

Even children can be good examples. Timothy was a young pastor. It would be easy for older Christians to look down on him because of his youth. He had to earn the respect of his elders by setting an example in his speech, life, love, faith, and purity. Regardless of your age, God can use you. Whether you are young or old, don't think of your age as a handicap. Live so others can see Christ in you.

▶ GOD'S CHILDREN
Who are God's children?

BIBLE READING: John 1:1-13
KEY BIBLE VERSE: *To all who believed him and accepted him, he gave the right to become children of God. They are reborn! This is not a physical birth resulting from human passion or plan—this rebirth comes from God.* (John 1:12-13)

Spiritual birth makes someone a child of God. All who welcome Jesus Christ as Lord of their lives are reborn spiritually, receiving new life from God. Through faith in Christ, this new birth changes us from the inside out—rearranging our attitudes, desires, and motives. Being born makes you physically alive and places you in your parents' family (1:13). Being born of God makes you spiritually alive and puts you in God's family (1:12). Have you asked Christ to make you a new person? This fresh start in life is available to all who believe in Christ.

BIBLE READING: 1 John 3:1-10
KEY BIBLE VERSE: *See how very much our heavenly Father loves us, for he allows us to be called his children, and we really are! But the people who belong to this world don't know God, so they don't understand that we are his children.* (1 John 3:1)

God offers us the opportunity to be his children. The self-worth of believers is based on the fact that God loves us and calls us his children. We are his children *now*, not just sometime in the distant future. Knowing that we are his children should encourage us to live as Jesus did. For other references about being part of God's family, see Romans 8:14-17; Galatians 3:26-27; 4:6-7.

BIBLE READING: Romans 8:1-17
KEY BIBLE VERSE: *His Holy Spirit speaks to us deep in our hearts and tells us that we are God's children.* (Romans 8:16)

Christians are adopted into God's family. Paul uses adoption or "sonship" to illustrate the believer's new relationship with God. In Roman culture, the adopted person lost all rights in his old family and gained all the rights of a legitimate child in his new family. He became a full heir to his new father's estate. Likewise, when a person becomes a Christian, he or she gains all the privileges and responsibilities of a child in God's family. One of these outstanding privileges is being led by the Spirit (see Galatians 4:5-6). We may not always feel as though we belong to God, but the Holy Spirit is our witness. His inward presence reminds us of who we are and encourages us with his love (5:5).

We are no longer cringing and fearful slaves; instead, we are the Master's children. What a privilege! Because we are God's children, we share in great treasures as coheirs. God has already given us his best gifts: his Son, forgiveness, and eternal life; and he encourages us to ask him for whatever we need.

BIBLE READING: Luke 18:15-17
KEY BIBLE VERSE: *Jesus called for the children and said to the disciples, "Let the children come to me. Don't stop them! For the Kingdom of God belongs to such as these. I assure you, anyone who doesn't have their kind of faith will never get into the Kingdom of God."* (Luke 18:16-17)

Childlike trust is essential to kingdom living. It was customary for a mother to bring her children to a rabbi for a blessing, and that is why these mothers gathered around Jesus. The disciples, however, thought the children were unworthy of the Master's time—they were less important than whatever else he was doing. But Jesus welcomed them because little children have the kind of faith and trust needed to enter God's kingdom. It is important that we introduce our children to Jesus and that we ourselves approach him with childlike attitudes of acceptance, faith, and trust.

Related Topics: ADOPTION, PARENT(S), YOUTH

CHOICES (*Action, Alternative, Decision*)

How can we learn to make good choices?

 BIBLE READING: John 5:16-30

KEY BIBLE VERSE: *I assure you, the Son can do nothing by himself. He does only what he sees the Father doing. Whatever the Father does, the Son also does. . . . And the Father leaves all judgment to his Son, so that everyone will honor the Son, just as they honor the Father. But if you refuse to honor the Son, then you are certainly not honoring the Father who sent him.* (John 5:19, 22-23)

We can make the same kinds of choices Jesus made. Because of his unity with God, Jesus lived as God wanted him to live. Because of our identification with Jesus, we must honor him and live as he wants us to live. The questions What would Jesus do? and What would Jesus have me do? may help us make the right choices.

BIBLE READING: Proverbs 1:1-19

KEY BIBLE VERSE: *My child, if sinners entice you, turn your back on them!* (Proverbs 1:10)

We can be aware that attractive choices sometimes lead to sin. Sin is enticing because it offers a quick route to prosperity and makes us feel like one of the crowd. But when we go along with others and refuse to listen to the truth, our own appetite becomes our master, and we'll do anything to satisfy it. Sin, even when attractive, is deadly. We must learn to make choices not on the basis of flashy appeal or short-term pleasure, but in view of the long-range effects. Sometimes this means steering clear of people who want to draw us into activities that we know are wrong. We can't be friendly with sin and expect our life to remain unaffected.

BIBLE READING: Proverbs 13:1-6

KEY BIBLE VERSE: *Godliness helps people all through life, while the evil are destroyed by their wickedness.* (Proverbs 13:6)

We can remember that good choices have positive long-term results. Living right is like posting a guard for your life. Every choice for good sets into motion other opportunities for good. Evil choices follow the same pattern, but in the opposite direction. Each decision you make to obey God's Word will bring a greater sense of order to your life, while each decision to disobey will bring confusion and destruction. The right choices you make reflect your integrity. Obedience brings the greatest safety and security.

BIBLE READING: Matthew 9:9-13

KEY BIBLE VERSE: *As Jesus was going down the road, he saw Matthew sitting at his tax-collection booth. "Come, be my disciple," Jesus said to him. So Matthew got up and followed him.* (Matthew 9:9)

We can remember that right choices are sometimes difficult. When Jesus called Matthew to be one of his disciples, Matthew got up and followed, leaving a lucrative career. When God calls you to follow or obey him, do you do it with as much abandon as Matthew? Sometimes the decision to follow Christ requires difficult or painful choices. Like Matthew, we must decide to leave behind those things that would keep us from following Christ.

Related Topics: CONSEQUENCES, DECISIONS, WISDOM

CHRIST *(see* JESUS CHRIST)

CHRISTIANITY

What makes Christianity unique among religions?

BIBLE READING: Luke 1:1-4

KEY BIBLE VERSE: *Having carefully investigated all of these accounts from the beginning, I have decided to write a careful summary for you, to reassure you of the truth of all you were taught.* (Luke 1:3-4)

Christianity encourages honest investigation. There was a lot of interest in Jesus, and many people had written firsthand accounts about him. Luke may have used these accounts and all other available resources as material for an accurate and complete account of Jesus' life, teachings, and ministry. Because truth was important to Luke, he relied heavily on eyewitness accounts. Christianity doesn't say, "Close your eyes and believe," but rather, "Check it out for yourself." The Bible encourages you to investigate its claims thoroughly (John 1:46; 21:24; Acts 17:11-12), because your conclusion about Jesus is a life-and-death matter.

BIBLE READING: Luke 24:1-12

KEY BIBLE VERSE: *He isn't here! He has risen from the dead! Don't you remember what he told you back in Galilee, that the Son of Man must be betrayed into the hands of sinful men and be crucified, and that he would rise again the third day?* (Luke 24:6-7)

Christianity is based on Jesus' resurrection. The resurrection of Jesus from the dead is the central fact of Christian history. On it the church is built; without it there would be no Christian church today. Jesus' resurrection is unique. Other religions have strong ethical systems, concepts about paradise and afterlife, and various holy scriptures. Only Christianity has a God who became human, literally died for his people, and was raised again in power and glory to rule his church forever.

Why is the resurrection so important? (1) Because Christ was raised from the dead, we know that the kingdom of heaven has broken into earth's history. Our world is now headed for redemption, not disaster. God's mighty power is at work destroying sin, creating new lives, and preparing us for Jesus' second coming. (2) Because of the Resurrection, we know that death has been conquered, and we too will be raised from the dead to live forever with Christ. (3) The Resurrection gives authority to the church's witness in the world. Look at the early evangelistic sermons in the book of Acts: the apostles' most important message was the proclamation that Jesus Christ had been raised from the dead! (4) The Resurrection gives meaning to the church's regular feast, the

Lord's Supper. Like the disciples on the Emmaus Road, we break bread with our risen Lord, who comes in power to save us. (5) The Resurrection helps us find meaning even in great tragedy. No matter what happens to us as we walk with the Lord, the Resurrection gives us hope for the future. (6) The Resurrection assures us that Christ is alive and ruling his kingdom. He is not a legend; he is alive and real. (7) God's power that brought Jesus back from the dead is available to us so that we can live for him in an evil world.

Christians can look very different from one another, and they can hold widely varying beliefs about politics, lifestyle, and even theology. But one central belief unites and inspires all true Christians—Jesus Christ rose from the dead! (For more on the importance of the Resurrection, see 1 Corinthians 15:12-58.)

How does someone become a Christian?

BIBLE READING: Romans 8:1-11

KEY BIBLE VERSE: *You are not controlled by your sinful nature. You are controlled by the Spirit if you have the Spirit of God living in you. (And remember that those who do not have the Spirit of Christ living in them are not Christians at all.)* (Romans 8:9)

Your relationship with Jesus Christ makes you a Christian. Have you ever worried about whether or not you really are a Christian? A Christian is anyone who has the Spirit of God living in him. If you have sincerely trusted Christ for your salvation and acknowledged him as Lord, then the Holy Spirit has come into your life, and you are a Christian. You won't know that the Holy Spirit has come if you are waiting for a certain feeling; you will know he has come because Jesus promised he would. When the Holy Spirit is working within you, you will believe that Jesus Christ is God's Son and that eternal life comes through him (1 John 5:5); you will begin to act as Christ directs (Romans 8:5; Galatians 5:22-23); you will find help in your daily problems and in your praying (Romans 8:26-27); you will be empowered to serve God and do his will (Acts 1:8; Romans 12:6ff.); and you will become part of God's plan to build up his church (Ephesians 4:12-13).

Related Topics: BELIEVERS, FAITH, SALVATION

CHRISTIANS (*see* BELIEVERS)

CHURCH (*Believers, Body of Christ, Disciples*)

▶ CHURCH PROFILE
What is the church?

BIBLE READING: Acts 17:22-34

KEY BIBLE VERSE: *He is the God who made the world and everything in it. Since he is Lord of heaven and earth, he doesn't live in man-made temples.* (Acts 17:24)

The church is not a building. Paul's address is a good example of how to communicate the gospel. Paul did not begin by reciting Jewish history, as he usually did, for this would have been meaningless to his Greek audience. He began by building a case for the one true God, using examples they understood (17:22-23). Then he established common ground by emphasizing what they agreed on about God (17:24-29). Finally he moved his message to the person of Christ, centering on the resurrection (17:30-31). When you witness to others, you can use Paul's approach: use examples, establish common ground, and then move people toward a decision about Jesus Christ.

BIBLE READING: Ephesians 2:14-22
KEY BIBLE VERSE: *We who believe are carefully joined together, becoming a holy temple for the Lord.* (Ephesians 2:21)

The church is people who believe. A church building is sometimes called God's house. In reality, God's household is not a building but a group of people. He lives in us and shows himself to a watching world through us. People can see that God is love and that Christ is Lord as we live in harmony with each other and with what God says in his Word. We are citizens of God's kingdom and members of his household.

BIBLE READING: 1 Corinthians 3:10-17
KEY BIBLE VERSE: *Don't you realize that all of you together are the temple of God and that the Spirit of God lives in you?* (1 Corinthians 3:16)

The church is a living building. Just as our bodies are the "temple of the Holy Spirit" (1 Corinthians 6:19), the local church or Christian community is God's temple. Just as the Jews' temple in Jerusalem was not to be defiled, the church is not to be spoiled and ruined by divisions, controversy, or other sins as members come together to worship God.

Two ways to destroy a building are to tamper with the foundation or to build with inferior materials. The church must be built on Christ, not on any other person or principle. Christ will evaluate each person's contribution to the life of the church, and the Day of judgment will reveal the sincerity of each one's work. God will determine whether or not he has been faithful to Jesus' instructions. Good work will be rewarded; unfaithful or inferior work will be discounted. The builder "will be saved, but like someone escaping through a wall of flames" means that unfaithful workers will be saved, but like people escaping from a burning building. All their possessions (accomplishments) will be lost.

BIBLE READING: Revelation 2:1-7
KEY BIBLE VERSE: *Anyone who is willing to hear should listen to the Spirit and understand what the Spirit is saying to the churches. Everyone who is victorious will eat from the tree of life in the paradise of God.* (Revelation 2:7)

God cares deeply about the church. Does God care about your church? If you are tempted to doubt it, look more closely at these seven letters. The Lord of the universe knew each of these churches and their precise situation. In each letter, Jesus told John to write about specific people, places, and events. He praised believers for their successes and told them how to correct their failures. Just as Jesus cared for each of these churches, he cares for yours. He wants it to reach its greatest potential. The group of believers with whom you worship and serve is God's vehicle for changing the world. Take it seriously—God does.

▶ **CHURCH PRIORITIES**
What does the church do?

BIBLE READING: 2 Timothy 4:1-8
KEY BIBLE VERSE: *Preach the word of God. Be persistent, whether the time is favorable or not. Patiently correct, rebuke, and encourage your people with good teaching.* (2 Timothy 4:2)

The church spreads the gospel. It was important for Timothy to preach the gospel so that the Christian faith could spread throughout the world. We believe in Christ today because people like Timothy were faithful to their mission. It is still vitally important for believers to spread the gospel. Half the people who have ever lived are alive today, and most of them do not know Christ. He is coming soon, and he wants to find his faithful believers ready for him. It may be inconvenient to take a stand for Christ or to tell others about his love, but preaching the Word of God is the most important responsibility the church and its members have been given. Be prepared, courageous, and sensitive to God-given opportunities to share the Good News.

BIBLE READING: Ephesians 4:1-16
KEY BIBLE VERSE: *Their responsibility is to equip God's people to do his work and build up the church, the body of Christ.* (Ephesians 4:12)

The church has God-given responsibilities. God has given his church an enormous responsibility—to make disciples in every nation (Matthew 28:18-20). This involves preaching, teaching, healing, nurturing, giving, administering, building, and many other tasks. If we had to fulfill this command as individuals, we might as well give up without trying—it would be impossible. But God calls us as members of his body. Some of us can do one task; some can do another. Together we can obey God more fully than any of us could alone. It is a human tendency to overestimate what we can do by ourselves and to underestimate what we can do as a group. But as the body of Christ, we can do more by functioning together than we would dream possible working by ourselves. Working together, the church can express the fullness of Christ.

BIBLE READING: Psalm 84:1-12
KEY BIBLE VERSE: *How happy are those who can live in your house, always singing your praises.* (Psalm 84:4)

The church is a place of refuge. The psalm writer longed to get away from the bustling world to meet God inside his dwelling place, his holy temple. We can meet God anywhere, at any time. But we know that going into a church building can help us step aside from the busy mainstream of life so we can quietly meditate and pray. We find joy not only in the beautiful building but also in the prayers, music, lessons, sermons, and fellowship.

▶ **CHURCH PARTICIPATION**
How does the church work?

BIBLE READING: Nehemiah 2:11–3:2
KEY BIBLE VERSE: *Then Eliashib the high priest and the other priests started to rebuild at the Sheep Gate. They dedicated it and set up its doors, building the wall as far as the Tower of the Hundred, which they dedicated, and the Tower of Hananel.* (Nehemiah 3:1)

Everyone has a role in the church. The high priest is the first person mentioned who pitched in and helped with the work. Spiritual leaders must lead not only by word but also by action. The Sheep Gate was the gate used to bring sheep into the city for temple sacrifices. Nehemiah had the priests repair this gate and section of the wall, respecting the priests' area of interest and at the same time emphasizing the priority of worship.

All the citizens of Jerusalem did their part on the huge job of rebuilding the city wall. Similarly, the work of the church requires every member's effort in order for the body of Christ to function effectively (1 Corinthians 12:12-27). The body needs you! Are you doing your part? Find a place to serve God and start contributing whatever time, talent, and money is needed.

BIBLE READING: 1 Corinthians 12:12-31

KEY BIBLE VERSE: *Some of us are Jews, some are Gentiles, some are slaves, and some are free. But we have all been baptized into Christ's body by one Spirit, and we have all received the same Spirit.* (1 Corinthians 12:13)

Each believer has a significant contribution to make. Using the analogy of the body, Paul emphasizes the importance of each church member. If a seemingly insignificant part is taken away, the whole body becomes less effective. Thinking that your gift is more important than someone else's is spiritual pride. We should not look down on those who seem unimportant, and we should not be jealous of others who have impressive gifts. Instead, we should use the gifts we have been given and encourage others to use theirs. If we don't, the body of believers will be less effective.

BIBLE READING: Hebrews 10:19-39

KEY BIBLE VERSE: *And let us not neglect our meeting together, as some people do, but encourage and warn each other, especially now that the day of his coming back again is drawing near.* (Hebrews 10:25)

Believers encourage each other. We have significant privileges with our new life in Christ: (1) we have personal access to God through Christ and can draw near to him without an elaborate system (10:22); (2) we may grow in faith, overcome doubts and questions, and deepen our relationship with God (10:23); (3) we may enjoy encouragement from one another (10:24); (4) we may worship together (10:25).

To neglect Christian meetings is to give up the encouragement and help of other Christians. We gather together to share our faith and to strengthen one another in the Lord. As we get closer to the "day of his coming," we will face many spiritual struggles and even persecution. Anti-Christian forces will grow in strength. Difficulties should never be excuses for missing church services. Rather, as difficulties arise, we should make an even greater effort to be faithful in attendance.

Related Topics: BELIEVERS, EVANGELISM, GIFTS

CIRCUMSTANCES (*Environment, Happening, Situation*)

How does God expect us to handle our circumstances?

BIBLE READING: 2 Chronicles 32:1-23

KEY BIBLE VERSE: *Be strong and courageous! Don't be afraid of the king of Assyria or his mighty army, for there is a power far greater on our side!* (2 Chronicles 32:7)

Difficult circumstances require work and trust in God. When Hezekiah was confronted with the frightening prospect of an Assyrian invasion, he made two important decisions. He did everything he could to deal with the situation, and he trusted God for the outcome. That is exactly what we must do when faced with difficult or frightening situations. Take all the steps you possibly can to solve the problem or improve the situation. But also commit the situation to God in prayer, trusting him for the solution.

BIBLE READING: Psalm 16:1-11

KEY BIBLE VERSE: *I know the LORD is always with me. I will not be shaken, for he is right beside me.* (Psalm 16:8)

Believers must expect and respond to a full range of circumstances. By saying that he will "not by shaken," David was talking about the unique sense of security felt by believers. God does not exempt believers from the day-to-day circumstances of life. Believers and unbelievers alike experience pain, trouble, and failure at times (Matthew 5:45). Unbelievers have a sense of hopelessness about life and confusion over their true purpose on earth. Those who seek God, however, can move ahead confidently with what they know is right and important in God's eyes. They know that God will keep them from being moved off of his chosen path.

BIBLE READING: 1 Samuel 17:1-58

KEY BIBLE VERSE: *David talked to some others standing there to verify the report. "What will a man get for killing this Philistine and putting an end to his abuse of Israel?" he asked them. "Who is this pagan Philistine anyway, that he is allowed to defy the armies of the living God?"* (1 Samuel 17:26)

We must look at circumstances from God's perspective. What a difference perspective can make. Most of the onlookers saw only a giant. David, however, saw a mortal man defying almighty God. He knew he would not be alone when he faced Goliath; God would fight with him. He looked at his situation from God's point of view. Viewing impossible situations from God's point of view helps us put giant problems in perspective. Once we see clearly, we can fight more effectively.

How does God use circumstances to accomplish his purposes?

BIBLE READING: Esther 4:1-17

KEY BIBLE VERSE: *If you keep quiet at a time like this, deliverance for the Jews will arise from some other place, but you and your relatives will die. What's more, who can say but that you have been elevated to the palace for just such a time as this?* (Esther 4:14)

Circumstances remind us of our dependence upon God. After the decree to kill the Jews was given, Mordecai and Esther could have despaired, decided to save only themselves, or just waited for God's intervention. Instead, they saw that God had placed them in their positions for a purpose, so they seized the moment and acted. When it is within our reach to save others, we must do so. In a life-threatening situation, don't withdraw, behave selfishly, wallow in despair, or wait for God to fix everything. Instead, ask God for his direction, and *act!* God may have placed you where you are "for just such a time as this."

BIBLE READING: James 1:1-18

KEY BIBLE VERSE: *Dear brothers and sisters, whenever trouble comes your way, let it be an opportunity for joy. For when your faith is tested, your endurance has a chance to grow.* (James 1:2-3)

Even difficult circumstances can be God's training tools. James doesn't say *if* you face trials, but *whenever* you face them. He assumes we will have trials and that it is possible to profit from them. The point is not to pretend to be happy when we face pain, but to have a positive outlook ("let it be an opportunity for joy") because of what trials can produce in our life. James tells us to turn our hardships into times of learning. Tough times can teach us perseverance. We can't really know the depth of our character until we see how we react under pressure. It is easy to be kind to others when everything is going well, but can we still be kind when others are treating us unfairly? God wants to make us mature and complete, not to keep us from all pain. Instead of complaining about our struggles, we should see them as opportunities for growth. Thank God for promising to be with you in rough times. Ask him to help you solve your problems or give you the strength to endure them. Then be patient. God will not leave you alone with your problems; he will stay close and help you grow.

For other passages dealing with perseverance (also called patience and steadfastness), see Romans 2:7; 5:3-5; 8:24-25; 2 Corinthians 6:3-7; 2 Peter 1:2-9.

Related Topics: BLESSING, SUFFERING, TESTING

CITIZENSHIP *(Belonging, Country, Membership)*

▶ **CITIZENSHIP IN EARTHLY KINGDOMS**
What kind of earthly citizens does God expect us to be?

BIBLE READING: Matthew 17:24-27
KEY BIBLE VERSE: *However, we don't want to offend them, so go down to the lake and throw in a line. Open the mouth of the first fish you catch, and you will find a coin. Take the coin and pay the tax for both of us.* (Matthew 17:27)

Christians are required to be responsible earthly citizens. As God's people, we are foreigners on earth because our real home is in heaven. Still we have to cooperate with the authorities and be responsible citizens. An ambassador to another country keeps the local laws in order to represent well the one who sent him. We are Christ's ambassadors (2 Corinthians 5:20). Are you being a good foreign ambassador for him to this world?

BIBLE READING: Romans 13:1-14
KEY BIBLE VERSE: *Obey the government, for God is the one who put it there. All governments have been placed in power by God.* (Romans 13:1)

Christians are required to take their earthly citizenship very seriously. Christians understand Romans 13 in different ways. All Christians agree that we are to live at peace with the state as long as the state allows us to live by our religious convictions. For hundreds of years, however, there have been at least three interpretations of how we are to do this.

(1) Some Christians believe that the state is so corrupt that Christians should have as little to do with it as possible. Although they should be good citizens as long as they can do so without compromising their beliefs, they should not work for the government, vote, or serve in the military.

(2) Others believe that God has given the state authority in certain areas and the church authority in others. Christians can be loyal to both and can work for either. They should not, however, confuse the two. In this view, church and state are concerned with two totally different spheres—the spiritual and the physical—and thus complement each other but do not work together.

(3) Still others believe that Christians have a responsibility to make the state better. They can do this politically, by electing Christian or other high-principled leaders. They can also do this morally, by serving as an influence for good in society. In this view, church and state ideally work together for the good of all.

None of these views advocate rebelling against or refusing to obey the government's laws or regulations unless they clearly require you to violate the moral standards revealed by God. Wherever we find ourselves we must be responsible citizens as well as responsible Christians.

▶ **CITIZENSHIP IN THE KINGDOM OF GOD**
What are the benefits of being a citizen of God's kingdom?

BIBLE READING: Revelation 21:15-27
KEY BIBLE VERSE: *Nothing evil will be allowed to enter—no one who practices shameful idolatry and dishonesty—but only those whose names are written in the Lamb's Book of Life.* (Revelation 21:27)

Citizenship in God's kingdom brings eternal benefits. Not everyone will be allowed into the new Jerusalem, "only those whose names are written in the Lamb's Book of Life." Don't think that you will get in because of your background, personality, or good behavior. Eternal life is available to you only because of what Jesus, the Lamb, has done. Trust him today to secure your citizenship in his new creation.

BIBLE READING: Colossians 1:1-14
KEY BIBLE VERSE: *For he has rescued us from the one who rules in the kingdom of darkness, and he has brought us into the Kingdom of his dear Son. God has purchased our freedom with his blood and has forgiven all our sins.* (Colossians 1:13-14)

Citizenship in God's kingdom brings immediate benefits. Paul lists five benefits God gives all believers through Christ: (1) he made us qualified to share his inheritance (see also 2 Corinthians 5:21); (2) he rescued us from Satan's dominion of darkness and made us his children (see also 2:15); (3) he brought us into his eternal kingdom (see also Ephesians 1:5-6); (4) he redeemed us—bought our freedom from sin and judgment (see also Hebrews 9:12); and (5) he forgave all our sins (see also Ephesians 1:7). Thank God for what you have received in Christ.

Related Topics: GOVERNMENT, KINGDOM OF GOD/KINGDOM OF HEAVEN, OBEDIENCE

COMFORT/COMFORTABLE *(Assistance, Relief, Security)*

▶ **NEGATIVE COMFORT**
When is comfort a danger?

BIBLE READING: Genesis 12:1-9
KEY BIBLE VERSE: *So Abram departed as the LORD had instructed him, and Lot went with him. Abram was seventy-five years old when he left Haran.* (Genesis 12:4)

Comfort may keep us from obeying God. God promised to bless Abram and make him great, but there was one condition. Abram had to do what God wanted him to do. This meant leaving his home and friends and traveling to a new land where God promised to build a great nation from Abram's family. Abram obeyed, walking away from his home for God's promise of even greater blessings in the future. God may be trying to lead you to a place of greater service and usefulness for him. Don't let the comfort and security of your present position make you miss God's plan for you.

BIBLE READING: Luke 12:1-12

KEY BIBLE VERSE: *Dear friends, don't be afraid of those who want to kill you. They can only kill the body; they cannot do any more to you.* (Luke 12:4)

Comfort may damage our relationship with Christ. Fear of opposition or ridicule can weaken our witness for Christ. Often we cling to peace and comfort, even at the cost of our walk with God. Jesus reminds us here that we should fear God who controls eternal, not merely temporal, consequences. Don't allow fear of a person or group to keep you from standing up for Christ.

▶ **POSITIVE COMFORT**
When is comfort part of God's plan for us?

BIBLE READING: Isaiah 40:1-11

KEY BIBLE VERSE: *"Comfort, comfort my people," says your God.* (Isaiah 40:1)

God comforts us when we face trials. The book of Isaiah makes a dramatic shift at this point. The following chapters discuss the majesty of God, who is coming to rule the earth and judge all people. God will reunite Israel and Judah and restore them to glory. Instead of warning the people of impending judgment here, Isaiah comforts them. Chapter 40 refers to the restoration after the exile. But Judah still had one hundred years of trouble before Jerusalem would fall, then seventy years of exile. So God tells Isaiah to speak tenderly and to comfort Jerusalem.

The seeds of comfort may take root in the soil of adversity. When your life seems to be falling apart, ask God to comfort you. You may not escape adversity, but you may find God's comfort as you face it. Sometimes, however, the only comfort we have is in the knowledge that someday we will be with God. Appreciate the comfort and encouragement found in his Word, his presence, and his people.

BIBLE READING: 2 Corinthians 1:3-11

KEY BIBLE VERSE: *All praise to the God and Father of our Lord Jesus Christ. He is the source of every mercy and the God who comforts us. He comforts us in all our troubles so that we can comfort others. When others are troubled, we will be able to give them the same comfort God has given us.* (2 Corinthians 1:3-4)

God offers us comfort even during our difficulties. Many think that when God comforts us, our hardships should go away. But if that were always so, people would turn to God only to be relieved of pain and not out of love for him. We must understand that being *comforted* can also mean receiving strength, encouragement, and hope to deal with our hardships. The more we suffer, the more comfort God gives us. If you are feeling overwhelmed, allow God to comfort you. Remember that every trial you endure will help you comfort other people who are suffering similar hardships.

BIBLE READING: Job 16:1-22

KEY BIBLE VERSE: *I could say the same things if you were in my place. I could spout off my criticisms against you and shake my head at you. But that's not what I would do. I would speak in a way that helps you. I would try to take away your grief.* (Job 16:4-5)

God comforts us so that we may help comfort others. Job's friends were supposed to be comforting him in his grief. Instead they condemned him for causing his own suffering. Job began his reply to Eliphaz by calling him and his friends "miserable comforters." Job's words reveal several ways to become a better comforter to those in pain: (1) don't talk just for the sake of talking; (2) don't sermonize by giving pat answers; (3) don't accuse or criticize; (4) put yourself in the other person's place; and (5) offer help and encouragement. Try Job's suggestions, knowing that they are given by a person who needed great comfort. The best comforters are those who know something about personal suffering.

Related Topics: FORGIVENESS, HELP, SUFFERING

COMMANDMENTS (*see* GOD'S WILL, LAW OF GOD)

COMMITMENT (*Faithfulness, Promise, Vow*)

What does the Bible teach us about commitments?

BIBLE READING: Matthew 8:18-27

KEY BIBLE VERSE: *But Jesus told him, "Follow me now! Let those who are spiritually dead care for their own dead."* (Matthew 8:22)

Our commitment to Christ must be complete. It is possible that this disciple was not asking permission to go to his father's funeral, but rather to put off following Jesus until his elderly father died. Perhaps he was the firstborn son and wanted to be sure to claim his inheritance. Perhaps he didn't want to face his father's wrath if he left the family business to follow an itinerant preacher. Whether his concern was financial security, family approval, or something else, he did not want to commit himself to Jesus just yet. Jesus, however, would not accept his excuse.

Jesus was always direct with those who wanted to follow him. He made sure they counted the cost and set aside any conditions they might have for following him. As God's Son, Jesus did not hesitate to demand complete loyalty. Even family loyalty was not to take priority over the demands of obedience. His direct challenge forces us to ask ourselves about our own priorities in following him. The decision to follow Jesus should not be put off, even though other loyalties compete for our attention. Nothing should be placed above a total commitment to living for him.

BIBLE READING: Joshua 24:14-27

KEY BIBLE VERSE: *If you are unwilling to serve the LORD, then choose today whom you will serve. Would you prefer the gods your ancestors served beyond the Euphrates? Or will it be the gods of the Amorites in whose land you now live? But as for me and my family, we will serve the LORD.* (Joshua 24:15)

Our commitment to God must be consistent. The people had to decide whether they would obey the Lord, who had proven his trustworthiness, or obey the local gods, which were only man-made idols. It's easy to slip into a quiet rebellion—going about life in your own way. But the time comes when you have to choose who or what will control you. In taking a definite stand for the Lord, Joshua again displayed his spiritual leadership. Regardless of what others decided, Joshua had made a commitment to God, and he was willing to set the example of living by that decision. The way we live shows others the strength of our commitment to serving God.

BIBLE READING: Romans 5:1-11

KEY BIBLE VERSE: *God showed his great love for us by sending Christ to die for us while we were still sinners.* (Romans 5:8)

Christ committed himself to us first. *While we were still sinners*—these are amazing words. God sent Jesus Christ to die for us, not because we were good enough, but because he loved us. Whenever you feel uncertain about God's love for you, remember that he loved you even before you turned to him. If God loved you when you were a rebel, he can surely strengthen you now that you love him in return.

BIBLE READING: Luke 16:16-18

KEY BIBLE VERSE: *Anyone who divorces his wife and marries someone else commits adultery, and anyone who marries a divorced woman commits adultery.* (Luke 16:18)

Life commitments should be lifelong. Most religious leaders of Jesus' day permitted a man to divorce his wife for nearly any reason. Jesus' teaching about divorce went beyond Moses' (Deuteronomy 24:1-4). Stricter than any of the then-current schools of thought, Jesus' teachings shocked his hearers (see Matthew 19:10) just as they shake today's readers. Jesus says in no uncertain terms that marriage is a lifetime commitment. To leave your spouse for another person may be legal, but it is adultery in God's eyes. As you think about marriage, remember that God intends it to be a permanent commitment.

BIBLE READING: Psalm 37:1-39

KEY BIBLE VERSE: *Commit everything you do to the LORD. Trust him, and he will help you.* (Psalm 37:5)

Commitment is the beginning of trusting God. David calls us to take delight in the Lord and to commit everything we have and do to him. But how do we do this? To *be delighted* in someone means to experience great pleasure and joy in his or her presence. This happens only when we know that person well. Thus, to delight in the Lord, we must know him better. Knowledge of God's great love for us will indeed give us delight.

To *commit* everything to the Lord means entrusting our life, family, job, and possessions to his control and guidance. To commit ourselves to the Lord means to trust in him (37:5), believing that he can care for us better than we can ourselves. We should be willing to wait patiently (37:7) for him to work out what is best for us.

Related Topics: COVENANT, FAITHFULNESS, PROMISE(S)

COMMUNION (*see* LORD'S SUPPER)

COMMUNITY (*see* CHURCH)

COMPARISONS (*Evaluation, Measurement, Similarities*)

▶ **COMPARISONS THAT HURT**
What types of comparison do us harm?

BIBLE READING: Genesis 31:1-16

KEY BIBLE VERSE: *Jacob soon learned that Laban's sons were beginning to grumble. "Jacob has robbed our father!" they said. "All his wealth has been gained at our father's expense."* (Genesis 31:1)

Comparisons can make us jealous. Jacob's wealth made Laban's sons jealous. It is sometimes difficult to be happy when others are doing better than we are. To compare our success with that of others is a dangerous way to judge the quality of our life. By comparing ourselves to others, we may be giving jealousy a foothold. We can avoid jealousy by rejoicing in others' successes (see Romans 12:15).

BIBLE READING: John 21:15-25

KEY BIBLE VERSE: *Jesus replied, "If I want him to remain alive until I return, what is that to you? You follow me."* (John 21:22)

Comparisons can discourage us. Peter asked Jesus how John would die. Jesus replied that Peter should not concern himself with that. We tend to compare our life with the lives of others, either to rationalize our own level of devotion to Christ or to question God's justice. Jesus responds to us as he did to Peter: "What is that to you? You follow me."

▶ **COMPARISONS THAT HELP**
When are comparisons helpful?

BIBLE READING: 2 Corinthians 10:1-18

KEY BIBLE VERSE: *We will not boast of authority we do not have. Our goal is to stay within the boundaries of God's plan for us, and this plan includes our working there with you.* (2 Corinthians 10:13)

Comparisons with God's standards are the most helpful. Paul criticized the false teachers who were trying to prove their goodness by comparing themselves with others rather than with God's standards. When we compare ourselves with others, we may feel pride because we think we're better. But when we measure ourselves against God's standards, it becomes obvious that we have no basis for pride. Don't worry about other people's accomplishments. Instead, continually ask: How does my life measure up to what God wants? How does my life compare to Jesus Christ?

Related Topics: MOTIVES, SELF-ESTEEM, SUCCESS

COMPASSION (*Assistance, Care, Understanding*)

How important is it to practice compassion?

BIBLE READING: Mark 5:21-43

KEY BIBLE VERSE: *Jesus ignored their comments and said to Jairus, "Don't be afraid. Just trust me."* (Mark 5:36)

Jesus demonstrated compassion. Jesus not only demonstrated great power; he also showed tremendous compassion. Jesus' power over nature, evil spirits, and death was motivated by compassion—for a demon-possessed man who lived among tombs, for a diseased woman, and for the family of a dead girl. The rabbis of the day considered such people unclean. Polite society avoided them. But Jesus reached out and helped anyone in need.

BIBLE READING: Mark 2:1-12

KEY BIBLE VERSE: *Seeing their faith, Jesus said to the paralyzed man, "My son, your sins are forgiven."* (Mark 2:5)

Jesus responded to compassion in others. The paralytic's need moved his friends to action, and they brought him to Jesus. When you recognize someone's need, do you act? Many people have physical and spiritual needs you can meet, either by yourself or with others who are also concerned. Human need moved these four men; let it also move you to compassionate action.

BIBLE READING: Job 6:1-30
KEY BIBLE VERSE: *One should be kind to a fainting friend, but you have accused me without the slightest fear of the Almighty.* (Job 6:14)

Compassion goes beyond words. Job said that Eliphaz's advice was like eating the tasteless white of an egg. When people are going through severe trials, ill-advised counsel is distasteful. They may listen politely, but inside they are upset. Be slow to give advice to those who are hurting. They often need compassion more than they need advice.

BIBLE READING: Lamentations 3:1-66
KEY BIBLE VERSE: *The unfailing love of the LORD never ends! By his mercies we have been kept from complete destruction.* (Lamentations 3:22)

God is compassionate. Jeremiah saw one ray of hope in all the sin and sorrow surrounding him: "The unfailing love of the Lord never ends! By his mercies we have been kept from complete destruction." God willingly responds with help when we ask. Perhaps there is some sin in your life that you thought God would not forgive. God's steadfast love and mercy are greater than any sin, and he promises forgiveness.

Related Topics: GRACE, LOVE, UNDERSTANDING

COMPLACENCY *(Apathy, Inattentiveness, Unconcern)*

How does complacency affect our spiritual life?

BIBLE READING: Isaiah 32:9-20
KEY BIBLE VERSE: *Listen, you women who lie around in lazy ease. Listen to me, and I will tell you of your reward.* (Isaiah 32:9)

Complacency grows out of a false security in our spiritual life. The people turned their backs on God and concentrated on their own pleasures. This warning is not just to the women of Jerusalem (see Isaiah 3:16–4:1) but to all who sit back in their thoughtless complacency, enjoying crops, clothes, land, and cities while an enemy approaches. Wealth and luxury bring false security, lulling us into thinking all is well when disaster is around the corner. By abandoning God's purpose for our life, we also abandon his help.

BIBLE READING: Joel 1:1-20
KEY BIBLE VERSE: *Wake up, you drunkards, and weep! All the grapes are ruined, and all your new wine is gone!* (Joel 1:5)

Complacency is evidence of spiritual laziness. The people's physical and moral senses were dulled, making them oblivious to sin. Joel called them to awaken from their complacency and confess their sins before it was too late. Otherwise, everything would be destroyed, even the grapes that caused their drunkenness. Our times of peace and prosperity can lull us to sleep. We must never let material abundance hinder our spiritual readiness.

BIBLE READING: Malachi 2:1-12

KEY BIBLE VERSE: *Are we not all children of the same Father? Are we not all created by the same God? Then why are we faithless to each other, violating the covenant of our ancestors?* (Malachi 2:10)

Complacency often degenerates into sin. After the temple had been rebuilt and the walls completed, the people were excited to see past prophecies coming true. But as time passed, the prophecies about the destruction of God's enemies and a coming messiah were not immediately fulfilled. The people became discouraged, and they grew complacent about obeying all of God's laws. This complacency gradually led to blatant sin, such as marriage to those who worshiped idols. Ezra and Nehemiah also had confronted this problem years earlier (Ezra 9–10; Nehemiah 13:23-31).

BIBLE READING: Revelation 3:14-22

KEY BIBLE VERSE: *I know all the things you do, that you are neither hot nor cold. I wish you were one or the other!* (Revelation 3:15)

Complacency creates a lukewarm faith. Lukewarm water makes a disgusting drink. The church in Laodicea had become lukewarm and thus distasteful and repugnant. The believers didn't stand for anything; indifference had led them to idleness. By neglecting to do anything for Christ, the church had become hardened and self-satisfied, and it was destroying itself. There is nothing more disgusting than a halfhearted, in-name-only Christian who is self-sufficient. Don't settle for following God halfway. Let Christ fire up your faith and get you into the action.

Complacency brings God's loving discipline. God said he would discipline this lukewarm church unless it turned from its indifference toward him. God's purpose in discipline is not to punish but to bring people back to him. Are you lukewarm in your devotion to God? God may discipline you to help you out of your uncaring attitude; but he uses only loving discipline. You can avoid God's discipline by drawing near to him through confession, service, worship, and studying his Word. Just as the spark of love can be rekindled in marriage, so the Holy Spirit can reignite our zeal for God when we allow him to work in our heart.

Related Topics: ABANDON, FAITH, SECURITY

COMPLAINING *(Discontent, Griping, Whining)*

Why do we complain?

BIBLE READING: Exodus 16:1-10

KEY BIBLE VERSE: *There, too, the whole community of Israel spoke bitterly against Moses and Aaron.* (Exodus 16:2)

Complaining can become a habitual response to stress. It happened again. As the Israelites encountered danger, shortages, and inconvenience, they complained bitterly and longed to be back in Egypt. But as always, God provided for their needs. Difficult circumstances often lead to stress, and complaining is a natural response. The Israelites didn't really want to be back in Egypt; they just wanted life to get a little easier. In the pressure of the moment, they could not focus on the cause of their stress (in this case, lack of trust in God); they could only think about the quickest way of escape. When pressure comes your way, resist the temptation to make a quick escape. Instead, focus on God's power and wisdom to help you deal with the cause of your stress.

BIBLE READING: Numbers 11:1-17

KEY BIBLE VERSE: *And Moses said to the LORD, "Why are you treating me, your servant, so miserably? What did I do to deserve the burden of a people like this?"* (Numbers 11:11)

Some complaints are valid. The Israelites complained, and then Moses complained. But God responded positively to Moses and negatively to the rest of the people. Why? The people complained *to one another*, and nothing was accomplished. Moses took his complaint *to God*, who could solve any problem. Many of us are good at complaining to each other. We need to learn to take our problems to the one who can do something about them.

Some complaints come from focusing on unfulfilled desires. Dissatisfaction comes when our attention shifts from what we have to what we don't have. The people of Israel didn't seem to notice what God was doing for them—setting them free, making them a nation, giving them a new land—because they were so wrapped up in what God wasn't doing for them. They could think of nothing but the delicious Egyptian food they had left behind. Somehow they forgot that the brutal whip of Egyptian slavery was the cost of eating that food. Before we judge the Israelites too harshly, it's helpful to think about what occupies our attention most of the time. Are we grateful for what God has given us, or are we always thinking about what we would like to have? We should not allow our unfulfilled desires to cause us to forget God's gifts of life, food, health, work, and friends.

Some complaints come from a lack of trust in God. Every morning the Israelites drew back their tent doors and witnessed a miracle. Covering the ground was white, fluffy manna—food from heaven. But soon that wasn't enough. Feeling it was their right to have more, they forgot what they already had. They didn't ask God to fill their need; instead they demanded meat, and they stopped trusting God to care for them. "Oh, for some meat!" they complained to Moses as they reminisced about the good food they had in Egypt. God gave them what they asked for, but they paid dearly for it when a plague struck the camp (see Numbers 11:18-20, 31-34). When you ask God for something, he may grant your request. But if you approach him with a sinful attitude, getting what you want may prove costly.

What happens when we complain?

BIBLE READING: Philippians 2:12-18

KEY BIBLE VERSE: *In everything you do, stay away from complaining and arguing.* (Philippians 2:14)

Complaining harms others as well as ourselves. Why are complaining and arguing so harmful? If all that people know about a church is that its members constantly argue, complain, and gossip, they get a false impression of Christ and the gospel. Belief in Christ should unite those who trust him. If the people in your church are always complaining and arguing, it lacks the unifying power of Jesus Christ. Stop arguing with other Christians or complaining about people and conditions within the church and let the world see Christ.

Our life should be characterized by moral purity, patience, and peacefulness, so that we will "shine brightly" in a dark and perverse world. A transformed life is an effective witness to the power of God's Word. Are you shining brightly, or are you clouded by complaints and arguing? Shine out for God.

Related Topics: ARGUMENTS, EXAMPLE, TESTING

COMPLICATIONS (*see* PROBLEMS)

COMPLIMENT (*see* ENCOURAGEMENT)

COMPOSURE (*Calmness, Self-Control, Serenity*)

How can we develop composure?

BIBLE READING: 2 Samuel 16:5-14
KEY BIBLE VERSE: *Perhaps the* LORD *will see that I am being wronged and will bless me because of these curses.* (2 Samuel 16:12)

Composure develops under pressure. Shimei kept up a steady tirade against David. Although his curses were unjustified because David had no part in Saul's death, David and his followers quietly tolerated the abuse. Maintaining your composure in the face of unjustified criticism can be a trying experience and an emotional drain, but if you can't stop criticism, it is best just to ignore it. Remember that God knows what you are enduring, and he will vindicate you if you are in the right.

BIBLE READING: John 19:1-16
KEY BIBLE VERSE: *"You won't talk to me?" Pilate demanded. "Don't you realize that I have the power to release you or to crucify you?"* (John 19:10)

Composure develops when we trust God. Throughout the trial we see that Jesus was in control, not Pilate or the religious leaders. Pilate vacillated, the Jewish leaders reacted out of hatred and anger, but Jesus remained composed. He knew the truth, he knew God's plan, and he knew the reason for his trial. Despite the pressure and persecution, Jesus remained unmoved. It was really Pilate and the religious leaders who were on trial, not Jesus. When you are questioned or ridiculed because of your faith, remember that while you may be on trial before your accusers, they are on trial before God.

Related Topics: DISCIPLINE, PRESSURE, TRUST

COMPROMISE (*Agreement, Bargain, Negotiation*)

What are the dangers of compromise?

BIBLE READING: 1 Kings 11:1-13
KEY BIBLE VERSE: *In Solomon's old age, they turned his heart to worship their gods instead of trusting only in the* LORD *his God, as his father, David, had done.* (1 Kings 11:4)

Compromise can be the first step towards disobedience. Solomon handled great pressures in running the government, but he could not handle the pressure from his wives who wanted him to worship their gods. In marriage and close friendships, it is difficult to resist pressure to compromise. Our love leads us to identify with the desires of those we care about.

Faced with such pressure, Solomon at first *resisted* it, maintaining pure faith. Then he *tolerated* a more widespread practice of idolatry. Finally he became involved in idolatrous worship, *rationalizing* away the potential danger to himself and to the kingdom. It is because we want to please and identify with our loved ones that God asks us not to marry those who do not share our commitment to him.

BIBLE READING: Mark 15:1-15

KEY BIBLE VERSE: *Pilate, anxious to please the crowd, released Barabbas to them. He ordered Jesus flogged with a lead-tipped whip, then turned him over to the Roman soldiers to crucify him.* (Mark 15:15)

Compromise limits our ability to do what is right. Although Jesus was innocent according to Roman law, Pilate caved in to political pressure. He abandoned what he knew was right. Trying to second-guess the Jewish leaders, Pilate made a decision that would please everyone while keeping himself safe. When we lay aside God's clear statements of right and wrong and make decisions based on the preferences of our audience, we fall into compromise and lawlessness. God promises to honor those who do right, not those who make everyone happy.

BIBLE READING: 2 Corinthians 6:14-18

KEY BIBLE VERSE: *Don't team up with those who are unbelievers. How can goodness be a partner with wickedness? How can light live with darkness?* (2 Corinthians 6:14)

Compromise can weaken and destroy faith. Paul urges believers not to form binding relationships with nonbelievers because this might weaken their Christian commitment, integrity, or standards. It would be a mismatch. Earlier, Paul had explained that this did not mean isolating oneself from non-believers (see 1 Corinthians 5:9-10). Paul even tells Christians to stay with their nonbelieving spouses (1 Corinthians 7:12-13). He wants believers to be active in their witness for Christ to nonbelievers, but they should not lock themselves into personal or business relationships that could cause them to compromise their faith. Believers should avoid situations that could force them to divide their loyalties.

BIBLE READING: Galatians 2:11-21

KEY BIBLE VERSE: *When I saw that they were not following the truth of the Good News, I said to Peter in front of all the others, "Since you, a Jew by birth, have discarded the Jewish laws and are living like a Gentile, why are you trying to make these Gentiles obey the Jewish laws you abandoned?"* (Galatians 2:14)

Compromise can weaken our respect for truth. The Judaizers accused Paul of watering down the gospel to make it easier for Gentiles to accept, while Paul accused the Judaizers of nullifying the truth of the gospel by adding conditions to it. The basis of salvation was the issue: Is salvation through Christ alone, or does it come through Christ *and* adherence to the law? The argument came to a climax when Peter, Paul, the Judaizers, and some Gentile Christians all gathered together in Antioch to share a meal. Peter probably thought that by staying away from the Gentiles, he was promoting harmony—he did not want to offend James and the Jewish Christians. James had a very prominent position and presided over the council (Acts 15). But Paul charged that Peter's action violated the gospel. By joining the Judaizers, Peter implicitly was supporting their claim that Christ was not sufficient for salvation. Compromise is an important element in getting along with others, but we should never compromise the truth of God's Word. If we feel we have to change our Christian beliefs to match those of our companions, we are on dangerous ground.

Related Topics: CONSISTENCY, FAITHFULNESS, TRUTH

CONDUCT (*see* ACTIONS)

CONFESSION (*Admission, Honesty, Truth*)

How does confession help us?

BIBLE READING: 2 Samuel 12:1-14

KEY BIBLE VERSE: *Then David confessed to Nathan, "I have sinned against the LORD." Nathan replied, "Yes, but the LORD has forgiven you, and you won't die for this sin."* (2 Samuel 12:13)

Confession clears the way for forgiveness. During this incident, David wrote Psalm 51, giving valuable insight into his character and offering hope for us as well. No matter how miserable guilt makes you feel or how terribly you have sinned, you can pour out your heart to God and seek his forgiveness as David did. There is forgiveness for us when we sin. David also wrote Psalm 32 to express the joy he felt after he was forgiven.

BIBLE READING: Nehemiah 9:1-38

KEY BIBLE VERSE: *The Book of the Law of the LORD their God was read aloud to them for about three hours. Then for three more hours they took turns confessing their sins and worshiping the LORD their God.* (Nehemiah 9:3)

Confession clears the way for worship. The Hebrews practiced open confession, admitting their sins to one another. Reading and studying God's Word should precede confession (see Nehemiah 8:18) because God can show us where we are sinning. Honest confession should precede worship because we cannot have a right relationship with God if we hold on to sin.

BIBLE READING: James 5:13-20

KEY BIBLE VERSE: *Confess your sins to each other and pray for each other so that you may be healed. The earnest prayer of a righteous person has great power and wonderful results.* (James 5:16)

Confession clears the way for real fellowship. Christ has made it possible for us to go directly to God for forgiveness. But confessing our sins to one another still has an important place in the life of the church. (1) If we have sinned against an individual, we must ask him or her to forgive us. (2) If our sin has affected the church, we must confess it publicly. (3) If we need loving support as we struggle with a sin, we should confess it to those who are able to provide that support. (4) If, after confessing a private sin to God, we still don't feel his forgiveness, we may wish to confess that sin to a fellow believer and hear him or her assure us of God's pardon. In Christ's kingdom, every believer is a priest to other believers (1 Peter 2:9).

BIBLE READING: 1 John 1:1-10

KEY BIBLE VERSE: *If we confess our sins to him, he is faithful and just to forgive us and to cleanse us from every wrong.* (1 John 1:9)

Confession clears the way for freedom. Confession is supposed to free us to enjoy fellowship with Christ. It should ease our conscience and lighten our cares. But some Christians do not understand how it works. They feel so guilty that they confess the same sins over and over; then they wonder if they might have forgotten something. Other Christians believe that God forgives them when they confess, but if they died with unconfessed sins, they would be forever lost. These Christians do not understand that God *wants* to forgive us. He allowed his beloved Son to die just so he could pardon us. When we come to Christ, he forgives all the sins we have committed or will ever commit. We don't need to confess the sins of the past all over again, and we don't need to fear that God will reject us if we don't keep our slate perfectly clean. Of course we should continue to confess our sins, but not because failure to do so will make us lose our salvation. Our relationship with Christ is secure. Instead, we should confess our sins so that we can enjoy maximum fellowship and joy with him.

True confession also involves a commitment not to continue in sin. We wouldn't be genuinely confessing our sins to God if we planned to commit them again and just wanted temporary forgiveness. We should also pray for strength to defeat temptation the next time we face it.

Related Topics: FORGIVENESS, GRACE, SIN

CONFIDENCE (*Assurance, Boldness, Trust*)

What is the source of confidence?

BIBLE READING: Judges 7:1-25

KEY BIBLE VERSE: *The LORD said to Gideon, "You have too many warriors with you. If I let all of you fight the Midianites, the Israelites will boast to me that they saved themselves by their own strength. Therefore, tell the people, 'Whoever is timid or afraid may leave and go home.'" Twenty-two thousand of them went home, leaving only ten thousand who were willing to fight.* (Judges 7:2-3)

Confidence grows out of our reliance upon God. Self-sufficiency is an enemy when it causes us to believe we can always do what needs to be done in our own strength. To prevent this attitude among Gideon's soldiers, God reduced their number from thirty-two thousand to three hundred. With an army this small, there could be no doubt that victory was from God. The men could not take the credit. Like Gideon, we must recognize the danger of fighting in our own strength. We can be confident of victory only if we put our confidence in God and not ourselves.

BIBLE READING: 1 Corinthians 2:1-5

KEY BIBLE VERSE: *My message and my preaching were very plain. I did not use wise and persuasive speeches, but the Holy Spirit was powerful among you.* (1 Corinthians 2:4)

Confidence is a gift of God's Spirit. Paul's confidence was not in his keen intellect or speaking ability but in the knowledge that the Holy Spirit was helping and guiding him. Paul is not denying the importance of study and preparation for preaching—he had a thorough education in the Scriptures. Effective preaching must combine studious preparation with the work of the Holy Spirit. Don't use Paul's statement as an excuse for not studying or preparing.

What is the purpose of confidence?

BIBLE READING: Matthew 10:26-42

KEY BIBLE VERSE: *Don't be afraid; you are more valuable to him than a whole flock of sparrows.* (Matthew 10:31)

Confidence from God means a new perspective on life's problems. Jesus said that God is aware of everything that happens even to sparrows, and you are far more valuable to him than they are. You are so valuable that God sent his only

Son to die for you (John 3:16). Because God places such value on you, you need never fear personal threats or difficult trials. These can't shake God's love or dislodge his Spirit from within you.

But this doesn't mean that God will take away all your troubles (see Matthew 10:16). The real test of value is how well something holds up under the wear, tear, and abuse of everyday life. Those who stand up for Christ in spite of their troubles truly have lasting value and will receive great rewards (see Matthew 5:11-12).

BIBLE READING: Acts 5:17-26

KEY BIBLE VERSE: *The apostles entered the Temple about daybreak and immediately began teaching. When the high priest and his officials arrived, they convened the high council, along with all the elders of Israel. Then they sent for the apostles to be brought for trial.* (Acts 5:21)

Confidence is required in Christ's service. The apostles had power to do miracles, great boldness in preaching, and God's presence in their lives; yet they were not free from hatred and persecution. They were arrested, put in jail, beaten, and slandered by community leaders. Faith in God does not make troubles disappear; it makes troubles appear less fearsome because it puts them in the right perspective. Don't expect everyone to react favorably when you share something as dynamic as your faith in Christ. Some will be jealous, frightened, or threatened. Expect some negative reactions, and remember that you must be more concerned about serving God than the reactions of people (see Acts 5:29).

Related Topics: DOUBT, HOLY SPIRIT, TRUST

CONFLICTS *(Adversity, Disagreement, Opposition)*

▶ **AVOIDING CONFLICTS**
How can conflicts be avoided?

BIBLE READING: Joshua 22:9-34

KEY BIBLE VERSE: *The whole community of the LORD demands to know why you are betraying the God of Israel. How could you turn away from the LORD and build an altar in rebellion against him?* (Joshua 22:16)

Conflicts can be avoided through negotiation. When the tribes of Reuben and Gad and the half-tribe of Manasseh built an altar at the Jordan River, the rest of Israel feared that these tribes were starting their own religion and rebelling against God. But before beginning an all-out war, Phinehas led a delegation to learn the truth, following the principle taught in Deuteronomy 13:12-19. He was prepared to negotiate rather than fight if a battle was not necessary. When he learned that the altar was for a memorial rather than for pagan sacrifice, war was averted and unity restored.

As nations and as individuals, we would benefit from a similar approach to resolving conflicts. Assuming the worst about the intentions of others only brings trouble. Israel averted the threat of civil war by asking before assaulting. Beware of reacting before you hear the whole story.

BIBLE READING: 2 Samuel 3:1-39

KEY BIBLE VERSE: *That was the beginning of a long war between those who had been loyal to Saul and those who were loyal to David. As time passed David became stronger and stronger, while Saul's dynasty became weaker and weaker.* (2 Samuel 3:1)

Conflicts can be avoided by finding a common goal. The events recorded in 2 Samuel 2 led to a long war between David's followers and the troops loyal to Abner and Ish-bosheth. Civil war rocked the country at great cost to both sides. This war occurred because Israel and Judah had lost sight of God's vision and purpose: to settle the land (Genesis 12:7), to drive out the Canaanites (Deuteronomy 7:1-4), and to obey God's laws (Deuteronomy 8:1). Instead of uniting to accomplish these goals, they fought each other. When you face conflict, step back from the hostilities and consider whether you and your enemy have common goals that are bigger than your differences. Appeal to those interests as you work for a settlement.

BIBLE READING: James 4:1-12
KEY BIBLE VERSE: *What is causing the quarrels and fights among you? Isn't it the whole army of evil desires at war within you?* (James 4:1)

Conflicts can be avoided by remembering their source. Conflicts and disputes among believers are always harmful. James explains that these quarrels result from evil desires battling within us—we want more possessions, more money, higher status, more recognition. When we want badly enough to fulfill these desires, we fight in order to do so. Instead of aggressively grabbing what we want, we should submit ourselves to God, ask God to help us get rid of our selfish desires, and trust him to give us what we really need.

▶ **FACING CONFLICTS**
What can we learn from conflicts?

BIBLE READING: Acts 5:17-42
KEY BIBLE VERSE: *Peter and the apostles replied, "We must obey God rather than human authority."* (Acts 5:29)

Sometimes conflict is inevitable. The apostles knew their priorities. While we should try to keep peace with everyone (Romans 12:18), conflict with the world and its authorities is sometimes inevitable for a Christian (John 15:18). There will be situations where you cannot obey both God and man. Then you must obey God and trust his Word. Let Jesus' words in Luke 6:22 encourage you: "Blessed are you when men hate you, when they exclude you and insult you and reject your name as evil because of the Son of Man!"

BIBLE READING: Luke 12:49-53
KEY BIBLE VERSE: *Do you think I have come to bring peace to the earth? No, I have come to bring strife and division!* (Luke 12:51)

Real allegiance to Christ will create conflicts. In these strange and unsettling words, Jesus revealed that his coming often results in conflict. He demands a response, so intimate groups may be torn apart when some choose to follow him and others refuse to do so. There is no middle ground with Jesus. Loyalties must be declared and commitments made, sometimes to the point of severing other relationships. Are you willing to risk your family's approval in order to gain eternal life?

BIBLE READING: Acts 15:36-41
KEY BIBLE VERSE: *Barnabas agreed and wanted to take along John Mark. But Paul disagreed strongly, since John Mark had deserted them in Pamphylia and had not shared in their work.* (Acts 15:37-38)

God can often use conflict for his purposes. Paul and Barnabas disagreed sharply over Mark. Paul didn't want to take him along because he had left them earlier (Acts 13:13). This disagreement caused the two great preachers to form two teams, opening up two missionary endeavors instead of one. God works even through conflict and disagreements. Later, Mark became a vital part of Paul's ministry (Colossians 4:10). Christians do not always agree, but problems can be solved by agreeing to disagree and letting God work his will.

BIBLE READING: Genesis 14:13-24

KEY BIBLE VERSE: *Abram and his allies recovered everything—the goods that had been taken, Abram's nephew Lot with his possessions, and all the women and other captives.* (Genesis 14:16)

We must prepare for conflicts in advance. These incidents portray two of Abram's characteristics: (1) He had courage that came from God. Facing a powerful foe, he attacked. (2) He was prepared. He had taken time to train his men for a potential conflict. We never know when we will be called upon to complete difficult tasks. Like Abram, we should prepare for those times and take courage from God when they come.

When Abram learned that Lot was a prisoner, he immediately tried to rescue his nephew. It would have been easier and safer not to become involved, but with Lot in serious trouble, Abram acted at once. Sometimes we must get involved in a messy or painful situation in order to help others. We should be willing to act immediately when others need our help.

Related Topics: ANGER, ENVY, PEACE

CONFORMITY (*see* PEER PRESSURE)

CONFRONTATION (*see* CORRECTION)

CONFUSION (*Complication, Disorder, Problem*)

What causes confusion in our life?

BIBLE READING: Mark 7:1-13

KEY BIBLE VERSE: *You break the law of God in order to protect your own tradition. And this is only one example. There are many, many others.* (Mark 7:13)

Disregarding God's Word creates confusion. The Pharisees added hundreds of their own petty rules and regulations to God's holy laws, and then they tried to force people to follow these rules. These men claimed to know God's will in every detail of life. There are still religious leaders today who add rules and regulations to God's Word, causing much confusion among believers. It is idolatry to claim that your interpretation of God's Word is as important as God's Word itself. It is especially dangerous to set up unbiblical standards for *others* to follow. Instead, look to Christ for guidance about your own behavior, and let him lead others in the details of their lives.

BIBLE READING: Romans 7:7-25

KEY BIBLE VERSE: *It seems to be a fact of life that when I want to do what is right, I inevitably do what is wrong.* (Romans 7:21)

Confusion is one by-product of our sinful nature. The "law at work within me" is the sin deep within us. This is our vulnerability to sin; it refers to everything within us that is more loyal to our old way of selfish living than to God.

This inward struggle with sin was as real for Paul as it is for us. From Paul we learn what to do about it. Whenever Paul felt lost, he would return to the beginning of his spiritual life, remembering that he had already been freed by Jesus Christ. When you feel confused and overwhelmed by sin's appeal, follow Paul's example: thank God that he has given you freedom through Jesus Christ. Let the reality of Christ's power lift you up to real victory over sin.

BIBLE READING: Deuteronomy 22:13-30

KEY BIBLE VERSE: *If a man is discovered committing adultery, both he and the other man's wife must be killed. In this way, the evil will be cleansed from Israel.* (Deuteronomy 22:22)

Sexual sin leads to confusion in relationships. Why did God include all these laws about sexual sins? Instructions about sexual behavior would have been vital for 3 million people on a forty-year camping trip. But they would be equally important when they entered the Promised Land and settled down as a nation. Paul, in Colossians 3:5-8, recognizes the importance of strong rules about sex for believers, because sexual sins have the power to disrupt and destroy the church. Sins involving sex are not innocent dabblings in forbidden pleasures, as is so often portrayed, but powerful destroyers of relationships. They confuse and tear down the climate of respect, trust, and credibility so essential for solid marriages and secure children.

Related Topics: OBEDIENCE, SIN, TRUTH

CONSCIENCE *(Convictions, Guilt, Memories)*

How dependable is our conscience?

BIBLE READING: Jonah 1:1-17

KEY BIBLE VERSE: *Fearing for their lives, the desperate sailors shouted to their gods for help and threw the cargo overboard to lighten the ship. And all this time Jonah was sound asleep down in the hold.* (Jonah 1:5)

We cannot depend on our conscience alone. While the storm raged, Jonah was sound asleep below deck. Even as he ran from God, Jonah's actions apparently didn't bother his conscience. But the absence of guilt isn't always a barometer of whether we are doing right. Because we can deny reality, we cannot measure obedience by our feelings. Instead, we must compare what we do with God's standards for living.

BIBLE READING: Proverbs 28:13-18

KEY BIBLE VERSE: *People who cover over their sins will not prosper. But if they confess and forsake them, they will receive mercy.* (Proverbs 28:13)

Our conscience moves us to repent or resist. A sinner's conscience will drive him either into guilt resulting in repentance, or to death itself because of a refusal to repent. It is no act of kindness to try to make him feel better; the more guilt he feels, the more likely he is to turn to God and repent. If we interfere with the natural consequences of his act, we may make it easier for him to continue in sin.

BIBLE READING: Romans 14:1-23

KEY BIBLE VERSE: *Let us aim for harmony in the church and try to build each other up.* (Romans 14:19)

We must be sensitive to the consciences of others. What is weak faith? In this passage, Paul is speaking about immature faith that has not yet developed the muscle it needs to stand against external pressures. For example, if a person who once worshiped idols were to become a Christian, he might understand perfectly well that Christ saved him through faith and that idols have no real power. Still, because of his past associations, he might be badly shaken if he knowingly ate meat that had been used in idol worship as part of a pagan ritual. If a person who once worshiped God on the required Jewish holy days were to become a Christian, he might well know that Christ saved him through faith, not through his keeping of the law. Still, when the feast days came, he might feel empty and unfaithful if he didn't dedicate them to God.

Paul responds to both weak brothers in love. Both are acting according to their conscience, but their honest scruples do not need to be made into rules for the church. Certainly some issues are central to the faith and worth fighting for—but many are based on individual differences and should not be legislated. Our principle should be: In essentials, unity; in nonessentials, liberty; in everything, love.

In nonessential matters, conscience must be taken into account. Eating "everything" refers to meat offered to idols; while the person weaker in the faith eats only vegetables and refuses to eat meat that has been offered to idols. But how would Christians end up eating meat that had been offered to idols? The ancient system of sacrifice was at the center of the religious, social, and domestic life of the Roman world. After a sacrifice was presented to a god in a pagan temple, only part of it was burned. The remainder was often sent to the market to be sold. Thus a Christian might easily—even unknowingly—buy such meat in the marketplace or eat it at the home of a friend. Should a Christian question the source of his meat? Some thought there was nothing wrong with eating meat that had been offered to idols because idols were not real gods. Others carefully checked the source of their meat, or gave up meat altogether, in order to avoid a guilty conscience. The problem was especially acute for Christians who had once been idol worshipers. For them, such a strong reminder of their pagan days might weaken their newfound faith. Paul also deals with this problem in 1 Corinthians 8.

Sometimes, our conscience is our best guide. We try to steer clear of actions forbidden by Scripture, of course; but sometimes Scripture is silent. Then we should follow our conscience. "If you do anything you believe is not right, you are sinning" means that to go against a conviction will leave a person with a guilty or uneasy conscience. When God shows us that something is wrong for us, we should avoid it. But we should not look down on other Christians who exercise their freedom in those areas.

How can our conscience be protected?

BIBLE READING: 1 Timothy 1:12-20

KEY BIBLE VERSE: *Timothy, my son, here are my instructions for you, based on the prophetic words spoken about you earlier. May they give you the confidence to fight well in the Lord's battles. Cling tightly to your faith in Christ, and always keep your conscience clear. For some people have deliberately violated their consciences; as a result, their faith has been shipwrecked.* (1 Timothy 1:18-19)

Depend on God to train our conscience. How can you hold on to a good conscience? Treasure your faith in Christ more than anything else and do what you know is right. Each time you deliberately ignore your conscience, you are hardening your heart. Over time your capacity to tell right from wrong will diminish. As you walk with God, he will speak to you through your conscience, letting you know the difference between right and wrong. Be sure to act on those inner tugs to do what is right—then your conscience will remain clear.

Related Topics: BIBLE, GUIDANCE, GUILT

CONSEQUENCES (*Effects, Results, Rewards*)

Why does the Bible record so many examples of the consequences of sin?

BIBLE READING: 2 Samuel 12:1-14

KEY BIBLE VERSE: *From this time on, the sword will be a constant threat to your family, because you have despised me by taking Uriah's wife to be your own.* (2 Samuel 12:10)

The Bible exposes the painful consequences of sin. The predictions in these verses came true. Because David murdered Uriah and stole his wife, (1) murder was a constant threat in his family (13:26-30; 18:14-15; 1 Kings 2:23-25); (2) his household rebelled against him (15:13); (3) his wives were given to another in public view (16:20-23); (4) his first child by Bathsheba died (12:18). If David had known the painful consequences of his sin, he might not have pursued the pleasures of the moment. Remember that the consequences of your actions reach farther and deeper than you can ever foresee. Because sin has consequences, God has set up moral guidelines to help us avoid sin in the first place. Be careful to do what God says.

BIBLE READING: Genesis 3:1-24

KEY BIBLE VERSE: *"Of course we may eat it," the woman told him. "It's only the fruit from the tree at the center of the garden that we are not allowed to eat. God says we must not eat it or even touch it, or we will die."* (Genesis 3:2-3)

The Bible exposes the ongoing nature of the consequences of sin. One of the realities of sin is that its effects spread. After Eve sinned, she involved Adam in her wrongdoing. When we do something wrong, often we try to relieve our guilt by involving someone else. Like toxic waste spilled in a river, sin swiftly spreads. Recognize and confess your sin to God before you are tempted to pollute those around you.

The Bible exposes the painful nature of the consequences of sin. After sinning, Adam and Eve felt guilt and embarrassment over their nakedness. Their guilty feelings made them try to hide from God. A guilty conscience is a warning signal God placed inside you that goes off when you've done wrong. The worst step you could take is to eliminate the guilty feelings without eliminating the cause. That would be like using a pain killer but not treating the disease. Be glad those guilty feelings are there. They make you aware of your sin so you can ask God's forgiveness and then correct your wrongdoing.

In his holiness, God punishes our sins. Adam and Eve chose their course of action (disobedience), and then God chose his. As a holy God, he could respond only in a way consistent with his perfect moral nature. He could not allow sin to go unchecked; he had to punish it. If the consequences of Adam and Eve's sin seem extreme, remember that their sin set in motion the world's tendency toward disobeying God. That is why we sin today: Every human being ever born, with the exception of Jesus, has inherited the sinful nature of Adam and Eve (Romans 5:12-21). Adam and Eve's punishment reflects how seriously God views sin of any kind.

In his compassion, God forgives our sins. Adam and Eve learned by painful experience that because God is holy and hates sin, he must punish sinners. The rest of the book of Genesis recounts painful stories of lives ruined as a result of the Fall. Disobedience is sin, and it breaks our fellowship with God. But, fortunately, when we disobey, God is willing to forgive us and to restore our relationship with him.

BIBLE READING: 1 Chronicles 21:1-30

KEY BIBLE VERSE: *And David said to God, "I am the one who called for the census! I am the one who has sinned and done wrong! But these people are innocent—what have they done? O LORD my God, let your anger fall against me and my family, but do not destroy your people."* (1 Chronicles 21:17)

We should consider the consequences before we act. Sin has a domino effect; once a sin is committed, a series of consequences follow. God will forgive our sin if we ask him, but the consequences of that sin have already been set in motion. David pled for mercy, and God responded by stopping the angel before his mission of death was complete. The consequences of David's sin, however, had already caused severe damage. God will always forgive our sins and will often intervene to make their bitter consequences less severe, but the scars will remain. Thinking through the possible consequences before we act can stop us and thus save us much sorrow and suffering.

Related Topics: GRACE, PUNISHMENT, SIN

CONSISTENCY (*Dependability, Integrity, Reliability*)

In what areas of life is consistency important?

BIBLE READING: 1 Samuel 31:1-13

KEY BIBLE VERSE: *When the people of Jabesh-gilead heard what the Philistines had done to Saul, their warriors traveled all night to Beth-shan and took the bodies of Saul and his sons down from the wall. They brought them to Jabesh, where they burned the bodies.* (1 Samuel 31:11-12)

God expects consistent obedience. Consider the difference between the last judge of Israel and its first king. Saul, the king, was characterized by inconsistency, disobedience, and self-will. He did not have a heart for God. Samuel, the judge, was characterized by consistency, obedience, and a deep desire for God's will. He had a genuine desire for God.

When God called Samuel, he said, "Yes, I'm listening" (3:9). But when God, through Samuel, called Saul, he replied, "You must have the wrong man!" (9:21). Saul was dedicated to himself; Samuel was dedicated to God.

BIBLE READING: 1 Kings 11:1-13

KEY BIBLE VERSE: *Now the LORD said to him, "Since you have not kept my covenant and have disobeyed my laws, I will surely tear the kingdom away from you and give it to one of your servants."* (1 Kings 11:11)

God expects consistent faithfulness. Solomon didn't turn away from God all at once or in a brief moment. His spiritual coldness started with a minor departure from God's laws (3:1). Over the years, that little sin grew until it resulted in Solomon's downfall. A little sin can be the first step in turning away from God. It is not the sins we don't know about but the sins we excuse that cause us the greatest trouble. We must never let any sin go unchallenged. In your life, is an unchallenged sin spreading like a deadly cancer? Don't excuse it. Confess this sin to God and ask him for strength to resist temptation.

God expects consistent follow-through on our promises. Solomon's powerful and glorious kingdom could have been blessed for all time; instead, it was approaching its end. Solomon had God's promises, guidance, and answers to prayer, and yet he allowed sin to remain all around him. Eventually it corrupted him so much that he was no longer interested in God. Psalm 127, written by Solomon, says, "Unless the Lord builds a house, the work of the builders is useless." Solomon began by laying the foundation with God, but he did not follow through in his later years. As a result, he lost everything. It is not enough to get off to a right start in building our marriage, career, or church on God's principles; we must remain faithful to God to the end (Mark 13:13). God must be in control of our life from start to finish.

BIBLE READING: Psalm 33:1-22

KEY BIBLE VERSE: *The LORD's plans stand firm forever; his intentions can never be shaken.* (Psalm 33:11)

We must remember God's consistency. "The Lord's plans stand firm forever." Are you frustrated by inconsistencies you see in others, or even in yourself? God is completely trustworthy—his intentions never change. There is a promise that good and perfect gifts come to us from the Creator who never changes (James 1:17). When you wonder if there is anyone in whom you can trust, remember that God is completely consistent. Let him counsel you.

What are the benefits of consistency?

BIBLE READING: Ruth 2:1-23

KEY BIBLE VERSE: *"Yes, I know," Boaz replied. "But I also know about the love and kindness you have shown your mother-in-law since the death of your husband. I have heard how you left your father and mother and your own land to live here among complete strangers."* (Ruth 2:11)

Consistency in good qualities brings an excellent reputation. Ruth's life exhibited admirable qualities: she was hardworking, loving, kind, faithful, and brave. These qualities gained for her a good reputation, but only because she displayed them *consistently* in all areas of her life. Wherever Ruth went or whatever she did, her character remained the same.

Your reputation is formed by the people who watch you at work, in town, at home, in church. A good reputation comes by *consistently* living out the qualities you believe in—no matter what group of people or surroundings you are in.

BIBLE READING: Psalm 125:1-5

KEY BIBLE VERSE: *Those who trust in the LORD are as secure as Mount Zion; they will not be defeated but will endure forever.* (Psalm 125:1)

Consistency based on trust in God develops a life not easily shaken. Have you ever known people who were drawn to every new fad or idea? Such people are inconsistent and therefore unreliable. The secret to consistency is trust in God because he never changes. He cannot be shaken by the changes in our world, and he endures forever. The fads and ideas of our world, and even our world itself, will not last.

 BIBLE READING: Proverbs 29:15-21
KEY BIBLE VERSE: *To discipline and reprimand a child produces wisdom, but a mother is disgraced by an undisciplined child.* (Proverbs 29:15)

Consistency is a key in personal and parental life. Parents of young children often weary of disciplining them. They feel like all they do is nag, scold, and punish. When you're tempted to give up and let your children do what they want, or when you wonder if you've ruined every chance for a loving relationship with them, remember—kind, firm correction helps them learn, and learning makes them wise. Consistent, loving discipline will ultimately teach them to discipline themselves.

Related Topics: DISCIPLINE, INTEGRITY, OBEDIENCE

CONTENTMENT (*Happiness, Joy, Peace*)

▶ **SOURCES OF CONTENTMENT**
What brings contentment?

BIBLE READING: Psalm 131:1-3
KEY BIBLE VERSE: *LORD, my heart is not proud; my eyes are not haughty. I don't concern myself with matters too great or awesome for me.* (Psalm 131:1)

Contentment grows out of humility and trust in God. Pride results from overvaluing ourselves and undervaluing others. It leads to restlessness because it makes us dissatisfied with what we have and concerned about what everyone else is doing. It keeps us always hungering for more attention and adoration. By contrast, humility puts others first and allows us to be content with God's leading in our lives. Such contentment gives us security so that we no longer have to prove ourselves to others. Let humility and trust affect your perspective and give you the strength and freedom to serve God and others.

BIBLE READING: Matthew 6:19-24
KEY BIBLE VERSE: *No one can serve two masters. For you will hate one and love the other, or be devoted to one and despise the other. You cannot serve both God and money.* (Matthew 6:24)

Contentment grows out of devotion to Christ. Jesus says we can have only one master. We live in a materialistic society where many people serve money. They spend all their lives collecting and storing it, only to die and leave it behind. Their desire for money and what it can buy far outweighs their commitment to God and spiritual matters. Whatever you store up you will spend much of your time and energy thinking about. Don't fall into the materialistic trap, because "the love of money is at the root of all kinds of evil" (1 Timothy 6:10). Can you honestly say that God, and not money, is your master? One test is to ask which one occupies more of your thoughts, time, and efforts.

Contentment grows out of eternal values. Jesus contrasted heavenly values with earthly values when he explained that our first loyalty should be to those things that do not fade, cannot be stolen or used up, and never wear out. We should not be fascinated with our possessions lest *they* possess *us.* This means we may have to do some cutting back if our possessions are becoming too important to us. Jesus is calling for a decision that allows us to live contentedly with whatever we have because we have chosen what is eternal and lasting.

BIBLE READING: Philippians 4:10-23

KEY BIBLE VERSE: *I know how to live on almost nothing or with everything. I have learned the secret of living in every situation, whether it is with a full stomach or empty, with plenty or little.* (Philippians 4:12)

Contentment is a gift from God. Are you content in any circumstances you face? Paul knew how to be content whether he had plenty or was in need. The secret was drawing upon Christ's power for strength. Do you have great needs, or are you discontented because you don't have what you want? Learn to rely on God's promises and Christ's power to help you be content. If you always want more, ask God to remove that desire and teach you contentment in every circumstance. He will supply all your needs, but in a way that he knows is best for you.

Contentment grows out of having God's perspective on life. Paul was content because he could see life from God's point of view. He focused on what he was supposed to *do*, not what he felt he should *have*. Paul had his priorities straight and was grateful for everything God had given him. He had detached himself from nonessentials so that he could concentrate on the eternal. Often the desire for more or better possessions is really a longing to fill an empty place in a person's life. To what are you drawn when you feel empty inside? How can you find true contentment? The answer lies in your perspective, your priorities, and your source of power.

▶ **BARRIERS TO CONTENTMENT**
What keeps us from contentment?

BIBLE READING: Genesis 33:1-20

KEY BIBLE VERSE: *"No, please accept them," Jacob said, "for what a relief it is to see your friendly smile. It is like seeing the smile of God!"* (Genesis 33:10)

Bitterness is a barrier to contentment. It is refreshing to see Esau's change of heart when the two brothers meet again. The bitterness over losing his birthright and blessing (25:29-34) seems gone. Instead, Esau was content with what he had. Jacob even said how great it was to see his brother obviously pleased with him (33:10).

Life can bring us some bad situations. We can feel cheated, as Esau did, but we don't have to remain bitter. We can remove bitterness from our life by honestly expressing our feelings to God, forgiving those who have wronged us, and being content with what we have.

BIBLE READING: Exodus 20:1-21

KEY BIBLE VERSE: *Do not covet your neighbor's house. Do not covet your neighbor's wife, male or female servant, ox or donkey, or anything else your neighbor owns.* (Exodus 20:17)

Coveting is a barrier to contentment. To covet is to wish to have the possessions of others. It goes beyond simply admiring someone else's possessions or thinking, *I'd like to have one of those.* Coveting includes envy—resenting the fact that others have what you don't. God knows, however, that possessions never make anyone happy for long. Since only God can supply all our needs, true contentment is found only in him. When you begin to covet, try to determine if a more basic need is leading you to envy others. For example, you may covet someone's success, not because you want to take it away from him, but because you would like to feel as appreciated by others as he is. If this is the case, pray that God will help you deal with your resentment and meet your basic needs.

BIBLE READING: 1 Timothy 6:3-10

KEY BIBLE VERSE: *People who long to be rich fall into temptation and are trapped by many foolish and harmful desires that plunge them into ruin and destruction.* (1 Timothy 6:9)

Materialism is a barrier to contentment. Despite overwhelming evidence to the contrary, most people still believe that money brings happiness. Rich people craving greater riches can be caught in an endless cycle that only ends in ruin and destruction. How can you keep away from the love of money? Paul gives us some guidelines: (1) realize that one day riches will all be gone (6:7, 17); (2) be content with what you have (6:8); (3) monitor what you are willing to do to get more money (6:9-10); (4) love people more than money (6:11); (5) love God's work more than money (6:11); (6) freely share what you have with others (6:18). (See Proverbs 30:7-9 for more on avoiding the love of money.)

Wants can be a barrier to contentment. It is often helpful to distinguish between *needs* and *wants*. We may have all we need to live but let ourselves become anxious and discontent over what we merely want. Like Paul, we can choose to be content without having all we want. The only alternative is to be a slave to our desires.

Related Topics: MONEY, NEEDS, POSSESSIONS

CONTROL (*see* DISCIPLINE)

CONVERSATION (*Dialogue, Discussion, Talk*)

▶ **WORTHWHILE CONVERSATIONS**
What makes a conversation worthwhile?

BIBLE READING: Colossians 4:2-6

KEY BIBLE VERSE: *Let your conversation be gracious and effective so that you will have the right answer for everyone.* (Colossians 4:6)

Conversations about our faith are worthwhile when we are gracious. When we tell others about Christ, it is important to always be gracious in what we say. No matter how much sense the message makes, we lose our effectiveness if we are not courteous. Just as we like to be respected, we must respect others if we want them to listen to what we have to say. "Gracious and effective" means that what we say should encourage further dialogue.

BIBLE READING: James 1:19-27

KEY BIBLE VERSE: *My dear brothers and sisters, be quick to listen, slow to speak, and slow to get angry.* (James 1:19)

Active listening makes a worthwhile conversation. When we talk too much and listen too little, we communicate to others that we think our ideas are much more important than theirs. James wisely advises us to reverse this process. Put a mental stopwatch on your conversations and keep track of how much you talk and how much you listen. When people talk with you, do they feel that their viewpoints and ideas have value?

Worthwhile conversations come when we are slow to be offended. These verses speak of anger that erupts when our egos are bruised—I *am hurt;* my *opinions are not being heard.* When injustice and sin occur, we *should* become angry because others are being hurt. But we should not become angry when we fail to win an argument or when we feel offended or neglected. Selfish anger never helps anybody.

▶ WORTHLESS CONVERSATIONS
What makes a conversation worthless?

BIBLE READING: James 3:1-18
KEY BIBLE VERSE: *We all make many mistakes, but those who control their tongues can also control themselves in every other way.* (James 3:2)

Worthless conversations are destructive. What you say and what you *don't* say are both important. Proper speech is not only saying the right words at the right time, but also controlling your desire to say what you shouldn't. Examples of an untamed tongue include gossiping, putting others down, bragging, manipulating, false teaching, exaggerating, complaining, flattering, and lying. Before you speak, ask yourself, Is what I want to say true? Is it necessary? Is it kind?

Worthless conversations demonstrate lack of self-control. James compares the damage the tongue can do to a raging fire—the tongue's wickedness has its source in hell itself. The uncontrolled tongue can do terrible damage. Satan uses the tongue to divide people and pit them against one another. Idle and hateful words are damaging because they spread destruction quickly, and no one can stop the results once they are spoken. We dare not be careless with what we say, thinking we can apologize later, because even if we do, the scars remain. A few words spoken in anger can destroy a relationship that took years to build. Before you speak, remember that words are like fire—you can neither control nor reverse the damage they do.

Worthless conversations remind us of our disobedient tendencies. If no human being can control the tongue, why bother trying? Even if we may not achieve perfect control of our tongue, we can still learn enough control to reduce the damage it can do. It is better to fight a fire than to go around setting new ones! Remember that we are not fighting the tongue's fire in our own strength. The Holy Spirit will give us increasing power to monitor and control what we say so that when we are offended, we will be reminded of God's love and won't react. When we are criticized, the Spirit will heal the hurt, and we won't lash out.

Worthless conversations remind us of our need for God's help. Our contradictory speech often puzzles us. At times our words are right and pleasing to God, but at other times they are violent and destructive. Which of these speech patterns reflects our true nature? The tongue gives us a picture of our basic human nature. We were made in God's image; but we have also fallen into sin. God works to change us from the inside out. When the Holy Spirit purifies a heart, he gives self-control so that a person can speak words that please God.

Related Topics: ARGUMENTS, CRITICISM, WORDS

CONVICTIONS (Beliefs, Principles, Values)

How do we develop and maintain godly convictions?

BIBLE READING: Daniel 1:8-21
KEY BIBLE VERSE: *Daniel made up his mind not to defile himself by eating the food and wine given to them by the king. He asked the chief official for permission to eat other things instead.* (Daniel 1:8)

Convictions—standing alone when necessary. Daniel resolved not to eat the royal food, either because the meat was some food forbidden by Jewish law, like pork (see Leviticus 11), or because accepting the king's food and drink was the first step toward depending on his gifts and favors. Although Daniel was in a culture that did not honor God, he still obeyed God's laws.

Convictions—choosing what is right in the midst of wrong. *Resolve* is a strong word that means to be devoted to principle and to be committed to a course of action. When Daniel resolved not to defile himself, he was being true to a life-long determination to do what was right and not to give in to the pressures around him. We, too, are often assaulted by pressures to compromise our standards and live more like the world around us. Merely wanting or preferring God's will and way is not enough to stand against the onslaught of temptation. Like Daniel, we must resolve to obey God.

Convictions require thoughtful preparation. It is easier to resist temptation if you have thought through your convictions well before the temptation arrives. Daniel and his friends made their decision to be faithful to the laws of God before they were faced with the king's delicacies, so they did not hesitate to stick with their convictions. We will get into trouble if we have not previously decided where to draw the line. Before such situations arise, decide on your commitments. Then when temptation comes, you will be ready to say no.

BIBLE READING: Acts 21:18-27
KEY BIBLE VERSE: *Go with them to the Temple and join them in the purification ceremony, and pay for them to have their heads shaved. Then everyone will know that the rumors are all false and that you yourself observe the Jewish laws.* (Acts 21:24)

Convictions must be held with humility. Evidently these four men had made a religious vow. Because Paul was going to participate with them in the vow (apparently he was asked to pay for some part of it), he would need to be sprinkled with water as part of the purification ceremony for entering the temple. Paul submitted himself to this Jewish custom to keep peace in the Jerusalem church. Although Paul was a man of strong convictions, he was willing to compromise on nonessential points, becoming all things to all men that he might win some (1 Corinthians 9:19-23). Often a church is split over disagreements about minor issues or traditions. Like Paul, we should remain firm on Christian essentials but flexible on nonessentials. Of course, no one should violate his true convictions, but sometimes we need to exercise the gift of mutual submission for the sake of the gospel.

Related Topics: CONSCIENCE, FAITH, TRUTH

CORRECTION *(Advice, Counsel, Teaching)*

When is correction a helpful gift?

BIBLE READING: Galatians 2:11-21
KEY BIBLE VERSE: *But when Peter came to Antioch, I had to oppose him publicly, speaking strongly against what he was doing, for it was very wrong.* (Galatians 2:11)

Correction is helpful when someone is compromising. Although Peter was a leader of the church, he was acting like a hypocrite. He knew better, yet he was driven by fear of what James and the others would think. Proverbs 29:25 says, "Fearing people is a dangerous trap." Paul knew that he had to confront Peter before his actions damaged the church. So Paul publicly opposed Peter. Note, however, that Paul did not go to the other leaders, nor did he write letters to the churches telling them not to follow Peter's example. Instead, he opposed Peter face to face. Sometimes sincere Christians, even Christian leaders, make mistakes. And it may take other sincere Christians to get them back on track. If you are convinced that someone is doing harm to himself or the church, try the direct approach. There is no place for backstabbing in the body of Christ.

BIBLE READING: 1 Corinthians 4:14-21

KEY BIBLE VERSE: *I am not writing these things to shame you, but to warn you as my beloved children.* (1 Corinthians 4:14)

Correction is helpful when motivated by love. In Paul's day, a guardian was a slave who was assigned as a special tutor and caretaker of a child. Paul was portraying his special affection for the Corinthians (greater than a slave) and his special role (more than a tutor). In an attempt to unify the church, Paul appealed to his relationship with them. By *father* he meant he was the church's founder. Because he started the church, he could be trusted to have its best interests at heart. Paul's tough words were motivated by love— like the love a good father has for his children (see also 1 Thessalonians 2:11).

BIBLE READING: 1 Corinthians 1:4-9

KEY BIBLE VERSE: *Now you have every spiritual gift you need as you eagerly wait for the return of our Lord Jesus Christ.* (1 Corinthians 1:7)

Correction is helpful when accompanied by affirmation. In this letter, Paul wrote some strong words to the Corinthians, but he began on a positive note. He affirmed their membership in God's family, the power God gave them to speak out for him and understand his truth, and the reality of their spiritual gifts. When we must correct others, it helps to begin by affirming what God has already accomplished in them.

BIBLE READING: Hebrews 12:1-13

KEY BIBLE VERSE: *As you endure this divine discipline, remember that God is treating you as his own children. Whoever heard of a child who was never disciplined?* (Hebrews 12:7)

Correction is helpful for those who want to grow spiritually. Who loves his child more—the father who allows the child to do what will harm him, or the one who corrects, trains, and even punishes the child to help him learn what is right? It's never pleasant to be corrected and disciplined by God, but his discipline is a sign of his deep love for us. When God corrects you, see it as proof of his love and ask him what he is trying to teach you.

We may respond to discipline in several ways: (1) we can accept it with resignation; (2) we can accept it with self-pity, thinking we really don't deserve it; (3) we can be angry and resent God for it; or (4) we can accept it gratefully as the appropriate response toward a loving Father.

Related Topics: DISCIPLINE, TEACHING, TRAINING

COST (*see* SACRIFICE)

COUNSEL (*see* ADVICE)

COURAGE (*Boldness, Bravery, Trust*)

▶ **EXAMPLES OF COURAGE**
What do courageous people do?

BIBLE READING: Exodus 1:15-22
KEY BIBLE VERSE: *Because the midwives feared God, they refused to obey the king and allowed the boys to live, too.* (Exodus 1:17)

Courageous people risk their lives to do what is right. Shiphrah and Puah may have been supervisors over the midwives, or else these two were given special mention. Hebrew midwives helped women give birth and cared for the baby until the mother was stronger. When Pharaoh ordered the midwives to kill the Hebrew baby boys, he was asking the wrong group of people. Midwives were committed to helping babies be born, not to killing them. These women showed great courage and love for God by risking their lives to disobey Pharaoh's command. (Note: A delivery stool was the stool upon which a woman crouched when delivering her baby.)

Against Pharaoh's orders, the midwives spared the Hebrew babies. Their faith in God gave them the courage to take a stand for what they knew was right. In this situation, disobeying the authority was proper. God does not expect us to obey those in authority when they ask us to disobey him or his Word. The Bible is filled with examples of those who were willing to sacrifice their very lives in order to obey God or save others. Esther and Mordecai (Esther 3:2; 4:13-16) and Shadrach, Meshach, and Abednego (Daniel 3:16-18) are some of the people who took a bold stand for what was right. Whole nations can be caught up in immorality (racial hatred, slavery, prison cruelty); thus following the majority or the authority is not always right. Whenever we are ordered to disobey God's Word, "we must obey God rather than human authority" (Acts 5:29).

BIBLE READING: Luke 23:50-56
KEY BIBLE VERSE: *Now there was a good and righteous man named Joseph. He was a member of the Jewish high council, but he had not agreed with the decision and actions of the other religious leaders. He was from the town of Arimathea in Judea, and he had been waiting for the Kingdom of God to come.* (Luke 23:50-51)

Courageous people risk their reputations to do what is right. Joseph of Arimathea was a wealthy and honored member of the Jewish Council. He was also a secret disciple of Jesus (John 19:38). The disciples who had publicly followed Jesus fled, but Joseph boldly took a stand that could cost him dearly. He cared enough about Jesus to ask for his body so he could give it a proper burial.

BIBLE READING: Acts 4:23-31
KEY BIBLE VERSE: *After this prayer, the building where they were meeting shook, and they were all filled with the Holy Spirit. And they preached God's message with boldness.* (Acts 4:31)

Courageous people are bold in representing Christ. Boldness is not reckless impulsiveness. Boldness requires courage to press through our fears and do what we know is right. How can we be more bold? Like the disciples, we need to pray with others for that courage. To gain boldness, you can (1) pray for the power of the Holy Spirit to give you courage, (2) look for opportunities in your family and neighborhood to talk about Christ, (3) realize that rejection, social discomfort, and embarrassment are not persecution, and (4) start where you are by being bolder in small ways.

▶ LESSONS OF COURAGE
How can we gain courage?

BIBLE READING: Deuteronomy 33:26-29
KEY BIBLE VERSE: *The eternal God is your refuge, and his everlasting arms are under you. He thrusts out the enemy before you; it is he who cries, "Destroy them!"* (Deuteronomy 33:27)

Courage grows as we trust God. Moses' song declares that God is our refuge, our only true security. How often we entrust our lives to other things—perhaps money, career, a noble cause, or a lifelong dream. But our only true refuge is the eternal God, who always holds out his arms to catch us when the shaky supports that we trust collapse and we fall. No storm can destroy us when we take refuge in him. Those without God, however, must forever be cautious. One mistake may wipe them out. Living for God in this world may look like risky business. But it is the godless who are on shaky ground. Because God is our refuge, we can dare to be bold.

BIBLE READING: John 16:16-33
KEY BIBLE VERSE: *I have told you all this so that you may have peace in me. Here on earth you will have many trials and sorrows. But take heart, because I have overcome the world.* (John 16:33)

Courage grows from the presence of Christ. Jesus summed up all he had told them this night, tying together themes from 14:27-29; 16:1-4; and 16:9-11. With these words he told his disciples to take courage. In spite of the inevitable struggles they would face, they would not be alone. Jesus does not abandon us to our struggles either. If we remember that the ultimate victory has already been won, we can claim the peace of Christ in the most troublesome times.

Related Topics: FAITH, FEAR, TRUST

COVENANT (*Agreement, Promise, Vow*)

What can we learn from God's covenants?

BIBLE READING: Genesis 9:1-17
KEY BIBLE VERSE: *God said to Noah, "Yes, this is the sign of my covenant with all the creatures of the earth."* (Genesis 9:17)

God keeps his promises. Noah stepped out of the ark onto an earth devoid of human life. But God gave him a reassuring promise. This covenant had three parts: (1) never again will a flood do such destruction; (2) as long as the earth remains, the seasons will always come as expected; (3) a rainbow will be visible when it rains as a sign to all that God will keep his promises. The earth's order and seasons are still preserved, and rainbows still remind us of God's faithfulness to his Word.

📖 BIBLE READING: Genesis 12:1-9

KEY BIBLE VERSE: *The LORD told Abram, "Leave your country, your relatives, and your father's house, and go to the land that I will show you. I will cause you to become the father of a great nation. I will bless you and make you famous, and I will make you a blessing to others."* (Genesis 12:1-2)

Many of God's covenants include us. When God called Abram, he moved out in faith from Ur to Haran and finally to Canaan. God then established a covenant with Abram, telling him that he would found a great nation. Not only would this nation be blessed, God said, but the other nations of the earth would be blessed through Abram's descendants. Israel, the nation that would come from Abram, was to follow God and influence those with whom it came in contact. Through Abram's family tree, Jesus Christ was born to save humanity. Through Christ, people can have a personal relationship with God and be blessed beyond measure.

God's covenants require a personal response. God promised to bless Abram and make him great, but there was one condition. Abram had to do what God wanted him to do. This meant leaving his home and friends and traveling to a new land where God promised to build a great nation from Abram's family. Abram obeyed, walking away from his home for God's promise of even greater blessings in the future. God may be trying to lead you to a place of greater service and usefulness for him. Don't let the comfort and security of your present position make you miss God's plan for you.

📖 BIBLE READING: Luke 22:7-23

KEY BIBLE VERSE: *After supper he took another cup of wine and said, "This wine is the token of God's new covenant to save you—an agreement sealed with the blood I will pour out for you."* (Luke 22:20)

Jesus established a new covenant between us and God. In Old Testament times, God agreed to forgive people's sins if they brought animals for the priests to sacrifice. When this sacrificial system was inaugurated, the agreement between God and man was sealed with the blood of animals (Exodus 24:8). But animal blood did not in itself remove sin (only God can forgive sin), and animal sacrifices had to be repeated day by day and year after year. Jesus instituted a "new covenant" or agreement between humans and God. Under this new covenant, Jesus would die in the place of sinners. Unlike the blood of animals, his blood (because he is God) would truly remove the sins of all who put their faith in him. And Jesus' sacrifice would never have to be repeated; it would be good for all eternity (Hebrews 9:23-28). The prophets looked forward to this new covenant that would fulfill the old sacrificial agreement (Jeremiah 31:31-34), and John the Baptist called Jesus "the Lamb of God, who takes away the sin of the world" (John 1:29).

📖 BIBLE READING: Hebrews 8:1-13

KEY BIBLE VERSE: *Our High Priest has been given a ministry that is far superior to the ministry of those who serve under the old laws, for he is the one who guarantees for us a better covenant with God, based on better promises.* (Hebrews 8:6)

God's new covenant in Christ offers us forgiveness. This passage contains a quotation from Jeremiah 31:31-34 and compares the new covenant with the old. The old covenant was the covenant of law between God and Israel. The new and better way is the covenant of grace—Christ's offer to forgive our sins and bring us to God through his sacrificial death. This covenant is new in extent—

it goes beyond Israel and Judah to all the Gentile nations. It is new in application because it is written in our hearts and minds. It offers a new way to forgiveness, not through animal sacrifice, but through faith. Have you entered into this new covenant and begun walking in the better way?

Related Topics: LAW, PROMISE(S), VOWS

COVETING (*see* JEALOUSY)

CRAFTSMANSHIP (*Ability, Skill, Talent*)

▶ **HUMAN CRAFTSMANSHIP**
What does the Bible say about special human skills?

📖 BIBLE READING: Exodus 31:1-11
KEY BIBLE VERSE: *Look, I have chosen Bezalel son of Uri, grandson of Hur, of the tribe of Judah. I have filled him with the Spirit of God, giving him great wisdom, intelligence, and skill in all kinds of crafts. He is able to create beautiful objects from gold, silver, and bronze. He is skilled in cutting and setting gemstones and in carving wood. Yes, he is a master at every craft!* (Exodus 31:2-5)

Skills are gifts from God. God regards all the skills of his people, not merely those with theological or ministerial abilities. Our tendency is to regard only those who are up front and in leadership roles. God gave Bezalel and Oholiab Spirit-filled abilities in artistic craftsmanship. Take notice of all the abilities God gives his people. Don't diminish your skills if they are not like Moses' and Aaron's.

📖 BIBLE READING: Jeremiah 10:1-10
KEY BIBLE VERSE: *The wisest of people who worship idols are stupid and foolish. The things they worship are made of wood!* (Jeremiah 10:8)

Craftsmanship is to be enjoyed and appreciated, but never worshiped. Those who put their trust in a chunk of wood, even though it is carved well and clothed beautifully, are foolish. The simplest person who worships God is wiser than the wisest person who worships a worthless substitute, because this person has discerned who God really is. In what or whom do you place your trust?

📖 BIBLE READING: Proverbs 31:10-31
KEY BIBLE VERSE: *Reward her for all she has done. Let her deeds publicly declare her praise.* (Proverbs 31:31)

Craftsmanship is a many-sided gift for both sexes. Proverbs has a lot to say about women. How fitting that the book ends with a picture of a woman of strong character, great wisdom, many skills, and great compassion.

Some people have the mistaken idea that the ideal woman in the Bible is retiring, servile, and entirely domestic. Not so! This woman is an excellent wife and mother. She is also a manufacturer, importer, manager, realtor, farmer, seamstress, upholsterer, and merchant. Her strength and dignity do not come from her amazing achievements, however. They are the result of her reverence for God. In our society where physical appearance counts for so much, it may surprise us to realize that her appearance is never mentioned. Her attractiveness comes entirely from her character.

The woman described in this chapter has outstanding abilities. Her family's social position is high. In fact, she may not be one woman at all—she may be a composite portrait of ideal womanhood. Do not see her as a model to imitate in every detail; your days are not long enough to do everything she does! See her instead as an inspiration to be all you can be. We can't be just like her, but we can learn from her industry, integrity, and resourcefulness.

▶ GOD'S CRAFTSMANSHIP
How does God demonstrate his craftsmanship?

BIBLE READING: Ephesians 2:1-10
KEY BIBLE VERSE: *We are God's masterpiece. He has created us anew in Christ Jesus, so that we can do the good things he planned for us long ago.* (Ephesians 2:10)

God demonstrates his craftsmanship in our salvation. We are God's workmanship (work of art, masterpiece). Our salvation is something only God can do. It is his powerful, creative work in us. If God considers us his works of art, we dare not treat ourselves or others with disrespect or as inferior work.

We become Christians through God's unmerited grace, not as the result of any effort, ability, intelligent choice, or act of service on our part. However, out of gratitude for this free gift, we will seek to help and serve others with kindness, charity, and goodness, and not merely to please ourselves. While no action or work we do can help us obtain salvation, God's intention is that our salvation will result in works of service. We are not saved merely for our own benefit but to serve him and build up the church (Ephesians 4:12).

BIBLE READING: Psalm 19:1-14
KEY BIBLE VERSE: *The heavens tell of the glory of God. The skies display his marvelous craftsmanship.* (Psalm 19:1)

God demonstrates his craftsmanship in creation. We are surrounded by fantastic displays of God's craftsmanship—the heavens give dramatic evidence of his existence, his power, his love, his care. To say that the universe happened by chance is absurd. Its design, intricacy, and orderliness point to a personally involved Creator. As you look at God's handiwork in nature and the heavens, thank him for such magnificent beauty and the truth it reveals about the Creator.

BIBLE READING: Psalm 139:1-24
KEY BIBLE VERSE: *Thank you for making me so wonderfully complex! Your workmanship is marvelous—and how well I know it.* (Psalm 139:14)

God demonstrates his craftsmanship in creating us. God's character goes into the creation of every person. His personal attention and awesome skill was applied to your creation. When you feel worthless or even begin to hate yourself, remember that God's Spirit is ready and willing to work within you. We should have as much respect for ourselves as our Maker has for us.

BIBLE READING: Jeremiah 18:1-12
KEY BIBLE VERSE: *O Israel, can I not do to you as this potter has done to his clay? As the clay is in the potter's hand, so are you in my hand.* (Jeremiah 18:6)

God demonstrates his craftsmanship in shaping our lives. As the potter molded or shaped a clay pot on the potter's wheel, defects often appeared. The potter had power over the clay, to permit the defects to remain or to reshape the pot. Likewise, God had power to reshape the nation to conform to his purposes. Our strategy should not be to become mindless and passive—one aspect of clay—

but to be willing and receptive to God's impact upon us. As we yield to God, he begins reshaping us into valuable vessels.

Our society admires assertiveness, independence, and defiance of authority. In a relationship with God these qualities become stubbornness, self-importance, and refusal to listen or change. Left unchecked, stubbornness becomes a way of life hostile to God.

Related Topics: ABILITIES, SERVING, SPIRITUAL GIFTS

CREATION *(Birth, Universe, World)*

What does the Bible teach us about creation?

BIBLE READING: Genesis 1:1–2:2

KEY BIBLE VERSE: *In the beginning God created the heavens and the earth.* (Genesis 1:1)

Creation teaches us about God and ourselves. The creation story teaches us much about God and ourselves. First, we learn about God: (1) he is creative; (2) as the Creator he is distinct from his creation; (3) he is eternal and in control of the world. We also learn about ourselves: (1) since God chose to create us, we are valuable in his eyes; (2) we are more important than the animals. (See 1:28 for more on our role in the created order.)

BIBLE READING: Psalm 19:1-14

KEY BIBLE VERSE: *The heavens tell of the glory of God. The skies display his marvelous craftsmanship.* (Psalm 19:1)

God reveals himself through creation. In this psalm, David's steps of meditation take him from creation, through God's Word, through David's own sinfulness, to salvation. As God reveals himself through nature (19:1-6), we learn about his power and our finiteness. As God reveals himself through Scripture (19:7-11), we learn about his holiness and our sinfulness. As God reveals himself through daily experiences (19:12-14), we learn about his gracious forgiveness and our salvation.

BIBLE READING: Romans 1:18-32

KEY BIBLE VERSE: *From the time the world was created, people have seen the earth and sky and all that God made. They can clearly see his invisible qualities—his eternal power and divine nature. So they have no excuse whatsoever for not knowing God.* (Romans 1:20)

Creation points to God's existence and our responsibility. Does anyone have an excuse for not believing in God? The Bible answers an emphatic *no.* God has revealed what he is like in his creation. Every person, therefore, either accepts or rejects God. Don't be fooled. When the day comes for God to judge your response to him, there will be no excuses. Begin today to give your devotion and worship to him.

BIBLE READING: Romans 8:18-28

KEY BIBLE VERSE: *All creation is waiting eagerly for that future day when God will reveal who his children really are.* (Romans 8:19)

Creation suffers from the results of sin. Sin has caused all creation to fall from the perfect state in which God created it. So the world is subject to futility and bondage by God so that it cannot fulfill its intended purpose. One day all creation will be transformed. Until that time it looks forward to the resurrection of God's children.

Christians see the world as it is—physically decaying and spiritually infected with sin. But Christians do not need to be pessimistic because they have hope in future glory. They look forward to the new heaven and new earth that God has promised, and they wait for God's new order that will free the world of sin, sickness, and evil. In the meantime, Christians go with Christ into the world, where they heal people's bodies and souls and fight the evil effects of sin in the world.

Related Topics: GOD, SIN, WORLD

CREATIVITY *(see* CRAFTSMANSHIP)

CRIME *(see* SIN)

CRISIS *(see* PROBLEMS)

CRITICISM *(Correction, Evaluation, Judgment)*

▶ **CONSTRUCTIVE CRITICISM**
What guidelines does the Bible give about constructive criticism?

BIBLE READING: Job 19:1-28
KEY BIBLE VERSE: *Ten times now you have meant to insult me. You should be ashamed of dealing with me so harshly.* (Job 19:3)

Constructive criticism is motivated by love. It is easy to point out someone else's faults or sins. Job's friends accused him of sin to make him feel guilty, not to encourage or correct him. If we feel we must admonish someone, we should be sure we are confronting that person because we love him, not because we are annoyed, inconvenienced, or seeking to blame him.

BIBLE READING: Deuteronomy 13:1-18
KEY BIBLE VERSE: *Suppose you hear in one of the towns the LORD your God is giving you that some worthless rabble among you have led their fellow citizens astray by encouraging them to worship foreign gods. In such cases, you must examine the facts carefully. If you find it is true and can prove that such a detestable act has occurred among you, you must attack that town and completely destroy all its inhabitants, as well as all the livestock.* (Deuteronomy 13:12-15)

Constructive criticism has the facts straight. A city that completely rejected God was to be destroyed so as not to lead the rest of the nation astray. But Israel was not to take action against a city until the rumor about its rejecting God was proven true. This guideline saved many lives when the leaders of Israel wrongly accused three tribes of falling away from their faith (Joshua 22). If we hear of friends who have wandered from the Lord or of entire congregations that have fallen away, we should check the facts and find the truth before doing or saying anything that could prove harmful. There are times, of course, when God wants us to take action—to rebuke a wayward friend, to discipline a child, to reject false teaching—but first we must be sure we have all the facts straight.

BIBLE READING: Luke 17:1-10

KEY BIBLE VERSE: *I am warning you! If another believer sins, rebuke him; then if he repents, forgive him.* (Luke 17:3)

Constructive criticism is tied to forgiveness. To rebuke does not mean to point out every sin we see; it means to bring sin to a person's attention with the purpose of restoring him or her to God and to others. When you feel you must rebuke another Christian for a sin, check your attitude before you speak. Do you love the person? Are you willing to forgive? Unless rebuke is tied to forgiveness, it will not help the sinning person.

▶ **DESTRUCTIVE CRITICISM**
What are the characteristics of destructive criticism?

BIBLE READING: Numbers 12:1-16

KEY BIBLE VERSE: *They said, "Has the LORD spoken only through Moses? Hasn't he spoken through us, too?" But the LORD heard them.* (Numbers 12:2)

Destructive criticism misses the real issue. Moses didn't have a Jewish wife because he lived with the Egyptians the first forty years of his life, and he was in the desert the next forty years. The woman is probably not Zipporah, his first wife, who was a Midianite (see Exodus 2:21). A Cushite was an Ethiopian. There is no explanation given for why Miriam objected to this woman.

People often argue over minor disagreements, leaving the real issue untouched. Such was the case when Miriam and Aaron came to Moses with a complaint. They represented the priests and the prophets, the two most powerful groups next to Moses. The real issue was their growing jealousy of Moses' position and influence. Since they could not find fault with the way Moses was leading the people, they chose to criticize his wife. Rather than face the problem squarely by dealing with their envy and pride, they chose to create a diversion from the real issue. When you are in a disagreement, stop and ask yourself if you are arguing over the real issue or if you have introduced a smoke screen by attacking someone's character. If you are unjustly criticized, remember that your critics may be afraid to face the real problem. Don't take this type of criticism personally. Ask God to help you identify the real issue and deal with it.

BIBLE READING: Matthew 7:1-6

KEY BIBLE VERSE: *Others will treat you as you treat them. Whatever measure you use in judging others, it will be used to measure how you are judged.* (Matthew 7:2)

Destructive criticism often covers the need for self-criticism. Jesus' statement, "Do not judge," is against the kind of hypocritical, judgmental attitude that tears others down in order to build oneself up. It is not a blanket statement against all critical thinking, but a call to be *discerning* rather than negative. Jesus said to expose false teachers (7:15-23), and Paul taught that we should exercise church discipline (1 Corinthians 5:1-2) and trust God to be the final Judge (1 Corinthians 4:3-5).

Jesus tells us to examine our own motives and conduct instead of judging others. The traits that bother us in others are often the habits we dislike in ourselves. Our untamed bad habits and behavior patterns are the very ones that we most want to change in others. Do you find it easy to magnify others' faults while excusing your own? If you are ready to criticize someone, check to see if you deserve the same criticism. Judge yourself first, and then lovingly forgive and help your neighbor.

📖 BIBLE READING: Galatians 5:13-26
KEY BIBLE VERSE: *If instead of showing love among yourselves you are always biting and devouring one another, watch out! Beware of destroying one another.* (Galatians 5:15)

Destructive criticism indicates a lack of love. When we are not motivated by love, we become critical of others. We stop looking for good in them and see only their faults. Soon the unity of believers is broken. Have you talked behind someone's back? Have you focused on others' shortcomings instead of their strengths? Remind yourself of Jesus' command to love others as you love yourself (Matthew 22:39). When you begin to feel critical of someone, make a list of that person's positive qualities. If there are problems that need to be addressed, it is better to confront in love than to gossip.

Related Topics: CORRECTION, FAILURE, PATIENCE

CROSS (*see* SUFFERING)

CRYING (*see* SORROW)

CULTURE (*Customs, Lifestyle, Society*)

What part does culture play in our obedience to God?

📖 BIBLE READING: Daniel 1:1-21
KEY BIBLE VERSE: *At the end of the ten days, Daniel and his three friends looked healthier and better nourished than the young men who had been eating the food assigned by the king.* (Daniel 1:15)

Cultural changes require creative adjustments. The Babylonians were trying to change the *thinking* of these Jews by giving them a Babylonian education, their *loyalty* by changing their names, and their *lifestyle* by changing their diet. Without compromising, Daniel found a way to live by God's standards in a culture that did not honor God. Wisely choosing to negotiate rather than to rebel, Daniel suggested an experimental ten-day diet of vegetables and water, instead of the royal foods and wine the king offered. Without compromising, Daniel quickly thought of a practical, creative solution that saved his life and the lives of his companions. As God's people, we may adjust to our culture as long as we do not compromise God's laws.

Real excellence is recognized in any culture. Daniel and his friends learned all they could about their new culture so they could do their work with excellence. But while they learned, they maintained steadfast allegiance to God, and God gave them skill and wisdom. Culture need not be God's enemy. If it does not violate his commands, it can aid in accomplishing his purpose. We who follow God are free to be competent leaders in our culture, but we are required to pledge our allegiance to God first.

📖 BIBLE READING: John 4:1-26
KEY BIBLE VERSE: *The woman was surprised, for Jews refuse to have anything to do with Samaritans. She said to Jesus, "You are a Jew, and I am a Samaritan woman. Why are you asking me for a drink?"* (John 4:9)

Cultural practices must be evaluated by Christ's standards. This woman (1) was a Samaritan, a member of the hated mixed race, (2) was known to be living in sin, and (3) was in a public place. No respectable Jewish man would talk to a woman under such circumstances. But Jesus did. The gospel is for every person, no matter what his or her race, social position, or past sins. We must be prepared to share this gospel at any time and in any place. Jesus crossed all barriers to share the gospel, and we who follow him must do no less.

Related Topics: COMPROMISE, LIFESTYLE, SOCIETY

CURIOSITY *(Inquisitiveness, Interest, Questions)*

How does God make use of natural curiosity?

BIBLE READING: Matthew 3:1-17

KEY BIBLE VERSE: *John's clothes were woven from camel hair, and he wore a leather belt; his food was locusts and wild honey. People from Jerusalem and from every section of Judea and from all over the Jordan Valley went out to the wilderness to hear him preach. (Matthew 3:4-5)*

Curiosity is sometimes the first step that leads us to God. John must have presented a strange image! Many people came to hear this preacher who wore odd clothes and ate unusual food. Some probably came simply out of curiosity and ended up repenting of their sins as they listened to his powerful message. People may be curious about your Christian lifestyle and values. You can use their simple curiosity as an opener to share how Christ makes a difference in you.

BIBLE READING: John 4:1-42

KEY BIBLE VERSE: *Many Samaritans from the village believed in Jesus because the woman had said, "He told me everything I ever did!" (John 4:39)*

A genuinely changed life makes people curious about the gospel. The Samaritan woman immediately shared her experience with others. Despite her reputation, many accepted her invitation and came out to meet Jesus. Perhaps there are sins in our past of which we're ashamed. But Christ changes us. As people see these changes, they become curious. Use these opportunities to introduce them to Christ.

Related Topics: ANSWERS, HUMILITY, LEARNING

DANGER (*Exposure, Risk, Threat*)

How should we think about danger?

 BIBLE READING: Nehemiah 4:1-23

KEY BIBLE VERSE: *From then on, only half my men worked while the other half stood guard with spears, shields, bows, and coats of mail. The officers stationed themselves behind the people of Judah.* (Nehemiah 4:16)

Danger requires that we depend on other Christians. The workers were spread out along the wall, so Nehemiah devised a plan of defense that would unite and protect his people—half the men worked while the other half stood guard. Christians need to help one another in the same way because we can become so afraid of possible dangers that we can't get anything done. By looking out for each other, we will be free to put forth our best efforts, confident that others are ready to offer help when needed. Don't cut yourself off from others; instead, join together for mutual benefit. You need others as much as they need you.

BIBLE READING: Esther 4:1–5:2

KEY BIBLE VERSE: *Go and gather together all the Jews of Susa and fast for me. Do not eat or drink for three days, night or day. My maids and I will do the same. And then, though it is against the law, I will go in to see the king. If I must die, I am willing to die.* (Esther 4:16)

Danger requires preparation. Esther risked her life by coming before the king. Her courageous act gives us a model to follow in approaching a difficult or dangerous task. Like Esther, we can: (1) *Calculate the cost.* Esther realized her life was at stake. (2) *Set priorities.* She believed that the safety of the Jewish race was more important than her life. (3) *Prepare.* She gathered support and fasted. (4) *Determine a course of action and move ahead boldly.* She didn't think too long about it, allowing the interlude to lessen her commitment to what she had to do.

Do you have to face a hostile audience, confront a friend on a delicate subject, or talk to your family about changes to be made? Rather than dreading difficult situations or putting them off, take action with confidence by following Esther's inspiring example.

Related Topics: CONFIDENCE, FEAR, TRUST

DARKNESS *(Dirty, Evil, Stained)*

What is darkness in the Bible?

BIBLE READING: John 1:1-9
KEY BIBLE VERSE: *The light shines through the darkness, and the darkness can never extinguish it.* (John 1:5)

The darkness is sin and its effects. "The darkness can never extinguish it" means the darkness of evil never has and never will overcome or extinguish God's light. Jesus Christ is the Creator of life, and his life brings light to mankind. In his light, we see ourselves as we really are (sinners in need of a Savior). When we follow Jesus, the true Light, we can avoid walking blindly and falling into sin. He lights the path ahead of us so we can see how to live. He removes the darkness of sin from our life. Have you allowed the light of Christ to shine into your life? Let Christ guide your life, and you'll never need to stumble in darkness.

BIBLE READING: 1 John 1:1-10
KEY BIBLE VERSE: *This is the message he has given us to announce to you: God is light and there is no darkness in him at all.* (1 John 1:5)

Darkness is opposed to light. Light represents what is good, pure, true, holy, and reliable. Darkness represents sin and evil. The statement "God is light" means that God is perfectly holy and true and that he alone can guide us out of the darkness of sin. Light is also related to truth in that it exposes whatever exists, whether it is good or bad. In the dark, good and evil look alike; in the light, they can be clearly distinguished. Just as darkness cannot exist in the presence of light, sin cannot exist in the presence of a holy God. If we want to have a relationship with God, we must put aside our sinful ways of living. To claim that we belong to him but live for ourselves is hypocrisy. Christ will expose and judge such deceit.

How can darkness be defeated?

BIBLE READING: Psalm 43:1-5
KEY BIBLE VERSE: *Send out your light and your truth; let them guide me. Let them lead me to your holy mountain, to the place where you live.* (Psalm 43:3)

Darkness can be defeated by depending on God. The psalmist asked God to send his light and truth to guide him to the holy mountain, the temple, where he would meet God. God's truth (see 1 John 2:27) provides the right path to follow, and God's light (see 1 John 1:5) provides the clear vision to follow it. If you feel surrounded by darkness and uncertainty, follow God's light and truth. He will guide you.

BIBLE READING: Psalm 119:105-112
KEY BIBLE VERSE: *Your word is a lamp for my feet and a light for my path.* (Psalm 119:105)

Darkness can be defeated by obeying God's Word. To walk safely in the woods at night we need a light so we don't trip over tree roots or fall into holes. In this life, we walk through a dark forest of evil. But the Bible can be our light to show us the way ahead so we won't stumble as we walk. It reveals the entangling roots of false values and philosophies. Study the Bible, so you will be able to see your way clear enough to stay on the right path.

Related Topics: EVIL, LIGHT, SIN

DEATH *(End, Failure, Passing)*

▶ DYING

Why do people die?

BIBLE READING: Romans 5:12-21

KEY BIBLE VERSE: *What a difference between our sin and God's generous gift of forgiveness. For this one man, Adam, brought death to many through his sin. But this other man, Jesus Christ, brought forgiveness to many through God's bountiful gift.* (Romans 5:15)

We die because Adam brought death into the world. We were all born into Adam's physical family—the family line that leads to certain death. All of us have reaped the results of Adam's sin. We have inherited his guilt, a sinful nature (the tendency to sin), and God's punishment. Because of Jesus, however, we can trade judgment for forgiveness. We can trade our sin for Jesus' goodness. Christ offers us the opportunity to be born into his spiritual family—the family line that begins with forgiveness and leads to eternal life. If we do nothing, we have death through Adam; but if we come to God by faith, we have life through Christ. Which family line do you now belong to?

We confirm our link with sinful human nature by our own sins. Death is the result of Adam's sin and of the sins we all commit, even if they don't resemble Adam's. Paul reminds his readers that for thousands of years the law had not yet been explicitly given, and yet people died. The law was added, he explains in Romans 5:20, to help people see their sinfulness, to show them the seriousness of their offenses, and to drive them to God for mercy and pardon. This was true in Moses' day, and it is still true today. Sin is a deep rupture between who we are and who we were created to be. The law points out our sin and places the responsibility for it squarely on our shoulders. But the law offers no remedy. When we are convicted of sin, we must turn to Jesus Christ for healing.

How can we face death?

BIBLE READING: Psalm 23:1-6

KEY BIBLE VERSE: *Even when I walk through the dark valley of death, I will not be afraid, for you are close beside me. Your rod and your staff protect and comfort me.* (Psalm 23:4)

God alone can lead us through death to eternal life. Death casts a frightening shadow over us because we are entirely helpless in its presence. We can struggle with other enemies—pain, suffering, disease, injury—but strength and courage cannot overcome death. It has the final word. Only one person can walk with us through death's dark valley and bring us safely to the other side—the God of life, our shepherd. Because life is uncertain, we should follow this shepherd who offers us eternal comfort.

BIBLE READING: Hebrews 9:23-28

KEY BIBLE VERSE: *Just as it is destined that each person dies only once and after that comes judgment, so also Christ died only once as a sacrifice to take away the sins of many people. He will come again but not to deal with our sins again. This time he will bring salvation to all those who are eagerly waiting for him.* (Hebrews 9:27-28)

Since death is unavoidable, we should be prepared. All people die physically, but Christ died so that we would not have to die spiritually. We can have wonderful confidence in his saving work for us past, present, and future. He has forgiven our past sin—when he died on the cross, he sacrificed himself once for all (9:26); he has given us the Holy Spirit to help us deal with present sin; he appears for us now in heaven as our high priest (9:24); and he promises to return (9:28) and raise us to eternal life in a world where sin will be banished.

BIBLE READING: 1 Corinthians 15:50-58

KEY BIBLE VERSE: *When this happens—when our perishable earthly bodies have been transformed into heavenly bodies that will never die—then at last the Scriptures will come true: "Death is swallowed up in victory. O death, where is your victory? O death, where is your sting?" For sin is the sting that results in death, and the law gives sin its power.* (1 Corinthians 15:54-56)

Christ has defeated death for us. Satan seemed to be victorious in the Garden of Eden (Genesis 3) and when Jesus died on the cross. But God turned Satan's apparent victory into defeat when Jesus Christ rose from the dead (Colossians 2:15; Hebrews 2:14-15). Death is no longer a source of dread or fear. Christ overcame it, and one day we will also. The law will no longer make sinners out of us because we cannot keep it. Death has been defeated, and we have hope beyond the grave.

▶ **CHRIST'S DEATH**
Why did Jesus die?

BIBLE READING: Matthew 20:20-28

KEY BIBLE VERSE: *Even I, the Son of Man, came here not to be served but to serve others, and to give my life as a ransom for many.* (Matthew 20:28)

Jesus died to ransom us from the bondage of sin. A ransom was the price paid to release a slave from bondage. Jesus often told his disciples that he must die, but here he told them why—to redeem all people from the bondage of sin and death. The disciples thought that as long as Jesus was alive, he could save them. But Jesus revealed that only his death would save them and the world.

BIBLE READING: John 12:20-36

KEY BIBLE VERSE: *Jesus replied, "The time has come for the Son of Man to enter into his glory. The truth is, a kernel of wheat must be planted in the soil. Unless it dies it will be alone—a single seed. But its death will produce many new kernels—a plentiful harvest of new lives."* (John 12:23-24)

Jesus died to prove his power over death. This is a beautiful picture of the necessary sacrifice of Jesus. Unless a kernel of wheat is buried in the ground, it will not become a blade of wheat producing many more seeds. Jesus had to die not only to pay the penalty for our sin, but also to show his power over death. His resurrection proves he has eternal life. Because Jesus is God, he can give this same eternal life to all who believe in him.

BIBLE READING: 1 Corinthians 1:18-31

KEY BIBLE VERSE: *When we preach that Christ was crucified, the Jews are offended, and the Gentiles say it's all nonsense.* (1 Corinthians 1:23)

Jesus died to give us hope. Many Jews considered the Good News of Jesus Christ to be foolish because they thought the Messiah would be a conquering king accompanied by signs and miracles. Jesus had not restored David's throne as they expected. Besides, he was executed as a criminal, and how could a criminal be a savior? Greeks, too, considered the gospel foolish: they did not believe in a bodily resurrection; they did not see in Jesus the powerful characteristics of their mythological gods; and they thought no reputable person would be crucified. To them, death was defeat, not victory.

The Good News of Jesus Christ still sounds foolish to many. Our society worships power, influence, and wealth. Jesus came as a humble, poor servant, and he offers his kingdom to those with faith, not works. This looks foolish to the world, but Christ is our power, the only way we can be saved. Knowing Christ personally is the greatest wisdom anyone could have.

Related Topics: ETERNAL LIFE, LIFE, RESURRECTION

DEBTS *(Borrowing, Obligation, Payments)*

What debts should we be concerned about?

BIBLE READING: Romans 1:8-17

KEY BIBLE VERSE: *I have a great sense of obligation to people in our culture and to people in other cultures, to the educated and uneducated alike.* (Romans 1:14)

We owe Christ a debt of grateful obedience. By "people in our culture and people in other cultures" Paul meant the Greeks and non-Greeks. Paul also refers to "educated and uneducated" people. What was Paul's obligation? After his experience with Christ on the road to Damascus (Acts 9), his whole life was consumed with spreading the Good News of salvation. His first obligation was to Christ for being his Savior, and his second was to the entire world. This is why he proclaimed Christ's salvation to *all* people—both Jews and Gentiles, across all cultural, social, racial, and economic lines. We also are obligated to Christ because he took on the punishment we deserve for our sin. Although we cannot repay Christ for all he has done, we can demonstrate our gratitude by showing his love to others.

BIBLE READING: Romans 13:8-14

KEY BIBLE VERSE: *Pay all your debts, except the debt of love for others. You can never finish paying that! If you love your neighbor, you will fulfill all the requirements of God's law.* (Romans 13:8)

We owe a debt of love. Why is love for others called a debt? We are permanently in debt to Christ for the lavish love he has poured out on us. The only way we can even begin to repay this debt is by loving others in turn. Because Christ's love is infinitely greater than ours, we will always have the obligation to love our neighbors.

How should we repay our debts?

BIBLE READING: Proverbs 3:21-35

KEY BIBLE VERSE: *Do not withhold good from those who deserve it when it's in your power to help them. If you can help your neighbor now, don't say, "Come back tomorrow, and then I'll help you."* (Proverbs 3:27-28)

The way in which we repay any kind of debt is a mark of character. To delay doing good is inconsiderate and unfair, whether it is repaying a loan, returning a tool, or fulfilling a promise. Withholding destroys trust and creates a great inconvenience. Be as eager to do good as you are to have good done to you.

Related Topics: HONESTY, LOVE, MONEY

DECAY (*see* SIN)

DECEIT (*Dishonesty, Lying, Tricking*)

▶ **THE DECEIVER**
Who does the Bible call the deceiver?

BIBLE READING: Revelation 12:1-9
KEY BIBLE VERSE: *This great dragon—the ancient serpent called the Devil, or Satan, the one deceiving the whole world—was thrown down to the earth with all his angels.* (Revelation 12:9)

The Bible describes Satan as the deceiver. The devil is not a symbol or legend; he is very real. Originally Satan was an angel of God, but through his pride, he became corrupt. The devil is God's enemy and he constantly tries to hinder God's work, but he is limited by God's power and can do only what he is permitted to do (Job 1:6–2:8). The name *Satan* means "adversary" or "accuser" (12:10). He actively looks for people to attack (1 Peter 5:8-9). Satan likes to seek out believers who are vulnerable in their faith, who are spiritually weak, or who are isolated from other believers.

　　Even though God permits the devil to do his work in this world, God is still in control. Jesus has complete power over Satan—he defeated Satan when he died and rose again for the sins of mankind. One day Satan will be bound forever, never again to do his evil work (see 20:10).

BIBLE READING: John 8:42-47
KEY BIBLE VERSE: *You are the children of your father the Devil, and you love to do the evil things he does. He was a murderer from the beginning and has always hated the truth. There is no truth in him. When he lies, it is consistent with his character; for he is a liar and the father of lies.* (John 8:44)

Jesus called Satan the father of lies. The attitudes and actions of these leaders clearly identified them as followers of Satan. They may not have been conscious of this, but their hatred of truth, their lies, and their murderous intentions indicated how much control the devil had over them. They were his tools in carrying out his plans; they spoke the very same language of lies. Satan still uses people to obstruct God's work (Genesis 4:8; Romans 5:12; 1 John 3:12).

▶ **DECEPTIONS**
What happens when we deceive others?

BIBLE READING: Luke 8:16-18
KEY BIBLE VERSE: *Everything that is hidden or secret will eventually be brought to light and made plain to all.* (Luke 8:17)

We cannot hide our sins from God. In God's eyes, people's hearts—their thoughts and motives—are as visible as a lamp mounted in the open. No matter how hard we try to cover up bad attitudes, deeds, or words, we cannot deceive God. Instead of hiding our faults, we should ask God to change our life so we no longer have to be ashamed. If you are trying to hide anything from God, it won't work. Only when you confess your hidden sins and seek God's forgiveness will you have the help you need to do right.

BIBLE READING: Exodus 20:1-21
KEY BIBLE VERSE: *Do not testify falsely against your neighbor.* (Exodus 20:16)

Deception weakens the foundations of our life. Giving false testimony means lying in court. God knew that Israel could not survive unless its system of justice was incorruptible. We should be honest in our private dealings as well as in our public statements. In either situation, we "testify falsely" by leaving something out of a story, telling a half-truth, twisting the facts, or inventing a falsehood. God warns us against deception. Even though deception is a way of life for many people, God's people must not give in to it!

BIBLE READING: Judges 16:1-30
KEY BIBLE VERSE: *Then Delilah pouted, "How can you say you love me when you don't confide in me? You've made fun of me three times now, and you still haven't told me what makes you so strong!"* (Judges 16:15)

The ugliness and danger of deceit are easier to see in others than in ourselves. Delilah was a deceitful woman with honey on her lips and poison in her heart. Cold and calculating, she toyed with Samson, pretending to love him while looking for personal gain. How could Samson be so foolish? Four times Delilah took advantage of him. If he didn't realize what was happening after the first or second experience, surely he should have understood the situation by the fourth time! We think Samson was foolish; but how many times do we allow ourselves to be deceived by flattery and give in to temptation and wrong beliefs? Avoid falling prey to deceit by asking God to help you distinguish between deception and truth.

BIBLE READING: Joshua 7:1-26
KEY BIBLE VERSE: *The LORD said to Joshua, "Get up! Why are you lying on your face like this? Israel has sinned and broken my covenant! They have stolen the things that I commanded to be set apart for me. And they have not only stolen them; they have also lied about it and hidden the things among their belongings."* (Joshua 7:10-11)

One person's deception can cause many to suffer. Why did Achan's sin bring judgment on the entire nation? Although it was one man's failure, God saw it as national disobedience to a national law. God needed the entire nation to be committed to the job it had agreed to do—conquer the land. Thus, when one person failed, everyone failed. If Achan's sin went unpunished, unlimited looting could break out. The nation as a whole had to take responsibility for preventing this undisciplined disobedience.

Achan's sin was not merely his keeping some of the plunder (God allowed it in some cases), but his disobeying God's explicit command to destroy everything connected with Jericho. His sin was indifference to the evil and idolatry of the city, not just a desire for money and clothes. God would not protect Israel's army again until the sin was removed and the army returned to obeying him without reservation. God is not content with our doing what is right some of the time. He wants us to do what is right all the time. We are under his orders to eliminate any thoughts, practices, or possessions that hinder our devotion to him.

Related Topics: INTEGRITY, LYING, TRUTH

DECISIONS *(Actions, Choices, Judgments)*

Why does God allow us the freedom to make choices?

BIBLE READING: Genesis 2:15-25
KEY BIBLE VERSE: *The LORD God gave him this warning: "You may freely eat any fruit in the garden except fruit from the tree of the knowledge of good and evil. If you eat of its fruit, you will surely die."* (Genesis 2:16-17)

We can learn from our mistakes. God gave Adam responsibility for the garden and told him not to eat from "the tree of the knowledge of good and evil," also called the "Tree of Conscience." Rather than physically preventing him from eating, God gave Adam a choice, and thus the possibility of choosing wrongly. God still gives us choices, and we, too, often choose wrongly. These wrong choices may cause us pain, but they can help us learn and grow and make better choices in the future. Living with the consequences of our choices teaches us to think and choose more carefully.

We can demonstrate our obedience to God through the choices we make. Why would God place a tree in the garden and then forbid Adam to eat from it? God wanted Adam to obey, but God gave Adam the freedom to choose. Without choice, Adam would have been like a prisoner, and his obedience would have been hollow. The two trees provided an exercise in choice, with rewards for choosing to obey and sad consequences for choosing to disobey. When you are faced with the choice, always choose to obey God.

How can we make good decisions?

 BIBLE READING: Nehemiah 1:1-11
KEY BIBLE VERSE: *When I heard this, I sat down and wept. In fact, for days I mourned, fasted, and prayed to the God of heaven.* (Nehemiah 1:4)

Prayer is an essential resource in good decision making. Nehemiah fasted and prayed for several days, expressing his sorrow for Israel's sin and his desire that Jerusalem would again come alive with the worship of the one true (1) praise, (2) thanksgiving, (3) repentance, (4) specific request, and (5) commitment. Heartfelt prayers like Nehemiah's can help clarify (1) any problem you may be facing, (2) God's great power to help you, and (3) the job you have to do. By the end of his prayer time, Nehemiah knew what action he had to take (1:11). When God's people pray, difficult decisions fall into proper perspective, and appropriate actions follow.

 BIBLE READING: Proverbs 18:10-17
KEY BIBLE VERSE: *Intelligent people are always open to new ideas. In fact, they look for them.* (Proverbs 18:15)

Wise decisions result from seeking information. Among these concise statements, there are three basic principles for making sound decisions: (1) get the facts before answering; (2) be open to new ideas; (3) make sure you hear both sides of the story before judging. All three principles center around seeking additional information. This is difficult work, but the only alternative is prejudice—judging before getting the facts.

 BIBLE READING: John 5:16-30
KEY BIBLE VERSE: *Jesus replied, "My Father never stops working, so why should I?"* (John 5:17)

Jesus is our best model for good decision making. Because of his unity with God, Jesus lived as God wanted him to live. Because of our identification with Jesus, we must honor him and live as he wants us to live. Asking ourselves the questions, What would Jesus do? and What would Jesus have me do? may help us make the right choices.

BIBLE READING: James 1:2-8

KEY BIBLE VERSE: *When you ask him, be sure that you really expect him to answer, for a doubtful mind is as unsettled as a wave of the sea that is driven and tossed by the wind.* (James 1:6)

Good decisions can be made in spite of doubts. If you have ever seen the constant rolling of huge waves at sea, you know how restless they are—subject to the forces of wind, gravity, and tide. Doubt leaves a person as unsettled as the restless waves. If you want to stop being tossed about, rely on God to show you what is best for you. Ask him for wisdom, and trust that he will give it to you. Then your decisions will be sure and solid.

Related Topics: ACTIONS, BELIEF/BELIEVE, CHOICES

DEDICATION (*Concentration, Devotion, Focus*)

What does it mean to be dedicated to God?

BIBLE READING: 2 Chronicles 7:1-22

KEY BIBLE VERSE: *King Solomon offered a sacrifice of 22,000 oxen and 120,000 sheep. And so the king and all the people dedicated the Temple of God.* (2 Chronicles 7:5)

God's purposes become our priorities. The temple was dedicated to God, and Solomon and the people prepared to worship him. Dedication means setting apart a place, an object, or a person for an exclusive purpose. The purpose of this dedication was to set apart the temple as a special place to worship God. Today, our bodies are God's temple (2 Corinthians 6:16). Solomon's dedication of the temple shows us that we should dedicate ourselves to carry out God's special purpose (Ephesians 1:11-12).

BIBLE READING: Luke 17:7-10

KEY BIBLE VERSE: *When you obey me you should say, "We are not worthy of praise. We are servants who have simply done our duty."* (Luke 17:10)

Dedication to God is our duty. If we have obeyed God, we have only done our duty. We should regard it as a privilege. Do you sometimes feel that you deserve extra credit for serving God? Remember, obedience is not something extra we do; it is our duty. Jesus is not saying that our service is meaningless or useless, nor is he doing away with rewards. He is attacking unwarranted self-esteem and spiritual pride.

BIBLE READING: Luke 9:51-62

KEY BIBLE VERSE: *Jesus told him, "Anyone who puts a hand to the plow and then looks back is not fit for the Kingdom of God."* (Luke 9:62)

Jesus commands our dedication. What does Jesus want from us? Total dedication, not halfhearted commitment. We can't pick and choose among Jesus' ideas and follow him selectively; we have to accept the cross along with the crown, judgment as well as mercy. We must count the cost and be willing to abandon everything else that has given us security. With our focus on Jesus, we should allow nothing to distract us from the manner of living that he calls good and true.

Related Topics: DEVOTION, DISCIPLINE, FAITHFULNESS

DEFEAT (*see* FAILURE)

DEFENSE (*see* PROTECTION)

DELAY (*Pause, Postpone, Wait*)

What can we learn from delays?

BIBLE READING: Joshua 18:1-10

KEY BIBLE VERSE: *Then Joshua asked them, "How long are you going to wait before taking possession of the remaining land the LORD, the God of your ancestors, has given to you?"* (Joshua 18:3)

Procrastination can be disobedience. Joshua asked why some of the tribes were putting off the job of possessing the land. Often we delay doing jobs that seem large, difficult, boring, or disagreeable. To continue putting them off shows lack of discipline, poor stewardship of time, and in some cases disobedience to God. Jobs we don't enjoy require concentration, teamwork, twice as much time, lots of encouragement, and accountability. Remember this when you are tempted to procrastinate.

BIBLE READING: 1 Samuel 13:1-15

KEY BIBLE VERSE: *Saul waited there seven days for Samuel, as Samuel had instructed him earlier, but Samuel still didn't come. Saul realized that his troops were rapidly slipping away. So he demanded, "Bring me the burnt offering and the peace offerings!" And Saul sacrificed the burnt offering himself.* (1 Samuel 13:8-9)

Delays beyond our control test our patience and obedience. It is difficult to trust God when you feel your resources slipping away. When Saul felt that time was running out, he became impatient with God's timing. In thinking that the ritual was all he needed, he substituted the ritual for faith in God.

When faced with a difficult decision, don't allow impatience to drive you to disobey God. When you know what God wants, follow his plan regardless of the consequences. God often uses delays to test our obedience and patience.

Related Topics: CIRCUMSTANCES, PATIENCE, WAITING

DELEGATION (*Appointing, Mission, Sharing*)

How does the Bible illustrate the importance of delegation?

BIBLE READING: Exodus 18:1-27

KEY BIBLE VERSE: *You're going to wear yourself out—and the people, too. This job is too heavy a burden for you to handle all by yourself.* (Exodus 18:18)

Moses had to learn to delegate. Moses was spending so much time and energy hearing the Hebrews' complaints that he could not get to other important work. Jethro suggested that Moses delegate most of this work to others and focus his efforts on jobs only he could do. People in positions of responsibility sometimes feel they are the only ones who can do necessary tasks, but others are capable of handling part of the load. Delegation relieved Moses' stress and improved the quality of the government. It helped prepare the Israelites for the system of government later set up in Canaan. Proper delegation can multiply your effectiveness while giving others a chance to grow.

Related Topics: CHURCH, LEADERSHIP, SERVING

DELIGHT (*see* JOY)

DELIVERANCE (*see* SALVATION)

DEMONS (*Evil, Possession, Satanic*)

▶ **DEMONIC CHARACTERISTICS**
What does the Bible say about demons?

BIBLE READING: Matthew 8:28-34
KEY BIBLE VERSE: *They began screaming at him, "Why are you bothering us, Son of God? You have no right to torture us before God's appointed time!"* (Matthew 8:29)

Demons are fallen angels who serve Satan. Demon-possessed people are under the control of one or more demons. Demons are fallen angels who joined Satan in his rebellion against God and are now evil spirits under Satan's control. They help Satan tempt people to sin and have great destructive powers. But whenever they are confronted by Jesus, they lose their power.

These demons recognized Jesus as God's Son, but they didn't think they had to obey him. Just believing is not enough (see James 2:19 for a discussion of belief and devils). Faith is more than belief. By faith, you accept what Jesus has done for you, receive him as the only one who can save you from sin, and live out your faith by obeying his commands.

The fate of demons is sealed. The Bible tells us that at the end of the world the devil and his angels will be thrown into the lake of burning sulfur (Revelation 20:10). When the demons asked if Jesus had come to torment them "before God's appointed time," they showed they knew their ultimate fate.

The goal of demons is destruction. When the demons entered the pigs, they drove the animals into the sea. The demons' action proves their destructive intent—if they could not destroy the men, they would destroy the pigs. Jesus' action, by contrast, shows the value he places on each human life.

BIBLE READING: Mark 1:21-28
KEY BIBLE VERSE: *Amazement gripped the audience, and they began to discuss what had happened. "What sort of new teaching is this?" they asked excitedly. "It has such authority! Even evil spirits obey his orders!"* (Mark 1:27)

Demons are powerful, but limited. Evil spirits, or demons, are ruled by Satan. They work to tempt people to sin. They were not created by Satan—because God is the Creator of all. Rather they are fallen angels who joined Satan in his rebellion. Though not all disease comes from Satan, demons can cause a person to become mute, deaf, blind, or insane. But in every case where demons confronted Jesus, they lost their power. Thus God limits what evil spirits can do; they can do nothing without his permission. During Jesus' life on earth, demons were allowed to be very active to demonstrate once and for all Christ's power and authority over them.

Demon possession can be similar to mental illness. Many psychologists dismiss all accounts of demon possession as a primitive way to describe mental illness. Although throughout history mental illness has often been wrongly diagnosed as demon possession, clearly a hostile outside force controlled the man described in Mark 1. Mark emphasized Jesus' conflict with evil powers to show his superiority over them, so he recorded many stories about Jesus driving out evil spirits. Jesus didn't have to conduct an elaborate exorcism ritual. His word was enough to send out the demons.

▶ JESUS AND DEMONS
How did Jesus confront demons?

BIBLE READING: Mark 3:7-12
KEY BIBLE VERSE: *Whenever those possessed by evil spirits caught sight of him, they would fall down in front of him shrieking, "You are the Son of God!"* (Mark 3:11)

Jesus confronted demons without compromise. The evil spirits knew that Jesus was the Son of God, but they refused to turn from their evil purposes. Knowing about Jesus, or even believing that he is God's Son, does not guarantee salvation. You must also want to follow and obey him (see James 2:17).

Jesus warned the evil spirits not to reveal his identity as Messiah because he did not want them to reinforce a popular misconception. The huge crowds were looking for a political and military leader who would free them from Rome's control, and they thought that the Messiah predicted by the Old Testament prophets would be this kind of man. Jesus wanted to teach the people about the kind of Messiah he really was—one who was far different from their expectations. Christ's kingdom is spiritual. It begins not with the overthrow of governments, but with the overthrow of sin in a person's heart.

BIBLE READING: Luke 8:26-39
KEY BIBLE VERSE: *"What is your name?" Jesus asked. "Legion," he replied—for the man was filled with many demons.* (Luke 8:30)

Jesus confronted demons with absolute authority. These demons recognized Jesus and his authority immediately. They knew who Jesus was and what his great power could do to them. Demons, Satan's messengers, are powerful and destructive. Still active today, they attempt to distort and destroy people's relationship with God. Demons and demon possession are real. It is vital that believers recognize the power of Satan and his demons, but we shouldn't let curiosity lead us to get involved with demonic forces (Deuteronomy 18:10-12). Demons are powerless against those who trust in Jesus. If we resist the devil, he will leave us alone (James 4:7).

BIBLE READING: Luke 9:37-45
KEY BIBLE VERSE: *As the boy came forward, the demon knocked him to the ground and threw him into a violent convulsion. But Jesus rebuked the evil spirit and healed the boy. Then he gave him back to his father.* (Luke 9:42)

Jesus' authority over the demonic continues today. As the disciples came down from the mountain with Jesus following the transfiguration, they passed from a reassuring experience of God's presence to a frightening experience of evil. The beauty they had just seen must have made the ugliness seem even uglier. As our spiritual vision improves and allows us to see and understand God better, we will also be able to see and understand evil better. We would be overcome by its horror if we did not have Jesus with us to take us through it safely.

▶ **DEMONS TODAY**
How are demons present today?

BIBLE READING: Ephesians 6:10-18
KEY BIBLE VERSE: *We are not fighting against people made of flesh and blood, but against the evil rulers and authorities of the unseen world, against those mighty powers of darkness who rule this world, and against wicked spirits in the heavenly realms.* (Ephesians 6:12)

The enemy is unseen, but the battle is real. In the Christian life we battle against rulers and authorities (the powerful evil forces of fallen angels headed by Satan, who is a vicious fighter; see 1 Peter 5:8). To withstand their attacks, we must depend on God's strength and use every piece of his armor. Paul is not only giving this counsel to the church as a whole, but to all individuals within the church. The whole body needs to be armed. As you do battle against "the powers of of darkness who rule this world," fight in the strength of the body of Christ—and remember, its power comes from the Holy Spirit.

The enemy is unseen, but the struggle is personal. These enemies who are not "flesh and blood" are demons over whom Satan has control. They are not mere fantasies—they are very real. We face a powerful army whose goal is to defeat Christ's church. When we believe in Christ, these beings become our enemies, and they try every device to turn us away from him and back to sin. Although we are assured of victory, we must engage in the struggle until Christ returns because Satan is constantly battling against all who are on the Lord's side. We need supernatural power to defeat Satan, and God has provided this by giving us his Holy Spirit within us and his armor surrounding us. If you feel discouraged, remember Jesus' words to Peter: "Upon this rock I will build my church, and the powers of hell will not conquer it" (Matthew 16:18).

Related Topics: EVIL, POWER, SATAN

DENIAL *(Excuse, Refuse, Rejection)*

How are Christians tempted to deny Jesus?

BIBLE READING: Matthew 26:69-75
KEY BIBLE VERSE: *Suddenly, Jesus' words flashed through Peter's mind: "Before the rooster crows, you will deny me three times." And he went away, crying bitterly.* (Matthew 26:75)

Denial usually isn't a sudden act. There were three stages to Peter's denial. First he acted confused and tried to divert attention from himself by changing the subject. Second, he denied that he knew Jesus, using an oath. Third, he began to curse and swear. Believers who deny Christ often begin doing so subtly by pretending not to know him. When opportunities to discuss religious issues come up, they walk away or pretend they don't know the answers. With only a little more pressure, they can be induced to deny flatly their relationship with Christ. If you find yourself subtly diverting conversation so you don't have to talk about Christ, watch out. You may be on the road to disowning him.

Denial comes when we don't anticipate its effects on us. Peter wept bitterly, not only because he realized that he had denied his Lord, the Messiah, but also because he had turned away from a very dear friend, a person who had loved and taught him for three years. Peter had said that he would *never* disown

Christ, despite Jesus' prediction (Mark 14:29-31; Luke 22:33-34). But when frightened, he went against all he had boldly promised. Unable to stand up for his Lord for even twelve hours, he had failed as a disciple and as a friend. We need to be aware of our own breaking points and not become overconfident or self-sufficient. If we fail him, we must remember that Christ can use those who recognize their failure. From this humiliating experience Peter learned much that would help him later when he assumed leadership of the young church.

Related Topics: ABANDON, FAITHFULNESS, SUFFERING

DEPEND *(Need, Rely, Trust)*

What does it mean to depend on God?

BIBLE READING: 1 Chronicles 29:10-25
KEY BIBLE VERSE: *Yours, O LORD, is the greatness, the power, the glory, the victory, and the majesty. Everything in the heavens and on earth is yours, O LORD, and this is your kingdom. We adore you as the one who is over all things.* (1 Chronicles 29:11)

Dependence on God means counting on his control. David acknowledged God's greatness. Our constantly changing world is controlled by a constant and unchanging God. As we see life come and go, materials decay, and friends change, the only thing on which we can truly depend is God's control. His love and purpose for us never change. Only when we understand this can we have real peace and security.

BIBLE READING: 2 Corinthians 1:3-11
KEY BIBLE VERSE: *We expected to die. But as a result, we learned not to rely on ourselves, but on God who can raise the dead.* (2 Corinthians 1:9)

Dependence on God means counting on him for our daily needs. Paul does not give details about their hardships in Asia, although his accounts of all three missionary journeys record many difficult trials he faced (Acts 13:2–14:28; Acts 15:40–21:17). He does write that they felt doomed to die, and realized that they could do nothing to help themselves—they simply had to trust in God.

We often depend on our own skills and abilities when life seems easy, but we turn to God when we feel unable to help ourselves. Depending on God is not defeat or weakness, but a realization of our own powerlessness without him and our need for his constant contact. God is our source of power, and we receive his help by keeping in touch with him. With this attitude, problems will drive us to God rather than away from him. Learn how to rely on God daily.

BIBLE READING: Mark 9:14-29
KEY BIBLE VERSE: *Jesus replied, "This kind can be cast out only by prayer."* (Mark 9:29)

Dependence on God means counting on the power of prayer. The disciples would often face difficult situations that could be resolved only through prayer. Prayer is the key that unlocks faith in our life. Effective prayer needs both an attitude—complete dependence—and an action—asking. Prayer demonstrates our reliance on God as we humbly invite him to fill us with faith and power. There is no substitute for prayer, especially in circumstances that seem impossible.

Related Topics: FAITH, PRAYER, TRUST

DEPRESSION (*Apathy, Boredom, Sadness*)

What are some common causes of depression?

BIBLE READING: Judges 15:1-20
KEY BIBLE VERSE: *Now Samson was very thirsty, and he cried out to the* LORD, *"You have accomplished this great victory by the strength of your servant. Must I now die of thirst and fall into the hands of these pagan people?"* (Judges 15:18)

Depression often follows exhaustion. Samson was physically and emotionally exhausted. After a great personal victory, his attitude declined quickly into self-pity—"Must I now die of thirst?" Emotionally, we are most vulnerable after a great effort or when faced with real physical needs. Severe depression often follows great achievements, so don't be surprised if you feel drained after a personal victory.

During these times of vulnerability, avoid the temptation to think that God owes you for your efforts. It was *his* strength that gave you victory. Concentrate on keeping your attitudes, actions, and words focused on God instead of yourself.

BIBLE READING: 1 Kings 19:1-9
KEY BIBLE VERSE: *Elijah was afraid and fled for his life. He went to Beersheba, a town in Judah, and he left his servant there. Then he went on alone into the desert, traveling all day. He sat down under a solitary broom tree and prayed that he might die. "I have had enough,* LORD," *he said. "Take my life, for I am no better than my ancestors."* (1 Kings 19:3-4)

Depression sometimes follows great success. Elijah experienced the depths of fatigue and discouragement just after his two great spiritual victories: the defeat of the prophets of Baal and the answered prayer for rain. Often discouragement sets in after great spiritual experiences, especially those requiring physical effort or involving great emotion. To lead him out of depression, God first let Elijah rest and eat. Then God confronted him with the need to return to his mission—to speak God's words in Israel. Elijah's battles were not over; there was still work for him to do. When you feel let down after a great spiritual experience, remember that God's purpose for your life is not yet over.

What are some Biblical cures for common depression?

BIBLE READING: Psalm 42:1-11
KEY BIBLE VERSE: *Why am I discouraged? Why so sad? I will put my hope in God! I will praise him again—my Savior and my God! Now I am deeply discouraged, but I will remember your kindness—from Mount Hermon, the source of the Jordan, from the land of Mount Mizar.* (Psalm 42:5-6)

Depression can be relieved by meditating on God's Word. Depression is one of the most common emotional ailments. One antidote for depression is to meditate on the record of God's goodness to his people. This will take your mind off the present situation and give you hope that it will improve. It will focus your thoughts on God's ability to help you rather than on your inability to help yourself. When you feel depressed, take advantage of this psalm's antidepressant. Read the Bible's accounts of God's goodness and meditate on them.

Depression can be relieved by patience. Later in this psalm, the writer tells his own soul to be patient. There are plenty of reasons from the past to trust God. In spite of the discouragement of the moment, the author is convinced that God has plans for tomorrow that are better. That fact may not make the darkness bright, but it may make it more bearable until the morning.

Depression can be relieved by expecting God to act. The psalmist confidently closes this song with a statement of hope in the midst of difficult emotions. He may not *feel* like it, but he *knows* that he will again have plenty of reason to praise him for all that he will do (42:11).

Related Topics: DISCOURAGEMENT, PATIENCE, STRENGTH

DESERTION (*see* ABANDON)

DESERVE (*Earn, Merit, Worthy*)

Why does God give us what we don't deserve?

BIBLE READING: Judges 2:10-23
KEY BIBLE VERSE: *Every time Israel went out to battle, the LORD fought against them, bringing them defeat, just as he promised. And the people were very distressed. Then the LORD raised up judges to rescue the Israelites from their enemies.* (Judges 2:15-16)

God is merciful in spite of sin. Despite Israel's disobedience, God showed his great mercy by raising up judges to save the people from their oppressors. Mercy has been defined as "not giving a person what he or she deserves." This is exactly what God did for Israel and what he does for us. Our disobedience demands judgment! But God shows mercy toward us by providing an escape from sin's penalty through Jesus Christ, who alone saves us from sin. When we pray for forgiveness, we are asking for what we do not deserve. Yet when we take this step and trust in Christ's saving work on our behalf, we can experience God's forgiveness.

BIBLE READING: Isaiah 48:1-11
KEY BIBLE VERSE: *For my own sake and for the honor of my name, I will hold back my anger and not wipe you out.* (Isaiah 48:9)

God is merciful in keeping with his own character. There was nothing in Israel's actions, attitudes, or accomplishments to compel God to love and to save them. But for his own sake, to show who he is and what he can do, he saved them. God does not save us because we are good, but because he loves us and because of his forgiving nature.

God is merciful in the midst of trials. Do you find it easy to complain when your life becomes complicated or difficult? Why would a loving God allow all kinds of unpleasant experiences to come to his children? Verse 10 shows us plainly that God tests us in the "furnace of suffering." Rather than complain, we should turn to God in faith for the strength to endure, and rejoice in our sufferings (see Romans 5:3; James 1:2-4). For without the testing, we would never know what we are capable of doing, nor would we grow. And without the refining, we will not become more pure and more like Christ. What kinds of adversity are you currently facing?

BIBLE READING: Romans 5:1-11
KEY BIBLE VERSE: *God showed his great love for us by sending Christ to die for us while we were still sinners.* (Romans 5:8)

God is merciful even before we turn to him. *While we were still sinners*—these are amazing words. God sent Jesus Christ to die for us, not because we were good enough, but because he loved us. Whenever you feel uncertain about God's love for you, remember that he loved you even before you turned to him. If God loved you when you were a rebel, he can surely strengthen you now that you love him in return.

Related Topics: GRACE, MERCY, TRAINING

DESIRES *(Needs, Wants, Wishes)*

▶ **APPROPRIATE DESIRES**
What desires meet with God's approval?

BIBLE READING: Genesis 29:1-30
KEY BIBLE VERSE: *Jacob spent the next seven years working to pay for Rachel. But his love for her was so strong that it seemed to him but a few days.* (Genesis 29:20)

Some desires require a real investment of ourselves. People often wonder if working a long time for something they desire is worth it. Jacob worked seven years to marry Rachel. After being tricked, he agreed to work seven more years for her (although he did get to marry Rachel shortly after he married Leah)! The most important goals and desires are worth working and waiting for. Movies and television have created the illusion that people have to wait only about an hour to solve their problems or get what they want. Don't be trapped into thinking the same is true in real life. Patience is hardest when we need it the most, but it is the key to achieving our goals.

BIBLE READING: Psalm 97:1-12
KEY BIBLE VERSE: *You who love the LORD, hate evil! He protects the lives of his godly people and rescues them from the power of the wicked.* (Psalm 97:10)

Our desires should not go against what God desires. A sincere desire to please God will result in an alignment of your desires with God's desires. You will love what God loves and hate what God hates. If you love the Lord, you will hate evil. If you do not despise the actions of people who take advantage of others, if you admire people who only look out for themselves, or if you envy those who get ahead using any means to accomplish their ends, then your primary desire in life is not to please God. Learn to love God's ways and hate evil in every form—not only the obvious sins but also the socially acceptable ones.

BIBLE READING: Acts 21:1-16
KEY BIBLE VERSE: *But [Paul] said, "Why all this weeping? You are breaking my heart! For I am ready not only to be jailed at Jerusalem but also to die for the sake of the Lord Jesus."* (Acts 21:13)

When desires are in conflict, the right choice is obedience to God. Paul knew he would be imprisoned in Jerusalem. Although his friends pleaded with him not to go there, he knew that he had to because God wanted him to. No one enjoys pain, but a faithful disciple wants above all else to please God. Our desire to please God should overshadow our desire to avoid hardship and suffering. When we really want to do God's will, we must accept all that comes with it—even the pain. Then we can say with Paul, "The Lord's will be done."

BIBLE READING: Hebrews 9:11-28
KEY BIBLE VERSE: *Just think how much more the blood of Christ will purify our hearts from deeds that lead to death so that we can worship the living God. For*

by the power of the eternal Spirit, Christ offered himself to God as a perfect sacrifice for our sins. (Hebrews 9:14)

The Holy Spirit will reshape our desires to match God's. If our hearts are not changed, following God's rules is unpleasant and difficult. We rebel against being told how to live. The Holy Spirit, however, gives us new desires. He helps us want to obey God (see Philippians 2:12-13). With new hearts, we find that serving God is our greatest joy.

▶ **INAPPROPRIATE DESIRES**

What happens when our desires clash with God's desires?

BIBLE READING: Galatians 5:13-26
KEY BIBLE VERSE: *The old sinful nature loves to do evil, which is just opposite from what the Holy Spirit wants. And the Spirit gives us desires that are opposite from what the sinful nature desires. These two forces are constantly fighting each other, and your choices are never free from this conflict.* (Galatians 5:17)

We need God's help to settle the conflict. Paul describes the two forces conflicting within us—the Holy Spirit and the sinful nature (our evil desires or inclinations; see also 5:16, 19, 24). Paul is not saying that these forces are equal—the Holy Spirit is infinitely stronger. But if we rely on our own wisdom, we will make wrong choices. If we try to follow the Spirit by our own human effort, we will fail. Our only way to freedom from our evil desires is through the empowering of the Holy Spirit (see Romans 8:9; Ephesians 4:23-24; Colossians 3:3-8).

We must not ignore the tendency to follow our own way. We all have evil desires, and we can't ignore them. In order for us to follow the Holy Spirit's guidance, we must deal with them decisively (crucify them—5:24). These desires include obvious sins such as sexual immorality and witchcraft. They also include less obvious sins such as selfish ambition, hatred, and jealousy. Those who ignore such sins or refuse to deal with them reveal that they have not received the gift of the Spirit leading to a transformed life.

BIBLE READING: Matthew 5:27-30
KEY BIBLE VERSE: *Anyone who even looks at a woman with lust in his eye has already committed adultery with her in his heart.* (Matthew 5:28)

Uncontrolled desires can themselves be sinful. The Old Testament law said that it is wrong for a person to have sex with someone other than his or her spouse (Exodus 20:14). But Jesus said that the *desire* to have sex with someone other than your spouse is mental adultery and thus sin. Jesus emphasized that if the *act* is wrong, then so is the *intention*. To be faithful to your spouse with your body but not your mind is to break the trust so vital to a strong marriage. Jesus is not condemning natural interest in the opposite sex or even healthy sexual desire, but the deliberate and repeated filling of one's mind with fantasies that would be evil if acted out.

Uncontrolled desires can lead to sin. Some think that if lustful thoughts are sin, why shouldn't a person go ahead and carry out the lustful actions too? Acting out sinful desires is harmful in several ways: (1) it causes people to excuse sin rather than to stop sinning; (2) it destroys marriages; (3) it is deliberate rebellion against God's Word; and (4) it always hurts someone else in addition to the sinner. Sinful action is more dangerous than sinful desire, and that is why desires should not be acted out. Nevertheless, sinful desire is just as damaging to righteousness. Left unchecked, wrong desires will result in wrong actions and turn people away from God.

Related Topics: GOALS, OBEDIENCE, SIN

DESPAIR (Give up, Grief, Hopelessness)

▶ **EXAMPLES OF DESPAIR**
What makes people reach a point of despair?

📖 BIBLE READING: Isaiah 59:1-21
KEY BIBLE VERSE: *There is a problem—your sins have cut you off from God. Because of your sin, he has turned away and will not listen anymore.* (Isaiah 59:2)

Despair comes most easily from realizing our alienation from God. Sin offends our holy God and separates us from him. Because God is holy, he cannot ignore, excuse, or tolerate sin as though it didn't matter. Sin cuts people off from him, forming a wall to isolate God from the people he loves. No wonder this long list of wretched sins makes God angry and forces him to look the other way. People who die with their sin unforgiven separate themselves eternally from God. God wants them to live with him forever, but he cannot take them into his holy presence unless their sin is removed. Have you confessed your sin to God, allowing him to remove it? The Lord can save you if you turn to him.

📖 BIBLE READING: Joel 1:1-12
KEY BIBLE VERSE: *The grapevines and the fig trees have all withered. The pomegranate trees, palm trees, and apple trees—yes, all the fruit trees—have dried up. All joy has dried up with them.* (Joel 1:12)

Despair can overcome a nation. This prophet described a people ripe for despair. Their physical and moral senses were dulled, making them oblivious to sin. Joel called them to awaken from their complacency and admit their sins before it was too late. Otherwise, everything would be destroyed, even the grapes that caused their drunkenness. Our times of peace and prosperity can lull us to sleep. We must never let material abundance hinder our spiritual readiness.

📖 BIBLE READING: Revelation 16:1-21
KEY BIBLE VERSE: *Then the fifth angel poured out his bowl on the throne of the beast, and his kingdom was plunged into darkness. And his subjects ground their teeth in anguish, and they cursed the God of heaven for their pains and sores. But they refused to repent of all their evil deeds.* (Revelation 16:10-11)

Despair can turn us away from our real source of hope. We know that the people realized that these judgments came from God because they cursed him for sending them. But they still refused to recognize God's authority and repent of their sins. Christians should not be surprised at the hostility and hardness of heart of unbelievers. Even when the power of God is fully and completely revealed, many will still refuse to repent. If you find yourself ignoring God more and more, turn back to him now before your heart becomes too hard to repent.

▶ **ESCAPES FROM DESPAIR**
How can God help us handle times of despair?

BIBLE READING: Psalm 40:1-17

KEY BIBLE VERSE: *Troubles surround me—too many to count! They pile up so high I can't see my way out. They are more numerous than the hairs on my head. I have lost all my courage.* (Psalm 40:12)

Overcoming despair often requires patience. Waiting for God to help us is not easy, but David received four benefits from waiting: God (1) lifted him out of his despair, (2) set his feet on a rock, (3) gave him a firm place to stand, and (4) put a new song of praise in his mouth. Often blessings cannot be received unless we go through the trial of waiting.

BIBLE READING: Genesis 48:1-22

KEY BIBLE VERSE: *Then Jacob said to Joseph, "I never thought I would see you again, but now God has let me see your children, too."* (Genesis 48:11)

God can always provide hope to lift us out of despair. When Joseph became a slave, Jacob thought he was dead and wept in despair (37:30). But eventually God's plan allowed Jacob to regain not only his son, but his grandchildren as well. Circumstances are never so bad that they are beyond God's help. Jacob regained his son. Job got a new family (Job 42:10-17). Mary regained her brother Lazarus (John 11:1-44). We need never despair, because we belong to a loving God. We never know what good he will bring out of a seemingly hopeless situation.

BIBLE READING: Exodus 14:1-14

KEY BIBLE VERSE: *Moses told the people, "Don't be afraid. Just stand where you are and watch the LORD rescue you. The Egyptians that you see today will never be seen again. The LORD himself will fight for you. You won't have to lift a finger in your defense!"* (Exodus 14:13-14)

Trusting God is the most reliable weapon against despair. Trapped against the sea, the Israelites faced the Egyptian army sweeping in for the kill. The Israelites thought they were doomed. After watching God's powerful hand deliver them from Egypt, their only response was fear, whining, and despair. Where was their trust in God? Israel had to learn from repeated experience that God was able to provide for them. God has preserved these examples in the Bible so that we can learn to trust him the first time. By focusing on God's faithfulness in the past we can face crises with confidence rather than with fear and complaining.

Related Topics: FAITH, FEAR, HOPE

DETAILS (*Data, Parts, Pieces*)

How does God relate to the details of our lives?

BIBLE READING: Exodus 39:32-43

KEY BIBLE VERSE: *Moses inspected all their work and blessed them because it had been done as the LORD had commanded him.* (Exodus 39:43)

God cares about details. The tabernacle was finally complete to the last detail. God was keenly interested in every minute part. The Creator of the universe was concerned about even the little things. Matthew 10:30 says that God knows the number of hairs on our head. This shows that God is greatly interested in you. Don't be afraid to talk with him about any of your concerns—no matter how small or unimportant they might seem.

BIBLE READING: Luke 16:1-15

KEY BIBLE VERSE: *Unless you are faithful in small matters, you won't be faithful in large ones. If you cheat even a little, you won't be honest with greater responsibilities.* (Luke 16:10)

God expects us to care about the details of our life. Our integrity is often tested in money matters. God calls us to be honest even in small details we could easily rationalize away. Heaven's riches are far more valuable than earthly wealth. But if we are not trustworthy with our money here (no matter how much or little we have), we will be unfit to handle the vast riches of God's kingdom. Don't let your integrity slip in small matters, and it will not fail you in crucial decisions either.

Related Topics: EXCUSES, FAITHFULNESS, OBEDIENCE

DETERIORATION (*see* SIN)

DETERMINATION (*Concentration, Plan, Purpose*)

What kind of determination is important to have?

BIBLE READING: 1 Samuel 7:3-17

KEY BIBLE VERSE: *Samuel said to all the people of Israel, "If you are really serious about wanting to return to the LORD, get rid of your foreign gods and your images of Ashtoreth. Determine to obey only the LORD; then he will rescue you from the Philistines."* (1 Samuel 7:3)

Determine to obey God. Samuel told the people they had to "determine to obey only the Lord." *To determine* means to set your mind on a course of action. This kind of commitment means that you don't back out, but you work toward the goal you have set. If you have made a decision to follow God, don't allow excuses, distractions, or second thoughts to deter you from your goal.

BIBLE READING: Luke 9:51-56

KEY BIBLE VERSE: *As the time drew near for his return to heaven, Jesus resolutely set out for Jerusalem.* (Luke 9:51)

Determine to follow Jesus in spite of obstacles. Although Jesus knew he would face persecution and death in Jerusalem, he was determined to go there. That kind of resolve should characterize our life too. When God gives us a course of action, we must move steadily toward our destination, no matter what potential hazards await us there.

Related Topics: DEVOTION, FAITHFULNESS, OBEDIENCE

DEVOTION (*Adoration, Dedication, Worship*)

What kind of devotion should we have towards God?

BIBLE READING: Exodus 33:7-23

KEY BIBLE VERSE: *Moses said to the LORD, "You have been telling me, 'Take these people up to the Promised Land.' But you haven't told me whom you will send with me. You call me by name and tell me I have found favor with you. Please, if this is really so, show me your intentions so I will understand you more fully and do exactly what you want me to do. Besides, don't forget that this nation is your very own people."* (Exodus 33:12-13)

We should treat God as our closest friend. God and Moses talked face to face in the Tent of Meeting, just as friends do. Why did Moses find such favor with God? It certainly was not because he was perfect, gifted, or powerful. Rather, it was because God chose Moses, and Moses in turn relied wholeheartedly on God's wisdom and direction. Friendship with God was a true privilege for Moses, out of reach for the other Hebrews. But it is not out of reach for us today. Jesus called his disciples—and, by extension, all of his followers—his friends (John 15:15). He has called you to be his friend. Will you trust him as Moses did?

 BIBLE READING: 1 Chronicles 28:1-10
KEY BIBLE VERSE: *Solomon, my son, get to know the God of your ancestors. Worship and serve him with your whole heart and with a willing mind. For the LORD sees every heart and understands and knows every plan and thought. If you seek him, you will find him. But if you forsake him, he will reject you forever.* (1 Chronicles 28:9)

Our devotion to God should be wholehearted. Nothing can be hidden from God. He sees and understands everything in our heart. David found this out the hard way when God sent Nathan to expose David's sins of adultery and murder (2 Samuel 12). David told Solomon to be completely open with God and dedicated to him. It makes no sense to try to hide any thoughts or actions from an all-knowing God. This should cause us joy, not fear, because God knows even the worst about us and loves us anyway.

 BIBLE READING: Mark 15:42-47
KEY BIBLE VERSE: *Mary Magdalene and Mary the mother of Joseph saw where Jesus' body was laid.* (Mark 15:47)

Even small things can be acts of devotion. These women could do very little. They couldn't speak before the Sanhedrin in Jesus' defense; they couldn't appeal to Pilate; they couldn't stand against the crowds; they couldn't overpower the Roman guards. But they did what they could. They stayed at the cross when the disciples had fled; they followed Jesus' body to the tomb; and they prepared spices for his body. Because these women used the opportunities they had, they were the first to witness the Resurrection. God blessed their devotion and diligence. As believers, we should take advantage of the opportunities we have and do what we *can* for Christ, instead of worrying about what we *cannot* do.

Related Topics: DEDICATION, OBEDIENCE, WORSHIP

DIFFERENCES *(Characteristics, Uniqueness, Variety)*

How do differences affect the way we relate to others?

 BIBLE READING: Genesis 19:1-29
KEY BIBLE VERSE: *When Lot still hesitated, the angels seized his hand and the hands of his wife and two daughters and rushed them to safety outside the city, for the LORD was merciful.* (Genesis 19:16)

A God-centered life will be different from others. Lot had lived so long and so contentedly among ungodly people that he was no longer a believable witness for God. He had allowed his environment to shape him, rather than shaping his environment. Do those who know you see you as a witness for God, or are you just one of the crowd, blending in unnoticed? Lot had compromised to the point that he was almost useless to God. When he finally made a stand, nobody listened. Have you too become useless to God because you are too much like your environment? To make a difference, you must first decide to be different in your faith and your conduct.

 BIBLE READING: Luke 6:12-26
KEY BIBLE VERSE: *At daybreak he called together all of his disciples and chose twelve of them to be apostles.* (Luke 6:13)

Some differences are actually strengths. Jesus selected "ordinary" men with a mixture of backgrounds and personalities to be his disciples. Today, God calls "ordinary" people together to build his church, teach salvation's message, and serve others out of love. Alone we may feel unqualified to serve Christ effectively, but together we make up a group strong enough to serve God in any way. Ask for patience to accept the diversity of people in your church, and build on the variety of strengths represented in your group.

BIBLE READING: Romans 14:1-13
KEY BIBLE VERSE: *Accept Christians who are weak in faith, and don't argue with them about what they think is right or wrong.* (Romans 14:1)

Differences can enrich our relationships. This verse assumes there will be differences of opinion in the church (in disputable matters). Paul says we are not to quarrel about issues that are matters of opinion. Differences should not be feared or avoided, but accepted and handled with love. Don't expect everyone, even in the best church, to agree on every subject. Through sharing ideas we can come to a fuller understanding of what the Bible teaches. Accept, listen to, and respect others. Differences of opinion need not cause division. They can be a source of learning and richness in our relationships.

Related Topics: CRITICISM, FELLOWSHIP, JUDGMENT

DIFFICULTIES (*see* PROBLEMS)

DIGNITY (*Honor, Value, Worth*)

How can we claim people have dignity?

BIBLE READING: Genesis 1:1-31
KEY BIBLE VERSE: *God created people in his own image; God patterned them after himself; male and female he created them.* (Genesis 1:27)

Being a special part of God's creation gives us dignity. How important is it to believe God created the earth? This is still a subject of great debate. Some say that there was a sudden explosion and the universe appeared. Others say God started the process, and the universe evolved over billions of years. Almost every ancient religion has its own story to explain how the earth came to be. And almost every scientist has an opinion on the origin of the universe. But only the

Bible shows one supreme God creating the earth out of his great love and giving all people a special place in it. We will never know all the answers to how God created the earth, but the Bible tells us that God did create it. That fact alone gives worth and dignity to all people.

 BIBLE READING: Leviticus 26:1-13

KEY BIBLE VERSE: *I, the LORD, am your God, who brought you from the land of Egypt so you would no longer be slaves. I have lifted the yoke of slavery from your neck so you can walk free with your heads held high.* (Leviticus 26:13)

God's personal care for us gives us dignity. Imagine the joy of a slave set free. God took the children of Israel out of bitter slavery and gave them freedom and dignity. We too are set free when we accept Christ's payment that redeems us from sin's slavery. We no longer need to be bogged down in shame over our past sins; we can walk with dignity because God has forgiven us and forgotten them. But just as the Israelites were still in danger of returning to a slave mentality, we need to beware of the temptation to return to our former sinful patterns.

BIBLE READING: 1 Samuel 2:1-11

KEY BIBLE VERSE: *Elkanah and Hannah returned home to Ramah without Samuel. And the boy became the LORD's helper, for he assisted Eli the priest.* (1 Samuel 2:11)

Even insignificant jobs done for God carry dignity. Samuel was Eli's helper, or assistant. In this role, Samuel's responsibilities would have included opening the tabernacle doors each morning (3:15), cleaning the furniture, and sweeping the floors. As he grew older, Samuel would have assisted Eli in offering sacrifices. The fact that he was wearing a linen ephod (a garment worn only by priests) shows that he was a priest-in-training (2:18). Because Samuel was Eli's helper, he was God's helper too. When you serve others—even in carrying out ordinary tasks—you are serving God. Because ultimately we serve God, every job has dignity.

Related Topics: CREATION, HONOR, SELF-ESTEEM

DILIGENCE (*see* DEVOTION)

DIRECTION (*Counsel, Guidance, Purpose*)

What are our best sources for direction in life?

BIBLE READING: Psalm 25:1-22

KEY BIBLE VERSE: *He leads the humble in what is right, teaching them his way.* (Psalm 25:9)

If we will humble ourselves before him, God will guide us. We are bombarded today with relentless appeals to go in various directions. Television advertising alone places hundreds of options before us, in addition to appeals made by political parties, cults, false religions, and dozens of other groups. Numerous organizations, including Christian organizations, seek to motivate us to support a cause. Add to that the dozens of decisions we must make concerning our job, our family, our money, our society, and we become desperate for someone to show us the right way. If you find yourself pulled in several directions, remember that God teaches the humble his way.

BIBLE READING: Matthew 2:1-12

KEY BIBLE VERSE: *When it was time to leave, they went home another way, because God had warned them in a dream not to return to Herod.* (Matthew 2:12)

Following Jesus involves taking a completely new direction in life. After finding Jesus and worshiping him, the magi were warned by God not to return through Jerusalem as they had intended. Finding Jesus may mean that your life must take a different direction, one that is responsive and obedient to God's Word. Are you willing to be led a different way?

BIBLE READING: John 12:12-19

KEY BIBLE VERSE: *His disciples didn't realize at the time that this was a fulfillment of prophecy. But after Jesus entered into his glory, they remembered that these Scriptures had come true before their eyes.* (John 12:16)

The longer we know Jesus, the better we will understand his ways. After Jesus' resurrection, the disciples understood for the first time many of the prophecies that they had missed along the way. Jesus' words and actions took on new meaning and made more sense. In retrospect, the disciples saw how Jesus had led them into a deeper and better understanding of his truth. Stop now and think about the events in your life leading up to where you are now. How has God led you to this point? As you grow older, you will look back and see God's involvement more clearly than you do now.

Related Topics: BIBLE, GUIDANCE, LEADERSHIP

DISAGREEMENTS (*Arguments, Opinions, Quarrels*)

How can disagreements be avoided or resolved?

BIBLE READING: Numbers 12:1-16

KEY BIBLE VERSE: *While they were at Hazeroth, Miriam and Aaron criticized Moses because he had married a Cushite woman. They said, "Has the LORD spoken only through Moses? Hasn't he spoken through us, too?" But the LORD heard them.* (Numbers 12:1-2)

In disagreements, focus on the issue at hand. People often argue over minor disagreements, leaving the real issue untouched. Such was the case when Miriam and Aaron came to Moses with a complaint. They represented the priests and the prophets, the two most powerful groups next to Moses. The real issue was their growing jealousy of Moses' position and influence. Since they could not find fault with the way Moses was leading the people, they chose to criticize his wife. Rather than face the problem squarely by dealing with their envy and pride, they chose to create a diversion from the real issue. When you are in a disagreement, stop and ask yourself if you are arguing over the real issue or if you have introduced a smoke screen by attacking someone's character. If you are unjustly criticized, remember that your critics may be afraid to face the real problem. Don't take this type of criticism personally. Ask God to help you identify the real issue and deal with it.

BIBLE READING: Matthew 5:21-26

KEY BIBLE VERSE: *Come to terms quickly with your enemy before it is too late and you are dragged into court, handed over to an officer, and thrown in jail.* (Matthew 5:25)

When disagreements occur, they should be resolved quickly. In Jesus' day, someone who couldn't pay a debt was thrown into prison until the debt was paid. Unless someone came to pay the debt for the prisoner, he or she would probably die there. It is practical advice to resolve our differences with our enemies before their anger causes more trouble (Proverbs 25:8-10). You may not get into a disagreement that takes you to court, but even small conflicts mend more easily if you try to make peace right away. In a broader sense, these verses advise us to get things right with our brothers and sisters before we have to stand before God.

BIBLE READING: Genesis 13:1-18

KEY BIBLE VERSE: *Then Abram talked it over with Lot. "This arguing between our herdsmen has got to stop," he said. "After all, we are close relatives!"* (Genesis 13:8)

Maturity is measured by the way disagreements are resolved. Facing a potential conflict with his nephew Lot, Abram took the initiative in settling the dispute. He gave Lot first choice, even though Abram, being older, had the right to choose first. Abram also showed a willingness to risk being cheated. Abram's example shows us how to respond to difficult family situations: (1) take the initiative in resolving conflicts; (2) let others have first choice, even if that means not getting what we want; (3) put family peace above personal desires.

Rivalries, arguments, and disagreements among believers can be destructive in three ways. (1) They damage goodwill, trust, and peace—the foundations of good human relations. (2) They hamper progress toward important goals. (3) They make us self-centered rather than love-centered. Jesus understood how destructive arguments among brothers could be. In his final prayer before being betrayed and arrested, Jesus asked God that his followers be "one" (John 17:21).

Related Topics: ARGUMENTS, CONFLICTS, PEACE

DISAPPOINTMENT (*see* DISCOURAGEMENT)

DISCERNMENT (*Experience, Understanding, Wisdom*)

When is discernment a helpful resource?

BIBLE READING: James 1:2-8

KEY BIBLE VERSE: *If you need wisdom—if you want to know what God wants you to do—ask him, and he will gladly tell you. He will not resent your asking.* (James 1:5)

Discernment is essential in making wise decisions. By *wisdom,* James is talking not only about knowledge, but about the ability to make wise decisions in difficult circumstances. Whenever we need wisdom, we can pray to God, and he will generously supply what we need. Christians don't have to grope around in the dark, hoping to stumble upon answers. We can ask for God's wisdom to guide our choices.

Wisdom here also means practical discernment. It begins with respect for God, leads to right living, and results in increased ability to tell right from wrong. God is willing to give us this wisdom; but we will be unable to receive it if our goals are self-centered instead of God centered. To learn God's will, we need to read his Word and ask him to show us how to obey it. Then we must do what he tells us.

BIBLE READING: Matthew 7:1-12

KEY BIBLE VERSE: *Others will treat you as you treat them. Whatever measure you use in judging others, it will be used to measure how you are judged.* (Matthew 7:2)

Having discernment means judging correctly. Jesus' statement, "Stop judging others," is aimed at the kind of hypocritical, judgmental attitude that tears others down in order to build oneself up. It is not a blanket statement against all critical thinking, but a call to be *discerning* rather than negative. Jesus said to expose false teachers (7:15-23), and Paul taught that we should exercise church discipline (1 Corinthians 5:1-2) and trust God to be the final Judge (1 Corinthians 4:3-5).

Having discernment means knowing when to speak and when to be silent. Pigs were unclean animals according to God's law (Deuteronomy 14:8). Anyone who touched an unclean animal became "ceremonially unclean" and could not go to the temple to worship until the uncleanness was removed. Jesus says that we should not entrust holy teachings to unholy or unclean people. It is futile to try to teach holy concepts to people who don't want to listen and will only tear apart what we say. We should not stop giving God's Word to unbelievers, but we should be wise and discerning in what we teach and to whom, so that we will not be wasting our time.

Having discernment means wanting what God wants. The child in Jesus' example (7:9) asked his father for bread and fish—good and necessary items. If the child had asked for a poisonous snake, would the wise father have granted his request? Sometimes God knows we are praying for "snakes" and does not give us what we ask for, even though we persist in our prayers. As we come to know God better as a loving Father, we learn to ask for what is good for us, and then he grants it.

BIBLE READING: Hebrews 5:11-14

KEY BIBLE VERSE: *Solid food is for those who are mature, who have trained themselves to recognize the difference between right and wrong and then do what is right.* (Hebrews 5:14)

Discernment is essential for spiritual growth. In order to grow from infant Christians to mature Christians, we must learn discernment. We must train our consciences, our senses, our minds, and our bodies to distinguish good from evil. Can you recognize temptation before it traps you? Can you tell the difference between a correct use of Scripture and a mistaken one?

Our capacity to feast on the deeper knowledge of God ("solid spiritual food") is determined by our spiritual growth. Too often we want God's banquet before we are spiritually capable of digesting it. As you grow in the Lord and put into practice what you have learned, your capacity to understand will also grow.

Related Topics: PRAYER, UNDERSTANDING, WISDOM

DISCIPLE (*see* BELIEVERS)

DISCIPLINE (*Correction, Practice, Training*)

▶ DISCIPLINING CHILDREN
What does the Bible say about disciplining children?

BIBLE READING: 1 Kings 1:1-8
KEY BIBLE VERSE: *His father, King David, had never disciplined him at any time, even by asking, "What are you doing?" Adonijah was a very handsome man and had been born next after Absalom.* (1 Kings 1:6)

Even children of godly parents require specific attention and training. God-fearing people like David and Samuel were used by God to lead nations; nevertheless they had problems in family relationships. God-fearing leaders cannot take for granted the spiritual well-being of their children. They are used to having others follow their orders, but they cannot expect their children to manufacture faith upon request. Moral and spiritual character takes years to build, and it requires constant attention and patient discipline.

David served God well as a king, but as a parent he often failed both God and his children. Don't let your service to God, even in leadership positions, take up so much of your time and energy that you neglect your other God-given responsibilities.

Children need limits for their own good. Because David had never interfered by opposing or even questioning his son, Adonijah did not know how to work within limits. The result was that he always wanted his own way, regardless of how it affected others. Adonijah did whatever he wanted and paid no respect to God's wishes. Undisciplined children may look cute to their parents, but undisciplined adults destroy themselves and others. As you set limits for your children, you make it possible for them to develop the self-discipline they will need in order to control themselves later. Discipline your children carefully while they are young, so that they will grow into self-disciplined adults.

BIBLE READING: Proverbs 13:18-25
KEY BIBLE VERSE: *If you refuse to discipline your children, it proves you don't love them; if you love your children, you will be prompt to discipline them.* (Proverbs 13:24)

Careful discipline is an expression of parental love. It is not easy for a loving parent to discipline a child, but it is necessary. The greatest responsibility that God gives parents is the nurture and guidance of their children. Lack of discipline puts parents' love in question because it shows a lack of concern for the character development of their children. Disciplining children averts long-range disaster. Without correction, children grow up with no clear understanding of right and wrong and with little direction to their lives. Don't be afraid to discipline your children. It is an act of love. Remember, however, that your efforts cannot make your children wise; they can only encourage your children to seek God's wisdom above all else!

BIBLE READING: Proverbs 29:15-19
KEY BIBLE VERSE: *To discipline and reprimand a child produces wisdom, but a mother is disgraced by an undisciplined child.* (Proverbs 29:15)

Disciplining children is a painstaking responsibility. Parents of young children often become weary of disciplining them. They feel like all they do is nag, scold, and punish. When you're tempted to give up and let your children do what they want, or when you wonder if you've ruined every chance for a loving relationship with them, remember—kind, firm correction helps them learn, and learning makes them wise. Consistent, loving discipline will ultimately teach them to discipline themselves.

BIBLE READING: Ephesians 6:1-4

KEY BIBLE VERSE: *Now a word to you fathers. Don't make your children angry by the way you treat them. Rather, bring them up with the discipline and instruction approved by the Lord.* (Ephesians 6:4)

Discipline is an unavoidable part of responsible parenting. The purpose of parental discipline is to help children grow, not to exasperate and provoke them to anger or discouragement (see also Colossians 3:21). Parenting is not easy—it takes lots of patience to raise children in a loving, Christ-honoring manner. But frustration and anger should not be causes for discipline. Instead, parents should act in love, treating their children as Jesus treats the people he loves. This is vital to children's development and to their understanding of what Christ is like.

▶ CHURCH DISCIPLINE

How does the Bible describe the use of discipline in the church?

BIBLE READING: 1 Corinthians 5:1-13

KEY BIBLE VERSE: *How terrible that you should boast about your spirituality, and yet you let this sort of thing go on. Don't you realize that if even one person is allowed to go on sinning, soon all will be affected?* (1 Corinthians 5:6)

The Bible gives directions for caring discipline within the church. The church must discipline flagrant sin among its members—such actions, left unchecked, can polarize and paralyze a church. The correction, however, should never be vengeful. Instead, it should be given to help bring about a cure. There was a specific sin in the church, but the Corinthian believers had refused to deal with it. In this case, a man was having an affair with his mother (or stepmother), and the church members were trying to ignore the situation. Paul was telling the church that it had a responsibility to maintain the standards of morality found in God's Word. God tells us not to judge others. But he also tells us not to tolerate flagrant sin because it is a dangerous influence on other believers (5:6).

Discipline may involve shunning a person until there is repentance. To "cast" this man "into Satan's hands" means to exclude him from the fellowship of believers. Without the spiritual support of Christians, this man would be left alone with his sin and Satan, and perhaps this emptiness would drive him to repentance. Putting someone out of the church should be a last resort in disciplinary action. It should not be done out of vengeance but out of love, just as parents punish children to correct them. The church's role should be to help, not hurt, the offender, motivating him to repent of his sins and to return to the fellowship of the church.

BIBLE READING: 2 Corinthians 2:5-11

KEY BIBLE VERSE: *Now it is time to forgive him and comfort him. Otherwise he may become so discouraged that he won't be able to recover. Now show him that you still love him.* (2 Corinthians 2:7-8)

Church discipline must include the opportunity for confession and restoration. Paul explained that it was time to forgive the man who had been punished by the church and had subsequently repented. He needed friendship and comfort. Satan would gain an advantage if they permanently separated this man from the congregation rather than forgiving and restoring him. This may be the man who had required the disciplinary action described in 1 Corinthians 5 or the chief opponent of Paul who had caused him the anguish described in this passage. The sorrowful letter taken by Titus had finally brought about the repentance of the Corinthians (2 Corinthians 7:8-14), and their discipline of the man had led to his repentance. Church discipline should seek restoration. Two mistakes in church discipline should be avoided—being too lenient and not correcting mistakes, or being too harsh and not forgiving. There is a time to confront and a time to comfort.

Church discipline requires humility. We use church discipline to help keep the church pure and to help wayward people repent. But Satan tries to harm the church by tempting it to use discipline in an unforgiving way. This causes those exercising discipline to become proud of their purity, and it causes the person who is being disciplined to become bitter and perhaps leave the church entirely. We must remember that our purpose in discipline is to *restore* a person to the fellowship, not to destroy him or her. We must be cautious that personal anger is not vented under the guise of church discipline.

▶ **SELF-DISCIPLINE**

How does God help us with self-discipline?

📖 BIBLE READING: Hebrews 12:1-13
KEY BIBLE VERSE: *As you endure this divine discipline, remember that God is treating you as his own children. Whoever heard of a child who was never disciplined?* (Hebrews 12:7)

God allows some things to happen to us in order to train us. Who loves his child more—the father who allows the child to do what will harm him, or the one who corrects, trains, and even punishes the child to help him learn what is right? It's never pleasant to be corrected and disciplined by God, but his discipline is a sign of his deep love for us. When God corrects you, see it as proof of his love and ask him what he is trying to teach you.

Our response to discipline will determine how much we benefit from it. We may respond to discipline in several ways: (1) we can accept it with resignation; (2) we can accept it with self-pity, thinking we really don't deserve it; (3) we can be angry and resent God for it; or (4) we can accept it gratefully as the appropriate response toward a loving Father.

God is more loving and demanding than any parent. God is not only a disciplining parent but also a demanding coach who pushes us to our limits and requires our life to be disciplined. Although we may not feel strong enough to push on to victory, we will be able to obtain it as we follow Christ and draw upon his strength. Then we can use our growing strength to help those around us who are weak and struggling.

Related Topics: CIRCUMSTANCES, MATURITY, SUFFERING

DISCOURAGEMENT *(Depression, Disappointment, Tiredness)*

What counsel does the Bible give for responding to discouragement?

📖 BIBLE READING: 1 Samuel 1:1-28
KEY BIBLE VERSE: *Hannah was in deep anguish, crying bitterly as she prayed to the LORD.* (1 Samuel 1:10)

Prayer is the key to handling discouragement. Hannah had good reason to feel discouraged and bitter. She was unable to bear children; she shared her husband with a woman who ridiculed her (1:7); her loving husband could not solve her problem (1:8); and even the high priest misunderstood her motives (1:14). But instead of retaliating or giving up hope, Hannah prayed. She brought her problem honestly before God.

Each of us may face times of barrenness when nothing "comes to birth" in our work, service, or relationships. It is difficult to pray in faith when we feel so ineffective. But, as Hannah discovered, prayer opens the way for God to work (1:19-20).

Others can also help in handling discouragement. Earlier Hannah had been discouraged to the point of being physically sick and unable to eat. At this point, she returned home well and happy. The change in her attitude may be attributed to three factors: (1) she honestly prayed to God (1:11); (2) she received encouragement from Eli (1:17); and (3) she resolved to leave the problem with God (1:18). This is the antidote for discouragement: tell God how you really feel and leave your problems with him. Then rely upon the support of good friends and counselors.

BIBLE READING: Nehemiah 4:1-14

KEY BIBLE VERSE: *As I looked over the situation, I called together the leaders and the people and said to them, "Don't be afraid of the enemy! Remember the Lord, who is great and glorious, and fight for your friends, your families, and your homes!"* (Nehemiah 4:14)

Remember that God is able to do wonders even in discouraging situations. Accomplishing any large task is tiring. There are always pressures that foster discouragement—the task seems impossible, it can never be finished, or too many factors are working against us. The only cure for fatigue and discouragement is focusing on God's purposes. Nehemiah reminded the workers of their calling, their goal, and God's protection. If you are overwhelmed by an assignment, tired, and discouraged, remember God's purpose for your life and his special purpose for the project.

BIBLE READING: Philippians 1:12-30

KEY BIBLE VERSE: *Because of my imprisonment, many of the Christians here have gained confidence and become more bold in telling others about Christ.* (Philippians 1:14)

God can use discouraging situations to bring glory to himself. Being imprisoned would cause many people to become bitter or to give up, but Paul saw it as one more opportunity to spread the Good News of Christ. Paul realized that his current circumstances weren't as important as what he did with them. Turning a bad situation into a good one, he reached out to the Roman soldiers who made up the palace guard and encouraged those Christians who were afraid of persecution. We may not be in prison, but we still have plenty of opportunities to be discouraged—times of indecision, financial burdens, family conflict, church conflict, or the loss of our jobs. How we act in such situations will reflect what we believe. Like Paul, look for ways to demonstrate your faith even in bad situations. Whether or not the situation improves, your faith will grow stronger.

Related Topics: DEPRESSION, DESPAIR, HOPE

DISEASE (*see* SICKNESS)

DISHONESTY *(Cheating, Deceiving, Lying)*

What are some of the consequences of dishonesty?

BIBLE READING: Genesis 27:1-29

KEY BIBLE VERSE: *What if my father touches me? He'll see that I'm trying to trick him, and then he'll curse me instead of blessing me.* (Genesis 27:12)

Fear and dishonesty are closely related. How we react to a moral dilemma often exposes our real motives. Frequently we are more worried about getting caught than about doing what is right. Jacob did not seem concerned about the deceitfulness of his mother's plan; instead he was afraid of getting in trouble while carrying it out. If you are worried about getting caught, you are probably in a position that is less than honest. Let your fear of getting caught be a warning to do right. Jacob paid a huge price for carrying out this dishonest plan.

BIBLE READING: 1 Samuel 15:1-23

KEY BIBLE VERSE: *When Samuel finally found him, Saul greeted him cheerfully. "May the LORD bless you," he said. "I have carried out the LORD's command!"* (1 Samuel 15:13)

Small areas of dishonesty are not overlooked by God. Saul thought he had won a great victory over the Amalekites, but God saw it as a great failure because Saul had disobeyed him and then lied to Samuel about the results of the battle. Saul may have thought his lie wouldn't be detected, or that what he did was not wrong. Saul was deceiving himself.

Dishonesty begins to seem like the truth after a while. Dishonest people soon begin to believe their own lies. Then they lose the ability to tell the difference between truth and falsehood. By believing your own lies you will deceive yourself, alienate yourself from God, and lose credibility in all your relationships. In the long run, honesty wins out.

BIBLE READING: Proverbs 20:23-30

KEY BIBLE VERSE: *The LORD despises double standards; he is not pleased by dishonest scales.* (Proverbs 20:23)

Persistent dishonesty affects us deeply. "Double standards" refers to the loaded scales a merchant might use in order to cheat the customers. Dishonesty is a difficult sin to avoid. It is easy to cheat if we think no one else is looking. But dishonesty affects the very core of a person. It makes him untrustworthy and untrusting. It eventually makes him unable to know himself or relate to others. Don't take dishonesty lightly. Even the smallest portion of dishonesty contains enough of the poison of deceit to kill your spiritual life. If there is any dishonesty in your life, tell God about it now.

Related Topics: DISOBEDIENCE, HONESTY, TRUTH

DISOBEDIENCE *(Defiance, Sin, Willfulness)*

What is God's response to disobedience?

BIBLE READING: Genesis 3:1-24

KEY BIBLE VERSE: *To Adam he said, "Because you listened to your wife and ate the fruit I told you not to eat, I have placed a curse on the ground. All your life you will struggle to scratch a living from it."* (Genesis 3:17)

Disobedience receives God's judgment. Adam and Eve chose their course of action (disobedience), and then God chose his. As a holy God, he could respond only in a way consistent with his perfect moral nature. He could not allow sin to go unchecked; he had to punish it. If the consequences of Adam and Eve's sin seem extreme, remember that their sin set in motion the world's tendency toward disobeying God. That is why we sin today. Every human being ever born, with the exception of Jesus, has inherited the sinful nature of Adam and Eve (Romans 5:12-21). Adam and Eve's punishment reflects how seriously God views sin of any kind.

God defines disobedience as sin. Adam and Eve learned by painful experience that because God is holy and hates sin, he must punish sinners. The rest of the book of Genesis recounts painful stories of lives ruined as a result of the Fall. Disobedience is sin, and it breaks our fellowship with God. But fortunately, when we disobey, God is willing to forgive us and to restore our relationship with him.

BIBLE READING: Numbers 20:1-13

KEY BIBLE VERSE: *The LORD said to Moses and Aaron, "Because you did not trust me enough to demonstrate my holiness to the people of Israel, you will not lead them into the land I am giving them!"* (Numbers 20:12)

Disobedience can limit future opportunities. The Lord had told Moses to speak to the rock; however, Moses struck it, not once, but twice. God did the miracle; yet Moses was taking credit for it when he said, "Must we bring you water from this rock?" For this he was forbidden to enter the Promised Land. Was God's punishment of Moses too harsh? After all, the people had nagged him, slandered him, and rebelled against both him and God. Now they were at it again (20:5). But Moses was the leader and model for the entire nation. Because of this great responsibility to the people, he could not be let off lightly. By striking the rock, Moses disobeyed God's direct command and dishonored God in the presence of his people.

BIBLE READING: 1 Chronicles 13:1-14

KEY BIBLE VERSE: *The LORD's anger blazed out against Uzzah, and he struck him dead because he had laid his hand on the Ark. So Uzzah died there in the presence of God.* (1 Chronicles 13:10)

Disobedience can sometimes lead to death. Uzza died instantly for touching the ark, but God blessed Obed-edom's home where the ark was stored. This demonstrates the two-edged aspect of God's power: he is perfectly loving and perfectly just. Great blessings come to those who obey his commands, but severe punishment comes to those who disobey him. This punishment may come swiftly or over time, but it will come. Sometimes we focus only on the blessings God gives us, while forgetting that when we sin, "It is a fearful thing to fall into the hands of the living God" (Hebrews 10:31). At other times, however, we concentrate so much on judgment that we miss his blessings. Don't fall into a one-sided view of God. Along with God's blessings comes the responsibility to live up to his demands for fairness, honesty, and justice.

Related Topics: DISCIPLINE, OBEDIENCE, SIN

DISRESPECT (*see* HONOR)

DISSATISFACTION (*see* CONTENTMENT)

DISTINCTION (*see* DIFFERENCES)

DISTRACTIONS (*see* COMMITMENT)

DISTRESS (*see* CONFLICTS)

DIVISIONS (*Break, Disagreement, Split*)

What causes divisions between people?

BIBLE READING: Genesis 26:12-22
KEY BIBLE VERSE: *He acquired large flocks of sheep and goats, great herds of cattle, and many servants. Soon the Philistines became jealous of him.* (Genesis 26:14)

Divisions often arise from jealousy. God kept his promise to bless Isaac. The neighboring Philistines grew jealous because everything Isaac did seemed to go right. So they plugged his wells and tried to get rid of him. Jealousy is a dividing force strong enough to tear apart the mightiest of nations or the closest of friends. It forces you to separate yourself from what you were longing for in the first place. When you find yourself becoming jealous of others, try thanking God for their good fortune. Before striking out in anger, consider what you could lose (a friend? a job? a spouse?).

BIBLE READING: John 6:60-71
KEY BIBLE VERSE: *At this point many of his disciples turned away and deserted him. Then Jesus turned to the Twelve and asked, "Are you going to leave, too?"* (John 6:66-67)

Division can arise when we take a stand for truth. There is no middle ground with Jesus. When he asked the disciples if they would also leave, he was showing that they could either accept or reject him. Jesus was not trying to repel people with his teachings. He was simply telling the truth. The more the people heard Jesus' real message, the more they divided into two camps—the honest seekers who wanted to understand more, and those who rejected Jesus because they didn't like what they had heard.

After many of Jesus' followers had deserted him, he asked the twelve disciples if they were also going to leave. Peter replied, "To whom would we go?" In his straightforward way, Peter answered for all of us—there is no other way. Though there are many philosophies and self-styled authorities, Jesus alone has the words of eternal life. People look everywhere for eternal life and miss Christ, the only source. Stay with him, especially when you are confused or feel alone.

BIBLE READING: 1 Corinthians 4:6-13
KEY BIBLE VERSE: *Dear brothers and sisters, I have used Apollos and myself to illustrate what I've been saying. If you pay attention to the Scriptures, you won't brag about one of your leaders at the expense of another.* (1 Corinthians 4:6)

Divisions can arise from misplaced loyalty. The Corinthians had split into various cliques, each following its favorite preacher (Paul, Apollos, Peter, etc.). Each clique really believed it was the only one to have the whole truth and thus felt spiritually proud. But Paul told the groups not to boast about being tied to a particular preacher because each preacher was simply a humble servant who had suffered for the same message of salvation in Jesus Christ. No preacher of God has more status than another.

How easy it is for us to become attached to a spiritual leader. When someone has helped us, it's natural to feel loyalty. But Paul warns against having such pride in our favorite leaders that we cause divisions in the church. Any true spiritual leader is a representative of Christ and has nothing to offer that God hasn't given him or her. Don't let your loyalty cause fighting, slander, or broken relationships. Make sure that your deepest loyalties are to Christ and not to his human agents. Those who spend more time debating church leadership than declaring Christ's message don't have Christ as their top priority.

Related Topics: CRITICISM, DISAGREEMENTS, LOYALTY

DIVORCE (*see* MARRIAGE)

DOCTRINE (*Basics, Foundation, Teaching*)

Where does a Christian learn the basics of Christianity?

BIBLE READING: 2 Timothy 3:10-17
KEY BIBLE VERSE: *All Scripture is inspired by God and is useful to teach us what is true and to make us realize what is wrong in our lives. It straightens us out and teaches us to do what is right.* (2 Timothy 3:16)

Christian doctrine comes from the Bible. The whole Bible is God's inspired Word. Because it is inspired and trustworthy, we should *read* it and *apply* it to our life. The Bible is our standard for testing everything else that claims to be true. It is our safeguard against false teaching and our source of guidance for how we should live. It is our only source of knowledge about how we can be saved. God wants to show you what is true and equip you to live for him. How much time do you spend in God's Word? Read it regularly to discover God's truth and to become confident in your life and faith. Develop a plan for reading the whole Bible, not just the familiar passages.

BIBLE READING: 2 Timothy 2:1-7
KEY BIBLE VERSE: *You have heard me teach many things that have been confirmed by many reliable witnesses. Teach these great truths to trustworthy people who are able to pass them on to others.* (2 Timothy 2:2)

Biblical doctrines are passed from believer to believer. If the body of Christ were to consistently follow this advice, the church would expand as well-taught believers would teach others and commission them, in turn, to teach still others. Disciples need to be equipped to pass on their faith; our work is not done until new believers are able to make disciples of others (see Ephesians 4:12-13).

BIBLE READING: Colossians 2:1-5
KEY BIBLE VERSE: *My goal is that they will be encouraged and knit together by strong ties of love. I want them to have full confidence because they have complete understanding of God's secret plan, which is Christ himself.* (Colossians 2:2)

Biblical teachings will always be under attack. The problem that Paul was combating in the Colossian church was similar to *Gnosticism* (from the Greek word for *knowledge*). This *heresy* (a teaching contrary to Biblical doctrine) undermined Christianity in several basic ways: (1) It insisted that important secret knowledge was hidden from most believers; Paul, however, said that Christ provides all the knowledge we need. (2) It taught that the body was evil; Paul countered that God himself dwelt in a body—that is, he was embodied in Jesus Christ. (3) It contended that Christ only seemed to be human, but was not; Paul insisted that Jesus is fully human and fully God.

Gnosticism became fashionable in the second century. But even in Paul's day, these ideas sounded attractive to many and they could easily seduce a church that didn't know Christian doctrine well. Similar teachings still pose significant problems for many in the church today. We combat heresy by becoming thoroughly acquainted with God's Word through personal study and sound Bible teaching.

BIBLE READING: 2 Timothy 1:1-14
KEY BIBLE VERSE: *Hold on to the pattern of right teaching you learned from me. And remember to live in the faith and love that you have in Christ Jesus. With the help of the Holy Spirit who lives within us, carefully guard what has been entrusted to you. (2 Timothy 1:13-14)*

The truth of the Bible can be guarded with the Holy Spirit's help. Timothy was in a time of transition. He had been Paul's bright young helper; soon he would be on his own as leader of a church in a difficult environment. Although his responsibilities were changing, Timothy was not without help. He had everything he needed to face the future if he would hold on tightly to it. He even had the Holy Spirit's help for hanging on. When you are facing difficult transitions, it is good to follow Paul's advice to Timothy and look back at your experience. Who is the foundation of your faith? How can you build on that foundation? What gifts has the Holy Spirit given you? Use the gifts you have already been given.

Related Topics: BIBLE, HERESY, TRUTH

DOUBLE STANDARD (*see* UNFAIRNESS)

DOUBT (*Confusion, Perplexity, Questions*)

How can doubts be overcome?

BIBLE READING: Genesis 3:1-24
KEY BIBLE VERSE: *Now the serpent was the shrewdest of all the creatures the LORD God had made. "Really?" he asked the woman. "Did God really say you must not eat any of the fruit in the garden?" (Genesis 3:1)*

Realize that doubts can weaken our trust in God. The serpent, Satan, tempted Eve by getting her to doubt God's goodness. He implied that God was strict, stingy, and selfish for not wanting Eve to share his knowledge of good and evil. Satan made Eve forget all that God had given her and instead focus on the one thing she couldn't have. We fall into trouble, too, when we dwell on the few things we don't have rather than on the countless things God has given us. The next time you are feeling sorry for yourself and what you don't have, consider all you *do* have and thank God. Then your doubts won't lead you into sin.

BIBLE READING: Numbers 11:1-35
KEY BIBLE VERSE: *Moses said, "There are 600,000 foot soldiers here with me, and yet you promise them meat for a whole month!"* (Numbers 11:21)

Doubts can remind us we are relying on ourselves. Moses had witnessed God's power in spectacular miracles, yet at this time he questioned God's ability to feed the wandering Israelites. If Moses doubted God's power, how much easier it is for us to do the same. But completely depending upon God is essential, regardless of our level of spiritual maturity. When we begin to rely on our own understanding, we are in danger of ignoring God's assessment of the situation. By remembering his past works and his present power, we can be sure that we are not cutting off his potential help.

BIBLE READING: Job 23:1-17
KEY BIBLE VERSE: *He knows where I am going. And when he has tested me like gold in a fire, he will pronounce me innocent.* (Job 23:10)

Occasional doubts must not be allowed to erode our trust in God. In chapter 22, Eliphaz had tried to condemn Job by identifying some secret sin which he may have committed. Here Job declares his confidence in his integrity and God's justice. We are always likely to have hidden sin in our life, sin we don't even know about because God's standards are so high and our performance is so imperfect. If we are true believers, however, all our sins are forgiven because of what Christ did on the cross in our behalf (Romans 5:1; 8:1). His forgiveness and cleansing are sufficient; they overrule our nagging doubts. The Holy Spirit in us is our proof that we are forgiven in God's eyes even though we may *feel* guilty. If we, like Job, are truly seeking God, we can stand up to others' accusations as well as our own nagging doubts. If God has forgiven and accepted us, we are forgiven indeed.

BIBLE READING: Luke 4:1-13
KEY BIBLE VERSE: *The Devil said to him, "If you are the Son of God, change this stone into a loaf of bread."* (Luke 4:3)

Beware of temptations that often come with doubt. Satan may tempt us to doubt Christ's true identity. He knows that once we begin to question whether or not Jesus was God, it's far easier to get us to do what he wants. Times of questioning can help us sort out our beliefs and strengthen our faith, but those times can also be dangerous. If you are dealing with doubt, realize that you are especially vulnerable to temptation. Even as you search for answers, protect yourself by meditating on the unshakable truths of God's Word.

BIBLE READING: Luke 7:18-35
KEY BIBLE VERSE: *John's two disciples found Jesus and said to him, "John the Baptist sent us to ask, 'Are you the Messiah we've been expecting, or should we keep looking for someone else?'"* (Luke 7:20)

Admitting our doubts often helps resolve them. John was confused because the reports he received about Jesus were unexpected and incomplete. John's doubts were natural, and Jesus didn't rebuke him for them. Instead, Jesus responded in a way that John would understand: Jesus explained that he had accomplished what the Messiah was supposed to accomplish. God can handle our doubts, and he welcomes our questions. Do you have questions about Jesus—about who he is or what he expects of you? Admit them to yourself and to God, and

begin looking for answers. Only as you face your doubts honestly can you begin
to resolve them.

 BIBLE READING: Matthew 17:14-23
KEY BIBLE VERSE: *"You didn't have enough faith," Jesus told them. "I assure you,
even if you had faith as small as a mustard seed you could say to this mountain,
'Move from here to there,' and it would move. Nothing would be impossible."*
(Matthew 17:20)

Doubts may remind us that our faith must grow. Once again Jesus predicted his
death (see also 16:21); but more important, he told of his resurrection. Unfortunately, the disciples heard only the first part of Jesus' words and became discouraged. They couldn't understand why Jesus wanted to go back to Jerusalem
where he would walk right into trouble.

The disciples didn't fully comprehend the purpose of Jesus' death and resurrection until Pentecost (Acts 2). We shouldn't get upset at ourselves for being slow
to understand everything about Jesus. After all, the disciples were with him, saw
his miracles, heard his words, and still had difficulty understanding. Despite their
questions and doubts, however, they believed. We should do no less.

BIBLE READING: James 1:2-8
KEY BIBLE VERSE: *When you ask him, be sure that you really expect him to answer,
for a doubtful mind is as unsettled as a wave of the sea that is driven and tossed
by the wind.* (James 1:6)

We resist doubts by practicing trust. To believe and not doubt means more than
believing in the existence of God. It also means believing in his loving care. It
includes relying on God and expecting that he will hear and answer when we
pray. We must put away our critical attitude when we come to him. God does
not grant every thoughtless or selfish request. We must have confidence that
God will align our desires with his purposes.

Trust in God grows as we faithfully seek him on a daily basis. A mind that
wavers is not completely convinced that God's way is best. It treats God's Word
like any human advice, and it retains the option to disobey. It vacillates between
feelings, the world's ideas, and God's commands. If your faith is new, weak, or
struggling, remember that you can trust God. Then be loyal to him. To stabilize
your wavering or doubtful mind, commit yourself wholeheartedly to God.

The uncertainties of doubt should remind us to pray. If you have ever seen the
constant rolling of huge waves at sea, you know how restless they are—subject
to the forces of wind, gravity, and tide. Doubt leaves a person as unsettled as
the restless waves. If you want to stop being tossed about, rely on God to show
you what is best. Ask him for wisdom, and trust that he will give it to you. Then
your decisions will be sure and solid.

Related Topics: COMMITMENT, CONSISTENCY, FAITH

DRINKING *(Alcoholism, Drunkenness, Inebriation)*

What warnings about drinking are in the Bible?

BIBLE READING: Genesis 9:20-29
KEY BIBLE VERSE: *One day he became drunk on some wine he had made and lay
naked in his tent.* (Genesis 9:21)

Drinking can lead to many negative consequences. Noah, the great hero of faith, got drunk—a poor example of godliness to his sons. Perhaps this story is included to show us that even godly people can sin and that their bad influence affects their families. Although the wicked people had all been killed, the possibility of evil still existed in the hearts of Noah and his family. Ham's mocking attitude revealed a severe lack of respect for his father and for God.

BIBLE READING: Proverbs 23:29-35

KEY BIBLE VERSE: *Who has anguish? Who has sorrow? Who is always fighting? Who is always complaining? Who has unnecessary bruises? Who has bloodshot eyes? It is the one who spends long hours in the taverns, trying out new drinks.* (Proverbs 23:29-30)

Drinking is only a temporary escape. The soothing comfort of alcohol is only temporary. Real relief comes from dealing with the cause of the anguish and sorrow and turning to God for peace. Don't lose yourself in alcohol; find yourself in God.

The Bible is cautious about the use of alcohol. Israel was a wine-producing country. In the Old Testament, winepresses bursting with new wine were considered a sign of blessing (3:10). Wisdom is even said to have set her table with wine (9:2, 5). But the Old Testament writers were alert to the dangers of wine. It dulls the senses; it limits clear judgment (31:1-9); it lowers the capacity for control (4:17); it destroys a person's efficiency (21:17). To make wine an end in itself, a means of self-indulgence, or as an escape from life is to misuse it and invite the consequences of the drunkard.

BIBLE READING: Ephesians 5:15-20

KEY BIBLE VERSE: *Don't be drunk with wine, because that will ruin your life. Instead, let the Holy Spirit fill and control you.* (Ephesians 5:18)

The Bible offers a powerful alternative to drinking. Paul contrasts getting drunk with wine, which produces a temporary "high," to being filled with the Spirit, which produces lasting joy. Getting drunk with wine is associated with the old way of life and its selfish desires. In Christ, we have a better joy, higher and longer lasting to cure our depression, monotony, or tension. We should not be concerned with how much of the Holy Spirit we have, but how much of us the Holy Spirit has. Submit yourself daily to his leading and draw on his power.

Related Topics: CELEBRATION, ESCAPE, TEMPTATION

EARTH (*Creation, Environment, World*)

What is our responsibility to the world in which we live?

 BIBLE READING: Genesis 1:1-31

KEY BIBLE VERSE: *God blessed them and told them, "Multiply and fill the earth and subdue it. Be masters over the fish and birds and all the animals."* (Genesis 1:28)

We are the caretakers of God's creation. To "be masters over" something is to have absolute authority and control over it. God has ultimate rule over the earth, and he exercises his authority with loving care. When God delegated some of his authority to the human race, he expected us to take responsibility for the environment and the other creatures that share our planet. We must not be careless and wasteful as we fulfill this charge. God was careful how he made this earth. We must not be careless about how we take care of it.

 BIBLE READING: Job 38:1–39:30

KEY BIBLE VERSE: *Where were you when I laid the foundations of the earth? Tell me, if you know so much.* (Job 38:4)

We, who are part of creation, are allowed to know our Creator. God stated that he has all the forces of nature at his command and can unleash or restrain them at will. No one completely understands such common occurrences as rain or snow, and no one can command them—only God who created them has that power. God's point was that if Job could not explain such common events in nature, how could he possibly explain or question God? And if nature is beyond our grasp, God's moral purposes may not be what we imagine either.

God asked Job questions about the universe and the animal kingdom in order to demonstrate how limited Job's knowledge really was. God was not seeking answers from Job. Instead, he was getting Job to recognize and submit to his power and sovereignty. Only then could he hear what God was really saying to him.

 BIBLE READING: Psalm 8:1-9

KEY BIBLE VERSE: *You put us in charge of everything you made, giving us authority over all things.* (Psalm 8:6)

God holds us responsible for how we use his creation. God gave human beings tremendous authority—to be in charge of the whole earth. But with great authority comes great responsibility. If we own a pet, we have the legal authority to do with it as we wish, but we also have the responsibility to feed and care for it. How do you treat God's creation? Use your resources wisely because God holds you accountable for your stewardship.

Related Topics: CREATION, RESPONSIBILITY, WORLD

EDUCATION (*Learning, Observing, School*)

What is God's desire for education?

 BIBLE READING: Deuteronomy 6:1-9
KEY BIBLE VERSE: *You must commit yourselves wholeheartedly to these commands I am giving you today. Repeat them again and again to your children. Talk about them when you are at home and when you are away on a journey, when you are lying down and when you are getting up again.* (Deuteronomy 6:6-7)

We need to be personally involved in our children's training. The Hebrews were extremely successful at making religion an integral part of life. The reason for their success was that religious education was life-oriented, not information-oriented. They used the context of daily life to teach about God. The key to teaching your children to love God is stated simply and clearly in these verses. If you want your children to follow God, you must make God a part of your everyday experiences. You must teach your children diligently to see God in all aspects of life, not just those that are church related.

BIBLE READING: Psalm 78:1-8
KEY BIBLE VERSE: *For he issued his decree to Jacob; he gave his law to Israel. He commanded our ancestors to teach them to their children, so the next generation might know them—even the children not yet born—that they in turn might teach their children.* (Psalm 78:5-6)

Children need spiritual roots. God commanded that the stories of his mighty acts in Israel's history and his laws be passed on from parents to children. This shows the purpose and importance of religious education—to help each generation obey God and set their hope on him. It is important to keep children from repeating the same mistakes as their ancestors. What are you doing to pass on the history of God's work to the next generation?

Related Topics: DISCIPLINE, PARENT(S), TEACHING

EFFECTIVENESS (*Accomplishments, Achievements, Success*)

What are God's guidelines for effective living?

BIBLE READING: 1 Kings 4:1-28
KEY BIBLE VERSE: *Solomon also had twelve district governors who were over all Israel. They were responsible for providing food from the people for the king's household. Each of them arranged provisions for one month of the year.* (1 Kings 4:7)

Effectiveness is a by-product of order. Solomon was well organized, with eleven chief officials with specific responsibilities and twelve district governors, and a manager in charge of the district officers. Each person had a specific responsibility or territory to manage. This organization was essential to maintain the government's effectiveness: it was a wise move by a wise man. It is good stewardship to be well organized. Good organization helps people work together in harmony and insures that the desired goal will be reached.

BIBLE READING: 2 Kings 1:1-18

KEY BIBLE VERSE: *Once more the king sent a captain with fifty men. But this time the captain fell to his knees before Elijah. He pleaded with him, "O man of God, please spare my life and the lives of these, your fifty servants." (2 Kings 1:13)*

Effective living is based on a humble regard for God. Notice how the third captain went to Elijah. Although the first two captains called Elijah "man of God," they were not being genuine—God was not in their hearts. The third captain also called him "man of God," but he humbly begged for mercy. His attitude showed respect for God and his power and saved the lives of his men. Effective living begins with a right attitude toward God. Before religious words come to your mouth, make sure they are from your heart. Let respect, humility, and servanthood characterize your attitude toward God and others.

BIBLE READING: Acts 1:1-11

KEY BIBLE VERSE: *When the Holy Spirit has come upon you, you will receive power and will tell people about me everywhere—in Jerusalem, throughout Judea, in Samaria, and to the ends of the earth. (Acts 1:8)*

Effectiveness is based on God's power and timing. Jesus instructed his disciples to witness to people of all nations about him. But they were told to wait first for the Holy Spirit. God has important work for you to do for him, but you must do it by the power of the Holy Spirit. We often like to get on with the job, even if it means running ahead of God. But waiting is sometimes part of God's plan. Are you waiting and listening for God's complete instructions, or are you running ahead of his plans? We need God's timing and power to be truly effective.

Related Topics: ACCOMPLISHMENTS, FAILURE, SUCCESS

EFFORT *(Energy, Involvement, Performance)*

When does God expect special effort from us?

BIBLE READING: Exodus 36:1-38

KEY BIBLE VERSE: *The skilled weavers first made ten sheets from fine linen. One of the craftsmen then embroidered blue, purple, and scarlet cherubim into them. Each sheet was exactly the same size—forty-two feet long and six feet wide. (Exodus 36:8-9)*

Beauty often requires effort to produce. Making cloth (spinning and weaving) took a great deal of time in Moses' day. To own more than two or three changes of clothes was a sign of wealth. The effort involved in making enough cloth for the tabernacle was staggering. The tabernacle would never have been built without tremendous community involvement. Today, churches and neighborhoods often require this same kind of pulling together. Without it, many essential services wouldn't get done.

BIBLE READING: Joshua 23:1-16

KEY BIBLE VERSE: *Be strong! Be very careful to follow all the instructions written in the Book of the Law of Moses. Do not deviate from them in any way. (Joshua 23:6)*

Effort is required in remaining obedient to God. Joshua knew the nation's weak spots. Before dying, he called the people together and gave commands to help them where they were most likely to slip: (1) follow all that is written in the Book of the Law of Moses without turning aside; (2) don't associate with the pagan nations or worship their gods; (3) don't intermarry with the pagan nations. These temptations were right in their backyard. Our associations and relationships can be temptations to us as well. It's wise to identify our weak spots *before* we break down. Then we can develop strategies to overcome these temptations instead of being overcome by them.

BIBLE READING: Matthew 7:7-12
KEY BIBLE VERSE: *Keep on asking, and you will be given what you ask for. Keep on looking, and you will find. Keep on knocking, and the door will be opened. For everyone who asks, receives. Everyone who seeks, finds. And the door is opened to everyone who knocks.* (Matthew 7:7-8)

Jesus tells us to persist in pursuing God. People often give up after a few half-hearted efforts and conclude that God cannot be found. But knowing God takes faith, focus, and follow-through, and Jesus assures us that we will be rewarded. Don't give up in your efforts to seek God. Continue to ask him for more knowledge, patience, wisdom, love, and understanding. He will give them to you.

BIBLE READING: Colossians 3:18-25
KEY BIBLE VERSE: *Work hard and cheerfully at whatever you do, as though you were working for the Lord rather than for people.* (Colossians 3:23)

The quality of our effort can be honoring to God. Since the creation, God has given us work to do. If we could regard our work as an act of worship or service to God, such an attitude would take some of the drudgery and boredom out of it. We could work without complaining or resentment if we would treat our job problems as the cost of discipleship.

Related Topics: DISCIPLINE, OBEDIENCE, WORK

EGO (*Identity, Personality, Self*)

In what ways is our ego a challenge in spiritual life?

BIBLE READING: Judges 15:1-20
KEY BIBLE VERSE: *Samson said, "With the jawbone of a donkey, I've made heaps on heaps! With the jawbone of a donkey, I've killed a thousand men!"* (Judges 15:16)

It is from our ego that pride most readily rises. The Lord's strength came upon Samson, but he was proud and boasted only of his own strength. "With the jawbone of a donkey, I've made heaps on heaps!" he said, and later asked God to refresh him because of *his* accomplishments (15:16-18). Pride can cause us to take credit for work we've done only because of God's strength. Our ego must learn its place of obedience to God.

BIBLE READING: 1 Samuel 15:1-35
KEY BIBLE VERSE: *Then Saul pleaded again, "I know I have sinned. But please, at least honor me before the leaders and before my people by going with me to worship the LORD your God."* (1 Samuel 15:30)

Ego problems stem from worrying about the opinions of others. Saul was more concerned about what others would think of him than he was about the status of his relationship with God (15:24). He begged Samuel to go with him to worship as a public demonstration that Samuel still supported him. If Samuel had refused, the people probably would have lost all confidence in Saul.

BIBLE READING: Matthew 3:1-17

KEY BIBLE VERSE: *I baptize with water those who turn from their sins and turn to God. But someone is coming soon who is far greater than I am—so much greater that I am not even worthy to be his slave. He will baptize you with the Holy Spirit and with fire.* (Matthew 3:11)

Genuine humility is the sign of a healthy ego. Put yourself in John's shoes. Your work is going well, people are taking notice, everything is growing. But you know that the purpose of your work is to prepare the people for Jesus (John 1:35-37). Then Jesus arrives, and his coming tests your integrity. Will you be able to turn your followers over to him? John passed the test by publicly baptizing Jesus. Soon he would say, "He must become greater and greater; I must become less and less" (John 3:30). Can we, like John, put our egos and profitable work aside in order to point others to Jesus? Are we willing to lose some of our status so that everyone will benefit?

Related Topics: HUMILITY, PEOPLE, SELF-CENTEREDNESS

ELDERLY (*see* AGE)

EMBARRASSMENT (*Guilt, Humiliation, Shame*)

What can we learn from embarrassment?

BIBLE READING: Genesis 2:18-25

KEY BIBLE VERSE: *Although Adam and his wife were both naked, neither of them felt any shame.* (Genesis 2:25)

Embarrassment is sometimes the result of sin. Have you ever noticed how little children can run naked through a room full of strangers without embarrassment? They are not aware of their nakedness, just as Adam and Eve were not embarrassed in their innocence. But after Adam and Eve sinned, shame and awkwardness followed, creating barriers between themselves and God. We often experience these same barriers in marriage. Ideally a husband and wife have no barriers between them and feel no embarrassment in exposing themselves to each other or to God. But, like Adam and Eve (3:7), we put on fig leaves (barriers) because we have areas we don't want our spouse, or God, to know about. Then we hide, just as Adam and Eve hid from God. In marriage, lack of spiritual, emotional, and intellectual intimacy usually precedes a breakdown of physical intimacy. In the same way, when we fail to expose our secret thoughts to God, we break our lines of communication with him.

BIBLE READING: Numbers 22:21-36

KEY BIBLE VERSE: *"Why did you beat your donkey those three times?" the angel of the LORD demanded. "I have come to block your way because you are stubbornly resisting me."* (Numbers 22:32)

Embarrassment is a signal our pride has been hurt. The donkey saved Balaam's life but made him look foolish in the process, so Balaam lashed out at the donkey. We sometimes strike out at blameless people who get in our way because we are embarrassed or our pride is hurt. Lashing out at others can be a sign that something is wrong with us. Don't allow your own hurt pride to lead you to hurt others.

BIBLE READING: Matthew 14:1-12
KEY BIBLE VERSE: *The king was sorry, but because of his oath and because he didn't want to back down in front of his guests, he issued the necessary orders.* (Matthew 14:9)

Fear of embarrassment can lead to sinful actions. Herod did not want to kill John the Baptist, but he gave the order so that he wouldn't be embarrassed in front of his guests. How easy it is to give in to the crowd and to let ourselves be pressured into doing wrong. Don't get in a situation where it will be too embarrassing to do what is right. Determine to do what is right, no matter how embarrassing or painful it may be.

BIBLE READING: Romans 1:8-17
KEY BIBLE VERSE: *For I am not ashamed of this Good News about Christ. It is the power of God at work, saving everyone who believes—Jews first and also Gentiles.* (Romans 1:16)

Embarrassment may indicate lack of genuine belief. Paul was not ashamed because his message was the gospel of Christ, the Good News. It was a message of salvation, it had life-changing power, and it was for everyone. When you are tempted to be ashamed, remember what the Good News is all about. If you focus on God and on what God is doing in the world rather than on your own inadequacy, you won't be ashamed or embarrassed.

Related Topics: GUILT, SHAME, TRUTH

EMOTIONS *(Affections, Feelings, Reactions)*

How should we handle our emotions?

BIBLE READING: Genesis 1:1-31
KEY BIBLE VERSE: *So God created people in his own image; God patterned them after himself; male and female he created them.* (Genesis 1:27)

Emotions are part of the image of God we share. In what ways are we made in God's image? God obviously did not create us exactly like himself, because God has no physical body. Instead, we are reflections of God's glory. Some feel that our reason, creativity, speech, or self-determination are the image of God. More likely, it is our entire self that reflects the image of God. We will never be totally like God, because he is our supreme Creator. But we do have the ability to reflect his character in our love, patience, forgiveness, kindness, and faithfulness.

Knowing that we are made in God's image and thus share many of his characteristics provides a solid basis for self-worth. Human worth is not based on possessions, achievements, physical attractiveness, or public acclaim. Instead it is based on being made in God's image. Because we bear God's image, we can feel positive about ourselves. Criticizing or downgrading ourselves is criticizing what God has made and the abilities he has given us. Knowing that you are a person of worth helps you love God, know him personally, and make a valuable contribution to those around you.

BIBLE READING: Numbers 14:1-45
KEY BIBLE VERSE: *Then all the people began weeping aloud, and they cried all night.* (Numbers 14:1)

Uncontrolled emotions can lead to bad decisions. When the chorus of despair went up, everyone joined in. Their greatest fears were being realized. Losing their perspective, the people were caught up in the emotion of the moment, forgetting what they knew about God's character. What if the people had spent as much energy moving forward as they did moving back? They could have enjoyed their land—instead, they never even entered it. When a cry of despair goes up around you, consider the larger perspective before you join in. You have better ways to use your energy than to complain.

BIBLE READING: Judges 11:1-40
KEY BIBLE VERSE: *When he saw her, he tore his clothes in anguish. "My daughter!" he cried out. "My heart is breaking! What a tragedy that you came out to greet me. For I have made a vow to the LORD and cannot take it back."* (Judges 11:35)

Uncontrolled emotions can lead to rash promises. Jephthah's rash vow brought him unspeakable grief. In the heat of emotion or personal turmoil it is easy to make foolish promises to God. These promises may sound very spiritual when we make them, but they may produce only guilt and frustration when we are forced to fulfill them. Making spiritual "deals" only brings disappointment. God does not want promises for the future, but obedience for today.

BIBLE READING: Ezra 3:1-13
KEY BIBLE VERSE: *The joyful shouting and weeping mingled together in a loud commotion that could be heard far in the distance.* (Ezra 3:13)

True worship includes the full range of emotions. The celebration after laying the temple foundation was marked by contrasts of emotion—shouts of joy and sounds of weeping. Both were appropriate. The Holy Spirit can stimulate us both to rejoice over the goodness of his grace and to grieve over the sins that required him to correct us. When we come into the presence of almighty God, we may feel full of joy and thanksgiving, yet at the same time feel sobered by our shortcomings.

BIBLE READING: John 11:32-45
KEY BIBLE VERSE: *Then Jesus wept.* (John 11:35)

Jesus expressed the full range of emotions, under control. John stresses that we have a God who cares. This portrait contrasts with the Greek concept of God that was popular in that day—a God with no emotions and no messy involvement with humans. Here we see many of Jesus' emotions—compassion, indignation, sorrow, even frustration. He often expressed deep emotion, and we must never be afraid to reveal our true feelings to him. He understands them, for he experienced them. Be honest, and don't try to hide anything from your Savior. He cares.

When Jesus saw the weeping and wailing, he too wept openly. Perhaps he empathized with their grief, or perhaps he was troubled at their unbelief. In either case, Jesus showed that he cares enough for us to weep with us in our sorrow.

Related Topics: FEELINGS, HUMANNESS, JESUS

EMPLOYMENT (Job, Labor, Work)

What does the Bible teach about employee/employer relationships?

BIBLE READING: Ephesians 6:5-9
KEY BIBLE VERSE: *Work with enthusiasm, as though you were working for the Lord rather than for people. Remember that the Lord will reward each one of us for the good we do, whether we are slaves or free.* (Ephesians 6:7-8)

Employers and employees are ultimately responsible to Christ. Paul's instructions encourage responsibility and integrity on the job. Christian employees should do their jobs as if Jesus Christ were their supervisor. And Christian employers should treat their employees fairly and with respect. Can you be trusted to do your best, even when the boss is not around? Do you work hard and with enthusiasm? Do you treat your employees as people, not machines? Remember that no matter whom you work for, and no matter who works for you, the one you ultimately should want to please is your Father in heaven.

BIBLE READING: Proverbs 25:11-15
KEY BIBLE VERSE: *Faithful messengers are as refreshing as snow in the heat of summer. They revive the spirit of their employer.* (Proverbs 25:13)

Employees should be trustworthy. It is often difficult to find people you can really trust. A faithful employee ("messenger") is punctual, responsible, honest, and hardworking. This person is invaluable as he or she helps take some of the pressure off his or her employer. Find out what your employer needs from you to make his or her job easier, and do it.

BIBLE READING: Titus 2:1-15
KEY BIBLE VERSE: *Slaves must obey their masters and do their best to please them. They must not talk back or steal, but they must show themselves to be entirely trustworthy and good. Then they will make the teaching about God our Savior attractive in every way.* (Titus 2:9-10)

Christians should be known as those who do their best. Slavery was common in Paul's day. Paul did not condemn slavery in any of his letters, but he advised slaves and masters to be loving and responsible in their conduct (see also Ephesians 6:5-9). The standards set by Paul can help any employee/ employer relationship. Employees should always do their best work and be trustworthy, not just when the employer is watching. Businesses in the United States lose millions of dollars a year to employees stealing and wasting time. If all Christian employees would follow Paul's advice at work, what a transformation it would make!

Related Topics: PURPOSE, SERVING, WORK

EMPTINESS (*see* DEPRESSION)

ENCOURAGEMENT (Cheering, Feedback, Motivation)

How can we get encouragement?

BIBLE READING: Joshua 24:1-15
KEY BIBLE VERSE: *So honor the LORD and serve him wholeheartedly. Put away*

forever the idols your ancestors worshiped when they lived beyond the Euphrates River and in Egypt. Serve the LORD alone. (Joshua 24:14)

God's faithfulness in the past offers encouragement. Joshua knew the nation's weak spots. Before dying, he called the people together and gave commands to help them where they were most likely to slip: (1) follow all that is written in the Book of the Law of Moses without turning aside; (2) don't associate with the pagan nations or worship their gods; (3) don't intermarry with the pagan nations. These temptations were right in their backyard. Our associations and relationships can be temptations to us as well. It's wise to identify our weak spots *before* we break down. Then we can develop strategies to overcome these temptations instead of being overcome by them.

Joshua knew his life was ending. So he called all the leaders of the nation together to give them his final words of encouragement and instruction. His whole message can be summarized in 23:8, "Be faithful to the Lord your God." Joshua had been a living example of those words, and he wanted that to be his legacy. For what do you want to be remembered, and what do you want to pass on to your children and associates? You can leave them nothing better than the admonition to hold on to God and to the memory of a person who did.

BIBLE READING: 1 Thessalonians 3:6-13
KEY BIBLE VERSE: *So we have been greatly comforted, dear brothers and sisters, in all of our own crushing troubles and suffering, because you have remained strong in your faith.* (1 Thessalonians 3:7)

We can be encouraged by the example of others. During times of persecution or pressure, believers should encourage one another. Christians who stand firm in the Lord encourage both ministers and teachers (who can see the benefit of their work in those who remain faithful), and also those who are new in their faith (who can learn from the steadfastness of the mature).

BIBLE READING: 1 Thessalonians 5:1-28
KEY BIBLE VERSE: *So encourage each other and build each other up, just as you are already doing.* (1 Thessalonians 5:11)

We gain encouragement by the words of others. As you near the end of a long race, your legs ache, your throat burns, and your whole body cries out for you to stop. This is when friends and fans are most valuable. Their encouragement helps you push through the pain to the finish. In the same way, Christians are to encourage one another. A word of encouragement offered at the right moment can be the difference between finishing well and collapsing along the way. Look around you. Be sensitive to others' need for encouragement and be supportive with your words and actions.

BIBLE READING: 1 Peter 1:1-12
KEY BIBLE VERSE: *So be truly glad! There is wonderful joy ahead, even though it is necessary for you to endure many trials for a while.* (1 Peter 1:6)

Reflecting on our eternal hope in Christ offers encouragement. Do you need encouragement? Peter's words offer joy and hope in times of trouble, and he bases his confidence on what God has done for us in Christ Jesus. We're called into a *living* hope of eternal life (1:3). Our hope is not only for the future: eternal life begins when we trust Christ and join God's family. No matter what pain or trial we face in this life, we know it is not our final experience. Eventually we will live with Christ forever.

How can we be encouraging?

BIBLE READING: Acts 14:1-28

KEY BIBLE VERSE: *After preaching the Good News in Derbe and making many disciples, Paul and Barnabas returned again to Lystra, Iconium, and Antioch of Pisidia, where they strengthened the believers. They encouraged them to continue in the faith, reminding them that they must enter into the Kingdom of God through many tribulations. (Acts 14:21-22)*

Consistently encourage young believers. Paul and Barnabas returned to visit the believers in all the cities where they had recently been threatened and physically attacked. These men knew the dangers they faced, yet they believed that they had a responsibility to encourage the new believers. No matter how inconvenient or uncomfortable the task may seem, we must always support new believers who need our help and encouragement. It was not convenient or comfortable for Jesus to go to the cross for us!

BIBLE READING: Romans 1:8-17

KEY BIBLE VERSE: *For I long to visit you so I can share a spiritual blessing with you that will help you grow strong in the Lord. I'm eager to encourage you in your faith, but I also want to be encouraged by yours. In this way, each of us will be a blessing to the other. (Romans 1:11-12)*

We are encouraged through encouraging others. Paul prayed for the chance to visit these Christians so that he could encourage them with his gift of faith and be encouraged by theirs. As God's missionary, he could help them understand the meaning of the Good News about Jesus. As God's devoted people, they could offer him fellowship and comfort. When Christians gather, everyone should give *and* receive. Our mutual faith gives us a common language and a common purpose for encouraging one another.

BIBLE READING: 1 Thessalonians 4:13-18

KEY BIBLE VERSE: *So comfort and encourage each other with these words.* (1 Thessalonians 4:18)

Take time to be with those who suffer. Because Jesus Christ came back to life, so will all believers. All Christians, including those living when Christ returns, will live with Christ forever. Therefore, we need not despair when loved ones die or world events take a tragic turn. God will turn our tragedies to triumphs, our poverty to riches, our pain to glory, and our defeat to victory. All believers throughout history will stand reunited in God's very presence, safe and secure. As Paul comforted the Thessalonians with the promise of the Resurrection, so we should comfort and reassure one another with this great hope.

BIBLE READING: 2 Timothy 1:1-18

KEY BIBLE VERSE: *Timothy, I thank God for you. He is the God I serve with a clear conscience, just as my ancestors did. Night and day I constantly remember you in my prayers. (2 Timothy 1:3)*

We should be faithful in praying for others. Paul constantly prayed for Timothy, his friend, his fellow traveler, his son in the faith, and a strong leader in the Christian church. Although the two men were separated from each other, their prayers provided a source of mutual encouragement. We too should pray consistently for others, especially for those who do God's work.

Related Topics: CHURCH, DISCOURAGEMENT, FELLOWSHIP

END TIMES (*see* LAST DAYS)

ENDURANCE (*Consistency, Patience, Strength*)

Why is endurance an important spiritual quality?

BIBLE READING: Matthew 10:16-42

KEY BIBLE VERSE: *And everyone will hate you because of your allegiance to me. But those who endure to the end will be saved.* (Matthew 10:22)

Endurance requires preparation. Jesus told the disciples that when arrested for preaching the gospel, they should not worry about what to say in their defense—God's Spirit would speak through them. This promise was fulfilled in Acts 4:8-14 and elsewhere. Some mistakenly think this means we don't have to prepare to present the gospel because God will take care of everything. Scripture teaches, however, that we are to make carefully prepared, thoughtful statements (Colossians 4:6). Jesus is not telling us to stop preparing, but to stop worrying.

Endurance grows out of commitment to Jesus Christ. Jesus predicted that his followers would be severely persecuted by those who hated what he stood for. In the midst of terrible persecutions, however, they could have hope, knowing that salvation was theirs. Times of trial serve to sift true Christians from false or fair-weather Christians. When you are pressured to give up and turn your back on Christ, don't do it. Remember the benefits of standing firm, and continue to live for Christ.

Standing firm to the end is not a way to be saved but the evidence that a person is really committed to Jesus. Persistence is not a means to earn salvation; it is the by-product of a truly devoted life.

BIBLE READING: Hebrews 3:1-6

KEY BIBLE VERSE: *But Christ, the faithful Son, was in charge of the entire household. And we are God's household, if we keep up our courage and remain confident in our hope in Christ.* (Hebrews 3:6)

Endurance is the means to joy in Christ. Because Christ lives in us as believers, we can remain courageous and hopeful to the end. We are not saved by being steadfast and firm in our faith, but our courage and hope reveal that our faith is real. Without this enduring faithfulness, we could easily be blown away by the winds of temptation, false teaching, or persecution. (See also 3:14.)

BIBLE READING: 2 Timothy 4:1-8

KEY BIBLE VERSE: *But you should keep a clear mind in every situation. Don't be afraid of suffering for the Lord. Work at bringing others to Christ. Complete the ministry God has given you.* (2 Timothy 4:5)

God will make our endurance worthwhile. To keep cool when you are jarred and jolted by people or circumstances, don't react quickly. In any work of ministry that you undertake, keeping your head makes you morally alert to temptation, resistant to pressure, and vigilant when facing heavy responsibility.

As he neared the end of his life, Paul could confidently say he had been faithful to his call. Thus he faced death calmly, knowing that he would be rewarded by Christ. Is your life preparing you for death? Do you share Paul's confident expectation of meeting Christ? The Good News is that the heavenly reward is not just for giants of the faith, like Paul, but for all who are eagerly

looking forward to Jesus' second coming. Paul gave these words to encourage
Timothy, and us, to keep fighting—no matter how difficult the fight seems.
When we are with Jesus Christ, we will discover that it was all worth it.

 BIBLE READING: Revelation 14:1-20
KEY BIBLE VERSE: *Let this encourage God's holy people to endure persecution
patiently and remain firm to the end, obeying his commands and trusting in
Jesus.* (Revelation 14:12)

Our endurance is related to the quality of our relationship with God. This news
about God's ultimate triumph should encourage God's people to remain firm
through every trial and persecution. They can do this, God promises, by trusting
in Jesus and obeying the commands in his Word. The secret to enduring, therefore, is trust and obedience. Trust God to give you patience to endure even the
small trials you face daily; obey him, even when obedience is unattractive or
dangerous.

Related Topics: CONSISTENCY, PATIENCE, STRENGTH

ENEMIES (*Antagonist, Attackers, Opponents*)

How does God expect us to treat our enemies?

 BIBLE READING: Exodus 23:1-9
KEY BIBLE VERSE: *"If you come upon your enemy's ox or donkey that has strayed
away, take it back to its owner. If you see the donkey of someone who hates you
struggling beneath a heavy load, do not walk by. Instead, stop and offer to help.*
(Exodus 23:4-5)

Loving one's enemies is a mark of a transformed life. The thought of being kind
to enemies was new and startling in a world where revenge was the common
form of justice. God not only introduced this idea to the Israelites, he made it
law! If a man found a lost animal owned by his enemy, he was to return it at
once, even if his enemy might use it to harm him. Jesus clearly taught in Luke
10:30-37 to reach out to all people in need, even our enemies. Following the
laws of right living is hard enough with friends. When we apply God's laws of
fairness and kindness to our enemies, we show how different we are from the
world.

 BIBLE READING: 1 Samuel 18:1-30
KEY BIBLE VERSE: *Saul was afraid of him, and he was jealous because the LORD had
left him and was now with David.* (1 Samuel 18:12)

Jealousy often produces enemies. Saul tried to kill David because he was jealous
of David's popularity, yet David continued to protect and comfort Saul. Perhaps
people have been jealous of you and have even attacked you in some way. They
may be intimidated by your strengths, which make them conscious of their
own shortcomings. It would be natural to strike back or to avoid them. A better
response is to befriend them (Matthew 5:43-44) and to ask God for the strength
to continue to love them, as David kept on loving Saul.

 BIBLE READING: Matthew 5:21-26
KEY BIBLE VERSE: *Come to terms quickly with your enemy before it is too late and
you are dragged into court, handed over to an officer, and thrown in jail.*
(Matthew 5:25)

An enemy should be treated honorably. Broken relationships can hinder our relationship with God. If we have a problem or grievance with a friend, we should resolve the problem as soon as possible. We are hypocrites if we claim to love God while we hate others. Our attitudes toward others reflect our relationship with God (1 John 4:20).

In Jesus' day, someone who couldn't pay a debt was thrown into prison until the debt was paid. Unless someone came to pay the debt for the prisoner, he or she would probably die there. It is practical advice to resolve differences with our enemies before their anger causes more trouble (Proverbs 25:8-10). You may not get into a disagreement that takes you to court, but even small conflicts mend more easily if you try to make peace right away. In a broader sense, these verses advise us to get things right with our brothers and sisters before we have to stand before God.

BIBLE READING: Matthew 5:43-48

KEY BIBLE VERSE: *You have heard that the law of Moses says, "Love your neighbor" and hate your enemy. But I say, love your enemies! Pray for those who persecute you!* (Matthew 5:43-44)

Jesus commands us to love our enemies. By telling us not to retaliate, Jesus keeps us from taking the law into our own hands. By loving and praying for our enemies, we can overcome evil with good.

The Pharisees interpreted Leviticus 19:18 as teaching that they should love only those who love in return, and Psalm 139:19-22 and 140:9-11 as meaning that they should hate their enemies. But Jesus says we are to love our enemies. If you love your enemies and treat them well, you will truly show that Jesus is Lord of your life. This is possible only for those who give themselves fully to God because only he can deliver people from natural selfishness. We must trust the Holy Spirit to help us *show* love to those for whom we may not *feel* love.

BIBLE READING: 1 John 2:1-11

KEY BIBLE VERSE: *Anyone who loves other Christians is living in the light and does not cause anyone to stumble.* (1 John 2:10)

Loving one's enemies is a mark of spiritual maturity. The commandment to love others is both old and new. It is old because it comes from the Old Testament (Leviticus 19:18). It is new because Jesus interpreted it in a radically new way (John 13:34-35). In the Christian church, love is not only showing respect; it is also self-sacrifice and servanthood (John 15:13). In fact, it can be defined as "selfless giving," reaching beyond friends to enemies and persecutors (Matthew 5:43-48). Love should be the unifying force and the identifying mark of the Christian community. It is the key to walking in the light because we cannot grow spiritually while we hate others. Our growing relationship with God will result in growing relationships with others.

Love is a choice, not a feeling. Does this passage mean that if you dislike anyone you aren't a Christian? These verses are not talking about disliking a disagreeable Christian brother or sister. There will always be people we will not like as well as others. John's words focus on the attitude that causes us to ignore or despise others, to treat them as irritants, competitors, or enemies. Christian love is not a feeling but a choice. We can choose to be concerned with people's well-being and treat them with respect, whether or not we feel affection toward them. If we choose to love others, God will help us express our love.

Related Topics: FRIENDSHIP, OPPOSITION, REJECTION

ENERGY (*see* STRENGTH)

ENTHUSIASM (*Excitement, Expressiveness, Intensity*)

▶ **BENEFITS OF ENTHUSIASM**
When is enthusiasm appropriate?

BIBLE READING: Exodus 35:20-35
KEY BIBLE VERSE: *Both men and women came, all whose hearts were willing. Some brought to the LORD their offerings of gold—medallions, earrings, rings from their fingers, and necklaces. They presented gold objects of every kind to the LORD.* (Exodus 35:22)

Giving should be done with enthusiasm. Those whose hearts were stirred gave cheerfully to the tabernacle building project. With great enthusiasm they gave because they knew how important their giving was to the completion of God's house. Airline pilots and computer operators can push test buttons to see if their equipment is functioning properly. God has a quick test button he can push to see the level of our commitment—our pocketbooks. Generous people aren't necessarily faithful to God. But faithful people are always generous.

BIBLE READING: Mark 5:1-20
KEY BIBLE VERSE: *So the man started off to visit the Ten Towns of that region and began to tell everyone about the great things Jesus had done for him; and everyone was amazed at what he told them.* (Mark 5:20)

We should speak of God's grace with enthusiasm. Jesus told this man to tell his friends about the miraculous healing. Most of the time, Jesus urged those he healed to keep quiet. Why the difference? Here are possible answers: (1) The demon-possessed man had been alone and unable to speak. Telling others what Jesus did for him would prove that he was healed. (2) This was mainly a Gentile and pagan area, so Jesus was not expecting great crowds to follow him or religious leaders to hinder him. (3) By sending the man away with this good news, Jesus was expanding his ministry to people who were not Jews.

This man had been demon-possessed but became a living example of Jesus' power. He wanted to go with Jesus, but Jesus told him to go home and share his story with his friends. If you have experienced Jesus' power, you too are a living example. Are you, like this man, enthusiastic about sharing the Good News with those around you? Just as we would tell others about a doctor who cured a physical disease, we should tell about Christ who cures our sin.

BIBLE READING: Colossians 3:18-25
KEY BIBLE VERSE: *Work hard and cheerfully at whatever you do, as though you were working for the Lord rather than for people.* (Colossians 3:23)

Everything we do for Christ ought to be with enthusiasm. Since the creation, God has given us work to do. If we could regard our work as an act of worship or service to God, such an attitude would take some of the drudgery and boredom out of it. In fact, working for Christ instead of a boss or a paycheck ought to bring a definite enthusiasm to our efforts. We could work without complaining or resentment if we would treat our job problems as the cost of discipleship.

▶ **CAUTIONS ABOUT ENTHUSIASM**
When should we be cautious about enthusiasm?

BIBLE READING: Ecclesiastes 12:1-14

KEY BIBLE VERSE: *Don't let the excitement of youth cause you to forget your Creator. Honor him in your youth before you grow old and no longer enjoy living.* (Ecclesiastes 12:1)

Youthful enthusiasm for life may lead us away from God. A life without God can produce a bitter, lonely, and hopeless old age. A life centered around God is fulfilling; it will make the days of old age—when disabilities, sickness, and handicaps bring barriers to enjoying life—satisfying because of the hope of eternal life. Being young is exciting. But the excitement of youth can become a barrier to closeness with God if it makes young people focus on passing pleasures instead of eternal values. Make your strength available to God when it is still yours—during your youthful years. Don't waste it on evil or meaningless activities that become bad habits and make you callous. Seek God now.

BIBLE READING: John 13:31-38

KEY BIBLE VERSE: *"But why can't I come now, Lord?"* he asked. *"I am ready to die for you."* (John 13:37)

Enthusiasm may lead us to make promises we can't keep. Peter proudly told Jesus that he was ready to die for him. But Jesus corrected him. He knew Peter would deny that he knew him that very night to protect himself (18:25-27). In our enthusiasm, it is easy to make promises, but God knows the extent of our commitment. Paul tells us not to think of ourselves more highly than we ought (Romans 12:3). Instead of bragging, demonstrate your commitment step by step as you grow in your knowledge of God's Word and in your faith.

BIBLE READING: Revelation 2:1-7

KEY BIBLE VERSE: *But I have this complaint against you. You don't love me or each other as you did at first!* (Revelation 2:4)

Enthusiasm by itself will not carry us far in faith. Just as when a man and woman fall in love, so also new believers rejoice at their newfound forgiveness. But when we lose sight of the seriousness of sin, we begin to lose the thrill of our forgiveness (see 2 Peter 1:9). In the first steps of your Christian life, you may have had enthusiasm without knowledge. Do you now have knowledge without enthusiasm? Both are necessary if we are to keep love for God intense and untarnished (see Hebrews 10:32, 35). Do you love God with the same fervor as when you were a new Christian?

Related Topics: DEVOTION, JOY, STRENGTH

ENVIRONMENT *(Home, Place, World)*

How should we relate to the environment in which we live?

BIBLE READING: Genesis 19:1-29

KEY BIBLE VERSE: *"Stand back!" they shouted. "Who do you think you are? We let you settle among us, and now you are trying to tell us what to do! We'll treat you far worse than those other men!" And they lunged at Lot and began breaking down the door.* (Genesis 19:9)

Believers should not let their social environment shape their lives. Lot had lived so long and so contentedly among ungodly people that he was no longer a believable witness for God. He had allowed his environment to shape him, rather than shaping his environment. Do those who know you see you as a witness for God, or are you just one of the crowd, blending in unnoticed? Lot had compromised to the point that he was almost useless to God. When he finally made a stand, nobody listened. Have you become useless to God because you are too much like your environment? To make a difference, you must first decide to be different in your faith and your conduct.

BIBLE READING: Romans 12:1-8

KEY BIBLE VERSE: *Don't copy the behavior and customs of this world, but let God transform you into a new person by changing the way you think. Then you will know what God wants you to do, and you will know how good and pleasing and perfect his will really is.* (Romans 12:2)

Christians must resist the pressure to conform to their environment. Christians are called to "not conform any longer to the pattern of this world" with its behavior and customs that are usually selfish and often corrupting. Many Christians wisely decide that much worldly behavior is off-limits for them. Our refusal to conform to this world's values, however, must go even deeper than the level of behavior and customs—it must be firmly founded in our minds—"let God transform you by changing the way you think." It is possible to avoid most worldly customs and still be proud, covetous, selfish, stubborn, and arrogant. Only when the Holy Spirit renews, reeducates, and redirects our minds are we truly transformed (see 8:5).

Related Topics: EARTH, HOME, WORLD

ENVY *(Coveting, Jealousy, Wanting)*

Why does God command us not to envy others?

BIBLE READING: Deuteronomy 5:1-33

KEY BIBLE VERSE: *Do not covet your neighbor's wife. Do not covet your neighbor's house or land, male or female servant, ox or donkey, or anything else your neighbor owns.* (Deuteronomy 5:21)

Envy demonstrates a lack of trust in God. To covet is to desire another person's property. We are not to set our desires on anything that belongs to someone else. Not only can such desires make us miserable, they can also lead us to other sins such as adultery and stealing. Envying others is a useless exercise because God is able to provide everything we really need, even if he does not always give us everything we want. To stop coveting, we need to practice being content with what we have. The apostle Paul emphasizes the significance of contentment in Philippians 4:11. It's a matter of perspective. Instead of thinking about what we don't have, we should thank God for what he has given and strive to be content. After all, our most important possession is free and available to everyone—eternal life through Christ.

BIBLE READING: 1 Kings 21:1-29

KEY BIBLE VERSE: *So Ahab went home angry and sullen because of Naboth's answer. The king went to bed with his face to the wall and refused to eat!* (1 Kings 21:4)

Envy can easily lead to other sins. Envy and desire for another's property led the way to murder in this case. But Ahab refused to admit his sin against God. Instead he accused Elijah of being his enemy for bringing him God's warning of punishment. When we are blinded by envy and hatred, it is almost impossible to see our own sin.

Related Topics: JEALOUSY, LUST, MATERIALISM

EQUALITY *(Fairness, Impartiality, Justice)*

Where can we find equality?

BIBLE READING: Ephesians 2:11-22

KEY BIBLE VERSE: *So now you Gentiles are no longer strangers and foreigners. You are citizens along with all of God's holy people. You are members of God's family.* (Ephesians 2:19)

There is equality for all in Jesus Christ. Before Christ's coming, Gentiles and Jews kept apart from one another. Jews considered Gentiles beyond God's saving power and therefore without hope. Gentiles resented Jewish claims. Christ revealed the total sinfulness of both Jews and Gentiles, and then he offered his salvation to both. Only Christ breaks down the walls of prejudice, reconciles all believers to God, and unifies us in one body.

The cross is the great equalizer. Christ has destroyed the barriers people build between themselves. Because these walls have been removed, we can have real unity with people who are not like us. This is true reconciliation. Because of Christ's death, we are all one (2:14); our hostility against each other has been put to death (2:16); we can all have access to the Father by the Holy Spirit (2:18); we are no longer foreigners or aliens to God (2:19); and we are all being built into a holy temple with Christ as our chief cornerstone (2:20-21).

BIBLE READING: Philemon 1:1-25

KEY BIBLE VERSE: *Perhaps you could think of it this way: Onesimus ran away for a little while so you could have him back forever. He is no longer just a slave; he is a beloved brother, especially to me. Now he will mean much more to you, both as a slave and as a brother in the Lord.* (Philemon 1:15-16)

Equality in Christ can affect every social relationship. What a difference Onesimus's status as a Christian made in his relationship to Philemon. He was no longer merely a servant, he was also a brother. That meant that both Onesimus and Philemon were members of God's family—equals in Christ. A Christian's status as a member of God's family transcends all other distinctions among believers. Do you look down on any fellow Christians? Remember, they are your equals before Christ (Galatians 3:28). How you treat your brothers and sisters in Christ's family reflects your true Christian commitment.

Related Topics: FAIRNESS, JUSTICE, SELF-ESTEEM

ESCAPE *(Avoidance, Breakout, Flight)*

What does God's provision of escape teach us about his character?

BIBLE READING: Exodus 14:1-31

KEY BIBLE VERSE: *But Moses told the people, "Don't be afraid. Just stand where you are and watch the LORD rescue you. The Egyptians that you see today will never be seen again."* (Exodus 14:13)

God opens escape routes to show us his power. The people were hostile and despairing, but Moses encouraged them to watch the wonderful way God would rescue them. Moses had a positive attitude! When it looked as if they were trapped, Moses called upon God to intervene. We may not be chased by an army, but we may still feel trapped. Instead of giving in to despair, we should adopt Moses' attitude to stand firm and "watch the Lord rescue you."

There was no apparent way of escape, but the Lord opened up a dry path through the sea. Sometimes we find ourselves caught in a problem and see no way out. Don't panic; God can open up a way.

BIBLE READING: 1 Corinthians 10:1-13

KEY BIBLE VERSE: *But remember that the temptations that come into your life are no different from what others experience. And God is faithful. He will keep the temptation from becoming so strong that you can't stand up against it. When you are tempted, he will show you a way out so that you will not give in to it.* (1 Corinthians 10:13)

God opens escape routes to show us he cares. In a culture filled with moral depravity and pressures, Paul gave strong encouragement to the Corinthians about temptation. He said: (1) wrong desires and temptations happen to everyone, so don't feel you've been singled out; (2) others have resisted temptation, and so can you; (3) any temptation can be resisted because God will help you resist it. God helps you resist temptation by helping you (1) recognize those people and situations that give you trouble, (2) run from anything you know is wrong, (3) choose to do only what is right, (4) pray for God's help, and (5) seek friends who love God and can offer help when you are tempted. Running from a tempting situation is your first step to victory (see 2 Timothy 2:22).

When should the possibility of escape be refused?

BIBLE READING: 1 Kings 22:29-40

KEY BIBLE VERSE: *Now King Ahab said to Jehoshaphat, "As we go into battle, I will disguise myself so no one will recognize me, but you wear your royal robes." So Ahab disguised himself, and they went into battle.* (1 Kings 22:30)

The temptation to escape from God is futile. Ahab could not escape God's judgment. The king of Aram sent thirty-two of his best chariot commanders with the sole purpose of killing Ahab. Thinking he could escape, Ahab tried a disguise, but a random arrow struck him while the chariots chased the wrong king, Jehoshaphat. It was foolish for Ahab to think he could escape by wearing a disguise. Sometimes people try to escape reality by disguising themselves—changing jobs, moving to a new town, even changing spouses. But God sees and evaluates the motives of each person. Any attempted disguise is futile.

BIBLE READING: Isaiah 16:1-14

KEY BIBLE VERSE: *On the hilltops the people of Moab will pray in anguish to their idols, but it will do them no good. They will cry to the gods in their temples, but no one will come to save them.* (Isaiah 16:12)

Our own means of escape usually fail. When the people of Moab experienced God's wrath, they sought their own idols and gods. Nothing happened, however, because there was no one there to save them. When we seek our own ways of escape in order to get through our daily troubles, the effect is the same: no pleasure, pastime, or man-made religious idea will come to save us. Our hope lies in God, the only one who can hear and help.

BIBLE READING: Jonah 1:1-17

KEY BIBLE VERSE: *But Jonah got up and went in the opposite direction in order to get away from the LORD. He went down to the seacoast, to the port of Joppa, where he found a ship leaving for Tarshish. He bought a ticket and went on board, hoping that by going away to the west he could escape from the LORD.* (Jonah 1:3)

Trying to escape God makes things worse. Jonah knew that God had a specific job for him, but he didn't want to do it. Tarshish could be one of any number of Phoenicia's western ports. Nineveh was toward the east. Jonah decided to go as far west as he could. When God gives us directions through his Word, sometimes we run in fear or in stubbornness, claiming that God is asking too much. It may have been fear, or anger at the wideness of God's mercy, that made Jonah run. But running got him into worse trouble. In the end, Jonah understood that it is best to do what God asks in the first place. But by then he had paid a costly price for running. It is far better to obey from the start.

Related Topics: GUIDANCE, PROTECTION, SECURITY

ETERNAL LIFE *(Heaven, Resurrection, Salvation)*

What are the characteristics of eternal life?

BIBLE READING: Isaiah 32:1-20

KEY BIBLE VERSE: *And this righteousness will bring peace. Quietness and confidence will fill the land forever.* (Isaiah 32:17)

Eternal life is complete peace. God acts from above to change man's condition here on earth. Only when God's Spirit is among us can we achieve true peace and fruitfulness (Ezekiel 36:22-38; Galatians 5:22-23). The settings described here will happen in full only in the end times. But we can have God's Spirit with us now, for he is available to all believers through Christ (John 15:26). The outpouring mentioned here happens when the worldwide kingdom of God is established for all eternity (see Joel 2:28-29).

BIBLE READING: John 3:1-21

KEY BIBLE VERSE: *For God so loved the world that he gave his only Son, so that everyone who believes in him will not perish but have eternal life.* (John 3:16)

Eternal life will be radically different from this life. Some people are repulsed by the idea of eternal life because their lives are miserable. But eternal life is not an extension of a person's miserable, mortal life; eternal life is God's life embodied in Christ given to all believers now as a guarantee that they will live forever. In eternal life there is no death, sickness, enemy, evil, or sin. When we don't know Christ, we make choices as though this life is all we have. In reality, this life is just the introduction to eternity. Receive this new life by faith and begin to evaluate all that happens from an eternal perspective.

BIBLE READING: 2 Corinthians 5:1-10

KEY BIBLE VERSE: *For we know that when this earthly tent we live in is taken down— when we die and leave these bodies—we will have a home in heaven, an eternal body made for us by God himself and not by human hands.* (2 Corinthians 5:1)

Eternal life begins in this life. Paul contrasts our earthly bodies ("earthly tent") and our future resurrection bodies ("an eternal body made for us by God himself and not by human hands"). Paul clearly states that our present bodies make us groan, but when we die we will not be spirits without bodies. We will have new bodies that will be perfect for our everlasting life.

Paul wrote as he did because the church at Corinth was in the heart of Greek culture, and many believers had difficulty with the concept of bodily resurrection. Greeks did not believe in a bodily resurrection. Most held that the real person was the soul, imprisoned in a physical body and that the afterlife was something that happened only to the soul. They believed that at death the soul is released—there is no immortality for the body, and the soul enters an eternal state. But the Bible teaches that the body and soul are inseparable.

The Holy Spirit within us is our guarantee that God will give us everlasting bodies at the Resurrection (2 Corinthians 1:22). We have eternity in us now! This truth should give us great courage and patience to endure anything we might experience.

How can someone know he or she has eternal life?

BIBLE READING: John 17:1-26

KEY BIBLE VERSE: *And this is the way to have eternal life—to know you, the only true God, and Jesus Christ, the one you sent to earth.* (John 17:3)

Eternal life is ours when we know God. How do we get eternal life? Jesus tells us clearly here—by knowing God the Father himself through his Son, Jesus Christ. Eternal life requires entering into a personal relationship with God in Jesus Christ. When we admit our sin and turn away from it, Christ's love lives in us by the Holy Spirit.

BIBLE READING: John 6:60-71

KEY BIBLE VERSE: *Simon Peter replied, "Lord, to whom would we go? You alone have the words that give eternal life. We believe them, and we know you are the Holy One of God."* (John 6:68-69)

Eternal life is ours through Jesus Christ. After many of Jesus' followers had deserted him, he asked the twelve disciples if they were also going to leave. Peter replied, "To whom would we go?" In his straightforward way, Peter answered for all of us—there is no other way. Though there are many philosophies and self-styled authorities, Jesus alone has the words of eternal life. People look everywhere for eternal life and miss Christ, the only source. Stay with him, especially when you are confused or feel alone.

BIBLE READING: Luke 18:18-30

KEY BIBLE VERSE: *Once a religious leader asked Jesus this question: "Good teacher, what should I do to get eternal life?"* (Luke 18:18)

Eternal life is not something we earn. This ruler sought reassurance, some way of knowing for sure that he had eternal life. He wanted Jesus to measure and grade his qualifications, or to give him some task he could do to assure his own immortality. So Jesus gave him a task—the one thing the rich ruler knew he could not do. "Then who in the world can be saved?" the bystanders asked. No one can, by his or her own achievements, Jesus' answer implied. "What is impossible with men is possible with God." Salvation cannot be earned—it is God's gift (see Ephesians 2:8-10).

BIBLE READING: 1 John 5:1-12

KEY BIBLE VERSE: *And this is what God has testified: He has given us eternal life, and this life is in his Son. So whoever has God's Son has life; whoever does not have his Son does not have life.* (1 John 5:11-12)

Eternal life belongs to those who trust in Jesus. Whoever believes in God's Son has eternal life. He is all you need. You don't need to *wait* for eternal life because it begins the moment you believe. You don't need to *work* for it because it is already yours. You don't need to *worry* about it because you have been given eternal life by God himself—and it is guaranteed.

Some people *hope* that they will receive eternal life. John says we can *know* we have it. Our certainty is based on God's promise that he has given us eternal life through his Son. This is true whether you feel close to God or distant from him. Eternal life is not based on feelings, but on facts. You can know that you have eternal life if you believe God's truth. If you aren't sure that you are a Christian, ask yourself: Have I honestly committed my life to him as my Savior and Lord? If so, you know by faith that you are indeed a child of God.

Related Topics: HEAVEN, KINGDOM OF GOD/KINGDOM OF HEAVEN, SALVATION

ETERNAL PUNISHMENT (*see* HELL)

ETERNITY (*see* ETERNAL LIFE)

EUCHARIST (*see* LORD'S SUPPER)

EVANGELISM (*Explaining, Gospel, Sharing*)

▶ **PRINCIPLES OF EVANGELISM**
How should the gospel be presented?

BIBLE READING: Matthew 13:1-23
KEY BIBLE VERSE: *But some seeds fell on fertile soil and produced a crop that was thirty, sixty, and even a hundred times as much as had been planted.* (Matthew 13:8)

The gospel message cannot be reduced to a simple formula. This parable should encourage spiritual "sowers"—those who teach, preach, and lead others. The farmer sowed good seed, but not all the seed sprouted, and even the plants that grew had varying yields. Don't be discouraged if you do not always see results as you faithfully teach the Word. Belief cannot be forced to follow a mathematical formula (i.e., a 4:1 ratio of seeds planted to seeds sprouted). Rather, it is a miracle of God's Holy Spirit as he uses your words to lead others to him.

The gospel message must be given to create some response. The four types of soil represent different responses to God's message. People respond differently because they are in different states of readiness. Some are hardened, others are shallow, others are contaminated by distracting worries, and some are receptive. How has God's Word taken root in your life? What kind of soil are you?

BIBLE READING: John 4:1-26
KEY BIBLE VERSE: *"Please, sir," the woman said, "give me some of that water! Then I'll never be thirsty again, and I won't have to come here to haul water."* (John 4:15)

Sometimes results of evangelism take time and patience. The woman mistakenly believed that if she received the water Jesus offered, she would not have to return to the well each day. She was interested in Jesus' message because she thought it could make her life easier. But if that were always the case, people would accept Christ's message for the wrong reasons. Christ did not come to take away challenges, but to change us on the inside and to empower us to deal with problems from God's perspective.

This woman did not immediately understand what Jesus was talking about. It takes time to accept something that changes the very foundations of your life. Jesus allowed the woman time to ask questions and put pieces together for herself. Sharing the gospel will not always have immediate results. When you ask people to let Jesus change their lives, give them time to weigh the matter.

▶ PEOPLE IN EVANGELISM
How can Christians be involved in evangelism?

BIBLE READING: Matthew 9:35-38
KEY BIBLE VERSE: *He said to his disciples, "The harvest is so great, but the workers are so few. So pray to the Lord who is in charge of the harvest; ask him to send out more workers for his fields."* (Matthew 9:37-38)

Christians should be personally responsible to pass on the gospel. Jesus needs workers who know how to deal with people's problems. We can comfort others and show them the way to live because we have been helped with our problems by God and his laborers (2 Corinthians 1:3-7).

Jesus looked at the crowds following him and referred to them as a field ripe for harvest. Many people are ready to give their lives to Christ if someone would show them how. Jesus commands us to pray that people will respond to this need for workers. Often, when we pray for something, God answers our prayers by using *us.* Be prepared for God to use you to show another person the way to him.

BIBLE READING: Matthew 28:16-20
KEY BIBLE VERSE: *Therefore, go and make disciples of all the nations, baptizing them in the name of the Father and the Son and the Holy Spirit. Teach these new disciples to obey all the commands I have given you. And be sure of this: I am with you always, even to the end of the age.* (Matthew 28:19-20)

Jesus commanded his followers to carry out evangelism. God gave Jesus authority over heaven and earth. On the basis of that authority, Jesus told his disciples to make more disciples as they preached, baptized, and taught. With this same authority, Jesus still commands us to tell others the Good News and make them disciples for the kingdom.

Evangelism is worldwide work. When someone is dying or leaving us, his or her last words are very important. Jesus left the disciples with these last words of instruction: they were under his authority; they were to make more disciples; they were to baptize and teach these new disciples to obey Christ; Christ would be with them always. Whereas in previous missions Jesus had sent his disciples only to the Jews (Matthew 10:5-6), their mission from now on would be worldwide. Jesus is Lord of the earth, and he died for the sins of people from all nations.

Evangelism is for all Christians. We are to go—whether it is next door or to another country—and make disciples. It is not an option, but a command to all who call Jesus "Lord." We are not all evangelists in the formal sense, but we have all received gifts that we can use to help fulfill the great commission. As we obey, we have comfort in the knowledge that Jesus is always with us.

Related Topics: GOSPEL, MISSION, WITNESSING

EVIDENCE *(Clues, Proof, Reasons)*

Upon what evidence do we base our faith in Jesus?

BIBLE READING: Luke 11:29-32

KEY BIBLE VERSE: *The people of Nineveh, too, will rise up against this generation on judgment day and condemn it, because they repented at the preaching of Jonah. And now someone greater than Jonah is here—and you refuse to repent.* (Luke 11:32)

The evidence for faith is actually overwhelming! The Ninevites and the queen of the South had turned to God with far less evidence than Jesus was giving his listeners—and far less than we have today. We have eyewitness reports of the risen Jesus, the continuing power of the Holy Spirit unleashed at Pentecost, easy access to the Bible, and knowledge of two thousand years of Christ's acts through his church. With the knowledge and insight available to us, our response to Christ ought to be even more complete and wholehearted.

BIBLE READING: John 12:37-50

KEY BIBLE VERSE: *But despite all the miraculous signs he had done, most of the people did not believe in him.* (John 12:37)

Some won't believe in spite of the evidence. Jesus had performed many miracles, but most people still didn't believe in him. Likewise, many today won't believe despite all God does. Don't be discouraged if your witness for Christ doesn't turn as many to him as you'd like. Your job is to continue as a faithful witness. You are responsible to reach out to others, but they are responsible for their own decisions.

BIBLE READING: Acts 14:8-20

KEY BIBLE VERSE: *Friends, why are you doing this? We are merely human beings like yourselves! We have come to bring you the Good News that you should turn from these worthless things to the living God, who made heaven and earth, the sea, and everything in them.* (Acts 14:15)

The evidence is enough for anyone who wants to believe. Responding to the people of Lystra, Paul and Barnabas reminded them that God never leaves himself "without a witness." Rain and crops, for example, are evidence of his goodness. Later Paul wrote that this evidence in nature leaves people without an excuse for unbelief (Romans 1:20). When in doubt about God, look around and you will see abundant evidence that he is at work in our world.

Related Topics: BELIEF/BELIEVE, EVANGELISM, RESURRECTION

EVIL *(Sin, Wickedness, Wrong)*

▶ **GOD AND EVIL**
Why does God allow evil to exist?

BIBLE READING: Judges 9:1-57

KEY BIBLE VERSE: *In the events that followed, God punished Abimelech and the men of Shechem for murdering Gideon's seventy sons.* (Judges 9:24)

God's punishment of evil is not on our timetable. Abimelech was the opposite of what God wanted in a judge, but it was three years before God moved against him, fulfilling Jotham's parable. Those three years must have seemed like forever to Jotham. Why wasn't Abimelech punished sooner for his evil ways?

We are not alone when we wonder why evil seems to prevail (Job 10:3; 21:1-18; Jeremiah 12:1; Habakkuk 1:2-4, 12-17). God promises to deal with sin, but in his time, not ours. Actually it is good news that God doesn't punish *us* immediately because we all have sinned and deserve God's punishment. God, in his mercy, often spares us from immediate punishment and allows us time to turn from our sins and turn to him in repentance. Trusting God for justice means (1) we must first recognize our own sins and repent, and (2) we may face a difficult time of waiting for the wicked to be punished. But in God's time, all evil will be destroyed.

BIBLE READING: Job 21:1-34

KEY BIBLE VERSE: *But I tell you to ask those who have been around, and they can tell you the truth. Evil people are spared in times of calamity and are allowed to escape. No one rebukes them openly. No one repays them for what they have done. When they are carried to the grave, an honor guard keeps watch at their tomb.* (Job 21:29-32)

God has not guaranteed complete justice in this life. If wicked people become wealthy despite their sin, why should we try to be good? The wicked may *seem* to get away with sin, but there is a higher Judge and a future judgment (Revelation 20:11-15). The final settlement of justice will come not in this life, but in the next. What is important is how a person views God in prosperity or poverty, not the prosperity or poverty itself.

BIBLE READING: Habakkuk 2:1-20

KEY BIBLE VERSE: *But these things I plan won't happen right away. Slowly, steadily, surely, the time approaches when the vision will be fulfilled. If it seems slow, wait patiently, for it will surely take place. It will not be delayed.* (Habakkuk 2:3)

Evil will come to an end. This chapter records God's answers to Habakkuk's questions: (1) How long would evil prevail (1:2-3)? (2) Why was Babylon chosen to punish Judah (1:13)? God said that the judgment, though slow to come, was certain. Although God used Babylon against Judah, he knew Babylon's sins and would bring judgment in due time.

Evil requires that we trust God. Evil and injustice seem to have the upper hand in the world. Like Habakkuk, Christians often feel angry and discouraged as they see what goes on. Habakkuk complained vigorously to God about the situation. God's answer to Habakkuk is the same answer he would give us, "Be patient! I will work out my plans in my perfect timing." It isn't easy to be patient, but it helps to remember that God hates sin even more than we do. Punishment of sin will certainly come. As God told Habakkuk, "Wait patiently." To trust God fully means to trust him even when we don't understand why events occur as they do.

▶ **PEOPLE AND EVIL**

How can people resist evil?

BIBLE READING: Genesis 3:1-24

KEY BIBLE VERSE: *God knows that your eyes will be opened when you eat it. You will become just like God, knowing everything, both good and evil.* (Genesis 3:5)

The mistake of our first parents must be avoided. Adam and Eve got what they wanted: an intimate knowledge of both good and evil. But they got it by doing evil, and the results were disastrous. Sometimes we have the illusion that freedom is doing anything we want. But God says that true freedom comes from obedience and knowing what *not* to do. The restrictions he gives us are for our good, helping us avoid evil. We have the freedom to walk in front of a speeding car, but we don't need to be hit to realize it would be foolish to do so. Don't listen to Satan's temptations. You don't have to do evil to gain more experience and learn more about life.

BIBLE READING: Exodus 2:1-10

KEY BIBLE VERSE: *During this time, a man and woman from the tribe of Levi got married. The woman became pregnant and gave birth to a son. She saw what a beautiful baby he was and kept him hidden for three months.* (Exodus 2:1-2)

Even small victories against evil are worthwhile. Moses' mother knew how wrong it would be to destroy her child. But there was little she could do to change Pharaoh's new law. Her only alternative was to hide the child and later place him in a tiny papyrus basket on the river. God used her courageous act to place her son, the Hebrew of his choice, in the house of Pharaoh. Do you sometimes feel surrounded by evil and frustrated by how little you can do about it? When faced with evil, look for ways to act against it. Then trust God to use your effort, however small it seems, in his war against evil.

BIBLE READING: 1 Chronicles 4:9-10

KEY BIBLE VERSE: *He was the one who prayed to the God of Israel, "Oh, that you would bless me and extend my lands! Please be with me in all that I do, and keep me from all trouble and pain!" And God granted him his request.* (1 Chronicles 4:10)

Evil can be resisted through trusting prayer. Jabez is remembered for a prayer request rather than a heroic act. In his prayer, he asked God to (1) bless him, (2) help him in his work, (3) be with him in all he did, and (4) keep him from evil and harm. Jabez acknowledged God as the true center of his work. When we pray for God's blessing, we should also pray that he will take his rightful position as Lord over our work, our family time, and our recreation. Obeying him in daily responsibilities *is* heroic living.

Evil can be resisted through specific prayer. Jabez prayed specifically to be protected from harm and pain. We live in a fallen world filled with sin, and it is important to ask God to keep us safe from the unavoidable evil that comes our way. But we must also avoid evil motives, desires, and actions that begin within us. Therefore, not only must we seek God's protection from evil, but we must also ask God to guard our thoughts and actions. We can begin to utilize his protection by filling our minds with positive thoughts and attitudes.

BIBLE READING: Luke 9:37-45

KEY BIBLE VERSE: *I begged your disciples to cast the spirit out, but they couldn't do it.* (Luke 9:40)

We cannot deal with evil in our own strength. As the disciples came down from the mountain with Jesus, they passed from a reassuring experience of God's presence to a frightening experience of evil. The beauty they had just seen must have made the ugliness seem even uglier. As our spiritual vision improves and allows us to see and understand God better, we will also be able to see and understand evil better. We would be overcome by its horror if we did not have Jesus with us to take us through it safely.

BIBLE READING: Ephesians 6:10-20
KEY BIBLE VERSE: *For we are not fighting against people made of flesh and blood, but against the evil rulers and authorities of the unseen world, against those mighty powers of darkness who rule this world, and against wicked spirits in the heavenly realms.* (Ephesians 6:12)

Jesus gives us weapons to use against evil. These who are not "flesh and blood" are demons over whom Satan has control. They are not mere fantasies—they are very real. We face a powerful army whose goal is to defeat Christ's church. When we believe in Christ, these beings become our enemies, and they try every device to turn us away from him and back to sin. Although we are assured of victory, we must engage in the struggle until Christ returns because Satan is constantly battling against all who are on the Lord's side. We need supernatural power to defeat Satan, and God has provided this by giving us his Holy Spirit within us and his armor surrounding us. If you feel discouraged, remember Jesus' words to Peter: "Upon this rock I will build my church, and all the powers of hell will not conquer it" (Matthew 16:18).

Related Topics: GOOD, POWER, SIN

EVOLUTION *(Change, Development, Expansion)*

What does the Bible say about the origin of the universe?

BIBLE READING: Genesis 1:1-31
KEY BIBLE VERSE: *In the beginning God created the heavens and the earth.* (Genesis 1:1)

The Bible says that God is the Creator of the universe. Just how did God create the earth? This is still a subject of great debate. Some say that there was a sudden explosion and the universe appeared. Others say God started the process, and the universe evolved over billions of years. Almost every ancient religion has its own story to explain how the earth came to be. And almost every scientist has an opinion on the origin of the universe. But only the Bible shows one supreme God creating the earth out of his great love and giving all people a special place in it. We will never know all the answers to how God created the earth, but the Bible tells us that God did create it. That fact alone gives worth and dignity to all people.

Related Topics: CREATION, EARTH, GOD

EXAMPLE *(Demonstrating, Modeling, Showing)*

How are others impacted by our actions?

BIBLE READING: Genesis 26:1-35
KEY BIBLE VERSE: *And when the men there asked him about Rebekah, he said, "She is my sister." He was afraid to admit that she was his wife. He thought they would kill him to get her, because she was very beautiful.* (Genesis 26:7)

Children are deeply affected by their parents' example. Isaac was afraid that the men in Gerar would kill him to get his beautiful wife, Rebekah. So he lied, claiming that Rebekah was his sister. Where did he learn that trick? He may have known about the actions of his father, Abraham (see 12:10-14 and 20:1-4). Parents help shape the world's future by the way they shape their children's values. The first step toward helping children live rightly is for the parents to live rightly. Your actions are often copied by those closest to you. What kind of example are you setting for your children?

BIBLE READING: Proverbs 1:8-19
KEY BIBLE VERSE: *Listen, my child, to what your father teaches you. Don't neglect your mother's teaching.* (Proverbs 1:8)

Parenting includes both words and actions. Our actions speak louder than our words. This is especially true in the home. Children learn values, morals, and priorities by observing how their parents act and react every day. If parents exhibit a deep reverence for and dependence on God, the children will catch these attitudes. Let them see your reverence for God. Teach them right living by giving worship an important place in your family life and by reading the Bible together.

BIBLE READING: Matthew 4:1-11
KEY BIBLE VERSE: *Then Jesus was led out into the wilderness by the Holy Spirit to be tempted there by the Devil.* (Matthew 4:1)

Jesus lived as a perfect example. This temptation by the devil shows us that Jesus was human, and it gave Jesus the opportunity to reaffirm God's plan for his ministry. It also gives us an example to follow when we are tempted. Jesus' temptation was an important demonstration of his sinlessness. He faced temptation and did not give in.

BIBLE READING: Hebrews 12:1-13
KEY BIBLE VERSE: *So take a new grip with your tired hands and stand firm on your shaky legs. Mark out a straight path for your feet. Then those who follow you, though they are weak and lame, will not stumble and fall but will become strong.* (Hebrews 12:12-13)

We are responsible for following Christ, the supreme example. God is not only a disciplining parent, but also a demanding coach who pushes us to our limits and requires our life to be disciplined. Although we may not feel strong enough to push on to victory, we will be able to obtain it as we follow Christ and draw upon his strength. Then we can use our growing strength to help those around us who are weak and struggling.

We are responsible for the example we set. The word *so* is a clue that what follows is important! We must not live with only our own survival in mind. Others will follow our example, and we have a responsibility to them if we claim to live for Christ. Does your example make it easier for others to believe, follow, and mature in Christ? Or would those who follow you end up confused and misled?

Related Topics: GUIDANCE, LEADERSHIP, TEACHING

EXCITEMENT (*see* ENTHUSIASM)

EXCUSES (*Allowing, Avoiding, Explaining*)

What's wrong with making excuses?

BIBLE READING: Exodus 3:1-18

KEY BIBLE VERSE: *"But who am I to appear before Pharaoh?" Moses asked God. "How can you expect me to lead the Israelites out of Egypt?"* (Exodus 3:11)

Sometimes we make excuses to avoid serving God. Moses made excuses because he felt inadequate for the job God asked him to do. It was natural for him to feel that way. He *was* inadequate all by himself. But God wasn't asking Moses to work alone. He offered other resources to help (God himself, Aaron, and the ability to do miracles). God often calls us to tasks that seem too difficult, but he doesn't ask us to do them alone. God offers us his resources, just as he did to Moses. We should not hide behind our inadequacies, as Moses did, but look beyond ourselves to the great resources available. Then we can allow God to use our unique contributions.

BIBLE READING: Matthew 11:20-30

KEY BIBLE VERSE: *What horrors await you, Korazin and Bethsaida! For if the miracles I did in you had been done in wicked Tyre and Sidon, their people would have sat in deep repentance long ago, clothed in sackcloth and throwing ashes on their heads to show their remorse.* (Matthew 11:21)

Excuses will not turn away God's punishment. Tyre, Sidon, and Sodom were ancient cities with long-standing reputations for wickedness (Genesis 18–19; Ezekiel 27–28). Each was destroyed by God for its evil. The people of Bethsaida, Chorazin, and Capernaum saw Jesus firsthand, and yet they stubbornly refused to repent of their sins and believe in him. Jesus said that if some of the wickedest cities in the world had seen him, they would have repented. Because Bethsaida, Korazin, and Capernaum saw Jesus and didn't believe, they would suffer even greater punishment than that of the wicked cities who didn't see Jesus. Similarly, nations and cities with churches on every corner and Bibles in every home will have no excuse on judgment day if they do not repent and believe.

BIBLE READING: Mark 7:1-37

KEY BIBLE VERSE: *You let them disregard their needy parents. As such, you break the law of God in order to protect your own tradition. And this is only one example. There are many, many others.* (Mark 7:12-13)

We should not make excuses to avoid meeting the needs of others. The Pharisees used God as an excuse to avoid helping their families. They thought it was more important to put money in the temple treasury than to help their needy parents, although God's law specifically says to honor fathers and mothers (Exodus 20:12) and to care for those in need (Leviticus 25:35-43). We should give money and time to God, but we must never use God as an excuse to neglect our responsibilities. Helping those in need is one of the most important ways to honor God.

BIBLE READING: James 1:1-27

KEY BIBLE VERSE: *And remember, no one who wants to do wrong should ever say, "God is tempting me." God is never tempted to do wrong, and he never tempts anyone else either.* (James 1:13)

We should confess our sins rather than make excuses. It is easy to blame others and make excuses for evil thoughts and wrong actions. Excuses include (1) it's the other person's fault; (2) I couldn't help it; (3) everybody's doing it; (4) it was just a mistake; (5) nobody's perfect; (6) the devil made me do it; (7) I was pressured into it; (8) I didn't know it was wrong; (9) God is tempting me. A person who makes excuses is trying to shift the blame from himself or herself to something or someone else. A Christian, on the other hand, accepts responsibility for his or her wrongs, confesses them, and asks God for forgiveness.

BIBLE READING: Romans 7:7-25

KEY BIBLE VERSE: *I don't understand myself at all, for I really want to do what is right, but I don't do it. Instead, I do the very thing I hate.* (Romans 7:15)

When we make excuses we underestimate the power of sin. This is more than the cry of one desperate man—it describes the experience of any Christian struggling against sin or trying to please God by keeping rules and laws without the Spirit's help. We must never underestimate the power of sin. We must never attempt to fight it in our own strength. Satan is a crafty tempter, and we have a great ability to make excuses. Instead of trying to overcome sin with human willpower, we must take hold of the tremendous power of Christ that is available to us. This is God's provision for victory over sin—he sends the Holy Spirit to live in us and give us power. And when we fall, he lovingly reaches out to help us up.

Related Topics: DECEIT, DISOBEDIENCE, OBEDIENCE

EXPECTATIONS *(Hopes, Plans, Wishes)*

What does God expect of us?

BIBLE READING: Deuteronomy 10:12-22

KEY BIBLE VERSE: *And now, Israel, what does the LORD your God require of you? He requires you to fear him, to live according to his will, to love and worship him with all your heart and soul, and to obey the LORD's commands and laws that I am giving you today for your own good.* (Deuteronomy 10:12-13)

God's expectations are specific. Often we ask, "What does God expect of me?" Here Moses gives a summary that is simple in form and easy to remember. Here are the essentials: (1) fear God; (2) live according to his will; (3) love him; (4) worship him with all your heart and soul; (5) obey his commands. How often we complicate faith with man-made rules, regulations, and requirements. Are you frustrated and burned out from trying hard to please God? Concentrate on his real requirements and find peace. Respect, follow, love, serve, and obey him.

How should our expectations be measured?

BIBLE READING: Mark 9:1-13

KEY BIBLE VERSE: *Jesus responded, "Elijah is indeed coming first to set everything in order. Why then is it written in the Scriptures that the Son of Man must suffer and be treated with utter contempt? But I tell you, Elijah has already come, and he was badly mistreated, just as the Scriptures predicted."* (Mark 9:12-13)

Our expectations must not limit God. It was difficult for the disciples to grasp the idea that their Messiah would have to suffer. The Jews who studied the Old Testament prophecies expected the Messiah to be a great king like David, who would overthrow the enemy, Rome. Their vision was limited to their own time and experience. They could not understand that the values of God's eternal kingdom were different from the values of the world. They expected relief from their present problems. But deliverance from sin is far more important than deliverance from physical suffering or political oppression. Our understanding of and appreciation for Jesus must go beyond what he can do for us here and now. Our expectations of what God will do must always include the fact that our perspective is very limited, too.

 BIBLE READING: John 6:16-21
KEY BIBLE VERSE: *Soon a gale swept down upon them as they rowed, and the sea grew very rough. They were three or four miles out when suddenly they saw Jesus walking on the water toward the boat. They were terrified, but he called out to them, "I am here! Don't be afraid."* (John 6:18-20)

Faith ought to include great expectation. The terrified disciples probably thought they were seeing a ghost (Mark 6:49). But if they had thought about all they had already seen Jesus do, they could have accepted this miracle. They were frightened—they didn't expect Jesus to come, and they weren't prepared for his help. Faith is a mind-set that *expects* God to act. When we act on this expectation, we can overcome our fears.

 BIBLE READING: Romans 1:8-17
KEY BIBLE VERSE: *One of the things I always pray for is the opportunity, God willing, to come at last to see you.* (Romans 1:10)

God's answers won't always fit our expectations. When you pray continually about a concern, don't be surprised at how God answers. Paul prayed to visit Rome so he could teach the Christians there. When he finally arrived in Rome, it was as a prisoner (see Acts 28:16). Paul prayed for a safe trip, and he did arrive safely—after getting arrested, slapped in the face, shipwrecked, and bitten by a poisonous snake. God's ways of answering our prayers are often far from what we expect. When you sincerely pray, God will answer—although sometimes with timing and in ways you do not expect.

Related Topics: HELP, HOPE, PROMISE(S)

EXPERIENCE (*Circumstances, Events, Lessons*)

How does God make use of the various experiences in our life?

BIBLE READING: Psalm 34:1-22
KEY BIBLE VERSE: *Taste and see that the LORD is good. Oh, the joys of those who trust in him!* (Psalm 34:8)

Every experience is an opportunity for spiritual growth. *Taste and see* does not mean, "Check out God's credentials." Instead it is a warm invitation: "Try this; I know you'll like it." When we take that first step of obedience in following God, we cannot help discovering that he is good and kind. When we begin the Christian life, our knowledge of God is partial and incomplete. As we trust him daily, we experience how good he is.

Experiences bring depth to our knowledge of God. You say you belong to the Lord, but do you fear him? To fear the Lord means to show deep respect and honor to him. We demonstrate true reverence by our humble attitude and genuine worship. Reverence was shown by Abraham (Genesis 17:2-4), Moses (Exodus 3:5-6), and the Israelites (Exodus 19:16-24). Their reactions to God's presence varied, but all deeply respected him.

Experiences teach us that God knows what we really need. At first we may question David's statement in verse 10, because we seem to lack many good things. This is not a blanket promise that all Christians will have everything they want. Instead, this is David's praise for God's goodness—all those who call upon God in their need will be answered, sometimes in unexpected ways.

Remember, God knows what we need, and our deepest needs are spiritual. Many Christians, even though they face unbearable poverty and hardship, still have enough spiritual nourishment to live for God. David was saying that to have God is to have all you really need. God is enough. If you feel you don't have everything you need, ask: (1) Is this really a need? (2) Is this really good for me? (3) Is this the best time for me to have what I desire? Even if you answer yes to all three questions, God may allow you to go without to help you grow more dependent on him. He may want you to learn that you need *him* more than your immediate desires.

BIBLE READING: Proverbs 6:20-35

KEY BIBLE VERSE: *My son, obey your father's commands, and don't neglect your mother's teaching. Keep their words always in your heart. Tie them around your neck.* (Proverbs 6:20-21)

Experiences allow us to counsel others from what God has taught us. This process is important in the family. It is natural and good for children, as they grow toward adulthood, to become increasingly independent of their parents. Young adults, however, should take care not to turn a deaf ear to their parents—to reject their advice just when it is needed most. If you are struggling with a decision or looking for insight, check with your parents or other older adults who know you well. Their extra years of experience may have given them the wisdom you seek.

BIBLE READING: John 1:35-42

KEY BIBLE VERSE: *The first thing Andrew did was to find his brother, Simon, and tell him, "We have found the Messiah" (which means the Christ).* (John 1:41)

Experience with Christ allows us to know him better. These new disciples used several names for Jesus: Lamb of God (1:36), Rabbi (1:38), Messiah (1:41), Son of God (1:49), and King of Israel (1:49). As they got to know Jesus, their appreciation for him grew. The more time we spend getting to know Christ, the more we will understand and appreciate who he is. We may be drawn to him for his teaching, but we will come to know him as the Son of God. Although these disciples made this verbal shift in a few days, they would not fully understand Jesus until three years later (Acts 2). What they so easily professed had to be worked out in experience. We may find that words of faith come easily, but deep appreciation for Christ comes with living by faith.

Related Topics: CIRCUMSTANCES, CONSEQUENCES, SPIRITUAL GROWTH

EXTRAMARITAL SEX (*see* ADULTERY, MARRIAGE, SEX)

F

FAILURE (*Defeats, Errors, Mistakes*)

What lessons can be learned from failure?

BIBLE READING: Joshua 8:1-29
KEY BIBLE VERSE: *The LORD said to Joshua, "Do not be afraid or discouraged. Take the entire army and attack Ai, for I have given to you the king of Ai, his people, his city, and his land." (Joshua 8:1)*

Failure should teach us not to make the same mistake twice. After Israel had been cleansed from Achan's sin, Joshua prepared to attack Ai again—this time to win. Joshua had learned some lessons that we can follow: (1) confess your sins when God reveals them to you (7:19-21); and (2) when you fail, refocus on God, deal with the problem, and move on (7:22-25; 8:1). God wants the cycle of sin, repentance, and forgiveness to strengthen us, not weaken us. The lessons we learn from our failures should make us better able to handle the same situation the second time around. Because God is eager to give us cleansing, forgiveness, and strength, the only way to lose is to give up. We can tell what kind of people we are by what we do on the second and third attempts.

BIBLE READING: Luke 22:54-62
KEY BIBLE VERSE: *At that moment the Lord turned and looked at Peter. Then Peter remembered that the Lord had said, "Before the rooster crows tomorrow morning, you will deny me three times." And Peter left the courtyard, crying bitterly. (Luke 22:61-62)*

Failure can help us become humble and useful. Peter wept bitterly, not only because he realized that he had denied his Lord, the Messiah, but also because he had turned away from a very dear friend, a person who had loved and taught him for three years. Peter had said that he would *never* disown Christ, despite Jesus' prediction (Mark 14:29-31; Luke 22:33-34). But when frightened, he went against all he had boldly promised. Unable to stand up for his Lord for even twelve hours, he had failed as a disciple and as a friend. We need to be aware of our own breaking points and not become overconfident or self-sufficient. If we fail him, we must remember that Christ can use those who recognize their failure. From this humiliating experience Peter learned much that would help him later when he assumed leadership of the young church.

BIBLE READING: Matthew 1:1-17
KEY BIBLE VERSE: *This is a record of the ancestors of Jesus the Messiah, a descendant of King David and of Abraham. (Matthew 1:1)*

God works in spite of failures. In the first seventeen verses of Matthew we meet forty-six people whose lifetimes span two thousand years. All were ancestors of Jesus, but they varied considerably in personality, spirituality, and experience. Some were heroes of faith—like Abraham, Isaac, Ruth, and David. Some had shady reputations—like Rahab and Tamar. Many were very ordinary—like Hezron, Aram, Nahshon, and Achim. And others were evil—like Manasseh and Abijah. God's work in history is not limited by human failures or sins, and he works through ordinary people. Just as God used all kinds of people to bring his Son into the world, he uses all kinds today to accomplish his will. And God wants to use you.

Related Topics: ACTIONS, MISTAKES, VICTORY

FAIRNESS (*Equality, Impartiality, Justice*)

How much fairness should be exercised and expected in life?

 BIBLE READING: Proverbs 16:1-33
KEY BIBLE VERSE: *The LORD demands fairness in every business deal; he sets the standard.* (Proverbs 16:11)

God expects fairness from us. Whether we buy or sell, make a product or offer a service, we know what is honest and what is dishonest. Sometimes we feel pressure to be dishonest in order to advance ourselves or gain more profit. But if we want to obey God, there is no middle ground: God demands honesty in every business transaction. No amount of rationalizing can cover up a dishonest business practice. Honesty and fairness are not always easy, but they are what God demands. Ask him for discernment and courage to be consistently honest and fair.

BIBLE READING: Isaiah 11:1-16
KEY BIBLE VERSE: *He will be clothed with fairness and truth.* (Isaiah 11:5)

Fairness is a part of God's character. God will judge with righteousness and justice. How we long for fair treatment from others, but do we give it? We hate those who base their judgments on appearance, false evidence, or hearsay, but are we quick to judge others using those standards? Only Christ can be the perfectly fair judge. Only as he governs our hearts can we learn to be as fair in our treatment of others as we expect others to be toward us.

In Isaiah's day, Judah had become corrupt and was surrounded by hostile, foreign powers. The nation desperately needed a revival of righteousness, justice, and faithfulness. They needed to turn from selfishness and show justice to the poor and the oppressed. The righteousness that God values is more than refraining from sin. It is actively turning toward others and offering them the help they need.

BIBLE READING: Isaiah 33:1-24
KEY BIBLE VERSE: *The ones who can live here are those who are honest and fair, who reject making a profit by fraud, who stay far away from bribes, who refuse to listen to those who plot murder, who shut their eyes to all enticement to do wrong.* (Isaiah 33:15)

Fairness should characterize those who wish to please God. These sinners realized that they could not live in the presence of the holy God, for he is like a fire that consumes evil. Only those who walk righteously and speak what is right can live with God. Isaiah gives examples of how to demonstrate our righteousness and uprightness: we can reject gain from extortion and bribes, refuse to listen to plots of wrong actions, and shut our eyes to evil. If we are fair and honest in our relationships, we will dwell with God, and he will supply our needs.

Related Topics: EQUALITY, JUSTICE, LEADERSHIP

FAITH *(Belief, Confidence, Trust)*

▶ **INEFFECTIVE FAITH**
How can we know our faith is ineffective?

BIBLE READING: Genesis 16:1-16
KEY BIBLE VERSE: *Sarai, Abram's wife, took Hagar the Egyptian servant and gave her to Abram as a wife. (This happened ten years after Abram first arrived in the land of Canaan.)* (Genesis 16:3)

Ineffective faith attempts to anticipate God's plan. Sarai took matters into her own hands by giving Hagar to Abram. Like Abram she had trouble believing God's promise that was apparently directed specifically toward Abram and Sarai. Out of this lack of faith came a series of problems. This invariably happens when we take over for God, trying to make his promise come true through efforts that are not in line with his specific directions. In this case, time was the greatest test of Abram and Sarai's willingness to let God work in their lives. Sometimes we too must simply wait. When we ask God for something and have to wait, it is a temptation to take matters into our own hands and interfere with God's plans.

BIBLE READING: Exodus 14:1-31
KEY BIBLE VERSE: *As Pharaoh and his army approached, the people of Israel could see them in the distance, marching toward them. The people began to panic, and they cried out to the LORD for help. Then they turned against Moses and complained, "Why did you bring us out here to die in the wilderness? Weren't there enough graves for us in Egypt? Why did you make us leave?"* (Exodus 14:10-11)

Ineffective faith is marked by a lack of trust in God. Trapped against the sea, the Israelites faced the Egyptian army sweeping in for the kill. The Israelites thought they were doomed. After watching God's powerful hand deliver them from Egypt, their only response was fear, whining, and despair. Where was their trust in God? Israel had to learn from repeated experience that God was able to provide for them. God has preserved these examples in the Bible so that we can learn to trust him the first time. By focusing on God's faithfulness in the past we can face crises with confidence rather than with fear and complaining.

BIBLE READING: Matthew 3:1-17
KEY BIBLE VERSE: *Prove by the way you live that you have really turned from your sins and turned to God.* (Matthew 3:8)

Ineffective faith is marked by an unchanged life. God's message hasn't changed since the Old Testament—people will be judged for their unproductive lives. God calls us to be *active* in our obedience. John compared people who claim they believe in God but don't live for him to unproductive trees that will be cut down. Just as a fruit tree is expected to bear fruit, God's people should produce a crop of good deeds. God has no use for people who call themselves Christians but do nothing about it. Like many people in John's day who were God's people in name only, we are of no value if we are Christians in name only. If others can't see our faith in the way we treat them, we may not be God's people at all. To be productive for God, we must obey his teachings, resist temptation, actively serve and help others, and share our faith. How productive are you for God?

BIBLE READING: 1 Corinthians 4:1-21

KEY BIBLE VERSE: *I will come—and soon—if the Lord will let me, and then I'll find out whether these arrogant people are just big talkers or whether they really have God's power.* (1 Corinthians 4:19)

Ineffective faith seldom goes beyond words. Some people talk a lot about faith, but that's all it is—talk. They may know all the right words to say, but their lives don't reflect God's power. Paul says that the kingdom of God is to be *lived*, not just discussed. There is a big difference between knowing the right words and living them out. Don't be content to have the right answers about Christ. Let your life show that God's power is really working in you.

▶ WEAK FAITH

How can we know our faith is weak?

BIBLE READING: Matthew 14:22-33

KEY BIBLE VERSE: *Then Peter called to him, "Lord, if it's really you, tell me to come to you by walking on water."* (Matthew 14:28)

Weak faith tends to lack endurance. Peter was not putting Jesus to the test, something we are told not to do (Matthew 4:7). Instead he was the only one in the boat to react in faith. His impulsive request led him to experience a rather unusual demonstration of God's power. Peter started to sink because he took his eyes off Jesus and focused on the high waves around him. His faith wavered when he realized what he was doing. We may not walk on water, but we do walk through tough situations. If we focus on the waves of difficult circumstances around us without looking to Jesus for help, we too may despair and sink. To maintain your faith when situations are difficult, keep your eyes on Jesus' power rather than on your inadequacies.

Weak faith often falters. Although we start out with good intentions, sometimes our faith falters. This doesn't necessarily mean we have failed. When Peter's faith faltered, he reached out to Christ, the only one who could help. He was afraid, but he still looked to Christ. When you are apprehensive about the troubles around you and doubt Christ's presence or ability to help, you must remember that he is the *only* one who can really help.

BIBLE READING: Luke 24:1-12

KEY BIBLE VERSE: *Peter ran to the tomb to look. Stooping, he peered in and saw the empty linen wrappings; then he went home again, wondering what had happened.* (Luke 24:12)

Even weak faith is a part of the process of belief. People who hear about the Resurrection for the first time may need time before they can comprehend this amazing story. Like the disciples, they may pass through four stages of belief. (1) At first, they may think it is a fairy tale, impossible to believe. (2) Like Peter, they may check out the facts but still be puzzled about what happened.

(3) Only when they encounter Jesus personally will they be able to accept the fact of the Resurrection. (4) Then, as they commit themselves to Jesus and devote their lives to serving him, will they begin fully to understand the reality of his presence with them.

BIBLE READING: Mark 9:14-29

KEY BIBLE VERSE: *The father instantly replied, "I do believe, but help me not to doubt!"* (Mark 9:24)

Weak faith can become strong faith with God's help. The attitude of trust and confidence that the Bible calls *belief* or *faith* (Hebrews 11:1, 6) is not something we can obtain without help. Faith is a gift from God (Ephesians 2:8-9). No matter how much faith we have, we never reach the point of being self-sufficient. Faith is not stored away like money in the bank. Growing in faith is a constant process of daily renewing our trust in Jesus.

BIBLE READING: Romans 14:1-23

KEY BIBLE VERSE: *Accept Christians who are weak in faith, and don't argue with them about what they think is right or wrong.* (Romans 14:1)

Those with weak faith need to recognize their limitations. Who is weak in faith and who is strong? We are all weak in some areas and strong in others. Our faith is strong if we can survive contact with sinners without falling into their patterns. It is weak if we must avoid certain activities, people, or places in order to protect our spiritual life. It is important to take a self-inventory in order to find out our strengths and weaknesses. In areas of strength, we should not fear being defiled by the world; rather we should go and serve God. In areas of weakness, we need to be cautious. If we have a strong faith but shelter it, we are not doing Christ's work in the world. If we have a weak faith but expose it, we are being extremely foolish. Whenever in doubt, we should ask, Can I do that without sinning? Can I influence others for good, rather than being influenced by them?

▶ **EFFECTIVE FAITH**

How can we know our faith is effective?

BIBLE READING: Luke 17:1-10

KEY BIBLE VERSE: *One day the apostles said to the Lord, "We need more faith; tell us how to get it."* (Luke 17:5)

Effective faith depends on God. The disciples' request was genuine; they wanted the faith necessary for radical forgiveness. But Jesus didn't directly answer their question because the amount of faith is not as important as its genuineness. What is faith? It is total dependence on God and a willingness to do his will. Faith is not something we use to put on a show for others. It is complete and humble obedience to God's will, readiness to do whatever he calls us to do. The amount of faith isn't as important as the right kind of faith—faith in our all-powerful God.

Effective faith is more concerned with its life than its size. A mustard seed is small, but it is alive and growing. Like a tiny seed, a small amount of genuine faith in God will take root and grow. Almost invisible at first, it will begin to spread, first under the ground and then visibly. Although each change will be gradual and imperceptible, soon this faith will have produced major results that will uproot and destroy competing loyalties. We don't need more faith; a tiny seed of faith is enough, if it is alive and growing.

BIBLE READING: Romans 5:1-11

KEY BIBLE VERSE: *Since we have been made right in God's sight by faith, we have peace with God because of what Jesus Christ our Lord has done for us.* (Romans 5:1)

Effective faith rests on what Christ has done. As Paul states clearly in 1 Corinthians 13:13, faith, hope, and love are at the heart of the Christian life. Our relationship with God begins with *faith*, which helps us realize that we are delivered from our past by Christ's death. *Hope* grows as we learn all that God has in mind for us; it gives us the promise of the future. And God's *love* fills our life and gives us the ability to reach out to others.

BIBLE READING: Hebrews 10:19-39

KEY BIBLE VERSE: *A righteous person will live by faith. But I will have no pleasure in anyone who turns away.* (Hebrews 10:38)

Effective faith grows under pressure. Hebrews encourages believers to persevere in their Christian faith and conduct when facing persecution and pressure. We don't usually think of suffering as good for us, but it can build our character and our patience. During times of great stress, we may feel God's presence more clearly and find help from Christians we never thought would care. Knowing that Jesus is with us in our suffering and that he will return one day to put an end to all pain helps us grow in our faith and our relationship with him (see Romans 5:3-5).

Effective faith becomes stronger through endurance. The writer encourages his readers not to abandon their faith in times of persecution, but to show by their endurance that their faith is real. Faith means resting in what Christ has done for us in the past, but it also means hoping for what he will do for us in the future (see Romans 8:12-25; Galatians 3:10-13).

BIBLE READING: Hebrews 11:1-40

KEY BIBLE VERSE: *What is faith? It is the confident assurance that what we hope for is going to happen. It is the evidence of things we cannot yet see.* (Hebrews 11:1)

Effective faith is hopeful anticipation. Do you remember how you felt when you were very young and your birthday approached? You were excited and anxious. You knew you would certainly receive gifts and other special treats. But some things would be a surprise. Birthdays combine assurance and anticipation, and so does faith! Faith is the conviction based on past experience that God's new and fresh surprises will surely be ours.

Effective faith is quiet certainty. Two words describe faith: *sure* and *certain*. These two qualities need a secure beginning and ending point. The beginning point of faith is believing in God's character—he *is* who he says. The end point is believing in God's promises—he will *do* what he says. When we believe that God will fulfill his promises even though we don't see those promises materializing yet, we demonstrate true faith (see John 20:24-31).

Related Topics: BELIEF/BELIEVE, CONFIDENCE, TRUST

FAITHFULNESS (*Consistency, Endurance, Perseverance*)

What examples of faithfulness do we find in the Bible?

BIBLE READING: Lamentations 3:1-66

KEY BIBLE VERSE: *The unfailing love of the LORD never ends! By his mercies we have been kept from complete destruction. Great is his faithfulness; his mercies begin afresh each day. (Lamentations 3:22-23)*

In the midst of despair, Jeremiah clung to God's faithfulness. Jeremiah saw one ray of hope in all the sin and sorrow surrounding him: "The unfailing love of the Lord never ends! By his mercies we have been kept from complete destruction." Jeremiah knew from personal experience about God's faithfulness. God had promised that punishment would follow disobedience, and it did. But God also had promised future restoration and blessing, and Jeremiah knew that God would keep that promise also. Trusting in God's faithfulness day by day makes us confident in his great promises for the future.

God willingly responds with help when we ask. Perhaps there is some sin in your life that you thought God would not forgive. God's steadfast love and mercy are greater than any sin, and he promises forgiveness.

BIBLE READING: 1 Kings 19:1-21

KEY BIBLE VERSE: *Elijah replied, "I have zealously served the LORD God Almighty. But the people of Israel have broken their covenant with you, torn down your altars, and killed every one of your prophets. I alone am left, and now they are trying to kill me, too." (1 Kings 19:10)*

God always has a remnant of faithful followers. Elijah thought he was the only person left who was still faithful to God. He had seen both the king's court and the priesthood become corrupt. After experiencing great victory at Mount Carmel, he had to run for his life. Lonely and discouraged, he forgot that others had remained faithful during the nation's wickedness. When you are tempted to think that you are the only one remaining faithful to a task, don't stop to feel sorry for yourself. Self-pity will dilute the good you are doing. Be assured that even if you don't know who they are, others are faithfully obeying God and fulfilling their duties.

BIBLE READING: Mark 9:42-50

KEY BIBLE VERSE: *Salt is good for seasoning. But if it loses its flavor, how do you make it salty again? You must have the qualities of salt among yourselves and live in peace with each other. (Mark 9:50)*

Faithfulness should be characteristic of God's people. Jesus used salt to illustrate three qualities that should be found in his people: (1) *We should remember God's faithfulness,* just as salt used with a sacrifice recalled God's covenant with his people (Leviticus 2:13). (2) *We should make a difference in the "flavor" of the world we live in,* just as salt changes meat's flavor (see Matthew 5:13). (3) *We should counteract the moral decay in society,* just as salt preserves food from decay. When we lose this desire to "salt" the earth with the love and message of God, we become useless to him.

Related Topics: CONSISTENCY, ENDURANCE, PERSEVERANCE

FAME (*see* POPULARITY)

FAMILY (*Home, Household, Relatives*)

▶ FAMILY TROUBLES
What actions cause the most problems for the family?

BIBLE READING: Genesis 37:1-11
KEY BIBLE VERSE: *Jacob loved Joseph more than any of his other children because Joseph had been born to him in his old age. So one day he gave Joseph a special gift—a beautiful robe.* (Genesis 37:3)

Favoritism destroys family unity. In Joseph's day, everyone had a robe or cloak. Robes were used to warm oneself, to bundle up belongings for a trip, to wrap babies in, to sit on, or even to serve as security for a loan. Most robes were knee length, short sleeved, and plain. In contrast, Joseph's robe was probably of the kind worn by royalty—long sleeved, ankle length, and colorful. The robe became a symbol of Jacob's favoritism toward Joseph, and it aggravated the already strained relations between Joseph and his brothers. Favoritism in families may be unavoidable, but its divisive effects should be minimized. Parents may not be able to change their feelings toward a favorite child, but they can change their actions toward the others.

BIBLE READING: Exodus 34:1-35
KEY BIBLE VERSE: *I show this unfailing love to many thousands by forgiving every kind of sin and rebellion. Even so I do not leave sin unpunished, but I punish the children for the sins of their parents to the third and fourth generations.* (Exodus 34:7)

Children often bear the consequences of their parents' sins. Why would sins affect grandchildren and great-grandchildren? This is no arbitrary punishment. Children still suffer for the sins of their parents. Consider child abuse or alcoholism, for example. While these sins are obvious, sins like selfishness and greed can be passed along as well. The dire consequences of sin are not limited to the individual family member. Be careful not to treat sin casually, but repent and turn from it. The sin may cause you little pain now, but it could sting in a most tender area of your life later—your children and grandchildren.

BIBLE READING: 1 Timothy 3:1-16
KEY BIBLE VERSE: *For if a man cannot manage his own household, how can he take care of God's church?* (1 Timothy 3:5)

Family responsibilities must be a priority for Christians. Christian workers and volunteers sometimes make the mistake of thinking their work is so important that they are justified in ignoring their families. Spiritual leadership, however, must begin at home. If a man is not willing to care for, discipline, and teach his children, he is not qualified to lead the church. Don't allow your volunteer activities to detract from your family responsibilities.

▶ **FAMILY TRIUMPHS**
What actions most strengthen family unity?

BIBLE READING: Exodus 10:1-29
KEY BIBLE VERSE: *You will be able to tell wonderful stories to your children and grandchildren about the marvelous things I am doing among the Egyptians to prove that I am the LORD.* (Exodus 10:2)

Retelling stories of God's faithfulness builds up the family. God told Moses that his miraculous experiences with Pharaoh should be retold to his descendants. What stories Moses had to tell! Living out one of the greatest dramas in biblical history, he witnessed events few people would ever see. It is important to tell our children about God's work in our past and to help them see what he is doing right now. What are the turning points in your life where

God intervened? What is God doing for you now? Your stories will form the foundations of your children's belief in God.

BIBLE READING: Deuteronomy 6:1-25

KEY BIBLE VERSE: *And you must commit yourselves wholeheartedly to these commands I am giving you today. Repeat them again and again to your children. Talk about them when you are at home and when you are away on a journey, when you are lying down and when you are getting up again.* (Deuteronomy 6:6-7)

Consistent living makes the deepest impression on children. This passage provides the central theme of Deuteronomy. It sets a pattern that helps us relate the Word of God to our daily lives. We are to love God, think constantly about his commandments, teach his commandments to our children, and live each day by the guidelines in his Word. God emphasized the importance of parents teaching the Bible to their children. The church and Christian schools cannot be used to escape from this responsibility. The Bible provides so many opportunities for object lessons and practical teaching that it would be a shame to study it only one day a week. Eternal truths are most effectively learned in the loving environment of a God-fearing home.

BIBLE READING: Luke 2:41-52

KEY BIBLE VERSE: *Then he returned to Nazareth with them and was obedient to them; and his mother stored all these things in her heart.* (Luke 2:51)

Family members should honor one another. This is the first time we are told that Jesus was aware that he was God's Son. But even though he knew his real Father, he did not reject his earthly parents. He went back to Nazareth with them and lived under their authority for another eighteen years. God's people should not despise human relationships or family responsibilities. If the Son of God obeyed his human parents, how much more should we honor our family members! Don't use commitment to God's work to justify neglecting your family.

BIBLE READING: Acts 16:1-5

KEY BIBLE VERSE: *Paul and Silas went first to Derbe and then on to Lystra. There they met Timothy, a young disciple whose mother was a Jewish believer, but whose father was a Greek.* (Acts 16:1)

Christian parents can pass on their faith to their children. Timothy is the first second-generation Christian mentioned in the New Testament. His mother, Eunice, and grandmother, Lois (2 Timothy 1:5), had become believers and had faithfully influenced him for the Lord. Although Timothy's father apparently was not a Christian, the faithfulness of his mother and grandmother prevailed. Never underestimate the far-reaching consequences of raising one small child to love the Lord.

BIBLE READING: Ephesians 6:1-4

KEY BIBLE VERSE: *"Honor your father and mother." This is the first of the Ten Commandments that ends with a promise.* (Ephesians 6:2)

God's commands apply to both parents and children. If our faith in Christ is real, it will usually prove itself at home, in our relationships with those who know us best. Children and parents have a responsibility to each other. Children should honor their parents even if the parents are demanding and unfair. Parents should gently care for their children, even if the children are disobedient and unpleasant. Ideally, of course, Christian parents and Christian children will relate to each other with thoughtfulness and love. This will happen if both parents and children put the others' interests above their own—that is, if they submit to one another.

Children have important God-given responsibilities within the family. There is a difference between obeying and honoring. To obey means to do as one is told; to honor means to respect and love. Children are not commanded to disobey God in obeying their parents. Adult children are not asked to be subservient to domineering parents. Children are to obey while under their parents' care, but the responsibility to honor parents is for life.

Some societies honor their elders. They respect their wisdom, defer to their authority, and pay attention to their comfort and happiness. This is how Christians should act. Where elders are respected, long life is a blessing, not a burden to them.

Parents are not to take unfair advantage of their authority. The purpose of parental discipline is to help children grow, not to exasperate and provoke them to anger or discouragement (see also Colossians 3:21). Parenting is not easy—it takes lots of patience to raise children in a loving, Christ-honoring manner. But frustration and anger should not be causes for discipline. Instead, parents should act in love, treating their children as Jesus treats the people he loves. This is vital to children's development and to their understanding of what Christ is like.

▶ OUR SPIRITUAL FAMILY
How do human families exemplify spiritual relationships?

BIBLE READING: Matthew 12:46-50
KEY BIBLE VERSE: *Anyone who does the will of my Father in heaven is my brother and sister and mother!* (Matthew 12:50)

Those who share the same spiritual Father are related to each other. Jesus was not denying his responsibility to his earthly family. On the contrary, he criticized the religious leaders for not following the Old Testament command to honor their parents (15:1-9). He provided for his mother's security as he hung on the cross (John 19:25-27). His mother and brothers were present in the upper room at Pentecost (Acts 1:14). Instead, Jesus was pointing out that spiritual relationships are as binding as physical ones, and he was paving the way for a new community of believers (the universal church), our spiritual family.

BIBLE READING: Romans 2:17-29
KEY BIBLE VERSE: *No, a true Jew is one whose heart is right with God. And true circumcision is not a cutting of the body but a change of heart produced by God's Spirit. Whoever has that kind of change seeks praise from God, not from people.* (Romans 2:29)

Membership in God's family is marked by heartfelt commitment. To be a Jew meant you were in God's family, an heir to all his promises. Yet Paul made it clear that membership in God's family is based on internal, not external, qualities. All whose hearts are right with God are real Jews—that is, part of God's family (see also Galatians 3:7). Attending church or being baptized, confirmed, or accepted for membership are not enough, just as circumcision was not enough for the Jews. God desires our devotion and obedience. (See also Deuteronomy 10:16; Jeremiah 4:4 for more on "circumcising the heart.")

BIBLE READING: Ephesians 3:14-21
KEY BIBLE VERSE: *When I think of the wisdom and scope of God's plan, I fall to my*

knees and pray to the Father, the Creator of everything in heaven and on earth. (Ephesians 3:14-15)

God's family is eternal. The family of God includes all who have believed in him in the past, all who believe in the present, and all who will believe in the future. We are all a family because we have the same Father. He is the source of all creation, the rightful owner of everything. God promises his love and power to his family, the church (3:16-21). If we want to receive God's blessings, it is important that we stay in contact with other believers in the body of Christ. Those who isolate themselves from God's family and try to go it alone cut themselves off from God's power.

Related Topics: CHILDREN, HOME, PARENT(S)

FASTING *(Abstaining, Discipline, Hunger)*

How is fasting used as a spiritual discipline?

BIBLE READING: 2 Chronicles 20:1-30
KEY BIBLE VERSE: *Jehoshaphat was alarmed by this news and sought the LORD for guidance. He also gave orders that everyone throughout Judah should observe a fast.* (2 Chronicles 20:3)

Fasting can be part of repentance. When the nation was faced with disaster, Jehoshaphat called upon the people to get serious with God by going without food (fasting) for a designated time. By separating themselves from the daily routine of food preparation and eating, they could devote that extra time to considering their sin and praying to God for help. Hunger pangs would reinforce their feelings of penitence and remind them of their weakness and their dependence upon God. Fasting still can be helpful today as we seek God's will in special situations.

BIBLE READING: Ezra 8:15-36
KEY BIBLE VERSE: *And there by the Ahava Canal, I gave orders for all of us to fast and humble ourselves before our God. We prayed that he would give us a safe journey and protect us, our children, and our goods as we traveled.* (Ezra 8:21)

Fasting can be part of prayer. Ezra knew God's promises to protect his people, but he didn't take them for granted. He also knew that God's blessings are appropriated through prayer; so Ezra and the people humbled themselves by fasting and praying. And their prayers were answered. Fasting humbled them because going without food was a reminder of their complete dependence on God. Fasting also gave them more time to pray and meditate on God.

Too often we pray glibly and superficially. Serious prayer, by contrast, requires concentration. It puts us in touch with God's will and can really change us. Without serious prayer, we reduce God to a quick-service pharmacist with painkillers for our every ailment.

BIBLE READING: Matthew 6:16-18
KEY BIBLE VERSE: *But when you fast, comb your hair and wash your face. Then no one will suspect you are fasting, except your Father, who knows what you do in secret. And your Father, who knows all secrets, will reward you.* (Matthew 6:17-18)

Fasting needs to be done for the right reasons. Fasting—going without food in order to spend time in prayer—is noble *and* difficult. It gives us time to pray, teaches self-discipline, reminds us that we can live with a lot less, and helps us appreciate God's gifts. Jesus was not condemning fasting, but hypocrisy—fasting in order to gain public approval. Fasting was mandatory for the Jewish people once a year, on the Day of Atonement (Leviticus 23:32). The Pharisees voluntarily fasted twice a week to impress the people with their "holiness." Jesus commended acts of self-sacrifice done quietly and sincerely. He wanted people to adopt spiritual disciplines for the right reasons, not from a selfish desire for praise.

Related Topics: DISCIPLINE, PRAYER, SPIRITUAL DISCIPLINES

FATHERS (*see* PARENT[S])

FATIGUE (*see* DEPRESSION)

FAULTS (*Flaws, Problems, Weakness*)

How should we respond to faults in ourselves and others?

 BIBLE READING: Matthew 7:1-6
KEY BIBLE VERSE: *Stop judging others, and you will not be judged. For others will treat you as you treat them. Whatever measure you use in judging others, it will be used to measure how you are judged.* (Matthew 7:1-2)

Judgment must be discerning and loving. Jesus' statement, "Stop judging others," is against the kind of hypocritical, judgmental attitude that tears others down in order to build oneself up. It is not a blanket statement against all critical thinking, but a call to be *discerning* rather than negative. Jesus said to expose false teachers (7:15-23), and Paul taught that we should exercise church discipline (1 Corinthians 5:1-2) and trust God to be the final Judge (1 Corinthians 4:3-5).

The motives behind criticism must always be examined. Jesus tells us to examine our own motives and conduct instead of judging others. The traits that bother us in others are often the habits we dislike in ourselves. Our untamed bad habits and behavior patterns are the very ones that we most want to change in others. Do you find it easy to magnify others' faults while excusing your own? If you are ready to criticize someone, check to see if you deserve the same criticism. Judge yourself first, and then lovingly forgive and help your neighbor.

BIBLE READING: Ephesians 4:1-16
KEY BIBLE VERSE: *Be humble and gentle. Be patient with each other, making allowance for each other's faults because of your love.* (Ephesians 4:2)

We should respond to others' faults with mercy and patience. God has chosen us to be Christ's representatives on earth. In light of this truth, Paul challenges us to live worthy of the calling we have received, to be called Christ's very own. This includes being humble, gentle, patient, understanding, and peaceful. People are watching your life. Can they see Christ in you? How well are you doing as his representative?

No one is ever going to be perfect here on earth, so we must accept and love other Christians in spite of their faults. When we see faults in fellow believers, we should be patient and gentle. Is there someone whose actions or personality really annoys you? Rather than dwelling on that person's weaknesses or looking for faults, pray for him or her. Then do even more—spend time together and see if you can learn to like him or her.

Related Topics: COMPASSION, PATIENCE, SIN

FAVORITISM *(Dishonesty, Partiality, Unfairness)*

Why does God condemn favoritism?

BIBLE READING: Malachi 2:1-17

KEY BIBLE VERSE: *I have made you despised and humiliated in the eyes of all the people. For you have not obeyed me but have shown partiality in your interpretation of the law.* (Malachi 2:9)

Favoritism reveals a destructive double standard. Malachi was angry at the priests because, though they were to be God's messengers, they did not know God's will. And this lack of knowledge caused them to lead God's people astray. Their ignorance was willful and inexcusable. The priests had allowed influential and favored people to break the law. The priests were so dependent on these people for support that they could not afford to confront them when they did wrong. In your church, are certain people allowed to do wrong without criticism? There should be no double standard based on wealth or position. Let your standards be those presented in God's Word. Playing favorites is contemptible in God's sight (see James 2:1-9).

BIBLE READING: James 2:1-13

KEY BIBLE VERSE: *My dear brothers and sisters, how can you claim that you have faith in our glorious Lord Jesus Christ if you favor some people more than others?* (James 2:1)

Favoritism betrays Christ. James condemns acts of favoritism. Often we treat a well-dressed, impressive-looking person better than someone who looks poor. We do this because we would rather identify with successful people than with apparent failures. The irony, as James reminds us, is that the supposed winners may have gained their impressive lifestyle at our expense. In addition, the rich find it difficult to identify with the Lord Jesus who came as a humble servant. Are you easily impressed by status, wealth, or fame? Are you partial to the "haves" while ignoring the "have nots"? This attitude is sin. God views all people as equals; and if he favors anyone, it is the poor and the powerless. We should follow his example.

Favoritism devalues people for whom Christ died. Why is it wrong to judge a person by his or her economic status? Wealth may indicate intelligence, wise decision-making, and hard work. On the other hand, it may mean only that a person had the good fortune of being born into a wealthy family. Or it can even be the sign of greed, dishonesty, and selfishness. By honoring someone just because he or she dresses well, we are making appearance more important than character. Sometimes we do this because (1) poverty makes us uncomfortable; we don't want to face our responsibilities to those who have less than we do; (2) we want to be wealthy too, and we hope to use the rich person as a means to that end; (3) we want the rich person to join our church and help support it financially. All these motives are selfish; they view neither the rich nor the poor person as a human being in need of fellowship. If we say that Christ is our Lord, then we must live as he requires, showing no favoritism and loving all people regardless of whether they are rich or poor.

Favoritism indicates an ignorance of God's values. We are often partial to the rich because we mistakenly assume that riches are a sign of God's blessing and approval. But God does not promise us earthly rewards or riches; in fact, Christ calls us to be ready to suffer for him and give up everything in order to hold on to eternal life (Matthew 6:19-21; 19:28-30; Luke 12:14-34; Romans 8:15-21; 1 Timothy 6:17-19). We will have untold riches in eternity if we are faithful in our present life (Luke 6:35; John 12:23-25; Galatians 6:7-10; Titus 3:4-8).

Related Topics: EQUALITY, FAIRNESS, HONESTY

FEAR *(Awe, Scared, Timid)*

▶ **APPROPRIATE FEAR**
What does it mean to fear God?

BIBLE READING: Deuteronomy 10:12-22
KEY BIBLE VERSE: *And now, Israel, what does the LORD your God require of you? He requires you to fear him, to live according to his will, to love and worship him with all your heart and soul, and to obey the LORD's commands and laws that I am giving you today for your own good.* (Deuteronomy 10:12-13)

Fear of God is motivated by his awesome power and justice. In saying that the Lord is God of gods and Lord of lords, Moses was distinguishing the true God from all the local gods worshiped throughout the land. Then Moses went a step further, calling God "mighty and awesome." He has such awesome power and justice that people cannot stand before him without his mercy. Fortunately, his mercy toward his people is unlimited. When we begin to grasp the extent of God's mercy toward us, we see what true love is and how deeply God loves us. Our fear of what he might do to us is transformed into a reverence and awe before his great mercy. Although our sins deserve severe judgment, God has chosen to show love and mercy to all who seek him.

BIBLE READING: Psalm 25:1-22
KEY BIBLE VERSE: *Who are those who fear the LORD? He will show them the path they should choose.* (Psalm 25:12)

Knowing God increases reverent fear. To fear the Lord is to recognize God for who he is: holy, almighty, righteous, pure, all-knowing, all-powerful, and all-wise. When we regard God correctly, we gain a clearer picture of ourselves: sinful, weak, frail, and needy. When we recognize who God is and who we are, we will fall at his feet in humble respect. Only then will he show us how to choose his way.

Fearing God leads to knowing him more fully. "Friendship with the Lord is reserved for those who fear him." God offers intimate and lasting friendship to those who revere him, who hold him in highest honor. What relationship could ever compare with having the Lord of all creation for a friend? Your everlasting friendship with God will grow as you revere him.

BIBLE READING: Exodus 20:1-26
KEY BIBLE VERSE: *"Don't be afraid," Moses said, "for God has come in this way to show you his awesome power. From now on, let your fear of him keep you from sinning!"* (Exodus 20:20)

Fearing God does not mean being terrified of him. Throughout the Bible we find this phrase, "Don't be afraid." God wasn't trying to scare the people. He was showing his mighty power so the Israelites would know he was the true God and would therefore obey him. If they would do this, he would make his power available to them. God wants us to follow him out of love rather than fear. To overcome fear, we must think more about his love. First John 4:18 says that, "perfect love expels all fear."

▶ AVOIDABLE FEAR
How can we handle our fears?

BIBLE READING: Genesis 15:1-21
KEY BIBLE VERSE: *Afterward the LORD spoke to Abram in a vision and said to him, "Do not be afraid, Abram, for I will protect you, and your reward will be great."* (Genesis 15:1)

The promise of God's protection can keep us from fear. Why would Abram be afraid? Perhaps he feared revenge from the kings he had just defeated (14:15). God gave him two good reasons for courage: (1) he promised to defend Abram, and (2) he promised to give Abram great blessings. When you fear what lies ahead, remember that God will stay with you through difficult times and that he has promised you great blessings.

BIBLE READING: Joshua 1:1-18
KEY BIBLE VERSE: *I command you—be strong and courageous! Do not be afraid or discouraged. For the LORD your God is with you wherever you go.* (Joshua 1:9)

Be careful not to leave God out of your thinking. Joshua's new job consisted of leading more than 2 million people into a strange new land and conquering it. What a challenge—even for a man of Joshua's caliber! Every new job is a challenge. Without God it can be frightening. With God it can be a great adventure. Just as God was with Joshua, he is with us as we face our new challenges. We may not conquer nations, but every day we face tough situations, difficult people, and temptations. However, God promises that he will never abandon us or fail to help us. By asking God to direct us we can conquer many of life's challenges.

BIBLE READING: Nehemiah 2:1-20
KEY BIBLE VERSE: *The king asked, "Well, how can I help you?" With a prayer to the God of heaven, I replied, "If it please Your Majesty and if you are pleased with me, your servant, send me to Judah to rebuild the city where my ancestors are buried."* (Nehemiah 2:4-5)

Fears can be resisted by remembering God's greatness. The king noticed Nehemiah's sad appearance. This frightened Nehemiah because it was dangerous to show sorrow before the king, who could execute anyone who displeased him. Anyone wearing sackcloth (mourning clothes) was barred from the palace (Esther 4:2).

Nehemiah wasn't ashamed to admit his fear, but he refused to allow fear to stop him from doing what God had called him to do. When we allow our fears to rule us, we make fear more powerful than God. Is there a task God wants you to do, but fear is holding you back? God is greater than all your fears. Recognizing why you are afraid is the first step in committing it to God. Realize that if God has called you to a task, he will help you accomplish it.

BIBLE READING: Proverbs 29:18-27
KEY BIBLE VERSE: *Fearing people is a dangerous trap, but to trust the LORD means safety.* (Proverbs 29:25)

It is far better to fear God than to fear man. Fear of people can hamper everything you try to do. In extreme forms, it can make you afraid to leave your home. By contrast, fear of God—respect, reverence, and trust—is liberating. Why fear people who can do no eternal harm? Instead, fear God who can turn the harm intended by others into good for those who trust him.

Related Topics: AWE, COURAGE, FEELINGS

FEELINGS *(Attitudes, Emotions, Passions)*

What are appropriate ways of dealing with our feelings?

BIBLE READING: Job 6:1–7:21
KEY BIBLE VERSE: *I cannot keep from speaking. I must express my anguish. I must complain in my bitterness.* (Job 7:11)

Honestly expressing our feelings to God keeps things in perspective. Job felt deep anguish and bitterness, and he spoke honestly to God about his feelings to let out his frustrations. If we express our feelings to God, we can deal with them without exploding in harsh words and actions, possibly hurting ourself and others. The next time strong emotions threaten to overwhelm you, express them openly to God in prayer. This will help you gain an eternal perspective on the situation and give you greater ability to deal with it constructively.

BIBLE READING: John 11:17-36
KEY BIBLE VERSE: *When Jesus saw her weeping and saw the other people wailing with her, he was moved with indignation and was deeply troubled.* (John 11:33)

Jesus is our example of how to handle feelings. John stresses that we have a God who cares. This portrait contrasts with the Greek concept of God that was popular in that day—a God with no emotions and no messy involvement with humans. Here we see many of Jesus' emotions—compassion, indignation, sorrow, even frustration. He often expressed deep emotion, and we must never be afraid to reveal our true feelings to him. He understands them, for he experienced them. Be honest, and don't try to hide anything from your Savior. He cares.

BIBLE READING: Romans 12:9-21
KEY BIBLE VERSE: *Don't let evil get the best of you, but conquer evil by doing good.* (Romans 12:21)

God often asks us to act in spite of our feelings. In this day of constant lawsuits and incessant demands for legal rights, Paul's command sounds almost impossible. When someone hurts you deeply, instead of giving him what he deserves, Paul says to befriend him. Why does Paul tell us to forgive our enemies? (1) Forgiveness may break a cycle of retaliation and lead to mutual reconciliation. (2) It may make the enemy feel ashamed and change his or her ways. (3) By contrast, returning evil for evil hurts you just as much as it hurts your enemy. Even if your enemy never repents, forgiving him or her will free you of a heavy load of bitterness.

Forgiveness involves both attitudes and actions. If you find it difficult to *feel* forgiving of someone who has hurt you, try responding with kind actions. If appropriate, tell this person that you would like to heal your relationship. Give him a helping hand. Send him a gift. Smile at him. Many times you will discover that right actions lead to right feelings.

What are inappropriate ways of dealing with our feelings?

 BIBLE READING: Ezekiel 3:1-27

KEY BIBLE VERSE: *The Spirit lifted me up and took me away. I went in bitterness and turmoil, but the LORD's hold on me was strong. Then I came to the colony of Judean exiles in Tel-abib, beside the Kebar River. I sat there among them for seven days, overwhelmed.* (Ezekiel 3:14-15)

We should not allow feelings to keep us from obeying God. Ezekiel was bitter and angry, not at God, but at the sins and attitudes of the people. Ezekiel's extraordinary vision had ended, and he had to begin the tedious job of prophesying among his people, who cared little about God's messages. Before the exile, the people had heard Jeremiah, but they would not listen. Here Ezekiel had to give a similar message, and he expected to be rejected as well. But Ezekiel had the vision of the living creatures and the rumbling wheels on his side. He had nothing to fear because God was with him. Despite knowing the probable outcome, Ezekiel obeyed God.

As we grow, we will have times of great joy when we feel close to God, and times when sins, struggles, or everyday tasks overwhelm us. Like Ezekiel, we should obey God even when we don't feel like it. Don't let feelings hinder your obedience.

BIBLE READING: Galatians 5:1-26

KEY BIBLE VERSE: *The old sinful nature loves to do evil, which is just opposite from what the Holy Spirit wants. And the Spirit gives us desires that are opposite from what the sinful nature desires. These two forces are constantly fighting each other, and your choices are never free from this conflict.* (Galatians 5:17)

Feelings are not reliable guides. If your desire is to have the qualities listed in Galatians 5:22-23, then you know that the Holy Spirit is leading you. At the same time, be careful not to confuse your feelings with the Spirit's leading. Being led by the Holy Spirit involves the desire to hear, the readiness to obey God's Word, and the sensitivity to discern between your feelings and his promptings. Live each day controlled and guided by the Holy Spirit. Then the words of Christ will be in your mind, the love of Christ will be behind your actions, and the power of Christ will help you control your selfish desires.

Related Topics: EMOTIONS, FEAR, LOVE

FELLOWSHIP (*Community, Friendship, Warmth*)

Why is fellowship with God and others important?

BIBLE READING: Genesis 3:1-24

KEY BIBLE VERSE: *Toward evening they heard the LORD God walking about in the garden, so they hid themselves among the trees.* (Genesis 3:8)

God desires to have fellowship with us. The thought of two humans covered with fig leaves trying to hide from the all-seeing, all-knowing God is humorous. How could they be so silly as to think they could actually hide? Yet we do the same, acting as though God doesn't know what we're doing. Have the courage to share all you do and think with him. And don't try to hide—it can't be done. Honesty will strengthen your relationship with God.

These verses show God's desire to have fellowship with us. They also show why we are afraid to have fellowship with him. Adam and Eve hid from God when they heard him approaching. God wanted to be with them, but because of their sin, they were afraid to show themselves. Sin had broken their close relationship with God, just as it has broken ours. But Jesus Christ, God's Son, opens the way for us to renew our fellowship with him. God longs to be with us. He actively offers us his unconditional love. Our natural response is fear, because we feel we can't live up to his standards. But understanding that he loves us, regardless of our faults, can help remove that dread.

BIBLE READING: Acts 20:13-38

KEY BIBLE VERSE: *They wept aloud as they embraced him in farewell, sad most of all because he had said that they would never see him again. Then they accompanied him down to the ship.* (Acts 20:37-38)

Fellowship builds strong personal relationships. Paul's relationship with these believers is a beautiful example of Christian fellowship. He had cared for them and loved them, even cried over their needs. They responded with love and care for him and sorrow over his leaving. They had prayed together and comforted one another. Like Paul, you can build strong relationships with other Christians by sharing, caring, sorrowing, rejoicing, and praying with them. You will gather others around you only by giving yourself away to them.

BIBLE READING: Philippians 1:1-11

KEY BIBLE VERSE: *It is right that I should feel as I do about all of you, for you have a very special place in my heart. We have shared together the blessings of God, both when I was in prison and when I was out, defending the truth and telling others the Good News.* (Philippians 1:7)

Genuine fellowship fosters the love of Christ. Have you ever longed to see a friend with whom you share fond memories? Paul had such a longing to see the Christians at Philippi. His love and affection for them was based not merely on past experiences, but also upon the unity that comes when believers draw upon Christ's love. All Christians are part of God's family and thus share equally in the transforming power of his love. Do you feel a deep love for fellow Christians, friends and strangers alike? Let Christ's love motivate you to love other Christians, and to express that love in your actions toward them.

BIBLE READING: Hebrews 10:1-39

KEY BIBLE VERSE: *Let us not neglect our meeting together, as some people do, but encourage and warn each other, especially now that the day of his coming back again is drawing near.* (Hebrews 10:25)

Fellowship is a gift from Christ. We have significant privileges with our new life in Christ: (1) we have personal access to God through Christ and can draw near to him without an elaborate system (10:22); (2) we may grow in faith, overcome doubts and questions, and deepen our relationship with God (10:23); (3) we may enjoy encouragement from one another (10:24); (4) we may worship together (10:25).

Others benefit from fellowship with us. To neglect Christian meetings is to give up the encouragement and help of other Christians. We gather together to share our faith and to strengthen one another in the Lord. As we get closer to the day when Christ will return, we will face many spiritual struggles and even persecution. Anti-Christian forces will grow in strength. Difficulties should never be excuses for missing church services. Rather, as difficulties arise, we should make an even greater effort to be faithful in attendance.

Related Topics: BELIEVERS, CHURCH, WORSHIP

📖 FIGHTING (*see* CONFLICTS)

FLATTERY (*Complimenting, Lying, Tricking*)

What are the dangers in believing flattery?

📖 BIBLE READING: Psalm 12:1-8
KEY BIBLE VERSE: *The LORD's promises are pure, like silver refined in a furnace, purified seven times over.* (Psalm 12:6)

Flattery is an attempt to manipulate others. Sincerity and truth are extremely valuable because they are so rare. Many people are deceivers, liars, flatterers; they think they will get what they want by deception. As a king, David certainly faced his share of such people, who hoped to win his favor and gain advancement through flattery. When we feel as though sincerity and truth have nearly gone out of existence, we have one hope—the word of God. God's words are as flawless as refined silver. So listen carefully when he speaks.

📖 BIBLE READING: Luke 20:20-26
KEY BIBLE VERSE: *Watching for their opportunity, the leaders sent secret agents pretending to be honest men. They tried to get Jesus to say something that could be reported to the Roman governor so he would arrest Jesus.* (Luke 20:20)

Flattery is an attempt to deceive. Jesus turned his enemies' attempt to trap him into a powerful lesson: As God's followers, we have legitimate obligations to both God and the government. But it is important to keep our priorities straight. When the two authorities conflict, our duty to God always must come before our duty to the government.

These spies, pretending to be honest men, flattered Jesus before asking him their trick question, hoping to catch him off guard. But Jesus knew what they were trying to do and stayed out of their trap. Beware of flattery. With God's help, you can detect it and avoid the trap that often follows.

📖 BIBLE READING: 1 Thessalonians 2:1-20
KEY BIBLE VERSE: *Never once did we try to win you with flattery, as you very well know. And God is our witness that we were not just pretending to be your friends so you would give us money!* (1 Thessalonians 2:5)

Flattery distorts the truth. In trying to persuade people, we may be tempted to alter our position just enough to make our message more palatable or to use flattery or praise. Paul never changed his *message* to make it more acceptable, but he did tailor his *methods* to each audience. Although our presentation must be altered to be appropriate to the situation, the truth of the gospel must never be compromised.

Flattery hides real motives. It's disgusting to hear a person "butter up" someone. Flattery is phony and a false cover-up for a person's real intentions. Christians should not be flatterers. Those who proclaim God's truth have a special responsibility to be honest. Are you honest and straightforward in your words and actions? Or do you tell people what they want to hear in order to get what you want or to get ahead?

Flattery destroys integrity. When Paul was with the Thessalonians, he didn't flatter them, didn't take their money, didn't seek their praise, and wasn't a burden to them. He and Silas completely focused their efforts on presenting God's message of salvation. This was important! The Thessalonian believers had their lives changed by God, not Paul; it was Christ's message they believed, not Paul's.

When we witness for Christ, our focus should not be on the impressions we make. As true ministers of Christ, we should point to him, not to ourself.

Related Topics: DECEIT, ENCOURAGEMENT, PRAISE

FOCUS *(Concentration, Goals, Values)*

How can a person maintain the right kind of focus?

BIBLE READING: Numbers 13:1-33
KEY BIBLE VERSE: *But Caleb tried to encourage the people as they stood before Moses. "Let's go at once to take the land," he said. "We can certainly conquer it!"* (Numbers 13:30)

Do not allow fear to shift the focus from God. God told the Israelites that the promised land was rich and fertile. Not only that, he promised that this bountiful land would be theirs. When the spies reported back to Moses, they gave plenty of good reasons for entering the land, but they couldn't stop focusing on their fears. Talk of giants (descendants of Anak) and fortified cities made it easy to forget about God's promise to help. When facing a tough decision, don't let the negatives cause you to lose sight of the positives. Weigh both sides carefully. Don't let potential difficulties blind you to God's power to help and his promise to guide.

BIBLE READING: 2 Corinthians 11:1-15
KEY BIBLE VERSE: *I fear that somehow you will be led away from your pure and simple devotion to Christ, just as Eve was deceived by the serpent.* (2 Corinthians 11:3)

Identify and avoid destructive distractions. The Corinthians' pure and simple devotion to Christ was being threatened by false teaching. Paul did not want the believers to lose their single-minded love for Christ. Keeping Christ first in our life can be very difficult when we have so many distractions threatening to sidetrack our faith. Just as Eve lost her focus by listening to the serpent, we too can lose our focus by letting our life become overcrowded and confused. Is there anything that weakens your commitment to keep Christ first in your life? How can you minimize the distractions that threaten your devotion to him?

Identify and avoid destructive instruction. The Corinthian believers fell for smooth talk and messages that sounded good and seemed to make sense. Today there are many false teachings that seem to make sense. Don't believe someone simply because he or she sounds like an authority or says words you like to hear. Search the Bible and check his or her teachings with God's Word. The Bible should be your authoritative guide. Don't listen to any "authoritative preacher" who contradicts God's Word.

Related Topics: GOALS, GUIDANCE, PRIORITIES

FOLLOW *(Believe, Commit, Respond)*

What does it take to follow Jesus?

BIBLE READING: Matthew 4:18-22
KEY BIBLE VERSE: *Jesus called out to them, "Come, be my disciples, and I will show you how to fish for people!" And they left their nets at once and went with him.* (Matthew 4:19-20)

Following Christ involves radical change. Jesus told Peter and Andrew to leave their fishing business and become "fishers of people," to help others find God. Jesus was calling them away from their productive trades to be productive spiritually. We all need to fish for souls. If we practice Christ's teachings and share the gospel with others, we will be able to draw those around us to Christ like a fisherman who pulls fish into his boat with nets.

Following Christ involves a conscious decision. These men already knew Jesus. He had talked to Peter and Andrew previously (John 1:35-42) and had been preaching in the area. When Jesus called them, they knew what kind of man he was and were willing to follow him. They were not in a hypnotic trance when they followed him, but had been thoroughly convinced that following him would change their lives forever.

BIBLE READING: Matthew 16:21-28

KEY BIBLE VERSE: *Jesus said to the disciples, "If any of you wants to be my follower, you must put aside your selfish ambition, shoulder your cross, and follow me."* (Matthew 16:24)

Following Jesus is a radical commitment. When Jesus used this picture of his followers taking up their crosses to follow him, the disciples knew what he meant. Crucifixion was a common Roman method of execution, and condemned criminals had to carry their crosses through the streets to the execution site. Following Jesus, therefore, meant a true commitment, the risk of death, and no turning back (see Matthew 10:39).

Following Jesus is a costly commitment. The possibility of losing their lives was very real for the disciples as well as for Jesus. Real discipleship implies real commitment—pledging our whole existence to his service. If we try to save our physical life from death, pain, or discomfort, we may risk losing our true eternal life. If we protect ourself from pain, we begin to die spiritually and emotionally. Our life turns inward, and we lose our intended purpose. When we give our life in service to Christ, however, we discover the real purpose of living.

BIBLE READING: Mark 8:31-38

KEY BIBLE VERSE: *Then he called his disciples and the crowds to come over and listen. "If any of you wants to be my follower," he told them, "you must put aside your selfish ambition, shoulder your cross, and follow me."* (Mark 8:34)

Following Jesus is an all-encompassing commitment. We should be willing to lose our life for the sake of the gospel, not because our life is useless but because nothing—not even life itself—can compare to what we gain with Christ. Jesus wants us to *choose* to follow him rather than to lead a life of sin and self-satisfaction. He wants us to stop trying to control our own destiny and to let him direct us. This makes good sense because, as the Creator, Christ knows better than we do what real life is about. He asks for submission, not self-hatred; he asks us only to lose our self-centered determination to be in charge.

Related Topics: BELIEF/BELIEVE, FAITH, FAITHFULNESS

FOLLOW-THROUGH (*Commitment, Consistency, Faithfulness*)

What is important about following through on our decisions?

BIBLE READING: Nehemiah 7:1-4

KEY BIBLE VERSE: *I said to them, "Do not leave the gates open during the hottest part of the day. And while the gatekeepers are still on duty, have them shut and bar the doors. Appoint the residents of Jerusalem to act as guards, everyone on a regular watch. Some will serve at their regular posts and some in front of their own homes."* (Nehemiah 7:3)

Good decisions require follow-through. The wall was complete, but the work was not finished. Nehemiah assigned each family the task of protecting the section of wall next to their home. It is tempting to relax our guard and rest on past accomplishments after we have completed a large task. But we must continue to serve and to take care of all that God has entrusted to us. Following through after a project is completed is as vital as doing the project itself.

BIBLE READING: Exodus 39:1-43

KEY BIBLE VERSE: *Moses inspected all their work and blessed them because it had been done as the LORD had commanded him.* (Exodus 39:43)

Effective follow-through begins with careful delegation. Moses had learned his management lesson well. He gave important responsibilities to others and then trusted them to do the job. Great leaders, like Moses, give plans and direction while letting others participate on the team. If you are a leader, trust your assistants with key responsibilities.

Effective follow-through includes praise and appreciation. Moses inspected the finished work, saw that it was done the way God wanted, and then blessed the people. A good leader follows up on assigned tasks and gives rewards for good work. In whatever responsible position you find yourself, follow up to make sure that tasks are completed as intended, and show your appreciation to the people who have helped.

BIBLE READING: Galatians 4:8-20

KEY BIBLE VERSE: *Oh, my dear children! I feel as if I am going through labor pains for you again, and they will continue until Christ is fully developed in your lives.* (Galatians 4:19)

Effective follow-through includes ongoing concern. Paul led many people to Christ and helped them mature spiritually. Perhaps one reason for his success as a spiritual father was the deep concern he felt for his spiritual children; he compared his pain over their faithlessness to the pain of childbirth. We should have the same intense care for those to whom we are spiritual parents. When you lead people to Christ, remember to stand by them to help them grow.

Related Topics: COMMITMENT, CONSISTENCY, FAITHFULNESS

FOOLISHNESS *(Impulsiveness, Rashness, Silliness)*

What are the characteristics of foolish behavior?

BIBLE READING: Psalm 14:1-7

KEY BIBLE VERSE: *Only fools say in their hearts, "There is no God." They are corrupt, and their actions are evil; no one does good!* (Psalm 14:1)

It is foolish to deny God's existence. The true atheist is either foolish or wicked—foolish because he ignores the evidence that God exists, or wicked because he refuses to live by God's truths. We become atheists in practice when we rely more on ourself than on God. The fool mentioned here is someone who is aggressively perverse in his actions. To speak in direct defiance of God is utterly foolish according to the Bible.

It is foolish to believe we can live apart from God. No one but God is perfect; all of us stand guilty before him (see Romans 3:23) and need his forgiveness. No matter how well we perform or how much we achieve compared to others, none of us can boast of his or her goodness when compared to God's standard. God not only expects us to obey his guidelines, but he wants us to love him with all our heart. No one except Jesus Christ has done that perfectly. Because we all fall short we must turn to Christ to save us (Romans 10:9-11). Have you asked him to save you?

BIBLE READING: Proverbs 9:1-18
KEY BIBLE VERSE: *Leave your foolish ways behind, and begin to live; learn how to be wise.* (Proverbs 9:6)

Foolish behavior has no lasting value. Wisdom and Folly are portrayed in this chapter as rival young women, each preparing a feast and inviting people to it. But Wisdom is a responsible woman of character, while Folly is a prostitute serving stolen food. Wisdom appeals first to the mind; Folly to the senses. It is easier to excite the senses, but the pleasures of Folly are temporary. By contrast, the satisfaction that Wisdom brings lasts forever.

BIBLE READING: 1 Corinthians 2:6-16
KEY BIBLE VERSE: *People who aren't Christians can't understand these truths from God's Spirit. It all sounds foolish to them because only those who have the Spirit can understand what the Spirit means.* (1 Corinthians 2:14)

The greatest foolishness is to reject Jesus Christ. The "truths from God's Spirit" refers to God's unfathomable nature and his wonderful plan—Jesus' resurrection—and to the promise of salvation, revealed only to those who believe that what God says is true. Those who believe in the Resurrection and put their faith in Christ will know all they need to know to be saved. This knowledge, however, can't be grasped by even the wisest people unless they accept God's message. All who reject God's message are foolish, no matter how wise the world thinks they are.

Related Topics: DISCIPLINE, PRIDE, WISDOM

FORGET *(Lose, Misplace, Reject)*

Does God forget?

BIBLE READING: Exodus 2:11-25
KEY BIBLE VERSE: *God heard their cries and remembered his covenant promise to Abraham, Isaac, and Jacob.* (Exodus 2:24)

God will not forget his promises to us. God doesn't always rescue us the moment we want it. God had promised to bring the Hebrew slaves out of Egypt (Genesis 15:16; 46:3-4). The people had waited a long time for that promise to be kept, but God rescued them when he knew the right time had come. God knows the best time to act. When you feel that God has forgotten you in your troubles, remember that God has a time schedule we can't see.

BIBLE READING: Hebrews 10:1-18

KEY BIBLE VERSE: *Then he adds, "I will never again remember their sins and lawless deeds." Now when sins have been forgiven, there is no need to offer any more sacrifices.* (Hebrews 10:17-18)

God forgets our sins when he forgives us. The writer of Hebrews concludes his argument with this powerful statement that God will never remember our sins. Christ forgives completely, so there is no need to confess our past sins repeatedly. As believers, we can be confident that the sins we confess and renounce are forgiven and forgotten.

Why do we forget God so often?

BIBLE READING: Nehemiah 9:1-38

KEY BIBLE VERSE: *Even while they had their own kingdom, they did not serve you even though you showered your goodness on them. You gave them a large, fertile land, but they refused to turn from their wickedness.* (Nehemiah 9:35)

We often take God for granted. Sometimes the very blessings God has showered on us make us forget him (9:28). We are often tempted to rely on wealth for security rather than on God. As you see what happened to the Israelites, look at your own life. Do your blessings make you thankful to God and draw you closer to him, or do they make you feel self-sufficient and forgetful of God?

BIBLE READING: Psalm 106:1-48

KEY BIBLE VERSE: *Israel failed to destroy the nations in the land, as the LORD had told them to. Instead, they mingled among the pagans and adopted their evil customs. They worshiped their idols, and this led to their downfall.* (Psalm 106:34-36)

Giving in to the pressures of evil can make us forget God. Israel constantly turned away from God. How, after the great miracles they saw, could they turn from God and worship the idols of the land? We also have seen God's great miracles, but sometimes find ourself enticed by the world's gods—power, convenience, fame, sex, and pleasure. As Israel forgot God, so we are susceptible to forgetting him and giving in to the pressures of an evil world. Remember all that God has done for you so you won't be drawn away from him by the world's pleasures.

BIBLE READING: Jeremiah 2:1-37

KEY BIBLE VERSE: *Does a young woman forget her jewelry? Does a bride hide her wedding dress? No! Yet for years on end my people have forgotten me.* (Jeremiah 2:32)

Following our own desires can make us forget God. Forgetting can be dangerous, whether it is intentional or an oversight. Israel forgot God by focusing its affections on the allurements of the world. The more we focus on the pleasures of the world, the easier it becomes to forget God's care, his love, his dependability, his guidance, and most of all, God himself. What pleases you most? Have you been forgetting God lately?

Related Topics: ABANDON, FAITHFULNESS, REMEMBERING

FORGIVENESS (*Grace, Mercy, Pardon*)

▶ GOD'S FORGIVENESS

How can we experience God's forgiveness?

BIBLE READING: Psalm 51:1-19

KEY BIBLE VERSE: *For I recognize my shameful deeds—they haunt me day and night.* (Psalm 51:3)

Experiencing God's forgiveness comes through confession and repentance. This psalm was David's written confession to God after a particularly sinful episode in his life. David was truly sorry for his adultery with Bathsheba and for murdering her husband to cover it up. He knew that his actions had hurt many people. But because David repented of those sins, God mercifully forgave him. No sin is too great to be forgiven! Do you feel that you could never come close to God because you have done something terrible? God can and will forgive you of any sin. While God forgives us, however, he does not always erase the natural consequences of our sin—David's life and family were never the same as a result of what he had done (see 2 Samuel 12:1-23).

BIBLE READING: John 20:19-31

KEY BIBLE VERSE: *If you forgive anyone's sins, they are forgiven. If you refuse to forgive them, they are unforgiven.* (John 20:23)

We can be confident that our sins have been forgiven in Christ. Jesus was giving the disciples their Spirit-powered and Spirit-guided mission—to preach the Good News about Jesus so people's sins might be forgiven. The disciples did not have the power to forgive sins (only God can forgive sins), but Jesus gave them the privilege of telling new believers that their sins *have been* forgiven because they have accepted Jesus' message. All believers have this same privilege. We can announce the forgiveness of sin with certainty when we find repentance and faith.

BIBLE READING: John 13:31-38

KEY BIBLE VERSE: *Now I am giving you a new commandment: Love each other. Just as I have loved you, you should love each other.* (John 13:34)

God consistently forgives us each time we ask in repentance. John describes these few moments in clear detail. We can see that Jesus knew exactly what was going to happen. He knew about Judas and about Peter, but he did not change the course of events, nor did he stop loving them. In the same way, Jesus knows exactly what you will do to hurt him. Yet he still loves you unconditionally and will forgive you whenever you ask for it. Judas couldn't understand this, and his life ended tragically. Peter understood, and despite his shortcomings, his life ended triumphantly because he never let go of his faith in the one who loved him.

BIBLE READING: 1 John 1:1-10

KEY BIBLE VERSE: *If we confess our sins to him, he is faithful and just to forgive us and to cleanse us from every wrong.* (1 John 1:9)

Forgiveness is complete even when confession isn't. Confession is supposed to free us to enjoy fellowship with Christ. It should ease our consciences and lighten our cares. But some Christians do not understand how it works. They feel so guilty that they confess the same sins over and over; then they wonder if they might have forgotten something. Other Christians believe that God forgives them when they confess, but if they died with unconfessed sins, they would be forever lost. These Christians do not understand that God *wants* to forgive us. He allowed his beloved Son to die just so he could pardon us. When we come to Christ, he forgives all the sins we have committed or will ever commit. We don't need to confess the sins of the past all over again, and we don't need to fear that God will reject us if we don't keep our slate perfectly clean. Of course we should continue to confess our sins, but not because failure to do so will make us lose our salvation. Our relationship with Christ is secure. Instead, we should confess our sins so that we can enjoy maximum fellowship and joy with him.

Honest confession includes turning away from sin. True confession also involves a commitment not to continue in sin. We wouldn't be genuinely confessing our sins to God if we planned to commit them again and just wanted temporary forgiveness. We should also pray for strength to defeat temptation the next time we face it.

Confession reestablishes relationship with God. If God has forgiven us for our sins because of Christ's death, why must we confess our sins? In admitting our sins and receiving Christ's cleansing, we are: (1) agreeing with God that our sin truly was sin and that we are willing to turn from it, (2) ensuring that we don't conceal our sins from him and consequently, from ourself, and (3) recognizing our tendency to sin and relying on his power to overcome it.

▶ HUMAN FORGIVENESS
Why should we forgive one another and how can we do it?

BIBLE READING: Genesis 45:1-28
KEY BIBLE VERSE: *Don't be angry with yourselves that you did this to me, for God did it. He sent me here ahead of you to preserve your lives.* (Genesis 45:5)

Joseph is a model of genuine forgiveness. Joseph was rejected, kidnapped, enslaved, and imprisoned. Although his brothers had been unfaithful to him, he graciously forgave them and shared his prosperity. Joseph demonstrated how God forgives us and showers us with goodness even though we have sinned against him. The same forgiveness and blessings are ours if we ask for them.

BIBLE READING: Romans 12:1-21
KEY BIBLE VERSE: *Don't let evil get the best of you, but conquer evil by doing good.* (Romans 12:21)

Forgiveness is a mark of the Christian life. Verses 17-21 summarize the real core of Christian living. If we love someone the way Christ loves us, we will be willing to forgive. If we have experienced God's grace, we will want to pass it on to others. And remember, grace is *undeserved* favor. By giving an enemy a drink, we're not excusing his misdeeds. We're recognizing him, forgiving him, and loving him in spite of his sins—just as Christ did for us.

Forgiveness is contrary to the pattern of the world. In this day of constant lawsuits and incessant demands for legal rights, Paul's command sounds almost impossible. When someone hurts you deeply, instead of giving him what he deserves, Paul says to befriend him. Why does Paul tell us to forgive our enemies? (1) Forgiveness may break a cycle of retaliation and lead to mutual reconciliation. (2) It may make the enemy feel ashamed and change his or her ways. (3) By contrast, returning evil for evil hurts you just as much as it hurts your enemy. Even if your enemy never repents, forgiving him or her will free you of a heavy load of bitterness.

Forgiveness is an act of the will. Forgiveness involves both attitudes and actions. If you find it difficult to *feel* forgiving of those who have hurt you, try responding with kind actions. If appropriate, tell such people that you would like to heal your relationships. Give them a helping hand. Send them a gift. Smile at them. Many times you will discover that right actions lead to right feelings.

BIBLE READING: Matthew 6:5-15
KEY BIBLE VERSE: *If you forgive those who sin against you, your heavenly Father will*

forgive you. But if you refuse to forgive others, your Father will not forgive your sins. (Matthew 6:14-15)

If we expect to be forgiven, we need to practice forgiveness. Jesus gives a startling warning about forgiveness: if we refuse to forgive others, God will also refuse to forgive us. Why? Because when we don't forgive others, we are denying our common ground as sinners in need of God's forgiveness. God's forgiveness of sin is not the direct result of our forgiving others, but it is based on our realizing what forgiveness means (see Ephesians 4:32). It is easy to ask God for forgiveness, but difficult to grant it to others. Whenever we ask God to forgive us for sin, we should ask ourselves, Have I forgiven the people who have wronged me?

BIBLE READING: Matthew 18:21-35
KEY BIBLE VERSE: *Peter came to him and asked, "Lord, how often should I forgive someone who sins against me? Seven times?"* (Matthew 18:21)

Real forgiveness does not keep track of offenses. The rabbis taught that people should forgive those who offend them—but only three times. Peter, trying to be especially generous, asked Jesus if seven (the "perfect" number) was enough times to forgive someone. But Jesus answered, "Seventy times seven," meaning that we shouldn't even keep track of how many times we forgive someone. We should always forgive those who are truly repentant, no matter how many times they ask.

Real forgiveness follows God's pattern. Because God has forgiven all our sins, we should not withhold forgiveness from others. Realizing how completely Christ has forgiven us should produce a free and generous attitude of forgiveness toward others. When we don't forgive others, we are setting ourselves outside and above Christ's law of love.

Related Topics: GOSPEL, GRACE, SALVATION

FORSAKE *(Abandon, Betray, Leave)*

Why did Jesus say, "My God, my God, why have you forsaken me?"

BIBLE READING: Mark 15:33-41
KEY BIBLE VERSE: *At that time Jesus called out with a loud voice, "Eloi, Eloi, lema sabachthani?" which means, "My God, my God, why have you forsaken me?"* (Mark 15:34)

Jesus suffered separation from God on our behalf. Jesus did not ask this question in surprise or despair. He was quoting the first line of Psalm 22. The whole psalm is a prophecy expressing the deep agony of the Messiah's death for the world's sin. Jesus knew that he would be temporarily separated from God the moment he took upon himself the sins of the world. This separation was what he had dreaded as he prayed in Gethsemane. The physical agony was horrible, but the spiritual alienation from God was the ultimate torture.

Related Topics: ABANDON, FAITHFULNESS, SACRIFICE

FOUL LANGUAGE *(Crude, Dirty, Nasty)*

What should characterize our way of speaking?

BIBLE READING: Ephesians 5:1-20
KEY BIBLE VERSE: *Obscene stories, foolish talk, and coarse jokes—these are not for you. Instead, let there be thankfulness to God.* (Ephesians 5:4)

Foul language does not honor God. Obscenity and coarse joking are so common that we begin to take them for granted. Paul cautions, however, that improper language should have no place in the Christian's conversation because it does not reflect God's gracious presence in us. How can we praise God and remind others of his goodness when we are speaking coarsely?

BIBLE READING: Colossians 4:2-6
KEY BIBLE VERSE: *Let your conversation be gracious and effective so that you will have the right answer for everyone.* (Colossians 4:6)

What we believe is reflected in what we say. We should be wise in our contacts with non-Christians, making the most of our chances to tell them the Good News of salvation. When we tell others about Christ, it is important always to be gracious in what we say. No matter how much sense the message makes, we lose our effectiveness if we are not courteous. Just as we like to be respected, we must respect others if we want them to listen to what we have to say. "Gracious and effective" means that what we say should encourage further dialogue. Are you making the best of the opportunities you have?

BIBLE READING: 1 Timothy 4:1-16
KEY BIBLE VERSE: *Don't let anyone think less of you because you are young. Be an example to all believers in what you teach, in the way you live, in your love, your faith, and your purity.* (1 Timothy 4:12)

Our manner of speech will influence others. Timothy was a young pastor. It would be easy for older Christians to look down on him because of his youth. He had to earn the respect of his elders by setting an example in his speech, life, love, faith, and purity. Regardless of your age, God can use you. Whether you are young or old, don't think of your age as a handicap. Live so others can see Christ in you.

Related Topics: CHARACTER, ENCOURAGEMENT, GOSPEL

FOUNDATION *(Basic, Core, Reasons)*

What makes a dependable foundation for life?

BIBLE READING: Luke 6:46-49
KEY BIBLE VERSE: *But anyone who listens and doesn't obey is like a person who builds a house without a foundation. When the floods sweep down against that house, it will crumble into a heap of ruins.* (Luke 6:49)

The words of Christ are a dependable foundation. Obeying God is like building a house on a strong, solid foundation that stands firm when storms come. When life is calm, our foundations don't seem to matter. But when crises come, our foundations are tested. Be sure your life is built on the solid foundation of knowing and trusting Jesus Christ.

Failing to build on an enduring foundation leads to destruction. Why would people build a house without a foundation? Perhaps to save time and avoid the hard work of preparing a stone foundation. Possibly because the waterfront scenery is more attractive or because beach houses have higher social status than cliff houses. Perhaps because they want to join their friends who have already settled in sandy areas. Maybe they haven't heard about the violent storms coming, or because they have discounted the reports, or for some reason they think disaster can't happen to them. Whatever their reason, those with no foundation are shortsighted, and they will be sorry. When you find yourself listening but not obeying, what are your reasons?

BIBLE READING: 1 Corinthians 3:1-23

KEY BIBLE VERSE: *No one can lay any other foundation than the one we already have—Jesus Christ.* (1 Corinthians 3:11)

Obedience to Christ determines the quality of our foundation. The foundation of the church—of all believers—is Jesus Christ. Paul laid this foundation when he began the church at Corinth. Whoever builds the church—officers, teachers, preachers, parents, and others—must build with high-quality materials (right doctrine and right living, 3:12ff.) that meet God's standards. Paul is not criticizing Apollos, but challenging future church leaders to have sound preaching and teaching.

Developing a dependable foundation is a personal responsibility. In the church built on Jesus Christ, each church member would be mature, spiritually sensitive, and doctrinally sound. However, the Corinthian church was filled with those whose work was "wood, hay, or straw," members who were immature, insensitive to one another, and eagerly accepting wrong doctrine (3:1-4). No wonder they had so many problems. Local church members should be deeply committed to Christ. Can your Christian character stand the test?

Jesus Christ is the blueprint for our foundation. A building is only as solid as its foundation. The foundation of our life is Jesus Christ; he is our base, our reason for being. Everything we are and do must fit into the pattern provided by him. Are you building your life on the only real and lasting foundation, or are you building on a faulty foundation such as wealth, security, success, or fame?

Any foundation apart from Christ will not last. Two ways to destroy a building are to tamper with the foundation or to build with inferior materials. The church must be built on Christ, not on any other person or principle. Christ will evaluate each minister's contribution to the life of the church, and the Day of Judgment will reveal the sincerity of each person's work. God will determine whether or not they have been faithful to Jesus' instructions. Good work will be srewarded; unfaithful or inferior work will be discounted. The builder "will be saved, but like someone escaping through a wall of flames" means that unfaithful workers will be saved, but like people escaping from a burning building. All their possessions (accomplishments) will be lost.

Related Topics: BASICS OF THE FAITH, DOCTRINE, FAITH

FREEDOM *(Liberty, Privileges, Responsibilities)*

How do we know we are really free?

BIBLE READING: John 8:31-47

KEY BIBLE VERSE: *If the Son sets you free, you will indeed be free.* (John 8:36)

Knowing Jesus is knowing real freedom. Jesus himself is the truth that sets us free (8:36). He is the source of truth, the perfect standard of what is right. He frees us from the consequences of sin, from self-deception, and from deception by Satan. He shows us clearly the way to eternal life with God. Jesus does not give us freedom to do what we want, but freedom to follow God. As we seek to serve God, Jesus' perfect truth frees us to be all that God meant us to be.

Knowing Jesus is freedom from the power of sin. Sin has a way of enslaving us, controlling us, dominating us, and dictating our actions. Jesus can free you from this slavery that keeps you from becoming the person God created you to be. If sin is restraining, mastering, or enslaving you, Jesus can break its power over your life.

BIBLE READING: Romans 5:12-21
KEY BIBLE VERSE: *Just as sin ruled over all people and brought them to death, now God's wonderful kindness rules instead, giving us right standing with God and resulting in eternal life through Jesus Christ our Lord.* (Romans 5:21)

Freedom in Christ is the freedom to obey. As a sinner, separated from God, you see his law from below, as a ladder to be climbed to get to God. Perhaps you have repeatedly tried to climb it, only to fall to the ground every time you have advanced one or two rungs. Or perhaps the sheer height of the ladder seems so overwhelming that you have never even started up. In either case, what relief you should feel to see Jesus offering with open arms to lift you above the ladder of the law, to take you directly to God! Once Jesus lifts you into God's presence, you are free to obey—out of love, not necessity; through God's power, not your own. You know that if you stumble, you will not fall back to the ground. Instead, you will be caught and held in Christ's loving arms.

BIBLE READING: Galatians 5:1-26
KEY BIBLE VERSE: *Christ has really set us free. Now make sure that you stay free, and don't get tied up again in slavery to the law.* (Galatians 5:1)

Freedom in Christ is the freedom to serve. Christ died to set us free from sin and from a long list of laws and regulations. Christ came to set us free—not free to do whatever we want because that would lead back into slavery to our selfish desires. Rather, thanks to Christ, we are now free and able to do what was impossible before—to live unselfishly. Those who appeal to their freedom so that they can have their own way or indulge their desires are falling back into sin. But it is also wrong to put a burden of law keeping on Christians. We must stand against those who would enslave us with rules, methods, or special conditions for being saved or growing in Christ.

Related Topics: DISCIPLINE, GOSPEL, LAW

FRIENDSHIP *(Affection, Companionship, Jesus)*

What are the marks of real friendship?

BIBLE READING: Exodus 33:7-11
KEY BIBLE VERSE: *Inside the Tent of Meeting, the LORD would speak to Moses face to face, as a man speaks to his friend. Afterward Moses would return to the camp, but the young man who assisted him, Joshua son of Nun, stayed behind in the Tent of Meeting.* (Exodus 33:11)

Real friendship involves face-to-face honesty. God and Moses talked face to face in the Tent of Meeting, just as friends do. Why did Moses find such favor with God? It certainly was not because he was perfect, gifted, or powerful. Rather, it was because God chose Moses, and Moses in turn relied wholeheartedly on God's wisdom and direction. Friendship with God was a true privilege for Moses, out of reach for the other Hebrews. But it is not out of reach for us today. Jesus called his disciples—and, by extension, all of his followers—his friends (John 15:15). He has called you to be his friend. Will you trust him as Moses did?

BIBLE READING: Proverbs 17:1-28

KEY BIBLE VERSE: *A friend is always loyal, and a brother is born to help in time of need.* (Proverbs 17:17)

Real friendship involves loyalty. What kind of friend are you? There is a vast difference between knowing someone well and being a true friend. The greatest evidence of genuine friendship is loyalty ("always loyal," see 1 Corinthians 13:7)—being available to help in times of distress or personal struggles. Too many people are fair-weather friends. They stick around when the friendship helps them and leave when they're not getting anything out of the relationship. Think of your friends and assess your loyalty to them. Be the kind of true friend the Bible encourages.

BIBLE READING: John 15:1-17

KEY BIBLE VERSE: *I no longer call you servants, because a master doesn't confide in his servants. Now you are my friends, since I have told you everything the Father told me.* (John 15:15)

Real friendship is found with Jesus. Because Jesus Christ is Lord and Master, he should call us servants; instead he calls us friends. How comforting and reassuring to be chosen as Christ's friends. Because he is Lord and Master, we owe him our unqualified obedience, but most of all, Jesus asks us to obey him because we love him.

Real friendship is imitating Christ in our relationships. We are to love each other as Jesus loved us, and he loved us enough to give his life for us. We may not have to die for someone, but there are other ways to practice sacrificial love: listening, helping, encouraging, giving. Think of someone in particular who needs this kind of love today. Give all the love you can, and then try to give a little more.

Related Topics: CHURCH, JESUS, RELATIONSHIP(S)

FRUIT *(Goals, Products, Results)*

What kind of fruit does God expect from us?

BIBLE READING: John 15:1-17

KEY BIBLE VERSE: *Remain in me, and I will remain in you. For a branch cannot produce fruit if it is severed from the vine, and you cannot be fruitful apart from me.* (John 15:4)

Following Christ ought to yield fruitful results. Christ is the vine, and God is the gardener who cares for the branches to make them fruitful. The branches are all those who claim to be followers of Christ. The fruitful branches are true believers who by their living union with Christ produce much fruit. But those who become unproductive—those who turn back from following Christ after making a superficial commitment—will be separated from the vine. Unproductive followers are as good as dead and will be cut off and tossed aside.

God expects many different kinds of fruit. Fruit is not limited to winning souls. In this chapter, answered prayer, joy, and love are mentioned as fruit (15:7, 11, 12). Galatians 5:22-24 and 2 Peter 1:5-8 describe additional fruit: qualities of Christian character.

Apart from Christ, there is no real fruitfulness. Many people try to be good, honest people who do what is right. But Jesus says that the only way to live a truly good life is to stay close to him, like a branch attached to the vine. Apart from Christ our efforts are unfruitful. Are you receiving the nourishment and life offered by Christ, the vine? If not, you are missing a special gift he has for you.

 BIBLE READING: Galatians 5:16-26
KEY BIBLE VERSE: *When the Holy Spirit controls our lives, he will produce this kind of fruit in us: love, joy, peace, patience, kindness, goodness, faithfulness, gentleness, and self-control. Here there is no conflict with the law.* (Galatians 5:22-23)

The Spirit produces Christlike fruit in us. The fruit of the Spirit is the spontaneous work of the Holy Spirit in us. The Spirit produces these character traits that are found in the nature of Christ. They are the by-products of Christ's control—we can't obtain them by *trying* to get them without his help. If we want the fruit of the Spirit to grow in us, we must join our life to his (see John 15:4-5). We must know him, love him, remember him, and imitate him. As a result, we will fulfill the intended purpose of the law—loving God and man. Which of these qualities do you want the Spirit to produce in you?

BIBLE READING: Matthew 3:1-12
KEY BIBLE VERSE: *Even now the ax of God's judgment is poised, ready to sever your roots. Yes, every tree that does not produce good fruit will be chopped down and thrown into the fire.* (Matthew 3:10)

Spiritual fruit is a natural by-product of God's presence. Just as a fruit tree is expected to bear fruit, God's people should produce a crop of good deeds. God has no use for people who call themselves Christians but do nothing about it. Like many people in John's day who were God's people in name only, we are of no value if we are Christians in name only. If others can't see our faith in the way we treat them, we may not be God's people at all.

Active obedience produces spiritual fruit. God's message hasn't changed since the Old Testament—people will be judged for their unproductive lives. God calls us to be *active* in our obedience. John compared people who claim they believe God but don't live for God to unproductive trees that will be cut down. To be productive for God, we must obey his teachings, resist temptation, actively serve and help others, and share our faith. How productive are you for God?

Related Topics: ACHIEVEMENTS, GOALS, RESULTS

FRUSTRATION *(Anger, Hopelessness, Mistakes)*

How should we handle frustration?

BIBLE READING: Exodus 2:1-10
KEY BIBLE VERSE: *When she could no longer hide him, she got a little basket made of papyrus reeds and waterproofed it with tar and pitch. She put the baby in the basket and laid it among the reeds along the edge of the Nile River.* (Exodus 2:3)

In the midst of frustration, remain obedient to God. Moses' mother knew how wrong it would be to destroy her child. But there was little she could do to change Pharaoh's new law. Her only alternative was to hide the child and later place him in a tiny papyrus basket on the river. God used her courageous act to place her son, the Hebrew of his choice, in the house of Pharaoh. Do you sometimes feel surrounded by evil and frustrated by how little you can do about it? When faced with evil, look for ways to act against it. Then trust God to use your effort, however small it seems, in his war against evil.

 BIBLE READING: Job 10:1-22
KEY BIBLE VERSE: *Yet your real motive—I know this was your intent—was to watch me, and if I sinned, you would not forgive my iniquity.* (Job 10:13-14)

Avoid making important decisions when you're frustrated. In frustration, Job jumped to the false conclusion that God was out to get him. Wrong assumptions lead to wrong conclusions. We dare not take our limited experiences and jump to conclusions about life in general. If you find yourself doubting God, remember that you don't have all the facts. God wants only the very best for your life. Many people endure great pain, but ultimately they find some greater good came from it. When you're struggling, don't assume the worst.

BIBLE READING: Ephesians 6:1-4
KEY BIBLE VERSE: *Now a word to you fathers. Don't make your children angry by the way you treat them. Rather, bring them up with the discipline and instruction approved by the Lord.* (Ephesians 6:4)

Don't be the cause of frustration in others. The purpose of parental discipline is to help children grow, not to exasperate and provoke them to anger or discouragement (see also Colossians 3:21). Parenting is not easy—it takes lots of patience to raise children in a loving, Christ-honoring manner.

Don't be motivated by frustration. Frustration and anger should not be causes for discipline. Instead, parents should act in love, treating their children as Jesus treats the people he loves. This is vital to children's development and to their understanding of what Christ is like.

Related Topics: ANGER, PATIENCE, WAITING

FULFILLMENT (*see* CONTENTMENT)

FUTILITY (*see* HOPELESSNESS)

FUTURE (*Ahead, Eternity, Tomorrow*)

What should be our attitude toward the future?

BIBLE READING: Deuteronomy 29:1-29
KEY BIBLE VERSE: *There are secret things that belong to the LORD our God, but the revealed things belong to us and our descendants forever, so that we may obey these words of the law.* (Deuteronomy 29:29)

God reveals only what we need to know to obey him. There are some secrets God has chosen not to reveal to us, possibly for the following reasons: (1) our finite minds cannot fully understand the infinite aspects of God's nature and the universe (Ecclesiastes 3:11); (2) some things are unnecessary for us to know until we are more mature; and (3) God is infinite and all-knowing, and we do not have the capacity to know everything he does. This verse shows that although God has not told us everything there is to know about obeying him, he has told us enough. Thus disobedience comes from an act of the will, not a lack of knowledge. Through God's Word we know enough about him to be saved by faith and to serve him. We must not use the limitation of our knowledge as an excuse to reject his claim on our life.

BIBLE READING: Micah 4:1-13

KEY BIBLE VERSE: *But they do not know the LORD's thoughts or understand his plan. These nations don't know that he is gathering them together to be beaten and trampled like bundles of grain on a threshing floor.* (Micah 4:12)

Our future is under God's control. Micah predicted the end of the kings. This was a drastic statement to the people of Judah, who thought that their kingdom would last forever. Micah also said that Babylon would destroy the land of Judah and carry away its king, but that after a time God would help his people return to their land. This all happened just as Micah prophesied, and these events are recorded in 2 Chronicles 36:9-23 and Ezra 1–2.

When God reveals the future, his purpose goes beyond satisfying our curiosity. He wants us to change our present behavior because of what we know about the future. Forever begins now; and a glimpse of God's plan for his followers should motivate us to serve him, no matter what the rest of the world may do.

BIBLE READING: Mark 13:1-37

KEY BIBLE VERSE: *When will all this take place? And will there be any sign ahead of time to show us when all this will be fulfilled?* (Mark 13:4)

Knowledge about the future should lead to obedience in the present. The disciples wanted to know when the temple would be destroyed. Jesus gave them a prophetic picture of that time, including events leading up to it. He also talked about future events connected with his return to earth to judge all people. Jesus predicted both near and distant events without putting them in chronological order. Some of the disciples lived to see the destruction of Jerusalem in A.D. 70. This event would assure them that everything else Jesus predicted would also happen.

Jesus warned his followers about the future so that they could learn how to live in the present. Many predictions Jesus made in this passage have not yet been fulfilled. He did not make them so that we would guess when they might be fulfilled, but to help us remain spiritually alert and prepared at all times, as we wait for his return.

Obeying in the present is more important than guessing about the future. What are the signs of the end times? There have been people in every generation since Christ's resurrection claiming to know exactly when Jesus would return. No one has been right yet, however, because Christ will return on God's timetable, not ours. Jesus predicted that before his return, many believers would be misled by false teachers claiming to have revelations from God.

According to Scripture, the one clear sign of Christ's return will be his unmistakable appearance in the clouds, which will be seen by all people (Mark 13:26; Revelation 1:7). In other words, you do not have to wonder whether a certain person is the Messiah or whether these are the "end times." When Jesus returns, *you will know* beyond a doubt, because it will be evident to all true believers. Beware of groups who claim special knowledge of the last days, because no one knows when that time will be (Mark 13:32). Be cautious about saying, "This is it!," but be bold in your total commitment to have your heart and life ready for Christ's return.

BIBLE READING: John 21:15-25

KEY BIBLE VERSE: *Jesus replied, "If I want him to remain alive until I return, what is that to you? You follow me."* (John 21:22)

We don't need to fear the future as long as we trust God. This passage includes a prediction of Peter's death by crucifixion. Tradition indicates that Peter was crucified for his faith—upside down because he did not feel worthy of dying as his Lord did. Despite what Peter's future held, Jesus told him to follow him. We may be uncertain and fearful about our future. But if we know God is in control, we can confidently follow Christ.

Related Topics: ETERNAL LIFE, HISTORY, PLANS

GENEROSITY (*Giving, Kindness, Sharing*)

What are the biblical guidelines for generosity?

 BIBLE READING: Exodus 35:4–36:7

KEY BIBLE VERSE: *Moses gave the command, and this message was sent throughout the camp: "Bring no more materials! You have already given more than enough." So the people stopped bringing their offerings. Their contributions were more than enough to complete the whole project.* (Exodus 36:6-7)

Generosity means giving cheerfully. God did not require these special offerings, but he appealed to people with generous hearts. Only those who were willing to give were invited to participate. God loves cheerful givers (2 Corinthians 9:7). Our giving should be from love and generosity, not from a guilty conscience.

Generosity means giving enthusiastically. Those whose hearts were stirred gave cheerfully to the tabernacle. With great enthusiasm they gave because they knew how important their giving was to the completion of God's house. Airline pilots and computer operators can push test buttons to see if their equipment is functioning properly. God has a quick test button he can push to measure the level of our commitment—our pocketbooks. Generous people aren't necessarily faithful to God. But faithful people are always generous.

BIBLE READING: Acts 11:19-30

KEY BIBLE VERSE: *The believers in Antioch decided to send relief to the brothers and sisters in Judea, everyone giving as much as they could.* (Acts 11:29)

Generosity flows out of a concern for those in need. There were serious food shortages during the reign of the Roman emperor Claudius (A.D. 41–54) because of a drought that had extended across much of the Roman Empire for many years. It is significant that the church in Antioch assisted the church in Jerusalem. The daughter church had grown enough to be able to help the established church.

The people of Antioch were motivated to give generously because they cared about the needs of others. This is "cheerful" giving that the Bible commends (2 Corinthians 9:7). Reluctant giving reflects a lack of concern for people. Focus your concern on the needy, and you will be motivated to give.

BIBLE READING: Leviticus 19:1-37

KEY BIBLE VERSE: *When you harvest your crops, do not harvest the grain along the edges of your fields, and do not pick up what the harvesters drop. It is the same with your grape crop—do not strip every last bunch of grapes from the vines, and do not pick* up the grapes that fall to the ground. Leave them for the poor and the foreigners who live among you, for I, the LORD, am your God. (Leviticus 19:9-10)

Generosity takes preparation. This law was a protection for the poor and the foreigner and a reminder that God owned the land; the people were only caretakers. Laws such as this showed God's generosity and liberality. As people of God, the Israelites were to reflect his nature and characteristics in their attitudes and actions. Ruth and Naomi were two people who benefited from this merciful law (Ruth 2:2).

God instructed the Hebrews to provide for those in need. He required that the people leave the edges of their fields unharvested, providing food for travelers and the poor. It is easy to ignore the poor or forget about those who have less than we do. But God desires generosity. In what ways can you leave the "edges of your field" for those in need?

Related Topics: GIFTS, GIVING, SELFISHNESS

GENTLENESS (*Humility, Softness, Tenderness*)

What makes gentleness such a powerful character quality?

BIBLE READING: 1 Thessalonians 2:1-12
KEY BIBLE VERSE: *As for praise, we have never asked for it from you or anyone else. As apostles of Christ we certainly had a right to make some demands of you, but we were as gentle among you as a mother feeding and caring for her own children.* (1 Thessalonians 2:6-7)

Gentleness allows others to grow. Gentleness is often overlooked as a personal trait in our society. Power and assertiveness gain more respect, even though no one likes to be bullied. Gentleness is love in action—being considerate, meeting the needs of others, allowing time for the other person to talk, and being willing to learn. It is an essential trait for both men and women. Maintain a gentle attitude in your relationships with others.

BIBLE READING: 2 Timothy 2:14-26
KEY BIBLE VERSE: *The Lord's servants must not quarrel but must be kind to everyone. They must be able to teach effectively and be patient with difficult people.* (2 Timothy 2:24)

Gentleness makes learning possible. As a teacher, Timothy helped those who were confused about the truth. Paul's advice to Timothy, and to all who teach God's truth, is to be humble, patiently and courteously explaining the truth. Good teaching never promotes quarrels or foolish arguments. Whether you are teaching Sunday school, leading a Bible study, or preaching in church, remember to listen to people's questions and treat them gently and respectfully, while avoiding foolish debates. If you do this, they will be more willing to hear what you have to say and perhaps turn from their error.

BIBLE READING: James 3:1-18
KEY BIBLE VERSE: *The wisdom that comes from heaven is first of all pure. It is also peace loving, gentle at all times, and willing to yield to others. It is full of mercy and good deeds. It shows no partiality and is always sincere.* (James 3:17)

Gentleness is a mark of wisdom. Have you ever known anyone who claimed to be wise, but who acted foolishly? True wisdom can be measured by the depth of a person's character. Just as you can identify a tree by the type of fruit it produces, you can evaluate your wisdom by the way you act. Foolishness leads to disorder, but wisdom leads to peace and goodness. Are you tempted to escalate the conflict, pass on the gossip, or fan the fire of discord? Careful, winsome speech and wise, loving words are the seeds of peace. God loves peacemakers (Matthew 5:9).

"Jealousy and selfish ambition" are inspired by the devil. It is easy for us to be drawn into wrong desires by the pressures of society and sometimes even by well-meaning Christians. By listening to the advice: "Assert yourself. . . . Go for it. . . . Set high goals," we can be drawn into greed and destructive competitiveness. Seeking God's wisdom delivers us from the need to compare ourself to others and to want what they have.

Related Topics: HUMILITY, LOVE, SENSITIVITY

GIFTS *(Offering, Presents, Talents)*

What should be our attitude toward gifts?

BIBLE READING: Deuteronomy 33:1-29
KEY BIBLE VERSE: *How blessed you are, O Israel! Who else is like you, a people saved by the LORD? He is your protecting shield and your triumphant sword! Your enemies will bow low before you, and you will trample on their backs!* (Deuteronomy 33:29)

Gifts are gratefully received when they are wisely used. Note the difference in blessings God gave each tribe. To one he gave the best land, to another strength, to another safety. Too often we see someone with a particular blessing and think that God must love that person more than others. Think rather that God draws out in all people their unique talents. All these gifts are needed to complete his plan. Don't be envious of the gifts others have. Instead, look for the gifts God has given you, and resolve to do the tasks he has uniquely qualified you to do.

BIBLE READING: Judges 14:1-20
KEY BIBLE VERSE: *The Spirit of the LORD powerfully took control of [Samson]. He went down to the town of Ashkelon, killed thirty men, took their belongings, and gave their clothing to the men who had answered his riddle. But Samson was furious about what had happened, and he went back home to live with his father and mother.* (Judges 14:19)

Using gifts selfishly indicates a lack of appreciation for the giver. Samson impulsively used the special gift God gave him for selfish purposes. Today, God distributes abilities and skills throughout the church (1 Corinthians 12:1ff.). The apostle Paul states that these gifts are to be used "to equip God's people to do his work and build up the church, the body of Christ" (Ephesians 4:12). To use these abilities for selfish purposes is to rob the church and fellow believers of strength. As you use the gifts God has given you, be sure you are helping others, not just yourself.

BIBLE READING: Matthew 2:1-12
KEY BIBLE VERSE: *They entered the house where the child and his mother, Mary, were, and they fell down before him and worshiped him. Then they opened their treasure chests and gave him gifts of gold, frankincense, and myrrh.* (Matthew 2:11)

Giving can be an act of worship. The magi traveled thousands of miles to see the king of the Jews. When they finally found him, they responded with joy, worship, and gifts. This is so different from the approach people often take today. We expect God to come looking for us, to explain himself, prove who he is, and give *us* gifts. But those who are wise still seek and worship Jesus today, not for what they can get, but for who he is.

Gifts must be accompanied by a right attitude. The magi brought gifts and worshiped Jesus for who he was. This is the essence of true worship—honoring Christ for who he is and being willing to give him what is valuable to you. Worship God because he is the perfect, just, and almighty Creator of the universe, worthy of the best you have to give.

BIBLE READING: Luke 19:11-27

KEY BIBLE VERSE: *The crowd was listening to everything Jesus said. And because he was nearing Jerusalem, he told a story to correct the impression that the Kingdom of God would begin right away.* (Luke 19:11)

God expects us to use the gifts he's given us. This story showed Jesus' followers what they were to do during the time between Jesus' departure and his second coming. Because we live in that time period, it applies directly to us. We have been given excellent resources to build and expand God's kingdom. Jesus expects us to use these talents so that they multiply and the kingdom grows. He asks each of us to account for what we do with his gifts. While awaiting the coming of the kingdom of God in glory, we must do Christ's work.

We will give an account to God for how we have used our gifts. Why was the king so hard on this man who had not increased the money? He punished the man because (1) he didn't share his master's interest in the kingdom; (2) he didn't trust his master's intentions; (3) his only concern was for himself; and (4) he did nothing to use the money. Like the king in this story, God has given you gifts to use for the benefit of his kingdom. Do you want the kingdom to grow? Do you trust God to govern it fairly? Are you as concerned for others' welfare as you are for your own? Are you willing to use faithfully what he has entrusted to you?

Related Topics: ABILITIES, ATTITUDE, GENEROSITY

GIVING *(Caring, Helping, Sharing)*

What kind of giving does God want us to practice?

BIBLE READING: Exodus 35:1-35

KEY BIBLE VERSE: *Both men and women came, all whose hearts were willing. Some brought to the LORD their offerings of gold—medallions, earrings, rings from their fingers, and necklaces. They presented gold objects of every kind to the LORD.* (Exodus 35:22)

God is pleased with personal giving. Those who spun cloth made a beautiful contribution to the tabernacle. Good workers take pride in the quality and beauty of their work. God is concerned with the quality and beauty of what you do. Whether you are a corporate executive or a drugstore cashier, your work should reflect the creative abilities God has given you.

BIBLE READING: Ezra 2:64-70

KEY BIBLE VERSE: *When they arrived at the Temple of the LORD in Jerusalem, some of the family leaders gave generously toward the rebuilding of God's Temple on its original site, and each leader gave as much as he could. The total of their gifts came to 61,000 gold coins, 6,250 pounds of silver, and 100 robes for the priests.* (Ezra 2:68-69)

God is pleased when we give generously. As the temple reconstruction progressed, everyone contributed freewill offerings according to his or her ability. Some were able to give huge gifts and did so generously. Everyone's effort and cooperation were required, and the people gave as much as they could. Often we limit our giving to 10 percent of our income. The Bible, however, emphasizes that we should give from the heart *all* that we are able (2 Corinthians 8:12; 9:6). Let the amount of your gift be decided by God's call to give generously, not by the amount of your leftovers.

BIBLE READING: 2 Corinthians 8:1-15
KEY BIBLE VERSE: *Though they have been going through much trouble and hard times, their wonderful joy and deep poverty have overflowed in rich generosity.* (2 Corinthians 8:2)

God is pleased with regular giving. The Corinthian believers excelled in everything—they had faith, good preaching, much knowledge, much earnestness, much love. Paul wanted them to also be leaders in giving. Giving is a natural response of love. Paul did not order the Corinthians to give, but he encouraged them to prove that their love was sincere. When you love someone, you want to give him or her your time and attention and to provide for his or her needs. If you refuse to help, your love is not as genuine as you say.

Sacrificial giving imitates Christ. There is no evidence that Jesus was any poorer than most first-century Palestinians; rather, Jesus became poor by giving up his rights as God and becoming human. In his incarnation God voluntarily became man—the wholly human person, Jesus of Nazareth. As a man, Jesus was subject to place, time, and other human limitations. He did not give up his eternal power when he became human, but he did set aside his glory and his rights. In response to the Father's will, he limited his power and knowledge. Christ became "poor" when he became human, because he set aside so much. Yet by doing so, he made us "rich" because we received salvation and eternal life.

Giving requires careful planning. The Corinthian church had money, and apparently they had planned to collect money for the Jerusalem churches a year previously (2 Corinthians 9:2). Paul challenges them to act on their plans. Four principles of giving emerge here: (1) your willingness to give cheerfully is more important than the amount you give; (2) you should strive to fulfill your financial commitments; (3) if you give to others in need, they will, in turn, help you when you are in need; (4) you should give as a response to Christ, not for anything you can get out of it. How you give reflects your devotion to Christ.

Deciding how much to give. How do you decide how much to give? What about differences in the financial resources Christians have? Paul gives the Corinthian church several principles to follow: (1) each person should follow through on previous promises (8:10; 9:3); (2) each person should give as much as he or she is able (8:12; 9:6); (3) each person must make up his or her own mind how much to give (9:7); and (4) each person should give in proportion to what God has given (9:10). God gives to us so that we can give to others.

We should give responsibly. Paul says that we should give of what we have, not what we don't have. Sacrificial giving must be responsible. Paul wants believers to give generously, but not to the extent that those who depend on the givers (their families, for example) must go without having their basic needs met. Give until it hurts, but don't give so that it hurts your family and/or relatives who need your financial support.

Related Topics: GENEROSITY, MONEY, TITHING

GIVING UP *(Abandon, Quit, Surrender)*

What should we do when we feel like giving up?

 BIBLE READING: Psalm 13:1-6
KEY BIBLE VERSE: *O LORD, how long will you forget me? Forever? How long will you look the other way?* (Psalm 13:1)

Being honest with God about our feelings is our first step toward victory. Sometimes all we need to do is talk over a problem with a friend to help put it in perspective. In this psalm, the phrase *how long* occurs four times in the first two verses, indicating the depth of David's distress. David expressed his feelings to God and found strength. By the end of his prayer, he was able to express hope and trust in God. Through prayer we can express our feelings and talk our problems out with God. He helps us regain the right perspective, and this gives us peace (Habakkuk 3:17-19).

Real trust doesn't give up. David frequently claimed that God was slow to act on his behalf. We often feel this same impatience. It seems that evil and suffering go unchecked, and we wonder when God is going to stop them. David affirmed that he would continue to trust God no matter how long he had to wait for God's justice to be realized. When you feel impatient, remember David's steadfast faith in God's unfailing love.

BIBLE READING: Matthew 9:18-26
KEY BIBLE VERSE: *Jesus turned around and said to her, "Daughter, be encouraged! Your faith has made you well." And the woman was healed at that moment.* (Matthew 9:22)

God's absolute sovereignty is one reason to never give up. God changed a situation that had been a problem for years. Like the leper and the demon-possessed men, this diseased woman was considered unclean. For twelve years, she too had been one of the "untouchables" and had not been able to lead a normal life. But Jesus changed that and restored her. Sometimes we are tempted to give up on people or situations that have not changed for many years. God can change what seems unchangeable, giving new purpose and hope.

BIBLE READING: 2 Corinthians 4:1-18
KEY BIBLE VERSE: *Though our bodies are dying, our spirits are being renewed every day. For our present troubles are quite small and won't last very long. Yet they produce for us an immeasurably great glory that will last forever!* (2 Corinthians 4:16-17)

Giving up often causes us to miss the best God has to offer. It is easy to quit. We all have faced problems in our relationships or work that have caused us to want to think about laying down the tools and walking away. Rather than giving up when persecution wore him down, Paul concentrated on experiencing the inner strength from the Holy Spirit (Ephesians 3:16). Don't let fatigue, pain, or criticism force you off the job. Renew your commitment to serving Christ.

Don't forsake your eternal reward because of the intensity of today's pain. Your very weakness allows the resurrection power of Christ to strengthen you moment by moment.

Related Topics: ABANDON, ENDURANCE, FAITHFULNESS

GLORY *(Beauty, Majesty, Wonder)*

What is God's glory?

BIBLE READING: Isaiah 64:1-12

KEY BIBLE VERSE: *As fire causes wood to burn and water to boil, your coming would make the nations tremble. Then your enemies would learn the reason for your fame!* (Isaiah 64:2)

God's glory is his overwhelming presence. God's appearance is so intense that it is like a consuming fire that burns everything in its path. If we are so impure, how can we be saved? Only by God's mercy. The Israelites had experienced God's appearance at Mount Sinai (Exodus 19:16-19). When God met with Moses there was a thunderstorm, smoke, and an earthquake. If God were to meet us today, his glory would overwhelm us, especially when we look at our "filthy rags" (64:6).

BIBLE READING: Ezekiel 9:1-11

KEY BIBLE VERSE: *The glory of the God of Israel rose up from between the cherubim, where it had rested, and moved to the entrance of the Temple. And the LORD called to the man dressed in linen who was carrying the writer's case. He said to him, "Walk through the streets of Jerusalem and put a mark on the foreheads of all those who weep and sigh because of the sins they see around them."* (Ezekiel 9:3-4)

God's glory is a display of who he is. God's glory is the manifestation of God's character—his ultimate power, transcendence, and moral perfection. God is completely above man and his limitations. Yet God reveals himself to us so that we can worship and follow him.

The cherubim (*cherub* is singular) mentioned here are an order of powerful angelic beings created to glorify God. They are associated with God's absolute holiness and moral perfection. God placed cherubim at the entrance of Eden to keep Adam and Eve out after they sinned (Genesis 3:24). Representations of cherubim were used to decorate the tabernacle and temple. The lid of the ark of the covenant, called the atonement cover, was adorned with two gold cherubim (Exodus 37:6-9). It was a symbol of the very presence of God. The cherubim seen by Ezekiel left the temple along with the glory of God (chapter 10). Ezekiel then recognized them as the living creatures he had seen in his first vision (see Ezekiel 1).

How do we reflect God's glory?

BIBLE READING: John 17:1-26

KEY BIBLE VERSE: *I brought glory to you here on earth by doing everything you told me to do.* (John 17:4)

God's glory is displayed in Christ. If God's glory is the sense of his awesome presence, the more we understand of Jesus' mission and work on earth, the more we will be aware of God's glory. For in Christ, God was physically present in this world.

God's glory is reflected in the lives of his people. What did Jesus mean when he said in verse 10, "They are my glory"? God's glory is the revelation of his character and presence. The lives of Jesus' disciples reveal his character, and he is present to the world through them. Does your life reveal Jesus' character and presence?

BIBLE READING: 2 Corinthians 3:7-18

KEY BIBLE VERSE: *All of us have had that veil removed so that we can be mirrors that brightly reflect the glory of the Lord. And as the Spirit of the Lord works within us, we become more and more like him and reflect his glory even more.* (2 Corinthians 3:18)

The more we know Christ, the more we reflect his glory. The glory that the Spirit imparts to the believer is more excellent and lasts longer than the glory that Moses experienced. By beholding the nature of God with unveiled minds, we can be more like him. In the gospel, we see the truth about Christ, and it transforms us morally as we understand and apply it. Through Christ's life, we can understand how wonderful God is and what he is really like. As our knowledge deepens, the Holy Spirit helps us to change. Becoming Christlike is a progressive experience (see Romans 8:29; Galatians 4:19; Philippians 3:21; 1 John 3:2). The more closely we follow Christ, the more we will be like him.

Related Topics: GOD, HEAVEN, HOLINESS

GOALS *(Aims, Objectives, Purposes)*

How does God help us with our goals?

BIBLE READING: Exodus 13:17-22

KEY BIBLE VERSE: *When Pharaoh finally let the people go, God did not lead them on the road that runs through Philistine territory, even though that was the shortest way from Egypt to the Promised Land. God said, "If the people are faced with a battle, they might change their minds and return to Egypt."* (Exodus 13:17)

God knows the best way. God doesn't always work in the way that seems best to us. Instead of guiding the Israelites along the direct route from Egypt to the promised land, he took them by a longer route to avoid fighting with the Philistines. If God does not lead you along the shortest path to your goal, don't complain or resist. Follow him willingly, and trust him to lead you safely around unseen obstacles. He can see the end of your journey from the beginning, and he knows the safest and best route.

BIBLE READING: Numbers 14:1-9

KEY BIBLE VERSE: *Do not rebel against the LORD, and don't be afraid of the people of the land. They are only helpless prey to us! They have no protection, but the LORD is with us! Don't be afraid of them!* (Numbers 14:9)

God helps us reach and exceed our goals. With great miracles, God had led the Israelites out of slavery, through the desolate desert, and up to the very edge of the Promised Land. He had protected them, fed them, and fulfilled every promise. Yet when encouraged to take that last step of faith and enter the land, the people refused. After witnessing so many miracles, why did they stop trusting God? Why did they refuse to enter the Promised Land when that had been their goal since leaving Egypt? They were afraid. Often we do the same thing. We trust God to handle the smaller issues but doubt his ability to take care of the big problems, the tough decisions, the frightening situations. Don't stop trusting God just as you are ready to reach your goal. He brought you this far and won't let you down now. We can continue trusting God by remembering all he has done for us.

BIBLE READING: Romans 8:18-39

KEY BIBLE VERSE: *God knew his people in advance, and he chose them to become like his Son, so that his Son would be the firstborn, with many brothers and sisters.* (Romans 8:29)

God's goals should be our goals. God's ultimate goal for us is to make us like Christ (1 John 3:2). As we become more and more like him, we discover our true selves, the persons we were created to be. How can we be conformed to his likeness? By reading and heeding his Word, by studying his life on earth through the Gospels, by being filled with his Spirit, and by doing his work in the world.

BIBLE READING: Philippians 3:1-21

KEY BIBLE VERSE: *I don't mean to say that I have already achieved these things or that I have already reached perfection! But I keep working toward that day when I will finally be all that Christ Jesus saved me for and wants me to be.* (Philippians 3:12)

Our most important goal should be getting to know Christ better. Paul says that his goal is to know Christ, to be like Christ, and to be all Christ has in mind for him. This goal absorbs all of Paul's energy. This is a helpful example for us. We should not let anything take our eyes off our goal—Christ. With the single-mindedness of an athlete in training, we must lay aside everything harmful and forsake anything that may distract us from being effective Christians. What is holding you back?

Related Topics: ACHIEVEMENTS, MOTIVES, PURPOSE

GOD *(Creator, Heavenly Father, Lord)*

▶ **CREATOR**

Why should we recognize God as our Creator?

BIBLE READING: Genesis 1:1-31

KEY BIBLE VERSE: *In the beginning God created the heavens and the earth.* (Genesis 1:1)

God is our Creator. The creation story teaches us much about God and ourself. First, we learn about God: (1) he is creative; (2) as the Creator he is distinct from his creation; (3) he is eternal and in control of the world. We also learn about ourself: (1) since God chose to create us, we are valuable in his eyes; (2) we are more important than the animals. (See Genesis 1:28 for more on our role in the created order.)

The simple statement that God created the heavens and the earth is one of the most challenging concepts confronting the modern mind. The vast galaxy we live in is spinning at the incredible speed of 490,000 miles an hour. But even at this breakneck speed, our galaxy still needs 200 million years to make one rotation. And there are over one billion other galaxies just like ours in the universe.

God has created an incredible universe. Some scientists say that the number of stars in creation is equal to all the grains of all the sands on all the beaches of the world. Yet this complex sea of spinning stars functions with remarkable order and efficiency. To say that the universe "just happened" or "evolved" requires more faith than to believe that God is behind these amazing statistics. God truly did create a wonderful universe.

God created the universe out of love. Almost every ancient religion has its own story to explain how the earth came to be. And almost every scientist has an opinion on the origin of the universe. But only the Bible shows one supreme God creating the earth out of his great love and giving all people a special place in it. We will never know all the answers to how God created the earth, but the Bible tells us that God did create it. That fact alone gives worth and dignity to all people.

God did not *need* to create the universe; he *chose* to create it. Why? God is love, and love is best expressed toward something or someone else—so God created the world and people as an expression of his love. We should avoid reducing God's creation to merely scientific terms. Remember that God created the universe because he loves each of us.

Human beings are evidence of God's creativity. In what ways are we made in God's image? God obviously did not create us exactly like himself, because God has no physical body. Instead, we are reflections of God's glory. Some feel that our reason, creativity, speech, or self-determination are the image of God. More likely, it is our entire self that reflects the image of God. We will never be totally like God, because he is our supreme Creator. But we do have the ability to reflect his character in our love, patience, forgiveness, kindness, and faithfulness.

Knowing that we are made in God's image and thus share many of his characteristics provides a solid basis for self-worth. Human worth is not based on possessions, achievements, physical attractiveness, or public acclaim. Instead it is based on being made in God's image. Because we bear God's image, we can feel positive about ourself. Criticizing or downgrading ourself is criticizing what God has made and the abilities he has given us. Knowing that you are a person of worth helps you love God, know him personally, and make a valuable contribution to those around you.

BIBLE READING: Hebrews 11:1-3

KEY BIBLE VERSE: *By faith we understand that the entire universe was formed at God's command, that what we now see did not come from anything that can be seen.* (Hebrews 11:3)

Recognizing God as our Creator is our most basic step of faith. God called the universe into existence out of nothing; he declared that it was to be, and it was. Our faith is in the God who created the entire universe by his word. God's word has awesome power. When he speaks, do you listen and respond? How can you better prepare yourself to respond to God's Word?

▶ HEAVENLY FATHER

Why should we recognize God as our heavenly Father?

BIBLE READING: Genesis 3:1-24

KEY BIBLE VERSE: *"Who told you that you were naked?" the LORD God asked. "Have you eaten the fruit I commanded you not to eat?"* (Genesis 3:11)

As with our human parents, we can rebel against our heavenly Father. This is how Adam and Eve broke their relationship with God: (1) they became convinced that their way was better than God's; (2) they became self-conscious and hid; (3) they tried to excuse and defend themselves. To build a relationship with God we must reverse those steps: (1) we must drop our excuses and self-defenses; (2) we must stop trying to hide from God; (3) we must become convinced that God's way is better than our way.

BIBLE READING: Genesis 6:1-22

KEY BIBLE VERSE: *The LORD was sorry he had ever made them. It broke his heart.* (Genesis 6:6)

As with our human parents, we can grieve our heavenly Father. Does this mean that God regretted creating humanity? Was he admitting he made a mistake? No, God does not change his mind (1 Samuel 15:29). Instead, he was expressing sorrow for what the people had done to themselves, as a parent might express sorrow over a rebellious child. God was sorry that the people chose sin and death instead of a relationship with him.

The people's sin grieved God. Our sins break God's heart as much as sin did in Noah's day. Noah, however, pleased God, although he was far from perfect. We can follow Noah's example and find "favor with the LORD" in spite of the sin that surrounds us.

BIBLE READING: Genesis 18:1-33

KEY BIBLE VERSE: *The two other men went on toward Sodom, but the LORD remained with Abraham for a while. Abraham approached him and said, "Will you destroy both innocent and guilty alike?"* (Genesis 18:22-23)

Sometimes we don't understand our heavenly Father's purposes. Why did God let Abraham question his justice and intercede for a wicked city? Abraham knew that God must punish sin, but he also knew from experience that God is merciful to sinners. God knew there were not ten righteous people in the city, but he was merciful enough to allow Abraham to intercede. He was also merciful enough to help Lot, Abraham's nephew, get out of Sodom before it was destroyed. God does not take pleasure in destroying the wicked, but he must punish sin. He is both just and merciful. We should be thankful that God's mercy extends to us.

BIBLE READING: Numbers 14:1-45

KEY BIBLE VERSE: *Please pardon the sins of this people because of your magnificent, unfailing love, just as you have forgiven them ever since they left Egypt.* (Numbers 14:19)

God is revealed as a forgiving father. Moses pleaded with God, asking him to forgive his people. His plea reveals several characteristics of God: (1) God is immensely patient; (2) God's love is one promise we can always count on; (3) God forgives again and again; and (4) God is merciful, listening to and answering our requests. God has not changed since Moses' day. Like Moses, we can rely on God's love, patience, forgiveness, and mercy.

▶ LORD

Why should we recognize God as Lord?

BIBLE READING: Exodus 3:1-22

KEY BIBLE VERSE: *Suddenly, the angel of the LORD appeared to him as a blazing fire in a bush. Moses was amazed because the bush was engulfed in flames, but it didn't burn up.* (Exodus 3:2)

God expects people to serve him. God spoke to Moses from an unexpected source: a burning bush. When Moses saw it, he went to investigate. Many people in the Bible experienced God in visible (not necessarily human) form. Abraham saw the smoking firepot and blazing torch (Genesis 15:17); Jacob wrestled with a man (Genesis 32:24-29). When the slaves were freed from Egypt, God led them by pillars of cloud and fire (13:17-22). God made such appearances to encourage his new nation, to guide them, and to prove the reliability of his verbal message. God may use unexpected sources when communicating to us too, whether people, thoughts, or experiences. Be willing to investigate, and be open to God's surprises.

God deserves our humble respect. At God's command, Moses removed his sandals and covered his face. Taking off his shoes was an act of reverence, conveying his own unworthiness before God. God is our friend, but he is also our sovereign Lord. To approach him frivolously shows a lack of respect and sincerity. When you come to God in worship, do you approach him casually, or do you come as though you were an invited guest before a king? If necessary, adjust your attitude so it is suitable for approaching a holy God.

BIBLE READING: Psalm 36:1-12
KEY BIBLE VERSE: *Your righteousness is like the mighty mountains, your justice like the ocean depths. You care for people and animals alike, O LORD.* (Psalm 36:6)

As Lord, God rules and protects his creation. In contrast to evil people and their wicked plots that end in failure, God is faithful, righteous, and just. His love reaches to the heavens; his faithfulness reaches to the skies; his righteousness is as solid as mighty mountains; and his judgments are as full of wisdom as the oceans with water ("the ocean depths"). We need not fear evil people because we know God loves us, judges evil, and will care for us throughout eternity.

BIBLE READING: Matthew 6:9-15
KEY BIBLE VERSE: *Pray like this: Our Father in heaven, may your name be honored.* (Matthew 6:9)

As Lord, God deserves our highest honor. The phrase "Our Father in heaven" indicates that God is not only majestic and holy, but also personal and loving. The first line of this model prayer is a statement of praise and a commitment to hallow, or honor, God's holy name. We can honor God's name by being careful to use it respectfully. If we use God's name lightly, we aren't remembering God's holiness.

BIBLE READING: John 3:1-36
KEY BIBLE VERSE: *God so loved the world that he gave his only Son, so that everyone who believes in him will not perish but have eternal life.* (John 3:16)

As Lord, God deeply cares for his creation. The entire gospel comes to a focus in this verse. God's love is not static or self-centered; it reaches out and draws others in. Here God sets the pattern of true love, the basis for all love relationships—when you love someone dearly, you are willing to pay dearly for that person's responsive love. God paid dearly with the life of his Son, the highest price he could pay. Jesus accepted our punishment, paid the price for our sins, and then offered us the new life that he had bought for us. When we share the gospel with others, our love must be like Jesus'—willingly giving up our own comfort and security so that others might join us in receiving God's love.

▶ UNIQUENESS
Why should we recognize that God is unique?

BIBLE READING: Exodus 3:1-22
KEY BIBLE VERSE: *God replied, "I AM THE ONE WHO ALWAYS IS. Just tell them, 'I AM has sent me to you.' "* (Exodus 3:14)

God reveals himself as the only true God. The Egyptians had many gods by many different names. Moses wanted to know God's name so the Hebrew people would know exactly who had sent him to them. God called himself *I Am*, a name describing his eternal power and unchangeable character. In a world where values, morals, and laws change constantly, we can find stability and security in our unchanging God. The God who appeared to Moses is the same God who can live in us today. Hebrews 13:8 says God is the same "yesterday, today, and forever." Because God's nature is stable and trustworthy, we are free to follow and enjoy him rather than spend our time trying to figure him out.

BIBLE READING: 1 Peter 1:13-25
KEY BIBLE VERSE: *Now you must be holy in everything you do, just as God—who chose you to be his children—is holy.* (1 Peter 1:15)

God reveals himself as a holy God. The God of Israel and of the Christian church is holy—he sets the standard for morality. Unlike the Roman gods, he is not warlike, adulterous, or spiteful. Unlike the gods of the pagan cults popular in the first century, he is not bloodthirsty or promiscuous. He is a God of mercy and justice who cares personally for each of his followers. Our holy God expects us to imitate him by following his high moral standards. Like him, we should be both merciful and just; like him, we should sacrifice ourself for others.

Related Topics: DOCTRINE, JESUS CHRIST, KINGDOM OF GOD/KINGDOM OF HEAVEN

GODLINESS (*see* HOLINESS)

GODS (*see* IDOLATRY)

GOD'S WILL (*Desire, Guidance, Purpose*)

How can we know God's will for our lives?

BIBLE READING: Numbers 9:15-23
KEY BIBLE VERSE: *They camped or traveled at the LORD's command, and they did whatever the LORD told them through Moses.* (Numbers 9:23)

God guides his people moment by moment. A pillar of cloud by day and a pillar of fire by night guided and protected the Israelites as they traveled across the desert. Some have said this pillar may have been a burning bowl of pitch whose smoke was visible during the day and whose fire could be seen at night. However, a bowl of pitch would not have lifted itself up and moved ahead of the people, and the Bible is clear that the cloud and fire moved in accordance with the will of God. The cloud and the fire were not merely natural phenomena; they were the vehicle of God's presence and the visible evidence of his moving and directing his people.

What we learn is that the Israelites traveled and camped as God guided.

When you follow God's guidance, you know you are where God wants you, whether you're moving or staying in one place. You are physically somewhere right now. Instead of praying, "God, what do you want me to do next?" ask, "God, what do you want me to do while I'm right here?" Direction from God is not just for your next big move. He has a purpose in placing you where you are right now. Begin to understand God's purpose for your life by discovering what he wants you to do now!

BIBLE READING: Esther 4:1-17

KEY BIBLE VERSE: *If you keep quiet at a time like this, deliverance for the Jews will arise from some other place, but you and your relatives will die. What's more, who can say but that you have been elevated to the palace for just such a time as this?* (Esther 4:14)

God's will is worked out in everyday events. After the decree to kill the Jews was given, Mordecai and Esther could have despaired, decided to save only themselves, or just waited for God's intervention. Instead, they saw that God had placed them in their positions for a purpose, so they seized the moment and acted. When it is within our power to save others, we must do so. In a life-threatening situation, don't withdraw, behave selfishly, wallow in despair, or wait for God to fix everything. Instead, ask God for his direction, and *act!* God may have placed you where you are "for just such a time as this."

BIBLE READING: Matthew 21:18-22

KEY BIBLE VERSE: *If you believe, you will receive whatever you ask for in prayer.* (Matthew 21:22)

Our prayers must be in harmony with God's will. This verse is not a guarantee that we can get *anything* we want simply by asking Jesus and believing. God does not grant requests that would hurt us or others or that would violate his own nature or will. Jesus' statement is not a blank check. To be fulfilled, our requests must be in harmony with the principles of God's kingdom. The stronger our belief, the more likely our prayers will be in line with God's will, and then God will be happy to grant them.

BIBLE READING: Philippians 2:1-30

KEY BIBLE VERSE: *Dearest friends, you were always so careful to follow my instructions when I was with you. And now that I am away you must be even more careful to put into action God's saving work in your lives, obeying God with deep reverence and fear. For God is working in you, giving you the desire to obey him and the power to do what pleases him.* (Philippians 2:12-13)

Our greatest happiness is found in willingly obeying God. What do we do when we don't feel like obeying? God has not left us alone in our struggles to do his will. He wants to come alongside us and be within us to help. God helps us *want* to obey him and then gives us the *power* to do what he wants. The secret to a changed life is to submit to God's control and let him work. Next time, ask God to help you *want* to do his will.

It is God's will that we become like Christ. To be like Christ, we must train ourself to think like Christ. To change our desires to be more like Christ's, we need the power of the indwelling Spirit (1:19), the influence of faithful Christians, obedience to God's Word (not just exposure to it), and sacrificial service. Often it is in *doing* God's will that we gain the *desire* for it (see Philippians 4:8-9). Do what he wants, and trust him to change your desires.

Related Topics: FREEDOM, GUIDANCE, OBEDIENCE

GOD'S WORD (*see* BIBLE)

GOOD/GOODNESS (*Best, Positive, Right*)

Is there a good end to all that is wrong in the world?

BIBLE READING: Job 1:1-22

KEY BIBLE VERSE: *There was a man named Job who lived in the land of Uz. He was blameless, a man of complete integrity. He feared God and stayed away from evil.* (Job 1:1)

We can have faith in God's goodness despite our circumstances. As we see calamity and suffering in the book of Job, we must remember that we live in a fallen world where good behavior is not always rewarded and bad behavior is not always punished. When we see a notorious criminal prospering or an innocent child in pain, we say, "That's wrong." And it is. Sin has twisted justice and made our world unpredictable and ugly.

The book of Job shows a good man suffering for no apparent fault of his own. Sadly, our world is like that. But Job's story does not end in despair. Through Job's life we can see that faith in God is justified even when our situations look hopeless. Faith based on rewards or prosperity is hollow. To be unshakable, faith must be built on the confidence that God's ultimate purpose will come to pass.

BIBLE READING: Genesis 50:1-26

KEY BIBLE VERSE: *As far as I am concerned, God turned into good what you meant for evil. He brought me to the high position I have today so I could save the lives of many people.* (Genesis 50:20)

In spite of evil, God is working out his good purposes. When Joseph became a slave, Jacob thought he was dead and wept in despair (Genesis 37:30). But eventually God's plan allowed Jacob to regain not only his son, but his grandchildren as well. Circumstances are never so bad that they are beyond God's help. Jacob regained his son. Job got a new family (Job 42:10-17). Mary regained her brother Lazarus (John 11:1-44). We need never despair, because we belong to a loving God. We never know what good he will bring out of a seemingly hopeless situation.

In Joseph's life, God brought good from the brothers' evil deed, Potiphar's wife's false accusation, the cupbearer's neglect, and seven years of famine. Joseph's experiences taught him that God brings good from evil for those who trust him. Do you trust God enough to wait patiently for him to bring good out of bad situations? You can trust him because, as Joseph learned, God can overrule people's evil intentions to bring about his intended results.

BIBLE READING: John 11:1-16

KEY BIBLE VERSE: *When Jesus heard about it he said, "Lazarus's sickness will not end in death. No, it is for the glory of God. I, the Son of God, will receive glory from this."* (John 11:4)

God's ability to do good is not limited by our understanding. As their brother grew very sick, Mary and Martha turned to Jesus for help. They believed in his ability to help because they had seen his miracles. We too know of Jesus' miracles, both from Scripture and through changed lives we have seen. When we need extraordinary help, Jesus offers extraordinary resources. We should not hesitate to ask him for assistance.

Any trial a believer faces can ultimately bring glory to God, because God can bring good out of any bad situation (Genesis 50:20; Romans 8:28). When trouble comes, do you grumble, complain, and blame God, or do you see your problems as opportunities to honor him?

BIBLE READING: Romans 8:1-39
KEY BIBLE VERSE: *We know that God causes everything to work together for the good of those who love God and are called according to his purpose for them.* (Romans 8:28)

God is involved in all realms of life to bring about his good ends. God works in "everything"—not just isolated incidents—for our good. This does not mean that all that happens to us is good. Evil is prevalent in our fallen world, but God is able to turn every circumstance around for our long-range good. Note that God is not working to make us happy, but to fulfill his purpose. Note also that this promise is not for everybody. It can be claimed only by those who love God and are fitting into God's plans. Those who are "called" are those the Holy Spirit convinces and enables to receive Christ. Such people have a new perspective, a new mind-set on life. They trust in God, not life's treasures; they look to their security in heaven, not on earth; they learn to accept, not resent, pain and persecution because God is with them.

Related Topics: BENEFITS, BLESSING, GRACE

GOOD NEWS (*Encouragement, Gospel, Hope*)

What does the Bible mean by Good News?

BIBLE READING: Mark 1:14-20
KEY BIBLE VERSE: *After John was arrested by Herod Antipas, Jesus went to Galilee to preach God's Good News. "At last the time has come!" he announced. "The Kingdom of God is near! Turn from your sins and believe this Good News!"* (Mark 1:14-15)

The Good News is the announcement of the kingdom of God. What is the Good News of God? These first words spoken by Jesus in the book of Mark give the core of his teaching: that the long-awaited Messiah has come to break the power of sin and begin God's personal reign on earth. Most of the people who heard this message were oppressed, poor, and without hope. Jesus' words were good news because they offered freedom, justice, and hope.

BIBLE READING: Luke 4:38-44
KEY BIBLE VERSE: *[Jesus] replied, "I must preach the Good News of the Kingdom of God in other places, too, because that is why I was sent."* (Luke 4:43)

The Good News means hope for those who have all but lost hope. The kingdom of God was good news! It was good news to the Jews because they had been awaiting the coming of the promised Messiah ever since the Babylonian captivity. It is good news for us also because it means freedom from slavery to sin and selfishness. The kingdom of God is here and now because the Holy Spirit lives in the hearts of believers. Yet it is also in the future because Jesus will return to reign over a perfect kingdom where sin and evil no longer exist.

BIBLE READING: Romans 1:1-32
KEY BIBLE VERSE: *This Good News was promised long ago by God through his prophets in the holy Scriptures. It is the Good News about his Son, Jesus, who came as a man, born into King David's royal family line.* (Romans 1:2-3)

The Good News is a message about Jesus Christ. Here Paul summarizes the Good News about Jesus Christ, who (1) came as a human by natural descent, (2) was part of the Jewish royal line through David, (3) died and was raised from the dead, and (4) opened the door for God's kindness to be poured out on us. The book of Romans is an expansion of these themes.

The Good News is a message that can be passed on. Christians have both privilege and a great responsibility. Paul and the apostles received forgiveness (*grace*) as an undeserved privilege. They also received the responsibility to share the message of God's forgiveness with others. God also graciously forgives our sins when we believe in him as Lord. In doing this, we are committing ourself to begin a new life. Paul's new life also involved a God-given responsibility—to witness of God's Good News to the world as a missionary. God may or may not call you to be an overseas missionary, but he does call you (and all believers) to witness and be an example of the changed life that Jesus Christ has begun in you.

Related Topics: FORGIVENESS, GOSPEL, SALVATION

GOSPEL *(Good News, Evangelism, Message)*

▶ **RESPONDING TO THE GOSPEL**
What kind of response does the gospel require?

 BIBLE READING: John 1:1-18
KEY BIBLE VERSE: *To all who believed him and accepted him, he gave the right to become children of God.* (John 1:12)

The gospel requires a response of faith in Christ. All who welcome Jesus Christ as Lord of their lives are reborn spiritually, receiving new life from God. Through faith in Christ, this new birth changes us from the inside out—rearranging our attitudes, desires, and motives. Being born makes you physically alive and places you in your parents' family (John 1:13). Being born of God makes you spiritually alive and puts you in God's family (John 1:12). Have you asked Christ to make you a new person? This fresh start in life is available to all who believe in Christ.

BIBLE READING: John 4:1-26
KEY BIBLE VERSE: *Jesus replied, "People soon become thirsty again after drinking this water. But the water I give them takes away thirst altogether. It becomes a perpetual spring within them, giving them eternal life."* (John 4:13-14)

The gospel requires a response of acceptance. The woman mistakenly believed that if she received the water Jesus offered, she would not have to return to the well each day. She was interested in Jesus' message because she thought it could make her life easier. But if that were always the case, people would accept Christ's message for the wrong reasons. Christ did not come to take away challenges, but to change us on the inside and to empower us to deal with problems from God's perspective.

The woman did not immediately understand what Jesus was talking about. It takes time to accept something that changes the very foundations of your life. Jesus allowed the woman time to ask questions and put pieces together for herself. Sharing the gospel will not always have immediate results. When you ask people to let Jesus change their lives, give them time to weigh the matter.

BIBLE READING: Acts 24:1-27

KEY BIBLE VERSE: *As [Paul] reasoned with them about righteousness and self-control and the judgment to come, Felix was terrified. "Go away for now," he replied. "When it is more convenient, I'll call for you again." (Acts 24:25)*

The gospel requires a personal response. Paul's talk with Felix became so personal that Felix grew fearful. Felix, like Herod Antipas (Mark 6:17-18), had taken another man's wife. Paul's words were interesting until they focused on "righteousness and self-control and the judgment to come." Many people will be glad to discuss the gospel with you as long as it doesn't touch their lives too personally. When it does, some will resist or leave. But this is what the gospel is all about—God's power to change lives. The gospel is not effective until it moves from principles and doctrine into a life-changing dynamic. When someone resists or runs from your witness, you have made the gospel personal.

BIBLE READING: 1 Thessalonians 1:2-10

KEY BIBLE VERSE: *We know that God loves you, dear brothers and sisters, and that he chose you to be his own people. For when we brought you the Good News, it was not only with words but also with power, for the Holy Spirit gave you full assurance that what we said was true. And you know that the way we lived among you was further proof of the truth of our message. (1 Thessalonians 1:4-5)*

The gospel requires a life-changing response. The gospel came "with power"; it had a powerful effect on the Thessalonians. Whenever the Bible is heard and obeyed, lives are changed! Christianity is more than a collection of interesting facts; it is the power of God to everyone who believes. What has God's power done in your life since you first believed?

The Holy Spirit changes people when they believe the gospel. When we tell others about Christ, we must depend on the Holy Spirit to open their eyes and convince them that they need salvation. God's power—not our cleverness or persuasion—changes people. Without the work of the Holy Spirit, our words are meaningless. The Holy Spirit not only convicts people of sin but also assures them of the truth of the gospel.

To whom is the gospel addressed?

BIBLE READING: Luke 24:1-53

KEY BIBLE VERSE: *Yes, it was written long ago that the Messiah must suffer and die and rise again from the dead on the third day. With my authority, take this message of repentance to all the nations, beginning in Jerusalem: "There is forgiveness of sins for all who turn to me." (Luke 24:46-47)*

The gospel is for all people. Luke wrote to the Greek-speaking world. He wanted them to know that Christ's message of God's love and forgiveness should go to all the world. We must never ignore the worldwide scope of Christ's gospel. God wants all the world to hear the Good News of salvation.

BIBLE READING: Matthew 28:16-20

KEY BIBLE VERSE: *Jesus came and told his disciples, "I have been given complete authority in heaven and on earth. Therefore, go and make disciples of all the nations, baptizing them in the name of the Father and the Son and the Holy Spirit." (Matthew 28:18-19)*

Jesus commanded us to take the gospel around the world. God gave Jesus authority over heaven and earth. On the basis of that authority, Jesus told his disciples to make more disciples as they preached, baptized, and taught. With this same authority, Jesus still commands us to tell others the Good News and make them disciples for the kingdom.

When someone is dying or leaving us, his or her last words are very important. Jesus left the disciples with these last words of instruction: they were under his authority; they were to make more disciples; they were to baptize and teach these new disciples to obey Christ; Christ would be with them always. Whereas in previous missions Jesus had sent his disciples only to the Jews (Matthew 10:5-6), their mission from now on would be worldwide. Jesus is Lord of the earth, and he died for the sins of people from all nations.

BIBLE READING: Philippians 4:10-23

KEY BIBLE VERSE: *Give my greetings to all the Christians there. The brothers who are with me here send you their greetings. And all the other Christians send their greetings, too, especially those who work in Caesar's palace.* (Philippians 4:21-22)

The gospel speaks to the needs of all people. There were many Christians in Rome; some were even in Caesar's household. Perhaps Paul, while awaiting trial, was making converts of the Roman civil service! Paul sent greetings from these Roman Christians to the believers at Philippi. The gospel had spread to all strata of society, linking people who had no other bond but Christ. The Roman Christians and the Philippian Christians were brothers and sisters because of their unity in Christ. Believers today are also linked to others across cultural, economic, and social barriers. Because all believers are brothers and sisters in Christ, let us live like God's true family.

▶ COMMUNICATING THE GOSPEL
How should the gospel be communicated?

BIBLE READING: Acts 6:1-15

KEY BIBLE VERSE: *God's message was preached in ever-widening circles. The number of believers greatly increased in Jerusalem, and many of the Jewish priests were converted, too.* (Acts 6:7)

The gospel should be communicated to one person at a time. Jesus had told the apostles that they were to witness first in Jerusalem (Acts 1:8). In a short time, their message had infiltrated the entire city and all levels of society. Even some priests were being converted, going against the directives of the council and endangering their position.

The word of God spread like ripples on a pond where, from a single center, each wave touches the next, spreading wider and farther. The gospel still spreads this way today. You don't have to change the world single-handedly—it is enough just to be part of the wave, touching those around you, who in turn will touch others, until all have felt the movement. Don't ever feel that your part is insignificant or unimportant.

BIBLE READING: Romans 1:8-17

KEY BIBLE VERSE: *I am not ashamed of this Good News about Christ. It is the power of God at work, saving everyone who believes—Jews first and also Gentiles.* (Romans 1:16)

The gospel should be communicated without embarrassment. Paul was not ashamed because his message was the gospel of Christ, the Good News. It was a message of salvation, it had life-changing power, and it was for everyone. When you are tempted to be ashamed, remember what the Good News is all about. If you focus on God and on what God is doing in the world rather than on your own inadequacy, you won't be ashamed or embarrassed.

BIBLE READING: 2 Corinthians 4:1-18
KEY BIBLE VERSE: *We reject all shameful and underhanded methods. We do not try to trick anyone, and we do not distort the word of God. We tell the truth before God, and all who are honest know that.* (2 Corinthians 4:2)

The gospel should be communicated without distortion. Preachers, teachers, and anyone else who talks about Jesus Christ must remember that they stand in God's presence—he hears every word. When you tell people about Christ, be careful not to distort the message to please your audience. Proclaim the truth of God's Word.

Related Topics: EVANGELISM, GOOD NEWS, SALVATION

GOSSIP *(Deception, Lies, Rumors)*

What effect can gossip have?

BIBLE READING: Exodus 23:1-9
KEY BIBLE VERSE: *Do not pass along false reports. Do not cooperate with evil people by telling lies on the witness stand.* (Exodus 23:1)

Gossip breaks down relationships. Making up or spreading false reports was strictly forbidden by God. Gossip, slander, and false witnessing undermined families, strained neighborhood cooperation, and made chaos of the justice system. Destructive gossip still causes problems. Even if you do not initiate a lie, you become responsible if you pass it along. Don't circulate rumors; squelch them.

BIBLE READING: Proverbs 25:18-28
KEY BIBLE VERSE: *Telling lies about others is as harmful as hitting them with an ax, wounding them with a sword, or shooting them with a sharp arrow.* (Proverbs 25:18)

Gossip is often more harmful and lasting than physical wounds. Lying is vicious. Its effects can be as permanent as those of a stab wound. The next time you are tempted to pass on a bit of gossip, imagine yourself stabbing the victim of your remarks with a sword. This image may shock you into silence.

BIBLE READING: 2 Thessalonians 3:6-15
KEY BIBLE VERSE: *We hear that some of you are living idle lives, refusing to work and wasting time meddling in other people's business. In the name of the Lord Jesus Christ, we appeal to such people—no, we command them: Settle down and get to work. Earn your own living.* (2 Thessalonians 3:11-12)

Gossip wastes valuable time. A lazy person who doesn't work ends up filling his or her time with less than helpful activities, like gossip. Rumors and hearsay are tantalizing and exciting to hear, and they make us feel like insiders. But they tear people down. If you often find your nose in other people's business, you may be underemployed. Look for a task to do for Christ or for your family, and get to work.

Related Topics: CONVERSATION, LYING, RELATIONSHIP(S)

GOVERNMENT *(Kings, Leaders, Rulers)*

What are the responsibilities of those in authority?

BIBLE READING: Deuteronomy 17:1-20

KEY BIBLE VERSE: *When he sits on the throne as king, he must copy these laws on a scroll for himself in the presence of the Levitical priests. He must always keep this copy of the law with him and read it daily as long as he lives. That way he will learn to fear the LORD his God by obeying all the terms of this law.* (Deuteronomy 17:18-19)

Those in authority are ultimately responsible to God. The king was to be a man of God's Word. He was to (1) have a copy of the law made for his personal use, (2) keep it with him all the time, (3) read from it every day, and (4) obey it completely. Through this process he would learn respect for God, keep himself from feeling more important than others, and avoid neglecting God in times of prosperity. We can't know what God wants except through his Word, and his Word won't affect our life unless we read and think about it regularly. With the abundant availability of the Bible today, it is not difficult to gain access to the source of the king's wisdom. What is more of a challenge is following its directives.

BIBLE READING: 1 Samuel 8:1-22

KEY BIBLE VERSE: *Samuel was very upset with their request and went to the LORD for advice. "Do as they say," the LORD replied, "for it is me they are rejecting, not you. They don't want me to be their king any longer."* (1 Samuel 8:6-7)

Government cannot solve problems of faith. The people clamored for a king, thinking that a new system of government would bring about a change in the nation. But because their basic problem was disobedience to God, their other problems would only continue under the new administration. What they needed was a unified faith, not a uniform rule.

Had the Israelites submitted to God's leadership, they would have thrived beyond their expectations (Deuteronomy 28:1). Our obedience is weak if we ask God to lead our family or personal life but continue to live by the world's standards and values. Faith in God must touch all the practical areas of life.

What are the responsibilities for those under authority?

BIBLE READING: Deuteronomy 16:18-22

KEY BIBLE VERSE: *Appoint judges and officials for each of your tribes in all the towns the LORD your God is giving you. They will judge the people fairly throughout the land. You must never twist justice or show partiality. Never accept a bribe, for bribes blind the eyes of the wise and corrupt the decisions of the godly.* (Deuteronomy 16:18-19)

Those under authority are responsible for choosing good leaders. These verses anticipated a great problem the Israelites would face when they arrived in the Promised Land. Although they had Joshua as their national leader, they failed to complete the task and choose other spiritual leaders who would lead the tribes, districts, and cities with justice and God's wisdom. Because they did not appoint wise judges and faithful administrators, rebellion and injustice plagued their communities. It is a serious responsibility to appoint or elect wise and just officials. In your sphere of influence—home, church, school, job—are you ensuring that justice and godliness prevail? Failing to choose leaders who uphold justice can lead to much trouble, as Israel would discover.

BIBLE READING: Romans 13:1-14

KEY BIBLE VERSE: *Obey the government, for God is the one who put it there. All governments have been placed in power by God.* (Romans 13:1)

Those under authority are responsible to God, then the state. Christians understand Romans 13 in different ways. All Christians agree that we are to live at peace with the state as long as the state allows us to live by our religious convictions. For hundreds of years, however, there have been at least three interpretations of how we are to do this.

(1) Some Christians believe that the state is so corrupt that Christians should have as little to do with it as possible. Although they should be good citizens as long as they can do so without compromising their beliefs, they should not work for the government, vote, or serve in the military.

(2) Others believe that God has given the state authority in certain areas and the church authority in others. Christians can be loyal to both and can work for either. They should not, however, confuse the two. In this view, church and state are concerned with two totally different spheres—the spiritual and the physical— and thus complement each other but do not work together.

(3) Still others believe that Christians have a responsibility to make the state better. They can do this politically, by electing Christians or other high-principled leaders. They can also do this morally, by serving as an influence for good in society. In this view, church and state ideally work together for the good of all.

None of these views advocate rebelling against or refusing to obey the government's laws or regulations unless they clearly require you to violate the moral standards revealed by God. Wherever we find ourself, we must be responsible citizens, as well as responsible Christians.

Those under authority must be loyal to the source of all authority. Are there times when we should not obey the government? We should never allow government to force us to disobey God. Jesus and his apostles never disobeyed the government for personal reasons; when they disobeyed, it was in order to follow their higher loyalty to God. Their disobedience was not cheap: they were threatened, beaten, thrown into jail, tortured, and executed for their convictions. Like them, if we are compelled to disobey, we must be ready to accept the consequences.

BIBLE READING: Titus 3:1-8

KEY BIBLE VERSE: *Remind your people to submit to the government and its officers. They should be obedient, always ready to do what is good.* (Titus 3:1)

Believers should cooperate with the authorities wherever possible. As Christians, our first allegiance is to Jesus as Lord, but we must also obey our government and its leaders. Christians are not above the law. Obeying the civil law is only the beginning of our Christian responsibility; we must do what we can to be good citizens. In a democracy, this means participation and willingness to serve. (See Acts 5:29 and Romans 13:1ff. for more on the Christian's attitude toward government.)

Related Topics: AUTHORITY, OBEDIENCE, SUBMISSION

GRACE *(Forgiveness, Love, Mercy)*

What are some aspects of God's grace?

BIBLE READING: Nehemiah 9:1-38

KEY BIBLE VERSE: *In your great mercy, you did not destroy them completely or abandon them forever. What a gracious and merciful God you are!* (Nehemiah 9:31)

God's grace is our only hope! Israel was devastated by times of intense rebellion and sin. Yet when the people repented and returned to God, he delivered them. God puts no limit on the number of times we can come to him to obtain mercy, but we must *come* in order to obtain it, recognizing our need and asking him for help. This miracle of grace should inspire us to say, "What a gracious and merciful God you are!" If there is a recurring problem or difficulty in your life, continue to ask God for help, and be willing and ready to make changes in your attitude and behavior that will correct that situation.

BIBLE READING: Ephesians 1:3–2:10

KEY BIBLE VERSE: *He is so rich in kindness that he purchased our freedom through the blood of his Son, and our sins are forgiven. He has showered his kindness on us, along with all wisdom and understanding.* (Ephesians 1:7-8)

God's grace makes our salvation possible. Grace is God's voluntary and loving favor given to those he saves. We can't earn salvation, nor do we deserve it. No religious, intellectual, or moral effort can gain it, because it comes only from God's mercy and love. Without God's grace, no person can be saved. To receive it, we must acknowledge that we cannot save ourself, that only God can save us, and that our only way to receive this loving favor is by faith in Christ.

God's grace should lead us to serve others with love. We become Christians through God's unmerited grace, not as the result of any effort, ability, intelligent choice, or act of service on our part. However, out of gratitude for this free gift, we will seek to help and serve others with kindness, charity, and goodness, and not merely to please ourself. While no action or work we do can help us obtain salvation, God's intention is that our salvation will result in works of service. We are saved, not merely for our own benefit, but to serve him and build up the church (Ephesians 4:12).

BIBLE READING: Romans 2:1-16

KEY BIBLE VERSE: *Don't you realize how kind, tolerant, and patient God is with you? Or don't you care? Can't you see how kind he has been in giving you time to turn from your sin?* (Romans 2:4)

God's grace leaves no room for self-righteousness. When Paul's letter was read in the Roman church, no doubt many heads nodded as he condemned idol worshipers, homosexual practices, and violent people. But what surprise his listeners must have felt when he turned on them and said, "You are just as bad!" Paul was emphatically stressing that *nobody* is good enough to save himself or herself. If we want to avoid punishment and live eternally with Christ, all of us, whether we have been murderers and molesters or whether we have been honest, hardworking, solid citizens, must depend totally on God's grace. Paul is not discussing whether some sins are worse than others. Any sin is enough to cause us to depend on Jesus Christ for salvation and eternal life. We have all sinned repeatedly, and there is no way apart from Christ to be saved from sin's consequences.

Related Topics: FORGIVENESS, LOVE, MERCY

GRATITUDE (*see* THANKFULNESS)

GREATNESS *(Effectiveness, Fame, Reputation)*

How does God measure true greatness?

BIBLE READING: Mark 10:35-45

KEY BIBLE VERSE: *Jesus called them together and said, "You know that in this world kings are tyrants, and officials lord it over the people beneath them. But among you it should be quite different. Whoever wants to be a leader among you must be your servant, and whoever wants to be first must be the slave of all." (Mark 10:42-44)*

True greatness does not concern itself with being recognized. James and John wanted the highest positions in Jesus' kingdom. But Jesus told them that true greatness comes in serving others. Peter, one of the disciples who had heard this message, expands the thought in 1 Peter 5:1-4.

Most businesses, organizations, and institutions measure greatness by high personal achievement. In Christ's kingdom, however, service is the way to get ahead. The desire to be on top will hinder, not help. Rather than seeking to have your needs met, look for ways that you can minister to the needs of others.

BIBLE READING: Matthew 23:1-12

KEY BIBLE VERSE: *The greatest among you must be a servant. But those who exalt themselves will be humbled, and those who humble themselves will be exalted. (Matthew 23:11-12)*

True greatness is measured by service. Jesus challenged society's norms. To him, greatness comes from serving—giving of yourself to help God and others. Service keeps us aware of others' needs, and it stops us from focusing only on ourself. Jesus came as a servant. What kind of greatness do you seek?

BIBLE READING: John 1:19-34

KEY BIBLE VERSE: *John told them, "I baptize with water, but right here in the crowd is someone you do not know, who will soon begin his ministry. I am not even worthy to be his slave." (John 1:26-27)*

True greatness is characterized by profound humility. John the Baptist said he was not even worthy to be Christ's slave, to perform the humble task of unfastening his shoes. But according to Luke 7:28, Jesus said that John was the greatest of all prophets. If such a great person felt inadequate even to be Christ's slave, how much more should we lay aside our pride to serve Christ! When we truly understand who Christ is, our pride and self-importance melt away.

True greatness is content to serve without recognition. Although John was a well-known preacher who attracted large crowds, he was content for Jesus to take the higher place. This is true humility, the basis for greatness in preaching, teaching, or any other work we do for Christ. When you are content to do what God wants you to do and let Jesus Christ be honored for it, God will do great things through you.

Related Topics: POPULARITY, REPUTATION, WISDOM

GREED *(Coveting, Desiring, Wanting)*

How can greed be recognized and controlled?

BIBLE READING: Numbers 16:1-22

KEY BIBLE VERSE: *Moses spoke again to Korah: "Now listen, you Levites! Does it seem a small thing to you that the God of Israel has chosen you from among all the people of Israel to be near him as you serve in the LORD's Tabernacle and to stand before the people to minister to them?"* (Numbers 16:8-9)

Greed is often present behind ambition. Moses saw through Korah, Dathan, and Abiram's charge to their true motivation—some of the Levites wanted the power of the priesthood. Like Korah, we often desire the special qualities God has given others. Korah had significant, worthwhile abilities and responsibilities of his own. In the end, however, his ambition for more caused him to lose everything. Inappropriate ambition is greed in disguise. Concentrate on finding the special purpose God has for you.

BIBLE READING: Deuteronomy 6:1-25

KEY BIBLE VERSE: *The LORD your God will soon bring you into the land he swore to give your ancestors Abraham, Isaac, and Jacob. It is a land filled with large, prosperous cities that you did not build. The houses will be richly stocked with goods you did not produce. You will draw water from cisterns you did not dig, and you will eat from vineyards and olive trees you did not plant. When you have eaten your fill in this land, be careful not to forget the LORD, who rescued you from slavery in the land of Egypt.* (Deuteronomy 6:10-12)

Greed often accompanies prosperity. Moses warned the people not to forget God when they entered the promised land and became prosperous. Prosperity, more than poverty, can dull our spiritual vision, because it tends to make us self-sufficient and eager to acquire still more of everything—except God. Instead of leading to contentment, prosperity can just as easily lead to greed. The same thing can happen in our church. Once we become successful in terms of numbers, programs, and buildings, we can easily become self-sufficient and less sensitive to our need for God. This leads us to concentrate on self-preservation rather than thankfulness and service to God.

BIBLE READING: James 4:1-17

KEY BIBLE VERSE: *What is causing the quarrels and fights among you? Isn't it the whole army of evil desires at war within you? You want what you don't have, so you scheme and kill to get it. You are jealous for what others have, and you can't possess it, so you fight and quarrel to take it away from them. And yet the reason you don't have what you want is that you don't ask God for it.* (James 4:1-2)

Greed can be cured by humble reliance upon God. The cure for evil desires is humility (see Proverbs 16:18-19; 1 Peter 5:5-6). Pride makes us self-centered and leads us to conclude that we deserve all we can see, touch, or imagine. It creates greedy appetites for far more than we need. We can be released from our self-centered desires by humbling ourself before God, realizing that all we really need is his approval. When the Holy Spirit fills us, we see that this world's seductive attractions are only cheap substitutes for what God has to offer.

Related Topics: GENEROSITY, GIVING, SELFISHNESS

GRIEF *(Pain, Sadness, Sorrow)*

How should we handle grief?

BIBLE READING: 2 Samuel 1:1-16

KEY BIBLE VERSE: *David and his men tore their clothes in sorrow when they heard the news. They mourned and wept and fasted all day for Saul and his son Jonathan, and for the LORD's army and the nation of Israel, because so many had died that day.* (2 Samuel 1:11-12)

Expressing grief is an important part of healing. "They mourned and wept and fasted all day." David and his men were visibly shaken over Saul's death. Their actions showed their genuine sorrow over the loss of their king, their friend Jonathan, and the other soldiers of Israel who died that day. They were not ashamed to grieve. Today, some people consider expressing emotion to be a sign of weakness. Those who wish to appear strong try to hide their feelings. But expressing our grief can help us deal with our intense sorrow when a loved one dies.

BIBLE READING: Nehemiah 1:1-11

KEY BIBLE VERSE: *When I heard this, I sat down and wept. In fact, for days I mourned, fasted, and prayed to the God of heaven.* (Nehemiah 1:4)

Grief is overcome through prayer and action. Nehemiah was deeply grieved about the condition of Jerusalem, but he didn't just brood about it. After his initial grief, he prayed, pouring his heart out to God (Nehemiah 1:5-11), and he looked for ways to improve the situation. Nehemiah put all his knowledge, experience, and organizational skills into determining what should be done. When tragic news comes to you, first pray. Then seek ways to move beyond grief to specific action that helps those who need it.

BIBLE READING: Job 3:1-26

KEY BIBLE VERSE: *Why didn't I die at birth as I came from the womb?* (Job 3:11)

Be honest about your grief. Job was experiencing extreme physical pain as well as grief over the loss of his family and possessions. He can't be blamed for wishing he were dead. Job's grief placed him at the crossroads of his faith, shattering many misconceptions about God (such as: he makes you rich, always keeps you from trouble and pain, or protects your loved ones). Job was driven back to the basics of his faith in God. He had only two choices: (1) he could curse God and give up, or (2) he could trust God and draw strength from him to continue.

BIBLE READING: John 11:1-44

KEY BIBLE VERSE: *When Jesus saw her weeping and saw the other people wailing with her, he was moved with indignation and was deeply troubled.* (John 11:33)

Know that Jesus understands our grief firsthand. John stresses that we have a God who cares. This portrait contrasts with the Greek concept of God that was popular in that day—a God with no emotions and no messy involvement with humans. Here we see many of Jesus' emotions—compassion, indignation, sorrow, even frustration. He often expressed deep emotion, and we must never be afraid to reveal our true feelings to him. He understands them, for he experienced them. Be honest, and don't try to hide anything from your Savior. He cares.

When Jesus saw the weeping and wailing, he too wept openly. Perhaps he empathized with their grief, or perhaps he was troubled at their unbelief. In either case, Jesus showed that he cares enough for us to weep with us in our sorrow.

Related Topics: HEALING, PAIN, SORROW

GROWTH *(Development, Improvement, Maturity)*

What factors bring about growth in our life?

BIBLE READING: Genesis 35:1-15

KEY BIBLE VERSE: *God appeared to Jacob once again when he arrived at Bethel after traveling from Paddan-aram. God blessed him and said, "Your name is no longer Jacob; you will now be called Israel."* (Genesis 35:9-10)

Problems can be opportunities for growth. God reminded Jacob of his new name, Israel, which meant "one who prevails with God" or "one who struggles with God." Although Jacob's life was littered with difficulties and trials, his new name was a tribute to his desire to stay close to God despite life's disappointments.

Many people believe that Christianity should offer a problem-free life. Consequently, as life gets tough, they draw back disappointed. Instead, they should determine to prevail with God through life's storms. Problems and difficulties are painful but inevitable; you might as well see them as opportunities for growth. You can't prevail with God unless you have troubles to prevail over.

BIBLE READING: Deuteronomy 5:1-33

KEY BIBLE VERSE: *Moses called all the people of Israel together and said, "Listen carefully to all the laws and regulations I am giving you today. Learn them and be sure to obey them!"* (Deuteronomy 5:1)

Spiritual growth results from listening to and obeying God's Word. The people had entered into a covenant with God, and Moses commanded them to hear, learn, and follow his statutes. Christians also have entered into a covenant with God (through Jesus Christ) and should be responsive to what God expects. Moses' threefold command to the Israelites is excellent advice for all of God's followers. *Listening* is absorbing and accepting information about God. *Learning* is understanding its meaning and implications. *Following* is putting into action all we have learned and understood. All three parts are essential to a growing relationship with God.

BIBLE READING: Romans 14:1-23

KEY BIBLE VERSE: *Accept Christians who are weak in faith, and don't argue with them about what they think is right or wrong.* (Romans 14:1)

Recognizing weaknesses is often the beginning of growth. What is weak faith? Paul is speaking about immature faith that has not yet developed the muscle it needs to stand against external pressures. For example, if a person who once worshiped idols were to become a Christian, he might understand perfectly well that Christ saved him through faith and that idols have no real power. Still, because of his past associations, he might be badly shaken if he knowingly ate meat that had been used in idol worship as part of a pagan ritual. If a person who once worshiped God on the required Jewish holy days were to become a Christian, he might well know that Christ saved him through faith, not through his keeping of the law. Still, when the feast days came, he might feel empty and unfaithful if he didn't dedicate those days to God.

Our response to others' weaknesses is a measure of our personal growth. Paul responds to both weak brothers in love. Both are acting according to their consciences, but their honest scruples do not need to be made into rules for the church. Certainly some issues are central to the faith and worth fighting for—but many are based on individual differences and should not be legislated. Our principle should be: In essentials, unity; in nonessentials, liberty; in everything, love.

BIBLE READING: 1 Corinthians 9:1-27
KEY BIBLE VERSE: *All athletes practice strict self-control. They do it to win a prize that will fade away, but we do it for an eternal prize.* (1 Corinthians 9:25)

Spiritual growth results from discipline. Winning a race requires purpose and discipline. Paul uses this illustration to explain that the Christian life takes hard work, self-denial, and grueling preparation. As Christians, we are running toward our heavenly reward. The essential disciplines of prayer, Bible study, and worship equip us to run with vigor and stamina. Don't merely observe from the grandstand; don't just turn out to jog a couple of laps each morning. Train diligently—your spiritual progress depends upon it.

Spiritual growth results from self-denial. At times we must give up something good in order to do what God wants. Each person's special duties determine the discipline and denial that he or she must accept. Without a goal, discipline is nothing but self-punishment. With the goal of pleasing God, our denial seems like nothing compared to the eternal, imperishable reward that will be ours.

Related Topics: DISCIPLINE, GUIDANCE, OBEDIENCE

GRUMBLING (*see* COMPLAINING)

GUARANTEE (*see* PROMISE[S])

GUIDANCE (*Counsel, Direction, Help*)

▶ **SEEKING GOD'S GUIDANCE**
How can we experience God's guidance?

BIBLE READING: Numbers 9:15-23
KEY BIBLE VERSE: *They camped or traveled at the LORD's command, and they did whatever the LORD told them through Moses.* (Numbers 9:23)

Depend on God's guidance both now and in the future. A pillar of cloud by day and a pillar of fire by night guided and protected the Israelites as they traveled across the desert. Some have said this pillar may have been a burning bowl of pitch whose smoke was visible during the day and whose fire could be seen at night. However, a bowl of pitch would not have lifted itself up and moved ahead of the people, and the Bible is clear that the cloud and fire moved in accordance with the will of God. The cloud and the fire were not merely natural phenomena; they were the vehicle of God's presence and the visible evidence of his moving and directing his people.

The Israelites traveled and camped as God guided. When you follow God's guidance, you know you are where God wants you, whether you're moving or staying in one place. You are physically somewhere right now. Instead of praying, "God, what do you want me to do next?" ask, "God, what do you want me to do while I'm right here?" Direction from God is not just for your next big move. He has a purpose in placing you where you are right now. Begin to understand God's purpose for your life by discovering what he wants you to do now!

BIBLE READING: Ruth 2:1-23

KEY BIBLE VERSE: *"May the LORD bless him!" Naomi told her daughter-in-law. "He is showing his kindness to us as well as to your dead husband. That man is one of our closest relatives, one of our family redeemers."* (Ruth 2:20)

God guides us through everyday events of life. Though Ruth may not have always recognized God's guidance, he had been with her every step of the way. She went to glean and "just happened" to end up in the field owned by Boaz, who "just happened" to be a close relative. This was more than mere coincidence. As you go about your daily tasks, God is working in your life in ways you may not even notice. We must not close the door on what God can do. Events do not occur by luck or coincidence. We should have faith that God is directing our life for his purpose.

▶ SUBMITTING TO GOD'S GUIDANCE
How is our obedience related to God's guidance?

 BIBLE READING: Exodus 11:1-10

KEY BIBLE VERSE: *Now the LORD had told Moses, "Pharaoh will not listen to you. But this will give me the opportunity to do even more mighty miracles in the land of Egypt." Although Moses and Aaron did these miracles in Pharaoh's presence, the LORD hardened his heart so he wouldn't let the Israelites leave the country.* (Exodus 11:9-10)

Guidance for the future comes with obedience in the present. When Moses gave God's message to the people, they were too discouraged to listen. The Hebrews didn't want to hear any more about God and his promises, because the last time they listened to Moses, all they got was more work and greater suffering. Sometimes a clear message from God is followed by a period when no change in the situation is apparent. During that time, seeming setbacks may turn people away from wanting to hear more about God. If you are a leader, don't give up. Keep bringing people God's message as Moses did. By focusing on God, who must be obeyed, rather than on the results to be achieved, good leaders see beyond temporary setbacks and reversals.

 BIBLE READING: 2 Chronicles 18:1-34

KEY BIBLE VERSE: *The messenger who went to get Micaiah said to him, "Look, all the prophets are promising victory for the king. Be sure that you agree with them and promise success." But Micaiah replied, "As surely as the LORD lives, I will say only what my God tells me to say."* (2 Chronicles 18:12-13)

Seeking guidance with no intention of obedience is self-destructive. Wicked Ahab asked Jehoshaphat to join forces with him in battle (18:2-3). Before making that commitment, Jehoshaphat rightly sought God's advice. However, when God gave his answer through the prophet Micaiah (18:16), Jehoshaphat ignored it (18:28). It does us no good to seek God's advice if we ignore it when it is given. Real love for God is shown not by merely asking for direction, but by following that direction once it is given.

 BIBLE READING: Acts 8:26-40

KEY BIBLE VERSE: *As for Philip, an angel of the Lord said to him, "Go south down the desert road that runs from Jerusalem to Gaza."* (Acts 8:26)

God's guidance seldom follows our plans. Philip was having a successful preaching ministry to great crowds in Samaria (8:5-8), but he obediently left that ministry to travel on a desert road. Because Philip went where God sent him,

Ethiopia was opened up to the gospel. Follow God's leading, even if it seems like a demotion. At first you may not understand his plans, but the results will prove that God's way is right.

Related Topics: GOD'S WILL, HOLY SPIRIT, PURPOSE

GUILT *(Fear, Shame, Sorrow)*

▶ THE SOURCE OF GUILT
What makes us feel guilty?

BIBLE READING: Genesis 3:1-24

KEY BIBLE VERSE: *The woman was convinced. The fruit looked so fresh and delicious, and it would make her so wise! So she ate some of the fruit. She also gave some to her husband, who was with her. Then he ate it, too. At that moment, their eyes were opened, and they suddenly felt shame at their nakedness. So they strung fig leaves together around their hips to cover themselves.* (Genesis 3:6-7)

Guilt comes from giving in to temptation. Notice what Eve did: She looked, she took, she ate, and she gave. The battle is often lost at the first look. Temptation often begins by simply seeing something you want. Are you struggling with temptation because you have not learned that looking is the first step toward sin? You would win over temptation more often if you followed Paul's advice to run from those things that produce evil thoughts (2 Timothy 2:22).

Involving others in sin compounds guilt. One of the realities of sin is that its effects spread. After Eve sinned, she involved Adam in her wrongdoing. When we do something wrong, often we try to relieve our guilt by involving someone else. Like toxic waste spilled in a river, sin swiftly spreads. Recognize and confess your sin to God before you are tempted to pollute those around you.

Sin makes us feel guilty. After sinning, Adam and Eve felt guilt and embarrassment over their nakedness. Their guilty feelings made them try to hide from God. A guilty conscience is a warning signal God placed inside you that goes off when you've done wrong. The worst step you could take is to eliminate the guilty feelings without eliminating the cause. That would be like using a painkiller but not treating the disease. Be glad those guilty feelings are there. They make you aware of your sin so you can ask God's forgiveness and then correct your wrongdoing.

BIBLE READING: Jonah 1:1-17

KEY BIBLE VERSE: *Fearing for their lives, the desperate sailors shouted to their gods for help and threw the cargo overboard to lighten the ship. And all this time Jonah was sound asleep down in the hold.* (Jonah 1:5)

The absence of guilty feelings does not mean a lack of guilt. While the storm raged, Jonah was sound asleep below deck. Even as he ran from God, Jonah's actions apparently didn't bother his conscience. But the absence of guilty feelings isn't always a barometer of whether we are doing right. Because we can deny reality, we cannot measure obedience by our feelings. Instead, we must compare what we do with God's standards for living.

BIBLE READING: Romans 2:17-29

KEY BIBLE VERSE: *You are so proud of knowing the law, but you dishonor God by breaking it.* (Romans 2:23)

Guilt comes from failing to do what God expects. Paul continues to argue that all stand guilty before God. After describing the fate of the unbelieving, pagan Gentiles, he moves to that of the religiously privileged. Despite their knowledge of God's will, they are guilty because they too have refused to live by their beliefs. Those of us who have grown up in Christian families are the religiously privileged of today. Paul's condemnation applies to us if we do not live up to what we know.

▶ THE SOLUTION FOR GUILT
How can our guilt be removed?

📖 BIBLE READING: Romans 3:21-31
KEY BIBLE VERSE: *Now God has shown us a different way of being right in his sight—not by obeying the law but by the way promised in the Scriptures long ago. We are made right in God's sight when we trust in Jesus Christ to take away our sins. And we all can be saved in this same way, no matter who we are or what we have done.* (Romans 3:21-22)

Guilt can be removed through Christ. After all this bad news about our sinfulness and God's condemnation, Paul gives the wonderful news. There is a way to be declared "not guilty"—by trusting Jesus Christ to take away our sins. Trusting means putting our confidence in Christ to forgive our sins, to make us right with God, and to empower us to live the way he taught us. God's solution is available to all of us regardless of our background or past behavior.

We are declared "not guilty" because of Christ. When a judge in a court of law declares the defendant "not guilty," all the charges are removed from his record. Legally, it is as if the person had never been accused. When God forgives our sins, our record is wiped clean. From his perspective, it is as though we had never sinned.

📖 BIBLE READING: Romans 8:1-17
KEY BIBLE VERSE: *Now there is no condemnation for those who belong to Christ Jesus.* (Romans 8:1)

Christ frees us from the condemnation of sin. "Not guilty; let him go free"—what would those words mean to you if you were on death row? The fact is that the whole human race *is* on death row, justly condemned for repeatedly breaking God's holy law. Without Jesus we would have no hope at all. But thank God! He has declared us "not guilty" and has offered us freedom from sin and power to do his will.

📖 BIBLE READING: 1 John 3:11-24
KEY BIBLE VERSE: *It is by our actions that we know we are living in the truth, so we will be confident when we stand before the Lord, even if our hearts condemn us. For God is greater than our hearts, and he knows everything.* (1 John 3:19-20)

Christ can relieve our guilty conscience. Many are afraid that they don't love others as they should. They feel guilty because they think they are not doing enough to show proper love to Christ. Their consciences bother them. John has these people in mind in this letter. How do we escape the gnawing accusations of our conscience? Not by ignoring them or rationalizing our behavior, but by setting our heart on God's love. When we feel guilty, we should remind ourself that God knows our motives as well as our actions. His voice of assurance is stronger than the accusing voice of our conscience. If we are in Christ, he will not condemn us (Romans 8:1; Hebrews 9:14-15). So if you are living for the Lord but feeling that you are not good enough, remind yourself that God is greater than your conscience.

Related Topics: FORGIVENESS, REPENTANCE

HABITS *(Customs, Patterns, Traditions)*

▶ **BAD HABITS**
How can bad habits be avoided or eliminated?

 BIBLE READING: Numbers 33:50-56
KEY BIBLE VERSE: *If you fail to drive out the people who live in the land, those who remain will be like splinters in your eyes and thorns in your sides. They will harass you in the land where you live. And I will do to you what I had planned to do to them.* (Numbers 33:55-56)

Bad habits must be replaced by good ones. God told Moses that before the Israelites settled in the Promised Land, they should drive out the wicked inhabitants and destroy their idols. In Colossians 3, Paul encourages us to live as Christians in the same manner: throwing away our old way of living and moving ahead into our new life of obedience to God and faith in Jesus Christ. Like the Israelites moving into the Promised Land, we can destroy the wickedness in our life, or we can settle down and live with it. To move in and possess the new life, we must drive out the sinful thoughts and practices to make room for the new.

BIBLE READING: Deuteronomy 12:1-32
KEY BIBLE VERSE: *When you drive out the nations that live there, you must destroy all the places where they worship their gods—high on the mountains, up on the hills, and under every green tree. Break down their altars and smash their sacred pillars. Burn their Asherah poles and cut down their carved idols. Erase the names of their gods from those places!* (Deuteronomy 12:2-3)

Bad habits deserve no mercy. When taking over a nation, the Israelites were supposed to destroy every pagan altar and idol in the land. God knew it would be easy for them to change their beliefs if they started using those altars, so nothing was to remain that might tempt them to worship idols. We too should ruthlessly find and remove any centers of false worship in our life. These may be activities, attitudes, possessions, relationships, places, or habits—anything that tempts us to turn our hearts from God and do wrong. We should never flatter ourselves by thinking we're too strong to be tempted. Israel learned that lesson.

BIBLE READING: 1 John 3:1-24
KEY BIBLE VERSE: *Those who have been born into God's family do not sin, because God's life is in them. So they can't keep on sinning, because they have been born of God.* (1 John 3:9)

Depend on God's power to combat bad habits. We all have areas where temptation is strong and habits are hard to conquer. These weaknesses give the devil a
foothold, so we must deal with our areas of vulnerability. If we are struggling
with a particular sin, however, these verses are not directed at us, even if for the
time we seem to keep on sinning. John is not talking about people whose victories are still incomplete; he is talking about people who make a practice of sinning and look for ways to justify it.

Bad habits must be changed with determination and God's help. Three steps
are necessary to find victory over prevailing sin: (1) seek the power of the Holy
Spirit and God's Word; (2) stay away from tempting situations; and (3) seek the
help of the body of Christ—be open to their willingness to hold you accountable and to pray for you.

▶ GOOD HABITS

What good habits should we start and maintain?

BIBLE READING: Deuteronomy 14:22-29
KEY BIBLE VERSE: *You must set aside a tithe of your crops—one-tenth of all the crops
you harvest each year.* (Deuteronomy 14:22)

Tithing is an excellent habit to develop. The Bible makes the purpose of tithing
very clear—to put God first in our life. We are to give God the first and best of
what we earn. For example, what we do first with our money shows what we
value most. Giving the first part of our paycheck to God immediately focuses
our attention on him. It also reminds us that all we have belongs to him. A
habit of regular tithing can keep God at the top of our priority list and give us
a proper perspective on everything else we have.

BIBLE READING: Luke 4:14-30
KEY BIBLE VERSE: *When he came to the village of Nazareth, his boyhood home,
he went as usual to the synagogue on the Sabbath and stood up to read the
Scriptures.* (Luke 4:16)

Jesus modeled a habit of worship we should imitate. Jesus went to the synagogue "as usual." Even though he was the perfect Son of God, and his local synagogue undoubtedly left much to be desired, Jesus attended services every week.
His example makes our excuses for not attending church sound weak and self-
serving. Make regular worship a part of your life.

BIBLE READING: Matthew 6:5-15
KEY BIBLE VERSE: *Now about prayer. When you pray, don't be like the hypocrites who
love to pray publicly on street corners and in the synagogues where everyone can
see them. I assure you, that is all the reward they will ever get.* (Matthew 6:5)

Jesus modeled the habit of prayer for us. Some people, especially the religious
leaders, wanted to be seen as "holy," and public prayer was one way to get
attention. Jesus saw through their self-righteous acts, however, and taught that
the essence of prayer is not public style but private communication with God.
There is a place for public prayer, but to pray only where others will notice you
indicates that your real audience is not God.

Related Topics: DISCIPLINE, GROWTH, SIN

────

HALFHEARTEDNESS (*see* COMMITMENT)

HANDICAPPED (*Disabled, Impaired, Limited*)

How are the handicapped treated in the Bible?

BIBLE READING: Leviticus 21:1-24

KEY BIBLE VERSE: *The LORD said to Moses, "Tell Aaron that in all future generations, his descendants who have physical defects will not qualify to offer food to their God." (Leviticus 21:16-17)*

The handicapped were limited in service, but personally accepted. Was God unfairly discriminating against handicapped people when he said they were unqualified to offer sacrifices? Just as God demanded that no imperfect animals be used for sacrifice, he required that no handicapped priests offer sacrifices. This was not meant as an insult; rather, it had to do with the fact that the priest must match as closely as possible the perfect God he served. Of course, such perfection was not fully realized until Jesus Christ came. As Levites, the handicapped priests were protected and supported with food from the sacrifices. They were not abandoned, because they still performed many essential services within the tabernacle.

BIBLE READING: Mark 10:46-52

KEY BIBLE VERSE: *And so they reached Jericho. Later, as Jesus and his disciples left town, a great crowd was following. A blind beggar named Bartimaeus (son of Timaeus) was sitting beside the road as Jesus was going by. (Mark 10:46)*

Jesus treated the handicapped with dignity. Beggars were a common sight in most towns. Because most occupations of that day required physical labor, anyone with a crippling disease or disability was at a severe disadvantage and was usually forced to beg, even though God's laws commanded care for such needy people (Leviticus 25:35-38). Blindness was considered a curse from God for sin (John 9:2), but Jesus refuted this idea when he reached out to heal the blind.

BIBLE READING: John 9:1-12

KEY BIBLE VERSE: *"Teacher," his disciples asked him, "why was this man born blind? Was it a result of his own sins or those of his parents?" "It was not because of his sins or his parents' sins," Jesus answered. "He was born blind so the power of God could be seen in him." (John 9:2-3)*

For Jesus, handicaps were opportunities for God to display his power. A common belief in Jewish culture was that calamity or suffering was the result of some great sin. But Christ used this man's suffering to teach about faith and to glorify God. We live in a fallen world where good behavior is not always rewarded and bad behavior not always punished. Therefore, innocent people sometimes suffer. If God took suffering away whenever we asked, we would follow him for comfort and convenience, not out of love and devotion. Regardless of the reasons for our suffering, Jesus has the power to help us deal with it. When you suffer from a disease, tragedy, or disability, try not to ask, "Why did this happen to me?" or "What did I do wrong?" Instead, ask God to give you strength for the trial and a clearer perspective on what is happening.

Related Topics: BARRIERS, LIMITATIONS, SUFFERING

HAPPINESS (*Contentment, Gladness, Laughter*)

What does the Bible teach us about happiness?

BIBLE READING: Ecclesiastes 1:1-18

KEY BIBLE VERSE: *I, the Teacher, was king of Israel, and I lived in Jerusalem. I devoted myself to search for understanding and to explore by wisdom everything being done in the world. I soon discovered that God has dealt a tragic existence to the human race. Everything under the sun is meaningless, like chasing the wind. What is wrong cannot be righted. What is missing cannot be recovered.* (Ecclesiastes 1:12-15)

Happiness is ultimately measured by our relationship with God. Many people feel restless and dissatisfied. They wonder: (1) If I am in God's will, why am I so tired and unfulfilled? (2) What is the meaning of life? (3) When I look back on it all, will I be happy with my accomplishments? (4) Why do I feel burned out, disillusioned, dry? (5) What is to become of me? Solomon tests our faith, challenging us to find true and lasting meaning in God alone. As you take a hard look at your life, as Solomon did his, you will see how important serving God is over all other options. Perhaps God is asking you to rethink your purpose and direction in life, just as Solomon did in Ecclesiastes.

BIBLE READING: Matthew 5:1-12

KEY BIBLE VERSE: *God blesses you when you are mocked and persecuted and lied about because you are my followers. Be happy about it! Be very glad! For a great reward awaits you in heaven. And remember, the ancient prophets were persecuted, too.* (Matthew 5:11-12)

Happiness is much more than a feeling. Each Beatitude tells how to be *blessed*. *Blessed* means more than happiness. It implies the fortunate or enviable state of those who are in God's kingdom. The Beatitudes don't promise laughter, pleasure, or earthly prosperity. To Jesus, "blessed" means the experience of hope and joy, independent of outward circumstances. To find hope and joy, the deepest form of happiness, follow Jesus no matter what the cost.

BIBLE READING: 1 Timothy 6:3-10

KEY BIBLE VERSE: *True religion with contentment is great wealth.* (1 Timothy 6:6)

Money doesn't bring happiness. This statement is the key to spiritual growth and personal fulfillment. We should honor God and center our desires on him ("true religion," see Matthew 6:33), and we should be content with what God is doing in our life (see Philippians 4:11-13).

Despite overwhelming evidence to the contrary, most people still believe that money brings happiness. Rich people craving greater riches can be caught in an endless cycle that only ends in ruin and destruction. How can you keep away from the love of money? Paul gives us some guidelines: (1) realize that one day riches will all be gone (6:7, 17); (2) be content with what you have (6:8); (3) monitor what you are willing to do to get more money (6:9-10); (4) love people more than money (6:11); (5) love God's work more than money (6:11); (6) freely share what you have with others (6:18). (See Proverbs 30:7-9 for more on avoiding the love of money.)

Related Topics: JOY, OBEDIENCE, SUFFERING

HARD-HEARTEDNESS (*Indifference, Pride, Stubbornness*)

What brings about hard-heartedness?

BIBLE READING: Exodus 11:1-10

KEY BIBLE VERSE: *Although Moses and Aaron did these miracles in Pharaoh's presence, the LORD hardened his heart so he wouldn't let the Israelites leave the country.* (Exodus 11:10)

Hard-heartedness is the result of stubborn unbelief. You may wonder how Pharaoh could be so foolish as to see God's miraculous power and still not listen to Moses. But Pharaoh had his mind made up long before the plagues began. He couldn't believe that someone was greater than he. This stubborn unbelief led to a heart so hard that even a major catastrophe couldn't soften him. Finally, it took the greatest of all calamities, the loss of his son, to force him to recognize God's authority. But even then he wanted God to leave, not to rule his country. We must not wait for great calamities to drive us to God, but must open our hearts and minds to his direction now.

Hard-heartedness is the result of deliberate rejection of God. Did God really harden Pharaoh's heart and force him to do wrong? Before the ten plagues began, Moses and Aaron announced what God would do if Pharaoh didn't let the people go. But their message only made Pharaoh stubborn—he was hardening his own heart. In so doing, he defied both God and his messengers. Through the first six plagues, Pharaoh's heart grew even more stubborn. After the sixth plague, God passed judgment. Sooner or later, evil people will be punished for their sins. When it became evident that Pharaoh wouldn't change, God confirmed Pharaoh's prideful decision and set the painful consequences of his actions in motion. God didn't force Pharaoh to reject him; rather, he gave him every opportunity to change his mind. In Ezekiel 33:11, God says, "I take no pleasure in the death of wicked people."

BIBLE READING: Mark 8:10-21

KEY BIBLE VERSE: *Jesus knew what they were thinking, so he said, "Why are you so worried about having no food? Won't you ever learn or understand? Are your hearts too hard to take it in? 'You have eyes—can't you see? You have ears—can't you hear?' Don't you remember anything at all?"* (Mark 8:17-18)

Hard-heartedness is the result of persistent resistance to God. The Pharisees had tried to explain away Jesus' previous miracles by claiming they were done by luck, coincidence, or evil power. Here they demanded a sign from heaven—something only God could do. Jesus refused their demand because he knew that even this kind of miracle would not convince them. They had already decided not to believe. Hearts can become so hard that even the most convincing facts and demonstrations will not change them.

BIBLE READING: Hebrews 3:7-19

KEY BIBLE VERSE: *That is why the Holy Spirit says, "Today you must listen to his voice. Don't harden your hearts against him as Israel did when they rebelled, when they tested God's patience in the wilderness."* (Hebrews 3:7-8)

Hard-heartedness is the result of failing to obey God's Word. In many places, the Bible warns us not to "harden" our hearts. This means stubbornly setting ourselves against God so that we are no longer able to turn to him for forgiveness. The Israelites became hard-hearted when they disobeyed God's command to conquer the Promised Land ("when they rebelled," see Numbers 13; 14; 20; and Psalm 95). Be careful to obey God's Word, and do not allow your heart to become hardened.

Related Topics: HUMILITY, PRIDE, STUBBORNNESS

HARD TIMES (*see* PROBLEMS)

HARMONY (*see* UNITY)

HATRED (*Anger, Dislike, Hostility*)

What does the Bible say about hatred?

BIBLE READING: Esther 5:1-14

KEY BIBLE VERSE: *What a happy man Haman was as he left the banquet! But when he saw Mordecai sitting at the gate, not standing up or trembling nervously before him, he was furious.* (Esther 5:9)

Unresolved hatred can become an all-consuming obsession. Hatred and bitterness are like weeds with long roots that grow in the heart and corrupt all of life. Haman was so consumed with hatred toward Mordecai that he could not even enjoy the honor of being invited to Esther's party. Hebrews 12:15 warns us to watch out "that no bitter root of unbelief rises up among you, for whenever it springs up, many are corrupted by its poison." Don't let hatred and its resulting bitterness build in your heart. Like Haman, you will find it backfiring against you (see Esther 6:13; 7:9-10). If the mere mention of someone's name provokes you to anger, confess your bitterness as sin. Ignoring bitterness, hiding it from others, or making superficial changes in behavior is not enough. If bitterness isn't completely removed, it will grow back, making matters worse.

BIBLE READING: Psalm 139:1-24

KEY BIBLE VERSE: *Jonah got up and went in the opposite direction in order to get away from the LORD. He went down to the seacoast, to the port of Joppa, where he found a ship leaving for Tarshish. He bought a ticket and went on board, hoping that by going away to the west he could escape from the LORD.* (Jonah 1:3)

Hatred may lead us to disobey God. Nineveh was a powerful and wicked city. Jonah had grown up hating the Assyrians and fearing their atrocities. His hatred was so strong that he didn't want them to receive God's mercy. Jonah was actually afraid the people would repent (Jonah 4:2-3). Jonah's attitude is representative of Israel's reluctance to share God's love and mercy with others, even though this was their God-given mission (Genesis 12:3). They, like Jonah, did not want non-Jews (Gentiles) to obtain God's favor. When hatred is shifted from the evil that people do onto the people themselves, even more evil has been generated.

BIBLE READING: Ecclesiastes 3:1-8

KEY BIBLE VERSE: *There is a time for everything, a season for every activity under heaven. A time to be born and a time to die. A time to plant and a time to harvest. A time to kill and a time to heal. A time to tear down and a time to rebuild. A time to cry and a time to laugh. A time to grieve and a time to dance. A time to scatter stones and a time to gather stones. A time to embrace and a time to turn away. A time to search and a time to lose. A time to keep and a time to throw away. A time to tear and a time to mend. A time to be quiet and a time to speak up. A time to love and a time to hate. A time for war and a time for peace.* (Ecclesiastes 3:1-8)

There is a time to hate. Timing is important. All the experiences listed in these verses are appropriate at certain times. The secret to peace with God is to discover, accept, and appreciate God's perfect timing. The danger is to doubt or resent God's timing. This can lead to despair, rebellion, or moving ahead without his advice.

The capacity to hate can be a powerful motivation toward justice. When is there a time for hating? We shouldn't hate evil people, but we should hate what they do. We should also hate it when people are mistreated, when children are starving, and when God is being dishonored. In addition, we must hate sin in our life—this is God's attitude (see Psalm 5:5).

Related Topics: ANGER, FEELINGS, LOVE

HEALING *(Care, Health, Wholeness)*

What does the Bible say about healing?

BIBLE READING: Matthew 4:23-25
KEY BIBLE VERSE: *Jesus traveled throughout Galilee teaching in the synagogues, preaching everywhere the Good News about the Kingdom. And he healed people who had every kind of sickness and disease.* (Matthew 4:23)

Healing is an important part of Christ's ministry. Jesus was teaching, preaching, and healing. These were the three main aspects of his ministry. *Teaching* shows Jesus' concern for understanding; *preaching* shows his concern for commitment; and *healing* shows his concern for wholeness. His miracles of healing authenticated his teaching and preaching, proving that he truly was from God.

Jesus healed both physical and spiritual sickness. Jesus preached the gospel— the Good News—to everyone who wanted to hear it. The gospel is that the kingdom of heaven has come, that God is with us, and that he cares for us. Christ can heal us, not just of physical sickness, but of spiritual sickness as well. There's no sin or problem too great or too small for him to handle. Jesus' words were good news because they offered freedom, hope, peace of heart, and eternal life with God.

BIBLE READING: Matthew 9:1-8
KEY BIBLE VERSE: *Some people brought to him a paralyzed man on a mat. Seeing their faith, Jesus said to the paralyzed man, "Take heart, son! Your sins are forgiven."* (Matthew 9:2)

Physical healing is not the most important gift God can give. Among the first words Jesus said to the paralyzed man were "Your sins are forgiven." Then he healed the man. We must be careful not to concentrate on God's power to heal physical sickness more than on his power to forgive spiritual sickness in the form of sin. Jesus saw that even more than physical health, this man needed spiritual health. Spiritual health comes only from Jesus' healing touch.

God understands every aspect of healing. Both the man's body and his spirit were paralyzed—he could not walk, and he did not know Jesus. But the man's spiritual state was Jesus' first concern. If God does not heal us or someone we love, we need to remember that physical healing is not Christ's only concern. We will all be completely healed in Christ's coming kingdom; but first we have to come to know Jesus.

BIBLE READING: Matthew 14:22-36
KEY BIBLE VERSE: *The news of their arrival spread quickly throughout the whole surrounding area, and soon people were bringing all their sick to be healed. The sick begged him to let them touch even the fringe of his robe, and all who touched it were healed.* (Matthew 14:35-36)

Focusing on physical needs can keep us from knowing Christ. The people recognized Jesus as a great healer, but how many understood who he truly was? They came to Jesus for physical healing, but did they come for spiritual healing? They came to prolong their lives on earth, but did they come to secure their eternal lives? People may seek Jesus to learn valuable lessons from his life or in hopes of finding relief from pain. But we miss Jesus' whole message if we seek him to heal our bodies but not our souls, or if we look to him for help only in this life, rather than for his eternal plan for us. Only when we understand the real Jesus Christ can we appreciate how he can truly change our life.

Related Topics: HEALTH, MIRACLES, SICKNESS

HEALTH *(Fitness, Wellness, Wholeness)*

How does the importance of physical health parallel the importance of spiritual health?

BIBLE READING: Leviticus 14:1-57

KEY BIBLE VERSE: *These are the instructions for dealing with the various kinds of contagious skin disease and infectious mildew, whether in clothing, in a house, in a swollen area of skin, in a skin rash, or in a shiny patch of skin. These instructions must be followed when dealing with any contagious skin disease or infectious mildew, to determine when something is ceremonially clean or unclean.* (Leviticus 14:54-57)

God's concern for us covers every part of living. God told the Israelites how to diagnose infectious skin diseases and mildew so they could avoid them or treat them. These laws were given for the people's health and protection. They helped the Israelites avoid diseases that were serious threats in that time and place. Although they wouldn't have understood the medical reasons for some of these laws, their obedience to them made them healthier. Many of God's laws must have seemed strange to the Israelites. His laws, however, helped them avoid not only physical contamination, but also moral and spiritual infection.

The Word of God still provides a pattern for physically, spiritually, and morally healthy living. We may not always understand the wisdom of God's laws, but if we obey them, we will thrive. Does this mean we are to follow the Old Testament health and dietary restrictions? In general, the basic principles of health and cleanliness are still healthful practices, but it would be legalistic, if not wrong, to adhere to each specific restriction today. Some of these regulations were intended to mark the Israelites as different from the wicked people around them. Others were given to prevent God's people from becoming involved in pagan religious practices, one of the most serious problems of the day. Still others related to quarantines in a culture where exact medical diagnosis was impossible. Today, for example, physicians can diagnose the different forms of leprosy, and they know which ones are contagious. Treatment methods have greatly improved, and quarantine for leprosy is rarely necessary.

BIBLE READING: Matthew 15:1-20

KEY BIBLE VERSE: *From the heart come evil thoughts, murder, adultery, all other sexual immorality, theft, lying, and slander. These are what defile you. Eating with unwashed hands could never defile you and make you unacceptable to God!* (Matthew 15:19-20)

Spiritual health is more important than physical health. We work hard to keep
our outward appearance attractive, but what is in our hearts is even more
important. The way we are deep down (where others can't see) matters much to
God. What are you like inside? When people become Christians, God makes
them different on the inside. He will continue the process of change inside
them if they only ask. God wants us to have healthy thoughts and motives, not
just healthy food and exercise.

Related Topics: BALANCE, MIRACLES, SICKNESS

HEART *(Desires, Emotions, Feelings)*

What does the Bible say concerning matters of the heart?

BIBLE READING: 1 Samuel 16:1-13
KEY BIBLE VERSE: *The LORD said to Samuel, "Don't judge by his appearance or
height, for I have rejected him. The LORD doesn't make decisions the way you
do! People judge by outward appearance, but the LORD looks at a person's
thoughts and intentions.* (1 Samuel 16:7)

God's primary concern is with the heart. Saul was tall and handsome; he was an
impressive-looking man. Samuel may have been trying to find someone who
looked like Saul to be Israel's next king, but God warned him against judging
by appearance alone. When people judge by outward appearance, they may
overlook quality individuals who lack the particular physical qualities society
currently admires. Appearance doesn't reveal what people are really like or their
true value.

Fortunately, God judges by faith and character, not appearances. And
because only God can see on the inside, only he can accurately judge people.
Most people spend hours each week maintaining their outward appearance;
they should do even more to develop their inner character. While everyone can
see your face, only you and God know what your heart really looks like. What
steps are you taking to improve your heart's attitude?

BIBLE READING: Psalm 51:1-19
KEY BIBLE VERSE: *Create in me a clean heart, O God. Renew a right spirit within
me.* (Psalm 51:10)

Our heart is unclean and in need of cleansing. Because we are born as sinners
(51:5), our natural inclination is to please ourselves rather than God. David
followed that inclination when he took another man's wife. We also follow
it when we sin in any way. Like David, we must ask God to cleanse us from
within (51:7), clearing our hearts and spirits for new thoughts and desires.
Right conduct can come only from a clean heart and spirit. Ask God to create a
pure heart and spirit in you.

BIBLE READING: 1 John 3:11-24
KEY BIBLE VERSE: *It is by our actions that we know we are living in the truth, so we
will be confident when we stand before the Lord, even if our hearts condemn us.
For God is greater than our hearts, and he knows everything.* (1 John 3:19-20)

Our heart needs to be subject to God's Word. Many are afraid that they don't
love others as they should. They feel guilty because they think they are not
doing enough to show proper love to Christ. Their consciences bother them.

John has these people in mind in this letter. How do we escape the gnawing accusations of our consciences? Not by ignoring them or rationalizing our behavior, but by setting our hearts on God's love. When we feel guilty, we should remind ourselves that God knows our motives as well as our actions. His voice of assurance is stronger than the accusing voice of our conscience. If we are in Christ, he will not condemn us (Romans 8:1; Hebrews 9:14-15). So if you are living for the Lord but feeling that you are not good enough, remind yourself that God is greater than your conscience.

A heart focused on God will experience great power in prayer. If your conscience is clear, you can come to God without fear, confident that your requests will be heard. John reaffirms Jesus' promise that whatever we ask for will be given to us (Matthew 7:7; see also Matthew 21:22; John 9:31; 15:7). You will receive if you obey and do what pleases him because you will then be asking in line with God's will. Of course this does not mean that you can have anything you want, like instant riches. If you are truly seeking God's will, there are some requests you will not make.

BIBLE READING: Romans 6:1-23

KEY BIBLE VERSE: *Thank God! Once you were slaves of sin, but now you have obeyed with all your heart the new teaching God has given you.* (Romans 6:17)

Our commitment to God should be wholehearted. To obey "with all your heart" means to give yourself fully to God, to love him "with all your heart, all your soul, and all your mind" (Matthew 22:37). And yet so often our efforts to know and obey God's commands can best be described as "halfhearted." How do you rate your heart's obedience? God wants to give you the power to obey him with all your heart.

Related Topics: COMMITMENT, HARD-HEARTEDNESS, OBEDIENCE

HEAVEN *(Eternal Life, Paradise, Reward)*

What does the Bible say about heaven?

BIBLE READING: Matthew 22:23-33

KEY BIBLE VERSE: *Jesus replied, "Your problem is that you don't know the Scriptures, and you don't know the power of God."* (Matthew 22:29)

Our ideas about heaven must be based on the Bible. The Sadducees asked Jesus what marriage would be like in heaven. Jesus said it was more important to understand God's power than know what heaven will be like. In every generation and culture, ideas of eternal life tend to be based on images and experiences of present life. Jesus answered that these faulty ideas are caused by ignorance of God's Word. We must not make up our own ideas about God, eternity, and heaven by thinking of them in human terms. We should concentrate more on our relationship with God than about what heaven will look like. Eventually we will find out, and it will be far beyond our greatest expectations.

BIBLE READING: John 14:1-14

KEY BIBLE VERSE: *There are many rooms in my Father's home, and I am going to prepare a place for you. If this were not so, I would tell you plainly. When everything is ready, I will come and get you, so that you will always be with me where I am.* (John 14:2-3)

Heaven is open to those who believe in Christ. Jesus' words show that the way to eternal life, though unseen, is secure—as secure as your trust in Jesus. He has already prepared the way to eternal life. The only issue that may still be unsettled is your willingness to believe.

Jesus is preparing places in heaven for his followers. There are few verses in Scripture that describe eternal life, but these few verses are rich with promises. Here Jesus says, "I am going to prepare a place for you," and "I will come and get you." We can look forward to eternal life because Jesus has promised it to all who believe in him. Although the details of eternity are unknown, we need not fear, because Jesus is preparing for us and will spend eternity with us.

BIBLE READING: Colossians 3:1-17
KEY BIBLE VERSE: *Let heaven fill your thoughts. Do not think only about things down here on earth.* (Colossians 3:2)

Heaven's priorities can be part of life here on earth. Letting heaven fill our thoughts means striving to put heaven's priorities into daily practice and concentrating on the eternal rather than the temporal. (See Philippians 4:8-9 and Colossians 3:15 for more on Christ's rule in our hearts and minds.)

Focusing on heavenly things puts earthly things in perspective. The Christian's real home is where Christ lives (John 14:2-3). This truth gives us a different perspective on our life here on earth. To "let heaven fill your thoughts" means to look at life from God's perspective and to seek what he desires. This is the antidote to materialism; we gain the proper perspective on material goods when we take God's view of them. The more we regard the world around us as God does, the more we will live in harmony with him. We must not become too attached to what is only temporary.

BIBLE READING: Revelation 4:1–5:14
KEY BIBLE VERSE: *As I looked, I saw a door standing open in heaven, and the same voice I had heard before spoke to me with the sound of a mighty trumpet blast. The voice said, "Come up here, and I will show you what must happen after these things."* (Revelation 4:1)

It isn't *what*, but *who* is in heaven that matters. Chapters 4 and 5 of Revelation record glimpses into Christ's glory. Here we see into the throne room of heaven. God is on the throne and orchestrating all the events that John records. The world is not spinning out of control; the God of creation will carry out his plans as Christ initiates the final battle with the forces of evil. John shows us heaven before showing us earth so that we will not be frightened by future events.

Related Topics: ETERNAL LIFE, HELL, KINGDOM OF GOD/KINGDOM OF HEAVEN

HELL *(Judgment, Punishment, Suffering)*

What does the Bible say about hell?

BIBLE READING: Matthew 25:41-46
KEY BIBLE VERSE: *The King will turn to those on the left and say, "Away with you, you cursed ones, into the eternal fire prepared for the Devil and his demons!"* (Matthew 25:41)

The Bible speaks about eternal punishment using different terms. Eternal punishment takes place in hell (the lake of fire, or Gehenna), the place of punishment after death for all those who refuse to repent. In the Bible, three words are used in connection with eternal punishment.

(1) *Sheol* or "the grave" is used in the Old Testament to mean the place of the dead, generally thought to be under the earth. (See Job 24:19; Psalm 16:10; Isaiah 38:10.)

(2) *Hades* is the Greek word for the underworld, the realm of the dead. It is the word used in the New Testament for Sheol. (See Matthew 16:18; Revelation 1:18; 20:13-14.)

(3) *Gehenna*, or hell, was named after the Valley of Hinnom near Jerusalem where children were sacrificed by fire to the pagan gods (see 2 Kings 23:10; 2 Chronicles 28:3). This is the place of eternal fire (Matthew 5:22; 10:28; Mark 9:43; Luke 12:5; James 3:6; Revelation 19:20) prepared for the devil, his angels, and all those who do not believe in God (25:46; Revelation 20:9-10). This is the final and eternal state of the wicked after the Resurrection and the Last Judgment.

When Jesus warns against unbelief, he is trying to save us from agonizing punishment.

BIBLE READING: Romans 1:18-32
KEY BIBLE VERSE: *God shows his anger from heaven against all sinful, wicked people who push the truth away from themselves.* (Romans 1:18)

The punishment of hell is just. In these verses, Paul answers a common objection: How could a loving God send anyone to hell, especially someone who has never heard about Christ? In fact, says Paul, God has revealed himself plainly in the creation to *all* people. And yet people reject even this basic knowledge of God. Also, everyone has an inner sense of what God requires, but they choose not to live up to it. Put another way, people's moral standards are always better than their behavior. If people suppress God's truth in order to live their own way, they have no excuse. They know the truth, and they will have to endure the consequences of ignoring it.

BIBLE READING: Revelation 20:1-15
KEY BIBLE VERSE: *Death and the grave were thrown into the lake of fire. This is the second death—the lake of fire.* (Revelation 20:14)

There are no second chances in hell. Death and hell are thrown into the lake of fire. God's judgment is finished. The lake of fire is the ultimate destination of everything wicked—Satan, the beast, the false prophet, the demons, death, hades, and all those whose names are not recorded in the book of life because they did not place their faith in Jesus Christ. John's vision does not permit any gray areas in God's judgment. If by faith we have not identified with Christ, confessing him as Lord, there will be no hope, no second chance, no other appeal.

Related Topics: HEAVEN, JUDGMENT, PUNISHMENT

HELP *(Assist, Rescue, Save)*

▶ **HOW GOD HELPS**
In what ways can we expect God to help us?

BIBLE READING: Genesis 18:1-15

KEY BIBLE VERSE: *Is anything too hard for the LORD? About a year from now, just as I told you, I will return, and Sarah will have a son.* (Genesis 18:14)

We can expect God's help in every area of life. "Is anything too hard for the Lord?" The obvious answer is, "Of course not!" This question reveals much about God. Make it a habit to insert your specific needs into the question. "Is this day in my life too hard for the Lord?" "Is this habit I'm trying to break too hard for him?" "Is the communication problem I'm having too hard for him?" Asking the question this way reminds you that God is personally involved in your life and nudges you to ask for his power to help you.

BIBLE READING: Ezekiel 3:16-27

KEY BIBLE VERSE: *The LORD took hold of me, and he said to me, "Go out into the valley, and I will talk to you there."* (Ezekiel 3:22)

We can expect God's help in recognizing our need of him. Ezekiel recognized his helplessness before God and fell facedown in his presence. Sometimes our prosperity, popularity, or physical strength blinds us to our spiritual helplessness. But nothing we do on our own can accomplish much for God. Only when God is in control of our wills can we accomplish great tasks for him. The first step to being God's person is to admit that you need his help; then you can begin to see what God can really do in your life.

BIBLE READING: Psalm 46:1-11

KEY BIBLE VERSE: *God is our refuge and strength, always ready to help in times of trouble.* (Psalm 46:1)

We can expect God's help in times of trouble. The fear of mountains or cities suddenly crumbling into the sea as the result of a nuclear blast haunts many people today. But the psalmist says that even if the world ends, we need not fear. In the face of utter destruction, the writer expressed a quiet confidence in God's ability to save him. It seems impossible to consider the end of the world without becoming consumed by fear, but the Bible is clear—God is our refuge even in the face of total destruction. He is not merely a temporary retreat; he is our eternal refuge and can provide strength in any circumstances.

BIBLE READING: Matthew 1:18-25

KEY BIBLE VERSE: *This is how Jesus the Messiah was born. His mother, Mary, was engaged to be married to Joseph. But while she was still a virgin, she became pregnant by the Holy Spirit.* (Matthew 1:18)

God's help comes to us through Jesus Christ. Why is the Virgin Birth important to the Christian faith? Jesus Christ, God's Son, had to be free from the sinful nature passed on to all other human beings by Adam. Because Jesus was born of a woman, he was a human being; but as the Son of God, Jesus was born without any trace of human sin. Jesus is both fully human and fully divine.

Because Jesus lived as a man, we know that he fully understands our experiences and struggles (Hebrews 4:15-16). Because he is God, he has the power and authority to deliver us from sin (Colossians 2:13-15). We can tell Jesus all our thoughts, feelings, and needs. He has been where we are now, and he has the ability to help.

▶ **HOW PEOPLE HELP**
Why should we help each other?

BIBLE READING: Nehemiah 2:1-10

KEY BIBLE VERSE: *The king asked, "Well, how can I help you?"* (Nehemiah 2:4)

We need each other. After his prayer, Nehemiah asked the king for permission to go to Judah. As soon as he got a positive answer, he began asking for additional help. Sometimes when we have needs, we hesitate to ask the right people for help because we are afraid to approach them. Not Nehemiah! He went directly to the person who could help him the most. Don't be reluctant to ask those who are most able to help. They may be more interested and approachable than you think. God's answers to prayer may come as a result of our asking others.

BIBLE READING: Mark 9:38-41

KEY BIBLE VERSE: *John said to Jesus, "Teacher, we saw a man using your name to cast out demons, but we told him to stop because he isn't one of our group."* (Mark 9:38)

Meeting human needs is an opportunity to serve God. The disciples were jealous of a man who healed in Jesus' name because they were more concerned about their own group's position than in helping to free those troubled by demons. We do the same today when we refuse to participate in worthy causes because (1) other people or groups are not affiliated with our denomination, (2) these projects do not involve the kind of people with whom we feel most comfortable, (3) others don't do things the way we are used to doing things, or (4) our efforts won't receive enough recognition. Correct theology is important but should never be an excuse to avoid helping people in need.

BIBLE READING: Galatians 6:1-10

KEY BIBLE VERSE: *Share each other's troubles and problems, and in this way obey the law of Christ.* (Galatians 6:2)

Helping one another is an important part of Christian living. No Christian should ever think that he or she is totally independent and doesn't need help from others, and no one should feel excused from the task of helping others. The body of Christ—the church—functions only when the members work together for the common good. Do you know someone who needs help? Is there a Christian brother or sister who needs correction or encouragement? Humbly and gently reach out to that person (John 13:34-35).

Related Topics: BELIEVERS, HOLY SPIRIT, SALVATION

HERESY *(Errors, Lies, Mistakes)*

How do heresies get started?

BIBLE READING: Colossians 2:1-23

KEY BIBLE VERSE: *Just as you accepted Christ Jesus as your Lord, you must continue to live in obedience to him. Let your roots grow down into him and draw up nourishment from him, so you will grow in faith, strong and vigorous in the truth you were taught. Let your lives overflow with thanksgiving for all he has done.* (Colossians 2:6-7)

Heresies grow where knowledge of God's Word is weak. The problem that Paul was combating in the Colossian church was similar to *Gnosticism* from the Greek word for *knowledge*. This *heresy*, a teaching contrary to biblical doctrine, undermined Christianity in several basic ways: (1) It insisted that important secret knowledge was hidden from most believers; Paul, however, said that Christ provides all the knowledge we need. (2) It taught that the body was evil; Paul countered that God himself lived in a body—that is, he was embodied in Jesus Christ. (3) It contended that Christ only seemed to be human, but was not; Paul insisted that Jesus is fully human and fully God.

Gnosticism became fashionable in the second century. Even in Paul's day, these ideas sounded attractive to many, and exposure to such teachings could easily seduce a church that didn't know Christian doctrine well. Similar teachings still pose significant problems for many in the church today. We combat heresy by becoming thoroughly acquainted with God's Word through personal study and sound Bible teaching.

Heresies rely on human insight and wisdom rather than God's Word. Paul writes against any philosophy of life based only on human ideas and experiences. Paul himself was a gifted philosopher, so he is not condemning philosophy. He is condemning teaching that credits humanity, not Christ, with being the answer to life's problems. That approach becomes a false religion. There are many man-made approaches to life's problems that totally disregard God. To resist heresy you must use your mind, keep your eyes on Christ, and study God's Word.

Heresies are attempts to reach God by human means. We cannot reach up to God by following rules of self-denial, by observing rituals, or by practicing religion. Paul isn't saying all rules are bad. But no keeping of laws or rules will earn salvation. The Good News is that God reaches down to human beings, and he asks for our response. Man-made religions focus on human effort; Christianity focuses on Christ's work. Believers must put aside sinful desires, but doing so is the by-product of our new life in Christ, not the reason for our new life. Our salvation does not depend on our own discipline and rule-keeping, but on the power of Christ's death and resurrection.

Heresies can be discovered through asking probing questions. We can guard against man-made religions by asking these questions about any religious group: (1) Does it stress man-made rules and taboos rather than God's grace? (2) Does it foster a critical spirit toward others, or does it exercise discipline discreetly and lovingly? (3) Does it stress formulas, secret knowledge, or special visions more than the Word of God? (4) Does it elevate self-righteousness, honoring those who keep the rules, rather than elevating Christ? (5) Does it neglect Christ's universal church, claiming to be an elite group? (6) Does it teach humiliation of the body as a means to spiritual growth rather than focusing on the growth of the whole person? (7) Does it disregard the family rather than holding it in high regard as the Bible does?

Related Topics: BIBLE, TEACHING, TRUTH

HERITAGE *(Ancestors, Background, Family)*

What is valuable about our heritage?

BIBLE READING: Isaiah 38:1-22

KEY BIBLE VERSE: *Only the living can praise you as I do today. Each generation can make known your faithfulness to the next.* (Isaiah 38:19)

Our spiritual heritage is important to pass on. Hezekiah spoke of the significance of passing the joy of the Lord from father to child, from generation to generation. The heritage of our faith has come to us because of faithful men and women who have carried God's message to us across the centuries. Do you share with your children or other young people the excitement of your relationship with God?

BIBLE READING: Luke 19:1-10
KEY BIBLE VERSE: *Jesus responded, "Salvation has come to this home today, for this man has shown himself to be a son of Abraham. And I, the Son of Man, have come to seek and save those like him who are lost." (Luke 19:9-10)*

A good heritage is no substitute for a personal response to God. When Jesus said Zacchaeus was a son of Abraham and yet was lost, he must have shocked his hearers in at least two ways. They would not have liked to acknowledge that this unpopular tax collector was a fellow son of Abraham, and they would not have wished to admit that sons of Abraham could be lost. But a person is not saved by a good heritage or condemned by a bad one; faith is more important than genealogy. Jesus still loves to bring the lost into his kingdom, no matter what their background or previous way of life. Through faith, the lost can be forgiven and made new.

BIBLE READING: Hebrews 11:1–12:3
KEY BIBLE VERSE: *Since we are surrounded by such a huge crowd of witnesses to the life of faith, let us strip off every weight that slows us down, especially the sin that so easily hinders our progress. And let us run with endurance the race that God has set before us.* (Hebrews 12:1)

Believers in Christ have a powerful heritage of faith. This "huge cloud of witnesses" is composed of the people described in chapter 11. Their faithfulness is a constant encouragement to us. We do not struggle alone, and we are not the first to struggle with the problems we face. Others have run the race and won, and their witness stirs us to run and win also. What an inspiring heritage we have!

A Christian heritage focuses on Jesus Christ. The Christian life involves hard work. It requires us to give up whatever endangers our relationship with God, to run patiently, and to struggle against sin with the power of the Holy Spirit. To live effectively, we must keep our eyes on Jesus. We will stumble if we look away from him to stare at ourself or at the circumstances surrounding us. We should be running for Christ, not ourself, and we must always keep him in sight.

Related Topics: FAMILY, HISTORY, SPIRITUAL GROWTH

HEROES *(Examples, Idols, Models)*

What are the characteristics of real heroes?

BIBLE READING: Judges 21:1-25
KEY BIBLE VERSE: *In those days Israel had no king, so the people did whatever seemed right in their own eyes.* (Judges 21:25)

Real heroes submit to God's authority. During the time of the judges, the people of Israel experienced trouble because everyone became his own authority and acted on his own opinions of right and wrong. This produced horrendous results. Our world is similar. Individuals, groups, and societies have made themselves the final authorities without reference to God. When people selfishly satisfy their personal desires at all costs, everyone pays the price.

Real heroes are models in every area of life. It is the ultimate heroic act to submit all our plans, desires, and motives to God. Men like Gideon, Jephthah, and Samson are known for their heroism in battle. But their personal lives were far from heroic.

Real heroes maintain consistency throughout life. To be truly heroic, we must go into battle each day in our home, job, church, and society to make God's kingdom a reality. Our weapons are the standards, morals, truths, and convictions we receive from God's Word. We will lose the battle if we gather the spoils of earthly treasures rather than seeking the treasures of heaven.

BIBLE READING: Psalm 101:1-8
KEY BIBLE VERSE: *I will keep a protective eye on the godly, so they may dwell with me in safety. Only those who are above reproach will be allowed to serve me.* (Psalm 101:6)

Godly heroes avoid all forms of wickedness. David may have written this psalm early in his reign as king as he set down the standards he wanted to follow. David knew that to lead a blameless life he would need God's help (101:2). We can lead blameless lives if we avoid (1) looking at wickedness ("I will refuse to look at anything vile and vulgar," 101:3), (2) perverse ideas (101:4), (3) slander (101:5), and (4) pride (101:5). While avoiding the wrongs listed above, we must also let God's Word show us the standards by which to live.

Godly heroes are the best ones to have. David said that he would keep his eyes "on the godly." In other words, he would choose as models and as friends those who are truthful and who love God. Our friends and associates can have a profound influence on our life. Make sure to keep your eyes on those who are faithful to God and his Word.

BIBLE READING: Acts 28:1-31
KEY BIBLE VERSE: *For the next two years, Paul lived in his own rented house. He welcomed all who visited him, proclaiming the Kingdom of God with all boldness and teaching about the Lord Jesus Christ. And no one tried to stop him.* (Acts 28:30-31)

God does his greatest work through unsung heroes. The book of Acts deals with the history of the Christian church and its expansion in ever-widening circles touching Jerusalem, Antioch, Ephesus, and Rome—the most influential cities in the Western world. Acts also shows the mighty miracles and testimonies of the heroes and martyrs of the early church—Peter, Stephen, James, and Paul. All the ministry was prompted and held together by the Holy Spirit working in the lives of ordinary people—merchants, travelers, slaves, jailers, church leaders, males, females, Gentiles, Jews, rich, poor. Many unsung heroes of the faith continued the work, through the Holy Spirit, in succeeding generations, changing the world with a changeless message—that Jesus Christ is Savior and Lord for all who call on him. Today we can be the unsung heroes in the continuing story of the spread of the gospel. It is that same message that we Christians are to take to our world so that many more may hear and believe.

Related Topics: EXAMPLE, FOLLOW, TEACHING

HESITATION (*see* OBEDIENCE)

HIDING (*Avoiding, Fearing, Leaving*)

What causes people to try to hide from God?

BIBLE READING: Exodus 3:1-22

KEY BIBLE VERSE: *"Now go, for I am sending you to Pharaoh. You will lead my people, the Israelites, out of Egypt." "But who am I to appear before Pharaoh?" Moses asked God. "How can you expect me to lead the Israelites out of Egypt?"* (Exodus 3:10-11)

Our inadequacies lead us to hide from God. Moses made excuses because he felt inadequate for the job God asked him to do. It was natural for him to feel that way. He *was* inadequate all by himself. But God wasn't asking Moses to work alone. He offered other resources to help (God himself, Aaron, and the ability to do miracles). God often calls us to tasks that seem too difficult, but he doesn't ask us to do them alone. God offers us his resources, just as he did to Moses. We should not hide behind our inadequacies, as Moses did, but look beyond ourself to the great resources available. Then we can allow God to use our unique contributions.

BIBLE READING: 1 Samuel 10:1-27

KEY BIBLE VERSE: *They asked the LORD, "Where is he?" And the LORD replied, "He is hiding among the baggage."* (1 Samuel 10:22)

Our fears of failure lead us to hide from God. When the Israelites assembled to choose a king, Saul already knew he was the one (10:1). Instead of coming forward, however, he hid among the baggage. Often we hide from important responsibilities because we are afraid of failure, afraid of what others will think, or perhaps unsure about how to proceed. Prepare now to step up to your future responsibilities. Count on God's provision rather than your feelings of adequacy.

Related Topics: FEAR, GOD, RESPONSIBILITY

HISTORY (*Facts, Past, Records*)

What can we learn from history?

BIBLE READING: Deuteronomy 26:1-19

KEY BIBLE VERSE: *You must then say in the presence of the LORD your God, "My ancestor Jacob was a wandering Aramean who went to live in Egypt. His family was few in number, but in Egypt they became a mighty and numerous nation."* (Deuteronomy 26:5)

Our personal history can teach us about how God works. This recitation of God's dealings with his people helped the people remember what God had done for them. What is the history of your relationship with God? Can you put into clear and concise words what God has done for you? Find a friend with whom you can share your spiritual journey. Telling your stories to each other will help you clearly understand your personal spiritual history, as well as encouraging and inspiring you both.

BIBLE READING: Mark 1:1-8

KEY BIBLE VERSE: *In the book of the prophet Isaiah, God said, "Look, I am sending my messenger before you, and he will prepare your way." (Mark 1:2)*

History demonstrates our need for a Savior. Isaiah was one of the greatest prophets of the Old Testament. The second half of the book of Isaiah is devoted to the promise of salvation. Isaiah wrote about the coming of the Messiah, Jesus Christ, and the man who would announce his coming, John the Baptist. John called people to give up their selfish way of living, renounce their sins, seek God's forgiveness, and establish a relationship with the almighty God by believing and obeying his words as found in the Bible (Isaiah 1:18-20; 57:15).

History teaches us God's control over the world's events. Hundreds of years earlier, the prophet Isaiah had predicted that John the Baptist and Jesus would come. How did he know? God promised Isaiah that a Redeemer would come to Israel, and that a messenger calling in the desert would prepare the way for him. Isaiah's words comforted many people as they looked forward to the Messiah, and knowing that God keeps his promises can comfort you too. As you read the book of Mark, realize that it is more than just a story; it is part of God's Word. In it God is revealing to you his plans for human history.

BIBLE READING: Romans 5:1-11

KEY BIBLE VERSE: *When we were utterly helpless, Christ came at just the right time and died for us sinners. (Romans 5:6)*

History demonstrates the perfection of God's plan. We were weak and helpless because we could do nothing on our own to save ourself. Someone had to come and rescue us. Not only did Christ come at a good time in history, but he came at exactly the right time—according to God's own schedule. God controls all history, and he controlled the timing, methods, and results of Jesus' death.

Related Topics: BIBLE, GOD, JESUS

HOLINESS *(Godliness, Maturity, Spirituality)*

▶ GOD'S HOLINESS
What does the Bible say about God's holiness?

BIBLE READING: 1 Peter 1:14-25

KEY BIBLE VERSE: *Now you must be holy in everything you do, just as God—who chose you to be his children—is holy. (1 Peter 1:15)*

God's holiness is beyond comparison. The God of Israel and of the Christian church is holy—he sets the standard for morality. Unlike the Roman gods, he is not warlike, adulterous, or spiteful. Unlike the gods of the pagan cults popular in the first century, he is not bloodthirsty or promiscuous. He is a God of mercy and justice who cares personally for each of his followers. Our holy God expects us to imitate him by following his high moral standards. Like him, we should be both merciful and just; like him, we should sacrifice ourself for others.

God's holiness is our standard for holy living. After people commit their lives to Christ, they usually still feel a pull back to their old ways. Peter tells us to be like our heavenly Father—holy in everything we do. Holiness means being totally devoted or dedicated to God, set aside for his special use, and set apart from sin and its influence. We're to be set apart and different, not blending in with the crowd, yet not being different just for the sake of being different. What makes us different is having God's qualities in our life. Our focus and priorities must be his. All this is in direct contrast to our old ways (1:14). We cannot become holy on our own, but God gives us his Holy Spirit to help us obey and to give us power to overcome sin. Don't use the excuse that you can't help slipping into sin. Call on God's power to free you from sin's grip.

BIBLE READING: Psalm 93:1-5
KEY BIBLE VERSE: *Your royal decrees cannot be changed. The nature of your reign, O LORD, is holiness forever.* (Psalm 93:5)

God cannot be known apart from his holiness. The key to God's eternal reign is his holiness. God's glory is not only his strength but also his perfect moral character. God will never do anything that is not morally perfect. This reassures us that we can trust him, yet it places a demand on us. Our desire to be holy (dedicated to God and morally clean) is our only suitable response. We must never use unholy means to reach a holy goal, because God says, "You must be holy because I, the Lord your God, am holy" (Leviticus 19:2).

BIBLE READING: Isaiah 59:1-21
KEY BIBLE VERSE: *There is a problem—your sins have cut you off from God. Because of your sin, he has turned away and will not listen anymore.* (Isaiah 59:2)

God's holiness cannot tolerate sin. Sin offends our holy God and separates us from him. Because God is holy, he cannot ignore, excuse, or tolerate sin as though it didn't matter. Sin cuts people off from him, forming a wall to isolate God from the people he loves. No wonder this long list of wretched sins makes God angry and forces him to look the other way. People who die with their life of sin unforgiven separate themselves eternally from God. God wants them to live with him forever, but he cannot take them into his holy presence unless their sin is removed. Have you confessed your sin to God, allowing him to remove it? The Lord can save you if you turn to him.

BIBLE READING: Revelation 4:1-11
KEY BIBLE VERSE: *Each of these living beings had six wings, and their wings were covered with eyes, inside and out. Day after day and night after night they keep on saying, "Holy, holy, holy is the Lord God Almighty—the one who always was, who is, and who is still to come."* (Revelation 4:8)

God's holiness will eventually be recognized by all creation. Just as the Holy Spirit is seen symbolically in the seven lighted lamps, so the "living beings" represent the attributes (the qualities and character) of God. These creatures were not real animals. Like the cherubim (the highest order of the angels), they guard God's throne, lead others in worship, and proclaim God's holiness. God's attributes symbolized in the animal-like appearance of these four creatures are majesty and power (the lion), faithfulness (the ox), intelligence (the man), and sovereignty (the eagle). The Old Testament prophet Ezekiel saw four similar creatures in one of his visions (Ezekiel 1:5-10).

The point of this chapter is summed up in this verse: All creatures in heaven and earth will praise and honor God because he is the Creator and Sustainer of everything.

▶ **HUMAN HOLINESS**
How can we be holy?

BIBLE READING: Exodus 19:1-25

KEY BIBLE VERSE: *Now if you will obey me and keep my covenant, you will be my own special treasure from among all the nations of the earth; for all the earth belongs to me. And you will be to me a kingdom of priests, my holy nation.* (Exodus 19:5-6)

Holiness is a gift of God's grace. Why did God choose Israel as his nation? God knew that no nation on earth was good enough to deserve to be called his people, his "own little flock." He chose Israel, not because of anything they had done, but in his love and mercy he chose Israel in spite of the wrong the nation had done and would do. Why did he want to have a special nation on earth? To represent his way of life, to teach his Word, and to be an agent of salvation to the world. "All the nations of the earth" would be blessed through Abraham's descendants (Genesis 18:18). Gentiles and kings would come to the Lord through Israel, predicted Isaiah (Isaiah 60:3). Through the nation of Israel, the Messiah, God's chosen Son, would be born. God chose one nation and put it through a rigorous training program, so that one day it could be a channel for his blessings to the whole world.

Holiness requires covenant faithfulness. In Genesis 15 and 17, God made a covenant with Abraham, promising to make his descendants into a great nation. Now that promise was being realized as God restated his agreement with the Israelite nation, the descendants of Abraham. God promised to bless and care for them. The people promised to obey him. The covenant was thus sealed. But the good intentions of the people quickly wore off. Have you made a commitment to God? How are you holding up your end of the bargain?

BIBLE READING: Isaiah 4:1-6

KEY BIBLE VERSE: *All those whose names are written down, who have survived the destruction of Jerusalem, will be a holy people.* (Isaiah 4:3)

Holiness comes from wholehearted obedience to God. The "branch of the Lord" probably refers to the Messiah, although some believe it refers to Judah. The point is that during the distress predicted by Isaiah, some people will be protected by God's loving grace. Those protected will be set apart to God when the Messiah rules the earth (Jeremiah 23:5-6; Zechariah 6:12-13). Their distinctive mark will be their holiness, not wealth or prestige. This holiness comes from a sincere desire to obey God and from wholehearted devotion to him. Evil will not always continue as it does now. God will put an end to all evil, and his faithful followers will share in his glorious reign.

BIBLE READING: John 17:1-26

KEY BIBLE VERSE: *Make them pure and holy by teaching them your words of truth.* (John 17:17)

Holiness grows in response to God's Word. A follower of Christ becomes sanctified (set apart for sacred use, cleansed, and made holy) through believing and obeying the Word of God (Hebrews 4:12). He or she has already accepted forgiveness through Christ's sacrificial death (Hebrews 7:26-27). But daily application of God's Word has a purifying effect on our minds and hearts. Scripture points out sin, motivates us to confess our sins, renews our relationship with Christ, and guides us back to the right path.

We are to be holy in the midst of an evil world. Jesus didn't ask God to take believers *out* of the world but instead to use them *in* the world. Because Jesus sends us into the world, we should not try to escape from the world, nor should we avoid all relationships with non-Christians. We are called to be salt and light (Matthew 5:13-16), and we are to do the work that God sent us to do.

Jesus prayed for all who would follow him, including you and others you know. He prayed for unity (17:11), protection from the evil one (17:15), and sanctity (holiness) (17:17). Knowing that Jesus prayed for us should give us confidence as we work for his kingdom.

Related Topics: OBEDIENCE, RIGHTEOUSNESS, SIN

HOLY SPIRIT *(Comforter, Giver, God)*

▶ **THE IDENTITY OF THE HOLY SPIRIT**
Who is the Holy Spirit?

BIBLE READING: Mark 1:9-13
KEY BIBLE VERSE: *And when Jesus came up out of the water, he saw the heavens split open and the Holy Spirit descending like a dove on him. And a voice came from heaven saying, "You are my beloved Son, and I am fully pleased with you."* (Mark 1:10-11)

The Holy Spirit is a member of the Trinity. As Jesus was baptized, a revelation of God was given. The Spirit descended like a dove on Jesus, and the voice from heaven proclaimed the Father's approval of Jesus as his divine Son. That Jesus is God's divine Son is the foundation for all we read about Jesus in the Gospels. Here we see all three members of the Trinity together—God the Father, God the Son, and God the Holy Spirit.

BIBLE READING: Matthew 18:15-20
KEY BIBLE VERSE: *I also tell you this: If two of you agree down here on earth concerning anything you ask, my Father in heaven will do it for you. For where two or three gather together because they are mine, I am there among them.* (Matthew 18:19-20)

The Holy Spirit is God living in and among those who believe. Jesus looked ahead to a new day when he would be present with his followers not in body, but through his Holy Spirit. In the body of believers (the church), the sincere agreement of two people is more powerful than the superficial agreement of thousands, because Christ's Holy Spirit is with them. Two or more believers, filled with the Holy Spirit, will pray according to God's will, not their own; thus their requests will be granted.

BIBLE READING: John 3:1-21
KEY BIBLE VERSE: *The truth is, no one can enter the Kingdom of God without being born of water and the Spirit. Humans can reproduce only human life, but the Holy Spirit gives new life from heaven. So don't be surprised at my statement that you must be born again.* (John 3:5-7)

The Holy Spirit is God at work in believers. Who is the Holy Spirit? God is three persons in one—the Father, the Son, and the Holy Spirit. God became a man in Jesus so that Jesus could die for our sins. Jesus rose from the dead to offer salvation to all people through spiritual renewal and rebirth. When Jesus ascended into heaven, his physical presence left the earth, but he promised to send the Holy Spirit so that his spiritual presence would still be among mankind (see Luke 24:49). The Holy Spirit first became available to all believers at

Pentecost (Acts 2). Whereas in Old Testament days the Holy Spirit empowered specific individuals for specific purposes, now all believers have the power of the Holy Spirit available to them. (For more on the Holy Spirit, read John 14:16-28; Romans 8:9; 1 Corinthians 12:13; and 2 Corinthians 1:22.)

▶ THE WORK OF THE HOLY SPIRIT
What does the Holy Spirit do?

BIBLE READING: Judges 3:7-11
KEY BIBLE VERSE: *The Spirit of the LORD came upon him, and he became Israel's judge. He went to war against King Cushan-rishathaim of Aram, and the LORD gave Othniel victory over him.* (Judges 3:10)

The Holy Spirit empowers believers. This phrase, "The Spirit of the Lord came upon him," was also spoken of the judges Gideon, Jephthah, and Samson, among others. It expresses a temporary and spontaneous increase of physical, spiritual, or mental strength. This was an extraordinary and supernatural occurrence to prepare a person for a special task. The Holy Spirit is available to all believers today, but he will come upon believers in an extraordinary way for special tasks. We should ask the Holy Spirit's help as we face our daily problems as well as life's major challenges.

BIBLE READING: Matthew 10:16-42
KEY BIBLE VERSE: *When you are arrested, don't worry about what to say in your defense, because you will be given the right words at the right time. For it won't be you doing the talking—it will be the Spirit of your Father speaking through you.* (Matthew 10:19-20)

The Holy Spirit is present in times of hardship. Jesus told the disciples that when arrested for preaching the gospel, they should not worry about what to say in their defense—God's Spirit would speak through them. This promise was fulfilled in Acts 4:8-14 and elsewhere. Some mistakenly think this means we don't have to prepare to present the gospel because God will take care of everything. Scripture teaches, however, that we are to make carefully prepared, thoughtful statements (Colossians 4:6). Jesus is not telling us to stop preparing, but to stop worrying.

BIBLE READING: John 4:1-26
KEY BIBLE VERSE: *The time is coming and is already here when true worshipers will worship the Father in spirit and in truth. The Father is looking for anyone who will worship him that way. For God is Spirit, so those who worship him must worship in spirit and in truth.* (John 4:23-24)

The Holy Spirit helps us worship God. "God is spirit" means he is not a physical being limited to one place. He is present everywhere, and he can be worshiped anywhere, at any time. It is not where we worship that counts, but how we worship. Is your worship genuine and true? Do you have the Holy Spirit's help? How does the Holy Spirit help us worship? The Holy Spirit prays for us (Romans 8:26), teaches us the words of Christ (14:26), and tells us we are loved (Romans 5:5).

BIBLE READING: John 14:15-31
KEY BIBLE VERSE: *If you love me, obey my commandments. And I will ask the Father, and he will give you another Counselor, who will never leave you. He is the Holy Spirit, who leads into all truth. The world at large cannot receive him, because it isn't looking for him and doesn't recognize him. But you do, because he lives with you now and later will be in you.* (John 14:15-17)

The Holy Spirit transforms us from within. Jesus was soon going to leave the disciples, but he would remain with them. How could this be? The Counselor—the Spirit of God himself—would come after Jesus was gone to care for and guide the disciples. The regenerating power of the Spirit came on the disciples just before his ascension (20:22), and the Spirit was poured out on all the believers at Pentecost (Acts 2), shortly after Jesus ascended to heaven. The Holy Spirit is the very presence of God within us and all believers, helping us live as God wants and building Christ's church on earth. By faith we can appropriate the Spirit's power each day.

The Holy Spirit works in every part of our life. The following chapters teach these truths about the Holy Spirit: he will be with us forever (14:16); the world at large cannot accept him (14:17); he lives with us and in us (14:17); he teaches us (14:26); he reminds us of Jesus' words (14:26; 15:26); he convicts us of sin, shows us God's righteousness, and announces God's judgment on evil (16:8); he guides into truth and gives insight into future events (16:13); he brings glory to Christ (16:14). The Holy Spirit has been active among people from the beginning of time, but after Pentecost (Acts 2) he came to live in all believers. Many people are unaware of the Holy Spirit's activities, but to those who hear Christ's words and understand the Spirit's power, the Spirit gives a whole new way to look at life.

The Holy Spirit helps us understand and remember the Bible. Jesus promised the disciples that the Holy Spirit would help them remember what he had been teaching them. This promise ensures the validity of the New Testament. The disciples were eyewitnesses of Jesus' life and teachings, and the Holy Spirit helped them remember without taking away their individual perspectives. We can be confident that the Gospels are accurate records of what Jesus taught and did (see 1 Corinthians 2:10-14). The Holy Spirit can help us in the same way. As we study the Bible, we can trust him to plant truth in our mind, convince us of God's will, and remind us when we stray from it.

The Holy Spirit gives us peace. The end result of the Holy Spirit's work in our life is deep and lasting peace. Unlike worldly peace, which is usually defined as the absence of conflict, this peace is confident assurance in any circumstance; with Christ's peace, we have no need to fear the present or the future. If your life is full of stress, allow the Holy Spirit to fill you with Christ's peace (see Philippians 4:6-7 for more on experiencing God's peace).

Related Topics: GOD, POWER, SPIRITUAL GIFTS

HOME *(Family, Land, Shelter)*

What is God's plan for the home?

BIBLE READING: Deuteronomy 6:1-25

KEY BIBLE VERSE: *You must commit yourselves wholeheartedly to these commands I am giving you today. Repeat them again and again to your children. Talk about them when you are at home and when you are away on a journey, when you are lying down and when you are getting up again.* (Deuteronomy 6:6-7)

Home is a place to learn about God. This passage provides the central theme of Deuteronomy. It sets a pattern that helps us relate the Word of God to our daily lives. We are to love God, think constantly about his commandments, teach his commandments to our children, and live each day by the guidelines in his Word. God emphasized the importance of parents teaching the Bible to their children. The church and Christian schools cannot be used to escape from this responsibility. The Bible provides so many opportunities for object lessons and practical teaching that it would be a shame to study it only one day a week. Eternal truths are most effectively learned in the loving environment of a God-fearing home.

BIBLE READING: 1 Samuel 3:1–4:1

KEY BIBLE VERSE: *I have warned him continually that judgment is coming for his family, because his sons are blaspheming God and he hasn't disciplined them. So I have vowed that the sins of Eli and his sons will never be forgiven by sacrifices or offerings.* (1 Samuel 3:13-14)

Serving God does not exempt people from responsibilities at home. Eli had spent his entire life in service to God. His responsibility was to oversee all the worship in Israel. But in pursuing this great mission he neglected the responsibilities in his own home. Don't let your desire to do God's work cause you to neglect your family. If you do, your mission may degenerate into a quest for personal importance, and your family will suffer the consequences of your neglect.

BIBLE READING: Ephesians 6:1-4

KEY BIBLE VERSE: *Now a word to you fathers. Don't make your children angry by the way you treat them. Rather, bring them up with the discipline and instruction approved by the Lord.* (Ephesians 6:4)

Home is a place of mutual service and respect. If our faith in Christ is real, it will usually prove itself at home, in our relationships with those who know us best. Children and parents have a responsibility to each other. Children should honor their parents even if the parents are demanding and unfair. Parents should care gently for their children, even if the children are disobedient and unpleasant. Ideally, of course, Christian parents and Christian children will relate to each other with thoughtfulness and love. This will happen if both parents and children put the others' interests above their own—that is, if they submit to one another.

BIBLE READING: Acts 5:17-42

KEY BIBLE VERSE: *Every day, in the Temple and in their homes, they continued to teach and preach this message: "The Messiah you are looking for is Jesus."* (Acts 5:42)

Home is one place the church can gather together. Home Bible studies are not new. As the believers needed to grow in their new faith, home Bible studies met their needs, as well as serving as a means to introduce new people to the Christian faith. During later times of persecution, meeting in homes became the primary method of passing on Bible knowledge. Christians throughout the world still use this approach when under persecution and as a way to build up believers. Meeting in homes is a good reminder to believers that the church is not a building, but people.

Related Topics: DISCIPLINE, FAMILY, HOSPITALITY

HOMOSEXUALITY *(Alternative Lifestyle, Gay, Lesbian)*

What does the Bible teach about homosexuality?

BIBLE READING: Romans 1:18-32

KEY BIBLE VERSE: *That is why God abandoned them to their shameful desires. Even the women turned against the natural way to have sex and instead indulged in sex with each other. And the men, instead of having normal sexual relationships with women, burned with lust for each other. Men did shameful things with other men and, as a result, suffered within themselves the penalty they so richly deserved.* (Romans 1:26-27)

The Bible condemns homosexual behavior. God's plan for natural sexual relationships is his ideal for his creation. Unfortunately, sin distorts the natural use of God's gifts. Sin often means not only denying God, but also denying the way we are made. When people say that any sex act is acceptable as long as nobody gets hurt, they are fooling themselves. In the long run (and often in the short run), sin hurts people—individuals, families, whole societies. How sad it is that people who worship the things God made instead of the Creator so often distort and destroy the very things they claim to value!

Alongside God's condemnation of sin is his offer of forgiveness. Homosexuality (to exchange or abandon natural relations of sex) was as widespread in Paul's day as it is in ours. Many pagan practices encouraged it. God is willing to receive anyone who comes to him in faith, and Christians should love and accept others no matter what their background. Yet, homosexuality is strictly forbidden in Scripture (Leviticus 18:22). Homosexuality is considered an acceptable practice by many in our world today—even by some churches. But society does not set the standard for God's law. Many homosexuals believe that their desires are normal and that they have a right to express them. But God does not obligate nor encourage us to fulfill all our desires (even normal ones). Those desires that violate his laws must be controlled.

Temptation can be overcome by God's grace. If you have these desires, you can and must resist acting upon them. Consciously avoid places or activities you know will kindle temptations of this kind. Don't underestimate the power of Satan to tempt you nor the potential for serious harm if you yield to these temptations. Remember, God can and will forgive sexual sins just as he forgives other sins. Surrender yourself to the grace and mercy of God, asking him to show you the way out of sin and into the light of his freedom and his love. Prayer, Bible study, and strong support in a Christian church can help you to gain strength to resist these powerful temptations. If you are already deeply involved in homosexual behavior, seek help from a trustworthy, professional pastoral counselor.

BIBLE READING: 1 Timothy 1:1-11

KEY BIBLE VERSE: *They were not made for people who do what is right. They are for people who are disobedient and rebellious, who are ungodly and sinful, who consider nothing sacred and defile what is holy, who murder their father or mother or other people. These laws are for people who are sexually immoral, for homosexuals and slave traders, for liars and oath breakers, and for those who do anything else that contradicts the right teaching that comes from the glorious Good News entrusted to me by our blessed God.* (1 Timothy 1:9-11)

Like all sinners, homosexuals are called to repent. There are those who attempt to legitimize homosexuality as an acceptable alternative lifestyle. Even some Christians say people have a right to choose their sexual preference. But the Bible specifically calls homosexual behavior sin (see Leviticus 18:22; Romans 1:18-32; 1 Corinthians 6:9-11). We must be careful, however, to condemn only the practice, and not the people. Those who commit homosexual acts are not to be feared, ridiculed, or hated. They can be forgiven, and their lives can be transformed. The church should be a haven of forgiveness and healing for repentant homosexuals without compromising its stance against homosexual behavior.

BIBLE READING: 1 Corinthians 6:1-11

KEY BIBLE VERSE: *There was a time when some of you were just like that, but now your sins have been washed away, and you have been set apart for God. You have been made right with God because of what the Lord Jesus Christ and the Spirit of our God have done for you.* (1 Corinthians 6:11)

Sinful patterns of all kinds require God's forgiveness. Paul is describing characteristics of unbelievers. He doesn't mean that idolaters, adulterers, male prostitutes, homosexuals, thieves, greedy people, drunkards, abusers, or swindlers are automatically and irrevocably excluded from heaven. Christians come out of all kinds of different backgrounds, including these. They may still struggle with evil desires, but they should not continue in these practices. In 6:11, Paul clearly states that even those who sin in these ways can have their lives changed by Christ. However, those who say that they are Christians but persist in these practices with no sign of remorse or change of life will not inherit the kingdom of God. Such people need to reevaluate their lives to see if they truly believe in Christ.

Christians should not tolerate sin of any kind in their life. In a permissive society it is easy for Christians to overlook or tolerate some immoral behaviors (greed, drunkenness, etc.) while remaining outraged at others (homosexuality, thievery). We must not participate in sin or condone it in any way, nor may we be selective about what we condemn or excuse. Staying away from more "acceptable" forms of sin is difficult, but it is no harder for us than it was for the Corinthians. God expects his followers in any age to have high standards.

Related Topics: ACCEPTANCE, REPENTANCE, SIN

HONESTY (*Integrity, Purity, Truthfulness*)

What are the benefits of honesty?

BIBLE READING: Micah 7:1-20

KEY BIBLE VERSE: *They go about their evil deeds with both hands. How skilled they are at using them! Officials and judges alike demand bribes. The people with money and influence pay them off, and together they scheme to twist justice.* (Micah 7:3)

Honesty preserves society. Micah could not find an upright person anywhere in the land. Even today, uprightness (honesty, integrity) is difficult to find. Society rationalizes sin, and even Christians sometimes compromise Christian principles in order to do what they want. It is easy to convince ourself that we deserve a few breaks, especially when "everyone else" is doing it. But the standards for honesty come from God, not society. We are honest because God is truth, and we are to be like him.

Honesty preserves the family. Sin had affected the government leaders and society in general. Deceit and dishonesty had even ruined the family, the core of society. A family is only as strong as the level of honesty between its members. As a result, the only way left to purify the people was God's judgment. This would draw the nation back to God and restore them from the inside out.

BIBLE READING: 1 Thessalonians 2:1-20
KEY BIBLE VERSE: *You can see that we were not preaching with any deceit or impure purposes or trickery.* (1 Thessalonians 2:3)

Rejected honesty is better than accepted dishonesty. It's disgusting to hear a person "butter up" someone. Flattery is phony, and it is a cover-up for a person's real intentions. Christians should not be flatterers. Those who proclaim God's truth have a special responsibility to be honest. Are you honest and straightforward in your words and actions? Or do you tell people what they want to hear in order to get what you want or to get ahead?

BIBLE READING: James 5:1-12
KEY BIBLE VERSE: *Most of all, my brothers and sisters, never take an oath, by heaven or earth or anything else. Just say a simple yes or no, so that you will not sin and be condemned for it.* (James 5:12)

Honesty breeds trust. People with a reputation for exaggeration or lying often can't get anyone to believe them on their word alone. Christians should never become like that. Always be honest so that others will believe your simple yes or no. By avoiding lies, half-truths, and omissions of the truth, you will become known as a trustworthy person.

Related Topics: DISHONESTY, INTEGRITY, TRUTH

HONOR *(Devotion, Reputation, Respect)*

What does the Bible say about honor?

BIBLE READING: Ezra 7:11-28
KEY BIBLE VERSE: *Praise him for demonstrating such unfailing love to me by honoring me before the king, his council, and all his mighty princes! I felt encouraged because the gracious hand of the LORD my God was on me. And I gathered some of the leaders of Israel to return with me to Jerusalem.* (Ezra 7:28)

Those who honor God will be honored. Ezra praised God for all that God had done for him and through him. Ezra had honored God throughout his life, and God chose to honor him. Ezra could have assumed that his own greatness and charisma had won over the king and his princes, but he gave the credit to God. We, too, should be grateful to God for our success and not think that we did it in our own power.

BIBLE READING: Romans 12:1-21
KEY BIBLE VERSE: *Love each other with genuine affection, and take delight in honoring each other.* (Romans 12:10)

Giving honor is better than receiving honor. We can honor others in one of two ways. One involves ulterior motives. We honor our bosses so they will reward us, our employees so they will work harder, the wealthy so they will contribute to our cause, the powerful so they will use their power for us and not against us. God's other way involves love. As Christians, we honor people because they have been created in God's image, because they are our brothers and sisters in Christ, and because they have a unique contribution to make to Christ's church. Does God's way of honoring others sound too difficult for your competitive nature? Why not try to outdo one another in showing honor? Put others first!

BIBLE READING: Exodus 20:1-26
KEY BIBLE VERSE: *Honor your father and mother. Then you will live a long, full life in the land the LORD your God will give you.* (Exodus 20:12)

Honoring parents is particularly important to God. This is the first commandment with a promise attached. To live in peace for generations in the Promised Land, the Israelites would need to respect authority and build strong families. But what does it mean to "honor" parents? Partly, it means speaking well of them and politely to them. It also means acting in a way that shows them courtesy and respect (but not obeying them if it means disobeying God). It means following their teaching and example of putting God first. Parents have a special place in God's sight. Even those who find it difficult to get along with their parents are still commanded to honor them.

Related Topics: OBEDIENCE, RESPECT, WORSHIP

HOPE *(Anticipation, Confidence, Faith)*

What are the sources of a believer's hope?

BIBLE READING: Leviticus 26:1-46
KEY BIBLE VERSE: *Despite all this, I will not utterly reject or despise them while they are in exile in the land of their enemies. I will not cancel my covenant with them by wiping them out. I, the LORD, am their God.* (Leviticus 26:44)

A Christian's hope is based on God's faithfulness. These verses show what God meant when he said he is slow to anger (Exodus 34:6). Even if the Israelites chose to disobey and were scattered among their enemies, God would still give them the opportunity to repent and return to him. His purpose was not to destroy them, but to help them grow. Our day-to-day experiences and hardships are sometimes overwhelming; unless we can see that God's purpose is to bring about continual growth in us, we may despair. The hope we need is well expressed in Jeremiah 29:11-12: " 'For I know the plans I have for you,' says the Lord. 'They are plans for good and not for disaster, to give you a future and a hope. In those days when you pray, I will listen.' " Retaining hope while we suffer shows we understand God's merciful ways of relating to his people.

BIBLE READING: Mark 5:21-43
KEY BIBLE VERSE: *Jesus ignored their comments and said to Jairus, "Don't be afraid. Just trust me."* (Mark 5:36)

Hope comes from trusting Christ. Jairus's crisis made him feel confused, afraid, and without hope. Jesus' words to Jairus in the midst of crisis speak to us as well: "Don't be afraid. Just trust me." In Jesus' mind, there was both hope and promise. The next time you feel hopeless and afraid, look at your problem from Jesus' point of view. He is the source of all hope and promise.

BIBLE READING: Romans 5:1-11
KEY BIBLE VERSE: *Since we have been made right in God's sight by faith, we have peace with God because of what Jesus Christ our Lord has done for us. Because of our faith, Christ has brought us into this place of highest privilege where we now stand, and we confidently and joyfully look forward to sharing God's glory.* (Romans 5:1-2)

Hope comes from remembering all that God has done for us. As Paul states clearly in 1 Corinthians 13:13, faith, hope, and love are at the heart of the Christian life. Our relationship with God begins with *faith*, which helps us realize that we are delivered from our past by Christ's death. *Hope* grows as we learn all that God has in mind for us; it gives us the promise of the future. And God's *love* fills our life and gives us the ability to reach out to others.

Hope grows as we depend on God in the difficult times. For first-century Christians, suffering was the rule rather than the exception. Paul tells us that in the future we will *become*, but until then we must *overcome*. This means we will experience difficulties that help us grow. We rejoice in suffering not because we like pain or deny its tragedy, but because we know God is using life's difficulties and Satan's attacks to build our character. The problems that we run into will develop our perseverance—which in turn will strengthen our character, deepen our trust in God, and give us greater confidence about the future. You probably find your patience tested in some way every day. Thank God for those opportunities to grow, and deal with them in his strength (see also James 1:2-4; 1 Peter 1:6-7).

BIBLE READING: 1 Thessalonians 4:13-18
KEY BIBLE VERSE: *Brothers and sisters, I want you to know what will happen to the Christians who have died so you will not be full of sorrow like people who have no hope.* (1 Thessalonians 4:13)

Hope grows as we remember the promise of the Resurrection. Because Jesus Christ came back to life, so will all believers. All Christians, including those living when Christ returns, will live with Christ forever. Therefore, we need not despair when loved ones die or world events take a tragic turn. God will turn our tragedies to triumphs, our poverty to riches, our pain to glory, and our defeat to victory. All believers throughout history will stand reunited in God's very presence, safe and secure. As Paul comforted the Thessalonians with the promise of the Resurrection, so we should comfort and reassure each other with this great hope.

Related Topics: CONFIDENCE, FAITH, TRUST

HOPELESSNESS *(Depression, Desperation, Discouragement)*

How should we respond to feelings of hopelessness?

BIBLE READING: Job 1:1-22
KEY BIBLE VERSE: *Job stood up and tore his robe in grief. Then he shaved his head and fell to the ground before God. He said, "I came naked from my mother's womb, and I will be stripped of everything when I die. The LORD gave me everything I had, and the LORD has taken it away. Praise the name of the LORD!" In all of this, Job did not sin by blaming God.* (Job 1:20-22)

Remember that we live in a fallen world. As we see calamity and suffering in the book of Job, we must remember that we live in a fallen world where good behavior is not always rewarded and bad behavior is not always punished. When we see a notorious criminal prospering or an innocent child in pain, we say, "That's wrong." And it is. Sin has twisted justice and made our world unpredictable and ugly.

Remember that God is sovereign. The book of Job shows a good man suffering for no apparent fault of his own. Sadly, our world is like that. But Job's story does not end in despair. Through Job's life we can see that faith in God is justified even when our situations look hopeless. Faith based on rewards or prosperity is hollow. To be unshakable, faith must be built on the confidence that God's ultimate purpose will come to pass.

BIBLE READING: Psalm 69:1-36

KEY BIBLE VERSE: *I keep right on praying to you, LORD, hoping this is the time you will show me favor. In your unfailing love, O God, answer my prayer with your sure salvation.* (Psalm 69:13)

Hopelessness is an opportunity to trust God. What problems David faced! He was scoffed at, mocked, insulted, humiliated, and made the object of citywide gossip. But still he prayed. When we are completely beaten down, we are tempted to turn from God, give up, and quit trusting him. When your situation seems hopeless, determine that no matter how bad things become you will continue to pray. God will hear your prayer, and he will rescue you. When others reject us, we need God most. Don't turn from your most faithful friend.

BIBLE READING: Isaiah 22:1-25

KEY BIBLE VERSE: *You dance and play; you slaughter sacrificial animals, feast on meat, and drink wine. "Let's eat, drink, and be merry," you say. "What's the difference, for tomorrow we die."* (Isaiah 22:13)

Remember to keep God's promises in mind. The people said, "Let's eat, drink, and be merry" because they had given up hope. Attacked on every side (22:7), they should have repented (22:12), but they chose to feast instead. The root problem was that Judah did not trust God's power or his promises (see 56:12; 1 Corinthians 15:32). When you face difficulties, turn to God. Today we still see people giving up hope. There are two common responses to hopelessness: despair and self-indulgence. But this life is not all there is, so we are not to act as if we had no hope. Our proper response should be to trust God and his promise to include us in the perfect and just new world that he will create.

Related Topics: CONFIDENCE, DESPAIR, HOPE

HOSPITALITY (*Kindness, Sharing, Welcome*)

How important is it to show hospitality?

BIBLE READING: Genesis 18:1-33

KEY BIBLE VERSE: *"My lord," he said, "if it pleases you, stop here for a while. Rest in the shade of this tree while my servants get some water to wash your feet. Let me prepare some food to refresh you. Please stay awhile before continuing on your journey." "All right," they said. "Do as you have said."* (Genesis 18:3-5)

Hospitality is a practical way to serve God. Abraham was eager to show hospitality to these three visitors, as was Lot (19:2). In Abraham's day, a person's reputation was largely connected to his hospitality—the sharing of home and food. Even strangers were to be treated as highly honored guests. Meeting another's need for food or shelter was and still is one of the most immediate and practical ways to obey God. It is also a time-honored relationship builder. Hebrews 13:2 suggests that we, like Abraham, might actually entertain angels. This thought should be on our minds the next time we have the opportunity to meet a stranger's needs.

BIBLE READING: Luke 10:1-16

KEY BIBLE VERSE: *When you enter a town, don't move around from home to home. Stay in one place, eating and drinking what they provide you. Don't hesitate to accept hospitality, because those who work deserve their pay.* (Luke 10:7)

Accepting hospitality allows others to practice generosity. Jesus' instruction to stay in one house avoided certain problems. Shifting from house to house could offend the families who first took them in. Some families might begin to compete for the disciples' presence, and some might think they weren't good enough to hear their message. If the disciples appeared not to appreciate the hospitality offered them, the town might not accept Jesus when he followed them there. In addition, by staying in one place, the disciples did not have to worry continually about getting good accommodations. They could settle down and do their appointed task.

Hospitality is a way to serve those who serve us. Jesus told his disciples to accept hospitality graciously because their work entitled them to it. Ministers of the gospel deserve to be supported, and it is our responsibility to make sure they have what they need. There are several ways to encourage those who serve God in his church. First, see that they have an adequate salary. Second, see that they are supported emotionally; plan a time to express appreciation for something they have done. Third, lift their spirits with special surprises from time to time. Our ministers deserve to know we are giving to them cheerfully and generously.

BIBLE READING: Luke 10:38-42

KEY BIBLE VERSE: *As Jesus and the disciples continued on their way to Jerusalem, they came to a village where a woman named Martha welcomed them into her home.* (Luke 10:38)

Hospitality should flow out of wholehearted devotion to God. Mary and Martha both loved Jesus. On this occasion they were both serving him. But Martha thought Mary's style of serving was inferior to hers. She didn't realize that in her desire to serve, she was actually neglecting her guest. Are you so busy doing things *for* Jesus that you're not spending any time *with* him? Don't let your service become self-serving.

Jesus did not blame Martha for being concerned about household chores. He was only asking her to set priorities. It is possible for service to Christ to degenerate into mere busywork that is no longer full of devotion to God.

BIBLE READING: Romans 12:9-21

KEY BIBLE VERSE: *When God's children are in need, be the one to help them out. And get into the habit of inviting guests home for dinner or, if they need lodging, for the night.* (Romans 12:13)

Hospitality is a gift that improves with practice. Christian hospitality differs from social entertaining. Entertaining focuses on the host—the home must be spotless; the food must be well prepared and abundant; the host must appear relaxed and good-natured. Hospitality, by contrast, focuses on the guests. Their needs—whether for a place to stay, nourishing food, a listening ear, or acceptance—are the primary concern. Hospitality can happen in a messy home. It can happen around a dinner table where the main dish is canned soup. It can even happen while the host and the guest are doing chores together. Don't hesitate to offer hospitality just because you are too tired, too busy, or not wealthy enough to entertain.

Related Topics: GIVING, HELP, HOME

HUMANNESS *(Being, Personhood, Value)*

▶ **THE HUMANNESS OF JESUS**
Why is it important that Jesus was human?

BIBLE READING: Hebrews 2:14-18
KEY BIBLE VERSE: *Because God's children are human beings—made of flesh and blood—Jesus also became flesh and blood by being born in human form. For only as a human being could he die, and only by dying could he break the power of the Devil, who had the power of death. Only in this way could he deliver those who have lived all their lives as slaves to the fear of dying.* (Hebrews 2:14-15)

Jesus' humanity allowed him to destroy death. Jesus had to become human ("flesh and blood") so that he could die and rise again, in order to destroy the devil's power over death (Romans 6:5-11). Only then could Christ deliver those who had lived in constant fear of death, and free them to live for him. When we belong to God, we need not fear death, because we know that death is only the doorway into eternal life (1 Corinthians 15).

Jesus' resurrection from the dead gives us hope. Christ's death and resurrection set us free from the fear of death because death has been defeated. Every person must die, but death is not the end; instead, it is the doorway to a new life. All who dread death should have the opportunity to know the hope that Christ's victory brings. How can you share this truth with those close to you?

BIBLE READING: Matthew 4:1-11
KEY BIBLE VERSE: *Jesus was led out into the wilderness by the Holy Spirit to be tempted there by the Devil.* (Matthew 4:1)

Jesus demonstrated that temptation can be resisted. This temptation by the devil shows us that Jesus was human, and it gave Jesus the opportunity to reaffirm God's plan for his ministry. It also gives us an example to follow when we are tempted. Jesus' temptation was an important demonstration of his sinlessness. He faced temptation and did not give in.

Jesus experienced the limitations of being human. Jesus was hungry and weak after fasting for forty days, but he chose not to use his divine power to satisfy his natural desire for food. Food, hunger, and eating are good, but the timing was wrong. Jesus was in the desert to fast, not to eat. And because Jesus had given up the unlimited, independent use of his divine power in order to experience humanity fully, he wouldn't use his power to change the stones to bread. We also may be tempted to satisfy a perfectly normal desire in a wrong way or at the wrong time. If we indulge in sex before marriage or if we steal to get food, we are trying to satisfy God-given desires in wrong ways. Remember, many of your desires are normal and good, but God wants you to satisfy them in the right way and at the right time.

Jesus used Scripture to resist temptation. Jesus was able to resist all of the devil's temptations because he not only knew Scripture, he also obeyed it. Ephesians 6:17 says that God's Word is a sword to use in spiritual combat. Knowing Bible verses is an important step in helping us resist the devil's attacks, but we must also obey the Bible. Note that Satan had memorized Scripture, but he failed to obey it. Knowing and obeying the Bible helps us follow God's desires rather than the devil's.

BIBLE READING: Philippians 2:5-11
KEY BIBLE VERSE: *Your attitude should be the same that Christ Jesus had. Though he was God, he did not demand and cling to his rights as God. He made himself*

nothing; he took the humble position of a slave and appeared in human form.
(Philippians 2:5-7)

By being fully human, Jesus made God known to us as never before. The *incarnation* was the act of the preexistent Son of God voluntarily assuming a human body and human nature. Without ceasing to be God, he became a human being, the man called Jesus. He did not give up his deity to become human, but he set aside the right to his glory and power. In submission to the Father's will, Christ limited his power and knowledge. Jesus of Nazareth was subject to place, time, and many other human limitations. What made his humanity unique was his freedom from sin. In his full humanity, Jesus showed us everything about God's character that can be conveyed in human terms. The incarnation is explained further in these passages: John 1:1-14; Romans 1:2-5; 2 Corinthians 8:9; 1 Timothy 3:16; Hebrews 2:14; and 1 John 1:1-3.

▶ OUR HUMANNESS

How does God work through our human limitations?

BIBLE READING: 2 Corinthians 4:1-18
KEY BIBLE VERSE: *This precious treasure—this light and power that now shine within us—is held in perishable containers, that is, in our weak bodies. So everyone can see that our glorious power is from God and is not our own.*
(2 Corinthians 4:7)

God presents the gospel through frail human beings. The supremely valuable message of salvation in Jesus Christ has been entrusted by God to frail and fallible human beings. Paul's focus, however, was not on the perishable container but on its priceless contents—God's power dwelling in us. Though we are weak, God uses us to spread his Good News, and he gives us power to do his work. Knowing that the power is his, not ours, should keep us from pride and motivate us to keep daily contact with God, our power source. Our responsibility is to let people see God through us.

God displays his power through our limitations. Paul reminds us that though we may think we are at the end of the rope, we are never at the end of hope. Our perishable bodies are subject to sin and suffering, but God never abandons us. Because Christ has won the victory over death, we have eternal life. All our risks, humiliations, and trials are opportunities for Christ to demonstrate his power and presence in and through us.

BIBLE READING: Colossians 2:6-23
KEY BIBLE VERSE: *You were dead because of your sins and because your sinful nature was not yet cut away. Then God made you alive with Christ. He forgave all our sins. He canceled the record that contained the charges against us. He took it and destroyed it by nailing it to Christ's cross. In this way, God disarmed the evil rulers and authorities. He shamed them publicly by his victory over them on the cross of Christ.* (Colossians 2:13-15)

God gives us a new nature in Christ. Before we believed in Christ, our nature was evil. We disobeyed, rebelled, and ignored God (even at our best, we did not love him with all our heart, soul, and mind). The Christian, however, has a new nature. God has crucified the old rebellious nature (Romans 6:6) and replaced it with a new loving nature (3:9-10). The penalty of sin died with Christ on the cross. God has declared us "not guilty," and we need no longer live under sin's power. God does not take us out of the world or make us robots—we will still feel like sinning, and sometimes we will sin. The difference is that before we were saved, we were slaves to our sinful nature; but now we are free to live for Christ (see Galatians 2:20).

BIBLE READING: Romans 6:1-14

KEY BIBLE VERSE: *He died once to defeat sin, and now he lives for the glory of God. So you should consider yourselves dead to sin and able to live for the glory of God through Christ Jesus.* (Romans 6:10-11)

We can have fellowship with God through Christ. We can enjoy our new life in Christ because we are united with him in his death and resurrection. Our evil desires, our bondage to sin, and our love of sin died with him. Now, united by faith with him in his resurrection life, we have unbroken fellowship with God and freedom from sin's hold on us. (For more on the difference between our new life in Christ and our old sinful nature, read Ephesians 4:21-24 and Colossians 3:3-17.)

Related Topics: HUMILITY, JESUS CHRIST, SACRIFICE

HUMILIATION (*Discredit, Dishonor, Shame*)

Can anything good come from humiliation?

BIBLE READING: Ezekiel 7:1-27

KEY BIBLE VERSE: *I will bring the most ruthless of nations to occupy their homes. I will break down their proud fortresses and defile their sanctuaries.* (Ezekiel 7:24)

Humiliation can help us overcome pride. The people of Jerusalem took great pride in their buildings. The temple itself was a source of pride (Ezekiel 24:20-21). This pride would be crushed when the evil and godless Babylonians destroyed Jerusalem's houses and holy places. If you are going through a humiliating experience, God may be using that experience to weed out pride in your life.

BIBLE READING: Luke 15:11-32

KEY BIBLE VERSE: *The boy became so hungry that even the pods he was feeding the pigs looked good to him. But no one gave him anything.* (Luke 15:16)

Humiliation can be an opportunity for repentance. The younger son, like many who are rebellious and immature, wanted to be free to live as he pleased, and he had to hit bottom before he came to his senses. It often takes great sorrow and tragedy to cause people to look to the only one who can help them. Are you trying to live life your own way, selfishly pushing aside any responsibility or commitment that gets in your way? Stop and look before you hit bottom. You will save yourself and your family much grief.

BIBLE READING: Hebrews 13:11-16

KEY BIBLE VERSE: *Let us go out to him outside the camp and bear the disgrace he bore.* (Hebrews 13:13)

Humiliation can be suffering for Jesus Christ. The Jewish Christians were being ridiculed and persecuted by Jews who didn't believe in Jesus the Messiah. Most of the book of Hebrews told them how Christ is greater than the sacrificial system. Here the writer drives home the point of his lengthy argument: It may be necessary to leave the "camp" and suffer with Christ. To be outside the camp meant to be unclean—in the days of the Exodus, those who were ceremonially unclean had to stay outside the camp. But Jesus suffered humiliation and uncleanness outside the Jerusalem gates on their behalf. The time had come for Jewish Christians to declare their loyalty to Christ above any other loyalty, to choose to follow the Messiah whatever suffering that might entail. They needed to move outside the safe confinement of their past, their traditions, and their ceremonies to live for Christ. What holds you back from complete loyalty to Jesus Christ?

Related Topics: COMMITMENT, OBEDIENCE, SUFFERING

HUMILITY (*Goodness, Modesty, Quietness*)

Why is humility an important part of our spiritual life?

BIBLE READING: Joshua 7:1-26

KEY BIBLE VERSE: *Joshua and the leaders of Israel tore their clothing in dismay, threw dust on their heads, and bowed down facing the Ark of the LORD until evening.* (Joshua 7:6)

Humility is the proper attitude before God. Joshua and the elders tore their clothing and sprinkled dust on their heads as signs of deep mourning before God. They were confused by their defeat at the small city of Ai after the spectacular Jericho victory, so they went before God in deep humility and sorrow to receive his instructions. When our life falls apart, we also should turn to God for direction and help. Like Joshua and the elders, we should humble ourself so that we will be able to hear his words.

Humility keeps us from depending on our own strengths. When Joshua first went against Ai (7:3), he did not consult God but relied on the strength of his army to defeat the small city. Only after Israel was defeated did they turn to God and ask what happened.

Too often we rely on our own skills and strength, especially when the task before us seems easy. We go to God only when the obstacles seem too great. However, only God knows what lies ahead. Consulting him, even when we are on a winning streak, may save us from grave mistakes or misjudgments. God may want us to learn lessons, remove pride, or consult others before he will work through us.

Humility makes our prayers direct and honest. Imagine praying the way Joshua prayed to God. This is not a formal church prayer; it is the prayer of a man who is afraid and confused by what is happening around him. Joshua poured out his real thoughts to God. Hiding your needs from God is ignoring the only one who can really help. God welcomes your honest prayers and wants you to express your true feelings to him. Any believer can become more honest in prayer by remembering that God is all-knowing and all-powerful and that his love is everlasting.

BIBLE READING: 2 Kings 5:1-19

KEY BIBLE VERSE: *His officers tried to reason with him and said, "Sir, if the prophet had told you to do some great thing, wouldn't you have done it? So you should certainly obey him when he says simply to go and wash and be cured!"* (2 Kings 5:13)

Humility is good training in obedience. Naaman, a great hero, was used to getting respect, and he was outraged when Elisha treated him like an ordinary person. A proud man, he expected royal treatment. To wash in a great river would be one thing, but the Jordan was small and dirty. To wash in the Jordan, Naaman thought, was beneath a man of his position. But Naaman had to humble himself and obey Elisha's commands in order to be healed.

Humility clarifies our dependence on God. Obedience to God begins with humility. We must believe that his way is better than our own. We may not always understand his ways of working, but by humbly obeying, we will receive his blessings. We must remember that (1) God's ways are best; (2) God wants our obedience more than anything else; and (3) God can use anything to accomplish his purposes.

Humility challenges our pride. Naaman left in a rage because the cure for his disease seemed too simple. He was a hero, and he expected a heroic cure. Full of pride and self-will, he could not accept the simple cure of faith. Sometimes people react to God's offer of forgiveness in the same way. Just to *believe* in Jesus Christ somehow doesn't seem significant enough to bring eternal life. To obey God's commands doesn't seem heroic. What Naaman had to do to have his leprosy washed away is similar to what we must do to have our sin washed away—humbly accept God's mercy. Don't let your reaction to the way of faith keep you from the cure you need the most.

BIBLE READING: Psalm 8:1-9

KEY BIBLE VERSE: *When I look at the night sky and see the work of your fingers— the moon and the stars you have set in place—what are mortals that you should think of us, mere humans that you should care for us?* (Psalm 8:3-4)

Humility is a deep awareness of unworthiness, not worthlessness. When we look at the vast expanse of creation, we wonder how God could be concerned for people who constantly disappoint him. Yet God created us only a little lower than himself or the angels! The next time you question your worth as a person, remember that God considers you highly valuable. We have great worth because we bear the stamp of the Creator. (See Genesis 1:26-27 for the extent of worth God places on all people.) Because God has already declared how valuable we are to him, we can be set free from feelings of worthlessness.

Humility increases our appreciation for God. To respect God's majesty, we must compare ourself to his greatness. When we look at creation, we often feel small by comparison. To feel small is a healthy way to get back to reality, but God does not want us to dwell on our smallness. Humility means proper respect for God, not self-depreciation.

BIBLE READING: Luke 14:1-14

KEY BIBLE VERSE: *The proud will be humbled, but the humble will be honored.* (Luke 14:11)

Humility is essential for service to others. Jesus advised people not to rush for the best places at a feast. People today are just as eager to raise their social status, whether by being with the right people, dressing for success, or driving the right car. Whom do you try to impress? Rather than aiming for prestige, look for a place where you can serve. If God wants you to serve on a wider scale, he will invite you to take a higher place.

Jesus Christ is our model for humility. How can we humble ourself? Some people try to give the appearance of humility in order to manipulate others. Others think that humility means putting themselves down. Truly humble people compare themselves only with Christ, realize their sinfulness, and understand their limitations. On the other hand, they also recognize their gifts and strengths and are willing to use them as Christ directs. Humility is not self-degradation; it is realistic assessment and commitment to serve.

Related Topics: GENTLENESS, PRIDE, SERVING

HUNGER (*see* COMPASSION)

HURT (*see* SUFFERING)

HUSBANDS (*Lovers, Mates, Partners*)

What are the basic biblical guidelines for husbands?

BIBLE READING: Ephesians 5:21-33

KEY BIBLE VERSE: *You husbands must love your wives with the same love Christ showed the church. He gave up his life for her.* (Ephesians 5:25)

In Christ, all of our relationships are transformed. Why did Paul tell wives to submit and husbands to love? Perhaps Christian women, newly freed in Christ, found submission difficult; perhaps Christian men, used to the Roman custom of giving unlimited power to the head of the family, were not used to treating their wives with respect and love. Of course both husbands and wives should submit to each other (5:21), just as both should love each other.

In Paul's day, women, children, and slaves were to submit to the head of the family—slaves would submit until they were freed, male children until they grew up, and women and girls their whole lives. Paul emphasized the equality of all believers in Christ (Galatians 3:28), but he did not suggest overthrowing Roman society to achieve it. Instead, he counseled all believers to submit to one another by choice—wives to husbands and husbands to wives; slaves to masters and masters to slaves; children to parents and parents to children. This kind of mutual submission preserves order and harmony in the family while it increases love and respect among family members.

Spiritual leadership is based on service. Although some people have distorted Paul's teaching on submission by giving unlimited authority to husbands, we cannot get around it—Paul told wives to submit to their husbands. The fact that a teaching is not popular is no reason to discard it. According to the Bible, the man is the spiritual head of the family, and his wife should acknowledge his leadership. But real spiritual leadership involves service. Just as Christ served the disciples, even to the point of washing their feet, so the husband is to serve his wife. A wise and Christ-honoring husband will not take advantage of his leadership role, and a wise and Christ-honoring wife will not try to undermine her husband's leadership. Either approach causes disunity and friction in marriage.

A husband's primary responsibility is to love his wife. Paul devotes twice as many words to telling husbands to love their wives as to telling wives to submit to their husbands. How should a man love his wife? (1) He should be willing to sacrifice everything for her. (2) He should make her well-being of primary importance. (3) He should care for her as he cares for his own body. No wife needs to fear submitting to a man who treats her in this way.

God calls both husband and wife to self-sacrifice. The union of husband and wife merges two persons in such a way that little can affect one without also affecting the other. Oneness in marriage does not mean losing your personality in the personality of the other. Instead, it means caring for your spouse as you care for yourself, learning to anticipate his or her needs, helping the other person become all he or she can be. The creation story tells of God's plan that husband and wife should be one (Genesis 2:24), and Jesus also referred to this plan (Matthew 19:4-6).

BIBLE READING: 1 Peter 3:1-7

KEY BIBLE VERSE: *You husbands must give honor to your wives. Treat her with understanding as you live together. She may be weaker than you are, but she is your equal partner in God's gift of new life. If you don't treat her as you should, your prayers will not be heard.* (1 Peter 3:7)

Husbands should honor their wives. When Peter calls women the "weaker" partners, he does not imply moral or intellectual inferiority, but he is recognizing women's physical limitations. Women in his day, if unprotected by men, were vulnerable to attack, abuse, and financial disaster. Women's lives may be easier today, but women are still vulnerable to criminal attack and family abuse. And in spite of increased opportunities in the workplace, most women still earn considerably less than most men, and the vast majority of the nation's poor are single mothers and their children. A man who honors his wife as a member of the weaker sex will protect, respect, help, and stay with her. He will not expect her to work full-time outside the home and full-time at home; he will lighten her load wherever he can. He will be sensitive to her needs, and he will relate to her with courtesy, consideration, insight, and tact.

Related Topics: MARRIAGE, PARENT(S), SERVING

HYPOCRISY (*Deception, Fraud, Lying*)

What are the dangers of hypocrisy?

BIBLE READING: Matthew 5:21-26

KEY BIBLE VERSE: *If you are standing before the altar in the Temple, offering a sacrifice to God, and you suddenly remember that someone has something against you, leave your sacrifice there beside the altar. Go and be reconciled to that person. Then come and offer your sacrifice to God.* (Matthew 5:23-24)

Hypocrisy can lead to self-deception. Broken relationships can hinder our relationship with God. If we have a problem or grievance with a friend, we should resolve the problem as soon as possible. We are hypocrites if we claim to love God while we hate others. This kind of hypocrisy is pure self-deception. Our attitudes toward others reflect our relationship with God.

What are the signs of hypocrisy?

BIBLE READING: Matthew 6:1-4

KEY BIBLE VERSE: *When you give a gift to someone in need, don't shout about it as the hypocrites do—blowing trumpets in the synagogues and streets to call attention to their acts of charity! I assure you, they have received all the reward they will ever get.* (Matthew 6:2)

Hypocrisy means giving out of wrong motives. The term *hypocrites*, as used here, describes people who do good acts for appearances only—not out of compassion or other good motives. Their actions may be good, but their motives are hollow. These empty acts are their only reward, but God will reward those who are sincere in their faith.

BIBLE READING: Matthew 23:1-39

KEY BIBLE VERSE: *How terrible it will be for you teachers of religious law and you Pharisees. Hypocrites! For you won't let others enter the Kingdom of Heaven, and you won't go in yourselves.* (Matthew 23:13)

Hypocrisy is knowing the truth but not obeying it. Jesus repeatedly exposed the hypocritical attitudes of the religious leaders. They knew the Scriptures but did not live by them. They didn't care about *being* holy—just *looking* holy in order to receive the people's admiration and praise. Today, like the Pharisees, many people who know the Bible do not let it change their lives. They say they follow Jesus, but they don't live by his standards of love. People who live this way are hypocrites. We must make sure that our actions match our beliefs.

Hypocrisy is living a self-serving life. People desire positions of leadership not only in business but also in the church. It is dangerous when love for the position grows stronger than loyalty to God. This is what happened to the Pharisees and teachers of the law. Jesus is not against all leadership—we need Christian leaders—but against leadership that serves itself rather than others.

Hypocrisy is claiming Christ as Lord without following him. Jesus challenged society's norms. To him, greatness comes from serving—giving of yourself to help others. Service keeps us aware of others' needs, and it stops us from focusing only on ourself. Jesus came as a servant. What kind of greatness do you seek?

Hypocrisy reduces faith to rigid rules. Being a religious leader in Jerusalem was very different from being a pastor in a secular society today. Israel's history, culture, and daily life centered around its relationship with God. The religious leaders were the best known, most powerful, and most respected of all leaders. Jesus made these stinging accusations because the leaders' hunger for more power, money, and status had made them lose sight of God, and their blindness was spreading to the whole nation.

Hypocrisy is outer conformity without inner reality. It's possible to obey the details of the laws but still be disobedient in our general behavior. For example, we could be very precise and faithful about giving 10 percent of our money to God, but refuse to give one minute of our time in helping others. Tithing is important, but giving a tithe does not exempt us from fulfilling God's other directives.

The Pharisees strained their water so they wouldn't accidentally swallow a gnat—an unclean insect, according to the law. Meticulous about the details of ceremonial cleanliness, they nevertheless had lost their perspective on inner purity. Ceremonially clean on the outside, they had corrupt hearts.

Jesus condemned the Pharisees and religious leaders for outwardly appearing saintly and holy but inwardly remaining full of corruption and greed. Living our Christianity merely as a show for others is like washing a cup on the outside only. When we are clean on the inside, our cleanliness on the outside won't be a sham.

Related Topics: DECEIT, LYING, TRUTH

IDENTIFICATION (*see* HUMANNESS)

IDLENESS (*see* LAZINESS)

IDOLATRY (*Gods, Heroes, Images*)

Why does the Bible consistently condemn idolatry?

BIBLE READING: Genesis 35:1-15
KEY BIBLE VERSE: *Jacob told everyone in his household, "Destroy your idols, wash yourselves, and put on clean clothing."* (Genesis 35:2)

Idolatry reduces God to a deity that can be manipulated. Why did the people have these idols? Idols were sometimes seen more as good-luck charms than as gods. Some Israelites, even though they worshiped God, had idols in their homes, just as some Christians today own good-luck trinkets. Jacob believed that idols should have no place in his household. He wanted nothing to divert his family's spiritual focus.

Jacob ordered his household to get rid of their gods. Unless we remove idols from our life, they can ruin our faith. What idols do we have? An idol is anything we put before God. Idols don't have to be physical objects; they can be thoughts or desires. Like Jacob, we should get rid of anything that could stand between us and God.

BIBLE READING: Exodus 32:1-35
KEY BIBLE VERSE: *When Moses failed to come back down the mountain right away, the people went to Aaron. "Look," they said, "make us some gods who can lead us. This man Moses, who brought us here from Egypt, has disappeared. We don't know what has happened to him."* (Exodus 32:1)

Idolatry often arises out of conformity to our environment. Two popular Egyptian gods, Hapi (Apis) and Hathor, were thought of as a bull and a heifer. The Canaanites around them worshiped Baal, thought of as a bull. Baal was their sacred symbol of power and fertility and was closely connected to immoral sexual practices. No doubt the Israelites, fresh from Egypt, found it quite natural to make a golden calf to represent the God who had just delivered them from their oppressors. They were weary of a God without a face. But in doing so, they were ignoring the command he had just given them: "Do not make idols of any kind, whether in the shape of birds or animals or fish" (20:4). They may even have thought they were worshiping God. Their apparent sincerity was no substitute for obedience, nor excuse for disobedience.

Idolatry is an attempt to make God in our image. Even if we do not make idols, we are often guilty of trying to make God in our image, molding him to fit our expectations, desires, and circumstances. When we do this, we end up worshiping ourself rather than the God who created us—and self-worship, today as in the Israelites' time, leads to all kinds of immorality. What is your favorite image of God? Is it biblical? Is it adequate? Do you need to destroy it in order to worship the immeasurably powerful God who delivered you from bondage to sin?

BIBLE READING: Romans 1:18-32

KEY BIBLE VERSE: *Claiming to be wise, they became utter fools instead. And instead of worshiping the glorious, ever-living God, they worshiped idols made to look like mere people, or birds and animals and snakes.* (Romans 1:22-23)

Idolatry worships the creature rather than the Creator. How could intelligent people turn to idolatry? Idolatry begins when people reject what they know about God. Instead of looking to him as the Creator and Sustainer of life, they see themselves as the center of the universe. They soon invent "gods" that are convenient projections of their own selfish plans and decrees. These gods may be wooden figures, but they may also be goals or things we pursue such as money, power, or comfort. They may even be misrepresentations of God himself—making God in our image, instead of the reverse. The common denominator is this—idolaters worship the things God made rather than God himself. Is there anything you feel you can't live without? Is there any priority greater than God? Do you have a dream you would sacrifice everything to realize? Does God take first place? Do you worship God or idols of your own making?

Idolatry is part of an overall rejection of God. Paul clearly portrays the inevitable downward spiral into sin. First, people reject God; next, they make up their own ideas of what a god should be and do; then they fall into sin—sexual sin, greed, hatred, envy, murder, strife, deceit, malice, gossip. Finally, they grow to hate God and encourage others to do so. God does not cause this steady progression toward evil. Rather, when people reject him, he allows them to live as they choose. God gives them over or permits them to experience the natural consequences of their sin. Once caught in the downward spiral, no one can pull himself or herself out. Sinners must trust Christ alone to put them on the path of escape.

Related Topics: RELIGION, SIN, WORSHIP

IGNORANCE (*Defiance, Disobedience, Disregard*)

How does ignorance affect our relationship with God?

BIBLE READING: Job 38:1–41:34

KEY BIBLE VERSE: *The LORD answered Job from the whirlwind: "Who is this that questions my wisdom with such ignorant words?"* (Job 38:1-2)

What we don't know should cause us to trust God more, not less. Out of a mighty storm, God spoke. Surprisingly, he didn't answer any of Job's questions; Job's questions were not at the heart of the issue. Instead, God used Job's ignorance of the earth's natural order to reveal his ignorance of God's moral order. If Job did not understand the workings of God's physical creation, how could he possibly understand God's mind and character? There is no standard or criterion higher than God himself by which to judge. God himself is the standard. Our only option is to submit to his authority and rest in his care.

BIBLE READING: Malachi 2:1-9

KEY BIBLE VERSE: *"The priests' lips should guard knowledge, and people should go to them for instruction, for the priests are the messengers of the LORD Almighty. But not you! You have left God's paths. Your 'guidance' has caused many to stumble into sin. You have corrupted the covenant I made with the Levites,"* says the LORD Almighty. (Malachi 2:7-8)

Ignorance of God's Word will lead to trouble. Malachi was angry at the priests because, though they were to be God's messengers, they did not know God's will. And this lack of knowledge caused them to lead God's people astray. Their ignorance was willful and inexcusable. Pastors and other leaders of God's people *must* know God's Word—what it says, what it means, and how it applies to daily life. How much time do you spend in God's Word?

BIBLE READING: Matthew 27:11-26

KEY BIBLE VERSE: *Pilate saw that he wasn't getting anywhere and that a riot was developing. So he sent for a bowl of water and washed his hands before the crowd, saying, "I am innocent of the blood of this man. The responsibility is yours!"* (Matthew 27:24)

The choice to remain ignorant can be motivated by fear. At first Pilate hesitated to give the religious leaders permission to crucify Jesus. He thought they were simply jealous of a teacher who was more popular with the people than they were. He wasn't sure who Jesus was, but he knew the man before him was innocent. When the Jews threatened to report Pilate to Caesar (John 19:12), Pilate became afraid. Historical records indicate that the Jews had already threatened to lodge a formal complaint against Pilate for his stubborn flouting of their traditions—and such a complaint would most likely have led to his recall by Rome. His job was in jeopardy. The Roman government could not afford to put large numbers of troops in all the regions under their control, so one of Pilate's main duties was to do whatever was necessary to maintain peace.

Ignorance can be a means of rejecting the truth. In making no decision, Pilate made the decision to let the crowds crucify Jesus. Although he washed his hands, the guilt remained. Washing your hands of a tough situation doesn't cancel your guilt. It merely gives you a false sense of peace. Don't make excuses—take responsibility for the decisions you make.

Related Topics: KNOWLEDGE, QUESTIONS, TRUTH

IMAGE *(Idea, Pattern, Shape)*

What does the Bible mean when it speaks of God's image?

BIBLE READING: Genesis 1:1-31

KEY BIBLE VERSE: *God said, "Let us make people in our image, to be like ourselves. They will be masters over all life—the fish in the sea, the birds in the sky, and all the livestock, wild animals, and small animals." So God created people in his own image; God patterned them after himself; male and female he created them.* (Genesis 1:26-27)

Being made in God's image refers to characteristics God shares with us. In what ways are we made in God's image? God obviously did not create us exactly like himself, because God has no physical body. Instead, we are reflections of God's glory. Some feel that the *image of God* refers to our reason, creativity, speech, or self-determination. More likely, it is our entire self that reflects the image of God. We will never be totally like God, because he is our supreme Creator. But we do have the ability to reflect his character in our love, patience, forgiveness, kindness, and faithfulness.

God's image is the basis for human self-worth. Knowing that we are made in God's image and thus share many of his characteristics provides a solid basis for self-worth. Human worth is not based on possessions, achievements, physical attractiveness, or public acclaim. Instead it is based on being made in God's image. Because we bear God's image, we can feel positive about ourself. Criticizing or downgrading ourself is criticizing what God has made and the abilities he has given us. Knowing that you are a person of worth helps you love God, know him personally, and make a valuable contribution to those around you.

God's image is shared equally by women and men. God made both man and woman in his image. Neither man nor woman is made more in the image of God than the other. From the beginning the Bible places both man and woman at the pinnacle of God's creation. Neither sex is exalted, and neither is depreciated.

BIBLE READING: Genesis 9:1-7
KEY BIBLE VERSE: *Yes, you must execute anyone who murders another person, for to kill a person is to kill a living being made in God's image.* (Genesis 9:6)

God's image is an important factor in all human relationships. Here God explains why murder is so wrong: To kill a person is to kill one made in God's image. Because all human beings are made in God's image, all people possess the qualities that distinguish them from animals: morality, reason, creativity, and self-worth. When we interact with others, we are interacting with beings made by God, beings to whom God offers eternal life. God wants us to recognize his image in all people.

BIBLE READING: Mark 12:13-17
KEY BIBLE VERSE: *When they handed it to him, he asked, "Whose picture and title are stamped on it?" "Caesar's," they replied. "Well, then," Jesus said, "give to Caesar what belongs to him. But everything that belongs to God must be given to God." This reply completely amazed them.* (Mark 12:16-17)

God's image in us means that we belong to him. The Pharisees and Herodians thought they had the perfect question to trap Jesus. But Jesus answered wisely, once again exposing their self-interest and wrong motives. Jesus said that the coin bearing the emperor's image should be given to the emperor. But our life, which bears God's image, belongs to God. Are you giving God all that is rightfully his? Give your life to God—you bear his image.

Related Topics: CREATION, HUMANNESS, SELF-ESTEEM

IMMORALITY (*Disobedience, Impurity, Wrong*)

How can we avoid falling into immoral practices?

📖 BIBLE READING: Judges 3:1-11

KEY BIBLE VERSE: *So Israel lived among the Canaanites, Hittites, Amorites, Perizzites, Hivites, and Jebusites, and they intermarried with them. Israelite sons married their daughters, and Israelite daughters were given in marriage to their sons. And the Israelites worshiped their gods.* (Judges 3:5-6)

Be aware of the subtle compromises that lead to immorality. The Israelites discovered that relationships affect faith. The men and women of the surrounding nations were attractive to the Israelites. Soon they intermarried, and the Israelites accepted their pagan gods. This was clearly prohibited by God (Exodus 34:15-17; Deuteronomy 7:1-4). By accepting these gods into their homes, the Israelites gradually began to accept the immoral practices associated with them. Most Israelites didn't start out determined to be idolaters; they just added the idols to the worship of God. But before long they found themselves absorbed in pagan worship.

A similar danger faces us. We want to befriend those who don't know God, but through those friendships we can become entangled in unhealthy practices. Friendships with unbelievers are important, but we must accept people without compromising our beliefs or adopting their patterns of behavior.

📖 BIBLE READING: 1 Corinthians 6:1-20

KEY BIBLE VERSE: *Don't you know that your body is the temple of the Holy Spirit, who lives in you and was given to you by God? You do not belong to yourself, for God bought you with a high price. So you must honor God with your body.* (1 Corinthians 6:19-20)

Do not use the past as an excuse for immoral behavior. Paul is describing characteristics of unbelievers. He doesn't mean that idolaters, adulterers, male prostitutes, homosexuals, thieves, greedy people, drunkards, abusers, and swindlers are automatically and irrevocably excluded from heaven. Christians come out of all kinds of different backgrounds, including these. They may still struggle with evil desires, but they should not continue in these practices. In 6:11, Paul clearly states that even those who sin in these ways can have their lives changed by Christ. However, those who say that they are Christians but persist in these practices with no sign of repentance will not inherit the kingdom of God. Such people need to reevaluate their lives to see if they truly believe in Christ.

Do not become selective about morality. In a permissive society it is easy for Christians to overlook or tolerate some immoral behaviors (greed, drunkenness, etc.) while remaining outraged at others (homosexuality, thievery). We must not participate in sin or condone it in any way, nor may we be selective about what we condemn or excuse. Staying away from more "acceptable" forms of sin is difficult, but it is no harder for us than it was for the Corinthians. God expects his followers in any age to have high standards.

📖 BIBLE READING: Revelation 9:13-21

KEY BIBLE VERSE: *The people who did not die in these plagues still refused to turn from their evil deeds. They continued to worship demons and idols made of gold, silver, bronze, stone, and wood—idols that neither see nor hear nor walk! And they did not repent of their murders or their witchcraft or their immorality or their thefts.* (Revelation 9:20-21)

Do not allow immorality to take root in your life. These people were so hardhearted that even plagues did not drive them to God. People don't usually fall into immorality and evil suddenly—they slip into it a little bit at a time until, hardly realizing what has happened, they are irrevocably mired in their wicked ways. Any person who allows sin to take root in his or her life can find himself or herself in this predicament. Temptation entertained today becomes sin tomorrow, then a habit the next day, then death and separation from God forever (see James 1:15). To think you could never become this evil is the first step toward a hard heart.

Related Topics: INTEGRITY, MORALITY, SIN

IMPARTIALITY (*see* FAIRNESS)

IMPATIENCE (*see* PATIENCE)

IMPORTANT *(Priority, Significant, Valued)*

How are we supposed to evaluate what's really important?

 BIBLE READING: Psalm 62:1-12
KEY BIBLE VERSE: *From the greatest to the lowliest—all are nothing in his sight. If you weigh them on the scales, they are lighter than a puff of air.* (Psalm 62:9)

What God considers important is really important. It is tempting to use honor, power, wealth, or prestige to measure people. We may even think that such people are really getting ahead in life. But these are human measures of importance. On God's scales, these people are a puff of air. What, then, can tilt the scales when God weighs us? Trusting God and working for him (62:12). Wealth, honor, power, and prestige add nothing to our value in God's eyes, but the faithful work we do for him has eternal value.

BIBLE READING: Malachi 2:1-9
KEY BIBLE VERSE: *"Listen, you priests; this command is for you! Listen to me and take it to heart. Honor my name," says the* LORD *Almighty, "or I will bring a terrible curse against you. I will curse even the blessings you receive. Indeed, I have already cursed them, because you have not taken my warning seriously."* (Malachi 2:1-2)

We must heed God's warnings. God warned the priests that if they did not honor his name, he would punish them. Like these priests, we are called to honor God's name—to worship him. This means acknowledging God for who he is—the almighty Creator of the universe who alone is perfect and who reaches down to sinful mankind with perfect love. According to this definition, are you honoring God's name?

The Bible is God's record of what is most important to him. The priests didn't take seriously (set their hearts to) God's priority, even though he had reminded them through his Word many times. How do you find out what is most important to God? Begin by loving him with all your heart, soul, and strength (Deuteronomy 6:5). This means listening to what God says in his Word and then setting your heart, mind, and will on doing what he says. When we love God, his Word becomes a shining light that guides our daily activities. The priests in Malachi's day had stopped loving God, and thus they did not know or care what he wanted.

Related Topics: BIBLE, LAW OF GOD, MORALITY

IMPOSSIBLE *(Hopeless, Incredible, Unthinkable)*

Why should we trust God even in impossible situations?

BIBLE READING: Exodus 2:1-10

KEY BIBLE VERSE: *The baby's sister approached the princess. "Should I go and find one of the Hebrew women to nurse the baby for you?" she asked. "Yes, do!" the princess replied. So the girl rushed home and called the baby's mother.* (Exodus 2:7-8)

God can make possible the impossible. Moses' mother was reunited with her baby! God used her courageous act of saving and hiding her baby to begin his plan to rescue his people from Egypt. God doesn't need much from us to accomplish his plan for our life. Focusing on our human predicament may paralyze us, because the situation may appear humanly impossible. But concentrating on God and his power will help us see the way out. Right now you may feel unable to see through your troubles. Focus instead on God, and trust him for the way out. That is all he needs to begin his work in you.

BIBLE READING: Mark 6:30-44

KEY BIBLE VERSE: *Late in the afternoon his disciples came to him and said, "This is a desolate place, and it is getting late. Send the crowds away so they can go to the nearby farms and villages and buy themselves some food." But Jesus said, "You feed them." "With what?" they asked. "It would take a small fortune to buy food for all this crowd!"* (Mark 6:35-37)

Impossibilities limit people, but not God. In this chapter, Jesus' life and ministry have been examined by various people: his neighbors and family, Herod the king, and the disciples. Yet none of these appreciated Jesus for who he was. The disciples were still pondering, still confused, still unbelieving. They did not realize that Jesus could provide for them. They were so preoccupied with the immensity of the task that they could not see what was possible with God. Do you let what seems impossible about Christianity keep you from believing?

Impossibilities are simply God's opportunities to work. When Jesus asked the disciples to provide food for over five thousand people, they asked in astonishment if they should go and spend eight months' wages on bread. How do you react when you are given an impossible task? A situation that seems impossible with human resources is simply an opportunity for God. The disciples did everything they could by gathering the available food and organizing the people into groups. Then, in answer to prayer, God did the impossible. When facing a seemingly impossible task, do what you can and ask God to do the rest. He may see fit to make the impossible happen.

BIBLE READING: Luke 18:18-30

KEY BIBLE VERSE: *Those who heard this said, "Then who in the world can be saved?" He replied, "What is impossible from a human perspective is possible with God."* (Luke 18:26-27)

In Christ, God has made possible the impossible. Because money represents power, authority, and success, often it is difficult for wealthy people to realize their need and their powerlessness to save themselves. Those rich in talent or intelligence suffer the same difficulty. Unless God reaches down into their lives, they will not come to him. Jesus surprised some of his hearers by offering salvation to the poor; he may surprise some people today by offering it to the rich. It is difficult for a self-sufficient person to realize his or her need and come to Jesus, but "What is impossible from a human perspective is possible with God."

Related Topics: GOD, POWER, SALVATION

IMPRESSIONS (*Idea, Image, Perception*)

Can we trust impressions?

BIBLE READING: 1 Samuel 16:1-13
KEY BIBLE VERSE: *The LORD said to Samuel, "Don't judge by his appearance or height, for I have rejected him. The LORD doesn't make decisions the way you do! People judge by outward appearance, but the LORD looks at a person's thoughts and intentions."* (1 Samuel 16:7)

Outward impressions can be misleading. Saul was tall and handsome; he was an impressive-looking man. Samuel may have been trying to find someone who looked like Saul to be Israel's next king, but God warned him against judging by appearance alone. When people judge by outward appearance, they may overlook quality individuals who lack the particular physical qualities society currently admires. Appearance doesn't reveal what people are really like or what their true value is.

God always looks beyond mere outward impressions. Fortunately, God judges by faith and character, not appearances. And because only God can see on the inside, only he can accurately judge people. Most people spend hours each week maintaining their outward appearance; they should do even more to develop their inner character. While everyone can see your face, only you and God know what your heart really looks like. What steps are you taking to improve your heart's attitude?

BIBLE READING: Luke 14:7-14
KEY BIBLE VERSE: *The proud will be humbled, but the humble will be honored.* (Luke 14:11)

False impressions will crumble sooner or later. Jesus advised people not to rush for the best places at a feast. People today are just as eager to raise their social status, whether by being with the right people, dressing for success, or driving the right car. Whom do you try to impress? Rather than aiming for prestige, look for a place where you can serve. If God wants you to serve on a wider scale, he will invite you to take a higher place.

BIBLE READING: Luke 16:1-18
KEY BIBLE VERSE: *He said to them, "You like to look good in public, but God knows your evil hearts. What this world honors is an abomination in the sight of God."* (Luke 16:15)

Our impressions don't fool God. The Pharisees acted piously to get praise from others, but God knew what was in their hearts. They considered their wealth to be a sign of God's approval. God detested their wealth because it caused them to abandon true spirituality. Though prosperity may earn people's praise, it must never substitute for devotion and service to God.

Related Topics: HONESTY, HONOR, IMAGE

IMPULSIVENESS *(Careless, Hasty, Rash)*

What does the Bible say about impulsiveness?

BIBLE READING: Genesis 25:19-34
KEY BIBLE VERSE: *Jacob gave Esau some bread and lentil stew. Esau ate and drank and went on about his business, indifferent to the fact that he had given up his birthright.* (Genesis 25:34)

Impulsiveness fails to consider the consequences of actions. Esau traded the lasting benefits of his birthright for the immediate pleasure of food. He acted on impulse, satisfying his immediate desires without pausing to consider the long-range consequences of what he was about to do. We can fall into the same trap. When we see something we want, our first impulse is to get it. At first we feel intensely satisfied and sometimes even powerful because we have obtained what we set out to get. But with the immediate pleasure we often lose sight of the future. We can avoid making Esau's mistake by comparing the short-term satisfaction with its long-range consequences before we act.

Impulsiveness is a reaction from a distorted perspective. Esau exaggerated his hunger, saying that he was "dying of starvation." This thought made his choice much easier, because if he was starving, what good was an inheritance anyway? The pressure of the moment distorted his perspective and made his decision seem urgent. We often experience similar pressures. For example, when we feel sexual pressure, a marriage vow may seem unimportant. We might feel such great pressure in one area that nothing else seems to matter and we lose our perspective. Getting through that short, pressure-filled moment is often the most difficult part of overcoming a temptation.

BIBLE READING: Judges 14:1-20
KEY BIBLE VERSE: *The Spirit of the LORD powerfully took control of [Samson]. He went down to the town of Ashkelon, killed thirty men, took their belongings, and gave their clothing to the men who had answered his riddle. But Samson was furious about what had happened, and he went back home to live with his father and mother.* (Judges 14:19)

Impulsiveness sometimes springs from self-centeredness. Samson impulsively used the special gift God gave him for selfish purposes. Today, God distributes abilities and skills throughout the church (1 Corinthians 12:1ff.). The apostle Paul states that these gifts are to be used to build up the church, the body of Christ" (Ephesians 4:12). To use these abilities for selfish purposes is to rob the church and fellow believers of strength. As you use the gifts God has given you, be sure you are helping others, not just yourself.

BIBLE READING: Matthew 14:22-33
KEY BIBLE VERSE: *Peter called to him, "Lord, if it's really you, tell me to come to you by walking on water." "All right, come," Jesus said. So Peter went over the side of the boat and walked on the water toward Jesus.* (Matthew 14:28-29)

Impulsiveness can be an expression of faith. Peter was not putting Jesus to the test, something we are told not to do (Matthew 4:7). Instead he was the only one in the boat to react in faith. His impulsive request led him to experience a rather unusual demonstration of God's power. Peter started to sink because he took his eyes off Jesus and focused on the high waves around him. His faith wavered when he realized what he was doing. We may not walk on water, but we do walk through tough situations. If we focus on the waves of difficult circumstances around us without looking to Jesus for help, we too may despair and sink. To maintain your faith when situations are difficult, keep your eyes on Jesus' power rather than on your inadequacies.

Related Topics: ACTIONS, DECISIONS, FAITH

INADEQUACY (*Doubts, Inabilities, Uncertainty*)

How can we overcome our inadequacies?

BIBLE READING: Genesis 50:22-26
KEY BIBLE VERSE: *"Soon I will die,"* Joseph told his brothers, *"but God will surely come for you, to lead you out of this land of Egypt. He will bring you back to the land he vowed to give to the descendants of Abraham, Isaac, and Jacob."* (Genesis 50:24)

We can be encouraged by God's work in others. The book of Genesis gives us rich descriptions of the lives of many great men and women who walked with God. They sometimes succeeded and often failed. Yet we learn much by reading the biographies of these people. Where did they get their motivation and courage? They got it by realizing God was with them despite their inadequacies. Knowing this should encourage us to be faithful to God, to rely on him for guidance, and to utilize the potential he has given us.

BIBLE READING: Exodus 3:1-22
KEY BIBLE VERSE: *"Now go, for I am sending you to Pharaoh. You will lead my people, the Israelites, out of Egypt." "But who am I to appear before Pharaoh?" Moses asked God. "How can you expect me to lead the Israelites out of Egypt?"* (Exodus 3:10-11)

We shouldn't hide behind our inadequacies. Moses made excuses because he felt inadequate for the job God asked him to do. It was natural for him to feel that way. He *was* inadequate all by himself. But God wasn't asking Moses to work alone. He offered other resources to help (God himself, Aaron, and the ability to do miracles). God often calls us to tasks that seem too difficult, but he doesn't ask us to do them alone. God offers us his resources, just as he did to Moses. We should not hide behind our inadequacies, as Moses did, but look beyond ourself to the great resources available. Then we can allow God to use our unique contributions.

BIBLE READING: Matthew 14:13-21
KEY BIBLE VERSE: *"Impossible!" they exclaimed. "We have only five loaves of bread and two fish!" "Bring them here,"* he said. (Matthew 14:17-18)

Jesus can take our inadequacy and make it more than adequate. Jesus multiplied five loaves and two fish to feed over five-thousand people. What he was originally given seemed insufficient, but in his hands it became more than enough. We often feel that our contribution to Jesus is meager, but he can use and multiply whatever we give him, whether it is talent, time, or treasure. It is when we give them to Jesus that our resources are multiplied.

Related Topics: ADEQUACY, GIFTS, SELF-ESTEEM

INCARNATION (*see* JESUS CHRIST)

INCONSISTENCIES (*see* CONSISTENCY)

INDECISIVENESS *(Doubts, Hesitation, Uncertainty)*

What are the dangers of indecisiveness?

BIBLE READING: 2 Samuel 14:1-33
KEY BIBLE VERSE: *Joab told the king what Absalom had said. Then at last David summoned his estranged son, and Absalom came and bowed low before the king, and David kissed him.* (2 Samuel 14:33)

Indecisiveness increases the possibility of bad decisions. Discipline is hard—and sometimes painful—work. David only made halfhearted efforts to correct his children. He did not punish Amnon for his sin against Tamar, nor did he deal decisively with Absalom's murder of Amnon. He never took time to correct Adonijah. Such indecisiveness became David's undoing. David avoided necessary confrontations with his children. But the consequences were disastrous. When we ignore sin, we experience greater pain than if we deal with it immediately.

BIBLE READING: John 3:22-36
KEY BIBLE VERSE: *All who believe in God's Son have eternal life. Those who don't obey the Son will never experience eternal life, but the wrath of God remains upon them.* (John 3:36)

Indecisiveness itself can be a bad decision. Jesus says that those who believe in him *have* (not *will* have) everlasting life. To receive eternal life is to join in God's life, which by nature is eternal. Thus, eternal life begins at the moment of spiritual rebirth.

John, the author of this Gospel, has been demonstrating that Jesus is the true Son of God. Jesus sets before us the greatest choice in life. We are responsible to decide today whom we will obey (Joshua 24:15), and God wants us to choose him and choose life (Deuteronomy 30:15-20). The wrath of God is God's final judgment and rejection of the sinner. To put off the choice is to choose not to follow Christ. Indecision can be a fatal decision.

Related Topics: CHOICES, DECISIONS, WISDOM

INDEPENDENCE *(Freedom, Liberty, Self-Reliance)*

What are the limits of human independence?

BIBLE READING: Judges 17:1-13
KEY BIBLE VERSE: *One day [Micah] said to his mother, "I heard you curse the thief who stole eleven hundred pieces of silver from you. Well, here they are. I was the one who took them." "The LORD bless you for admitting it," his mother replied.* (Judges 17:2)

God's commands are limits for our independence. Micah and his mother seemed to be good and moral and may have sincerely desired to worship God, but they disobeyed God by following their own desires instead of doing what God wanted. The attitude that prevailed in Micah's day was this: "The people did whatever seemed right in their own eyes" (17:6). This is remarkably similar to today's prevailing attitudes. But God has given us standards.

He has not left our conduct up to us and our opinions. We can avoid conforming to society's low standards by taking God's commands seriously and applying them to life. Independence and self-reliance are positive traits, but only within the framework of God's standards.

BIBLE READING: Luke 2:41-52

KEY BIBLE VERSE: *[Jesus'] parents didn't know what to think. "Son!" his mother said to him. "Why have you done this to us? Your father and I have been frantic, searching for you everywhere."* (Luke 2:48)

Healthy parenting includes giving children healthy independence. Mary had to let go of her child and let him become a man, God's Son, the Messiah. Fearful that she hadn't been careful enough with this God-given child, she searched frantically for him. But she was looking for a boy, not the young man who was in the temple astounding the religious leaders with his questions. It is hard to let go of people or projects we have nurtured. It is both sweet and painful to see our children as adults, our students as teachers, our subordinates as managers, our inspirations as institutions. But when the time comes to step back and let go, we must do so in spite of the hurt. Then our protégés can exercise their wings, take flight, and soar to the heights God intended for them.

BIBLE READING: Ephesians 4:11-16

KEY BIBLE VERSE: *We will hold to the truth in love, becoming more and more in every way like Christ, who is the head of his body, the church. Under his direction, the whole body is fitted together perfectly. As each part does its own special work, it helps the other parts grow, so that the whole body is healthy and growing and full of love.* (Ephesians 4:15-16)

Human independence is an opportunity to help others. Our oneness in Christ does not destroy our individuality. There is great freedom in the body of Christ. One of the most important actions independent believers can take is to choose to invest their lives in service of others. The Holy Spirit has given each Christian special gifts for building up the church. Now that we have these gifts, it is crucial to use them. Are you spiritually mature, exercising the gifts God has given you? If you know what your gifts are, look for opportunities to serve. If you don't know, ask God to show you, perhaps with the help of your pastor or Christian friends. Then, as you begin to recognize your special area of service, use your gifts to strengthen and encourage the church.

Related Topics: CHURCH, FREEDOM, SERVING

INDIFFERENCE (*Apathy, Disinterest, Insensitivity*)

When can we not afford to be indifferent?

BIBLE READING: Mark 15:21-32

KEY BIBLE VERSE: *The leading priests and teachers of religious law also mocked Jesus. "He saved others," they scoffed, "but he can't save himself!"* (Mark 15:31)

We cannot be indifferent to Christ's sacrifice for us. Many of those who watched Jesus die had a hard-hearted indifference to everything he had said and done. Jesus could have saved himself, but he endured this suffering because of his love for us. He could have chosen not to take the pain and humiliation; he could have killed those who mocked him—but he suffered through it all because he loved even his enemies. We had a significant part in the drama that afternoon, because our sins were on the cross too. Jesus died on that cross for us, and the penalty for our sins was paid by his death. The only adequate response we can make is to confess our sin and freely accept the fact that Jesus paid for it so we wouldn't have to. Don't insult God with indifference toward the greatest act of genuine love in history.

BIBLE READING: Romans 13:1-14

KEY BIBLE VERSE: *Love does no wrong to anyone, so love satisfies all of God's requirements.* (Romans 13:10)

We cannot be indifferent to the needs of others. Christians must obey the law of love, which supersedes both religious and civil laws. How easy it is to excuse our indifference to others merely because we have no legal obligation to help them, and even to justify harming them if our actions are technically legal! But Jesus does not leave loopholes in the law of love. Whenever love demands it, we are to go beyond human legal requirements and imitate the God of love. (See James 2:8-9; 4:11; and 1 Peter 2:16-17 for more about this law of love.)

BIBLE READING: Revelation 3:14-22

KEY BIBLE VERSE: *I know all the things you do, that you are neither hot nor cold. I wish you were one or the other!* (Revelation 3:15)

We cannot afford to be indifferent in our obedience to Christ. Lukewarm water makes a disgusting drink. The church in Laodicea had become lukewarm and thus distasteful and repugnant. The believers didn't take a stand for anything; indifference had led to idleness. By neglecting to do anything for Christ, the church had become hardened and self-satisfied, and it was destroying itself. There is nothing more disgusting than a halfhearted, in-name-only Christian who is self-sufficient. Don't settle for following God halfway. Let Christ fire up your faith and get you into the action.

Related Topics: ACTIONS, FAITH, INSENSITIVITY

INFATUATION (*see* LOVE)

INFERIORITY (*see* INADEQUACY)

INFLUENCE (*Authority, Control, Power*)

How should we evaluate being influenced and influencing others?

BIBLE READING: 2 Kings 15:1-12

KEY BIBLE VERSE: *[Uzziah] did what was pleasing in the LORD's sight, just as his father, Amaziah, had done. But he did not destroy the pagan shrines, where the people offered sacrifices and burned incense.* (2 Kings 15:3-4)

We must seek to be influenced by Christlike models. Although Uzziah accomplished a great deal, he failed to destroy the high places, the location of pagan shrines in Judah, just as his father Amaziah and grandfather Joash had failed to do. Uzziah imitated the kings he had heard stories about and had watched while growing up. Although Uzziah's father and grandfather were basically good kings, they were poor models in some important areas. To rise above the influence of poor models, we must seek better ones. Christ provides a perfect model. No matter how you were raised or who has influenced your life, you can move beyond those limitations by taking Christ as your example and consciously trying to live as he did.

Our influence on others will be judged by God. Zechariah was an evil king because he encouraged Israel to sin by worshiping idols. Sin in our life is serious. But it is even more serious to encourage others to disobey God. We are responsible for the way we influence others. Beware of double sins: ones that not only hurt us, but also hurt others by encouraging them to sin.

BIBLE READING: Romans 1:18-32

KEY BIBLE VERSE: *They are fully aware of God's death penalty for those who do these things, yet they go right ahead and do them anyway. And, worse yet, they encourage others to do them, too.* (Romans 1:32)

We must evaluate influences by biblical standards. People tend to believe lies that reinforce their own selfish, personal beliefs. Today, more than ever, we need to be careful about the input we allow to form our beliefs. With TV, music, movies, and the rest of the media often presenting sinful lifestyles and unwholesome values, we find ourself constantly bombarded by attitudes and beliefs that are totally opposed to the Bible. Be careful about what you allow to form your opinions. The Bible is the only standard of truth. Evaluate all other opinions in light of its teachings.

Related Topics: AUTHORITY, POWER, SERVING

INITIATIVE *(Curiosity, Drive, Leadership)*

Why is initiative often a positive character quality?

BIBLE READING: Genesis 13:1-18

KEY BIBLE VERSE: *Abram talked it over with Lot. "This arguing between our herdsmen has got to stop," he said. "After all, we are close relatives!"* (Genesis 13:8)

Initiative is taking responsibility for solving a problem. Facing a potential conflict with his nephew Lot, Abram took the initiative in settling the dispute. He gave Lot first choice, even though Abram, being older, had the right to choose first. Abram also showed a willingness to risk being cheated. Abram's example shows us how to respond to difficult family situations: (1) take the initiative in resolving conflicts; (2) let others have first choice, even if that means not getting what we want; (3) put family peace above personal desires.

BIBLE READING: Ruth 2:1-13

KEY BIBLE VERSE: *One day Ruth said to Naomi, "Let me go out into the fields to gather leftover grain behind anyone who will let me do it." And Naomi said, "All right, my daughter, go ahead."* (Ruth 2:2)

Trusting God includes taking initiative. Ruth made her home in a foreign land. Instead of depending on Naomi or waiting for good fortune to happen, she took the initiative. She went to work. She was not afraid of admitting her need or working hard to supply it. When Ruth went out to the fields, God provided for her. If you are waiting for God to provide, consider this: He may be waiting for you to take the first step to demonstrate just how important your need is.

Taking initiative opens doors. Ruth's task, though menial, tiring, and perhaps degrading, was done faithfully. What is your attitude when the task you have been given is not up to your true potential? The task at hand may be all you can do, or it may be the work God wants you to do. Or, as in Ruth's case, it may be a test of your character that can open up new doors of opportunity.

 BIBLE READING: Joshua 3:1-17

KEY BIBLE VERSE: *Now it was the harvest season, and the Jordan was overflowing its banks. But as soon as the feet of the priests who were carrying the Ark touched the water at the river's edge, the water began piling up at a town upstream called Adam, which is near Zarethan. And the water below that point flowed on to the Dead Sea until the riverbed was dry. Then all the people crossed over near the city of Jericho.* (Joshua 3:15-16)

Initiative can demonstrate faith. The Israelites were eager to enter the Promised Land, conquer nations, and live peacefully. But first they had to cross the flood-level waters of the Jordan River. God gave them specific instructions: in order to cross, the priests had to step into the water. What if these priests had been afraid to take that first step? Often God provides no solution to our problems until we trust him and move ahead with what we know we should do. What are the rivers, or obstacles, in your life? In obedience to God, take that first step into the water.

Related Topics: ACTIONS, FAITH, OBEDIENCE

INJUSTICE (*Cheating, Dishonesty, Unfairness*)

Why is God so insistent in condemning injustice?

BIBLE READING: Deuteronomy 16:18-20

KEY BIBLE VERSE: *You must never twist justice or show partiality. Never accept a bribe, for bribes blind the eyes of the wise and corrupt the decisions of the godly.* (Deuteronomy 16:19)

Injustice undermines community peace. These verses anticipated a great problem the Israelites would face when they arrived in the Promised Land. Although they had Joshua as their national leader, they failed to complete the task and choose other spiritual leaders who would lead the tribes, districts, and cities with justice and God's wisdom. Because they did not appoint wise judges and faithful administrators, rebellion and injustice plagued their communities. It is a serious responsibility to appoint or elect wise and just officials. In your sphere of influence—home, church, school, job—are you ensuring that justice and godliness prevail? Failing to choose leaders who uphold justice can lead to much trouble, as Israel would discover.

BIBLE READING: Habakkuk 1:1-17

KEY BIBLE VERSE: *Must I forever see this sin and misery all around me? Wherever I look, I see destruction and violence. I am surrounded by people who love to argue and fight.* (Habakkuk 1:3)

Injustice can tempt us to believe that God does not care. Saddened by the violence and corruption he saw around him, Habakkuk poured out his heart to God. Today injustice is still rampant, but don't let your concern cause you to doubt God or rebel against him. Instead, consider the message that God gave Habakkuk, and recognize God's long-range plans and purposes. Realize that God is doing right, even when you do not understand why he works as he does.

Injustice can tempt us to believe God has forgotten. God responded to Habakkuk's questions and concerns by stating that he would do amazing acts that would astound Habakkuk. When circumstances around us become almost unbearable, we wonder if God has forgotten us. But remember, he is in control. God has a plan and will judge evildoers in his time. If we are truly humble, we will be willing to accept God's answers and await his timing.

History demonstrates that injustice has devastating consequences. God told the inhabitants of Jerusalem that they would be utterly amazed at what he was about to do. The people would, in fact, see a series of unbelievable events: (1) their own independent and prosperous kingdom, Judah, would suddenly become a vassal nation; (2) Egypt, a world power for centuries, would be crushed almost overnight; (3) Nineveh, the capital of the Assyrian empire, would be so completely ransacked that people would forget where it had been; and (4) the Babylonians would rise to power. Though these words were indeed amazing, the people saw them fulfilled during their lifetime.

How can we overcome injustice?

BIBLE READING: Matthew 5:38-48
KEY BIBLE VERSE: *You have heard that it was said, "Love your neighbor and hate your enemy." But I tell you: Love your enemies and pray for those who persecute you.* (Matthew 5:43-44, NIV)

We should not retaliate with injustice. When we are wronged, often our first reaction is to get even. Instead Jesus said we should do *good* to those who wrong us! Our desire should not be to keep score, but to love and forgive. This is not natural—it is supernatural. Only God can give us the strength to love as he does. Instead of planning vengeance, pray for those who hurt you.

Injustice must be met with justice. To many Jews of Jesus' day, these statements were offensive. Any Messiah who would turn the other cheek was not the military leader they wanted to lead a revolt against Rome. Since they were under Roman oppression, they wanted retaliation against their enemies, whom they hated. But Jesus suggested a new, radical response to injustice: instead of demanding rights, give them up freely! According to Jesus, it is more important to *give* justice and mercy than to receive it.

Injustice can be overcome by love. By telling us not to retaliate, Jesus keeps us from taking the law into our own hands. By loving and praying for our enemies, we can overcome evil with good.

The Pharisees interpreted Leviticus 19:18 as teaching that they should love only those who love in return, and Psalms 139:19-22 and 140:9-11 as meaning that they should hate their enemies. But Jesus says we are to love our enemies. If you love your enemies and treat them well, you will truly show that Jesus is Lord of your life. This is possible only for those who give themselves fully to God, because only he can deliver people from natural selfishness. We must trust the Holy Spirit to help us *show* love to those for whom we may not *feel* love.

Related Topics: EVIL, FAIRNESS, JUSTICE

INSECURITY (Anxiety, Nervousness, Worry)

How should we respond to feelings of insecurity?

BIBLE READING: Mark 9:33-37
KEY BIBLE VERSE: *They didn't answer, because they had been arguing about which of them was the greatest.* (Mark 9:34)

Faithful obedience to Christ controls insecurity. The disciples, caught up in their constant struggle for personal success, were embarrassed to answer Jesus' question. It is always painful to compare our motives with Christ's. It is not wrong for believers to be industrious or ambitious. But when ambition pushes obedience and service to one side, it becomes sin. Pride or insecurity can cause us to overvalue position and prestige. In God's kingdom, such motives are destructive. The only safe ambition is directed toward Christ's kingdom, not our own advancement.

BIBLE READING: Galatians 3:1-14
KEY BIBLE VERSE: *I ask you again, does God give you the Holy Spirit and work miracles among you because you obey the law of Moses? Of course not! It is because you believe the message you heard about Christ.* (Galatians 3:5)

Faith in Christ is the answer to insecurity. The Galatians knew that they had received the Holy Spirit when they believed, not when they obeyed the law. People still feel insecure in their faith, because faith alone seems too easy. People still try to get closer to God by following rules. While certain disciplines (Bible study, prayer) and service may help us grow, they must not take the place of the Holy Spirit in us or become ends in themselves. By asking these questions, Paul hoped to get the Galatians to focus again on Christ as the foundation of their faith.

Related Topics: CONFIDENCE, FAITH, SECURITY

INSENSITIVITY (Indifferent, Thoughtless, Unresponsive)

How can insensitivity be a self-destructive attitude?

BIBLE READING: Psalm 5:1-12
KEY BIBLE VERSE: *O God, you take no pleasure in wickedness; you cannot tolerate the slightest sin.* (Psalm 5:4)

We may become insensitive to sin. God cannot condone or excuse even the smallest sin. Therefore we cannot excuse ourself for sinning only a little bit. As we grow spiritually, our sensitivity to sin increases. What is your reaction to sin in your life? Are you insensitive, unconcerned, disappointed, or comfortable? As God makes us aware of sin, we must be intolerant toward it and be willing to change. All believers should strive to be more tolerant of people but less tolerant of the sin in others and in themselves.

BIBLE READING: Matthew 15:21-28
KEY BIBLE VERSE: *Jesus gave her no reply—not even a word. Then his disciples urged him to send her away. "Tell her to leave," they said. "She is bothering us with all her begging."* (Matthew 15:23)

Insensitivity may lead us to cut ourself off from others. The disciples asked Jesus to get rid of the woman because she was bothering them with her nagging persistence. They showed no compassion for her or sensitivity to her needs. It is possible to become so occupied with spiritual matters that we miss real needs right around us. This is especially likely if we are prejudiced against needy people or if they cause us inconvenience. Instead of being bothered, be aware of the opportunities that surround you. Be open to the beauty of God's message for *all* people, and make an effort not to shut out those who are different from you.

BIBLE READING: Matthew 23:37-39

KEY BIBLE VERSE: *O Jerusalem, Jerusalem, the city that kills the prophets and stones God's messengers! How often I have wanted to gather your children together as a hen protects her chicks beneath her wings, but you wouldn't let me.* (Matthew 23:37)

Persistent insensitivity blinds us to our own needs. Jesus wanted to gather his people together as a hen protects her chicks under her wings, but they wouldn't let him. Jesus also wants to protect us if we will just come to him. Many times we hurt and don't know where to turn. We reject Christ's help because we don't think he can give us what we need. But who knows our needs better than our Creator? Those who turn to Jesus will find that he helps and comforts as no one else can.

Insensitivity blinds us to God's presence. Jerusalem was the capital city of God's chosen people, the ancestral home of David, Israel's greatest king, and the location of the temple, the earthly dwelling place of God. It was intended to be the center of worship of the true God and a symbol of justice to all people. But Jerusalem had become blind to God and insensitive to human need. Here we see the depth of Jesus' feelings for lost people and for his beloved city, which would soon be destroyed.

Related Topics: DISOBEDIENCE, INDIFFERENCE, SIN

INSIGHT *(Knowledge, Understanding, Wisdom)*

What are the sources of dependable spiritual insight?

BIBLE READING: Matthew 6:19-24

KEY BIBLE VERSE: *Your eye is a lamp for your body. A pure eye lets sunshine into your soul. But an evil eye shuts out the light and plunges you into darkness. If the light you think you have is really darkness, how deep that darkness will be!* (Matthew 6:22-23)

Spiritual insight comes from focusing our life on God. Spiritual vision is our capacity to see clearly what God wants us to do and to see the world from his point of view. But this spiritual insight can be easily clouded. Self-serving desires, interests, and goals block that vision. Serving God is the best way to restore it. A "pure" eye is one that is fixed on God.

Our desire should be to discover what God wants and then invest ourselves in obedience. As we do, our understanding of God will increase. Our vision of God will become clearer.

BIBLE READING: Psalm 119:105-112

KEY BIBLE VERSE: *Your word is a lamp for my feet and a light for my path.* (Psalm 119:105)

God's Word is an inexhaustible source of insight. God's Word makes us wise—wiser than our enemies and wiser than any teachers who ignore it. True wisdom goes beyond amassing knowledge; it is *applying* knowledge in a life-changing way. Intelligent or experienced people are not necessarily wise. Wisdom comes from allowing what God teaches to guide us.

 BIBLE READING: Ephesians 1:15-23

KEY BIBLE VERSE: *I pray that your hearts will be flooded with light so that you can understand the wonderful future he has promised to those he called. I want you to realize what a rich and glorious inheritance he has given to his people.* (Ephesians 1:18)

Insight from God helps us see Christ for who he really is. Paul prayed that the Ephesians would know Christ better. Christ is our model, and the more we know of him, the more we will be like him. Study Jesus' life in the Gospels to see what he was like on earth two thousand years ago, and get to know him in prayer now. Personal knowledge of Christ will change your life.

Insight from God helps us see all of life from his point of view. The hope we have is not a vague feeling that the future will be positive, but it is complete assurance of certain victory through God. This hope remains in spite of the sometimes confusing events of history and the difficulties of our own lives. This complete certainty comes to us through the Holy Spirit who is working in us. (For more on hope, see Romans 8:23-24; Ephesians 4:4; Colossians 1:5; 1 Thessalonians 1:3; 1 Peter 3:15.)

Related Topics: KNOWLEDGE, UNDERSTANDING, WISDOM

INSPIRATION (*Example, Motivation, Source*)

What does inspiration mean when applied to the Bible?

BIBLE READING: 2 Timothy 3:10-17

KEY BIBLE VERSE: *All Scripture is inspired by God and is useful to teach us what is true and to make us realize what is wrong in our lives. It straightens us out and teaches us to do what is right.* (2 Timothy 3:16)

Inspiration refers to the way God guided those who wrote his Word. The Bible is not a collection of stories, fables, myths, or merely human ideas about God. It is not a human book. Through the Holy Spirit, God revealed his person and plan to certain believers, who wrote down his message for his people (2 Peter 1:20-21). This process is known as *inspiration.* The writers wrote from their own personal, historical, and cultural contexts. Although they used their own minds, talents, language, and style, they wrote what God wanted them to write.

Inspiration refers to the reliability of God's Word. Scripture is completely trustworthy because God was in control of its writing. The means God used were frail human beings, but the meanings he made sure were recorded are God's message to us. Its words are entirely authoritative for our faith and for our life. The Bible is "inspired by God." Read it, and use its teachings to guide your conduct.

God's inspired Word is one way he breathes his Spirit into our life. The whole Bible is God's inspired Word. Because it is inspired and trustworthy, we should *read* it and *apply* it to our life. The Bible is our standard for testing everything else that claims to be true. It is our safeguard against false teaching and our source of guidance for how we should live. It is our only source of knowledge about how we can be saved. God wants to show you what is true and equip you to live for him. How much time do you spend in God's Word? Read it regularly to discover God's truth and to become confident in your life and faith. Develop a plan for reading the whole Bible, not just the familiar passages.

BIBLE READING: 2 Peter 1:12-21

KEY BIBLE VERSE: *Above all, you must understand that no prophecy in Scripture ever came from the prophets themselves or because they wanted to prophesy. It was the Holy Spirit who moved the prophets to speak from God.* (2 Peter 1:20-21)

Inspiration means that God is the ultimate source of the Bible. "It was the Holy Spirit who moved the prophets to speak from God" means that Scripture did not come from the creative work of the prophets' own invention or interpretation. God inspired the writers; therefore their message is authentic and reliable. God used the talents, education, and cultural background of each writer (they were not mindless robots); and God cooperated with the writers in such a way to ensure that the message he intended was faithfully communicated in the very words they wrote.

Related Topics: BIBLE, HOLY SPIRIT, TRUTH

INSTRUCTIONS (*Commands, Directions, Orders*)

How should we respond to instructions we don't fully understand?

BIBLE READING: Joshua 6:1-21

KEY BIBLE VERSE: *Your entire army is to march around the city once a day for six days. Seven priests will walk ahead of the Ark, each carrying a ram's horn. On the seventh day you are to march around the city seven times, with the priests blowing the horns. When you hear the priests give one long blast on the horns, have all the people give a mighty shout. Then the walls of the city will collapse, and the people can charge straight into the city.* (Joshua 6:3-5)

Full understanding is not a prerequisite for obedience. Why did God give Joshua all these complicated instructions for the battle? Several answers are possible: (1) God was making it undeniably clear that the battle would depend upon him, and not upon Israel's weapons and expertise. This is why priests carrying the ark, not soldiers, led the Israelites into battle. (2) God's method of taking the city accentuated the terror already felt in Jericho (2:9). (3) This strange military maneuver was a test of the Israelites' faith and their willingness to follow God completely. The blowing of the trumpets in the battle had a special significance. They had been instructed to blow the same trumpets used in their religious festivals to remind them that victory would come from the Lord, not their own military might (Numbers 10:9).

BIBLE READING: 1 Samuel 31:1-13

KEY BIBLE VERSE: *Saul groaned to his armor bearer, "Take your sword and kill me before these pagan Philistines run me through and humiliate me." But his armor bearer was afraid and would not do it. So Saul took his own sword and fell on it.* (1 Samuel 31:4)

It is more important to obey God than any human commands. Saul's armor-bearer faced a moral dilemma—should he carry out a sinful order from a man he was supposed to obey? He knew he should obey his master, the king, but he also knew murder was wrong. He decided not to kill Saul.

There is a difference between following an order with which you don't agree and following one you know is wrong. It is never right or ethical to carry out a wrong act, no matter who gives the order or what the consequences for disobedience may be. What shapes your choice when you face a moral dilemma? Have the courage to follow God's law above human commands.

Related Topics: DIRECTION, GUIDANCE, OBEDIENCE

INSULT(S) *(Attack, Hurt, Slander)*

How should we respond to insults?

BIBLE READING: Judges 12:1-7
KEY BIBLE VERSE: *Then the tribe of Ephraim mobilized its army and crossed over to Zaphon. They sent this message to Jephthah: "Why didn't you call for us to help you fight against Ammon? We are going to burn down your house with you in it!"* (Judges 12:1)

We should not act in response to insults spoken against us. Israel had just won a great battle, but instead of joy, there was pettiness and quarreling. The tribe of Ephraim was angry and jealous that they were not invited to join in the fighting (although Jephthah said he had invited them). The insults of the Ephraimites enraged Jephthah, who called out his troops and killed forty-two thousand men from Ephraim.

Jephthah usually spoke before he acted, but this time his revenge was swift. It cost Israel dearly, and it might have been avoided. Insulting others and being jealous are not right responses when we feel left out. But seeking revenge for an insult is just as wrong, and very costly.

BIBLE READING: Proverbs 12:1-28
KEY BIBLE VERSE: *A fool is quick-tempered, but a wise person stays calm when insulted.* (Proverbs 12:16)

Our response to insults should be deliberate and controlled. When someone annoys or insults you, it is natural to retaliate. But this solves nothing and only encourages trouble. Instead, answer slowly and quietly. Your positive response will achieve positive results. Proverbs 15:1 says, "A gentle answer turns away wrath."

BIBLE READING: John 2:13-23
KEY BIBLE VERSE: *Then his disciples remembered this prophecy from the Scriptures: "Passion for God's house burns within me."* (John 2:17)

Every evil act is an insult against God. Jesus took the evil acts in the temple as an insult against God, and thus he did not deal with them halfheartedly. He was consumed with righteous anger against such flagrant disrespect for God. If we have been insulted without cause we can be sure that God has also been insulted. We must leave the final results in God's hands and respond as he has directed us to respond.

Related Topics: GENTLENESS, INJUSTICE, PATIENCE

INTEGRITY (*Dependability, Honesty, Trustworthiness*)

What does the Bible say about integrity?

📖 BIBLE READING: Joshua 14:1-15
KEY BIBLE VERSE: *I'm asking you to give me the hill country that the LORD promised me. You will remember that as scouts we found the Anakites living there in great, walled cities. But if the LORD is with me, I will drive them out of the land, just as the LORD said.* (Joshua 14:12)

Integrity is a long-term character trait. Caleb was faithful from the start. As one of the original spies sent into the Promised Land (Numbers 13:30-33), he saw great cities and giants, yet he knew God would help the people conquer the land. Because of his faith, God promised him a personal inheritance of land (Numbers 14:24; Deuteronomy 1:34-36). Here, forty-five years later, the land was given to him. His faith was still unwavering. The integrity with which he had boldly contradicted the cowardly advice of the ten spies years before was as strong as ever. Although his inherited land still had giants, Caleb knew the Lord would help him conquer them. Like Caleb, we must be faithful to God, not only at the start of our walk with him, but through our entire lives. We must never allow ourself to rest on our past accomplishments or reputations.

📖 BIBLE READING: Psalm 25:1-22
KEY BIBLE VERSE: *May integrity and honesty protect me, for I put my hope in you.* (Psalm 25:21)

Integrity is being what we say we are. If ever we needed two powerful forces to preserve us along life's way, we need integrity and honesty. The psalmist asks for these to protect him step-by-step. Honesty makes us learn God's requirements and strive to fulfill them. Integrity—being what we say we are—keeps us from claiming to be honest while living as if we do not know God. Honesty says, "This is the Shepherd's way," and integrity says, "I will walk consistently in it."

📖 BIBLE READING: Luke 16:1-15
KEY BIBLE VERSE: *Unless you are faithful in small matters, you won't be faithful in large ones. If you cheat even a little, you won't be honest with greater responsibilities. And if you are untrustworthy about worldly wealth, who will trust you with the true riches of heaven?* (Luke 16:10-11)

One of the most difficult tests of integrity is wealth. Our integrity often meets its match in money matters. God calls us to be honest even in small details we could easily rationalize away. Heaven's riches are far more valuable than earthly wealth. But if we are not trustworthy with our money here (no matter how much or how little we have), we will be unfit to handle the vast riches of God's kingdom. Don't let your integrity slip in small matters, and it will not fail you in crucial decisions either.

Related Topics: CONSISTENCY, FAITHFULNESS, HONESTY

INTENTIONS (*Motives, Purposes, Reasons*)

How does God measure our intentions?

BIBLE READING: Numbers 14:36-45

KEY BIBLE VERSE: *They got up early the next morning and set out for the hill country of Canaan. "Let's go," they said. "We realize that we have sinned, but now we are ready to enter the land the LORD has promised us."* (Numbers 14:40)

God knows our real intentions. When the Israelites realized their foolish mistake, they were suddenly ready to return to God. But God didn't confuse their admission of guilt with true repentance, because he knew their hearts. Sure enough, they soon went their own way again. Sometimes right actions or good intentions come too late. We must not only do what is right, but also do it at the right time. God wants complete and instant obedience.

BIBLE READING: Matthew 5:27-30

KEY BIBLE VERSE: *Anyone who even looks at a woman with lust in his eye has already committed adultery with her in his heart.* (Matthew 5:28)

The intention to do evil is sin. The Old Testament law said that it is wrong for a person to have sex with someone other than his or her spouse (Exodus 20:14). But Jesus said that the *desire* to have sex with someone other than your spouse is mental adultery and thus sin. Jesus emphasized that if the *act* is wrong, then so is the *intention*. To be faithful to your spouse with your body but not your mind is to break the trust so vital to a strong marriage. Jesus is not condemning natural interest in the opposite sex or even healthy sexual desire, but the deliberate and repeated filling of one's mind with fantasies that would be evil if acted out.

BIBLE READING: Matthew 14:22-33

KEY BIBLE VERSE: *"All right, come," Jesus said. So Peter went over the side of the boat and walked on the water toward Jesus. But when he looked around at the high waves, he was terrified and began to sink. "Save me, Lord!" he shouted.* (Matthew 14:29-30)

Good intentions can become a reality with Christ's help. Although we start out with good intentions, sometimes our faith falters. This doesn't necessarily mean we have failed. When Peter's faith faltered, he reached out to Christ, the only one who could help. He was afraid, but he still looked to Christ. When you are apprehensive about the troubles around you and doubt Christ's presence or ability to help, you must remember that he is the *only* one who can really help.

BIBLE READING: Matthew 21:28-32

KEY BIBLE VERSE: *"Which of the two was obeying his father?" They replied, "The first, of course." Then Jesus explained his meaning: "I assure you, corrupt tax collectors and prostitutes will get into the Kingdom of God before you do."* (Matthew 21:31)

God knows the real intentions of our heart. Like the first son, we are sometimes prone to say no to God and only then realize whom we have rejected. God loves us too much to settle for our superficial answers to his call. The second son, who said he would obey and then didn't, represented the nation of Israel in Jesus' day. They said they wanted to do God's will, but they constantly disobeyed. They were phony, just going through the motions. It is dangerous to pretend to obey God when our heart is far from him, because God knows our true intentions. Our actions must match our words.

Related Topics: ACTIONS, HEART, MOTIVES

INTERPRETATIONS (*Explanations, Impressions, Understandings*)

What guidelines should we follow when interpreting the Bible?

BIBLE READING: Matthew 23:1-36

KEY BIBLE VERSE: *Practice and obey whatever they say to you, but don't follow their example. For they don't practice what they teach. They crush you with impossible religious demands and never lift a finger to help ease the burden.* (Matthew 23:3-4)

The key to interpretation is practice. Jesus exposed the hypocritical attitudes of the religious leaders. They knew the Scriptures but did not live by them. They didn't care about *being* holy—just *looking* holy in order to receive the people's admiration and praise. Today, like the Pharisees, many people who know the Bible do not let it change their lives. They say they follow Jesus but don't live by his standards of love. People who live this way are hypocrites. We must make sure our actions match our beliefs.

BIBLE READING: John 16:5-16

KEY BIBLE VERSE: *When the Spirit of truth comes, he will guide you into all truth. He will not be presenting his own ideas; he will be telling you what he has heard. He will tell you about the future.* (John 16:13)

We must depend on the Holy Spirit to guide our interpretations. The truth into which the Holy Spirit guides us is the truth about Christ. The Spirit also helps us through patient practice to discern right from wrong. Those who do not depend on the guidance God offers will be limited and wrong in the understanding of God's Word.

Our interpretations must not go beyond or contradict God's Word. Jesus said the Holy Spirit would tell them "about the future"—the nature of their mission, the opposition they would face, and the final outcome of their efforts. They didn't fully understand these promises until the Holy Spirit came after Jesus' death and resurrection. Then the Holy Spirit revealed truths to the disciples that they wrote down in the books that now form the New Testament. Since that time, the Holy Spirit's guidance has emphasized helping believers understand and practice God's Word.

BIBLE READING: 2 Timothy 2:14-26

KEY BIBLE VERSE: *Work hard so God can approve you. Be a good worker, one who does not need to be ashamed and who correctly explains the word of truth.* (2 Timothy 2:15)

Our interpretations must be balanced. Paul urged Timothy to remind the believers not to argue over unimportant details ("fighting over words") or have foolish discussions, because such arguments are confusing, useless, and even harmful. False teachers loved to cause strife and divisions by their meaningless quibbling over unimportant details (see 1 Timothy 6:3-5). To handle the word of truth correctly, we must study what the Word of God says so we can understand what it means.

Related Topics: BIBLE, TRUTH, UNDERSTANDING

INTIMACY (*see* LOVE)

INTIMIDATION *(Bullying, Fear, Threatening)*

How should we respond to intimidation?

BIBLE READING: Ezra 5:1-5

KEY BIBLE VERSE: *They also asked for a list of the names of all the people who were working on the Temple. But because their God was watching over them, the leaders of the Jews were not prevented from building until a report was sent to Darius and he returned his decision.* (Ezra 5:4-5)

Intimidation must be met with confidence. The non-Jews who lived nearby attempted to hinder the construction of the temple. But while the legal debate went on and the decision was under appeal, the Jews continued to rebuild. When we are doing God's work, others may try to delay, confuse, or frustrate us, but we can proceed confidently. God will accomplish his purposes in our world, no matter who attempts to block them. Just as he watched over the Jewish elders, he watches over you. Concentrate on God's purpose, and don't be sidetracked by intrigues or slander.

Intimidation must be met by focusing on God. It is not always easy to speak up for our faith in an unbelieving world, but we must. The way to deal with pressure and intimidation is to recognize that we are workers for God. Our allegiance is to him first, people second. When we contemplate the reactions and criticisms of hostile people, we can become paralyzed with fear. If we try to offend no one or to please everyone, we won't be effective. God is our leader, and his rewards are most important. So don't be intimidated. Let others know by your words and actions whom you really serve.

BIBLE READING: 2 Timothy 1:1-18

KEY BIBLE VERSE: *God has not given us a spirit of fear and timidity, but of power, love, and self-discipline.* (2 Timothy 1:7)

Intimidation must be met by relying on the Holy Spirit. Timothy was experiencing great opposition to his message and to himself as a leader. His youth, his association with Paul, and his leadership had come under fire from believers and nonbelievers alike. Paul urged him to be bold. When we allow people to intimidate us, we neutralize our effectiveness for God. The power of the Holy Spirit can help us overcome our fear of what some might say or do to us, so that we can continue to do God's work.

Related Topics: CONFIDENCE, FEAR, TRUST

INVESTMENT *(Ownership, Purchase, Value)*

What kinds of investments are pleasing to God?

BIBLE READING: Psalm 49:1-20

KEY BIBLE VERSE: *Those who are wise must finally die, just like the foolish and senseless, leaving all their wealth behind.* (Psalm 49:10)

The best investments are made with eternity in mind. The rich and poor have one similarity—when they die, they leave all they own here on earth. At the moment of death (and all of us will face that moment), both rich and poor are naked and empty-handed before God. The only riches we have at that time are those we have already invested in our eternal heritage. At the time of death, each of us will wish we had invested less on earth, where we must leave it, and more in heaven, where we will retain it forever. To have treasure in heaven, we must place our faith in God, pledge ourself to obey him, and utilize our resources for the good of his kingdom. This is a good time to check up on your investments and see where you have invested the most. Then do whatever it takes to place your investments where they really count.

BIBLE READING: Matthew 25:14-30

KEY BIBLE VERSE: *Again, the Kingdom of Heaven can be illustrated by the story of a man going on a trip. He called together his servants and gave them money to invest for him while he was gone.* (Matthew 25:14)

We have a responsibility to invest God's resources wisely. The master divided the money (talents) among his servants according to their abilities. No one received more or less than he could handle. If he failed in his assignment, his excuse could not be that he was overwhelmed. Failure could come only from laziness or hatred toward the master. The talents represent any kind of resource we are given. God gives us time, gifts, and other resources according to our abilities, and he expects us to invest them wisely until he returns. We are responsible to use well what God has given us. The issue is not how much we have, but how well we use what we have.

Our investments must not be for selfish ends. This last man was thinking only of himself. He hoped to play it safe and protect himself from his hard master, but he was judged for his self-centeredness. We must not make excuses to avoid doing what God calls us to do. If God truly is our Master, we must obey him willingly. Our time, abilities, and money aren't ours in the first place—we are caretakers, not owners. When we ignore, squander, or abuse what we are given, we are rebellious and deserve to be punished.

Our investments must be centered on the kingdom of God. This parable describes the consequences resulting from two attitudes to Christ's return. The person who diligently prepares for it by investing his or her time and talent to serve God will be rewarded. The person who has no heart for the work of the kingdom will be punished. God rewards faithfulness. Those who bear no fruit for God's kingdom cannot expect to be treated the same as those who are faithful.

BIBLE READING: 2 Corinthians 9:6-15

KEY BIBLE VERSE: *Yes, you will be enriched so that you can give even more generously. And when we take your gifts to those who need them, they will break out in thanksgiving to God.* (2 Corinthians 9:11)

Giving is one of the best investments. God gives us resources to use and invest for him. Paul uses the illustration of seed to explain that the resources God gives us are not to be hidden, foolishly devoured, or thrown away. Instead, they should be cultivated in order to produce more crops. When we invest what God has given us in his work, he will provide us with even more to give in his service.

Related Topics: DEBTS, GIVING, RESOURCES

INVITATION *(Proposition, Request, Welcome)*

How should we respond to God's invitation?

BIBLE READING: Luke 14:1-24

KEY BIBLE VERSE: *His master said, "Go out into the country lanes and behind the hedges and urge anyone you find to come, so that the house will be full. For none of those I invited first will get even the smallest taste of what I had prepared for them." (Luke 14:23-24)*

We should accept God's invitation while it is offered. The man sitting at the table with Jesus saw the glory of God's kingdom, but he did not yet understand how to get in. In Jesus' story, many people turned down the invitation to the banquet because the timing was inconvenient. We too can resist or delay responding to God's invitation, and our excuses may sound reasonable—work duties, family responsibilities, financial needs, or whatever they may be. Nevertheless, God's invitation is the most important event in our life, no matter how inconveniently it may be timed. Are you making excuses to avoid responding to God's call? Jesus reminds us that the time will come when God will pull his invitation and offer it to others—then it will be too late to get into the banquet.

We should accept God's invitation wholeheartedly. It was customary to send two invitations to a party—the first to announce the event, the second to tell the guests that everything was ready. The guests in Jesus' story insulted the host by making excuses when he issued the second invitation. In Israel's history, God's first invitation came from Moses and the prophets; the second came from his Son. The religious leaders accepted the first invitation. They believed that God had called them to be his people, but they insulted God by refusing to accept his Son. Thus, as the master in the story sent his servant into the streets to invite the needy to his banquet, so God sent his Son to the whole world of needy people to tell them that God's kingdom had arrived and was ready for them.

We should accept God's invitation with joy. In this chapter we read Jesus' words against seeking status, and in favor of hard work and even suffering. Let us not lose sight of the end result of all our humility and self-sacrifice—a joyous banquet with our Lord! God never asks us to suffer for the sake of suffering. He never asks us to give up something good unless he plans to replace it with something even better. Jesus is not calling us to join him in a labor camp but in a feast—the wedding supper of the Lamb (Revelation 19:6-9), when God and his beloved church will be joined forever.

Related Topics: ETERNAL LIFE, GOSPEL, SALVATION

INVOLVEMENT (*Experience, Participation, Skill*)

What can we learn from God about the importance of involvement with others?

BIBLE READING: John 12:12-19

KEY BIBLE VERSE: *His disciples didn't realize at the time that this was a fulfillment of prophecy. But after Jesus entered into his glory, they remembered that these Scriptures had come true before their eyes. (John 12:16)*

Involvement with others should be consistent even when it goes unnoticed. After Jesus' resurrection, the disciples understood for the first time many of the prophecies that they had missed along the way. Jesus' words and actions took on new meaning and made more sense. In retrospect, the disciples saw how

Jesus had led them into a deeper and better understanding of his truth. Stop now and think about the events in your life leading up to where you are now. How has God led you to this point? As you grow older, you will look back and see God's involvement more clearly than you do now.

BIBLE READING: Matthew 25:31-46
KEY BIBLE VERSE: *The King will tell them, "I assure you, when you did it to one of the least of these my brothers and sisters, you were doing it to me!"* (Matthew 25:40)

Involvement with others is a daily challenge. This parable describes acts of mercy we all can do every day. These acts do not depend on wealth, ability, or intelligence; they are simple acts freely given and freely received. We have no excuse to neglect those who have deep needs, and we cannot hand over this responsibility to the church or government. Jesus demands our personal involvement in caring for others' needs (Isaiah 58:7). It is one of those ways in which we can imitate Christ in our daily lives.

BIBLE READING: John 17:13-19
KEY BIBLE VERSE: *I'm not asking you to take them out of the world, but to keep them safe from the evil one.* (John 17:15)

Involvement in the world is a God-given responsibility. Jesus didn't ask God to take believers *out* of the world but instead to use them *in* the world. Because Jesus sends us into the world, we should not try to escape from the world or avoid all relationships with non-Christians. We are called to be salt and light (Matthew 5:13-16), and we are to do the work God sent us to do.

Related Topics: ACTIONS, EXAMPLE, FAITH

ISOLATION (*Retreat, Seclusion, Solitude*)

How can we overcome isolation?

BIBLE READING: Psalm 130:1-8
KEY BIBLE VERSE: *From the depths of despair, O LORD, I call for your help.* (Psalm 130:1)

Isolation caused by despair can be overcome by focusing on God. In the depths of despair, the psalmist cried out to God. Despair makes us feel isolated and distant from God, but this is precisely when we need God most. Despair over sin should not lead to self-pity, causing us to think more about ourself than God. Instead, it should lead to confession and then to God's mercy, forgiveness, and redemption. When we feel overwhelmed by a problem, feeling sorry for ourself will only increase feelings of hopelessness; but crying out to God will turn our attention to the only one who can really help.

BIBLE READING: Isaiah 1:1-31
KEY BIBLE VERSE: *Oh, what a sinful nation they are! They are loaded down with a burden of guilt. They are evil and corrupt children who have turned away from the LORD. They have despised the Holy One of Israel, cutting themselves off from his help.* (Isaiah 1:4)

Isolation caused by sin can be overcome by repentance. As long as the people of Judah continued to sin, they cut themselves off from God's help and isolated themselves. When you feel lonely and separated from God, remember that God does not abandon you. Our sins cut us off from him. The only sure cure for this kind of loneliness is to restore a meaningful relationship with God by confessing your sin, obeying his instructions, and communicating regularly with him (see Psalm 140:13 and 1 John 1:9).

BIBLE READING: Ephesians 3:14-21

KEY BIBLE VERSE: *When I think of the wisdom and scope of God's plan, I fall to my knees and pray to the Father, the Creator of everything in heaven and on earth.* (Ephesians 3:14-15)

Realize that living in spiritual isolation leads to real problems. The family of God includes all who have believed in him in the past, all who believe in the present, and all who will believe in the future. We are all a family because we have the same Father. He is the source of all creation, the rightful owner of everything. God promises his love and power to his family, the church (3:16-21). If we want to receive God's blessings, it is important that we stay in contact with other believers in the body of Christ. Those who isolate themselves from God's family and try to go it alone cut themselves off from God's power.

Related Topics: QUIET, REST, SOLITUDE

JEALOUSY (*Coveting, Desire, Envy*)

▶ **GOD'S JEALOUSY**
Why is God a "jealous" God?

BIBLE READING: Nahum 1:1-15
KEY BIBLE VERSE: *The LORD is a jealous God, filled with vengeance and wrath. He takes revenge on all who oppose him and furiously destroys his enemies!* (Nahum 1:2)

God's jealousy is justified. God alone has the right to be jealous and to carry out vengeance. Jealousy and vengeance may be surprising terms to associate with God. When humans are jealous and take vengeance, they are usually acting in a spirit of selfishness. But it is appropriate for God to insist on our complete allegiance, and it is just for him to punish unrepentant evildoers. His jealousy and vengeance are not tainted with selfishness. Their purpose is to remove sin and restore peace to the world (Deuteronomy 4:24; 5:9).

BIBLE READING: Deuteronomy 4:15-31
KEY BIBLE VERSE: *Be careful not to break the covenant the LORD your God has made with you. You will break it if you make idols of any shape or form, for the LORD your God has absolutely forbidden this. The LORD your God is a devouring fire, a jealous God.* (Deuteronomy 4:23-24)

Only God deserves our undivided devotion. Jealousy is a demand for someone else's exclusive affection or loyalty. Some jealousy is bad. It is destructive for a man to get upset when his wife talks pleasantly with another man. But other jealousy is good. It is right for a man to demand that his wife treat him, and only him, as her husband. Usually we use the word *jealousy* only for the bad reaction. But God's kind of jealousy is appropriate and good. He is defending his word and his high honor. He makes a strong, exclusive demand on us: We must treat only the Lord—and no one else in all the universe—as God.

▶ **HUMAN JEALOUSY**
What are the results of human jealousy?

BIBLE READING: Genesis 26:12-35
KEY BIBLE VERSE: *He acquired large flocks of sheep and goats, great herds of cattle, and many servants. Soon the Philistines became jealous of him, and they filled*

up all of Isaac's wells with earth. These were the wells that had been dug by the servants of his father, Abraham. (Genesis 26:14-15)

Human jealousy is most often destructive rather than constructive. God kept his promise to bless Isaac. The neighboring Philistines grew jealous because everything Isaac did seemed to go right. So they plugged his wells and tried to get rid of him. Jealousy is a dividing force strong enough to tear apart the mightiest of nations or the closest of friends. It forces you to separate yourself from what you were longing for in the first place. When you find yourself becoming jealous of others, try thanking God for their good fortune. Before striking out in anger, consider what you could lose (a friend, a job, a spouse?).

BIBLE READING: 1 Samuel 18:1-16

KEY BIBLE VERSE: *This made Saul very angry. "What's this?" he said. "They credit David with ten thousands and me with only thousands. Next they'll be making him their king!" So from that time on Saul kept a jealous eye on David.* (1 Samuel 18:8-9)

Human jealousy can destroy relationships. Saul's appreciation for David turned to jealousy as people began to applaud David's exploits. In a jealous rage, Saul attempted to murder David by hurling his spear at him (18:11-12).

Jealousy may not seem to be a major sin, but in reality, it is one step short of murder. Jealousy starts as you resent a rival; it leads to your wishing he or she were removed; then it manifests itself in your seeking ways to harm that person in word or action. Beware of letting jealousy get a foothold in your life.

Love is the best weapon against jealousy. Saul tried to kill David because he was jealous of David's popularity, yet David continued to protect and comfort Saul. Perhaps people have been jealous of you and have even attacked you in some way. They may be intimidated by your strengths, which make them conscious of their own shortcomings. It would be natural to strike back or to avoid them. A better response is to befriend them (Matthew 5:43-44) and to ask God for the strength to continue to love them, as David kept on loving Saul.

BIBLE READING: Romans 13:1-14

KEY BIBLE VERSE: *We should be decent and true in everything we do, so that everyone can approve of our behavior. Don't participate in wild parties and getting drunk, or in adultery and immoral living, or in fighting and jealousy. But let the Lord Jesus Christ take control of you, and don't think of ways to indulge your evil desires.* (Romans 13:13-14)

Human jealousy leads to sin. The *night* refers to the present evil time. The *day* refers to the time of Christ's return. Some people are surprised that Paul lists fighting and jealousy with the gross and obvious sins of wild parties, drunkenness, and sexual immorality. Like Jesus in his Sermon on the Mount (Matthew 5–7), Paul considers attitudes as important as actions. Just as hatred leads to murder, so jealousy leads to strife and lust to adultery. When Christ returns, he wants to find his people clean on the inside as well as on the outside.

Becoming like Christ is the answer to the problem of human jealousy. How do we clothe ourselves with the armor of right living? First we identify with Christ by being baptized (Galatians 3:27). This shows our solidarity with other Christians and with the death, burial, and resurrection of Jesus Christ.

Second, we exemplify the qualities Jesus showed while he was here on earth (love, humility, truth, service). In a sense, we role-play what Jesus would do in our situation (see Ephesians 4:24-32; Colossians 3:10-17). We also must not give our desires any opportunity to lead us into sin. Avoid those situations that open the door to gratifying sinful desires.

Related Topics: ENVY, HUMILITY, LUST

JESUS CHRIST (*Lord, Messiah, Savior*)

▶ **THE IDENTITY OF JESUS CHRIST**
Who is Jesus?

BIBLE READING: John 1:1-18
KEY BIBLE VERSE: *In the beginning the Word already existed. He was with God, and he was God. . . . So the Word became human and lived here on earth among us. He was full of unfailing love and faithfulness. And we have seen his glory, the glory of the only Son of the Father.* (John 1:1, 14)

Jesus is the Son of God. What Jesus taught and what he did are tied inseparably to who he is. The Bible shows Jesus as fully human and fully God. Although Jesus took upon himself full humanity and lived as a man, he never ceased to be the eternal God who has always existed, the Creator and Sustainer of all things, and the source of eternal life. This is the truth about Jesus, and the foundation of all truth. If we cannot or do not believe this basic truth, we will not have enough faith to trust our eternal destiny to him. That is why John wrote this Gospel—to build faith and confidence in Jesus Christ so that we may believe that he truly was and is the Son of God (20:30-31).

Jesus is the light of the world. Jesus Christ is the Creator of life, and his life brings light to mankind. In his light, we see ourselves as we really are (sinners in need of a Savior). When we follow Jesus, the true Light, we can avoid walking blindly and falling into sin. He lights the path ahead of us so we can see how to live. He removes the darkness of sin from our life. Have you allowed the light of Christ to shine into your life? Let Christ guide your life, and you'll never need to stumble in darkness.

Jesus is both human and divine. By becoming human, Christ became (1) *the perfect teacher*—in Jesus' life we see how God thinks and, therefore, how we should think (Philippians 2:5-11); (2) *the perfect example*—as a model of what we are to become, he shows us how to live and gives us the power to live that way (1 Peter 2:21); (3) *the perfect sacrifice*—Jesus came as a sacrifice for all sins, and his death satisfied God's requirements for the removal of sin (Colossians 1:15-23).

BIBLE READING: Mark 1:9-13
KEY BIBLE VERSE: *A voice came from heaven saying, "You are my beloved Son, and I am fully pleased with you."* (Mark 1:11)

Jesus is a member of the Trinity. The Spirit descended like a dove on Jesus, and the voice from heaven proclaimed the Father's approval of Jesus as his divine Son. That Jesus is God's divine Son is the foundation for all we read about Jesus in the Gospels. Here we see all three members of the Trinity together—God the Father, God the Son, and God the Holy Spirit.

BIBLE READING: Matthew 16:13-20

KEY BIBLE VERSE: *[Jesus] asked them, "Who do you say I am?" Simon Peter answered, "You are the Messiah, the Son of the living God."* (Matthew 16:15-16)

Jesus is the Messiah. The disciples answered Jesus' question with the common view—that Jesus was one of the great prophets come back to life. This belief may have stemmed from Deuteronomy 18:18, where God said he would raise up a prophet from among the people. Peter, however, confessed Jesus as divine and as the promised and long-awaited Messiah. If Jesus were to ask you this question, how would you answer? Is he your Lord and Messiah?

BIBLE READING: Luke 8:40-56

KEY BIBLE VERSE: *When the woman realized that Jesus knew, she began to tremble and fell to her knees before him. The whole crowd heard her explain why she had touched him and that she had been immediately healed. "Daughter," he said to her, "your faith has made you well. Go in peace."* (Luke 8:47-48)

Jesus is the Great Physician. Many people surrounded Jesus as he made his way toward Jairus's house. It was virtually impossible to get through the multitude, but one woman fought her way desperately through the crowd in order to touch Jesus. As soon as she did so, she was healed. What a difference there is between the crowds that are curious about Jesus and the few that reach out and touch him! Today, many people are vaguely familiar with Jesus, but nothing in their lives is changed or bettered by this passing acquaintance. It is only faith that releases God's healing power. Are you just curious about God, or do you reach out to him in faith, knowing that his mercy will bring healing to your body, soul, and spirit?

▶ THE HUMANITY AND SUFFERING OF JESUS CHRIST

In what ways did Jesus demonstrate his humanity?

BIBLE READING: Isaiah 53:1-12

KEY BIBLE VERSE: *All of us have strayed away like sheep. We have left God's paths to follow our own. Yet the LORD laid on him the guilt and sins of us all.* (Isaiah 53:6)

Jesus demonstrated his human nature by dying for us. In this chapter Isaiah speaks of the Messiah, Jesus, who would suffer for the sins of all people. Such a prophecy is astounding! Who would believe that God would choose to save the world through a humble, suffering servant rather than a glorious king? The idea is contrary to human pride and worldly ways. But God often works in ways we don't expect. The Messiah's strength is shown by humility, suffering, and mercy.

BIBLE READING: Matthew 4:1-11

KEY BIBLE VERSE: *The Devil came and said to him, "If you are the Son of God, change these stones into loaves of bread."* (Matthew 4:3)

Jesus demonstrated his humanity and divinity in resisting temptation. This temptation by the devil shows us that Jesus was human, and it gave Jesus the opportunity to reaffirm God's plan for his ministry. It also gives us an example to follow when we are tempted. Jesus' temptation was an important demonstration of his sinlessness. He would face temptation and not give in.

This time of testing showed that Jesus really was the Son of God, able to overcome the devil and his temptations. A person has not shown true obedience if he or she has never had an opportunity to disobey. We read in Deuteronomy 8:2 that God led the Israelites into the desert to humble and test them. God wanted to see whether or not his people would really obey him. We too will be tested. Because we know that testing will come, we should be alert and ready for it. Remember, your convictions are strong only if they hold up under pressure!

▶ **THE DIVINITY OF JESUS CHRIST**
How is Jesus proved to be divine?

BIBLE READING: Mark 1:21-28
KEY BIBLE VERSE: *He began shouting, "Why are you bothering us, Jesus of Nazareth? Have you come to destroy us? I know who you are—the Holy One sent from God!"* (Mark 1:24)

Jesus demonstrated his divinity by his control over evil power. Evil spirits, or demons, are ruled by Satan. They work to tempt people to sin. They were not created by Satan—because God is the Creator of all. Rather, they are fallen angels who joined Satan in his rebellion. Though not all disease comes from Satan, demons can cause a person to become mute, deaf, blind, or insane. But in every case where demons confronted Jesus, they lost their power. Thus God limits what evil spirits can do; they can do nothing without his permission. During Jesus' life on earth, demons were allowed to be very active to demonstrate once and for all Christ's power and authority over them.

BIBLE READING: Luke 9:28-36
KEY BIBLE VERSE: *Even as he was saying this, a cloud came over them; and terror gripped them as it covered them. Then a voice from the cloud said, "This is my Son, my Chosen One. Listen to him."* (Luke 9:34-35)

God the Father identified Jesus as divine. As God's Son, Jesus has God's power and authority; thus his words should be our final authority. If a person's teaching is true, it will agree with Jesus' teachings. Test everything you hear against Jesus' words, and you will not be led astray. Don't be hasty to seek advice and guidance from merely human sources and thereby neglect Christ's message.

God clearly identified Jesus as his Son before saying that Peter and the others were to listen to Jesus and not to their own ideas and desires. The ability to follow Jesus comes from confidence about who he is. If we believe he is God's Son, then we surely will want to do what he says.

BIBLE READING: Mark 16:1-8
KEY BIBLE VERSE: *The angel said, "Do not be so surprised. You are looking for Jesus, the Nazarene, who was crucified. He isn't here! He has been raised from the dead! Look, this is where they laid his body."* (Mark 16:6)

Jesus demonstrated his divinity by his resurrection. The Resurrection is vitally important for many reasons: (1) Jesus kept his promise to rise from the dead, so we can believe he will keep all his other promises. (2) The Resurrection ensures that the ruler of God's eternal kingdom will be the living Christ, not just an idea, hope, or dream. (3) Christ's resurrection gives us the assurance that we also will be resurrected. (4) The power of God that brought Christ's body back from the dead is available to us to bring our morally and spiritually dead selves back to life so that we can change and grow (1 Corinthians 15:12-19). (5) The Resurrection provides the substance of the church's witness to the world. We do not merely tell lessons from the life of a good teacher; we proclaim the reality of the resurrection of Jesus Christ.

BIBLE READING: Philippians 2:1-11

KEY BIBLE VERSE: *Because of this, God raised him up to the heights of heaven and gave him a name that is above every other name, so that at the name of Jesus every knee will bow, in heaven and on earth and under the earth, and every tongue will confess that Jesus Christ is Lord, to the glory of God the Father.* (Philippians 2:9-11)

Christ's divinity will someday be known by all. These verses are probably from a hymn sung by the early Christian church. The passage holds many parallels to the prophecy of the suffering servant in Isaiah 53. As a hymn, it was not meant to be a complete statement about the nature and work of Christ. Several key characteristics of Jesus Christ, however, are praised in this passage: (1) Christ has always existed with God; (2) Christ is equal to God because he *is* God (John 1:1ff.; Colossians 1:15-19); (3) although Christ is God, he became a man in order to fulfill God's plan of salvation for all people; (4) Christ did not just have the appearance of being a man—he actually became human to identify with our sins; (5) Christ voluntarily laid aside his divine rights and privileges out of love for his Father; (6) Christ died on the cross for our sins so we wouldn't have to face eternal death; (7) God glorified Christ because of his obedience; (8) God raised Christ to his original position at the Father's right hand, where he will reign forever as our Lord and Judge. How can we do anything less than praise Christ as our Lord and dedicate ourselves to his service!

▶ **THE RESURRECTION OF JESUS CHRIST**
How do we know that Jesus rose from the dead?

BIBLE READING: Matthew 27:57-66

KEY BIBLE VERSE: *We request that you seal the tomb until the third day. This will prevent his disciples from coming and stealing his body and then telling everyone he came back to life! If that happens, we'll be worse off than we were at first.* (Matthew 27:64)

Christ's enemies confirm the truth of the Resurrection. The religious leaders took Jesus' resurrection claims more seriously than the disciples did. The disciples didn't remember Jesus' teaching about his resurrection (20:17-19); but the religious leaders did. Because of his claims, they were almost as afraid of Jesus after his death as when he was alive. They tried to take every precaution that his body would remain in the tomb.

The empty tomb was undeniable evidence. The Pharisees were so afraid of Jesus' predictions about his resurrection that they made sure the tomb was thoroughly sealed and guarded. Because the tomb was hewn out of rock in the side of a hill, there was only one entrance. The tomb was sealed by stringing a cord across the stone that was rolled over the entrance. The cord was sealed at each end with clay. But the religious leaders took a further precaution, asking that guards be placed at the tomb's entrance. With such precautions, the only way the tomb could be empty would be for Jesus to rise from the dead. The Pharisees failed to understand that no rock, seal, guard, or army could prevent the Son of God from rising again.

BIBLE READING: Luke 24:1-12

KEY BIBLE VERSE: *Very early on Sunday morning the women came to the tomb, taking the spices they had prepared. They found that the stone covering the entrance had been rolled aside. So they went in, but they couldn't find the body of the Lord Jesus.* (Luke 24:1-3)

The eyewitness testimonies confirm the truth of the Resurrection. The two angels (appearing as men "clothed in dazzling robes") asked the women why they were looking in a tomb for someone who was alive. Often we run into people who are looking for God among the dead. They study the Bible as a mere historical document and go to church as if going to a memorial service. But Jesus is not among the dead—he lives! He reigns in the hearts of Christians, and he is the head of his church. Do you look for Jesus among the living? Do you expect him to be active in the world and in the church? Look for signs of his power—they are all around you.

The Resurrection is an essential truth of Christianity. Why is the Resurrection so important? (1) Because Christ was raised from the dead, we know that the kingdom of heaven has broken into human history. Our world is now headed for redemption, not disaster. God's mighty power is at work destroying sin, creating new lives, and preparing us for Jesus' second coming. (2) Because of the Resurrection, we know that death has been conquered, and we, too, will be raised from the dead to live forever with Christ. (3) The Resurrection gives authority to the church's witness in the world. Look at the early evangelistic sermons in the book of Acts: the apostles' most important message was the proclamation that Jesus Christ had been raised from the dead! (4) The Resurrection gives meaning to the church's regular feast, the Lord's Supper. Like the disciples on the Emmaus Road, we break bread with our risen Lord, who comes in power to save us. (5) The Resurrection helps us find meaning even in great tragedy. No matter what happens to us as we walk with the Lord, the Resurrection gives us hope for the future. (6) The Resurrection assures us that Christ is alive and ruling his kingdom. He is not legend; he is alive and real. (7) God's power that brought Jesus back from the dead is available to us so that we can live for him in an evil world.

BIBLE READING: John 20:1-9

KEY BIBLE VERSE: *The other disciple also went in, and he saw and believed—for until then they hadn't realized that the Scriptures said he would rise from the dead.* (John 20:8-9)

The truth of the Resurrection can withstand serious inquiry. People who hear about the Resurrection for the first time may need time before they can comprehend this amazing story. Like Mary and the disciples, they may pass through four stages of belief. (1) At first, they may think the story is a fabrication, impossible to believe (20:2). (2) Like Peter, they may check out the facts and still be puzzled about what happened (20:6). (3) Only when they encounter Jesus personally are they able to accept the fact of the Resurrection (20:16). (4) Then, as they commit themselves to the risen Lord and devote their lives to serving him, they begin to understand fully the reality of his presence with them (20:28).

The Resurrection is confirmed by the surprise of the disciples. As further proof that the disciples did not fabricate this story, we find that Peter and John were surprised that Jesus was not in the tomb. When John saw the graveclothes looking like an empty cocoon from which Jesus had emerged, he believed that Jesus had risen. It wasn't until after they had seen the empty tomb that they remembered what the Scriptures and Jesus had said—he would die, but he would also rise again!

The Resurrection answers many more questions than it raises. Jesus' resurrection is the key to the Christian faith. Why? (1) Just as he said, Jesus rose from the dead. We can be confident, therefore, that he will accomplish all he has promised. (2) Jesus' bodily resurrection shows us that the living Christ, not a false prophet or impostor, is ruler of God's eternal kingdom. (3) We can be certain of our own resurrection because Jesus was resurrected. Death is not the end—there is future life. (4) The divine power that brought Jesus back to life is now available to us to bring our spiritually dead selves back to life. (5) The Resurrection is the basis for the church's witness to the world.

▶ THE TEACHING OF JESUS CHRIST
What did Jesus teach while here on earth?

BIBLE READING: Matthew 4:12-25
KEY BIBLE VERSE: *From then on, Jesus began to preach, "Turn from your sins and turn to God, because the Kingdom of Heaven is near."* (Matthew 4:17)

Jesus called people to repentance. Jesus started his ministry with the very word people had heard John the Baptist say: "Turn from your sins and turn to God." The message is the same today as when Jesus and John gave it. Becoming a follower of Christ means turning away from our self-centeredness and "self" control and turning our life over to Christ's direction and control.

The "kingdom of heaven" has the same meaning as the "kingdom of God" in Mark and Luke. Matthew uses this phrase because the Jews, out of their intense reverence and respect, did not pronounce God's name. The kingdom of heaven is still near because it has arrived in our hearts.

BIBLE READING: Matthew 5:1-20
KEY BIBLE VERSE: *Don't misunderstand why I have come. I did not come to abolish the law of Moses or the writings of the prophets. No, I came to fulfill them.* (Matthew 5:17)

Jesus demanded complete commitment from his hearers. Matthew 5–7 is called the Sermon on the Mount because Jesus gave it on a hillside near Capernaum. This "sermon" probably covered several days of preaching. In it, Jesus proclaimed his attitude toward the law. Position, authority, and money are not important in his kingdom—what matters is faithful obedience from the heart. The Sermon on the Mount challenged the proud and legalistic religious leaders of the day. It called them back to the messages of the Old Testament prophets who, like Jesus, taught that heartfelt obedience is more important than legalistic observance.

Jesus preached the values of the kingdom of God. There are at least four ways to understand the Beatitudes: (1) They are a code of ethics for the disciples and a standard of conduct for all believers. (2) They contrast kingdom values (what is eternal) with worldly values (what is temporary). (3) They contrast the superficial "faith" of the Pharisees with the real faith Christ wants. (4) They show how the Old Testament expectations will be fulfilled in the new kingdom. These Beatitudes are not multiple-choice—pick what you like and leave the rest. They must be taken as a whole. They describe what we should be like as Christ's followers.

Jesus taught his followers to live for the kingdom of God. With Jesus' announcement that the kingdom was near (4:17), people were naturally asking, "How do I qualify to be in God's kingdom?" Jesus said that God's kingdom is organized differently from worldly kingdoms. In the kingdom of heaven, wealth and power and authority are unimportant. Kingdom people seek different blessings and benefits, and they have different attitudes. Are your attitudes a carbon copy of the world's selfishness, pride, and lust for power, or do they reflect the humility and self-sacrifice of Jesus, your King?

BIBLE READING: John 14:1-14

KEY BIBLE VERSE: *Jesus told him, "I am the way, the truth, and the life. No one can come to the Father except through me." (John 14:6)*

Jesus proclaimed himself as the only way to God. This is one of the most basic and important passages in Scripture. How can we know the way to God? Only through Jesus. Jesus is the way because he is both God and man. By uniting our life with his, we are united with God. Trust Jesus to take you to the Father, and all the benefits of being God's child will be yours.

BIBLE READING: John 11:17-44

KEY BIBLE VERSE: *Jesus told her, "I am the resurrection and the life. Those who believe in me, even though they die like everyone else, will live again." (John 11:25)*

Jesus proclaimed and proved that he had power over death. Jesus has power over life and death as well as power to forgive sins. This is because he is the Creator of life (see John 14:6). He who *is* life can surely restore life. Whoever believes in Christ has a spiritual life that death cannot conquer or diminish in any way. When we realize his power and how wonderful his offer to us really is, how can we help but commit our life to him! To those of us who believe, what wonderful assurance and certainty we have: "I will live again, and you will, too" (14:19).

▶ THE WORK OF JESUS CHRIST
What did Jesus do while he was here on earth?

BIBLE READING: Matthew 1:18-25

KEY BIBLE VERSE: *She will have a son, and you are to name him Jesus, for he will save his people from their sins. (Matthew 1:21)*

Jesus established the way of salvation for the human race. *Jesus* means "the Lord saves." Jesus came to earth to save us because we can't save ourselves from sin and its consequences. No matter how good we are, we can't eliminate the sinful nature present in all of us. Only Jesus can do that. Jesus didn't come to help people save themselves; he came to be their Savior from the power and penalty of sin. Thank Christ for his death on the cross for your sin, and then ask him to take control of your life. Your new life begins at that moment.

BIBLE READING: Matthew 4:12-25

KEY BIBLE VERSE: *Jesus traveled throughout Galilee teaching in the synagogues, preaching everywhere the Good News about the Kingdom. And he healed people who had every kind of sickness and disease. (Matthew 4:23)*

Jesus' work touched people's lives at every level. Jesus was teaching, preaching, and healing. These were the three main aspects of his ministry. *Teaching* shows Jesus' concern for understanding; *preaching* shows his concern for commitment; and *healing* shows his concern for wholeness. His miracles of healing authenticated his teaching and preaching, proving that he truly was from God.

Jesus taught and preached with authority. Jesus soon developed a powerful preaching ministry and often spoke in the synagogues. Most towns that had ten or more Jewish families had a synagogue. The building served as a religious gathering place on the Sabbath and as a school during the week. The leader of the synagogue was not a preacher as much as an administrator. His job was to find and invite rabbis to teach and preach. It was customary to invite visiting rabbis like Jesus to speak.

Jesus healed people's diseases. Jesus preached the gospel—the Good News—to everyone who wanted to hear it. The Good News is that the kingdom of heaven has come, that God is with us, and that he cares for us. Christ can heal us, not just of physical sickness, but of spiritual sickness as well. There's no sin or problem too great or too small for him to handle. Jesus' words were good news because they offered freedom, hope, peace of heart, and eternal life with God.

BIBLE READING: Mark 10:13-16

KEY BIBLE VERSE: *He took the children into his arms and placed his hands on their heads and blessed them.* (Mark 10:16)

Jesus' actions overturned the world's priorities. Jesus was often criticized for spending too much time with the wrong people—children, tax collectors, and sinners (Matthew 9:11; Luke 15:1-2; 19:7). Some, including the disciples, thought Jesus should be spending more time with important leaders and the devout, because this was the way to improve his position and avoid criticism. But Jesus didn't need to improve his position. He was God, and he wanted to speak to those who needed him most.

Jesus loved little children. Adults are not as trusting as little children. To feel secure, all children need is a loving look and a gentle touch from someone who cares. Complete intellectual understanding is not one of their requirements. They believe us if they trust us. Jesus said that people should believe in him with this kind of childlike faith. We should not have to understand all the mysteries of the universe; it should be enough to know that God loves us and provides forgiveness for our sin. This doesn't mean that we should be childish or immature, but that we should trust God with a child's simplicity and receptivity.

▶ OUR RESPONSE TO JESUS CHRIST
What does Jesus expect from us?

BIBLE READING: Mark 3:7-19

KEY BIBLE VERSE: *[Jesus] selected twelve of them to be his regular companions, calling them apostles. He sent them out to preach, and he gave them authority to cast out demons.* (Mark 3:14-15)

Jesus expects wholehearted obedience from his followers. From the hundreds of people who followed him from place to place, Jesus chose twelve to be his *apostles. Apostle* means messenger or authorized representative. He did not choose these twelve to be his associates and companions because of their faith; their faith often faltered. He didn't choose them because of their talent and ability; no one stood out with unusual ability. The disciples represented a wide range of backgrounds and life experiences, but apparently they had no more leadership potential than those who were not chosen. The one characteristic they all shared was their willingness to obey Jesus. After Jesus' ascension, they were filled with the Holy Spirit and empowered to carry out special roles in the growth of the early church. We should not disqualify ourselves from service to Christ because we do not have the expected credentials. Being a good disciple is simply a matter of following Jesus with a willing heart.

BIBLE READING: Luke 9:18-27

KEY BIBLE VERSE: *[Jesus] said to the crowd, "If any of you wants to be my follower, you must put aside your selfish ambition, shoulder your cross daily, and follow me."* (Luke 9:23)

Jesus expects us to deny ourselves in following him. People are willing to pay a high price for something they value. Is it any surprise that Jesus would demand this much commitment from his followers? There are at least three conditions that must be met by people who want to follow Jesus. We must be willing to deny self, to take up our crosses, and to follow him. Anything less is superficial lip service.

Jesus expects us to imitate him. Christians follow their Lord by imitating his life and obeying his commands. To take up the cross meant to carry your own cross to the place where you would be killed. Many Galileans had been killed that way by the Romans. Applied to the disciples, it meant to identify completely with Christ's message, even if it meant death. We must deny our selfish desires to use our time and money our own way and to choose our own direction in life without regard to Christ. Following Christ is costly now, but in the long run, it is well worth the pain and effort.

Jesus expects the investment of our life in his service. If this present life is most important to you, you will do everything you can to protect it. You will not want to do anything that might endanger your safety, health, or comfort. By contrast, if following Jesus is most important, you may find yourself in unsafe, unhealthy, and uncomfortable places. You will risk death, but you will not fear it because you know that Jesus will raise you to eternal life. Nothing material can compensate for the loss of eternal life. Jesus' disciples are not to use their lives on earth for their own pleasure—they should spend their lives serving God and people.

BIBLE READING: Luke 11:29-32
KEY BIBLE VERSE: *The people of Nineveh, too, will rise up against this generation on judgment day and condemn it, because they repented at the preaching of Jonah. And now someone greater than Jonah is here—and you refuse to repent.* (Luke 11:32)

Jesus expects us to repent of our sins. The cruel, warlike men of Nineveh, capital of Assyria, repented when Jonah preached to them—and Jonah did not even care about them. The pagan queen of the South (Sheba) praised the God of Israel when she heard Solomon's wisdom, and Solomon was full of faults. By contrast, Jesus, the perfect Son of God, had come to people that he loved dearly—but they rejected him. Thus God's chosen people made themselves more liable to judgment than either a notoriously wicked nation or a powerful pagan queen. Compare Luke 10:12-15, where Jesus says the evil cities of Sodom, Tyre, and Sidon will be judged less harshly than the cities in Judea and Galilee that rejected Jesus' message.

Jesus expects us to act upon the knowledge we have. The Ninevites and the queen of the South had turned to God with far less evidence than Jesus was giving his listeners—and far less than we have today. We have eyewitness reports of the risen Jesus, the continuing power of the Holy Spirit unleashed at Pentecost, easy access to the Bible, and knowledge of two thousand years of Christ's acts through his church. With the knowledge and insight available to us, our response to Christ ought to be even more complete and wholehearted.

BIBLE READING: Galatians 2:11-21
KEY BIBLE VERSE: *I myself no longer live, but Christ lives in me. So I live my life in this earthly body by trusting in the Son of God, who loved me and gave himself for me.* (Galatians 2:20)

Jesus expects us to identify with his death. How have we been crucified with Christ? *Legally,* God looks at us as if we had died with Christ. Because our sins died with him, we are no longer condemned (Colossians 2:13-15). *Relationally,* we have become one with Christ, and his experiences are ours. Our Christian life began when, in unity with him, we died to our old life (see Romans 6:5-11). *In our daily life,* we must regularly crucify sinful desires that keep us from following Christ. This too is a kind of dying with him (Luke 9:23-25).

Jesus expects us to live for him. The focus of Christianity is not dying, but living. Because we have been crucified with Christ, we have also been raised with him (Romans 6:5). *Legally,* we have been reconciled with God (2 Corinthians 5:19) and are free to grow into Christ's likeness (Romans 8:29). And *in our daily life,* we have Christ's resurrection power as we continue to fight sin (Ephesians 1:19-20). We are no longer alone, for Christ lives in us—he is our power for living and our hope for the future (Colossians 1:27).

BIBLE READING: Philippians 2:5-11

KEY BIBLE VERSE: *Your attitude should be the same that Christ Jesus had.* (Philippians 2:5)

Jesus expects us to adopt a servant's attitude. Jesus Christ was humble, willing to give up his rights in order to obey God and serve people. Like Christ, we should have a servant's attitude, serving out of love for God and for others, not out of guilt or fear. Remember, you can choose your attitude. You can approach life expecting to be served, or you can look for opportunities to serve others. (See Mark 10:45 for more on Christ's attitude of servanthood.)

Jesus expects our life to be marked by his humility. Often people excuse selfishness, pride, or evil by claiming their rights. They think, *I can cheat on this test; after all, I deserve to pass this class,* or *I can spend all this money on myself—I worked hard for it,* or *I can get an abortion; I have a right to control my own body.* But as believers, we should have a different attitude, one that enables us to lay aside our rights in order to serve others. If we say we follow Christ, we must also say we want to live as he lived. We should develop his attitude of humility as we serve, even when we are not likely to get recognition for our efforts. Are you selfishly clinging to your rights, or are you willing to serve?

Related Topics: ATONEMENT, GOD, HUMILITY

JOBS *(Effort, Service, Work)*

How does God want us to view our jobs?

BIBLE READING: Ruth 2:1-23

KEY BIBLE VERSE: *She asked me this morning if she could gather grain behind the harvesters. She has been hard at work ever since, except for a few minutes' rest over there in the shelter.* (Ruth 2:7)

We should approach even the smallest job with faithfulness. Ruth's task, though menial, tiring, and perhaps degrading, was done faithfully. What is your attitude when the task you have been given is not up to your true potential? The task at hand may be all you can do, or it may be the work God wants you to do. Or, as in Ruth's case, it may be a test of your character that can open up new doors of opportunity.

Our work is an important way to develop character. Ruth's life exhibited admirable qualities: she was hardworking, loving, kind, faithful, and brave. These qualities gained for her a good reputation, but only because she displayed them *consistently* in all areas of her life. Wherever Ruth went or whatever she did, her character remained the same.

Whatever the task, our attitude should be consistent. Your reputation is formed by the people who watch you at work, in town, at home, in church. A good reputation comes by *consistently* living out the qualities you believe in—no matter what group of people or surroundings you are in.

BIBLE READING: Nehemiah 3:1-32

KEY BIBLE VERSE: *Eliashib the high priest and the other priests started to rebuild at the Sheep Gate. They dedicated it and set up its doors, building the wall as far as the Tower of the Hundred, which they dedicated, and the Tower of Hananel.* (Nehemiah 3:1)

Our attitude towards work impacts others. Note that the high priest is the first person mentioned who pitched in and helped with the work. Spiritual leaders must lead not only by word, but also by action. The Sheep Gate was the gate used to bring sheep into the city to the temple for sacrifices. Nehemiah had the priests repair this gate and section of the wall, respecting the priests' area of interest and at the same time emphasizing the priority of worship.

Our work should be done in an attitude of service to God. All the citizens of Jerusalem did their part in the huge job of rebuilding the city wall. Similarly, the work of the church requires every member's effort in order for the body of Christ to function effectively (1 Corinthians 12:12-27). The body needs you! Are you doing your part? Find a place to serve God and start contributing whatever time, talent, and money is needed.

Lazy leadership will not be respected. The nobles of Tekoa were lazy and wouldn't help. These men were the only ones who did not support the building project in Jerusalem. Every group, even churches, will have those who think they are too wise or important to work hard. Gentle encouragement doesn't seem to help. Sometimes the best policy is to ignore them. They may think they are getting away with something, but their inactivity will be remembered by all who worked hard.

BIBLE READING: Amos 1:1-15

KEY BIBLE VERSE: *This message was given to Amos, a shepherd from the town of Tekoa in Judah. He received this message in visions two years before the earthquake, when Uzziah was king of Judah and Jeroboam II, the son of Jehoash, was king of Israel.* (Amos 1:1)

God can use people, even in seemingly insignificant jobs. Amos raised sheep—not a particularly "spiritual" job—yet he became a prophet who proclaimed God's message to others. Your job may not cause you to feel spiritual or successful, but it is a vital work if you are in the place God wants you to be. God can work through you to do extraordinary things, no matter how ordinary your occupation.

BIBLE READING: Ephesians 6:5-9

KEY BIBLE VERSE: *Work with enthusiasm, as though you were working for the Lord rather than for people.* (Ephesians 6:7)

Our work should be marked by integrity. Paul's instructions encourage responsibility and integrity on the job. Christian employees should do their jobs as if

Jesus Christ were their supervisor. And Christian employers should treat their employees fairly and with respect. Can you be trusted to do your best, even when the boss is not around? Do you work hard and with enthusiasm? Do you treat your employees as people, not machines? Remember that no matter whom you work for, and no matter who works for you, the one you ultimately should want to please is your Father in heaven.

 BIBLE READING: Colossians 3:1-17

KEY BIBLE VERSE: *Whatever you do or say, let it be as a representative of the Lord Jesus, all the while giving thanks through him to God the Father.* (Colossians 3:17)

Everything we do should honor Christ. Doing everything "as a representative of the Lord Jesus" means bringing honor to Christ in every aspect and activity of daily living. As a Christian, you represent Christ at all times—wherever you go and whatever you say. What impression do people have of Christ when they see or talk with you? What changes would you make in your life in order to honor Christ?

Related Topics: ACHIEVEMENTS, EFFORT, WORK

JOY *(Contentment, Delight, Laughter)*

How can joy become characteristic of our life?

BIBLE READING: Leviticus 23:1-44

KEY BIBLE VERSE: *The LORD said to Moses, "Give the Israelites instructions regarding the LORD's appointed festivals, the days when all of you will be summoned to worship me."* (Leviticus 23:1-2)

Joy grows out of real worship. Worship involves both celebration and confession. But in Israel's national holidays, the balance seems heavily tipped in favor of celebration—five joyous occasions to two solemn ones. The God of the Bible encourages joy! God does not intend for religion to be only meditation and introspection. He also wants us to celebrate. Serious reflection and immediate confession of sin are essential, of course. But these should be balanced by celebrating who God is and what he has done for his people.

BIBLE READING: Psalm 16:1-11

KEY BIBLE VERSE: *I know the LORD is always with me. I will not be shaken, for he is right beside me. No wonder my heart is filled with joy, and my mouth shouts his praises! My body rests in safety.* (Psalm 16:8-9)

Joy comes from being in God's presence. David's heart was glad—he had found the secret to joy. True joy is far deeper than happiness; we can feel joy in spite of our deepest troubles. Happiness is temporary because it is based on external circumstances, but joy is lasting because it is based on God's presence within us. As we contemplate his daily presence, we will find contentment. As we understand the future he has for us, we will experience joy. Don't base your life on circumstances, but on God.

BIBLE READING: Galatians 5:16-26

KEY BIBLE VERSE: *When the Holy Spirit controls our lives, he will produce this kind of fruit in us: love, joy, peace, patience, kindness, goodness, faithfulness, gentleness, and self-control. Here there is no conflict with the law.* (Galatians 5:22-23)

Joy comes from having the Holy Spirit. The fruit of the Spirit is the spontaneous work of the Holy Spirit in us. The Spirit produces these character traits that are found in Christ. They are the by-products of Christ's control—we can't obtain them by *trying* to get them without his help. If we want the fruit of the Spirit to grow in us, we must join our life to his (see John 15:4-5). We must know him, love him, remember him, and imitate him. As a result, we will fulfill the intended purpose of the law—to love God and our neighbors. Which of these qualities do you want the Spirit to produce in you?

BIBLE READING: Philippians 4:1-23

KEY BIBLE VERSE: *Always be full of joy in the Lord. I say it again—rejoice!* (Philippians 4:4)

We can be joyful in spite of our circumstances. It seems strange that a man in prison would be telling a church to rejoice. But Paul's attitude teaches us an important lesson: our inner attitudes do not have to reflect our outward circumstances. Paul was full of joy because he knew that no matter what happened to him, Jesus Christ was with him. Several times in this letter, Paul urged the Philippians to be joyful, probably because they needed to hear this. It's easy to get discouraged about unpleasant circumstances or to take unimportant events too seriously. If you haven't been joyful lately, you may not be looking at life from the right perspective.

Ultimate joy comes from Christ dwelling within us. Christ is near, and at his second coming we will fully realize this ultimate joy. He who lives within us will fulfill his final purposes for us.

Related Topics: CONTENTMENT, HAPPINESS, PEACE

JUDGING *(Criticize, Evaluate, Test)*

In what situations might it be appropriate to judge another person?

BIBLE READING: Isaiah 11:1-16

KEY BIBLE VERSE: *He will delight in obeying the LORD. He will never judge by appearance, false evidence, or hearsay. He will defend the poor and the exploited. He will rule against the wicked and destroy them with the breath of his mouth. He will be clothed with fairness and truth.* (Isaiah 11:3-5)

We must judge others by God's standards of fairness. God will judge with righteousness and justice. How we long for fair treatment from others, but do we give it? We hate those who base their judgments on appearance, false evidence, or hearsay, but are we quick to judge others using those standards? Only Christ can be the perfectly fair judge. Only as he governs our heart can we learn to be as fair in our treatment of others as we expect others to be toward us.

BIBLE READING: Matthew 7:1-6

KEY BIBLE VERSE: *Stop judging others, and you will not be judged. For others will treat you as you treat them. Whatever measure you use in judging others, it will be used to measure how you are judged.* (Matthew 7:1-2)

Some types of judgment are necessary and appropriate. Jesus' statement, "Stop judging others," is against the kind of hypocritical, judgmental attitude that tears others down in order to build oneself up. It is not a blanket statement against all critical thinking, but a call to be *discerning* rather than negative. Jesus said to expose false teachers (Matthew 7:15-23), and Paul taught that we should exercise church discipline (1 Corinthians 5:1-2) and trust God to be the final Judge (1 Corinthians 4:3-5).

Our perception of others often tells us a lot about ourself. Jesus tells us to examine our own motives and conduct instead of judging others. The traits that bother us in others are often the habits we dislike in ourself. Our untamed bad habits and behavior patterns are the very ones that we most want to change in others. Do you find it easy to magnify others' faults while excusing your own? If you are ready to criticize someone, check to see if you deserve the same criticism. Judge yourself first, and then lovingly forgive and help your neighbor.

BIBLE READING: 1 Corinthians 5:1-13

KEY BIBLE VERSE: *It isn't my responsibility to judge outsiders, but it certainly is your job to judge those inside the church who are sinning in these ways.* (1 Corinthians 5:12)

Judgment is appropriate when confronting sin. The Bible consistently tells us not to criticize people by gossiping or making rash judgments. At the same time, however, we are to judge and deal with sin that can hurt others. Paul's instructions should not be used to handle trivial matters or to take revenge; nor should they be applied to individual problems between believers. These verses are instructions for dealing with open sin in the church, with a person who claims to be a Christian and yet who sins without remorse. The church is to confront and discipline such a person in love.

Related Topics: CHURCH, DISCIPLINE, TRUTH

JUDGMENT (GOD'S) *(Condemnation, Grace, Justice)*

▶ THE CERTAINTY OF GOD'S JUDGMENT
How sure can we be that God will judge the human race?

BIBLE READING: Deuteronomy 7:1-26

KEY BIBLE VERSE: *When the LORD your God hands these nations over to you and you conquer them, you must completely destroy them. Make no treaties with them and show them no mercy.* (Deuteronomy 7:2)

History teaches us that God's judgment is inevitable. God told the Israelites to destroy their enemies totally. How can a God of love and mercy wipe out everyone, even children? Although God is loving and merciful, he is also just. These enemy nations were as much a part of God's creation as Israel was, but God does not allow evil to continue unchecked. God had punished Israel by keeping out of the Promised Land all those who had disobeyed. The command to destroy these nations was both a judgment (9:4-6) and a safety measure. On one hand, the people living in the land were being judged for their sin, and Israel was God's instrument of judgment—just as God would one day use other nations to judge Israel for its sin (2 Chronicles 36:17; Isaiah 10:12). On the other hand, God's command was designed to protect the nation of Israel from being ruined by the idolatry and immorality of its enemies. To think that God is too "nice" to judge sin would be to underestimate him.

BIBLE READING: 1 Kings 22:29-40

KEY BIBLE VERSE: *An Aramean soldier, however, randomly shot an arrow at the*

Israelite troops, and the arrow hit the king of Israel between the joints of his armor. "Get me out of here!" Ahab groaned to the driver of his chariot. "I have been badly wounded!" (1 Kings 22:34)

God's judgment is unavoidable. Ahab could not escape God's judgment. The king of Aram sent thirty-two of his best chariot commanders with the sole purpose of killing Ahab. Thinking he could escape, Ahab tried to disguise himself, but a random arrow struck him while the chariots chased the wrong king, Jehoshaphat. It was foolish for Ahab to think he could escape by wearing a disguise. Sometimes people try to escape reality by disguising themselves—changing jobs, moving to a new town, even changing spouses. But God sees and evaluates the motives of each person. Any attempted disguise is futile.

BIBLE READING: Romans 2:1-16

KEY BIBLE VERSE: *But no, you won't listen. So you are storing up terrible punishment for yourself because of your stubbornness in refusing to turn from your sin. For there is going to come a day of judgment when God, the just judge of all the world, will judge all people according to what they have done.* (Romans 2:5-6)

God's judgment comes according to his own timing. Although God does not usually punish us immediately for sin, his eventual judgment is certain. We don't know exactly when it will happen, but we know that no one will escape that final encounter with the Creator. (For more on judgment, see John 12:48 and Revelation 20:11-15.)

God's judgment is fair and just. People are condemned not for what they don't know, but for what they do with what they know. Those who know God's written Word and his law will be judged by them. Those who have never seen a Bible still know right from wrong, and they will be judged because they did not keep even those standards that their own consciences dictated. Our modern-day sense of fair play and the rights of the individual often balks at God's judgment. But keep in mind that people violate the very standards they create for themselves.

God's judgment will be universal. If you traveled around the world, you would find evidence in every society and culture of God's moral law. For example, all cultures prohibit murder, and yet in all societies that law has been broken. We belong to a stubborn race. We know what's right, but we insist on doing what's wrong. It is not enough to know what's right; we must also do it. Admit to yourself and to God that you fit the human pattern and frequently fail to live up to your own standards (much less to God's standards). That's the first step to forgiveness and healing.

▶ THE CONSEQUENCES OF GOD'S JUDGMENT
What happens to those under God's judgment?

BIBLE READING: Obadiah 1:1-21

KEY BIBLE VERSE: *The day is near when I, the LORD, will judge the godless nations! As you have done to Israel, so it will be done to you. All your evil deeds will fall back on your own heads.* (Obadiah 1:15)

People in unrepentant rebellion towards God will be destroyed. Edom is an example to all the nations that are hostile toward God. Nothing can break God's promise to protect his people from complete destruction. In the book of Obadiah we see four aspects of God's message of judgment: (1) evil will certainly be punished; (2) those faithful to God have hope for a new future; (3) God is sovereign in human history; and (4) God's ultimate purpose is to establish his eternal kingdom. The Edomites had been cruel to God's people.

They were arrogant and proud, and they took advantage of others' misfortunes. Any nation that mistreats people who obey God will be punished, regardless of how invincible they appear. Similarly we, as individuals, cannot allow ourself to feel so comfortable with our wealth or security that we fail to help God's people. This is sin. And because God is just, sin will be punished.

BIBLE READING: Matthew 16:21-28

KEY BIBLE VERSE: *I, the Son of Man, will come in the glory of my Father with his angels and will judge all people according to their deeds.* (Matthew 16:27)

Christians will be judged by how they used God's gifts. Jesus Christ has been given the authority to judge all the earth (Romans 14:9-11; Philippians 2:9-11). Although his judgment is already working in our life, there is a future, final judgment when Christ returns (25:31-46) and everyone's life is reviewed and evaluated. This will not be confined to unbelievers; Christians too will face a judgment. Their eternal destiny is secure, but Jesus will look at how they handled gifts, opportunities, and responsibilities in order to determine their heavenly rewards. At the time of judgment, God will deliver the righteous and condemn the wicked. We should not judge others' salvation; that is God's work.

BIBLE READING: Matthew 25:31-46

KEY BIBLE VERSE: *They will go away into eternal punishment, but the righteous will go into eternal life.* (Matthew 25:46)

The final judgment for unbelievers will be eternal. Eternal punishment takes place in hell (the lake of fire, or Gehenna), the place of punishment after death for all those who refuse to repent. In the Bible, three words are used in connection with eternal punishment.

(1) *Sheol* or "the grave" is used in the Old Testament to mean the place of the dead, generally thought to be under the earth. (See Job 24:19; Psalm 16:10; Isaiah 38:10.)

(2) *Hades* is the Greek word for the underworld, the realm of the dead. It is the word used in the New Testament for *Sheol*. (See Matthew 16:18; Revelation 1:18; 20:13-14.)

(3) *Gehenna*, or hell, was named after the Valley of Hinnom near Jerusalem where children were sacrificed by fire to the pagan gods (see 2 Kings 23:10; 2 Chronicles 28:3). This is the place of eternal fire (Matthew 5:22; 10:28; Mark 9:43; Luke 12:5; James 3:6; Revelation 19:20) prepared for the devil, his angels, and all those who do not believe in God (Matthew 25:46; Revelation 20:9-10). This is the final and eternal state of the wicked after the Resurrection and the Last Judgment.

When Jesus warns against unbelief, he is trying to save us from agonizing punishment.

BIBLE READING: Revelation 20:11-15

KEY BIBLE VERSE: *I saw the dead, both great and small, standing before God's throne. And the books were opened, including the Book of Life. And the dead were judged according to the things written in the books, according to what they had done.* (Revelation 20:12)

God's judgment is complete. At the judgment, the books are opened. They represent God's verdict, and in them are recorded the deeds of everyone, good or evil. We are not saved by deeds, but deeds are seen as clear evidence of a person's actual relationship with God. The Book of Life contains the names of those who have put their trust in Christ to save them.

God's judgment is final. Death and hades are thrown into the lake of fire. God's judgment is finished. The lake of fire is the ultimate destination of everything wicked—Satan, the beast, the false prophet, the demons, death, hades, and all those whose names are not recorded in the Book of Life because they did not place their faith in Jesus Christ. John's vision does not permit any gray areas in God's judgment. If by faith we have not identified with Christ, confessing him as Lord, there will be no hope, no second chance, no other appeal.

Related Topics: FORGIVENESS, GRACE, HELL

JUSTICE *(Correctness, Fairness, Truth)*

How does God exercise both justice and mercy?

BIBLE READING: Genesis 18:20-33

KEY BIBLE VERSE: *Surely you wouldn't do such a thing, destroying the innocent with the guilty. Why, you would be treating the innocent and the guilty exactly the same! Surely you wouldn't do that! Should not the Judge of all the earth do what is right?* (Genesis 18:25)

God punishes sin, but offers mercy to the sinful. Why did God let Abraham question his justice and intercede for a wicked city? Abraham knew that God must punish sin, but he also knew from experience that God is merciful to sinners. God knew there were not ten righteous people in the city, but he was merciful enough to allow Abraham to intercede. He was also merciful enough to help Lot, Abraham's nephew, get out of Sodom before it was destroyed. God does not take pleasure in destroying the wicked, but he must punish sin. He is both just and merciful. We should be thankful that God's mercy extends to us.

God's justice is not changed by his mercy. Did Abraham change God's mind? Of course not. The more likely answer is that God changed Abraham's mind. Abraham knew that God is just and that he punishes sin, but he may have wondered about God's mercy. Abraham seemed to be probing God's mind to see how merciful he really was. He left his conversation with God convinced that God was both kind and fair. Our prayers won't change God's mind, but they may change ours just as Abraham's prayer changed his. Prayer helps us better understand the mind of God.

BIBLE READING: Isaiah 3:1-26

KEY BIBLE VERSE: *The leaders and the princes will be the first to feel the LORD's judgment. "You have ruined Israel, which is my vineyard. You have taken advantage of the poor, filling your barns with grain extorted from helpless people."* (Isaiah 3:14)

God guarantees justice. In the middle of this gloomy message, God gives hope—eventually the righteous will receive God's reward and the wicked will receive their punishment. It is disheartening to see the wicked prosper while we struggle to obey God and follow his plan. Yet we keep holding on to God's truth and take heart! God will bring about justice in the end, and he will reward those who have been faithful.

God despises injustice. The elders and leaders were responsible to help people, but instead they stole from the poor. Because they were unjust, Isaiah said the leaders would be the first to receive God's judgment. Leaders will be held accountable for how they lead. If you are in a position of leadership, you must lead according to God's just commands. Corruption will bring God's wrath, especially if others follow your example.

God is just. Why is justice so important in the Bible? (1) Justice is part of God's nature; it is the way he runs the universe. (2) It is a natural desire in every person. Even as sinners, we all want justice for ourself. (3) When government and church leaders are unjust, the poor and powerless suffer. Thus they are hindered from worshiping God. (4) God holds the poor in high regard. They are the ones most likely to turn to him for help and comfort. Injustice, then, attacks God's children. When we do nothing to help the oppressed, we are in fact joining with the oppressor. Because we follow a just God, we must uphold justice.

BIBLE READING: John 1:1-18

KEY BIBLE VERSE: *The law was given through Moses; God's unfailing love and faithfulness came through Jesus Christ.* (John 1:17)

God's justice and mercy work together. Law and grace are both aspects of God's nature that he uses in dealing with us. Moses emphasized God's law and justice, while Jesus Christ came to highlight God's mercy, love, and forgiveness. Moses could only be the giver of the law, while Christ came to fulfill the law (Matthew 5:17). The nature and will of God were revealed in the law; now the nature and will of God are revealed in Jesus Christ. Rather than coming through cold stone tablets, God's revelation now comes through a person's life. As we get to know Christ better, our understanding of God will increase.

Related Topics: GRACE, JUDGMENT (GOD'S), MERCY

KILL (*see* MURDER)

KINDNESS (*Gentleness, Goodness, Helpfulness*)

Why does God expect us to be kind?

 BIBLE READING: Luke 6:27-36

KEY BIBLE VERSE: *Love your enemies! Do good to them! Lend to them! And don't be concerned that they might not repay. Then your reward from heaven will be very great, and you will truly be acting as children of the Most High, for he is kind to the unthankful and to those who are wicked.* (Luke 6:35)

Showing undeserved kindness imitates God's character. Love means action. One way to put love to work is to take the initiative in meeting specific needs. This is easy to do with people who love us, people whom we trust; but love means doing this even to those who dislike us or plan to hurt us. The money we give others should be considered a gift, not a high-interest loan that will help us more than them. Give as though you are giving to God.

BIBLE READING: Romans 12:9-21

KEY BIBLE VERSE: *If people persecute you because you are a Christian, don't curse them; pray that God will bless them.* (Romans 12:14)

Genuine kindness is our response to God's love. Most of us have learned how to pretend to love others—how to speak kindly, avoid hurting their feelings, and appear to take an interest in them. We may even be skilled in pretending to feel moved with compassion when we hear of others' needs, or to become indignant when we learn of injustice. But God calls us to real and sincere love that goes far beyond pretense and politeness. Sincere love requires concentration and effort. It means helping others become better people. It demands our time, money, and personal involvement. No individual has the capacity to express love to a whole community, but the body of Christ in your town does. Look for people who need your love, and look for ways you and your fellow believers can love your community for Christ.

BIBLE READING: Colossians 3:1-17

KEY BIBLE VERSE: *Since God chose you to be the holy people whom he loves, you must clothe yourselves with tenderhearted mercy, kindness, humility, gentleness, and patience.* (Colossians 3:12)

Kindness is one of the characteristics of God's people. Paul offers a strategy to help us live for God day by day: (1) imitate Christ's compassionate, forgiving attitude (3:12-13); (2) let love guide your life (3:14); (3) let the peace of Christ rule in your heart (3:15); (4) always be thankful (3:15); (5) keep God's Word in you at all times (3:16); (6) live as Jesus Christ's representative (3:17).

Related Topics: GENEROSITY, GIVING, HELP

KINGDOM OF GOD/ KINGDOM OF HEAVEN (*Authority, Control, Rule*)

What is the kingdom of God?

 BIBLE READING: Mark 10:35-45

KEY BIBLE VERSE: *"In your glorious Kingdom, we want to sit in places of honor next to you," they said, "one at your right and the other at your left."* (Mark 10:37)

The kingdom of God is not a visible, earthly kingdom. The disciples, like most Jews of that day, had the wrong idea of the Messiah's kingdom as predicted by the Old Testament prophets. They thought Jesus would establish an earthly kingdom that would free Israel from Rome's oppression, and James and John wanted honored places in it. But Jesus' kingdom is not of this world; it is centered not in palaces and thrones, but in the hearts and lives of his followers. The disciples did not understand this until after Jesus' resurrection.

BIBLE READING: Matthew 6:5-15

KEY BIBLE VERSE: *May your Kingdom come soon. May your will be done here on earth, just as it is in heaven.* (Matthew 6:10)

The kingdom of God is a reality now. The phrase "May your Kingdom come soon" is a reference to God's spiritual reign, not Israel's freedom from Rome. God's kingdom was announced in the covenant with Abraham (8:11; Luke 13:28), is present in Christ's reign in believers' hearts (Luke 17:21), and will be complete when all evil is destroyed and God establishes the new heaven and earth (Revelation 21:1).

BIBLE READING: Matthew 13:1-58

KEY BIBLE VERSE: *[Jesus] explained to them, "You have been permitted to understand the secrets of the Kingdom of Heaven, but others have not."* (Matthew 13:11)

The values of the kingdom often run counter to our expectations. All the parables in this chapter teach us about God and his kingdom. For instance, Jesus gives the meaning of the first parable in verses 36-43. Each story explains what the kingdom is really like as opposed to our expectations of it. The kingdom of heaven is not a geographic location, but a spiritual realm where God rules and where we share in his eternal life. We join that kingdom when we trust in Christ as Savior.

The kingdom grows almost invisibly among its enemies. The young weeds and the young blades of wheat look the same and can't be distinguished until they are grown and ready for harvest. Weeds (unbelievers) and wheat (believers) must live side by side in this world. God allows unbelievers to remain for a while, just as a farmer allows weeds to remain in his field so the surrounding wheat isn't uprooted with them. At the harvest, however, the weeds will be uprooted and thrown away. God's harvest (judgment) of all people is coming. We are to make ourself ready by making sure that our faith is sincere.

The kingdom will ultimately be revealed in its fullness. At the end of the world, angels will separate the evil from the good. There are true and false believers in churches today, but we should be cautious in our judgments because only Christ is qualified to make the final separation. If you start judging, you may damage some of the good "plants." It's more important to judge our own response to God than to analyze others' responses.

Citizenship in God's kingdom is our most valuable possession. The kingdom of heaven is more valuable than anything else we can have, and a person must be willing to give up everything to obtain it. The man who discovered the treasure in the field stumbled upon it by accident but knew its value when he found it. The merchant was earnestly searching for the pearl of great value and, when he found it, sold everything he had to purchase it.

God determines who will be in his kingdom. The parable of the fishing net has the same meaning as the parable of the wheat and weeds. We are to obey God and tell others about his grace and goodness, but we cannot dictate who is part of the kingdom of heaven and who is not. This sorting will be done at the Last Judgment by those infinitely more qualified than we are.

We can live as citizens of the kingdom of heaven today. Anyone who understands God's real purpose in the law as revealed in the Old Testament has a real treasure. The Old Testament points the way to Jesus, the Messiah. Jesus always upheld its authority and relevance. But there is a double benefit to those who understand Jesus' teaching about the kingdom of heaven. This was a new treasure that Jesus was revealing. Both the old and the new teaching give practical guidelines for faith and for living in the world. The religious leaders, however, were trapped in the old and blind to the new. They were looking for a future kingdom *preceded* by judgment. Jesus, however, taught that the kingdom was *now* and the judgment was future. The religious leaders were looking for a physical and temporal kingdom (via military rebellion and physical rule), but they were blind to the spiritual significance of the kingdom that Christ brought.

BIBLE READING: Luke 12:22-34

KEY BIBLE VERSE: *He will give you all you need from day to day if you make the Kingdom of God your primary concern. So don't be afraid, little flock. For it gives your Father great happiness to give you the Kingdom.* (Luke 12:31-32)

The kingdom of God is the kingship of Christ. Seeking the kingdom of God means making Jesus the Lord and King of your life. He must control every area—your work, play, plans, relationships. Is the kingdom only one of your many concerns, or is it central to all you do? Are you holding back any areas of your life from God's control? As Lord and Creator, he wants to help provide what you need as well as guide how you use what he provides.

Related Topics: ETERNAL LIFE, HELL, SALVATION

KNOWLEDGE *(Ability, Awareness, Discipline)*

Why isn't having knowledge enough to please God?

BIBLE READING: Mark 3:7-12

KEY BIBLE VERSE: *Whenever those possessed by evil spirits caught sight of him, they would fall down in front of him shrieking, "You are the Son of God!"* (Mark 3:11)

Knowledge about Jesus is not the same as allegiance to him. The evil spirits knew that Jesus was the Son of God, but they refused to turn from their evil purposes. Knowing about Jesus, or even believing that he is God's Son, does not guarantee salvation. You must also want to follow and obey him (see also James 2:17).

Knowledge about Jesus is not the same as surrender to him. Jesus warned the evil spirits not to reveal his identity because he did not want them to reinforce a popular misconception. The huge crowds were looking for a political and military leader who would free them from Rome's control, and they thought that the Messiah predicted by the Old Testament prophets would be this kind of man. Jesus wanted to teach the people about the kind of Messiah he really was—one who was far different from their expectations. Christ's kingdom is spiritual. It begins not with the overthrow of governments, but with the overthrow of sin in people's hearts.

BIBLE READING: John 3:1-21

KEY BIBLE VERSE: *Jesus replied, "You are a respected Jewish teacher, and yet you don't understand these things? I assure you, I am telling you what we know and have seen, and yet you won't believe us."* (John 3:10-11)

Knowledge of the Bible is not the same as obedience to its message. This Jewish teacher of the Bible knew the Old Testament thoroughly, but he didn't understand what it said about the Messiah. Knowledge is not salvation. You should know the Bible, but even more important, you should understand the God whom the Bible reveals and the salvation that God offers.

BIBLE READING: Jeremiah 9:1-26

KEY BIBLE VERSE: *This is what the LORD says: "Let not the wise man gloat in his wisdom, or the mighty man in his might, or the rich man in his riches. Let them boast in this alone: that they truly know me and understand that I am the LORD who is just and righteous, whose love is unfailing, and that I delight in these things. I, the LORD, have spoken!"* (Jeremiah 9:23-24)

Knowing about God is not the same as knowing him personally. People tend to admire four qualities in others: human wisdom, power (strength), kindness, and riches. But God puts a higher priority on knowing him personally and living a life that reflects his justice and righteousness. What do you want people to admire most about you?

Related Topics: GOSPEL, TRUTH, WISDOM

L

LAND (*see* EARTH)

LANGUAGE (*see* WORDS)

LAST DAYS (*Completion, Conclusion, Ending*)

What does the Bible mean by the "last days"?

BIBLE READING: Acts 2:14-41

KEY BIBLE VERSE: *In the last days, God said, I will pour out my Spirit upon all people. Your sons and daughters will prophesy, your young men will see visions, and your old men will dream dreams.* (Acts 2:17)

The *last days* refers to the pouring out of God's Spirit on earth. Peter began his first message after the resurrection of Jesus Christ with a quote from the Old Testament. Not everything mentioned in Joel 2:28-29 was happening that particular morning. But God's Spirit filling the disciples was unmistakable and needed an explanation. "The last days" is another way of saying "from now on." All the days between Christ's first and second comings are included. "That great and glorious day of the Lord" (2:20) denotes the whole Christian age. Even Moses yearned for the Lord to put his Spirit on everyone (Numbers 11:29). At Pentecost the Holy Spirit was released throughout the entire world—to men, women, slaves, Jews, Gentiles. Now *everyone* can receive the Spirit. This was a revolutionary thought for first-century Jews. Even today, knowing we are living in the last days, this truth should deeply affect the way we live.

BIBLE READING: 2 Peter 3:1-18

KEY BIBLE VERSE: *First, I want to remind you that in the last days there will be scoffers who will laugh at the truth and do every evil thing they desire. This will be their argument: "Jesus promised to come back, did he? Then where is he? Why, as far back as anyone can remember, everything has remained exactly the same since the world was first created."* (2 Peter 3:3-4)

Non-Christians find it hard to believe we are living in the last days. "In the last days" scoffers will say that Jesus is never coming back, but Peter refutes their argument by explaining God's mastery over time. The "last days" is the time between Christ's first and second comings; thus we, like Peter, live in the last days. We must do the work to which God has called us and believe that he will return as he promised.

By our standards, the last days may be a long period of time. God may have seemed slow to these believers as they faced persecution every day and longed to be delivered. But God is not slow; he just is not on *our* timetable (Psalm 90:4). Jesus is waiting so that more sinners will repent and turn to him. We must not sit and wait for Christ to return, but we should live with the realization that time is short and that we have important work to do. Be ready to meet Christ any time, even today; yet plan your course of service as though he may not return for many years.

BIBLE READING: 1 John 2:18-29

KEY BIBLE VERSE: *Dear children, the last hour is here. You have heard that the Antichrist is coming, and already many such antichrists have appeared. From this we know that the end of the world has come.* (1 John 2:18)

The last days will not be an easy time for God's people. John is talking about the last days, the time between Christ's first and second comings. The first-century readers of 1 John lived in the last days, and so do we. During this time, antichrists (false teachers who pretend to be Christians and who lure weak members away from Christ) will appear. Finally, just before the world ends, one great antichrist will arise (Revelation 13; 19:20; 20:10). We do not need to fear these evil people. The Holy Spirit shows us their errors, so we will not be deceived. However, we must teach God's Word clearly and carefully to the peripheral, weak members among us so that they won't fall prey to these teachers who "come disguised as harmless sheep, but are really wolves that will tear you apart" (Matthew 7:15).

Related Topics: HISTORY, JUDGMENT, SECOND COMING OF JESUS

LAW OF GOD *(Commandments, Instructions, Requirements)*

Once we know Christ, what is the purpose for keeping God's law?

BIBLE READING: Exodus 20:1-26

KEY BIBLE VERSE: *"Don't be afraid," Moses said, "for God has come in this way to show you his awesome power. From now on, let your fear of him keep you from sinning!"* (Exodus 20:20)

God's law gives us direction for living a holy life. Why were the Ten Commandments necessary for God's new nation? At the foot of Mount Sinai, God showed his people the true function and beauty of his laws. The commandments were designed to lead Israel to a life of practical holiness. In them, people could see the nature of God and his plan for how they should live. The commands and guidelines were intended to direct the community to meet the needs of each individual in a loving and responsible manner. By Jesus' time, however, most people looked at the law the wrong way. They saw it as a means to prosperity in both this world and the next. And they thought that to obey every law was the way to earn God's protection from foreign invasion and natural disaster. Law keeping became an end in itself, not the means to fulfill God's ultimate law of love.

BIBLE READING: Matthew 5:1–7:29

KEY BIBLE VERSE: *Don't misunderstand why I have come. I did not come to abolish the law of Moses or the writings of the prophets. No, I came to fulfill them. I assure you, until heaven and earth disappear, even the smallest detail of God's law will remain until its purpose is achieved.* (Matthew 5:17-18)

God's law directs our love for him. God's moral and ceremonial laws were given to help people love God with all their hearts and minds. Throughout Israel's history, however, these laws had been often misquoted and misapplied. By Jesus' time, religious leaders had turned the laws into a confusing mass of rules. When Jesus talked about a new way to understand God's law, he was actually trying to bring people back to its *original* purpose. Jesus did not speak against the law itself, but against the abuses and excesses to which it had been subjected. (See John 1:17.)

Through Christ, our relationship to God's law is clarified. If Jesus did not come to abolish the law, does that mean all the Old Testament laws still apply to us today? In the Old Testament, there were three categories of law: ceremonial, civil, and moral.

(1) The *ceremonial law* related specifically to Israel's worship (see Leviticus 1:2-3, for example). Its primary purpose was to point forward to Jesus Christ; these laws, therefore, were no longer necessary after Jesus' death and resurrection. While we are no longer bound by ceremonial laws, the principles behind them—to worship and love a holy God—still apply. Jesus was often accused by the Pharisees of violating ceremonial law.

(2) The *civil law* applied to daily living in Israel (see Deuteronomy 24:10-11, for example). Because modern society and culture are so radically different from that time and setting, not all of these guidelines can be followed specifically. But the principles behind the commands are timeless and should guide our conduct. Jesus demonstrated these principles by example.

(3) The *moral law* (such as the Ten Commandments) is the direct command of God, and it requires strict obedience (see Exodus 20:13, for example). The moral law reveals the nature and will of God, and it still applies today. Jesus obeyed the moral law completely.

Obedience to God's law must always begin within us. Some of those in the crowd were experts at telling others what to do, but they missed the central point of God's laws themselves. Jesus made it clear, however, that obeying God's law is more important than explaining it. It's much easier to study God's laws and tell others to obey them than to put them into practice. How are you doing at obeying God *yourself?*

God expects from us wholehearted obedience to his commands. The Pharisees were exacting and scrupulous in their attempts to follow their laws. So how could Jesus reasonably call us to a greater righteousness than theirs? The Pharisees' weakness was that they were content to obey the laws outwardly without allowing God to change their hearts (or attitudes). Jesus was saying, therefore, that the *quality* of our goodness should be greater than that of the Pharisees. They looked pious, but they were far from the kingdom of God. God judges our hearts as well as our deeds, for it is in the heart that our real allegiance lies. Be just as concerned about your attitudes that people don't see as about your actions that are seen by all.

Shallow obedience to God's law is unacceptable. Jesus was saying that his listeners needed a different kind of righteousness altogether (love and obedience), not just a more intense version of the Pharisees' righteousness (legal compliance). Our righteousness must (1) come from what God does in us, not what we can do by ourselves, (2) be God-centered, not self-centered, (3) be based on reverence for God, not approval from people, and (4) go beyond keeping the law to living by the principles behind the law.

BIBLE READING: Galatians 2:11-21

KEY BIBLE VERSE: *You and I are Jews by birth, not "sinners" like the Gentiles. And yet we Jewish Christians know that we become right with God, not by doing what the law commands, but by faith in Jesus Christ. So we have believed in Christ Jesus, that we might be accepted by God because of our faith in Christ—and not because we have obeyed the law. For no one will ever be saved by obeying the law.* (Galatians 2:15-16)

God's law offers direction, not justification. If observing the Jewish laws cannot justify us, why should we still obey the Ten Commandments and other Old Testament laws? We know that Paul was not saying the law is bad, because in another letter he wrote, "the law itself is holy and right and good" (Romans 7:12). Instead, he is saying that the law can never make us acceptable to God. The law still has an important role to play in the life of a Christian. The law: (1) guards us from sin by giving us standards for behavior; (2) convicts us of sin, leaving us the opportunity to ask God's forgiveness; and (3) drives us to trust in the sufficiency of Christ, because we can never keep the Ten Commandments perfectly. The law cannot possibly save us. But after we have become Christians, it can guide us to live as God requires.

Related Topics: GRACE, OBEDIENCE, SALVATION

LAZINESS *(Apathy, Idleness, Listlessness)*

How should Christians respond to laziness?

BIBLE READING: 2 Thessalonians 3:1-18

KEY BIBLE VERSE: *We hear that some of you are living idle lives, refusing to work and wasting time meddling in other people's business. In the name of the Lord Jesus Christ, we appeal to such people—no, we command them: Settle down and get to work. Earn your own living.* (2 Thessalonians 3:11-12)

The return of Christ is a motivation for diligence, not laziness. Some people in the Thessalonian church were falsely teaching that because Christ would return any day, people should set aside their responsibilities, quit work, do no future planning, and just wait for the Lord. But their lack of activity only led them into sin. They became a burden to the church, which was supporting them; they wasted time that could have been used for helping others; and they started meddling in other people's business (3:11). These church members may have thought that they were being more spiritual by not working, but Paul tells them to be responsible and get back to work. Being ready for Christ means obeying him in every area of life. Because we know that Christ is coming, we must live in such a way that our faith and our daily practice will please him when he arrives.

There is an appropriate place for rest and relaxation. Paul was writing here about the person who is lazy. Paul explained that when he and his companions were in Thessalonica, they worked hard, buying what they needed rather than becoming a burden to any of the believers. The rule they followed was, "If a man will not work, he shall not eat." There's a difference between leisure and laziness. Relaxation and recreation provide a necessary and much-needed balance to our lives; but when it is time to work, Christians should jump right in. We should make the most of our talent and time, doing all we can to provide for ourselves and our dependents. Rest when you should be resting, and work when you should be working.

Persistent laziness should not be permitted. Paul counseled the church to stop supporting financially and associating with those who persisted in their idleness. Hunger and loneliness can be very effective ways to make the idle person become productive. Paul was not advising coldness or cruelty, but the kind of tough love that a person would show a brother or sister.

BIBLE READING: 2 Peter 3:1-18
KEY BIBLE VERSE: *Dear friends, while you are waiting for these things to happen, make every effort to live a pure and blameless life. And be at peace with God.* (2 Peter 3:14)

Obedience is true preparation for Christ's coming. We should not become lazy and complacent because Christ has not yet returned. Instead, we should live in eager expectation of his coming. What would you like to be doing when Christ returns? That is how you should be living each day.

Related Topics: ACTIONS, FAITH, WORK

LEADERSHIP *(Commanders, Guides, Models)*

▶ LEADERSHIP PRINCIPLES
What are some qualities of effective leaders?

BIBLE READING: Exodus 6:1-12
KEY BIBLE VERSE: *Therefore, say to the Israelites: "I am the LORD, and I will free you from your slavery in Egypt. I will redeem you with mighty power and great acts of judgment."* (Exodus 6:6)

Effective leaders persevere through tough times. When Moses gave God's message to the people, they were too discouraged to listen. The Hebrews didn't want to hear any more about God and his promises, because the last time they listened to Moses, all they got was more work and greater suffering. Sometimes a clear message from God is followed by a period when no change in the situation is apparent. During that time, seeming setbacks may turn people away from wanting to hear more about God. If you are a leader, don't give up. Keep bringing people God's message as Moses did. By focusing on God, who must be obeyed, rather than on the results to be achieved, good leaders see beyond temporary setbacks and reversals.

BIBLE READING: Exodus 39:32-43
KEY BIBLE VERSE: *Moses inspected all their work and blessed them because it had been done as the LORD had commanded him.* (Exodus 39:43)

Effective leaders delegate. Moses had learned his management lesson well. He gave important responsibilities to others and then trusted them to do the job. Great leaders, like Moses, give plans and direction while letting others participate on the team. If you are a leader, trust your assistants with key responsibilities.

Effective leaders appreciate the work of others. Moses inspected the finished work, saw that it was done the way God wanted, and then blessed the people. A good leader follows up on assigned tasks and gives rewards for good work. In whatever responsible position you find yourself, follow up to make sure that tasks are completed as intended, and show your appreciation to the people who have helped.

BIBLE READING: Deuteronomy 1:9-18

KEY BIBLE VERSE: *At that time I told you, "You are too great a burden for me to carry all by myself."* (Deuteronomy 1:9)

Effective leaders recognize their limitations. It was a tremendous burden for Moses to lead the nation by himself. He could not accomplish the task single-handedly. Like nations, as organizations and churches grow, they become increasingly complex. Conflicting needs and quarrels arise. No longer can one leader make all the decisions. Like Moses, you may have a natural tendency to try to do all the work alone. You may be afraid or embarrassed to ask for help. Moses made a wise decision to share the leadership with others. Rather than trying to handle larger responsibilities alone, look for ways of sharing the load so that others may exercise their God-given gifts and abilities.

Effective leaders cultivate good character qualities. Moses identified some of the inner qualities of good leaders: (1) wisdom, (2) understanding, and (3) respect. These characteristics differ markedly from the ones that often help elect leaders today: good looks, wealth, popularity, willingness to do anything to get to the top. The qualities Moses identified should be evident in us as we lead, and we should look for them in those we elect to positions of leadership.

BIBLE READING: Luke 22:7-38

KEY BIBLE VERSE: *Jesus told them, "In this world the kings and great men order their people around, and yet they are called 'friends of the people.' "* (Luke 22:25)

Effective leaders are servants. The world's system of leadership is very different from leadership in God's kingdom. Worldly leaders are often selfish and arrogant as they claw their way to the top. (Some kings in the ancient world gave themselves the title "Benefactor.") But among Christians, the leader is to be the one who *serves* best. There are different styles of leadership—some lead through public speaking, some through administering, some through relationships—but every Christian leader needs a servant's heart. Ask the people you lead how you can serve them better.

BIBLE READING: Hebrews 2:1-18

KEY BIBLE VERSE: *It was only right that God—who made everything and for whom everything was made—should bring his many children into glory. Through the suffering of Jesus, God made him a perfect leader, one fit to bring them into their salvation.* (Hebrews 2:10)

Christ demonstrated effective leadership through suffering. How was Jesus made perfect through suffering? Jesus' suffering made him a perfect leader, or pioneer, of our salvation. Jesus did not need to suffer for his own salvation, because he was God in human form. His perfect obedience (which led him down the road of suffering) demonstrates that he was the complete sacrifice for us. Through suffering, Jesus completed the work necessary for our own salvation. Our suffering can make us more sensitive servants of God. People who have known pain are able to reach out with compassion to others who hurt. If you have suffered, ask God how your experience can be used to help others.

Christ is the best model for effective leadership. God's grace to us led Christ to his death. Jesus did not come into the world to gain status or political power, but to suffer and die so that we could have eternal life ("glory"). If it is difficult for us to identify with Christ's servant attitude, perhaps we need to evaluate our own motives. Are we more interested in power or participation, domination or service, getting or giving?

▶ **LEADERSHIP IN THE CHURCH**
In what ways is leadership to be exercised in the church?

BIBLE READING: Nehemiah 3:1-32
KEY BIBLE VERSE: *Eliashib the high priest and the other priests started to rebuild at the Sheep Gate. They dedicated it and set up its doors, building the wall as far as the Tower of the Hundred, which they dedicated, and the Tower of Hananel.* (Nehemiah 3:1)

Church leadership works when all do their part. All the citizens of Jerusalem did their part on the huge job of rebuilding the city wall. Similarly, the work of the church requires every member's effort in order for the body of Christ to function effectively (1 Corinthians 12:12-27). The body needs you! Are you doing your part? Find a place to serve God, and start contributing whatever time, talent, and money is needed.

BIBLE READING: 1 Corinthians 12:12-31
KEY BIBLE VERSE: *The human body has many parts, but the many parts make up only one body. So it is with the body of Christ.* (1 Corinthians 12:12)

Every believer has an important area of service. Using the analogy of the body, Paul emphasizes the importance of each church member. If a seemingly insignificant part is taken away, the whole body becomes less effective. Thinking that your gift is more important than someone else's is an expression of spiritual pride. We should not look down on those who seem unimportant, and we should not be jealous of others who have impressive gifts. Instead, we should use the gifts we have been given and encourage others to use theirs. If we don't, the body of believers will be less effective.

Related Topics: OBEDIENCE, PASTORS, SERVING

LEADING (*see* GUIDANCE)

LEARNING (*Imitating, Observing, Remembering*)

Why is learning important to our relationship with God?

BIBLE READING: Deuteronomy 5:1-33
KEY BIBLE VERSE: *Moses called all the people of Israel together and said, "Listen carefully to all the laws and regulations I am giving you today. Learn them and be sure to obey them!"* (Deuteronomy 5:1)

Constant learning is one of the keys to spiritual growth. The people had entered into a covenant with God, and Moses commanded them to hear, learn, and follow his statutes. Christians also have entered into a covenant with God (through Jesus Christ) and should be responsive to what God expects. Moses' threefold command to the Israelites is excellent advice for all God's followers. *Listening* is absorbing and accepting information about God. *Learning* is understanding its meaning and implications. *Obeying* is putting into action all we have learned and understood. All three parts are essential to a growing relationship with God.

BIBLE READING: Proverbs 19:1-29
KEY BIBLE VERSE: *If you punish a mocker, the simpleminded will learn a lesson; if you reprove the wise, they will be all the wiser.* (Proverbs 19:25)

Learning is sometimes the result of suffering. There is a great difference between the person who learns from criticism and the person who refuses to accept correction. How we respond to criticism determines whether or not we grow in wisdom. The next time someone criticizes you, listen carefully to all that is said. You might learn something.

 BIBLE READING: Lamentations 3:1-66
KEY BIBLE VERSE: *It is good for the young to submit to the yoke of his discipline. Let them sit alone in silence beneath the LORD's demands. Let them lie face down in the dust; then at last there is hope for them.* (Lamentations 3:27-29)

Learning requires and develops humility. To "submit to the yoke of his discipline" means to willingly and humbly come before God to learn what he wants to teach us. This involves several important factors: (1) silent reflection on what God wants, (2) repentant humility, (3) self-control in the face of adversity, and (4) confident patience, depending on the divine Teacher to bring about loving lessons in our life. God has several long-term and short-term lessons for you right now. Are you doing your homework?

Related Topics: DISCIPLINE, KNOWLEDGE, TEACHING

LEGALISM *(Judgmental, Self-Righteous, Uncaring)*

How can legalism destroy our faith?

 BIBLE READING: Matthew 12:1-14
KEY BIBLE VERSE: *He went over to the synagogue, where he noticed a man with a deformed hand. The Pharisees asked Jesus, "Is it legal to work by healing on the Sabbath day?" (They were, of course, hoping he would say yes, so they could bring charges against him.)* (Matthew 12:9-10)

Legalism puts rules above God. As they pointed to the man with the shriveled hand, the Pharisees tried to trick Jesus by asking him if it was legal to heal on the Sabbath. Their Sabbath rules said that people could be helped on the Sabbath only if their lives were in danger. Jesus healed on the Sabbath several times, and none of those healings were in response to emergencies. If Jesus had waited until another day, he would have been submitting to the Pharisees' authority, showing that their petty rules were equal to God's law. If he healed the man on the Sabbath, the Pharisees could claim that because Jesus broke their rules, his power was not from God. But Jesus made it clear how ridiculous and petty their rules were. God is a God of people, not rules. The best time to reach out to someone is when he or she needs help.

Legalism puts rules above human needs. The Pharisees were so concerned about Jesus' breaking one of their rules that they did not care about the man's shriveled hand. What is your attitude toward others? If your convictions don't allow you to help certain people, your convictions may not be in tune with God's Word. Don't allow dogma to blind you to human need.

 BIBLE READING: Galatians 4:8-20
KEY BIBLE VERSE: *Before you Gentiles knew God, you were slaves to so-called gods that do not even exist. And now that you have found God (or should I say, now that God has found you), why do you want to go back again and become slaves once more to the weak and useless spiritual powers of this world?* (Galatians 4:8-9)

Legalism kills joy. Have you lost your joy? Paul sensed that the Galatians had lost the joy of their salvation because of legalism. Legalism can take away joy because (1) it makes people feel guilty rather than loved; (2) it produces self-hatred rather than humility; (3) it stresses performance over relationship; and (4) it points out how far short we fall rather than how far we've come because of what Christ did for us. If you feel guilty and inadequate, check your focus. Are you living by faith in Christ or by trying to live up to the demands and expectations of others?

BIBLE READING: Colossians 2:6-23
KEY BIBLE VERSE: *These rules may seem wise because they require strong devotion, humility, and severe bodily discipline. But they have no effect when it comes to conquering a person's evil thoughts and desires.* (Colossians 2:23)

Legalism is attractive, but destructive. To the Colossians, the discipline demanded by the false teachers seemed good, and legalism still attracts many people today. Following a long list of religious rules requires strong self-discipline and can make a person appear moral, but religious rules cannot change a person's heart. Only the Holy Spirit can do that.

Related Topics: FREEDOM, GROWTH, OBEDIENCE

LEISURE (*see* REST)

LIES (*see* LYING)

LIFE (*Awareness, Being, Existence*)

▶ THE VALUE OF HUMAN LIFE
What makes human life valuable?

BIBLE READING: Genesis 9:1-17
KEY BIBLE VERSE: *Yes, you must execute anyone who murders another person, for to kill a person is to kill a living being made in God's image.* (Genesis 9:6)

Human beings are made in the image of God. Here God explains why murder is so wrong: To kill a person is to kill one made in God's image. Because all human beings are made in God's image, all people possess the qualities that distinguish them from animals: morality, reason, creativity, and self-worth. When we interact with others, we are interacting with beings made by God, beings to whom God offers eternal life. God wants us to recognize his image in all people.

BIBLE READING: Psalm 39:1-13
KEY BIBLE VERSE: *LORD, remind me how brief my time on earth will be. Remind me that my days are numbered, and that my life is fleeing away.* (Psalm 39:4)

Each moment of life is a gift of God. Life is short no matter how long we live. If there is something important we want to do, we must not put it off for a better day. Ask yourself, If I had only six months to live, what would I do? Tell someone that you love him or her? Deal with an undisciplined area in your life? Tell someone about Jesus? Because life is short, don't neglect what is truly important.

Life stretches beyond earthly bounds into eternity. The brevity of life is a theme throughout the books of Psalms, Proverbs, and Ecclesiastes. Jesus also spoke about it (Luke 12:20). It is ironic that people spend so much time securing their lives on earth and spend little or no thought about what comes afterward. David realized that amassing riches and busily accomplishing worldly tasks would make no difference in eternity. Few people understand that their only hope is in the Lord. (For other verses on the brevity of life, see Ecclesiastes 2:18 and James 4:14.)

BIBLE READING: Psalm 90:1-17

KEY BIBLE VERSE: *Teach us to make the most of our time, so that we may grow in wisdom.* (Psalm 90:12)

Living in light of eternity makes life valuable. Realizing that life is short helps us use the little time we have more wisely, and for eternal good. Take time to number your days by asking yourself, What do I want to see happen in my life before I die? What small step could I take toward that purpose today?

Living for God makes life valuable. Because our days are numbered, we want our work to count, to be effective and productive. We desire to see God's eternal plan revealed now and for our work to reflect his permanence. If you feel dissatisfied with this life and all its imperfections, remember our desire to see our work established is given by God. But our desire can only be satisfied in eternity. Until then we must apply ourselves to loving and serving God.

BIBLE READING: Mark 8:31-38

KEY BIBLE VERSE: *If you try to keep your life for yourself, you will lose it. But if you give up your life for my sake and for the sake of the Good News, you will find true life.* (Mark 8:35)

Living for the gospel makes life valuable. We should be willing to lose our life for the sake of the gospel, not because our life is useless, but because nothing—not even life itself—can compare to what we gain with Christ. Jesus wants us to *choose* to follow him rather than to lead a life of sin and self-satisfaction. He wants us to stop trying to control our own destiny and to let him direct us. This makes good sense because Christ, as the Creator, knows better than we do what real life is about. He asks for submission, not self-hatred; he asks us only to lose our self-centered determination to be in charge.

Living unselfishly makes life valuable. Many people spend all their energy seeking pleasure. Jesus said, however, that a world of pleasure centered on possessions, position, or power is ultimately worthless. Whatever you have on earth is only temporary; it cannot be exchanged for your soul. If you work hard at getting what you want, you might eventually have a "pleasurable" life, but in the end you will find it hollow and empty. Are you willing to make the pursuit of God more important than the selfish pursuit of pleasure? Follow Jesus, and you will know what it means to live abundantly now and to have eternal life as well.

▶ **SPIRITUAL LIFE**

What are the characteristics of a spiritual life?

BIBLE READING: Deuteronomy 8:1-20

KEY BIBLE VERSE: *Yes, he humbled you by letting you go hungry and then feeding you with manna, a food previously unknown to you and your ancestors. He did it to teach you that people need more than bread for their life; real life comes by feeding on every word of the LORD.* (Deuteronomy 8:3)

Spiritual life is lived in pursuit of God. Jesus quoted this verse when the devil tempted him to turn stones into bread (Matthew 4:4). Many people think that life is based on satisfying their appetites. If they can earn enough money to dress, eat, and play in high style, they think they are living "the good life." But such things do not satisfy our deepest longings. In the end they leave us empty and dissatisfied. Real life, according to Moses, comes from total commitment to God, the one who created life itself. It requires discipline, sacrifice, and hard work, and that's why most people never find it.

BIBLE READING: Luke 9:18-27
KEY BIBLE VERSE: *How do you benefit if you gain the whole world but lose or forfeit your own soul in the process?* (Luke 9:25)

Spiritual life is self-sacrificing. If this present life is most important to you, you will do everything you can to protect it. You will not want to do anything that might endanger your safety, health, or comfort. By contrast, if following Jesus is most important, you may find yourself in unsafe, unhealthy, and uncomfortable places. You will risk death, but you will not fear it because you know that Jesus will raise you to eternal life. Nothing material can compensate for the loss of eternal life. Jesus' disciples are not to use their lives on earth for their own pleasure—they should spend their lives serving God and people.

BIBLE READING: John 1:1-18
KEY BIBLE VERSE: *To all who believed him and accepted him, he gave the right to become children of God.* (John 1:12)

Spiritual life is a gift of God. All who welcome Jesus Christ as Lord of their life are reborn spiritually, receiving new life from God. Through faith in Christ, this new birth changes us from the inside out—rearranging our attitudes, desires, and motives. Being born makes you physically alive and places you in your parents' family (1:13). Being born of God makes you spiritually alive and puts you in God's family (1:12). Have you asked Christ to make you a new person? This fresh start in life is available to all who believe in Christ.

BIBLE READING: John 4:1-26
KEY BIBLE VERSE: *Jesus replied, "People soon become thirsty again after drinking this water. But the water I give them takes away thirst altogether. It becomes a perpetual spring within them, giving them eternal life."* (John 4:13-14)

Spiritual life is eternal. Many spiritual functions parallel physical functions. As our body hungers and thirsts, so does our soul. But our soul needs *spiritual* food and water. The woman confused the two kinds of water, perhaps because no one had ever talked with her about her spiritual hunger and thirst before. We would not think of depriving our body of food and water when it is hungry or thirsty. Why then should we deprive our soul? The living Word, Jesus Christ, and the written Word, the Bible, can satisfy our hungry and thirsty soul.

BIBLE READING: Romans 6:1-14
KEY BIBLE VERSE: *Since we have been united with him in his death, we will also be raised as he was. Our old sinful selves were crucified with Christ so that sin might lose its power in our lives. We are no longer slaves to sin. For when we died with Christ we were set free from the power of sin.* (Romans 6:5-7)

Spiritual life is living in fellowship with Christ. We can enjoy our new life in Christ because we are united with him in his death and resurrection. Our evil desires, our bondage to sin, and our love of sin died with him. Now, united by faith with him in his resurrection life, we have unbroken fellowship with God and freedom from sin's hold on us. (For more on the difference between our new life in Christ and our old sinful nature, read Ephesians 4:21-24 and Colossians 3:3-15.)

Related Topics: CREATION, ETERNAL LIFE, SELF-ESTEEM

LIFESTYLE (*Customs, Habits, Patterns*)

How should we evaluate our lifestyle?

📖 BIBLE READING: Exodus 23:20-33
KEY BIBLE VERSE: *Do not worship the gods of these other nations or serve them in any way, and never follow their evil example. Instead, you must utterly conquer them and break down their shameful idols.* (Exodus 23:24)

Our lifestyle should reflect what we believe. If you're in the furnace, it's easy to catch fire. God warned the Israelites about their neighbors whose beliefs and actions could turn them away from him. We also live with neighbors whose values may be completely different from ours. We are called to maintain a life-style that shows our faith. This can be a struggle, especially if our Christian lifestyle differs from the norm. Our life should show that we put obeying God before doing what is praised and accepted by society.

📖 BIBLE READING: Matthew 5:1-12
KEY BIBLE VERSE: *God blesses you when you are mocked and persecuted and lied about because you are my followers. Be happy about it! Be very glad! For a great reward awaits you in heaven. And remember, the ancient prophets were perse-cuted, too.* (Matthew 5:11-12)

Our lifestyle should be a reflection of God's kingdom. With Jesus' recent announcement that the kingdom was near (4:17), people were naturally asking, "How do I qualify to be in God's kingdom?" Jesus said that God's kingdom is organized differently from worldly kingdoms. In the kingdom of heaven, wealth and power and authority are unimportant. Kingdom people seek different bless-ings and benefits, and they have different attitudes. Their entire lifestyle ought to be different. Are your attitudes a carbon copy of the world's selfishness, pride, and lust for power, or do they reflect the humility and self-sacrifice of Jesus, your King?

📖 BIBLE READING: 1 Corinthians 9:1-27
KEY BIBLE VERSE: *Remember that in a race everyone runs, but only one person gets the prize. You also must run in such a way that you will win. All athletes practice strict self-control. They do it to win a prize that will fade away, but we do it for an eternal prize.* (1 Corinthians 9:24-25)

Our lifestyle should be disciplined. Winning a race requires purpose and disci-pline. Paul uses this illustration to explain that the Christian life takes hard work, self-denial, and grueling preparation. As Christians, we are running toward our heavenly reward. The essential disciplines of prayer, Bible study, and worship equip us to run with vigor and stamina. Don't merely observe from the grandstand; don't just turn out to jog a couple of laps each morning. Train diligently—your spiritual progress depends upon it.

BIBLE READING: 2 Timothy 2:14-26

KEY BIBLE VERSE: *Work hard so God can approve you. Be a good worker, one who does not need to be ashamed and who correctly explains the word of truth.* (2 Timothy 2:15)

Our lifestyle should be consistent with God's Word. Because God will examine what kind of workers we have been for him, we should build our life on his Word and build his Word into our life—it alone tells us how to live for him and serve him. Believers who ignore the Bible will certainly be ashamed at the judgment. Consistent and diligent study of God's Word is vital; otherwise we will be lulled into neglecting God and our true purpose for living.

Related Topics: EXAMPLE, INFLUENCE, LEADERSHIP

LIGHT *(Clarity, Reality, Truth)*

What does light represent in the Bible?

BIBLE READING: Matthew 5:13-16

KEY BIBLE VERSE: *Don't hide your light under a basket! Instead, put it on a stand and let it shine for all. In the same way, let your good deeds shine out for all to see, so that everyone will praise your heavenly Father.* (Matthew 5:15-16)

Light may represent our relationship with Christ. Can you hide a city that is sitting on top of a hill? Its light at night can be seen for miles. If we live for Christ, we will glow like lights, showing others what Christ is like. We hide our light by (1) being quiet when we should speak, (2) going along with the crowd, (3) denying the light, (4) letting sin dim our light, (5) not explaining our light to others, or (6) ignoring the needs of others. Be a beacon of truth—don't shut your light off from the rest of the world.

BIBLE READING: Mark 4:21-25

KEY BIBLE VERSE: *Jesus asked them, "Would anyone light a lamp and then put it under a basket or under a bed to shut out the light? Of course not! A lamp is placed on a stand, where its light will shine."* (Mark 4:21)

Light may represent the effect of our life on others. If a lamp doesn't help people see, it is useless. Does your life show other people how to find God and how to live for him? If not, ask what "boxes" have extinguished your light. Complacency, resentment, stubbornness of heart, or disobedience could keep God's light from shining through you to others.

Light may represent growing in our knowledge of Christ. The light of Jesus' truth is revealed to us, not hidden. But we may not be able to see or to use all of that truth right now. Only as we put God's teachings into practice will we understand and see more of the truth. The truth is clear, but our ability to understand is imperfect. As we obey, we will sharpen our vision and increase our understanding (see James 1:22-25).

BIBLE READING: John 1:1-18

KEY BIBLE VERSE: *Life itself was in him, and this life gives light to everyone. The light shines through the darkness, and the darkness can never extinguish it.* (John 1:4-5)

Jesus is the light. Jesus Christ is the Creator of life, and his life brings light to humanity. In his light, we see ourselves as we really are (sinners in need of a

Savior). When we follow Jesus, the true light, we can avoid walking blindly and falling into sin. He lights the path ahead of us so we can see how to live. He removes the darkness of sin from our life. Have you allowed the light of Christ to shine into your life? Let Christ guide your life, and you'll never need to stumble in darkness.

Our light is only a reflection of Christ's presence. We, like John the Baptist, are not the source of God's light; we merely reflect that light. Jesus Christ is the true light; he helps us see our way to God and shows us how to walk along that way. But Christ has chosen to reflect his light through his followers to an unbelieving world, perhaps because unbelievers are not able to bear the full blazing glory of his light firsthand. The word *witness* indicates our role as reflectors of Christ's light. We are never to present ourselves as the light to others, but are always to point them to Christ, the light.

Related Topics: GOSPEL, JESUS CHRIST, TRUTH

LIMITATIONS (*Barriers, Handicaps, Restrictions*)

How does God want us to view our limitations?

BIBLE READING: Judges 6:1-40
KEY BIBLE VERSE: *"But Lord," Gideon replied, "how can I rescue Israel? My clan is the weakest in the whole tribe of Manasseh, and I am the least in my entire family!"* (Judges 6:15)

Our limitations are opportunities for God to work. "I will be with you," God told Gideon, and God promised to give him the strength he needed to overcome the opposition. In spite of this clear promise for strength, Gideon made excuses. Seeing only his limitations and weaknesses, he failed to see how God could work through him.

Our limitations are opportunities to trust God. Like Gideon, we are called to serve God in specific ways. Although God promises us the tools and strength we need, we often make excuses. But reminding God of our limitations only implies that he does not know all about us or that he has made a mistake in evaluating our character. Don't spend time making excuses. Instead spend it doing what God wants.

Our limitations are not God's limitations. After seeing the miracle of the wet fleece, why did Gideon ask for another miracle? Perhaps he thought the results of the first test could have happened naturally. A thick fleece could retain moisture long after the sun had dried the surrounding ground. "Putting out fleeces" is a poor decision-making method. Those who do this put limitations on God. They ask him to fit their expectations. The results of such experiments are usually inconclusive and thus fail to make us any more confident about our choices. Don't let a "fleece" become a substitute for God's wisdom that comes through Bible study and prayer.

BIBLE READING: 1 Corinthians 15:35-58
KEY BIBLE VERSE: *Our perishable earthly bodies must be transformed into heavenly bodies that will never die.* (1 Corinthians 15:53)

Our limitations are temporary. We all face limitations. Those who have physical, mental, or emotional disabilities are especially aware of this. Some may be blind, but they can see a new way to live. Some may be deaf, but they can hear

God's Good News. Some may be lame, but they can walk in God's love. In addition, they have the encouragement that those disabilities are only temporary. Paul tells us that we all will be given new bodies when Christ returns and that these bodies will be without disabilities, never to die or become sick. This can give us hope in our suffering.

Related Topics: BARRIERS, CHALLENGE, SUCCESS

LISTENING *(Attention, Concentration, Hearing)*

Why is listening an important spiritual skill?

BIBLE READING: Deuteronomy 5:1-33

KEY BIBLE VERSE: *Moses called all the people of Israel together and said, "Listen carefully to all the laws and regulations I am giving you today. Learn them and be sure to obey them!"* (Deuteronomy 5:1)

Listening to God is the first step toward obeying him. The people had entered into a covenant with God, and Moses commanded them to hear, learn, and follow his statutes. Christians also have entered into a covenant with God (through Jesus Christ) and should be responsive to what God expects. Moses' threefold command to the Israelites is excellent advice for all God's followers. *Listening* is absorbing and accepting information about God. *Learning* is understanding its meaning and implications. *Obeying* is putting into action all we have learned and understood. All three parts are essential to a growing relationship with God.

BIBLE READING: 1 Kings 19:1-18

KEY BIBLE VERSE: *After the earthquake there was a fire, but the LORD was not in the fire. And after the fire there was the sound of a gentle whisper. When Elijah heard it, he wrapped his face in his cloak and went out and stood at the entrance of the cave. And a voice said, "What are you doing here, Elijah?"* (1 Kings 19:12-13)

Listening for God is training in humility. Elijah knew that the sound of the gentle whisper was God's voice. He realized that God doesn't reveal himself only in powerful, miraculous ways. To look for God only in something big (rallies, churches, conferences, highly visible leaders) may be to miss him, because he is often found gently whispering in the quietness of a humbled heart. Are you listening for God? Step back from the noise and activity of your busy life, and listen humbly and quietly for his guidance. It may come when you least expect it.

BIBLE READING: Mark 4:1-20

KEY BIBLE VERSE: *He replied, "You are permitted to understand the secret about the Kingdom of God. But I am using these stories to conceal everything about it from outsiders, so that the Scriptures might be fulfilled: 'They see what I do, but they don't perceive its meaning. They hear my words, but they don't understand. So they will not turn from their sins and be forgiven.'"* (Mark 4:11-12)

Spiritual listening involves the heart and mind. We hear with our ears, but there is a deeper kind of listening with the mind and heart that is necessary in order to gain spiritual understanding from Jesus' words. Some people in the crowd were looking for evidence to use against Jesus; others truly wanted to learn and grow. Jesus' words were for the honest seekers.

Spiritual listening requires an openness to God. Some people do not understand God's truth because they are not ready for it. God reveals truth to people who will act on it, who will make it visible in their lives. When you talk with people about God, be aware that they will not understand if they are not yet ready. Be patient, taking every chance to tell them more of the truth about God, and praying that the Holy Spirit will open their minds and hearts to receive the truth and act on it.

BIBLE READING: James 1:19-27
KEY BIBLE VERSE: *My dear brothers and sisters, be quick to listen, slow to speak, and slow to get angry. Your anger can never make things right in God's sight.* (James 1:19-20)

Spiritual listening allows us to learn from others. When we talk too much and listen too little, we communicate to others that we think our ideas are much more important than theirs. James wisely advises us to reverse this process. Put a mental stopwatch on your conversations, and keep track of how much you talk and how much you listen. When people talk with you, do they feel that their viewpoints and ideas have value?

Spiritual listening is always followed by action. It is important to listen to what God's Word says, but it is much more important to obey it, to *do* what it says. We can measure the effectiveness of our Bible study time by the effect it has on our behavior and attitudes. Do you put into action what you have studied?

Related Topics: HONOR, LEARNING, OBEDIENCE

LONELINESS (Alone, Isolation, Separation)

How should we react to times of loneliness?

BIBLE READING: Mark 4:30-34
KEY BIBLE VERSE: *Jesus asked, "How can I describe the Kingdom of God? What story should I use to illustrate it? It is like a tiny mustard seed. Though this is one of the smallest of seeds, it grows to become one of the largest of plants, with long branches where birds can come and find shelter."* (Mark 4:30-32)

Seek out fellow Christians in times of loneliness. Jesus used this parable to explain that although Christianity had very small beginnings, it would grow into a worldwide community of believers. When you feel alone in your stand for Christ, realize that God is building a worldwide kingdom. He has faithful followers in every part of the world, and your faith, no matter how small, can join with that of others to accomplish great things.

BIBLE READING: 1 Kings 19:1-18
KEY BIBLE VERSE: *He replied again, "I have zealously served the LORD God Almighty. But the people of Israel have broken their covenant with you, torn down your altars, and killed every one of your prophets. I alone am left, and now they are trying to kill me, too."* (1 Kings 19:14)

Beware of self-pity in times of loneliness. Elijah thought he was the only person left who was still true to God. He had seen both the king's court and the priesthood become corrupt. After experiencing great victory at Mount Carmel, he had to run for his life. Lonely and discouraged, he forgot that others had remained faithful during the nation's wickedness. When you are tempted to think that you are the only one remaining faithful to a task, don't stop to feel sorry for yourself. Self-pity will dilute the good you are doing. Be assured that even if you don't know who they are, others are faithfully obeying God and fulfilling their duties.

BIBLE READING: John 16:1-16

KEY BIBLE VERSE: *It is actually best for you that I go away, because if I don't, the Counselor won't come. If I do go away, he will come because I will send him to you.* (John 16:7)

Remember that we are never really alone, because the Spirit is always with us. In his last moments with his disciples, Jesus (1) warned them about further persecution, (2) told them where, when, and why he was going, and (3) assured them that they would not be left alone, but that the Spirit would come. Jesus knew what lay ahead, and he did not want the disciples' faith shaken or destroyed. God wants you to know you are not alone. You have the Holy Spirit to comfort you, teach you truth, and help you.

BIBLE READING: 3 John 1:1-14

KEY BIBLE VERSE: *Dear friend, you are doing a good work for God when you take care of the traveling teachers who are passing through, even though they are strangers to you.* (3 John 1:5)

Caring for the lonely can be a cure for loneliness. In the church's early days, traveling prophets, evangelists, and teachers were helped on their way by people like Gaius, who housed and fed them. Hospitality is a lost art in many churches today. We would do well to invite more people for meals—fellow church members, young people, traveling missionaries, those in need, visitors. This is an active and much-appreciated way to show your love. In fact, it is probably more important today. Because of our individualistic, self-centered society, there are many lonely people who wonder if anyone cares whether they live or die. If you find such a lonely person, show him or her that *you* care!

Related Topics: ABANDON, CHURCH, FRIENDSHIP

LORDSHIP (*see* JESUS CHRIST)

LORD'S SUPPER (*Communion, Eucharist, Sacrament*)

What is the significance of the Lord's Supper?

BIBLE READING: Matthew 26:17-30

KEY BIBLE VERSE: *As they were eating, Jesus took a loaf of bread and asked God's blessing on it. Then he broke it in pieces and gave it to the disciples, saying, "Take it and eat it, for this is my body." And he took a cup of wine and gave thanks to God for it. He gave it to them and said, "Each of you drink from it, for this is my blood, which seals the covenant between God and his people. It is poured out to forgive the sins of many."* (Matthew 26:26-28)

The Lord's Supper has many important dimensions. Each name we use for this sacrament brings out a different dimension to it. It is the *Lord's Supper* because it commemorates the Passover meal Jesus ate with his disciples; it is the *Eucharist* (thanksgiving) because in it we thank God for Christ's work for us; it is *Communion* because through it we commune with God and with other believers. As we eat the bread and drink the wine, we should be quietly reflective as we recall Jesus' death and his promise to come again, grateful for God's wonderful gift to us, and joyful as we meet with Christ and the body of believers.

BIBLE READING: 1 Corinthians 11:17-34

KEY BIBLE VERSFE: *Every time you eat this bread and drink this cup, you are announcing the Lord's death until he comes again.* (1 Corinthians 11:26)

The Lord's Supper reminds us that Christ died for us. The Lord's Supper (11:20) is a visible representation of the Good News of the death of Christ for our sins. It reminds us of Christ's death and the glorious hope of his return. Our participation in it strengthens our faith through fellowship with Christ and with other believers.

The Lord's Supper is a spiritual meal. When the Lord's Supper was celebrated in the early church, it included a feast or fellowship meal followed by the celebration of Communion. In the church in Corinth, the fellowship meal had become a time when some ate and drank excessively while others went hungry. There was little sharing and caring. This certainly did not demonstrate the unity and love that should characterize the church, nor was it a preparation for Communion. Paul condemned these actions and reminded the church of the real purpose of the Lord's Supper.

The Lord's Supper has a variety of meanings within the church. The early church remembered that Jesus instituted the Lord's Supper on the night of the Passover meal (Luke 22:13-20). Just as Passover celebrated deliverance from slavery in Egypt, so the Lord's Supper celebrates deliverance from sin by Christ's death.

Christians pose several different possibilities for what Christ meant when he said, "This is my body." (1) Some believe that the wine and bread actually become Christ's physical blood and body. (2) Others believe that the bread and wine remain unchanged, but Christ is spiritually present with the bread and wine. (3) Still others believe that the bread and wine symbolize Christ's body and blood. Christians generally agree, however, that participating in the Lord's Supper is an important element in the Christian faith and that Christ's presence, however we understand it, strengthens us spiritually.

The Lord's Supper commemorates the New Covenant. What is this New Covenant? In the Old Covenant, people could approach God only through the priests and the sacrificial system. Jesus' death on the cross ushered in the New Covenant or agreement between God and us. Now all people can personally approach God and communicate with him. The people of Israel first entered into this agreement after their exodus from Egypt (Exodus 24), and it was designed to point to the day when Jesus Christ would come. The New Covenant completes the Old Covenant, fulfilling everything the old covenant looked forward to (see Jeremiah 31:31-34). Eating the bread and drinking the cup shows that we are remembering Christ's death for us and renewing our commitment to serve him.

The Lord's Supper is remembering. Jesus said, "Do this in remembrance of me." How do we remember Christ in the Lord's Supper? By thinking about what he did and why he did it. If the Lord's Supper becomes just a ritual or a pious habit, it no longer remembers Christ, and it loses its significance.

The Lord's Supper is a holy act. Paul gives specific instructions on how the Lord's Supper should be observed. (1) We should take the Lord's Supper thoughtfully, because we are proclaiming that Christ died for our sins (11:26). (2) We should take it worthily, with due reverence and respect (11:27). (3) We should examine ourselves for any unconfessed sin or resentful attitude (11:28). We are to be properly prepared, based on our belief in and love for Christ. (4) We should be considerate of others (11:33), waiting until everyone is there and then eating in an orderly and unified manner.

The Lord's Supper is not to be taken lightly. When Paul said that no one should take the Lord's Supper in an unworthy manner, he was speaking to the church members who were rushing into it without thinking of its meaning. Those who did so were "guilty of sinning against the body and the blood of the Lord." Instead of honoring his sacrifice, they were sharing in the guilt of those who crucified Christ. In reality, *no one* is worthy to take the Lord's Supper. We are all sinners saved by grace. This is why we should prepare ourselves for Communion through healthy introspection, confession of sin, and resolution of differences with others. These actions remove the barriers that affect our relationship with Christ and with other believers. Awareness of your sin should not keep you away from Communion but should drive you to participate in it.

Related Topics: FELLOWSHIP, NEW COVENANT, SACRIFICE

LOST *(Forgotten, Vanished, Wayward)*

Who are the "lost," and how does God respond to them?

BIBLE READING: Isaiah 53:1-12
KEY BIBLE VERSE: *All of us have strayed away like sheep. We have left God's paths to follow our own. Yet the LORD laid on him the guilt and sins of us all.* (Isaiah 53:6)

We are all lost until we belong to Christ. Isaiah speaks of Israel straying from God and compares them to wandering sheep. Yet God would send the Messiah to bring them back into the fold. We have the hindsight to see and know the identity of the promised Messiah who has come and died for our sins. But if we can see all that Jesus did and still reject him, our sin is much greater than that of the ancient Israelites, who could not see what we have seen. Have you given your life to Jesus Christ, the "good shepherd" (John 10:11-16), or are you still like a wandering sheep?

BIBLE READING: Luke 15:1-32
KEY BIBLE VERSE: *Heaven will be happier over one lost sinner who returns to God than over ninety-nine others who are righteous and haven't strayed away!* (Luke 15:7)

The lost are of great value to God. It may seem foolish for the shepherd to leave ninety-nine sheep to go search for just one. But the shepherd knew that the ninety-nine would be safe in the sheepfold, whereas the lost sheep was in danger. Because each sheep was of high value, the shepherd knew that it was worthwhile to search diligently for the lost one. God's love for each individual is so great that he seeks each one out and rejoices when he or she is "found." Jesus associated with sinners because he wanted to bring the lost sheep—people considered beyond hope—the gospel of God's kingdom. If you feel far from God, don't despair. He is searching for you.

God takes special effort in seeking out the lost. Palestinian women received ten silver coins as a wedding gift. Besides their monetary value, these coins held sentimental value like that of a wedding ring, and to lose one would be extremely distressing. Just as a woman would rejoice at finding her lost coin or ring, so the angels would rejoice over a repentant sinner. Each individual is precious to God. He grieves over every loss and rejoices whenever one of his children is found and brought into the kingdom. Perhaps we would have more joy in our churches if we shared Jesus' love and concern for the lost.

God is patient with the lost. In the two preceding stories, the seekers actively looked for the coin and the sheep, which could not return by themselves. In this story, the father watched and waited. He was dealing with a human being with a will of his own, but he was ready to greet his son if he returned. In the same way, God's love is constant and patient and welcoming. He will search for us and give us opportunities to respond, but he will not force us to come to him. Like the father in this story, God waits patiently for us to come to our senses.

Related Topics: JESUS CHRIST, MERCY, SALVATION

LOVE (*Affections, Commitment, Compassion*)

▶ **GOD'S LOVE**
How does the Bible describe God's love?

BIBLE READING: Luke 15:1-7
KEY BIBLE VERSE: *Heaven will be happier over one lost sinner who returns to God than over ninety-nine others who are righteous and haven't strayed away!* (Luke 15:7)

God's love is forgiving. We may be able to understand a God who would forgive sinners who come to him for mercy. But a God who tenderly searches for sinners and then joyfully forgives them must possess an extraordinary love! This is the kind of love that prompted Jesus to come to earth to search for lost people and save them. This is the kind of extraordinary love that God has for you. If you feel far from God, don't despair. He is searching for you.

BIBLE READING: Romans 8:28-39
KEY BIBLE VERSE: *I am convinced that nothing can ever separate us from his love. Death can't, and life can't. The angels can't, and the demons can't. Our fears for today, our worries about tomorrow, and even the powers of hell can't keep God's love away. Whether we are high above the sky or in the deepest ocean, nothing in all creation will ever be able to separate us from the love of God that is revealed in Christ Jesus our Lord.* (Romans 8:38-39)

God's love is beyond measure. These words were written to a church that would soon undergo terrible persecution. In just a few years, Paul's hypothetical situations would turn into painful realities. This passage reaffirms God's profound love for his people. No matter what happens to us, no matter where we are, we can never be lost to his love. Suffering should not drive us away from God; it should help us to identify with him further and allow his love to reach us and heal us.

God's love is eternal. These verses contain one of the most comforting promises in all Scripture. Believers have always had to face hardships in many forms: persecution, illness, imprisonment, even death. These could cause them to fear that they have been abandoned by Christ. But Paul exclaims that it is *impossible* to be separated from Christ. His death for us is proof of his unconquerable love. Nothing can stop Christ's constant presence with us. God tells us how great his love is so that we will feel totally secure in him. If we believe these overwhelming assurances, we will not be afraid.

BIBLE READING: John 3:1-21

KEY BIBLE VERSE: *God so loved the world that he gave his only Son, so that everyone who believes in him will not perish but have eternal life.* (John 3:16)

God's love is sacrificial. The entire gospel comes to a focus in this verse. God's love is not static or self-centered; it reaches out and draws others in. Here God sets the pattern of true love, the basis for all love relationships—when you love someone dearly, you are willing to pay dearly for that person's responsive love. God paid dearly with the life of his Son, the highest price he could pay. Jesus accepted our punishment, paid the price for our sins, and then offered us the new life that he had bought for us. When we share the gospel with others, our love must be like Jesus'. We must be willing to give up our own comfort and security so that others might join us in receiving God's love.

BIBLE READING: Psalm 136:1-26

KEY BIBLE VERSE: *Give thanks to the LORD, for he is good! His faithful love endures forever.* (Psalm 136:1)

God's love is inexhaustible. Repeated throughout this psalm is the phrase, "His faithful love endures forever." This psalm may have been a responsive reading, with the congregation saying these words in unison after each sentence. The repetition made this important lesson sink in. God's love includes aspects of love, kindness, mercy, and faithfulness. We never have to worry that God will run out of love, because it flows from a well that will never run dry.

▶ **HUMAN LOVE**

What are the biblical guidelines for human love?

BIBLE READING: 1 Corinthians 13:1-13

KEY BIBLE VERSE: *Love is patient and kind. Love is not jealous or boastful or proud or rude. Love does not demand its own way. Love is not irritable, and it keeps no record of when it has been wronged. It is never glad about injustice but rejoices whenever the truth wins out. Love never gives up, never loses faith, is always hopeful, and endures through every circumstance.* (1 Corinthians 13:4-7)

Love is more important than spiritual gifts. In chapter 12 Paul gave evidence of the Corinthians' lack of love in the utilization of spiritual gifts; chapter 13 defines real love; and chapter 14 shows how love works. Love is more important than all the spiritual gifts exercised in the church body. Great faith, acts of dedication or sacrifice, and miracle-working power produce very little without love. Love makes our actions and gifts useful. Although people have different gifts, love is available to everyone.

Love benefits others. Our society confuses love and lust. Unlike lust, God's kind of love is directed outward toward others, not inward toward ourselves. It is utterly unselfish. This kind of love goes against our natural inclinations. It is possible to practice this love only if God helps us set aside our own desires and instincts, so that we can give love while expecting nothing in return. Thus the more we become like Christ, the more love we will show to others.

BIBLE READING: 1 John 2:1-11

KEY BIBLE VERSE: *Dear friends, I am not writing a new commandment, for it is an old one you have always had, right from the beginning. This commandment— to love one another—is the same message you heard before. Yet it is also new. This commandment is true in Christ and is true among you, because the darkness is disappearing and the true light is already shining.* (1 John 2:7-8)

Love is a command. The commandment to love others is both old and new. It is old because it comes from the Old Testament (Leviticus 19:18). It is new because Jesus interpreted it in a radically new way (John 13:34-35). In the Christian church, love is not only expressed by showing respect; it is also expressed through self-sacrifice and servanthood (John 15:13). In fact, it can be defined as "selfless giving," reaching beyond friends to enemies and persecutors (Matthew 5:43-48). Love should be the unifying force and the identifying mark of the Christian community. Love is the key to walking in the light, because we cannot grow spiritually while we hate others. Our growing relationship with God will result in growing relationships with others.

Love is a choice. Does this mean that if you dislike someone you aren't a Christian? These verses are not talking about disliking a disagreeable Christian brother or sister. There will always be people we will not like as well as others. John's words focus on the attitude that causes us to ignore or despise others, to treat them as irritants, competitors, or enemies. Christian love is not a feeling, but a choice. We can choose to be concerned with people's well-being and treat them with respect, whether or not we feel affection toward them. If we choose to love others, God will help us express our love.

BIBLE READING: Mark 12:28-34

KEY BIBLE VERSE: *Jesus replied, "The most important commandment is this: 'Hear, O Israel! The Lord our God is the one and only Lord. And you must love the Lord your God with all your heart, all your soul, all your mind, and all your strength.' The second is equally important: 'Love your neighbor as yourself.' No other commandment is greater than these."* (Mark 12:29-31)

Loving God is the greatest human act. God's laws are not burdensome. They can be reduced to two simple principles: love God and love others. These commands are from the Old Testament (Deuteronomy 6:5; Leviticus 19:18). When you love God completely and care for others as you care for yourself, then you have fulfilled the intent of the Ten Commandments and the other Old Testament laws. According to Jesus, these two commandments summarize all of God's laws. Let them rule your thoughts, decisions, and actions. When you are uncertain about what to do, ask yourself which course of action best demonstrates love for God and love for others.

BIBLE READING: John 21:15-25

KEY BIBLE VERSE: *Once more he asked him, "Simon son of John, do you love me?" Peter was grieved that Jesus asked the question a third time. He said, "Lord, you know everything. You know I love you." Jesus said, "Then feed my sheep."* (John 21:17)

Loving God means serving him. Peter had disowned Jesus three times. Three times Jesus asked Peter if he loved him. When Peter answered yes, Jesus told him to feed his sheep. It is one thing to say you love Jesus, but the real test is willingness to serve him. Peter had repented, and here Jesus was asking him to commit his life. Peter's life changed when he finally realized who Jesus was. His occupation changed from fisherman to evangelist; his identity changed from impetuous to "rock"; and his relationship to Jesus changed—he was forgiven, and he finally understood the significance of Jesus' words about his death and resurrection.

Loving God requires everything we have and are. Jesus asked Peter three times if he loved him. The first time Jesus said, "Do you love [Greek *agape*: volitional, self-sacrificial love] me more than these?" The second time, Jesus still used the word translated from the Greek word *agape*. The third time, Jesus used the word translated from the Greek word *phileo* (signifying affection, affinity, or brotherly love) and asked, in effect, "Are you even my friend?" Each time Peter responded with the word translated into Greek as *phileo*. Jesus doesn't settle for quick, superficial answers. Peter had to face his true feelings and motives when Jesus confronted him. How would you respond if Jesus asked you, "Do you love me?" Are you even his friend?

Related Topics: GOD, OBEDIENCE, SERVING

LOYALTY (*Affections, Commitment, Compassion*)

How important is loyalty, and what does it mean in our relationships?

BIBLE READING: Proverbs 17:1-28
KEY BIBLE VERSE: *A friend is always loyal, and a brother is born to help in time of need.* (Proverbs 17:17)

Loyalty is an essential part of true friendship. There is a vast difference between knowing someone well and being a true friend. The greatest evidence of genuine friendship is loyalty (see 1 Corinthians 13:7)—being available to help in times of struggle. Too many people are fair-weather friends. They stick around when the friendship helps them and leave when they're not getting anything out of the relationship. Think of your friends, and assess your loyalty to them. Be the kind of true friend the Bible encourages.

BIBLE READING: Matthew 6:19-24
KEY BIBLE VERSE: *"No one can serve two masters. For you will hate one and love the other, or be devoted to one and despise the other. You cannot serve both God and money.* (Matthew 6:24)

Our loyalty to God cannot be divided. Jesus says we can have only one master. We live in a materialistic society where many people serve money. They spend all their lives collecting and storing it, only to die and leave it behind. Their desire for money and what it can buy far outweighs their commitment to God and spiritual matters. Whatever you store up, you will spend much of your time and energy thinking about. Don't fall into the materialistic trap, because "the love of money is at the root of all kinds of evil" (1 Timothy 6:10). Can you honestly say that God, and not money, is your master? One test is to ask which one occupies more of your thoughts, time, and efforts.

Our highest loyalty should be to God and his eternal values. Jesus contrasted heavenly values with earthly values when he explained that our first loyalty should be to those things that do not fade, cannot be stolen or used up, and never wear out. We should not be fascinated with our possessions, lest *they* possess *us*. This means we may have to do some cutting back if our possessions are becoming too important to us. Jesus is calling for a decision that allows us to live contentedly with whatever we have because we have chosen what is eternal and lasting.

BIBLE READING: Luke 12:49-53
KEY BIBLE VERSE: *Do you think I have come to bring peace to the earth? No, I have come to bring strife and division!* (Luke 12:51)

We can be completely loyal to only one person. In these strange and unsettling words, Jesus revealed that his coming often results in conflict. He demands a response so intimate that groups may be torn apart when some choose to follow him and others refuse to do so. There is no middle ground with Jesus. Loyalties must be declared and commitments made, sometimes to the point of severing other relationships. Are you willing to risk your family's approval in order to gain eternal life?

Related Topics: COMMITMENT, FAITHFULNESS, LOVE

LUST *(Craving, Desire, Passion)*

Why is lust such a dangerous tendency?

BIBLE READING: Numbers 11:4-35

KEY BIBLE VERSE: *So that place was called Kibroth-hattaavah—"the graves of craving"—because they buried the people there who had craved meat from Egypt.* (Numbers 11:34)

Lust can destroy any normal desire. Craving or lusting is more than inappropriate sexual desire. It can be an unnatural or greedy desire for anything (sports, knowledge, possessions, influence over others). In this circumstance, God punished the Israelites for craving good food! Their desire was not wrong; the sin was in allowing that desire to turn into greed. They felt it was their right to have fine food, and they could think of nothing else. When you become preoccupied with something until it affects your perspective on everything else, you have moved from desire to lust.

BIBLE READING: Judges 16:1-22

KEY BIBLE VERSE: *Then Delilah pouted, "How can you say you love me when you don't confide in me? You've made fun of me three times now, and you still haven't told me what makes you so strong!" So day after day she nagged him until he couldn't stand it any longer. Finally, Samson told her his secret. "My hair has never been cut," he confessed, "for I was dedicated to God as a Nazirite from birth. If my head were shaved, my strength would leave me, and I would become as weak as anyone else."* (Judges 16:15-17)

Lust can lead to bad decision making. Samson was deceived because he wanted to believe Delilah's lies. Although he could strangle a lion, he could not smother his burning lust and see Delilah for who she really was. How can you keep your desire for love and sexual pleasure from deceiving you? (1) You must decide what kind of person you will love *before* passion takes over. Determine whether a person's character and faith in God are as desirable as his or her physical appearance. (2) Because most of the time you spend with your spouse will *not* involve sex, your companion's personality, temperament, and commitment to solve problems must be as gratifying as his or her kisses. (3) Be patient. The second look often reveals what is beneath the pleasant appearance and attentive touch.

BIBLE READING: Matthew 5:27-30

KEY BIBLE VERSE: *But I say, anyone who even looks at a woman with lust in his eye has already committed adultery with her in his heart.* (Matthew 5:28)

Lust itself is a sinful behavior. The Old Testament law said that it is wrong for a person to have sex with someone other than his or her spouse (Exodus 20:14).

But Jesus said that the *desire* to have sex with someone other than your spouse is mental adultery and thus sin. Jesus emphasized that if the *act* is wrong, then so is the *intention*. To be faithful to your spouse with your body but not your mind is to break the trust so vital to a strong marriage. Jesus is not condemning natural interest in the opposite sex or even healthy sexual desire, but the deliberate and repeated filling of one's mind with fantasies that would be evil if acted out.

Lust is often used as an excuse for further sin. Some think that if lustful thoughts are sin, why shouldn't a person go ahead and do the lustful actions too? Acting out sinful desires is harmful in several ways: (1) it causes people to excuse sin rather than to stop sinning; (2) it destroys marriages; (3) it is deliberate rebellion against God's Word; and (4) it always hurts someone else in addition to the sinner. Sinful action is more dangerous than sinful desire, and that is why desires should not be acted out. Nevertheless, sinful desire is just as damaging to righteousness. Left unchecked, wrong desires will result in wrong actions and turn people away from God.

Related Topics: ADULTERY, MARRIAGE, SIN

LYING (*Deceit, Falsehood, Untruth*)

Why is God's judgment against lying so harsh?

BIBLE READING: 1 Samuel 15:1-35
KEY BIBLE VERSE: *When Samuel finally found him, Saul greeted him cheerfully. "May the LORD bless you," he said. "I have carried out the LORD's command!" "Then what is all the bleating of sheep and lowing of cattle I hear?" Samuel demanded.* (1 Samuel 15:13-14)

Lying is a form of self-deception. Saul thought he had won a great victory over the Amalekites, but God saw it as a great failure because Saul had disobeyed him and then lied to Samuel about the results of the battle. Saul may have thought his lie wouldn't be detected, or that what he did was not wrong. Saul was deceiving himself.

Lying destroys integrity. Dishonest people soon begin to believe the lies they construct around themselves. Then they lose the ability to tell the difference between truth and lies. By believing your own lies you deceive yourself, you alienate yourself from God, and you lose credibility in all your relationships. In the long run, honesty wins out.

BIBLE READING: 2 Chronicles 18:1-27
KEY BIBLE VERSE: *So King Ahab summoned his prophets, four hundred of them, and asked them, "Should we go to war against Ramoth-gilead or not?" They all replied, "Go ahead, for God will give you a great victory!"* (2 Chronicles 18:5)

Lying sometimes leads to injustice. When you want to please or impress someone, it is tempting to lie to make yourself look good. Ahab's four hundred prophets did just that, telling Ahab only what he wanted to hear. They were then rewarded for making Ahab happy. Micaiah, however, told the truth and got arrested (18:25-26). Obeying God doesn't always protect us from evil consequences. Obedience may, in fact, provoke them. But it is better to suffer from human's displeasure than from God's wrath (Matthew 10:28). If you are ridiculed for being honest, remember that this can be a sign that you are indeed doing what is right in God's eyes (Matthew 5:10-12; Romans 8:17, 35-39).

BIBLE READING: Ephesians 4:17-32
KEY BIBLE VERSE: *So put away all falsehood and "tell your neighbor the truth" because we belong to each other.* (Ephesians 4:25)

Lying undermines our freedom and unity in Christ. Lying to each other disrupts unity by creating conflicts and destroying trust. It tears down relationships and leads to open warfare in a church. Our old way of life before we believed in Christ, which may have included lying, is completely in the past. We should put it behind us like old clothes to be thrown away. We first make this choice when we decide to accept Christ's gift of salvation (2:8-10), and we must consciously renew this commitment every day. We are not to be driven by desire and impulse. We must put on the new role, head in the new direction, and have the new way of thinking that the Holy Spirit gives.

Related Topics: EXCUSES, HONESTY, TRUTH

MAGIC (*Incantation, Occultism, Trickery*)

What does magic have to do with Christianity?

BIBLE READING: Matthew 4:1-11

KEY BIBLE VERSE: *Jesus responded, "The Scriptures also say, 'Do not test the Lord your God.' "* (Matthew 4:7)

God cannot be manipulated. God is not our magician in the sky ready to perform on request. In response to Satan's temptations, Jesus said not to put God to a test (Deuteronomy 6:16). You may want to ask God to do something to prove his existence or his love for you. A man once asked Jesus that a special sign be sent to help people believe. Jesus told him that people who don't believe what is written in the Bible wouldn't believe even if someone were to come back from the dead to warn them (Luke 16:31)! God wants us to live by faith, not by magic. Don't try to manipulate God by asking for signs.

BIBLE READING: Matthew 6:5-15

KEY BIBLE VERSE: *When you pray, don't babble on and on as people of other religions do. They think their prayers are answered only by repeating their words again and again. Don't be like them, because your Father knows exactly what you need even before you ask him!* (Matthew 6:7-8)

Prayers are not magic. Repeating the same words over and over like a magic incantation is no way to ensure that God will hear your prayer. It's not wrong to come to God many times with the same requests—Jesus encourages *persistent* prayer. But he condemns the shallow repetition of words that are not offered with a sincere heart. We can never pray too much if our prayers are honest and sincere. Before you start to pray, make sure you mean what you say.

BIBLE READING: Acts 19:1-22

KEY BIBLE VERSE: *Many who became believers confessed their sinful practices. A number of them who had been practicing magic brought their incantation books and burned them at a public bonfire. The value of the books was several million dollars.* (Acts 19:18-19)

Black magic and the Christian faith are not compatible. The Jews mentioned earlier in this passage traveled from town to town making a living by claiming to heal the sick and drive out demons. Often they would recite a whole list of names in their incantation to be sure of including the right deity. Here they were trying to use Jesus' name in an effort to match Paul's power. They were dabbling with power they did not understand. It turned into a dangerous and evil experiment.

God's power is demonstrated through the Holy Spirit, not through magic. Many Ephesians engaged in exorcism and occult practices for profit. The sons of Sceva were impressed by the work of Paul, whose power to drive out demons came not from witchcraft, but from God's Holy Spirit. They wanted this power because it was obviously stronger than the power they had. They discovered, however, that no one can control or duplicate God's power. These men were calling on the name of Jesus without knowing the person. The power to change people comes from Christ. It cannot be tapped by reciting his name like a magic charm. God works his power only through those he chooses.

Occult magic is opposed to God. Ephesus was a center for black magic and other occult practices. The people cooked up magical formulas to give them wealth, happiness, and success in marriage. Superstition and sorcery were commonplace. God clearly forbids such practices (Deuteronomy 18:9-13). You cannot be a believer and hold on to the occult, black magic, or sorcery. Once you begin to dabble in these areas, it is extremely easy to become obsessed by them, because Satan is very powerful. But God's power is even greater (1 John 4:4; Revelation 20:10). If you are mixed up in the occult, learn a lesson from the Ephesians, and get rid of anything that could keep you trapped in such practices.

Related Topics: EVIL, MIRACLES, PRAYER

MAJORITY *(Greatest, Most, Power)*

When must the majority opinion be resisted?

BIBLE READING: Exodus 1:1-22

KEY BIBLE VERSE: *Because the midwives feared God, they refused to obey the king and allowed the boys to live, too.* (Exodus 1:17)

The majority must be resisted when it overrules God's commands. Against Pharaoh's orders, the midwives spared the Hebrew babies. Their faith in God gave them the courage to take a stand for what they knew was right. In this situation, disobeying the authority was proper. God does not expect us to obey those in authority when they ask us to disobey him or his Word. The Bible is filled with examples of those who were willing to sacrifice their very lives in order to obey God or save others. Esther and Mordecai (Esther 3:2; 4:13-16) and Shadrach, Meshach, and Abednego (Daniel 3:16-18) are some of the people who took a bold stand for what was right. Whole nations can be caught up in immorality (racial hatred, slavery, prison cruelty); thus, following the majority or the authority is not always right. Whenever we are ordered to disobey God's Word, we must "obey God rather than human authority" (Acts 5:29).

BIBLE READING: Numbers 13:26-33

KEY BIBLE VERSE: *Caleb tried to encourage the people as they stood before Moses. "Let's go at once to take the land," he said. "We can certainly conquer it!"* (Numbers 13:30)

Our reasons for resisting the majority must be clear. Imagine standing before a crowd and loudly voicing an unpopular opinion! Caleb was willing to take the unpopular stand to do as God had commanded. To be effective when you go against the crowd, you must (1) have the facts (Caleb had seen the land himself);

(2) have the right attitude (Caleb trusted God's promise to give Israel the land); and (3) state clearly what you believe (Caleb said, "We can certainly conquer it").

BIBLE READING: 2 Samuel 19:1-43

KEY BIBLE VERSE: *The king went out and sat at the city gate, and as the news spread throughout the city that he was there, everyone went to him. Meanwhile, the Israelites who supported Absalom had fled to their homes. And throughout the tribes of Israel there was much discussion and argument going on. The people were saying, "The king saved us from our enemies, the Philistines, but Absalom chased him out of the country. Now Absalom, whom we anointed to rule over us, is dead. Let's ask David to come back and be our king again." (2 Samuel 19:8-10)*

God's Word is dependable; public opinion is not. Just a few days before Absalom died, most of Israel was supporting him in his bid to become king. Now the people wanted David back as their king. Because crowds are often fickle, there must be a higher moral code to follow than the pleasure of the majority. Following the moral principles given in God's Word will help you avoid being swayed by the popular opinions of the crowd.

Related Topics: COURAGE, DECISIONS, LEADERSHIP

MAN (*see* IMAGE)

MANAGEMENT (*Control, Leadership, Supervision*)

What principles of management do we find illustrated in the Bible?

BIBLE READING: Exodus 18:1-27

KEY BIBLE VERSE: *Find some capable, honest men who fear God and hate bribes. Appoint them as judges over groups of one thousand, one hundred, fifty, and ten. (Exodus 18:21)*

Effective management includes sharing the work load. Moses was spending so much time and energy hearing the Hebrews' complaints that he could not get to other important work. Jethro suggested that Moses delegate most of this work to others and focus his efforts on jobs only he could do. People in positions of responsibility sometimes feel they are the only ones who can do necessary tasks; but others are capable of handling part of the load. Delegation relieved Moses' stress and improved the quality of the government. It helped prepare them for the system of government set up in Canaan. Proper delegation can multiply your effectiveness while giving others a chance to grow.

BIBLE READING: Exodus 39:32-43

KEY BIBLE VERSE: *The people of Israel followed all of the LORD's instructions to Moses. Moses inspected all their work and blessed them because it had been done as the LORD had commanded him. (Exodus 39:42-43)*

Effective management includes supervision and affirmation. Moses inspected the finished work, saw that it was done the way God wanted, and then blessed the people. A good leader follows up on assigned tasks and gives rewards for good work. In whatever responsible position you find yourself, follow up to make sure that tasks are completed as intended, and show your appreciation to the people who have helped.

Moses had learned his management lesson well. He gave important responsibilities to others and then trusted them to do the job. Great leaders, like Moses, make plans and give direction while letting others participate on the team. If you are a leader, trust your assistants with key responsibilities.

BIBLE READING: Romans 12:1-8

KEY BIBLE VERSE: *God has given each of us the ability to do certain things well. So if God has given you the ability to prophesy, speak out when you have faith that God is speaking through you. If your gift is that of serving others, serve them well. If you are a teacher, do a good job of teaching. If your gift is to encourage others, do it! If you have money, share it generously. If God has given you leadership ability, take the responsibility seriously. And if you have a gift for showing kindness to others, do it gladly.* (Romans 12:6-8)

Management is one of God's gifts. Look at this list of gifts and imagine the kinds of people who would have each gift. Prophets are often bold and articulate. Servers (those in ministry) are faithful and loyal. Teachers are clear thinkers. Encouragers know how to motivate others. Givers are generous and trusting. Leaders are good organizers and managers. Those who show mercy are caring people who are happy to give their time to others. It would be difficult for one person to embody all these gifts. An assertive prophet would not usually make a good counselor, and a generous giver might fail as a leader. When you identify your own gifts (and this list is far from complete), ask how you can use them to build up God's family. At the same time, realize that your gifts can't do the work of the church all alone. Be thankful for people whose gifts are completely different from yours. Let your strengths balance their weaknesses, and be grateful that their abilities make up for your deficiencies. Together you can build Christ's church.

Related Topics: ABILITIES, GIFTS, LEADERSHIP

MANIPULATION (*see* HONESTY)

MARRIAGE (*Covenant, Promises, Relationship*)

▶ MARRIAGE PRINCIPLES
What does the Bible teach about marriage?

BIBLE READING: Genesis 2:1-25

KEY BIBLE VERSE: *This explains why a man leaves his father and mother and is joined to his wife, and the two are united into one.* (Genesis 2:24)

Marriage is a committed partnership between a man and a woman. God's creative work was not complete until he made woman. He could have made her from the dust of the ground, as he made man. God chose, however, to make her from the man's flesh and bone. In so doing, he illustrated for us that in marriage, a man and a woman symbolically become one flesh. This is a mystical union of the couple's hearts and lives. Throughout the Bible, God treats this special partnership seriously. If you are married or planning to be married, are you willing to keep the commitment that makes the two of you one? The goal in marriage should be more than friendship; it should be oneness.

Marriage is a cooperative effort between equal partners. God forms and equips men and women for various tasks, but all these tasks lead to the same goal—

honoring God. Man gives life to woman; woman gives life to the world. Each role carries exclusive privileges; there is no room for thinking that one sex is superior to the other.

Marriage is a gift from God. God gave marriage as a gift to Adam and Eve. They were created perfect for each other. Marriage was not just for convenience, nor was it brought about by any culture.

Marriage was designed by God. The marriage relationship that God designed has three basic aspects: (1) the man leaves his parents and, in a public act, promises himself to his wife; (2) the man and woman are joined together by taking responsibility for each other's welfare and by loving the mate above all others; (3) the two become one flesh in the intimacy and commitment of sexual union that is reserved for marriage. Strong marriages include all three of these aspects.

Marriage is intended to be a relationship of growing openness. Have you ever noticed how little children can run naked through a room full of strangers without embarrassment? They are not aware of their nakedness, just as Adam and Eve were not embarrassed in their innocence. But after Adam and Eve sinned, shame and awkwardness followed, creating barriers between themselves and God. We often experience these same barriers in marriage. Ideally a husband and wife have no barriers, feeling no embarrassment in exposing themselves to each other or to God. But, like Adam and Eve (3:7), we put on fig leaves (barriers) because we have areas we don't want our spouse, or God, to know about. Then we hide, just as Adam and Eve hid from God. In marriage, lack of spiritual, emotional, and intellectual intimacy usually precedes a breakdown of physical intimacy. In the same way, when we fail to expose our secret thoughts to God, we break our lines of communication with him.

BIBLE READING: Ephesians 5:21-33

KEY BIBLE VERSE: *This is a great mystery, but it is an illustration of the way Christ and the church are one. So again I say, each man must love his wife as he loves himself, and the wife must respect her husband.* (Ephesians 5:32-33)

Marriage requires submission by both partners. Submitting to another person is a concept that is often misunderstood. It does not mean becoming a doormat. Christ—at whose name "every knee will bow, in heaven and on earth and under the earth" (Philippians 2:10)—submitted his will to the Father, and we honor Christ by following his example. When we submit to God, we become more willing to obey his command to submit to others, that is, to subordinate our rights to theirs. In a marriage relationship, both husband and wife are called to submit. For the wife, this means willingly following her husband's leadership in Christ. For the husband, it means putting aside his own interests in order to care for his wife. Submission is rarely a problem in homes where both partners have a strong relationship with Christ and where each is concerned for the happiness of the other.

Marriage is a challenge to each partner. Why did Paul tell wives to submit and husbands to love? Perhaps Christian women, newly freed in Christ, found submission difficult; perhaps Christian men, used to the Roman custom of giving unlimited power to the head of the family, were not used to treating their wives with respect and love. Of course both husbands and wives should submit to each other (5:21), just as both should love each other.

Marriage is a relationship in which both partners are servants. In Paul's day, women, children, and slaves were to submit to the head of the family—slaves would submit until they were freed, male children until they grew up, and women and girls their whole lives. Paul emphasized the equality of all believers in Christ (Galatians 3:28), but he did not suggest overthrowing Roman society to achieve it. Instead, he counseled all believers to submit to one another by choice—wives to husbands and also husbands to wives; slaves to masters and also masters to slaves; children to parents and also parents to children. This kind of mutual submission preserves order and harmony in the family while it increases love and respect among family members.

Marriage is a diversity of roles within a partnership of equals. Although some people have distorted Paul's teaching on submission by giving unlimited authority to husbands, we cannot get around it—Paul told wives to submit to their husbands. The fact that a teaching is not popular is no reason to discard it. According to the Bible, the man is the spiritual head of the family, and his wife should acknowledge his leadership. But real spiritual leadership involves service. Just as Christ served the disciples, even to the point of washing their feet, so the husband is to serve his wife. A wise and Christ-honoring husband will not take advantage of his leadership role, and a wise and Christ-honoring wife will not try to undermine her husband's leadership. Either approach causes disunity and friction in marriage.

Marriage is helping each partner grow. The union of husband and wife merges two persons in such a way that little can affect one without also affecting the other. Oneness in marriage does not mean losing your personality in the personality of the other. Instead, it means caring for your spouse as you care for yourself, learning to anticipate his or her needs, and helping the other person become all he or she can be. The creation story tells of God's plan that husband and wife should be one (Genesis 2:24), and Jesus also referred to this plan (Matthew 19:4-6).

▶ MARRIAGE PROBLEMS

What solutions does the Bible offer for common marriage problems?

BIBLE READING: Ezra 9:1-15

KEY BIBLE VERSE: *The men of Israel have married women from these people and have taken them as wives for their sons. So the holy race has become polluted by these mixed marriages. To make matters worse, the officials and leaders are some of the worst offenders.* (Ezra 9:2)

Marriage must be a spiritual as well as emotional and physical union. Some Israelites had married pagan spouses and lost track of God's purpose for them. The New Testament says that believers should not marry unbelievers (2 Corinthians 6:14). Such marriages cannot have unity in the most important issue in life—commitment and obedience to God. Because marriage involves two people becoming one, faith may become an issue, and one spouse may have to compromise beliefs for the sake of unity. Many people discount this problem only to regret it later. Don't allow emotion or passion to blind you to the ultimate importance of marrying someone with whom you can be united spiritually.

BIBLE READING: Matthew 5:31-32

KEY BIBLE VERSE: *You have heard that the law of Moses says, "A man can divorce his wife by merely giving her a letter of divorce." But I say that a man who divorces his wife, unless she has been unfaithful, causes her to commit adultery. And anyone who marries a divorced woman commits adultery.* (Matthew 5:31-32)

Look for ways to restore a marriage rather than leave it. Jesus said that divorce is not permissible except for unfaithfulness. This does not mean that divorce should automatically occur when a spouse commits adultery. The word translated "unfaithful" implies a sexually immoral lifestyle, not a confessed and repented act of adultery. Those who discover that their partner has been unfaithful should first make every effort to forgive, reconcile, and restore their relationship. We are always to look for reasons to restore the marriage relationship rather than for excuses to leave it.

BIBLE READING: 1 Corinthians 7:1-40

KEY BIBLE VERSE: *Now about the questions you asked in your letter. Yes, it is good to live a celibate life. But because there is so much sexual immorality, each man should have his own wife, and each woman should have her own husband.* (1 Corinthians 7:1-2)

Sex within marriage provides strength against temptation. Sexual temptations are difficult to withstand because they appeal to the normal and natural desires that God has given us. Marriage provides God's way to satisfy these natural sexual desires and to strengthen the partners against temptation. Married couples have the responsibility to care for each other; therefore, husbands and wives should not withhold themselves sexually from one another but should fulfill each other's needs and desires.

Spiritually, our bodies belong to God when we become Christians because Jesus Christ bought us by paying the price to release us from sin (see 6:19-20). Physically, our bodies belong to our spouses because God designed marriage so that, through the union of husband and wife, the two become one (Genesis 2:24). Paul stressed complete equality in sexual relationships. Neither male nor female should seek dominance or autonomy.

A Christian should be a positive influence on an unbelieving spouse. Because of their desire to serve Christ, some people in the Corinthian church thought they ought to divorce their pagan spouses and marry Christians. But Paul affirmed the marriage commitment. God's ideal is for marriages to stay together—even when one spouse is not a believer. The Christian spouse should try to win the other to Christ. It would be easy to rationalize leaving; however, Paul makes a strong case for staying with the unbelieving spouse and being a positive influence on the marriage. Paul, like Jesus, believed that marriage is permanent (see Mark 10:1-9).

Related Topics: ADULTERY, DIVORCE, LOVE

MASTER (*see* JESUS CHRIST)

MATERIALISM (*Acquisitiveness, Possessiveness, Worldliness*)

What are the dangers of materialism?

BIBLE READING: Genesis 14:1-24

KEY BIBLE VERSE: *They also captured Lot—Abram's nephew who lived in Sodom—and took everything he owned.* (Genesis 14:12)

Materialism can make us slaves to things. Lot's greedy desire for the best of everything led him into sinful surroundings. His burning desire for possessions and success cost him his freedom and enjoyment. As a captive to Kedorlaomer, he faced torture, captivity, or death. Lot's materialism had taken him from one form of slavery to another. In much the same way, we can be enticed into doing things or going places we shouldn't. The prosperity we long for is captivating; it can both entice us and enslave us if our motives are not in line with God's desires.

BIBLE READING: Matthew 4:1-11
KEY BIBLE VERSE: *The Devil took [Jesus] to the peak of a very high mountain and showed him the nations of the world and all their glory. "I will give it all to you," he said, "if you will only kneel down and worship me." (Matthew 4:8-9)*

Materialism is a temptation to evil. The devil offered the whole world to Jesus if Jesus would only bow down and worship him. Today the devil offers us the world by trying to entice us with materialism and power. We can resist temptations the same way Jesus did. If you find yourself craving something that the world offers, quote Jesus' words to the devil: "You must worship the Lord your God; serve only him."

BIBLE READING: Matthew 6:19-24
KEY BIBLE VERSE: *No one can serve two masters. For you will hate one and love the other, or be devoted to one and despise the other. You cannot serve both God and money.* (Matthew 6:24)

Materialism can take the place of God in our lives. Jesus says we can have only one master. We live in a materialistic society where many people serve money. They spend all their lives collecting and storing it, only to die and leave it behind. Their desire for money and what it can buy far outweighs their commitment to God and spiritual matters. Whatever you store up, you will spend much of your time and energy thinking about. Don't fall into the materialistic trap, because "the love of money is at the root of all kinds of evil" (1 Timothy 6:10). Can you honestly say that God, and not money, is your master? One test is to ask which one occupies more of your thoughts, time, and efforts.

The values of the kingdom are contrary to materialism. Jesus contrasted heavenly values with earthly values when he explained that our first loyalty should be to those things that do not fade, cannot be stolen or used up, and never wear out. We should not be fascinated with our possessions, lest *they* possess *us*. This means we may have to do some cutting back if our possessions are becoming too important to us. Jesus is calling for a decision that allows us to live contentedly with whatever we have because we have chosen what is eternal and lasting.

Related Topics: LUST, MONEY, POSSESSIONS

MATURITY *(Experience, Growth, Wisdom)*

What does the Bible say about spiritual maturity?

BIBLE READING: Deuteronomy 7:1-26
KEY BIBLE VERSE: *The LORD your God will drive those nations out ahead of you little by little. You will not clear them away all at once, for if you did, the wild animals would multiply too quickly for you.* (Deuteronomy 7:22)

Spiritual maturity is a gradual process. Moses told the Israelites that God would destroy Israel's enemies, but not all at once. God had the power to destroy those nations instantly, but he chose to do it in stages. In the same way and with the same power, God could miraculously and instantaneously change your life. Usually, however, he chooses to help you gradually, teaching you one lesson at a time. Rather than expecting instant spiritual maturity and solutions to all your problems, slow down and work one step at a time, trusting God to make up the difference between where you should be and where you are now. You'll soon look back and see that a miraculous transformation has occurred.

BIBLE READING: Colossians 1:15-29

KEY BIBLE VERSE: *Everywhere we go, we tell everyone about Christ. We warn them and teach them with all the wisdom God has given us, for we want to present them to God, perfect in their relationship to Christ.* (Colossians 1:28)

The goal of every believer is spiritual maturity. The word *perfect* means mature or complete, not flawless. Paul wanted to see each believer mature spiritually. Like Paul, we must work as wholeheartedly as an athlete, but we should not strive in our own strength alone. We have the power of his Spirit working in us. We can learn and grow daily, motivated by love, not by fear or pride, knowing that God gives the energy to become mature.

The first step toward spiritual maturity is faith in Christ. Christ's message is for everyone; so everywhere Paul and Timothy went they brought the Good News to all who would listen. An effective presentation of the gospel includes warning and teaching. The warning is that without Christ, people are doomed to eternal separation from God. The teaching is that salvation is available through faith in Christ. As Christ works in you, tell others about him, warning and teaching them in love. Who do you know that needs to hear this message?

BIBLE READING: Hebrews 6:1-20

KEY BIBLE VERSE: *Let us stop going over the basics of Christianity again and again. Let us go on instead and become mature in our understanding. Surely we don't need to start all over again with the importance of turning away from evil deeds and placing our faith in God.* (Hebrews 6:1)

Spiritual maturity begins with the basics of the faith. Certain elementary teachings are essential for all believers to understand. Those basics include the importance of faith, the foolishness of trying to be saved by good deeds, the meaning of baptism and spiritual gifts, and the facts of resurrection and eternal life. To go on to maturity in our understanding, we need to move beyond (but not away from) the elementary teachings to a more complete understanding of the faith. And this is what the author intends for them to do (6:3). Mature Christians should be teaching new Christians the basics. Then, acting on what they know, the mature will learn even more from God's Word.

BIBLE READING: Hebrews 13:1-25

KEY BIBLE VERSE: *May the God of peace, who brought again from the dead our Lord Jesus, equip you with all you need for doing his will. May he produce in you, through the power of Jesus Christ, all that is pleasing to him. Jesus is the great Shepherd of the sheep by an everlasting covenant, signed with his blood. To him be glory forever and ever. Amen.* (Hebrews 13:20)

Jesus Christ is the basis and goal of spiritual maturity. The letter to the Hebrews is a call to Christian maturity. It was addressed to first-century Jewish Christians, but it applies to Christians of any age or background. Christian maturity means making Christ the beginning and end of our faith. To grow in maturity, we must center our lives on him, not depending on religious ritual, not falling back into sin, not trusting in ourselves, and not letting anything come between us and Christ. Christ is sufficient and superior.

Related Topics: GROWTH, OBEDIENCE, WISDOM

MEDIATOR *(Advocate, Go-between, Representative)*

In what ways is Jesus Christ our mediator with God?

BIBLE READING: 1 Timothy 2:1-15
KEY BIBLE VERSE: *There is only one God and one Mediator who can reconcile God and people. He is the man Christ Jesus. He gave his life to purchase freedom for everyone. This is the message that God gave to the world at the proper time.* (1 Timothy 2:5-6)

Jesus bridges the chasm of sin separating us from God. We human beings are separated from God by sin, and only one person in the universe is our mediator and can stand between us and God and bring us together again—Jesus, who is both God and man. Jesus' sacrifice brought new life to all people. Have you let him bring you to the Father?

BIBLE READING: Romans 1:1-17
KEY BIBLE VERSE: *Let me say first of all that your faith in God is becoming known throughout the world. How I thank God through Jesus Christ for each one of you.* (Romans 1:8)

Jesus is the one through whom we give our thanks to God. Paul uses the phrase "I thank God through Jesus Christ" to emphasize the point that Christ is the one and only mediator between God and humans. Through Christ, God sends his love and forgiveness to us; through Christ, we send our thanks to God.

BIBLE READING: Hebrews 7:11-28
KEY BIBLE VERSE: *He is able, once and forever, to save everyone who comes to God through him. He lives forever to plead with God on their behalf.* (Hebrews 7:25)

Jesus represents us before God the Father. As our high priest, Christ is our advocate, the mediator between us and God. He looks after our interests and intercedes for us with God. The Old Testament high priest went before God once a year to plead for the forgiveness of the nation's sins; Christ makes perpetual intercession before God for us. Christ's continuous presence in heaven with the Father assures us that our sins have been paid for and forgiven (see Romans 8:33-34; Hebrews 2:17-18; 4:15-16; 9:24). This wonderful assurance frees us from guilt and from fear of failure.

Related Topics: GOSPEL, JESUS CHRIST, SALVATION

MEDITATION *(Contemplation, Reflection, Understanding)*

What is Christian meditation?

BIBLE READING: Joshua 1:1-18
KEY BIBLE VERSE: *Study this Book of the Law continually. Meditate on it day and night so you may be sure to obey all that is written in it. Only then will you succeed.* (Joshua 1:8)

Meditation is obedient reflection on God's Word. Many people think that prosperity and success come from having power, influential personal contacts, and a relentless desire to get ahead. But the strategy for gaining prosperity that God taught Joshua goes against such criteria. He said that to succeed, Joshua must (1) be strong and courageous because the task ahead would not be easy,

(2) obey God's law, and (3) constantly read and study the Book of the Law—God's Word. To be successful, follow God's words to Joshua. You may not succeed by the world's standards, but you will be a success in God's eyes—and his opinion lasts forever.

BIBLE READING: Psalm 1:1-6

KEY BIBLE VERSE: *They delight in doing everything the LORD wants; day and night they think about his law.* (Psalm 1:2)

Christian meditation is persistent reflection on God's Word. You can learn how to follow God by meditating on his Word. Meditating means spending time reading and thinking about what you have read. It means asking yourself how you should change so you're living as God wants. Knowing and meditating on God's Word are the first steps toward applying it to your everyday life. If you want to follow God more closely, you must know what he says.

BIBLE READING: Luke 5:12-16

KEY BIBLE VERSE: *Jesus often withdrew to the wilderness for prayer.* (Luke 5:16)

Christian meditation and prayer were exemplified by Jesus. People were flocking to hear Jesus preach and to have their diseases healed, but Jesus made sure he often withdrew to quiet, solitary places to pray. It was a habit. Many things clamor for our attention, and we often run ourselves ragged attending to them. Like Jesus, however, we should take time to withdraw to a quiet and deserted place to pray. Strength comes from God, and we can be strengthened only by spending time with him.

BIBLE READING: 2 Timothy 2:1-13

KEY BIBLE VERSE: *Think about what I am saying. The Lord will give you under-standing in all these things.* (2 Timothy 2:7)

Christian meditation is careful reflection on God's Word. Paul told Timothy to reflect on his words, and God would give him insight. God speaks through the Bible, his Word, but we need to be open and receptive to him. As you read the Bible, ask God to show you his timeless truths and the application to your life. Then consider what you have read by thinking it through and meditating on it. God will give you understanding.

Related Topics: BIBLE, DISCERNMENT, MEMORIZATION

MEMORIZATION (*Learn, Remember, Retain*)

What are the advantages of memorizing Scripture?

BIBLE READING: Psalm 119:9-16

KEY BIBLE VERSE: *I have hidden your word in my heart, that I might not sin against you.* (Psalm 119:11)

Scripture memorization is a defense against sin. Hiding (keeping) God's Word in our heart is a deterrent to sin. This alone should inspire us to memorize Scripture. But memorization alone will not keep us from sin; we must also put God's Word to work in our life, making it a vital guide for everything we do.

BIBLE READING: Deuteronomy 31:1-13

KEY BIBLE VERSE: *Call them all together—men, women, children, and the foreigners living in your towns—so they may listen and learn to fear the LORD your God and carefully obey all the terms of this law. Do this so that your children who have not known these laws will hear them and will learn to fear the LORD your God. Do this as long as you live in the land you are crossing the Jordan to occupy.* (Deuteronomy 31:12-13)

Memorization increases the possibility of obedience to God's Word. The laws were to be read to the whole assembly so that everyone, including the children, could hear them. Every seven years the entire nation would gather together and listen as a priest read the law to them. There were no books, Bibles, or newsstands to spread God's Word, so the people had to rely on word of mouth and an accurate memory. Memorization was an important part of worship, because if everyone knew the law, ignorance would be no excuse for breaking it. To fulfill God's purpose and will in our life, we need the content and substance of his Word in our heart and mind. For the Hebrews, this process began in childhood. Teaching our children and new believers should be one of our top priorities. Our finest teachers, best resources, and most careful thought should be directed toward showing young believers how to follow God in all of life's situations.

BIBLE READING: Matthew 4:1-11

KEY BIBLE VERSE: *Jesus told him, "No! The Scriptures say, 'People need more than bread for their life; they must feed on every word of God.' "* (Matthew 4:4)

Memorization allows God's Word to become a weapon against evil. Jesus was able to resist all of the devil's temptations because he not only knew Scripture, he also obeyed it. Ephesians 6:17 says that God's Word is a sword to use in spiritual combat. Knowing Bible verses is an important step in helping us resist the devil's attacks, but we must also obey the Bible. Note that Satan had memorized Scripture, but he failed to obey it. Knowing and obeying the Bible helps us follow God's desires rather than the devil's.

Related Topics: BIBLE, KNOWLEDGE, MEDITATION

MERCY *(Caring, Compassion, Kindness)*

In what ways do we experience God's mercy?

BIBLE READING: Genesis 20:1-18

KEY BIBLE VERSE: *"Yes, I know you are innocent," God replied. "That is why I kept you from sinning against me; I did not let you touch her."* (Genesis 20:6)

God is merciful even when we are not aware of it. Abimelech had unknowingly taken a married woman to be his wife and was about to commit adultery. But God somehow prevented him from touching Sarah and held him back from sinning. What mercy on God's part! How many times has God done the same for us, holding us back from sin in ways we can't even detect? We have no way of knowing—we just know from this story that he can. God works just as often in ways we can't see as in ways we can.

BIBLE READING: Psalm 6:1-10

KEY BIBLE VERSE: *Have compassion on me, LORD, for I am weak. Heal me, LORD, for my body is in agony.* (Psalm 6:2)

In times of disobedience we experience God's mercy. David accepted God's punishment, but he begged God not to discipline him in anger. Jeremiah also asked God to correct him gently and not in anger (Jeremiah 10:24). David recognized that if God treated him with justice alone and not with mercy, he would be wiped out by God's wrath. Often we want God to show mercy to us and justice to everyone else. God, in his kindness, forgives us instead of giving us what we deserve.

📖 BIBLE READING: Zechariah 3:1-10
KEY BIBLE VERSE: *Jeshua's clothing was filthy as he stood there before the angel. So the angel said to the others standing there, "Take off his filthy clothes." And turning to Jeshua he said, "See, I have taken away your sins, and now I am giving you these fine new clothes."* (Zechariah 3:3-4)

God's mercy does not come as a result of our worthiness. Zechariah's vision graphically portrays how we receive God's mercy. We do nothing ourselves. God removes our filthy clothes (sins), then provides us with new, clean, rich garments (the righteousness and holiness of God—2 Corinthians 5:21; Ephesians 4:24; Revelation 19:8). All we need to do is repent and ask God to forgive us. When Satan tries to make you feel dirty and unworthy, remember that the clean clothes of Christ's righteousness make you worthy to draw near to God.

📖 BIBLE READING: Luke 18:9-14
KEY BIBLE VERSE: *The tax collector stood at a distance and dared not even lift his eyes to heaven as he prayed. Instead, he beat his chest in sorrow, saying, "O God, be merciful to me, for I am a sinner." I tell you, this sinner, not the Pharisee, returned home justified before God. For the proud will be humbled, but the humble will be honored.* (Luke 18:13-14)

The proud do not experience God's mercy. The Pharisee did not go to the temple to pray to God but to announce to all within earshot how good he was. The tax collector went recognizing his sin and begging for mercy. Self-righteousness is dangerous. It leads to pride, causes a person to despise others, and prevents him or her from learning anything from God. The tax collector's prayer should be our prayer, because we all need God's mercy every day. Don't let pride in your achievements cut you off from God.

Related Topics: FORGIVENESS, GRACE, PRIDE

MESSIAH (*Christ, Lord, Savior*)

How does the title of Messiah fit Jesus?

📖 BIBLE READING: Isaiah 53:1-12
KEY BIBLE VERSE: *He was wounded and crushed for our sins. He was beaten that we might have peace. He was whipped, and we were healed! All of us have strayed away like sheep. We have left God's paths to follow our own. Yet the LORD laid on him the guilt and sins of us all.* (Isaiah 53:5-6)

Jesus is the suffering servant Messiah. This chapter in Isaiah speaks of the Messiah, Jesus, who would suffer for the sins of all people. Such a prophecy is astounding! Who would believe that God would choose to save the world through a humble, suffering servant rather than a glorious king? The idea is contrary to human pride and worldly ways. But God often works in ways we don't expect. The Messiah's strength is shown by humility, suffering, and mercy.

Jesus the Messiah fulfilled the Old Testament sacrificial system. How could an Old Testament person understand the idea of Christ dying for our sins (our transgressions and iniquities)—actually bearing the punishment that we deserved? The sacrifices suggested this idea, but it is one thing to kill a lamb, and something quite different to think of God's chosen servant as that Lamb. But God was pulling aside the curtain of time to let the people of Isaiah's day look ahead to the suffering of the future Messiah and the resulting forgiveness made available to all mankind.

BIBLE READING: Luke 2:21-40

KEY BIBLE VERSE: *Lord, now I can die in peace! As you promised me, I have seen the Savior you have given to all people. He is a light to reveal God to the nations, and he is the glory of your people Israel!* (Luke 2:29-32)

Jesus fully met the character and role requirements of the Messiah. The Jews were well acquainted with the Old Testament prophecies that spoke of the Messiah's blessings to their nation. They did not always give equal attention to the prophecies saying that he would bring salvation to the entire world, not just the Jews (see, for example, Isaiah 49:6). Many thought that Christ had come to save only his own people. Luke made sure his Greek audience understood that Christ had come to save *all* who believe, Gentiles as well as Jews.

BIBLE READING: Luke 7:18-35

KEY BIBLE VERSE: *John's two disciples found Jesus and said to him, "John the Baptist sent us to ask, 'Are you the Messiah we've been expecting, or should we keep looking for someone else?' " At that very time, he cured many people of their various diseases, and he cast out evil spirits and restored sight to the blind. Then he told John's disciples, "Go back to John and tell him what you have seen and heard—the blind see, the lame walk, the lepers are cured, the deaf hear, the dead are raised to life, and the Good News is being preached to the poor. And tell him, 'God blesses those who are not offended by me.' "* (Luke 7:20-23)

Jesus fully performed the ministry of the Messiah. The proofs listed here for Jesus' being the Messiah are significant. They consist of observable deeds, not theories—actions that Jesus' contemporaries saw and reported for us to read today. The prophets had said that the Messiah would do these very acts (see Isaiah 35:5-6; 61:1). These physical proofs helped John—and will help all of us—to recognize who Jesus is.

Related Topics: JESUS CHRIST, PROPHECY, SUFFERING

MIND *(Attitude, Reason, Thinking)*

According to the Bible, how should we develop our mind?

BIBLE READING: Romans 12:1-8

KEY BIBLE VERSE: *Don't copy the behavior and customs of this world, but let God transform you into a new person by changing the way you think. Then you will know what God wants you to do, and you will know how good and pleasing and perfect his will really is.* (Romans 12:2)

Our relationship with God needs to influence the way we think. Christians are told, "Don't copy the behavior and customs of this world," which are usually selfish and often corrupting. Many Christians wisely decide that much worldly behavior is off limits for them. Our refusal to conform to this world's values, however, must go even deeper than the level of behavior and customs—

it must be firmly planted in our mind. It is possible to avoid most worldly customs and still be proud, covetous, selfish, stubborn, and arrogant. Only when the Holy Spirit renews, reeducates, and redirects our mind are we truly transformed (see Romans 8:5).

BIBLE READING: 1 Corinthians 2:6-16

KEY BIBLE VERSE: *We who have the Spirit understand these things, but others can't understand us at all. How could they? For, "Who can know what the Lord is thinking? Who can give him counsel?" But we can understand these things, for we have the mind of Christ.* (1 Corinthians 2:15-16)

As Christians, we should have the "mind of Christ." No one can comprehend God (Romans 11:34), but through the guidance of the Holy Spirit, believers have insight into some of God's plans, thoughts, and actions—they, in fact, have the "mind of Christ." Through the Holy Spirit we can begin to know God's thoughts, talk with him, and expect his answers to our prayers. Are you spending enough time with Christ to have his very mind in you? An intimate relationship with Christ comes only from spending time consistently in his presence and in his Word.

BIBLE READING: Philippians 2:1-11

KEY BIBLE VERSE: *Your attitude should be the same that Christ Jesus had.* (Philippians 2:5)

The Christian mind is characterized by humility. Jesus Christ was humble, willing to give up his rights in order to obey God and serve people. Like Christ, we should have a servant's attitude, serving out of love for God and for others, not out of guilt or fear. Remember, you can choose your attitude. You can approach life expecting to be served, or you can look for opportunities to serve others. (See Mark 10:45 for more on Christ's attitude of servanthood.)

BIBLE READING: Philippians 4:1-9

KEY BIBLE VERSE: *Dear brothers and sisters, let me say one more thing as I close this letter. Fix your thoughts on what is true and honorable and right. Think about things that are pure and lovely and admirable. Think about things that are excellent and worthy of praise.* (Philippians 4:8)

The Christian mind is characterized by purity and truth. What you put into your mind determines what comes out in your words and actions. Paul tells us to program our mind with thoughts that are true, noble, right, pure, lovely, admirable, excellent, and praiseworthy. Do you have problems with impure thoughts and daydreams? Examine what you are putting into your mind through television, books, conversations, movies, and magazines. Replace harmful input with wholesome material. Above all, read God's Word and pray. Ask God to help you focus your mind on what is good and pure. It takes practice, but it can be done.

Related Topics: ATTITUDE, JESUS CHRIST, THINKING

MINISTRY *(Function, Service, Work)*

What is true ministry?

BIBLE READING: 1 Corinthians 1:10-17

KEY BIBLE VERSE: *Dear brothers and sisters, I appeal to you by the authority of the*

Lord Jesus Christ to stop arguing among yourselves. Let there be real harmony so there won't be divisions in the church. I plead with you to be of one mind, united in thought and purpose. (1 Corinthians 1:10)

True ministry is always a team effort. Paul was emphasizing that no one person should do everything. Paul's gift was preaching, and that's what he did. Christian ministry should be a team effort; no preacher or teacher is a complete link between God and people, and no individual can do all that the apostles did. We must be content with the contribution God has given us to make, and carry it out wholeheartedly. (For more on different gifts, see 1 Corinthians 12 and 13.)

True ministry centers on God's message. Some speakers use impressive words, but they are weak on content. Paul stressed solid content and practical help for his listeners. He wanted them to be impressed with his *message,* not just his style (see 1 Corinthians 2:1-5). You don't need to be a great speaker with a large vocabulary to share the gospel effectively. The persuasive power is in the story, not the storyteller. Paul was not against those who carefully prepare what they say (see 1 Corinthians 2:6), but against those who try to impress others with their own knowledge or speaking ability.

BIBLE READING: 1 Corinthians 9:1-27

KEY BIBLE VERSE: *When I am with those who are oppressed, I share their oppression so that I might bring them to Christ. Yes, I try to find common ground with everyone so that I might bring them to Christ.* (1 Corinthians 9:22)

True ministry considers the needs of others. Paul gives several important principles for ministry: (1) find common ground with those you contact; (2) avoid a know-it-all attitude; (3) make others feel accepted; (4) be sensitive to their needs and concerns; and (5) look for opportunities to tell them about Christ. These principles are just as valid for us as they were for Paul.

BIBLE READING: Galatians 2:1-10

KEY BIBLE VERSE: *Fourteen years later I went back to Jerusalem again, this time with Barnabas; and Titus came along, too.* (Galatians 2:1)

True ministry includes preparation and feedback. After his conversion, Paul spent many years preparing for the ministry to which God had called him. This preparation period included time alone with God (1:16-17), as well as time conferring with other Christians. Often new Christians, in their zeal, want to begin a full-time ministry without investing the necessary time studying the Bible and learning from qualified teachers. We need not wait to share Christ with our friends, but we may need more preparation before embarking on a special ministry, whether volunteer or paid. While we wait for God's timing, we should continue to study, learn, and grow.

Related Topics: PASTORS, SERVING, WORK

MIRACLES *(Unexpected, Unusual, Wonderful)*

How important are miracles to our understanding of Christianity?

BIBLE READING: Exodus 14:1-31

KEY BIBLE VERSE: *Moses raised his hand over the sea, and the LORD opened up a path through the water with a strong east wind. The wind blew all that night, turning the seabed into dry land. So the people of Israel walked through the sea on dry ground, with walls of water on each side!* (Exodus 14:21-22)

Miracles are an unavoidable part of the Christian faith. Some scholars believe the Israelites did not cross the main body of the Red Sea, but rather one of the shallow lakes or marshes north of it that dry up at certain times of the year, or perhaps a smaller branch of the Red Sea where the water would have been shallow enough to wade across. But the Bible clearly states that the Lord "opened up a path through the water with a strong east wind. The wind blew all that night, turning the seabed into dry land" (Exodus 14:21; see also Joshua 3:15-16 and 2 Kings 2:13-14). Also, the water was deep enough to cover the chariots (Exodus 14:28). The God who created the earth and water performed a mighty miracle at exactly the right time to demonstrate his great power and love for his people.

BIBLE READING: John 2:1-11

KEY BIBLE VERSE: *This miraculous sign at Cana in Galilee was Jesus' first display of his glory. And his disciples believed in him.* (John 2:11)

Miracles drew attention to Jesus' authority and uniqueness. When the disciples saw Jesus' miracle, they believed. The miracle showed his power over nature and revealed the way he would go about his ministry—helping others, speaking with authority, and being in personal touch with people.

Jesus' miracles drew attention to God's care for his creation. Miracles are not merely superhuman events, but events that demonstrate God's power. Almost every miracle Jesus did was a renewal of fallen creation—restoring sight, making the lame walk, even restoring life to the dead. Believe in Christ not because he is a superman, but because he is the God who continues his creation, even in those of us who are poor, weak, crippled, orphaned, blind, deaf, or with some other desperate need for re-creation.

BIBLE READING: John 20:24-31

KEY BIBLE VERSE: *Jesus told him, "You believe because you have seen me. Blessed are those who haven't seen me and believe anyway." Jesus' disciples saw him do many other miraculous signs besides the ones recorded in this book. But these are written so that you may believe that Jesus is the Messiah, the Son of God, and that by believing in him you will have life.* (John 20:29-31)

The miraculous never cancels the need for personal faith. Some people think they would believe in Jesus if they could see a definite sign or miracle. But Jesus says we are blessed if we can believe without seeing. We have all the proof we need in the words of the Bible and the testimony of believers. A physical appearance would not make Jesus any more real to us than he is now.

The Gospels, including the miracles of Jesus, provide a basis for faith. To understand the life and mission of Jesus more fully, all we need to do is study the Gospels. John tells us that his Gospel records only a few of the many events in Jesus' life on earth. But the gospel includes everything we need to know to believe that Jesus is the Christ, the Son of God, through whom we receive eternal life.

BIBLE READING: Acts 5:12-16

KEY BIBLE VERSE: *Crowds came in from the villages around Jerusalem, bringing their sick and those possessed by evil spirits, and they were all healed.* (Acts 5:16)

Miracles validated the ministry of the early church. What did these miraculous healings do for the early church? (1) They attracted new believers. (2) They confirmed the truth of the apostles' teaching. (3) They demonstrated that the power of the Messiah who had been crucified and risen was now with his followers.

Related Topics: GOD, HEALING, POWER

MISSION (*Assignment, Orders, Work*)

What is God's mission for us?

BIBLE READING: John 2:1-11

KEY BIBLE VERSE: *The next day Jesus' mother was a guest at a wedding celebration in the village of Cana in Galilee. Jesus and his disciples were also invited to the celebration.* (John 2:1-2)

Pleasure can be part of our mission. Jesus was on a mission to save the world, the greatest mission in the history of mankind. Yet he took time to attend a wedding and take part in its festivities. We may be tempted to think we should not take time out from our "important" work for social occasions. But maybe these social occasions are part of our mission. Jesus valued these wedding festivities because they involved people, and Jesus came to be with people. Our mission can often be accomplished in joyous times of celebration with others. Bring balance to your life by bringing Jesus into times of pleasure as well as times of work.

BIBLE READING: John 20:19-23

KEY BIBLE VERSE: *He spoke to them again and said, "Peace be with you. As the Father has sent me, so I send you."* (John 20:21)

Preaching the Good News is our mission. Jesus was giving the disciples their Spirit-powered and Spirit-guided mission—to preach the Good News about Jesus so people's sins might be forgiven. The disciples did not have the power to forgive sins (only God can forgive sins), but Jesus gave them the privilege of telling new believers that their sins *had been* forgiven because they had accepted Jesus' message. All believers have this same privilege. We can announce the forgiveness of sins with certainty when we ourselves repent and find faith.

BIBLE READING: Romans 1:18-32

KEY BIBLE VERSE: *God shows his anger from heaven against all sinful, wicked people who push the truth away from themselves. For the truth about God is known to them instinctively. God has put this knowledge in their hearts. From the time the world was created, people have seen the earth and sky and all that God made. They can clearly see his invisible qualities—his eternal power and divine nature. So they have no excuse whatsoever for not knowing God.* (Romans 1:18-20)

People throughout the world are our mission. Some people wonder why we need missionaries if people can know about God through nature (the Creation). The answer: (1) Although people know that God exists, they suppress that truth by their wickedness and thus refuse a relationship with him. Missionaries sensitively expose their error and point them to a new beginning. (2) Although people may believe there is a God, they refuse to commit themselves to him. Missionaries help persuade them, through both loving words and caring actions. (3) Missionaries convince people who reject God of the dangerous consequences of their actions. (4) Missionaries help the church obey the great commission of our Lord (Matthew 28:19-20). (5) Most important, though nature reveals God, people need to be told about Jesus and how, through him, they can have a personal relationship with God.

Knowing that God exists is not enough. People must learn that God is loving. They must understand what he did to demonstrate his love for us (5:8). They must be shown how to accept God's forgiveness of their sins. (See also 10:14-15.)

Related Topics: GOSPEL, OBEDIENCE, WITNESSING

MISTAKES *(Errors, Sin, Wrongdoing)*

What can we learn from our mistakes?

BIBLE READING: Genesis 4:1-26

KEY BIBLE VERSE: *"Why are you so angry?" the* LORD *asked him. "Why do you look so dejected? You will be accepted if you respond in the right way. But if you refuse to respond correctly, then watch out! Sin is waiting to attack and destroy you, and you must subdue it."* (Genesis 4:6-7)

Wisdom gained from past mistakes ought to guide our decisions. How do you react when someone suggests you have done something wrong? Do you move to correct the mistake or deny that you need to correct it? After Cain's sacrifice was rejected, God gave him the chance to right his wrong and try again. God even encouraged him to do this! But Cain refused, and the rest of his life is a startling example of what happens to those who refuse to admit their mistakes. The next time someone suggests you are wrong, take an honest look at yourself, and choose God's way instead of Cain's.

BIBLE READING: Nehemiah 9:1-38

KEY BIBLE VERSE: *In spite of all this, we are making a solemn promise and putting it in writing. On this sealed document are the names of our princes and Levites and priests.* (Nehemiah 9:38)

Reviewing the past can keep us from repeating mistakes. Many prayers and speeches in the Bible include a long summary of Israel's history because individuals did not have their own copies of the Bible as we do today. This summary of God's past works reminded the people of their great heritage and God's promises.

We should also remember our history to avoid repeating our mistakes so that we can serve God better. Reviewing our past helps us understand how to improve our behavior. It shows us the pattern to our spiritual growth. Learn from your past so that you will become the kind of person God wants you to be.

BIBLE READING: Ephesians 4:1-16

KEY BIBLE VERSE: *We will hold to the truth in love, becoming more and more in every way like Christ, who is the head of his body, the church. Under his direction, the whole body is fitted together perfectly. As each part does its own special work, it helps the other parts grow, so that the whole body is healthy and growing and full of love.* (Ephesians 4:15-16)

We must risk making mistakes to grow spiritually. Some Christians fear that any mistake will destroy their witness for the Lord. They see their own weaknesses, and they know that many non-Christians seem to have stronger character than they do. How can we grow up into Christ? The answer is that Christ forms us into a body—into a group of individuals who are united in their purpose and in their love for one another and for the Lord. If an individual stumbles, the rest of the group is there to pick him or her up and help him or her walk with God again. If an individual sins, restoration can be found through the church (Galatians 6:1), even as the rest of the body continues to witness to God's truth. As part of Christ's body, do you reflect part of Christ's character and carry out your special role in his work?

Related Topics: LEARNING, REPENTANCE, SIN

MOCKING *(see* INSULT[S]*)*

—

MODELING (*see* EXAMPLE)

—

MONEY (*Cash, Fortune, Treasure*)

▶ **MONEY DANGERS**

What does the Bible say concerning money?

 BIBLE READING: Ecclesiastes 10:1-20
KEY BIBLE VERSE: *A party gives laughter, and wine gives happiness, and money gives everything!* (Ecclesiastes 10:19)

Money does not solve problems. Government leaders, businesses, families, even churches get trapped into thinking money is the answer to every problem. We throw money at our problems. But just as the thrill of wine is only temporary, the soothing effect of the last purchase soon wears off, and we have to buy more. Scripture recognizes that money is necessary for survival, but it warns against the love of money (see Matthew 6:24; 1 Timothy 6:10; Hebrews 13:5). Money is dangerous because it deceives us into thinking that wealth is the easiest way to get everything we want. The love of money is sinful because we trust money, rather than God, to solve our problems. Those who pursue its empty promises will one day discover that they have nothing because they are spiritually bankrupt.

BIBLE READING: Mark 10:17-31
KEY BIBLE VERSE: *Jesus looked around and said to his disciples, "How hard it is for rich people to get into the Kingdom of God!"* (Mark 10:23)

The love of money is a barrier between us and God. This young man wanted to be sure he would get eternal life, so he asked what he could *do.* He said he had never once broken any of the laws Jesus mentioned (10:19), and perhaps he had even kept the Pharisees' loophole-filled version of them. But Jesus lovingly broke through the young man's pride with a challenge that brought out his true motives: "Go and sell all you have and give the money to the poor." This challenge exposed the barrier that could keep this young man out of the kingdom: his love of money. Money represented his pride of accomplishment and self-effort. Ironically, his attitude made him unable to keep the first commandment, to let nothing be more important than God (Exodus 20:3). He could not meet the one requirement Jesus gave—to turn his whole heart and life over to God. The man came to Jesus wondering what he could do; he left seeing what he was unable to do. What barriers are keeping you from turning your life over to Christ?

Our handling of money can be a way of service. What does your money mean to you? Although Jesus wanted this man to sell everything and give his money to the poor, this does not mean that all believers should sell all their possessions. Most of his followers did not sell everything, although they used their possessions to serve others. Instead, this story shows us that we must not let anything we have or desire keep us from following Jesus. We must remove all barriers to serving him fully. If Jesus asked you to, could you give up your house? your car? your level of income? your position on the ladder of promotion? Your reaction may show your attitude toward money—whether it is your servant or your master.

The love of money leads to a destructive self-reliance. Jesus said it was very difficult for the rich to enter the kingdom of God. This is true because the rich, with most of their basic physical needs met, often become self-reliant. When they feel empty, they can buy something new to dull the pain that was meant to drive them toward God. Their abundance and self-sufficiency become their deficiency. The person who has everything on earth can still lack what is most important—eternal life.

Money is not a measurement of our standing with God. The disciples were amazed. Was not wealth a blessing from God, a reward for being good? This misconception is still common today. Although many believers enjoy material prosperity, many others live in hardship. Wealth is not a sign of faith or of partiality on God's part.

▶ MONEY MANAGEMENT
What guidelines does the Bible give us for managing money?

BIBLE READING: Matthew 19:16-30
KEY BIBLE VERSE: *Jesus told him, "If you want to be perfect, go and sell all you have and give the money to the poor, and you will have treasure in heaven. Then come, follow me."* (Matthew 19:21)

God has given us all that we have. Should all believers sell everything they own? No. We are responsible to care for our own needs and the needs of our family so as not to be a burden on others. We should, however, be willing to give up anything if God asks us to do so. This kind of attitude allows nothing to come between us and God and keeps us from using our God-given wealth selfishly. If you are comforted by the fact that Christ did not tell all his followers to sell all their possessions, then you may be too attached to what you have.

We must use money in accordance with the love of God. We cannot love God with all our heart and yet keep our money to ourselves. Loving him totally means using our money in ways that please him.

BIBLE READING: Luke 16:1-15
KEY BIBLE VERSE: *No one can serve two masters. For you will hate one and love the other, or be devoted to one and despise the other. You cannot serve both God and money.* (Luke 16:13)

Our obedience to Christ is tested by how we use money. Here are some conclusions we can draw from this passage in Luke. (1) Let us use our resources wisely, because they belong to God and not to us. (2) Money can be used for good or evil; let us use ours for good. (3) Money has a lot of power, so we must use it carefully and thoughtfully. (4) We must use our material goods in a way that will foster faith and obedience (see 12:33-34).

Money can be a tool for helping others. We are to make wise use of our finances, spending our money to help those in need and to spread the gospel. In this way, our earthly investment will bring eternal benefit. When we obey God's will, the unselfish use of possessions will follow.

Our integrity often is tested in money matters. God calls us to be honest, even in small details we might think unimportant. Heaven's riches are far more valuable than earthly wealth. But if we are not trustworthy with our money here (no matter how much or how little we have), we will be unfit to handle the vast riches of God's kingdom. Guard your integrity in small matters, and it will not fail you in crucial decisions.

Money must be managed or it will manage. Money has the power to take God's place in your life. It can become your master. How can you tell if you

are a slave to money? (1) Do you think and worry about it frequently?
(2) Do you give up doing what you should do or would like to do in order
to make more money? (3) Do you spend a great deal of your time caring for
your possessions? (4) Is it hard for you to give money away? (5) Are you in
debt?

Money is a hard master and a deceptive one. Wealth promises power and
control, but often it cannot deliver. Great fortunes can be made—and lost—
overnight, and no amount of money can provide health, happiness, or eternal
life. How much better it is to let God be your Master. His servants have peace
of mind and security, both now and forever.

Related Topics: POOR, POSSESSIONS, WEALTH

MORALITY *(Goodness, Righteousness, Values)*

What is true morality?

BIBLE READING: Matthew 19:16-30

KEY BIBLE VERSE: *Many who seem to be important now will be the least important
then, and those who are considered least here will be the greatest then.* (Matthew 19:30)

Morality is following Jesus with humility. What many people call acceptable
behavior Jesus rejects as unacceptable. Consider the most powerful or well-
known people in our world—how many got where they are by being humble,
self-effacing, and gentle? Not many! But in the life to come, the last will be
first—if they got in last place by choosing to follow Jesus. Don't forfeit eternal
rewards for temporary benefits. Be willing to make sacrifices now for greater
rewards later. Be willing to accept human disapproval, while knowing that you
have God's approval.

BIBLE READING: Romans 2:1-16

KEY BIBLE VERSE: *It is not merely knowing the law that brings God's approval. Those
who obey the law will be declared right in God's sight. Even when Gentiles, who
do not have God's written law, instinctively follow what the law says, they show
that in their hearts they know right from wrong. They demonstrate that God's
law is written within them, for their own consciences either accuse them or tell
them they are doing what is right.* (Romans 2:13-15)

Morality is possible only with God's help. If you traveled around the world,
you would find evidence in every society and culture of God's moral law.
For example, all cultures prohibit murder, and yet in all societies that law has
been broken. We belong to a stubborn race. We know what's right, but we
insist on doing what's wrong. It is not enough to know what's right; we must
also do it. Admit to yourself and to God that you fit the human pattern and
frequently fail to live up to your own standards (much less to God's standards). That's the first step to forgiveness and healing.

BIBLE READING: Romans 12:1-8

KEY BIBLE VERSE: *Don't copy the behavior and customs of this world, but let God
transform you into a new person by changing the way you think. Then you will
know what God wants you to do, and you will know how good and pleasing and
perfect his will really is.* (Romans 12:2)

Morality is conformity to Christ. Christians are told, "Don't copy the behavior and customs of this world," which are usually selfish and often corrupting. Many Christians wisely decide that much worldly behavior is off limits for them. Our refusal to conform to this world's values, however, must go even deeper than the level of behavior and customs—it must be firmly planted in our mind. It is possible to avoid most worldly customs and still be proud, covetous, selfish, stubborn, and arrogant. Only when the Holy Spirit renews, reeducates, and redirects our mind are we truly transformed (see Romans 8:5).

Related Topics: ACTIONS, LOVE, RIGHTEOUSNESS

MOTIVES (*Goal, Purpose, Reason*)

How can we understand our own motives?

BIBLE READING: Genesis 27:1-46

KEY BIBLE VERSE: *"But Mother!" Jacob replied. "He won't be fooled that easily. Think how hairy Esau is and how smooth my skin is! What if my father touches me? He'll see that I'm trying to trick him, and then he'll curse me instead of blessing me."* (Genesis 27:11-12)

How we react to a moral dilemma often exposes our real motives. Frequently we are more worried about getting caught than about doing what is right. Jacob did not seem concerned about the deceitfulness of his mother's plan; instead he was afraid of getting in trouble while carrying it out. If you are worried about getting caught, you are probably in a position that is less than honest. Let your fear of getting caught be a warning to do right. Jacob paid a huge price for carrying out this dishonest plan.

BIBLE READING: Jeremiah 17:1-18

KEY BIBLE VERSE: *The human heart is most deceitful and desperately wicked. Who really knows how bad it is? But I know! I, the LORD, search all hearts and examine secret motives. I give all people their due rewards, according to what their actions deserve.* (Jeremiah 17:9-10)

Only God understands our real motives. God makes it clear why we sin—it's a matter of the heart. Our heart has been inclined toward sin from the time we were born. It is easy to fall into the routine of forgetting and forsaking God. But we can still choose whether or not to continue in sin. We can yield to a specific temptation, or we can ask God to help us resist temptation when it comes.

BIBLE READING: James 4:1-12

KEY BIBLE VERSE: *And even when you do ask, you don't get it because your whole motive is wrong—you want only what will give you pleasure.* (James 4:3)

Problems with people are often clues that wrong motives are at work. Conflicts and disputes among believers are always harmful. James explains that these quarrels result from evil desires battling within us—we want more possessions, more money, higher status, more recognition. We will even fight in order to fulfill these desires. Instead of aggressively grabbing what we want, we should submit ourselves to God, ask God to help us get rid of our selfish desires, and trust him to give us what we really need.

Problems in prayer are often clues that wrong motives are at work. James mentions the most common problems in prayer: not asking, asking for the wrong things, asking for the wrong reasons. Do you talk to God at all? When you do, what do you talk about? Do you ask only to satisfy your desires? Do you seek God's approval for what you already plan to do? Your prayers will become powerful when you allow God to change your desires so that they perfectly correspond to his will for you (1 John 3:21-22).

Related Topics: GOALS, PRAYER, PURPOSE

MOURNING *(Grief, Sadness, Sorrow)*

What does the Bible teach us about mourning?

BIBLE READING: Genesis 50:1-26
KEY BIBLE VERSE: *When they arrived at the threshing floor of Atad, near the Jordan River, they held a very great and solemn funeral, with a seven-day period of mourning for Joseph's father.* (Genesis 50:10)

Mourning takes time. When Jacob died at the age of 147, Joseph wept and mourned for months. When someone close to us dies, we need a long period of time to work through our grief. Crying and sharing our feelings with others helps us recover and go on with life. Allow yourself and others the freedom to grieve over the loss of a loved one, and give yourself time enough to complete your grieving process.

BIBLE READING: 2 Samuel 1:1-16
KEY BIBLE VERSE: *David and his men tore their clothes in sorrow when they heard the news. They mourned and wept and fasted all day for Saul and his son Jonathan, and for the LORD's army and the nation of Israel, because so many had died that day.* (2 Samuel 1:11-12)

Mourning is an appropriate response to the loss of a loved one. "They mourned and wept and fasted all day." David and his men were visibly shaken over Saul's and Jonathan's death. Their actions showed their genuine sorrow over the loss of their king, their friend Jonathan, and the other soldiers of Israel who died that day. They were not ashamed to grieve. Today, some people consider expressing emotions to be a sign of weakness. Those who wish to appear strong try to hide their feelings. But expressing our grief can help us deal with our intense sorrow when a loved one dies.

BIBLE READING: John 11:17-44
KEY BIBLE VERSE: *Then Jesus wept.* (John 11:35)

Jesus experienced grief. John stresses that we have a God who cares. This portrait contrasts with the Greek concept of God that was popular in that day—a god with no emotions and no messy involvement with humans. Here we see many of Jesus' emotions—compassion, indignation, sorrow, even frustration. He often expressed deep emotion, and we must never be afraid to reveal our true feelings to him. He understands them, for he experienced them. Be honest, and don't try to hide anything from your Savior. He cares.

Jesus did not hesitate to reveal his emotions. When Jesus saw the weeping and wailing, he too wept openly. Perhaps he empathized with their grief, or perhaps

he was troubled at their unbelief. In either case, Jesus showed that he cares
enough for us to weep with us in our sorrow.

Related Topics: EMOTIONS, GRIEF, JOY

MOVING *(Change, Travel, Uprooting)*

How can we handle life's changes?

BIBLE READING: Numbers 10:11-36
KEY BIBLE VERSE: *They marched for three days after leaving the mountain of the
LORD, with the Ark of the LORD's covenant moving ahead of them to show
them where to stop and rest. As they moved on each day, the cloud of the LORD
hovered over them.* (Numbers 10:33-34)

God's unchanging presence can help us cope with change. Those who travel,
move, or face new challenges know what it is to be uprooted. Life is full of
changes, and few things remain stable. The Israelites were constantly moving
through the desert. They were able to handle change only because God's presence in the tabernacle was always with them. The portable tabernacle signified
God and his people moving together. For us, stability does not mean lack of
change, but moving with God in every circumstance.

BIBLE READING: Esther 2:1-18
KEY BIBLE VERSE: *The king loved [Esther] more than any of the other young women.
He was so delighted with her that he set the royal crown on her head and
declared her queen instead of Vashti.* (Esther 2:17)

Remember that God has a purpose for our lives. God placed Esther on the
throne even before the Jews faced the possibility of complete destruction
(Esther 3:5ff.), so that when trouble came, a person would already be in
the position to help. No human effort could thwart God's plan to send the
Messiah to earth as a Jew. If you are changing jobs, position, or location
and can't see God's purpose in your situation, understand that God is in
control. He may be placing you in a position so you can help when the need
arises.

BIBLE READING: Matthew 2:1-18
KEY BIBLE VERSE: *When it was time to leave, they went home another way, because
God had warned them in a dream not to return to Herod. After the wise men
were gone, an angel of the Lord appeared to Joseph in a dream. "Get up and
flee to Egypt with the child and his mother," the angel said. "Stay there until
I tell you to return, because Herod is going to try to kill the child."* (Matthew
2:12-13)

Realize that God sometimes moves us to keep us safe. After finding Jesus and
worshiping him, the magi were warned by God not to return through Jerusalem
as they had intended. Finding Jesus may mean that your life must take a different direction, one that is responsive and obedient to God's Word. Are you willing to be led a different way?

Realize that God sometimes moves us to test our obedience. This was the
second dream or vision that Joseph received from God. Joseph's first dream
revealed that Mary's child would be the Messiah (1:20-21). His second dream
told him how to protect the child's life. Although Joseph was not Jesus' natural

father, he was Jesus' legal father and was responsible for his safety and well-being. Divine guidance comes only to prepared hearts. Joseph remained receptive to God's guidance.

Related Topics: GOD'S WILL, GUIDANCE, OBEDIENCE

MURDER (*Execute, Hurt, Kill*)

What does the Bible say about murder?

BIBLE READING: Genesis 4:1-26

KEY BIBLE VERSE: *Later Cain suggested to his brother, Abel, "Let's go out into the fields." And while they were there, Cain attacked and killed his brother.* (Genesis 4:8)

Murder is a crime against someone made in God's image. This is the first murder—taking a life by shedding human blood. Blood represents life (Leviticus 17:10-14). If the blood is removed from a living creature, it will die. Because God created life, only God should take life away.

Murder is a crime against our Creator and a fellow creature. Adam and Eve's disobedience brought sin into the human race. They may have thought their sin—eating a piece of fruit—wasn't very bad, but notice how quickly their sinful nature developed in their children. Simple disobedience quickly degenerated into outright murder. Adam and Eve acted only against God, but Cain acted against both God and humankind. A small sin has a way of growing out of control. Let God help you with your "little" sins before they turn into tragedies.

BIBLE READING: Deuteronomy 5:1-33

KEY BIBLE VERSE: *Do not murder.* (Deuteronomy 5:17)

Anger can be a form of murder. "But I don't murder people," you may say. Good. That fulfills the letter of the law. But Jesus explained that hateful anger breaks this commandment (Matthew 5:21-22). Have you ever been so angry with someone who mistreated you that for a moment you wished that person were dead? Have you ever fantasized that you could do someone in? Jesus' teaching concerning this law demonstrates that we are capable of murder in our heart. Even if we are legally innocent, we are all morally guilty of murder and need to ask God's forgiveness. We need to commit ourselves to the opposite of hatred and anger—love and reconciliation.

BIBLE READING: James 5:1-6

KEY BIBLE VERSE: *You have condemned and killed good people who had no power to defend themselves against you.* (James 5:6)

Oppression of the poor is a form of murder. "Good people" were defenseless persons, probably poor laborers. Poor people who could not pay their debts were thrown into prison or forced to sell all their possessions. At times they were even forced to sell their family members into slavery. With no opportunity to work off their debts, poor people often died of starvation. God called this murder. Hoarding money, exploiting employees, and living self-indulgently will not escape God's notice.

Related Topics: ANGER, HATRED, REVENGE

MUSIC *(Harmony, Melody, Tones)*

In what ways is music useful in worship?

BIBLE READING: Exodus 15:1-21

KEY BIBLE VERSE: *Moses and the people of Israel sang this song to the LORD: "I will sing to the LORD, for he has triumphed gloriously; he has thrown both horse and rider into the sea." (Exodus 15:1)*

Music can be an expression of worship. Music played an important part in Israel's worship and celebration. Singing was an expression of love and thanks, and it was a creative way to pass down oral traditions. Some say this song of Moses is the oldest recorded song in the world. It was a festive epic poem celebrating God's victory, lifting the hearts and voices of the people outward and upward. After having been delivered from great danger, they sang with joy! Psalms and hymns can be great ways to express relief, praise, and thanks when you have been through trouble.

BIBLE READING: Psalm 81:1-16

KEY BIBLE VERSE: *Sing praises to God, our strength. Sing to the God of Israel. Sing! Beat the tambourine. Play the sweet lyre and the harp. (Psalm 81:1-2)*

Music can help us focus our attention on God. David instituted music for the temple worship services (1 Chronicles 25). Music and worship go hand in hand. Worship should involve the whole person, and music helps lift a person's thoughts and emotions to God. Through music we can reflect upon our needs and shortcomings as well as celebrate God's greatness.

BIBLE READING: Colossians 3:1-17

KEY BIBLE VERSE: *Let the words of Christ, in all their richness, live in your hearts and make you wise. Use his words to teach and counsel each other. Sing psalms and hymns and spiritual songs to God with thankful hearts. (Colossians 3:16)*

Music can be a means of peace, opening the way for worship. Christians should live in peace. Living in peace does not mean that suddenly all differences in opinion are eliminated, but it does require that loving Christians work together despite their differences. Such love is not a feeling but a decision to meet others' needs (see 1 Corinthians 13). To live in love leads to peace between individuals and among the members of the body of believers. Do problems in your relationships with other Christians cause open conflicts or mutual silence? Consider what you can do to heal those relationships with love.

Related Topics: JOY, PRAISE, WORSHIP

NAMES (*Honor, Identity, Reputation*)

Why is so much attention given to names in the Bible?

BIBLE READING: Genesis 32:22-32

KEY BIBLE VERSE: *"What is your name?" the man asked. He replied, "Jacob." "Your name will no longer be Jacob," the man told him. "It is now Israel, because you have struggled with both God and men and have won."* (Genesis 32:27-28)

Names in the Bible often represented a person's character. God gave many Bible people new names (Abraham, Sarah, Peter). Their new names were symbols of how God had changed their lives. Here we see how Jacob's character had changed. Jacob, the ambitious deceiver, had now become Israel, the one who struggles with God and overcomes.

In Jacob's case, a quality that had been destructive was not being directed towards God and channeled for good. Jacob continued his wrestling match all night just to be blessed. He was persistent. God encourages persistence in all areas of our lives, including the spiritual. Where in your spiritual life do you need more persistence? Strong character develops as you struggle through tough conditions.

BIBLE READING: Exodus 3:1-22

KEY BIBLE VERSE: *God replied, "I AM THE ONE WHO ALWAYS IS. Just tell them, 'I AM has sent me to you.'" God also said, "Tell them, 'The LORD, the God of your ancestors—the God of Abraham, the God of Isaac, and the God of Jacob—has sent me to you.' This will be my name forever; it has always been my name, and it will be used throughout all generations."* (Exodus 3:14-15)

To honor God's name is to honor him. The Egyptians had many gods by many different names. Moses wanted to know God's name so the Hebrew people would know exactly who had sent him to them. God called himself *I Am*, a name describing his eternal power and unchangeable character. In a world where values, morals, and laws change constantly, we can find stability and security in our unchanging God. The God who appeared to Moses is the same God who can live in us today. Hebrews 13:8 says God is the same "yesterday, today, and forever." Because God's nature is stable and trustworthy, we are free to follow and enjoy him rather than spend our time trying to figure him out.

God's name is like his signature guarantee of his promises. *Yahweh* is derived from the Hebrew word for "I am." God reminded Moses of his covenant promises to Abraham (Genesis 12:1-3; 15; 17), Isaac (Genesis 26:2-5), and Jacob (Genesis 28:13-15), and used the name I Am to show his unchanging nature.

What God promised to the great patriarchs hundreds of years earlier he would fulfill through Moses.

BIBLE READING: Exodus 20:1-21

KEY BIBLE VERSE: *Do not misuse the name of the LORD your God. The LORD will not let you go unpunished if you misuse his name.* (Exodus 20:7)

Disrespectful use of God's name is an insult to him. God's name is special because it carries his personal identity. Using it frivolously or in a curse is so common today that we may fail to realize how serious it is. The way we use God's name conveys how we really feel about him. We should respect his name and use it appropriately, speaking it in praise or worship rather than in curse or jest. We should not take lightly the abuse or dishonor of his name.

BIBLE READING: Acts 3:1-26

KEY BIBLE VERSE: *The name of Jesus has healed this man—and you know how lame he was before. Faith in Jesus' name has caused this healing before your very eyes.* (Acts 3:16)

The name of Jesus merits the highest honor. Jesus, not the apostles, received the glory for the healing of the crippled man. In those days a man's name represented his character; it stood for his authority and power. By using Jesus' name, Peter showed who gave him the authority and power to heal. The apostles did not emphasize what *they* could do, but what God could do through them. Jesus' name is not to be used as magic—it must be used in faith. When we pray in Jesus' name, we must remember that it is Christ himself, not merely the sound of his name, who gives our prayers their power.

Related Topics: CHARACTER, HONOR, PRAYER

NATURE *(Creation, Universe, World)*

What lessons can we learn from nature?

BIBLE READING: Psalm 19:1-14

KEY BIBLE VERSE: *The heavens tell of the glory of God. The skies display his marvelous craftsmanship.* (Psalm 19:1)

Nature teaches us about God's character. In this psalm, David's steps of meditation take him from creation, through God's Word, through David's own sinfulness, to salvation. As God reveals himself through nature (19:1-6), we learn about his power and our finiteness. As God reveals himself through Scripture (19:7-11), we learn about his holiness and our sinfulness. As God reveals himself through daily experiences (19:12-14), we learn about his gracious forgiveness and our salvation.

Nature can teach us humility and wonder. We are surrounded by fantastic displays of God's craftsmanship—the heavens give dramatic evidence of his existence, his power, his love, his care. To say that the universe happened by chance is absurd. Its design, intricacy, and orderliness point to a personally involved Creator. As you look at God's handiwork in nature and the heavens, thank him for such magnificent beauty and the truth it reveals about the Creator.

Nature cannot teach us everything necessary for life. The apostle Paul referred to this psalm when he explained that everyone knows about God because nature proclaims God's existence and power (Romans 1:19-20). This does not cancel the need for missions, because the message of God's salvation found in his Word, the Bible, must still be told to the ends of the earth. While nature points to the existence of God, the Bible tells us about salvation. God's people must explain to others how they can have a relationship with God. Although people everywhere should believe in a Creator by just looking at the evidence of nature around them, God needs us to explain his love, mercy, and grace. What are you doing to take God's message to the world?

 BIBLE READING: Matthew 8:23-27

KEY BIBLE VERSE: *And Jesus answered, "Why are you afraid? You have so little faith!" Then he stood up and rebuked the wind and waves, and suddenly all was calm.* (Matthew 8:26)

Nature teaches us about God's power. Although the disciples had witnessed many miracles, they panicked in this storm. As experienced sailors, they knew its danger; what they did not know was that Christ could control the forces of nature. There is often a stormy area of our human nature where we feel God can't or won't work. When we truly understand who God is, however, we will realize that he controls both the storms of nature and the storms of the troubled heart. Jesus' power that calmed this storm can also help us deal with the problems we face. Jesus is willing to help if we only ask him. We should never discount his power, even in terrible trials.

 BIBLE READING: Romans 1:18-32

KEY BIBLE VERSE: *From the time the world was created, people have seen the earth and sky and all that God made. They can clearly see his invisible qualities—his eternal power and divine nature. So they have no excuse whatsoever for not knowing God.* (Romans 1:20)

Nature teaches us that God exists. What kind of God does nature reveal? Nature shows us a God of might, intelligence, and intricate detail; a God of order and beauty; a God who controls powerful forces. That is *general* revelation. Through *special* revelation (the Bible and the coming of Jesus), we learn about God's love and forgiveness, and the promise of eternal life. God has graciously given us both sources that we might more completely believe in him.

Nature's revelation is distorted. God reveals his divine nature and personal qualities through creation, even though creation's testimony has been distorted by the fall. Adam's sin resulted in a divine curse upon the whole natural order (Genesis 3:17-19); thorns and thistles were an immediate result, and natural disasters have been common from Adam's day to ours. In Romans 8:19-21, Paul says that nature itself is eagerly awaiting its own redemption from the effects of sin (see Revelation 22:3).

Related Topics: CREATION, EARTH, GOD

NEEDS (*Desires, Inadequacies, Lack*)

▶ **THE NEEDS OF OTHERS**
How does God demonstrate his concern for people's needs?

 BIBLE READING: Exodus 20:1-21

KEY BIBLE VERSE: *"Don't be afraid,"* Moses said, *"for God has come in this way to show you his awesome power. From now on, let your fear of him keep you from sinning!"* (Exodus 20:20)

God gives commands to insure that people's needs are met. Why were the Ten Commandments necessary for God's new nation? At the foot of Mount Sinai, God showed his people the true function and beauty of his laws. The commandments were designed to lead Israel to a life of practical holiness. In them, people could see the nature of God and his plan for how they should live. The commands and guidelines were intended to direct the community to meet the needs of each individual in a loving and responsible manner. By Jesus' time, however, most people looked at the law the wrong way. They saw it as a means to prosperity in both this world and the next. And they thought that to obey every law was the way to earn God's protection from foreign invasion and natural disaster. Lawkeeping became an end in itself, not the means to fulfill God's ultimate law of love.

BIBLE READING: 2 Kings 6:1-7

KEY BIBLE VERSE: *"Where did it fall?" the man of God asked. When he showed him the place, Elisha cut a stick and threw it into the water. Then the ax head rose to the surface and floated. "Grab it," Elisha said to him. And the man reached out and grabbed it.* (2 Kings 6:6-7)

God meets needs through people. The incident of the floating ax head is recorded to show God's care and provision for those who trust him, even in the insignificant events of everyday life. God is always present. Placed in the Bible between the healing of an Aramean general and the deliverance of Israel's army, this miracle also shows Elisha's personal contact with the students in the company of prophets. Although he had the respect of kings, Elisha never forgot to care for the faithful. Don't let the importance of your work drive out your concern for human need.

How are we to demonstrate our concern for people's needs?

BIBLE READING: Matthew 23:1-39

KEY BIBLE VERSE: *The greatest among you must be a servant. But those who exalt themselves will be humbled, and those who humble themselves will be exalted.* (Matthew 23:11-12)

We should be willing to meet the needs of others. Jesus challenged society's norms. To him, greatness comes from serving—giving of yourself to help God and others. Service keeps us aware of others' needs, and it stops us from focusing only on ourselves. Jesus came as a servant. What kind of greatness do you seek?

BIBLE READING: Matthew 25:31-46

KEY BIBLE VERSE: *The King will tell them, "I assure you, when you did it to one of the least of these my brothers and sisters, you were doing it to me!"* (Matthew 25:40)

Realize that meeting the needs of others is serving Christ. This parable describes acts of mercy we all can do every day. These acts do not depend on wealth, ability, or intelligence; they are simple acts freely given and freely received. We have no excuse to neglect those who have deep needs, and we cannot hand over this responsibility to the church or government. Jesus demands our personal involvement in caring for others' needs (Isaiah 58:7).

▶ **OUR NEEDS**

How does God want us to handle our own needs?

BIBLE READING: Ruth 2:1-23

KEY BIBLE VERSE: *One day Ruth said to Naomi, "Let me go out into the fields to gather leftover grain behind anyone who will let me do it." And Naomi said, "All right, my daughter, go ahead." So Ruth went out to gather grain behind the harvesters. And as it happened, she found herself working in a field that belonged to Boaz, the relative of her father-in-law, Elimelech.* (Ruth 2:2-3)

We should use the resources God has provided to meet our needs. Ruth made her home in a foreign land. Instead of depending on Naomi or waiting for good fortune to happen, she took the initiative. She went to work. She was not afraid of admitting her need or working hard to supply it. She made use of gifts and opportunities God had already given, like health and energy. When Ruth went out to the fields, God provided for her. If you are waiting for God to provide, consider this: He may be waiting for you to take the first step to demonstrate just how important your need is.

BIBLE READING: Psalm 104:1-35

KEY BIBLE VERSE: *Every one of these depends on you to give them their food as they need it. When you supply it, they gather it. You open your hand to feed them, and they are satisfied.* (Psalm 104:27-28)

We should recognize our dependence upon God for every need. Today many people are arrogant enough to think they don't need God. They don't realize that our every breath depends on the spirit he has breathed into us (Genesis 2:7; 3:19; Job 33:4; 34:14-15; Daniel 5:23). Not only do we depend on God for our very life, but he wants the best for us. We should also desire to learn more of his plans for us each day.

BIBLE READING: Mark 8:1-13

KEY BIBLE VERSE: *About this time another great crowd had gathered, and the people ran out of food again. Jesus called his disciples and told them, "I feel sorry for these people. They have been here with me for three days, and they have nothing left to eat. And if I send them home without feeding them, they will faint along the road. For some of them have come a long distance."* (Mark 8:1-3)

We must trust that God knows and cares for our needs. Do you ever feel that God is so busy with important concerns that he can't possibly be aware of your needs? Just as Jesus was concerned about these people's need for food, he is concerned about our daily needs. At another time Jesus said, "So don't worry about having enough food or drink or clothing. . . . Your heavenly Father already knows all your needs" (Matthew 6:31-32). Do you have concerns that you think would not interest God? There is nothing too large for him to handle and no need too small to escape his interest.

Related Topics: GENEROSITY, GIVING, SERVING

NEEDY (*see* POOR)

NEGATIVE(S) (*see* INFLUENCE)

NEGLECT (*Disregard, Forget, Ignore*)

How serious a sin is the habit of neglect?

BIBLE READING: Matthew 7:24-29

KEY BIBLE VERSE: *Anyone who hears my teaching and ignores it is foolish, like a person who builds a house on sand.* (Matthew 7:26)

Neglecting God and his Word can undermine all of life. Like a house of cards, the fool's life crumbles. Most people do not deliberately seek to build on a false or inferior foundation; instead, they just don't think about their life's purpose. Many people are headed for destruction, not out of stubbornness but out of thoughtlessness. Part of our responsibility as believers is to help others stop and think about where their lives are headed and to point out the consequences of ignoring Christ's message.

BIBLE READING: Mark 7:1-23

KEY BIBLE VERSE: *You reject God's laws in order to hold on to your own traditions.* (Mark 7:9)

Neglecting family responsibilities is disobedience to God. The Pharisees used God as an excuse to avoid helping their families. They thought it was more important to put money in the temple treasury than to help their needy parents, although God's law specifically says to honor fathers and mothers (Exodus 20:12) and to care for those in need (Leviticus 25:35-43). We should give money and time to God, but we must never use God as an excuse to neglect our responsibilities. Helping those in need is one of the most important ways to honor God.

BIBLE READING: James 4:1-17

KEY BIBLE VERSE: *Remember, it is sin to know what you ought to do and then not do it.* (James 4:17)

Neglecting to do right is as sinful as doing wrong. We tend to think that *doing* wrong is sin. But James tells us that sin is also *not* doing right. (These two kinds of sin are sometimes called sins of commission and sins of omission.) It is a sin to lie; it can also be a sin to know the truth and not tell it. It is a sin to speak evil of someone; it is also a sin to avoid that person when you know he or she needs your friendship. We should be willing to help as the Holy Spirit guides us. If God has directed you to do a kind act, to render a service, or to restore a relationship, do it. You will experience a renewed and refreshed vitality to your Christian faith.

Related Topics: ABANDON, DISOBEDIENCE, FAITHFULNESS

NEIGHBOR (*Acquaintance, Fellow Citizen, Friend*)

What kind of relationship should we have with our neighbors?

BIBLE READING: Luke 10:25-37

KEY BIBLE VERSE: *The man answered, "'You must love the Lord your God with all your heart, all your soul, all your strength, and all your mind.' And, 'Love your neighbor as yourself.'" "Right!" Jesus told him. "Do this and you will live!"* (Luke 10:27-28)

God expects us to be loving toward our neighbors. This expert in the law was quoting Deuteronomy 6:5 and Leviticus 19:18. He correctly understood that the law demanded total devotion to God and love for one's neighbor. From the parable Jesus told (verses 30-35), we learn three principles about loving our neighbor: (1) lack of love is often easy to justify, even though it is never right; (2) our neighbor is anyone of any race, creed, or social background who is in need; and (3) love means acting to meet the person's need. Wherever you live, there are needy people close by. There is no good reason for refusing to help.

BIBLE READING: Romans 13:8-14
KEY BIBLE VERSE: *The commandments against adultery and murder and stealing and coveting—and any other commandment—are all summed up in this one commandment: "Love your neighbor as yourself."* (Romans 13:9)

We should love our neighbors as ourselves. Somehow many of us have gotten the idea that self-love is wrong. But if this were the case, it would be pointless to love our neighbors as ourselves. But Paul explains what he means by self-love. Even if you have low self-esteem, you probably don't willingly let yourself go hungry. You clothe yourself reasonably well. You make sure there's a roof over your head if you can. You try not to let yourself be cheated or injured. And you get angry if someone tries to ruin your marriage. This is the kind of love we need to have for our neighbors. Do we see that others are fed, clothed, and housed as well as they can be? Are we concerned about issues of social justice? Loving others as ourselves means to be actively working to see that their needs are met. Interestingly, people who focus on others rather than on themselves rarely suffer from low self-esteem.

Related Topics: CHURCH, LOVE, SELF-ESTEEM

NEW COVENANT (*Agreement, Guarantee, Promise*)

What does the Bible mean when it speaks of a new covenant between us and God?

BIBLE READING: Jeremiah 31:1-40
KEY BIBLE VERSE: *"This is the new covenant I will make with the people of Israel on that day," says the LORD. "I will put my laws in their minds, and I will write them on their hearts. I will be their God, and they will be my people."* (Jeremiah 31:33)

The new covenant is the ultimate solution to human rebellion. The old covenant, broken by the people, would be replaced by a new covenant. The foundation of this new covenant is Christ (Hebrews 8:6). It is revolutionary, involving not only Israel and Judah, but even the Gentiles. It offers a unique personal relationship with God himself, with his laws written on individuals' hearts instead of on stone. Jeremiah looked forward to the day when Jesus would come to establish this covenant. But for us today, this covenant is here. We have the wonderful opportunity to make a fresh start and establish a permanent, personal relationship with God (see Jeremiah 29:11; 32:38-40).

The new covenant is a personal relationship between God and people. God would write his law on their hearts rather than on tablets of stone as the Ten Commandments were written. In Jeremiah 17:1, Judah's sins were said to be engraved on their hearts so that they wanted above all to disobey. For God to write his law on the hearts of his people seems to describe an experience very much like the new birth, with God taking the initiative. When we turn our life over to God, he, by his Holy Spirit, builds into us the desire to obey him.

BIBLE READING: Luke 22:1-38

KEY BIBLE VERSE: *After supper he took another cup of wine and said, "This wine is the token of God's new covenant to save you—an agreement sealed with the blood I will pour out for you."* (Luke 22:20)

The new covenant comes through the death of Jesus Christ. In Old Testament times, God agreed to forgive people's sins if they brought animals for the priests to sacrifice. When this sacrificial system was inaugurated, the agreement between God and man was sealed with the blood of animals (Exodus 24:8). But animal blood did not in itself remove sin (only God can forgive sin), and animal sacrifices had to be repeated day by day and year after year. Jesus instituted a "new covenant" or agreement between humans and God. Under this new covenant, Jesus would die in the place of sinners. Unlike the blood of animals, his blood (because he is God) would truly remove the sins of all who put their faith in him. And Jesus' sacrifice would never have to be repeated; it would be good for all eternity (Hebrews 9:23-28). The prophets looked forward to this new covenant that would fulfill the old sacrificial agreement (Jeremiah 31:31-34), and John the Baptist called Jesus "the Lamb of God who takes away the sin of the world" (John 1:29).

BIBLE READING: Hebrews 7:11-28

KEY BIBLE VERSE: *Because of God's oath, it is Jesus who guarantees the effectiveness of this better covenant.* (Hebrews 7:22)

The new covenant means we can go directly to God through Christ. This "better covenant" is also called the new covenant or testament. It is new and better because it allows us to go directly to God through Christ. We no longer need to rely on sacrificed animals and mediating priests to obtain God's forgiveness. This new covenant is better because, while all human priests die, Christ lives forever. Priests and sacrifices could not save people, but Christ truly saves. You have access to Christ. He is available to you, but do you go to him with your needs?

Related Topics: BIBLE, GRACE, JESUS CHRIST

NEW LIFE *(Beginning, Change, Start)*

How can we have new life now?

BIBLE READING: Matthew 1:18-25

KEY BIBLE VERSE: *She will have a son, and you are to name him Jesus, for he will save his people from their sins.* (Matthew 1:21)

The hope of new life begins with Jesus. *Jesus* means "the Lord saves." Jesus came to earth to save us because we can't save ourselves from sin and its consequences. No matter how good we are, we can't eliminate the sinful nature present in all of us. Only Jesus can do that. Jesus didn't come to help people save themselves; he came to be their Savior from the power and penalty of sin. Thank Christ for his death on the cross for your sin, and then ask him to take control of your life. Your new life begins at that moment.

BIBLE READING: Romans 6:1-14

KEY BIBLE VERSE: *Since we have been united with him in his death, we will also be raised as he was.* (Romans 6:5)

The hope of new life is guaranteed by Jesus' resurrection. We can enjoy our new life in Christ because we are united with him in his death and resurrection. Our evil desires, our bondage to sin, and our love of sin died with him. Now, united by faith with him in his resurrection life, we have unbroken fellowship with God and freedom from sin's hold on us. (For more on the difference between our new life in Christ and our old sinful nature, read Ephesians 4:21-24 and Colossians 3:3-15.)

BIBLE READING: Colossians 2:6-23

KEY BIBLE VERSE: *You were dead because of your sins and because your sinful nature was not yet cut away. Then God made you alive with Christ. He forgave all our sins. He canceled the record that contained the charges against us. He took it and destroyed it by nailing it to Christ's cross.* (Colossians 2:13-14)

The hope of new life is freedom from bondage to sin. Before we believed in Christ, our nature was evil. We disobeyed, rebelled, and ignored God (even at our best, we did not love him with all our heart, soul, and mind). The Christian, however, has a new nature. God has crucified the old, rebellious nature (Romans 6:6) and replaced it with a new, loving nature (3:9-10). The penalty of sin died with Christ on the cross. God has declared us not guilty, and we need no longer live under sin's power. God does not take us out of the world or make us robots—we will still feel like sinning, and sometimes we will sin. The difference is that before we were saved, we were slaves to our sinful nature; but now we are free to live for Christ (see Galatians 2:20).

Related Topics: CHANGE, SALVATION, SPIRITUAL REBIRTH

———

NEW TESTAMENT (*see* BIBLE)

OBEDIENCE (*Compliance, Cooperation, Submission*)

▶ **THE FREEDOM OF OBEDIENCE**
In what ways is obedience to God true freedom?

 BIBLE READING: Genesis 3:1-24
KEY BIBLE VERSE: *He replied, "I heard you, so I hid. I was afraid because I was naked." "Who told you that you were naked?" the LORD God asked. "Have you eaten the fruit I commanded you not to eat?"* (Genesis 3:10-11)

Obedience keeps our relationship with God open and free. Adam and Eve got what they wanted: an intimate knowledge of both good and evil. But they got it by doing evil, and the results were disastrous. Sometimes we have the illusion that freedom is doing anything we want. But God says that true freedom comes from obedience and knowing what *not* to do. The restrictions he gives us are for our good, helping us avoid evil. We have the freedom to walk in front of a speeding car, but we don't need to be hit to realize it would be foolish to do so. Don't listen to Satan's temptations. You don't have to do evil to gain more experience and learn more about life.

BIBLE READING: Deuteronomy 30:11-19
KEY BIBLE VERSE: *Now listen! Today I am giving you a choice between prosperity and disaster, between life and death. I have commanded you today to love the LORD your God and to keep his commands, laws, and regulations by walking in his ways. If you do this, you will live and become a great nation, and the LORD your God will bless you and the land you are about to enter and occupy.* (Deuteronomy 30:15-16)

Obeying God is in our best interest. God has called us to keep his commands, while reminding us that his laws are not hidden from us or beyond our reach. Have you ever said you would obey God if you knew what he wanted? Have you ever complained that obedience is too difficult for a mere human? These are unacceptable excuses. God's laws are written in the Bible and are clearly evident in the world around us. Obeying them is reasonable, sensible, and beneficial. The most difficult part of obeying God's laws is simply deciding to start now.

BIBLE READING: 1 Chronicles 15:11-29
KEY BIBLE VERSE: *Because you Levites did not carry the Ark the first time, the anger of the LORD our God burst out against us. We failed to ask God how to move it in the proper way.* (1 Chronicles 15:13)

Obeying God, even when we don't understand, is true freedom. When David's first attempt to move the ark failed (13:8-14), he learned an important lesson: when God gives specific instructions, it is wise to follow them precisely. This time David saw to it that the Levites carried the ark (Numbers 4:5-15). We may not fully understand the reasons behind God's instructions, but we do know that his wisdom is complete and his judgment infallible. The way to know God's instructions is to know his Word. But just as children do not understand the reasons for all their parents' instructions until they are older, we may not understand all of God's reasons in this life. It is far better to obey God first, and then discover the reasons. We are never free to disobey God just because we don't understand.

BIBLE READING: Romans 5:1-21

KEY BIBLE VERSE: *God's law was given so that all people could see how sinful they were. But as people sinned more and more, God's wonderful kindness became more abundant.* (Romans 5:20)

Freedom to obey comes through God's grace. As a sinner, separated from God, you see his law from below, as a ladder to be climbed to get to God. Perhaps you have repeatedly tried to climb it, only to fall to the ground every time you have advanced one or two rungs. Or perhaps the sheer height of the ladder seems so overwhelming that you have never even started up. In either case, what relief you should feel to see Jesus offering with open arms to lift you above the ladder of the law, to take you directly to God! Once Jesus lifts you into God's presence, you are free to obey—out of love, not necessity, and through God's power, not your own. You know that if you stumble, you will not fall back to the ground. Instead, you will be caught and held in Christ's loving arms.

▶ THE BENEFITS OF OBEDIENCE
What can we expect from God when we obey him?

BIBLE READING: Joshua 1:1-9

KEY BIBLE VERSE: *Study this Book of the Law continually. Meditate on it day and night so you may be sure to obey all that is written in it. Only then will you succeed.* (Joshua 1:8)

Obedience to God is pleasing to him. Many people think that prosperity and success come from having power, influential personal contacts, and a relentless desire to get ahead. But the strategy for gaining prosperity that God taught Joshua goes against such criteria. He said that to succeed Joshua must (1) be strong and courageous, because the task ahead would not be easy, (2) obey God's law, and (3) constantly read and study the Book of the Law—God's Word. To be successful, follow God's words to Joshua. You may not succeed by the world's standards, but you will be a success in God's eyes—and his opinion lasts forever.

BIBLE READING: 2 Chronicles 14:1-15

KEY BIBLE VERSE: *When Abijah died, he was buried in the City of David. Then his son Asa became the next king. There was peace in the land for ten years, for Asa did what was pleasing and good in the sight of the LORD his God.* (2 Chronicles 14:1-2)

Obedience to God often leads to peace. Asa's reign was marked by peace because he "did what was pleasing and good in the sight of the LORD his God." This refrain is often repeated in Chronicles—*obedience* to God leads to *peace* with God and others. In the case of Judah's kings, obedience to God led to national peace, just as God had promised centuries earlier. In our case, obedience may not always bring peace with our enemies, but it will bring peace with God and complete peace in his future kingdom. Obeying God is the first step on the path to peace.

▶ THE CHALLENGE OF OBEDIENCE
How is obedience challenged?

BIBLE READING: Exodus 5:4-9
KEY BIBLE VERSE: *Load them down with more work. Make them sweat! That will teach them to listen to these liars!* (Exodus 5:9)

Obedience is often challenged by difficulties. Moses and Aaron took their message to Pharaoh just as God directed. The unhappy result was harder work and more oppression for the Hebrews. Sometimes hardship comes as a result of obeying God. Are you following God, but still suffering—or suffering even worse than before? If your life is miserable, don't assume you have fallen out of God's favor. You may be suffering for doing good in an evil world.

BIBLE READING: Joshua 9:1-6
KEY BIBLE VERSE: *When they arrived at the camp of Israel at Gilgal, they told Joshua and the men of Israel, "We have come from a distant land to ask you to make a peace treaty with us."* (Joshua 9:6)

Obedience is often challenged by deception. As the news about their victory became widespread, the Israelites experienced opposition in two forms: direct (kings in the area began to unite against them) and indirect (the Gibeonites resorted to deception). We can expect similar opposition as we obey God's commands. To guard against these pressures, we must rely on God and communicate daily with him. He will give us strength to endure the direct pressures and wisdom to see through the trickery.

How does obedience challenge us?

BIBLE READING: Matthew 5:17-20
KEY BIBLE VERSE: *If you break the smallest commandment and teach others to do the same, you will be the least in the Kingdom of Heaven. But anyone who obeys God's laws and teaches them will be great in the Kingdom of Heaven.* (Matthew 5:19)

Obedience challenges us to go beyond mere understanding. Some of those in the crowd were experts at telling others what to do, but they missed the central point of God's laws themselves. Jesus made it clear, however, that obeying God's law is more important than explaining it. It's much easier to study God's laws and tell others to obey them than to put them into practice. How are you doing at obeying God *yourself?*

Obedience challenges us to go beyond mere outward conformity. The Pharisees were exacting and scrupulous in their attempts to follow their laws. So how could Jesus reasonably call us to a greater righteousness than theirs? The Pharisees' weakness was that they were content to obey the laws outwardly without allowing God to change their hearts (or attitudes). Jesus was saying, therefore, that the quality of our goodness should be greater than that of the Pharisees. They looked pious, but they were far from the kingdom of God. God judges our hearts as well as our deeds, for it is in the heart that our real allegiance lies. Be just as concerned about your attitudes that people don't see as about your actions that are seen by all.

Obedience challenges us to act out of love for God. Jesus was saying that his listeners needed a different kind of righteousness altogether (love and obedience), not just a more intense version of the Pharisees' righteousness (legal compliance). Our righteousness must (1) come from what God does in us, not what we can do by ourselves, (2) be God-centered, not self-centered, (3) be based on reverence for God, not approval from people, and (4) go beyond keeping the law to living by the principles behind the law.

Related Topics: ACTIONS, DISCIPLINE, SUBMISSION

OBLIGATION (*Debt, Promise, Responsibility*)

Can life truly be lived out of obligation?

BIBLE READING: Deuteronomy 5:1-33
KEY BIBLE VERSE: *Oh, that they would always have hearts like this, that they might fear me and obey all my commands! If they did, they and their descendants would prosper forever.* (Deuteronomy 5:29)

We cannot love God out of obligation. God told Moses that he wanted the people to incline their hearts to fear him—to *want* to respect and obey him. There is a difference between doing something because it is required and doing something because we want to. God is not interested in forced religious exercises and rule-keeping. He wants our hearts and lives completely dedicated to him. If we love him, obedience will follow.

BIBLE READING: 1 Samuel 25:1-44
KEY BIBLE VERSE: *Should I take my bread and water and the meat I've slaughtered for my shearers and give it to a band of outlaws who come from who knows where?* (1 Samuel 25:11)

True generosity goes beyond obligation. Nabal rudely refused David's request to feed his six hundred men. If we sympathize with Nabal, it is because customs are so different today. First, simple hospitality demanded that travelers—any number of them—be fed. Nabal was very rich and could have easily afforded to meet David's request. Second, David wasn't asking for a handout. He and his men had been protecting Nabal's work force, and part of Nabal's prosperity was due to David's vigilance. We should be generous with those who protect us and help us prosper, even if we are not obligated to do so by law or custom.

BIBLE READING: Romans 13:8-14
KEY BIBLE VERSE: *Pay all your debts, except the debt of love for others. You can never finish paying that! If you love your neighbor, you will fulfill all the requirements of God's law.* (Romans 13:8)

Because of God's love, we are obligated to love others. Why is love for others called a debt? We are permanently in debt to Christ for the lavish love he has poured out on us. The only way we can even begin to repay this debt is by loving others in turn. Because Christ's love will always be infinitely greater than ours, we will always have the obligation to love our neighbors.

Related Topics: GENEROSITY, LOVE, OBEDIENCE

OBSTACLES (*see* BARRIERS)

OCCULT (*Evil*, *Mysterious*, *Satanic*)

Why does God forbid our involvement in the occult?

 BIBLE READING: Deuteronomy 18:9-13

KEY BIBLE VERSE: *Never sacrifice your son or daughter as a burnt offering. And do not let your people practice fortune-telling or sorcery, or allow them to interpret omens, or engage in witchcraft, or cast spells, or function as mediums or psychics, or call forth the spirits of the dead.* (Deuteronomy 18:10-11)

The occult expresses spiritual rebellion against God. Child sacrifice and occult practices were strictly forbidden by God. These practices were common among the pagans. Some of Israel's neighbors actually sacrificed their children to the god Molech (Leviticus 20:2-5). Others of their neighbors used occult means, such as contacting the spirit world, to foretell the future and gain guidance. Because of these wicked practices, God would drive out the pagan nations (Deuteronomy 18:12). The Israelites were to replace their evil practices with the worship of the one true God.

The occult is a satanic trap. The Israelites were naturally curious about the occult practices of the Canaanite religions. But Satan is behind the occult, and God flatly forbade Israel to have anything to do with it. Today people are still fascinated by horoscopes, fortune-telling, witchcraft, and bizarre cults. Often their interest comes from a desire to know and control the future. But Satan is no less dangerous today than he was in Moses' time. In the Bible, God tells us all we need to know about what is going to happen. The information Satan offers is likely to be distorted or completely false. With the trustworthy guidance of the Holy Spirit through the Bible and the church, we don't need to turn to occult sources for faulty information.

BIBLE READING: 1 Samuel 28:1-25

KEY BIBLE VERSE: *He asked the LORD what he should do, but the LORD refused to answer him, either by dreams or by sacred lots or by the prophets. Saul then said to his advisers, "Find a woman who is a medium, so I can go and ask her what to do." His advisers replied, "There is a medium at Endor."* (1 Samuel 28:6-7)

The occult is deceptive and distorts God's truth. Did Samuel really come back from the dead at the medium's call? The medium shrieked at the appearance of Samuel—she knew too well that the spirits she usually contacted were either contrived or satanic. Somehow Samuel's appearance revealed to her that she was dealing with a power far greater than she had known. She did not call up Samuel by trickery or by the power of Satan; God brought Samuel back to give Saul a prediction regarding his fate, a message Saul already knew. This in no way justifies efforts to contact the dead or communicate with persons or spirits from the past. God is against all such practices (Galatians 5:19-21).

Related Topics: EVIL, FORGIVENESS, SATAN

OFFENSE (*Angering*, *Hurting*, *Insensitivity*)

How can we avoid offending others?

BIBLE READING: Mark 6:1-6

KEY BIBLE VERSE: *The next Sabbath he began teaching in the synagogue, and many who heard him were astonished. They asked, "Where did he get all his wisdom and the power to perform such miracles? He's just the carpenter, the son of Mary and brother of James, Joseph, Judas, and Simon. And his sisters live right here among us." They were deeply offended and refused to believe in him.* (Mark 6:2-3)

Sometimes offense is unavoidable. Jesus was teaching effectively and wisely, but the people of his hometown saw him as only a carpenter. "He's no better than we are—he's just a carpenter," they said. They were offended that others could be impressed by Jesus and follow him. They rejected his authority because he was one of their peers. They thought they knew him, but their preconceived notions about who he was made it impossible for them to accept his message. Don't let prejudice blind you to truth. As you learn more about Jesus, try to see him for who he really is. Realize also that anyone seeking to speak the truth runs the danger of offending others, no matter how sensitive he or she is to them.

BIBLE READING: Acts 21:17-26

KEY BIBLE VERSE: *Here's our suggestion. We have four men here who have taken a vow and are preparing to shave their heads. Go with them to the Temple and join them in the purification ceremony, and pay for them to have their heads shaved. Then everyone will know that the rumors are all false and that you yourself observe the Jewish laws.* (Acts 21:23-24)

Flexibility is often the key to avoiding unnecessary offense. The Jerusalem council (Acts 15) had settled the issue of circumcision of Gentile believers. Evidently there was a rumor that Paul had gone far beyond their decision, even forbidding Jews to circumcise their children. This, of course, was not true, and so Paul willingly submitted to Jewish custom to show that he was not working against the council's decision and that he was still Jewish in his lifestyle. Sometimes we must go the second mile to avoid offending others, especially when offending them would hinder God's work.

Willingness to compromise on nonessentials can also avoid offense. Evidently these four men had made a religious vow. Because Paul was going to participate with them in the vow (apparently he was asked to pay for some of the required expenses), he would need to take part in the purification ceremony for entering the temple (Numbers 6:9-20). Paul submitted himself to this Jewish custom to keep peace in the Jerusalem church. Although Paul was a man of strong convictions, he was willing to compromise on nonessential points, becoming all things to all people so that he might save some (1 Corinthians 9:19-23). Often a church is split over disagreements about minor issues or traditions. Like Paul, we should remain firm on Christian essentials but flexible on nonessentials. Of course, no one should violate his or her true convictions, but sometimes we need to exercise the gift of mutual submission for the sake of the gospel.

BIBLE READING: 1 Corinthians 8:1-13

KEY BIBLE VERSE: *You must be careful with this freedom of yours. Do not cause a brother or sister with a weaker conscience to stumble.* (1 Corinthians 8:9)

Abstaining from certain practices can avoid offense. Paul addressed these words to believers who weren't bothered by eating meat that had been sacrificed to idols. Although an idol was not really a god, and the pagan ritual of sacrificing to idols was meaningless, eating such meat offended some Christians with a sensitive conscience. Paul said, therefore, that if a weak or less mature believer misunderstood their actions, they should, out of consideration, avoid eating meat that had been offered to idols.

Limiting our freedom for the sake of others can avoid offense. Christian freedom does not mean that anything goes. It means that our salvation is not determined by good deeds or legalistic rules, but by the free gift of God (Ephesians 2:8-9). Christian freedom, then, is inseparably tied to Christian responsibility. New believers are often very sensitive to what is right or wrong, what they should or shouldn't do. Some actions may be perfectly all right for us to do, but they may harm a Christian brother or sister who is still young in the faith and learning what the Christian life is all about. We must be careful not to offend a sensitive or younger Christian or, by our example, cause him or her to sin. When we love others, our freedom should be less important to us than strengthening the faith of a brother or sister in Christ.

Related Topics: FREEDOM, LOVE, SENSITIVITY

OFFERING (*see* TITHING)

OLD TESTAMENT (*see* BIBLE)

ONENESS (*see* UNITY)

OPENNESS (*Honesty, Sincerity, Truthfulness*)

What are some characteristics of an open person?

BIBLE READING: Joshua 17:1-18

KEY BIBLE VERSE: *Manasseh's inheritance came to ten parcels of land, in addition to the land of Gilead and Bashan across the Jordan River, because the female descendants of Manasseh received an inheritance along with the male descendants. (The land of Gilead was given to the rest of the male descendants of Manasseh.)* (Joshua 17:5-6)

An open person is willing to change tradition for the sake of people. Although women did not traditionally inherit property in Israelite society, Moses put justice ahead of tradition and gave these five women the land they deserved (see Numbers 27:1-11). In fact, God told Moses to add a law that would help other women in similar circumstances inherit property as well. Joshua was now carrying out this law. It is easy to refuse to honor a reasonable request because "things have never been done that way before." But, just as Moses and Joshua did, it is best to look carefully at the purpose of the law and the merits of each case before deciding.

BIBLE READING: Matthew 2:1-23

KEY BIBLE VERSE: *When it was time to leave, they went home another way, because God had warned them in a dream not to return to Herod. After the wise men were gone, an angel of the Lord appeared to Joseph in a dream. "Get up and flee to Egypt with the child and his mother," the angel said. "Stay there until I tell you to return, because Herod is going to try to kill the child."* (Matthew 2:12-13)

An open person changes plans in accordance with God's direction. After finding Jesus and worshiping him, the magi were warned by God not to return through Jerusalem as they had intended. Finding Jesus may mean that your life must take a different direction, one that is responsive and obedient to God's Word. Are you willing to be led a different way?

An open person accepts the unexpected. This was the second dream or vision that Joseph received from God. Joseph's first dream revealed that Mary's child would be the Messiah (1:20-21). His second dream told him how to protect the child's life. Although Joseph was not Jesus' natural father, he was Jesus' legal father and was responsible for his safety and well-being. Divine guidance comes only to prepared hearts. Joseph remained receptive to God's guidance.

BIBLE READING: Mark 4:1-20

KEY BIBLE VERSE: *The good soil represents those who hear and accept God's message and produce a huge harvest—thirty, sixty, or even a hundred times as much as had been planted.* (Mark 4:20)

An open person is receptive to the gospel. The four soils represent four different ways people respond to God's message. Usually we think that Jesus was talking about four different kinds of people. But he may also have been talking about (1) different times or phases in a person's life, or (2) how we willingly receive God's message in some areas of our life and resist it in others. For example, you may be open to God about your future, but closed concerning how you spend your money. You may respond like good soil to God's demand for worship, but like rocky soil to his demand to give to people in need. We must strive to be like good soil in every area of our life at all times.

Related Topics: HONESTY, SINCERITY, TRUTH

OPINIONS (*Conclusions, Ideas, Philosophies*)

What role should opinions play in our decisions?

BIBLE READING: 1 Chronicles 13:1-14

KEY BIBLE VERSE: *David consulted with all his officials, including the generals and captains of his army.* (1 Chronicles 13:1)

The opinions of others can be helpful in making decisions. David took time to confer with all his officers. As king, he had ultimate authority and could have given orders on his own, but he chose to involve others in leadership. Perhaps this is why there was unanimous support for his decisions (13:1-5). When we are in charge, it is tempting to make unilateral decisions, pushing through our own opinions. But effective leaders listen carefully to others' opinions, and they encourage others to participate in making decisions. Of course, we should always consult God first. We can run into big problems if we don't talk to him.

BIBLE READING: Matthew 23:1-39

KEY BIBLE VERSE: *They crush you with impossible religious demands and never lift a finger to help ease the burden.* (Matthew 23:4)

Human opinions cannot take the place of God's Word. The Pharisees' traditions and their interpretations and applications of the laws had become as important to them as God's law itself. Their laws were not all bad—some were beneficial. The problem arose when the religious leaders (1) took man-made rules and opinions as seriously as God's laws, (2) told the people to obey these rules but did not do so themselves, or (3) obeyed the rules, not to honor God, but to make themselves look good. Usually Jesus did not condemn the Pharisees for their opinions but for their actions. They were hypocrites.

BIBLE READING: 2 Timothy 2:14-26
KEY BIBLE VERSE: *They have left the path of truth, preaching the lie that the resurrection of the dead has already occurred; and they have undermined the faith of some.* (2 Timothy 2:18)

Human opinions must be submitted to the correction of God's Word. The false teachers were denying the resurrection of the body. They believed that when a person became a Christian, he or she was spiritually reborn, and that was the only resurrection there would ever be. To them, resurrection was symbolic and spiritual, not physical. Paul clearly taught, however, that believers will be resurrected after they die, and that their bodies as well as their souls will live eternally with Christ (1 Corinthians 15:35ff.; 2 Corinthians 5:1-10; 1 Thessalonians 4:15-18). We cannot shape the doctrines of Scripture to match our opinions. If we do, we are putting ourselves above God. Instead, our beliefs should be consistent with God's Word.

Related Topics: BELIEF/BELIEVE, BIBLE, CONVICTIONS

OPPORTUNITIES (*Chance, Freedom, Opening*)

How does God want us to view new opportunities?

BIBLE READING: Numbers 14:1-45
KEY BIBLE VERSE: *Not one of these people will ever enter that land. They have seen my glorious presence and the miraculous signs I performed both in Egypt and in the wilderness, but again and again they tested me by refusing to listen. They will never even see the land I swore to give their ancestors. None of those who have treated me with contempt will enter it.* (Numbers 14:22-23)

With opportunity comes responsibility. The people of Israel had a clearer view of God than any people before them, for they had both his laws and his physical presence. Their refusal to follow God after witnessing his miraculous deeds and listening to his words made the judgment against them more severe. Increased opportunity brings increased responsibility. As Jesus said: "Much is required from those to whom much is given" (Luke 12:48). How much greater is our responsibility to obey and serve God—we have the whole Bible, and we know God's Son, Jesus Christ.

BIBLE READING: Mark 6:30-44
KEY BIBLE VERSE: *Jesus said, "You feed them." "With what?" they asked. "It would take a small fortune to buy food for all this crowd!"* (Mark 6:37)

A seemingly impossible task may be an opportunity for God to work. When Jesus asked the disciples to provide food for over five thousand people, they asked in astonishment if they should go and spend a small fortune on bread. How do you react when you are given an impossible task? A situation that seems impossible with human resources is simply an opportunity for God. The disciples did everything they could by gathering the available food and organizing the people into groups. Then, in answer to prayer, God did the impossible. When facing a seemingly impossible task, do what you can and ask God to do the rest. He may see fit to make the impossible happen.

BIBLE READING: Ephesians 3:1-13

KEY BIBLE VERSE: *By God's special favor and mighty power, I have been given the wonderful privilege of serving him by spreading this Good News.* (Ephesians 3:7)

Opportunities to share the gospel are given to us by God. When Paul became a servant of the gospel, God gave him the ability to share effectively the gospel of Christ. You may not be an apostle or even an evangelist, but God will give you opportunities to tell others about Christ. And with the opportunities he will provide the ability, courage, and power. Whenever an opportunity presents itself, make yourself available to God as his servant. As you focus on the other person and his or her needs, God will communicate your caring attitude. Your words will be natural, loving, and compelling.

BIBLE READING: Philippians 1:12-30

KEY BIBLE VERSE: *Because of my imprisonment, many of the Christians here have gained confidence and become more bold in telling others about Christ.* (Philippians 1:14)

Opportunities to share the gospel may come from hardships. Being imprisoned would cause many people to become bitter or to give up, but Paul saw it as one more opportunity to spread the Good News of Christ. Paul realized that his current circumstances weren't as important as what he did with them. Turning a bad situation into a good one, he reached out to the Roman soldiers who made up the palace guard and encouraged those Christians who were afraid of persecution. We may not be in prison, but we still have plenty of opportunities to be discouraged—times of indecision, financial burdens, family conflict, church conflict, or the loss of our jobs. How we act in such situations will reflect what we believe. Like Paul, look for ways to demonstrate your faith even in bad situations. Whether or not the situation improves, your faith will grow stronger.

Related Topics: CONSISTENCY, OBEDIENCE, SUFFERING

OPPOSITION *(Difficulties, Enemies, Resistance)*

What can we learn from opposition?

BIBLE READING: Ezra 4:1-24

KEY BIBLE VERSE: *They bribed agents to work against them and to frustrate their aims. This went on during the entire reign of King Cyrus of Persia and lasted until King Darius of Persia took the throne.* (Ezra 4:5)

Opposition is an unavoidable by-product of obedience to God. Believers can expect opposition when they do God's work (2 Timothy 3:12). Unbelievers and evil spiritual forces are always working against God and his people. The opposition may: offer compromising alliances (4:2), attempt to discourage and intimidate us (4:4-5), or accuse us unjustly (4:6). If you expect these tactics, you won't be halted by them. Move ahead with the work God has planned for you, and trust him to show you how to overcome the obstacles.

BIBLE READING: Luke 10:1-24

KEY BIBLE VERSE: *Go now, and remember that I am sending you out as lambs among wolves.* (Luke 10:3)

Opposition is an opportunity to show strength of character. Jesus said he was sending his disciples out like "lambs among wolves." They would have to be careful, because they would surely meet with opposition. We too are sent into the world like lambs among wolves. Be alert, and remember to face your enemies, not with aggression, but with love and gentleness. A dangerous mission requires sincere commitment.

BIBLE READING: John 3:1-21

KEY BIBLE VERSE: *Their judgment is based on this fact: The light from heaven came into the world, but they loved the darkness more than the light, for their actions were evil.* (John 3:19)

Opposition sometimes reveals people's fear of change. Many people don't want their lives exposed to God's light because they are afraid of what will be revealed. They don't want to be changed. Don't be surprised when these same people are threatened by your desire to obey God and do what is right, because they are afraid that the light in you may expose some of the darkness in their lives. Rather than giving in to discouragement, keep praying that they will come to see how much better it is to live in light than in darkness.

Related Topics: CONFLICTS, ENEMIES, PROBLEMS

OPPRESSED *(Downtrodden, Hurt, Needy)*

What can we do for those who are oppressed?

BIBLE READING: Exodus 22:16-31

KEY BIBLE VERSE: *Do not oppress foreigners in any way. Remember, you yourselves were once foreigners in the land of Egypt.* (Exodus 22:21)

We should be aware of the needs of strangers. God warned the Israelites not to treat aliens unfairly, because they themselves were once strangers in Egypt. It is not easy coming into a new environment where you feel alone and out of place. Are there strangers in your corner of the world? Refugees? New arrivals at school? Immigrants from another country? Be sensitive to their struggles, and express God's love by your kindness and generosity.

We should be aware of the needs of our neighbors. The Hebrew law code is noted for its fairness and social responsibility toward the poor. God insisted that the poor and powerless be well treated and given the chance to restore their fortunes. We should reflect God's concern for the poor by helping those less fortunate than ourselves.

We should be aware that oppression takes many forms. Why did the law insist on returning a person's cloak by evening? The cloak was one of an Israelite's most valuable possessions. Making clothing was difficult and time consuming. As a result, cloaks were expensive, and most people owned only one. The cloak was used as a blanket, a sack to carry things in, a pad to sit on, a pledge for a debt, and, of course, clothing.

BIBLE READING: 1 Timothy 5:1-25

KEY BIBLE VERSE: *If a Christian woman has relatives who are widows, she must take care of them and not put the responsibility on the church. Then the church can care for widows who are truly alone.* (1 Timothy 5:16)

We should care for those who are oppressed. Because there were no pensions, no social security, no life insurance, and few honorable jobs for women, widows were usually unable to support themselves. The responsibility for caring for widows naturally fell first on their families, the people whose lives were most closely linked with theirs. Paul stressed the importance of families caring for the needs of widows and not leaving this for the church to do, so the church could care for those widows who had no family. A widow who had no children or other family members to support her was doomed to poverty. From the beginning, the church took care of its widows, who in turn gave valuable service to the church.

The church should support those who have no family and should also help the elderly, young, disabled, ill, or poverty-stricken with their emotional and spiritual needs. Often families who are caring for their own helpless members have heavy burdens. They may need extra money, a listening ear, a helping hand, or a word of encouragement. Interestingly, those who are helped often turn around and help others, turning the church into more of a caring community. Don't wait for people to ask. Take the initiative and look for ways to serve them.

Related Topics: JUSTICE, MERCY, TRUTH

ORDINARY (*Common, Humble, Insignificant*)

How does God use things and people we call ordinary?

BIBLE READING: Exodus 4:1-17
KEY BIBLE VERSE: *"Perform this sign, and they will believe you," the* LORD *told him. "Then they will realize that the* LORD, *the God of their ancestors—the God of Abraham, the God of Isaac, and the God of Jacob—really has appeared to you."* (Exodus 4:5)

What we consider ordinary, God puts to good use. A shepherd's staff was commonly a three- to six-foot wooden rod with a curved hook at the top. The shepherd used it for walking, guiding his sheep, killing snakes, and many other tasks. Still, it was just a stick. But God used the simple shepherd's staff Moses carried as a sign to teach him an important lesson. God sometimes takes joy in using ordinary things for extraordinary purposes. What are the ordinary things in your life—your voice, a pen, a hammer, a broom, a musical instrument? While it is easy to assume God can use only special skills, you must not hinder his use of the everyday contributions you can make. Little did Moses imagine the power his simple staff would wield when it became the staff of God.

BIBLE READING: Luke 6:12-16
KEY BIBLE VERSE: *At daybreak he called together all of his disciples and chose twelve of them to be apostles.* (Luke 6:13)

Those we consider ordinary, God uses in significant ways. Jesus selected "ordinary" men with a mixture of backgrounds and personalities to be his disciples. Today, God calls "ordinary" people together to build his church, teach salvation's message, and serve others out of love. Alone we may feel unqualified to serve Christ effectively, but together we make up a group strong enough to serve God in any way. Ask for patience to accept the diversity of people in your church, and build on the variety of strengths represented in your group.

BIBLE READING: 1 Corinthians 1:18-31
KEY BIBLE VERSE: *God deliberately chose things the world considers foolish in order to shame those who think they are wise. And he chose those who are powerless to shame those who are powerful.* (1 Corinthians 1:27)

God chooses ordinary people for service in his kingdom. Is Christianity against rational thinking? Christians clearly do believe in using their minds to weigh the evidence and make wise choices. Paul is declaring that no amount of human knowledge can replace or bypass Christ's work on the cross. If it could, Christ would be accessible only to the intellectually gifted and well educated, and not to ordinary people or to children.

Paul emphasizes that the way to receive salvation is so simple that *any* person who wants to can understand it. Skill and wisdom do not get a person into God's kingdom—simple faith does—so no one can boast that his or her achievements helped him or her secure eternal life. Salvation is totally from God through Jesus' death. There is *nothing* we can do to earn our salvation; we need only accept what Jesus has already done for us.

Related Topics: IMAGE, SELF-ESTEEM, VALUE

ORGANIZATION (*see* PLANS)

PAGANS (*see* UNBELIEVERS)

PAIN (*Agony, Hurt, Suffering*)

Can pain serve any purpose in this world?

BIBLE READING: 1 Samuel 5:1-12

KEY BIBLE VERSE: *The LORD began to afflict the people of Ashdod and the nearby villages with a plague of tumors. When the people realized what was happening, they cried out, "We can't keep the Ark of the God of Israel here any longer! He is against us! We will all be destroyed along with our god Dagon." (1 Samuel 5:6-7)*

Sometimes pain is necessary to get our attention. Although the Philistines had just witnessed a great victory by Israel's God over their god, Dagon, they didn't act upon that insight until they were afflicted with bubonic plague. Similarly, today many people don't respond to biblical truth until they experience pain. Are you willing to listen to God for truth's sake, or do you turn to him only when you are hurting?

BIBLE READING: Matthew 16:21-28

KEY BIBLE VERSE: *If you try to keep your life for yourself, you will lose it. But if you give up your life for me, you will find true life. (Matthew 16:25)*

Sometimes pain tests our commitment. The possibility of losing their life was very real for the disciples as well as for Jesus. Real discipleship implies real commitment—pledging our whole existence to his service. If we try to save our physical life from death, pain, or discomfort, we may risk losing eternal life. If we protect ourself from pain, we begin to die spiritually and emotionally. Our life turns inward, and we lose our intended purpose. When we give our life in service to Christ, however, we discover the real purpose of living.

BIBLE READING: Hebrews 12:1-13

KEY BIBLE VERSE: *We do this by keeping our eyes on Jesus, on whom our faith depends from start to finish. He was willing to die a shameful death on the cross because of the joy he knew would be his afterward. Now he is seated in the place of highest honor beside God's throne in heaven. (Hebrews 12:2)*

Pain is often necessary for growth. When we face hardship and discouragement, it is easy to lose sight of the big picture. But we're not alone; there is help. Many have already made it through life, enduring far more difficult circumstances than we have experienced. Suffering is the training ground for Christian maturity. It develops our patience and makes our final victory sweet.

 BIBLE READING: Matthew 8:14-17
KEY BIBLE VERSE: *That evening many demon-possessed people were brought to Jesus. All the spirits fled when he commanded them to leave; and he healed all the sick. This fulfilled the word of the Lord through Isaiah, who said, "He took our sicknesses and removed our diseases."* (Matthew 8:16-17)

Through pain we experience God's power and grace. Matthew repeatedly shows Jesus' kingly nature. Through a single touch, Jesus healed (8:3, 15); when he spoke a single word, evil spirits fled his presence (8:16). Jesus has authority over all evil powers and all earthly disease. He also has power and authority to conquer sin. Sickness and evil are consequences of living in a fallen world. But in the future, when God removes all sin, there will be no more sickness, pain, or death. Jesus' healing miracles were a taste of what the whole world will one day experience in God's kingdom.

Related Topics: EVIL, SIN, SUFFERING

PANIC *(see* FEAR)

PARENT(S) *(Fathers, Guardians, Mothers)*

What are God's expectations for parents?

BIBLE READING: Proverbs 1:1-9
KEY BIBLE VERSE: *Listen, my child, to what your father teaches you. Don't neglect your mother's teaching.* (Proverbs 1:8)

Parents are to be good role models for their children. Our actions speak louder than our words. This is especially true in the home. Children learn values, morals, and priorities by observing how their parents act and react every day. If parents exhibit a deep reverence for and dependence on God, the children will catch these attitudes. Let them see your reverence for God. Teach them right living by giving worship an important place in your family life and by reading the Bible together.

BIBLE READING: Numbers 30:1-16
KEY BIBLE VERSE: *Now Moses summoned the leaders of the tribes of Israel and told them, "This is what the LORD has commanded: A man who makes a vow to the LORD or makes a pledge under oath must never break it. He must do exactly what he said he would do."* (Numbers 30:1-2)

Parents are to train their children in the art of decision making. Under Israelite law, parents could overrule their children's vows. This helped young people avoid the consequences of making foolish promises or costly commitments. From this law comes an important principle for both parents and children. Young people still living at home should seek their parents' help when they make decisions. A parent's experience could save a child from a serious mistake. Parents, however, should exercise their authority with caution and grace. They should let children learn from their mistakes, but protect them from disaster.

BIBLE READING: Deuteronomy 6:1-25

KEY BIBLE VERSE: *You must commit yourselves wholeheartedly to these commands I am giving you today. Repeat them again and again to your children. Talk about them when you are at home and when you are away on a journey, when you are lying down and when you are getting up again.* (Deuteronomy 6:6-7)

Parents are to teach their children the Scriptures. This passage provides the central theme of Deuteronomy. It sets a pattern that helps us relate the Word of God to our daily life. We are to love God, think constantly about his commandments, teach his commandments to our children, and live each day by the guidelines in his Word. God emphasized the importance of parents' teaching the Bible to their children. The church and Christian schools cannot be used as an escape from this responsibility. The Bible provides so many opportunities for object lessons and practical teaching that it would be a shame to study it only one day a week. Eternal truths are most effectively learned in the loving environment of a God-fearing home.

Parents are to train their children in applying the Scriptures. The Hebrews were extremely successful at making religion an integral part of life. The reason for their success was that religious education was life-oriented, not information-oriented. They used the context of daily life to teach about God. The key to teaching your children to love God is stated simply and clearly in these verses. If you want your children to follow God, you must make God a part of your everyday experiences. You must diligently teach your children to see God in all aspects of life, not just those that are church related.

BIBLE READING: Matthew 20:20-28

KEY BIBLE VERSE: *The mother of James and John, the sons of Zebedee, came to Jesus with her sons. She knelt respectfully to ask a favor. "What is your request?" he asked. She replied, "In your Kingdom, will you let my two sons sit in places of honor next to you, one at your right and the other at your left?"* (Matthew 20:20-21)

Parents are to seek God's will for their children. The mother of James and John asked Jesus to give her sons special positions in his kingdom. Parents naturally want to see their children promoted and honored, but this desire is dangerous if it causes them to lose sight of God's specific will for their children. God may have different work in mind—not as glamorous, but just as important. Thus parents' desires for their children's advancement must be held in check as they pray for God's will to be done in their children's lives.

Related Topics: CHILDREN, DISCIPLINE, FAMILY

PARTIALITY (*see* FAIRNESS)

PARTNERSHIPS (*Agreements, Contracts, Relationships*)

What does the Bible say about partnerships?

BIBLE READING: 2 Chronicles 20:31-37

KEY BIBLE VERSE: *But near the end of his life, King Jehoshaphat of Judah made an alliance with King Ahaziah of Israel, who was a very wicked man.* (2 Chronicles 20:35)

Unwise partnerships can have disastrous consequences. Jehoshaphat met disaster when he joined forces with wicked King Ahaziah. He did not learn from his disastrous alliance with Ahab (18:28-34) or from his father's alliance with Aram (16:2-9). The partnership stood on unequal footing because one man served the Lord and the other worshiped idols. We court disaster when we enter into partnership with unbelievers, because our very foundations differ (2 Corinthians 6:14-18). While one serves the Lord, the other does not recognize God's authority. Inevitably, the one who serves God is faced with the temptation to compromise values. When that happens, spiritual disaster results.

There are important basic guidelines for partnerships. Before entering into partnerships, ask: (1) What are my motives? (2) What problems am I avoiding by seeking this partnership? (3) Is this partnership the best solution, or is it only a quick fix to my problem? (4) Have I prayed or asked others to pray for guidance? (5) Are my partner and I really working toward the same goals? (6) Am I willing to settle for less financial gain in order to do what God wants?

BIBLE READING: Jeremiah 2:1-37

KEY BIBLE VERSE: *First here, then there—you flit from one ally to another asking for help. But your new friends in Egypt will let you down, just as Assyria did before.* (Jeremiah 2:36)

Some partnerships betray a lack of trust in God. God is not against alliances or working partnerships, but he is against people trusting others for the help that should come from him. This was the problem in Jeremiah's time. After the days of David and Solomon, Israel fell apart because the leaders turned to other nations and gods instead of the true God. They played power politics, thinking that their strong neighbors could protect them. But Judah would soon learn that its alliance with Egypt would be just as disappointing as its former alliance with Assyria (2 Kings 16:8-9; Isaiah 7:13-25).

Related Topics: COMPROMISE, RELATIONSHIP(S), TRUST

PAST *(Experience, History, Life)*

Why is our past important?

BIBLE READING: Genesis 49:1-28

KEY BIBLE VERSE: *Then Jacob called together all his sons and said, "Gather around me, and I will tell you what is going to happen to you in the days to come."* (Genesis 49:1)

Our past influences our future. Jacob blessed each of his sons and then made a prediction about each one's future. The way the men had lived played an important part in Jacob's blessing and prophecy. Our past also affects our present and future. By sunrise tomorrow, our actions of today will have become part of the past. Yet they will already have begun to shape the future. What actions can you choose or avoid that will positively shape your future?

BIBLE READING: 1 Samuel 7:1-17

KEY BIBLE VERSE: *Samuel then took a large stone and placed it between the towns of Mizpah and Jeshanah. He named it Ebenezer—"the stone of help"—for he said, "Up to this point the LORD has helped us!"* (1 Samuel 7:12)

Our past can be a reminder of God's grace. The Israelites had great difficulty with the Philistines, but God rescued them. In response, the people set up a stone as a memorial of God's great help and deliverance. During tough times, we may need to remember the crucial turning points in our past to help us through the present. Memorials can help us remember God's past victories and gain confidence and strength for the present.

BIBLE READING: 1 Corinthians 10:1-13
KEY BIBLE VERSE: *All these events happened to them as examples for us. They were written down to warn us, who live at the time when this age is drawing to a close.* (1 Corinthians 10:11)

The past is full of helpful lessons for today. Today's pressures make it easy to ignore or forget the lessons of the past. But Paul cautions us to remember the lessons the Israelites learned about God, so that we can avoid repeating their errors. The key to remembering is to study the Bible regularly so that these lessons remind us of how God wants us to live. We need not repeat their mistakes!

Related Topics: EXPERIENCE, HISTORY, MISTAKES

PASTORS *(Clergy, Ministers, Preachers)*

▶ **WHO PASTORS ARE**
What characteristics should mark a pastor's life?

BIBLE READING: Titus 1:5-9
KEY BIBLE VERSE: *I left you on the island of Crete so you could complete our work there and appoint elders in each town as I instructed you.* (Titus 1:5)

Pastors should model personal obedience to God. Paul briefly described some qualifications that the elders or overseers should have. Paul had given Timothy a similar set of instructions for the church in Ephesus (see 1 Timothy 3:1-7; 5:22). Notice that most of the qualifications involve character, not knowledge or skill. A person's lifestyle and relationships provide a window into his or her character. Consider these qualifications as you evaluate a person for a position of leadership in your church. It is important to have leaders who can effectively preach God's Word, but it is even more important to have those who can live out God's Word and be examples for others to follow.

BIBLE READING: 1 Corinthians 4:1-13
KEY BIBLE VERSE: *Dear brothers and sisters, I have used Apollos and myself to illustrate what I've been saying. If you pay attention to the Scriptures, you won't brag about one of your leaders at the expense of another.* (1 Corinthians 4:6)

Pastors are not to be status seekers. The Corinthians had split into various cliques, each following its favorite preacher (Paul, Apollos, Peter, etc.). The people in each clique believed they were the only ones to have the whole truth, and thus they felt spiritually superior. But Paul told the groups not to boast about being tied to a particular preacher, because each preacher was simply a humble servant who had suffered for the same message of salvation in Jesus Christ. No preacher of God has more status than another.

BIBLE READING: 1 Timothy 3:1-16
KEY BIBLE VERSE: *An elder must be a man whose life cannot be spoken against. He must be faithful to his wife. He must exhibit self-control, live wisely, and have a good reputation. He must enjoy having guests in his home and must be able to teach. He must not be a heavy drinker or be violent. He must be gentle, peace*

loving, and not one who loves money. He must manage his own family well, with children who respect and obey him. (1 Timothy 3:2-4)

Church leaders should be reflections of God's truth. To be a church leader ("elder") is a heavy responsibility because the church belongs to the living God. Church leaders should not be elected because they are popular, nor should they be allowed to push their way to the top. Instead, they should be chosen by the church because of the respect for the truth, both in what they believe and in how they live.

Church leaders should be faithful to family responsibilities. Christian workers and volunteers sometimes make the mistake of thinking their work is so important that they are justified in ignoring their families. Spiritual leadership, however, must begin at home. If a man is not willing to care for, discipline, and teach his children, he is not qualified to lead the church. Don't allow your volunteer activities to detract from your family responsibilities.

▶ WHAT PASTORS DO
What are the most important responsibilities of pastors?

BIBLE READING: Deuteronomy 18:1-8
KEY BIBLE VERSE: *The LORD your God chose the tribe of Levi out of all your tribes to minister in the LORD's name forever.* (Deuteronomy 18:5)

Pastors should serve the people. The priests and Levites served much the same function as our ministers today. Their duties included (1) teaching the people about God, (2) setting an example of godly living, (3) caring for the sanctuary and its workers, and (4) distributing the offerings. Because priests could not own property or pursue outside business interests, God made special arrangements so that people would not take advantage of them. Often churches take advantage of the men and women God has brought to lead them. For example, ministers may not be paid in accordance with their skills or the time they put in. Or pastors may be expected to attend every evening meeting, even to the detriment of their family life. As you look at your own church in light of God's Word, what ways do you see to honor the leaders God has given you?

BIBLE READING: Micah 3:1-12
KEY BIBLE VERSE: *You rulers govern for the bribes you can get; you priests teach God's laws only for a price; you prophets won't prophesy unless you are paid. Yet all of you claim you are depending on the LORD. "No harm can come to us," you say, "for the LORD is here among us."* (Micah 3:11)

Pastors are to lead others toward God. Micah denounced the sins of the leaders, priests, and prophets —those responsible for teaching the people right from wrong. These leaders, who should have known the law and taught it to the people, had set the law aside and had become the worst of sinners. They were taking advantage of the very people they were supposed to serve. All sin is bad, but the sin that leads others astray is the worst of all.

Pastors are to seek the good of others. The leaders had no compassion or respect for those they were supposed to serve. They were treating the people miserably in order to satisfy their own desires, and then they had the gall to ask for God's help when they found themselves in trouble. We, like the leaders, should not treat God like a light switch to be turned on only as needed. Instead, we should always rely on him.

Pastors should be committed to their ministry. Micah remained true to his calling and proclaimed God's words. In contrast, the false prophets' messages were geared to the favors they received. Not all those who claim to have messages from God really do. Micah prophesied that one day the false prophets would be shamed by their actions.

Pastors should rely on God for help and power. Micah attributed the power of his ministry to the Spirit of the Lord. Our power comes from the same source. Jesus told his followers they would receive power to witness about him when the Holy Spirit came on them (Acts 1:8). You can't witness effectively by relying on your own strength, because fear will keep you from speaking out for God. Only by relying on the power of the Holy Spirit can you live and witness for him.

Pastors must stand up for what is right. Micah warned the leaders, priests, and prophets of his day to avoid bribes. Pastors today accept bribes when they allow those who contribute much to control the church. When fear of losing money or members influences pastors to remain silent instead of speaking up for what is right, their churches are in danger. We should remember that Judah was finally destroyed because of the behavior of its religious leaders. A similar warning must be directed at those who have money—*never* use your resources to influence or manipulate God's ministers—that is bribery.

BIBLE READING: Acts 20:17-38
KEY BIBLE VERSE: *Now beware! Be sure that you feed and shepherd God's flock—his church, purchased with his blood—over whom the Holy Spirit has appointed you as elders.* (Acts 20:28)

Pastors are to teach God's people by word and example. These Ephesian elders were told by Paul to feed the believers under their care by teaching them God's Word and to shepherd them by being examples of God's love. All leaders of the church carry these two major responsibilities—to nourish others with God's truth and to exemplify God's truth at work in their lives. God's truth must be talked out and lived out.

Related Topics: CHURCH, LEADERSHIP, MINISTRY

PATIENCE *(Calmness, Endurance, Long-Suffering)*

▶ **GOD'S PATIENCE**
What does the Bible say about God's patience?

BIBLE READING: Nehemiah 9:1-38
KEY BIBLE VERSE: *They refused to listen and did not remember the miracles you had done for them. Instead, they rebelled and appointed a leader to take them back to their slavery in Egypt! But you are a God of forgiveness, gracious and merciful, slow to become angry, and full of unfailing love and mercy. You did not abandon them.* (Nehemiah 9:17)

God's patience is long-suffering. Seeing how God continued to be with his people shows that his patience is amazing! In spite of our repeated failings, pride, and stubbornness, he is always ready to pardon (9:17), and his Spirit is always ready to instruct (9:20). Realizing the extent of God's forgiveness helps us forgive those who fail us, even "seven times seven" if necessary (Matthew 18:21-22).

BIBLE READING: Joshua 23:1-16

KEY BIBLE VERSE: *If you break the covenant of the* LORD *your God by worshiping and serving other gods, his anger will burn against you, and you will quickly be wiped out from the good land he has given you.* (Joshua 23:16)

God's patience should not be taken for granted. This chilling prediction about the consequences of intermarriage with the Canaanite nations eventually became a reality. Numerous stories in the book of Judges show what Israel had to suffer because of failure to follow God wholeheartedly. God was supremely loving and patient with Israel, just as he is with us. But we must not confuse his patience with us as approval of or indifference to our sin. Beware of demanding your own way, because eventually you may get it—along with all its painful consequences.

BIBLE READING: Luke 15:11-32

KEY BIBLE VERSE: *So he returned home to his father. And while he was still a long distance away, his father saw him coming. Filled with love and compassion, he ran to his son, embraced him, and kissed him.* (Luke 15:20)

God's patience is an expression of his love. In two preceding stories in Luke's Gospel, the seeker actively looked for the coin and the sheep, which could not return by themselves. In this story, the father watched and waited. He was dealing with a human being with a will of his own, but he was ready to greet his son if he returned. In the same way, God's love is constant, patient, and welcoming. He will search for us and give us opportunities to respond, but he will not force us to come to him. Like the father in this story, God waits patiently for us to come to our senses.

▶ **HUMAN PATIENCE**
How can our patience be strengthened?

BIBLE READING: Esther 6:1-11

KEY BIBLE VERSE: *That night the king had trouble sleeping, so he ordered an attendant to bring the historical records of his kingdom so they could be read to him. In those records he discovered an account of how Mordecai had exposed the plot of Bigthana and Teresh, two of the eunuchs who guarded the door to the king's private quarters. They had plotted to assassinate the king.* (Esther 6:1-2)

Patience is developed through waiting. Mordecai had exposed a plot to assassinate Xerxes—thus he had saved the king's life (2:21-23). Although his good deed was recorded in the history books, Mordecai had gone unrewarded. But God was saving Mordecai's reward for the right time. Just as Haman was about to hang Mordecai unjustly, the king was ready to give the reward. Although God promises to reward our good deeds, we sometimes feel our "payoff" is too far away. Be patient. God steps in when it will do the most good.

BIBLE READING: 2 Thessalonians 1:1-12

KEY BIBLE VERSE: *We proudly tell God's other churches about your endurance and faithfulness in all the persecutions and hardships you are suffering.* (2 Thessalonians 1:4)

Patience is developed through hardships. Paul had been persecuted during his first visit to Thessalonica (Acts 17:5-9). No doubt those who had responded to his message and had become Christians were continuing to be persecuted by both Jews and Gentiles. In Paul's first letter to the Thessalonians, he said that Christ's return would bring deliverance from persecution and judgment on the persecutors. But this caused the people to expect Christ's return right away to rescue and vindicate them. So Paul had to point out that while waiting for God's kingdom, believers could and should learn perseverance and faith from their suffering.

Related Topics: ENDURANCE, PERSEVERANCE, WAITING

PEACE *(Calm, Quiet, Rest)*

▶ **PEACE DEFINED**
What is peace?

BIBLE READING: Psalm 122:1-9
KEY BIBLE VERSE: *Pray for the peace of Jerusalem. May all who love this city prosper. O Jerusalem, may there be peace within your walls and prosperity in your palaces.* (Psalm 122:6-7)

Peace is wholeness. The peace sought in these verses is much more than the mere absence of conflict. It suggests completeness, health, justice, prosperity, and protection. The world cannot provide this peace. Real peace comes from faith in God, because he alone embodies all the characteristics of peace. To find peace of mind and peace with others, you must find peace with God.

BIBLE READING: John 14:1-31
KEY BIBLE VERSE: *I am leaving you with a gift—peace of mind and heart. And the peace I give isn't like the peace the world gives. So don't be troubled or afraid.* (John 14:27)

Peace is resting in God's sovereignty. The end result of the Holy Spirit's work in our life is deep and lasting peace. Unlike worldly peace, which is usually defined as the absence of conflict, this peace is confident assurance in any circumstance. With Christ's peace, we have no need to fear the present or the future. If your life is full of stress, allow the Holy Spirit to fill you with Christ's peace (see Philippians 4:6-7 for more on experiencing God's peace).

Peace is the calming of internal conflict. Sin, fear, uncertainty, doubt, and numerous other forces are at war within us. The peace of God moves into our heart and life to restrain these hostile forces and offer comfort in place of conflict. Jesus says he will give us that peace if we are willing to accept it from him.

BIBLE READING: Romans 5:1-11
KEY BIBLE VERSE: *Since we have been made right in God's sight by faith, we have peace with God because of what Jesus Christ our Lord has done for us.* (Romans 5:1)

Peace is reconciliation with God. We now have peace *with God,* which may differ from peaceful feelings such as calmness and tranquility. There is no more hostility between us, no sin blocking our relationship with him. Peace with God is possible only because Jesus paid the price for our sins through his death on the cross.

▶ **PEACE ACHIEVED**
How can we find peace?

BIBLE READING: Genesis 21:1-7
KEY BIBLE VERSE: *Who would have dreamed that I would ever have a baby? Yet I have given Abraham a son in his old age!* (Genesis 21:7)

Peace is the by-product of trust in God. After repeated promises, a visit by two angels, and the appearance of the Lord himself, Sarah finally cried out with amazement and joy at the birth of her son. Because of her doubt, worry, and fear, she had forfeited the peace she could have felt in God's wonderful promise to her. The way to bring peace to a troubled heart is to focus on God's promises. Trust him to do what he says.

BIBLE READING: 2 Chronicles 14:1-15
KEY BIBLE VERSE: *Asa told the people of Judah, "Let us build towns and fortify them with walls, towers, gates, and bars. The land is ours because we sought the LORD our God, and he has given us rest from our enemies." So they went ahead with these projects and brought them to completion.* (2 Chronicles 14:7)

Peace is a by-product of obedience. Asa's reign was marked by peace because he "did what was pleasing and good in the sight of the Lord his God." This refrain is often repeated in Chronicles—*obedience* to God leads to *peace* with God and others. In the case of Judah's kings, obedience to God led to national peace, just as God had promised centuries earlier. In our case, obedience may not always bring peace with our enemies, but it will bring peace with God and complete peace in his future kingdom. Obeying God is the first step on the path to peace.

BIBLE READING: Psalm 3:1-8
KEY BIBLE VERSE: *I cried out to the LORD, and he answered me from his holy mountain. I lay down and slept. I woke up in safety, for the LORD was watching over me.* (Psalm 3:4-5)

Peace is the by-product of dependence on God. Sleep does not come easily during a crisis. David could have had sleepless nights when his son Absalom rebelled and gathered an army to kill him. But he slept peacefully, even during the rebellion. What made the difference? David cried out to the Lord, and the Lord heard him. The assurance of answered prayer brings peace. It is easier to sleep well when we have full assurance that God is in control of circumstances. If you are lying awake at night worrying about circumstances you can't change, pour out your heart to God, and thank him that he is in control. Then sleep will come.

BIBLE READING: Luke 21:1-38
KEY BIBLE VERSE: *When all these things begin to happen, stand straight and look up, for your salvation is near!* (Luke 21:28)

Complete peace will only come when Christ returns. The picture of the coming persecutions and natural disasters is gloomy, but ultimately it is cause not for worry, but for great joy. When believers see these events happening, they will know that the return of their Messiah is near, and they can look forward to his reign of justice and peace. Rather than being terrified by what is happening in our world, we should confidently await Christ's return to bring justice and restoration to his people.

Related Topics: CHRIST, GOSPEL, SECURITY

PEER PRESSURE *(Conformity, Expectations, Modeling)*

What are the dangers of giving in to peer pressure?

BIBLE READING: Matthew 14:1-12
KEY BIBLE VERSE: *The king was sorry, but because of his oath and because he*

didn't want to back down in front of his guests, he issued the necessary orders.
(Matthew 14:9)

Peer pressure often leads to bad decision making. Herod did not want to kill
John the Baptist, but he gave the order so that he wouldn't be embarrassed in
front of his guests. How easy it is to give in to the crowd and to be pressured
into doing wrong. Don't get in a situation where it will be too embarrassing
to do what is right. Determine to do what is right, no matter how embarrassing
or painful it may be.

BIBLE READING: Luke 23:13-25
KEY BIBLE VERSE: *The crowd shouted louder and louder for Jesus' death, and their
voices prevailed. So Pilate sentenced Jesus to die as they demanded.* (Luke
23:23-24)

Peer pressure can cause us to lose sight of the truth. When the stakes are high,
it is difficult to stand up for what is right, and it is easy to see our opponents as
problems to be solved rather than as people to be respected. Had Pilate been a
man of real courage, he would have released Jesus no matter what the consequences. But the crowd roared, and Pilate buckled. We are like Pilate when we
know what is right but decide not to do it. When you have a difficult decision
to make, don't discount the effects of peer pressure. Realize beforehand that
the right decision could have unpleasant consequences: social rejection, career
derailment, public ridicule. Then think of Pilate and resolve to stand up for
what is right, no matter what other people pressure you to do.

BIBLE READING: 2 Corinthians 6:3-13
KEY BIBLE VERSE: *We serve God whether people honor us or despise us, whether they
slander us or praise us. We are honest, but they call us impostors.* (2 Corinthians 6:8)

Peer pressure can rob us of our joy in Christ. What a difference it makes to know
Jesus! He cares for us in spite of what the world thinks. Christians don't have to
give in to public opinion and pressure. Paul stood faithful to God whether people praised him or condemned him. He remained active, joyous, and content in
the most difficult hardships. Don't let circumstances or people's expectations
control you. Be firm as you stand true to God, and refuse to compromise his
standards for living.

Related Topics: CONSISTENCY, HONESTY, TRUTH

PEOPLE *(Humans, Neighbors, Persons)*

How does God show that he values people?

BIBLE READING: 1 Kings 8:15-21
KEY BIBLE VERSE: *He told my father, "From the day I brought my people Israel out
of Egypt, I have never chosen a city among the tribes of Israel as the place where
a temple should be built to honor my name. But now I have chosen David to be
king over my people."* (1 Kings 8:16)

God chooses to work through people. For 480 years after Israel's escape from
Egypt, God did not ask them to build a temple for him. Instead he emphasized
the importance of his presence among them and their need for spiritual leaders.
It is easy to think of a building as the focus of God's presence and power, but

God chooses and uses *people* to do his work. He can use you more than he can use a building of wood and stone. Building or enlarging our place of worship may be necessary, but it should never take priority over developing spiritual leaders.

BIBLE READING: Luke 6:1-11
KEY BIBLE VERSE: *Jesus added, "I, the Son of Man, am master even of the Sabbath."* (Luke 6:5)

God puts people above traditions and regulations. Each week twelve consecrated loaves of bread, representing the twelve tribes of Israel, were placed on a table in the temple. This bread was called the bread of the Presence. After its use in the temple, it was to be eaten only by priests. Jesus, accused of Sabbath breaking, referred to a well-known story about David (1 Samuel 21:1-6). On one occasion, when fleeing from Saul, David and his men ate this consecrated bread. Their need was more important than ceremonial regulations. Jesus was appealing to the same principle: human need is more important than human regulations and rules. By comparing himself and his disciples with David and his men, Jesus was saying, "If you condemn me, you must also condemn David."

BIBLE READING: 2 Thessalonians 2:1-17
KEY BIBLE VERSE: *As for us, we always thank God for you, dear brothers and sisters loved by the Lord. We are thankful that God chose you to be among the first to experience salvation, a salvation that came through the Spirit who makes you holy and by your belief in the truth.* (2 Thessalonians 2:13)

God saves people from their sins and makes them new creatures. God worked through Paul and his companions to tell the Good News so that people could share in Christ's glory. It may seem strange that God works through us fallible, unfaithful, untrustworthy human creatures. But he has given us the fantastic privilege of accomplishing his great mission—telling the world how to find salvation.

Related Topics: CREATION, HUMANNESS, IMAGE

PERFECT (*Flawless, Mature, Whole*)

What does it mean for us to be perfect?

BIBLE READING: Matthew 5:43-48
KEY BIBLE VERSE: *You are to be perfect, even as your Father in heaven is perfect.* (Matthew 5:48)

Perfection is a goal toward which we move. How can we be perfect? (1) *In character.* In this life we cannot be flawless, but we can aspire to be as much like Christ as possible. (2) *In holiness.* Like the Pharisees, we are to separate ourself from the world's sinful values. But unlike the Pharisees, we are to be devoted to God's desires rather than our own and carry his love and mercy into the world. (3) *In maturity.* We can't achieve Christlike character and holy living all at once, but we must grow toward maturity and wholeness. Just as we expect different behavior from a baby, a child, a teenager, and an adult, so God expects different behavior from us, depending on our stage of spiritual development. (4) *In love.* We can seek to love others as completely as God loves us.

BIBLE READING: Colossians 1:24-29

KEY BIBLE VERSE: *Everywhere we go, we tell everyone about Christ. We warn them and teach them with all the wisdom God has given us, for we want to present them to God, perfect in their relationship to Christ.* (Colossians 1:28)

Perfection is God's work in us. The word *perfect* means mature or complete, not flawless. Paul wanted to see each believer mature spiritually. Like Paul, we must work wholeheartedly, like an athlete, but we should not strive in our strength alone. We have the power of his Spirit working in us. We can learn and grow daily, motivated by love and not by fear or pride, knowing that God gives the energy to become mature.

BIBLE READING: Jude 1:1-25

KEY BIBLE VERSE: *Now, all glory to God, who is able to keep you from stumbling, and who will bring you into his glorious presence innocent of sin and with great joy. All glory to him, who alone is God our Savior, through Jesus Christ our Lord. Yes, glory, majesty, power, and authority belong to him, in the beginning, now, and forevermore. Amen.* (Jude 1:24-25)

Perfection will be completed in us when we see Christ. When we finally see Christ face to face, we will be "innocent of sin and with great joy." When Christ appears, and we are given our new body, we will be like Christ (1 John 3:2). Coming into Christ's presence will be more wonderful than we could ever imagine!

Related Topics: GROWTH, HEAVEN, MATURITY

PERSECUTION *(Intimidation, Opposition, Oppression)*

Why does God allow his people to be persecuted?

BIBLE READING: Matthew 5:1-16

KEY BIBLE VERSE: *God blesses you when you are mocked and persecuted and lied about because you are my followers. Be happy about it! Be very glad! For a great reward awaits you in heaven. And remember, the ancient prophets were persecuted, too.* (Matthew 5:11-12)

Persecution builds character. Jesus said to rejoice when we're persecuted. Persecution can be good because (1) it takes our eyes off earthly rewards, (2) it strips away superficial belief, (3) it strengthens the faith of those who endure, and (4) our attitude through it serves as an example to others who follow. We can be comforted to know that God's greatest prophets were persecuted (Elijah, Jeremiah, Daniel). The fact that we are being persecuted proves that we have been faithful; faithless people would be unnoticed. In the future God will reward the faithful by receiving them into his eternal kingdom where there is no more persecution.

BIBLE READING: Matthew 24:1-51

KEY BIBLE VERSE: *Sin will be rampant everywhere, and the love of many will grow cold. But those who endure to the end will be saved.* (Matthew 24:12-13)

Persecution strengthens our faith. Jesus predicted that his followers would be severely persecuted by those who hated what he stood for. In the midst of terrible persecutions, however, they could have hope, knowing that salvation was theirs. Times of trial serve to sift true Christians from false or fair-weather Christians. When you are pressured to give up and turn your back on Christ, don't do it. Remember the benefits of standing firm, and continue to live for Christ.

BIBLE READING: 1 Peter 1:1-12

KEY BIBLE VERSE: *Be truly glad! There is wonderful joy ahead, even though it is necessary for you to endure many trials for a while.* (1 Peter 1:6)

Persecution brings maturity. Peter mentions suffering several times in this letter: 1:6-7; 3:13-17; 4:12-19; 5:9. When he speaks of trials, he is not talking about natural disasters or the experience of God's punishments, but the response of an unbelieving world to people of faith. All believers face such trials when they let their light shine into the darkness. We must accept trials as part of the refining process that burns away impurities and prepares us to meet Christ. Trials teach us patience (Romans 5:3-4; James 1:2-3) and help us grow to be the kind of people God wants.

Related Topics: EVIL, PERSEVERANCE, SUFFERING

PERSEVERANCE (*Endurance, Patience, Strength*)

What does perseverance show?

BIBLE READING: Nehemiah 4:1-23

KEY BIBLE VERSE: *At last the wall was completed to half its original height around the entire city, for the people had worked very hard.* (Nehemiah 4:6)

Perseverance reveals genuine commitment. The work of rebuilding the wall progressed well because the people had set their hearts and minds on accomplishing the task. They did not lose heart or give up, but persevered in the work. If God has called you to a task, determine to complete it, even if you face opposition or discouragement. The rewards of work well done will be worth the effort.

BIBLE READING: Mark 13:1-23

KEY BIBLE VERSE: *Everyone will hate you because of your allegiance to me. But those who endure to the end will be saved.* (Mark 13:13)

Perseverance reveals genuine believers. To believe in Jesus and "endure to the end" will take perseverance, because our faith will be challenged and opposed. Severe trials will sift true Christians from fair-weather believers. Enduring to the end does not earn salvation for us, but marks us as already saved. The assurance of our salvation will keep us going through the times of persecution.

BIBLE READING: Hebrews 3:1-19

KEY BIBLE VERSE: *Christ, the faithful Son, was in charge of the entire household. And we are God's household, if we keep up our courage and remain confident in our hope in Christ.* (Hebrews 3:6)

Perseverance reveals genuine faith. Because Christ lives in us, we can remain courageous and hopeful to the end. We are not saved by being steadfast and firm in our faith, but our courage and hope do reveal that our faith is real. Without this enduring faithfulness, we could easily be blown away by the winds of temptation, false teaching, or persecution. (See also Hebrews 3:14.)

Related Topics: ENDURANCE, PATIENCE, STRENGTH

PERSISTENCE (*Determination, Discipline, Self-Control*)

▶ GOD'S PERSISTENCE
How does God demonstrate his persistence?

BIBLE READING: Genesis 8:1-22
KEY BIBLE VERSE: *As long as the earth remains, there will be springtime and harvest, cold and heat, winter and summer, day and night.* (Genesis 8:22)

Creation is an expression of God's persistent grace. Countless times throughout the Bible we see God showing his love and patience toward men and women in order to save them. Although he realizes that their hearts are evil, he continues to try to reach them. God's love is unmistakably persistent. When we sin or fall away from God, we surely deserve to be destroyed by his judgment. But God has promised never again to destroy everything on earth until the Judgment Day, when Christ returns to destroy evil forever. Now every change of season is a reminder of his promise.

BIBLE READING: Hebrews 1:1-14
KEY BIBLE VERSE: *Lord, in the beginning you laid the foundation of the earth, and the heavens are the work of your hands. Even they will perish, but you remain forever. They will wear out like old clothing. You will roll them up like an old coat. They will fade away like old clothing. But you are always the same; you will never grow old.* (Hebrews 1:10-12)

Christ is an expression of God's persistent love. What does it mean that Christ is changeless ("you are always the same")? It means that Christ's character will never change. He persistently shows his love to us. He is always fair, just, and merciful to us who are so undeserving. Be thankful that Christ is changeless—he will always help you when you need it and offer forgiveness when you fall.

▶ OUR PERSISTENCE
How can persistence be both a strength and a weakness?

BIBLE READING: Genesis 32:22-32
KEY BIBLE VERSE: *"Your name will no longer be Jacob," the man told him. "It is now Israel, because you have struggled with both God and men and have won."* (Genesis 32:28)

Persistence in developing your spiritual life is a strength. Jacob continued this wrestling match all night just to be blessed. He was persistent. God encourages persistence in every area of our life, including the spiritual. Where in your spiritual life do you need more persistence? Strong character develops as you struggle through tough conditions.

BIBLE READING: 2 Samuel 2:1-32
KEY BIBLE VERSE: *Asahel would not give up, so Abner thrust the butt end of his spear through Asahel's stomach, and the spear came out through his back. He stumbled to the ground and died there. And everyone who came by that spot stopped and stood still when they saw Asahel lying there.* (2 Samuel 2:23)

Persistence that becomes mere stubbornness is a weakness. Abner repeatedly warned Asahel to turn back or risk losing his life, but Asahel refused to turn from his self-imposed duty. Persistence is a good trait if it is for a worthy cause. But if the goal is only personal honor or gain, persistence may be no more than stubbornness. Asahel's stubbornness not only cost him his life, but it also spurred unfortunate disunity in David's army for years to come (3:26-27; 1 Kings 2:28-35). Before you decide to pursue a goal, make sure it is worthy of your devotion.

 BIBLE READING: Matthew 7:7-12

KEY BIBLE VERSE: *Keep on asking, and you will be given what you ask for. Keep on looking, and you will find. Keep on knocking, and the door will be opened. For everyone who asks, receives. Everyone who seeks, finds. And the door is opened to everyone who knocks.* (Matthew 7:7-8)

Persistence in seeking after God is a strength. Jesus tells us to persist in pursuing God. People often give up after a few halfhearted efforts and conclude that God cannot be found. But knowing God takes faith, focus, and follow-through, and Jesus assures us that we will be rewarded. Don't give up in your efforts to seek God. Continue to ask him for more knowledge, patience, wisdom, love, and understanding. He will give them to you.

Related Topics: ENDURANCE, HOPE, PERSEVERANCE

PERSPECTIVE *(Outlook, View, Vision)*

How does human perspective differ from God's?

BIBLE READING: Exodus 4:1-17

KEY BIBLE VERSE: *"Now go, and do as I have told you. I will help you speak well, and I will tell you what to say." But Moses again pleaded, "Lord, please! Send someone else."* (Exodus 4:12-13)

Human perspective is limited; God's is unlimited. Moses pleaded with God to let him out of his mission. After all, he was not a good speaker and would probably embarrass both himself and God. But God looked at Moses' problem quite differently. All Moses needed was some help—and who better than God could help him say and do the right things? God made his mouth and would give him the words to say. It is easy for us to focus on our weaknesses, but if God asks us to do something, then he will help us get the job done. If the job involves some of our weak areas, then we can trust that he will provide words, strength, courage, and ability where needed.

BIBLE READING: Matthew 16:21-28

KEY BIBLE VERSE: *Jesus turned to Peter and said, "Get away from me, Satan! You are a dangerous trap to me. You are seeing things merely from a human point of view, and not from God's."* (Matthew 16:23)

Human perspective tends to be distorted; God's is always clear. In his desert temptations, Jesus heard the message that he could achieve greatness without dying (Matthew 4:6). Here he heard the same message from Peter. Peter had just recognized Jesus as Messiah. Here, however, he forsook God's perspective and evaluated the situation from a human one. Satan is always trying to get us to leave God out of the picture. Jesus rebuked Peter for this attitude.

BIBLE READING: Mark 5:21-43

KEY BIBLE VERSE: *He went inside and spoke to the people. "Why all this weeping and commotion?" he asked. "The child isn't dead; she is only asleep."* (Mark 5:39)

Human perspective is temporal; God's perspective is eternal. The mourners began to laugh at Jesus when he said, "The child isn't dead; she is only asleep." The girl was dead, but Jesus used the image of sleep to indicate that her condition was temporary and that she would be restored.

Jesus tolerated the crowd's abuse in order to teach an important lesson about maintaining hope and trust in him. Today, most of the world laughs at Christ's claims, which seem ridiculous to them. When you are belittled for expressing faith in Jesus and hope for eternal life, remember that unbelievers don't see from God's perspective.

Related Topics: FAITH, GOD, HOPE

PERSUASION (*see* WITNESSING)

PESSIMISM (*see* HOPELESSNESS)

PLANS (*Goals, Outline, Preparations*)

▶ **HUMAN PLANS**
What is important to know about making plans?

 BIBLE READING: Genesis 41:1-40
KEY BIBLE VERSE: *Joseph's suggestions were well received by Pharaoh and his advisers. As they discussed who should be appointed for the job, Pharaoh said, "Who could do it better than Joseph? For he is a man who is obviously filled with the spirit of God."* (Genesis 41:37-38)

We can make wise use of resources through planning. After interpreting Pharaoh's dream, Joseph gave the king a survival plan for the next fourteen years. The only way to prevent starvation was through careful planning; without a plan, Egypt would have turned from prosperity to ruin. Many find detailed planning boring and unnecessary. But planning is a responsibility, not an option. Joseph was able to save a nation by translating God's plan for Egypt into practical actions (implementation). We must take time to translate God's plan for us into practical actions too.

 BIBLE READING: Proverbs 13:1-25
KEY BIBLE VERSE: *Wise people think before they act; fools don't and even brag about it!* (Proverbs 13:16)

Planning can lead to freedom. Being spontaneous can be fun, but it is not the best way to approach every situation. There is a place for planning and self-discipline, especially when you have goals you want to reach. Some people think planning is too restrictive. In reality, it can set a person free to enjoy life and to be productive. Take time to set goals, to plan your course of action, and to set priorities before you launch into action.

Planning can lead to stubbornness. When you set your heart on something, you may lose your ability to assess it objectively (see verse 19). Your desire blinds your judgment, and you proceed with an unwise relationship, a wasteful purchase, or a poorly conceived plan in spite of the objections from others. Faithfulness is a virtue, but stubbornness is not. If your plans cause you to use people and love things rather than use things and love people, give up your plans immediately.

BIBLE READING: Matthew 6:25-34

KEY BIBLE VERSE: *Don't worry about tomorrow, for tomorrow will bring its own worries. Today's trouble is enough for today.* (Matthew 6:34)

Careful planning can keep us from worry. Planning for tomorrow is time well spent; worrying about tomorrow is time wasted. Sometimes it's difficult to tell the difference. Careful planning is thinking ahead about goals, steps, and schedules, and trusting in God's guidance. When done well, planning can help alleviate worry. Worriers, by contrast, are consumed with fear and find it difficult to trust God. They let their plans interfere with their relationship with God. Don't let worries about tomorrow affect your relationship with God today.

BIBLE READING: James 4:13-17

KEY BIBLE VERSE: *What you ought to say is, "If the Lord wants us to, we will live and do this or that." Otherwise you will be boasting about your own plans, and all such boasting is evil.* (James 4:15-16)

Careful planning should include submission to God. It is good to have goals, but goals will disappoint us if we leave God out of them. There is no point in making plans as though God does not exist, because the future is in his hands. What would you like to be doing ten years from now? One year from now? Tomorrow? How will you react if God steps in and rearranges your plans? Plan ahead, but hold your plans loosely. Put God's desires at the center of your planning; he will never disappoint you.

▶ GOD'S GREAT PLAN
What does the Bible say about God's plan?

BIBLE READING: Joshua 1:1-18

KEY BIBLE VERSE: *They answered Joshua, "We will do whatever you command us, and we will go wherever you send us."* (Joshua 1:16)

God's plan requires our submission to him. If everyone had tried to conquer the Promised Land his own way, chaos would have resulted. In order to complete the enormous task of conquering the land, everyone had to agree to the leader's plan and be willing to support and obey him. If we are going to complete the tasks God has given us, we must fully agree to his plan, pledge to obey it, and put his principles into action. Agreeing to God's plan means both knowing what the plan is (as found in the Bible) and carrying it out daily.

BIBLE READING: 1 Corinthians 2:6-16

KEY BIBLE VERSE: *The wisdom we speak of is the secret wisdom of God, which was hidden in former times, though he made it for our benefit before the world began.* (1 Corinthians 2:7)

God's plan is for our eternal benefit. God's "secret wisdom . . . which was hidden" was his offer of salvation to all people. Originally unknown to humanity, this plan became crystal clear when Jesus rose from the dead. His resurrection proved that he had power over sin and death and could offer us this power as well. God's plan, however, is still hidden to unbelievers because they either refuse to accept it, choose to ignore it, or simply haven't heard about it.

God's plan is more wonderful than we can imagine. We cannot imagine all that God has in store for us, both in this life and for eternity. He will create a new heaven and a new earth (Isaiah 65:17; Revelation 21:1), and we will live with him forever. Until then, his Holy Spirit comforts and guides us. Knowing the wonderful and eternal future that awaits us gives us hope and courage to press

on in this life, to endure hardship, and to avoid giving in to temptation. This
world is not all there is. The best is yet to come.

BIBLE READING: Ephesians 1:1-14
KEY BIBLE VERSE: *God's secret plan has now been revealed to us; it is a plan centered
on Christ, designed long ago according to his good pleasure. And this is his
plan: At the right time he will bring everything together under the authority
of Christ—everything in heaven and on earth.* (Ephesians 1:9-10)

God's plan cannot be understood apart from Christ. God was not just keeping
a secret; he was keeping it until the right moment. His plan for the world could
not be fully understood until Christ rose from the dead. His purpose for sending Christ was to unite Jews and Gentiles in one body with Christ as the head.
Many people still do not understand God's plan; but when the time is right, he
will bring us together to be with him forever. Then everyone will understand.
On that day, all people will bow to Jesus as Lord, either because they love him
or because they fear his power (see Philippians 2:10-11).

Related Topics: BIBLE, JESUS, SALVATION

PLEASURE *(Delight, Enjoyment, Feelings)*

What are God's instructions about his gift of pleasure?

BIBLE READING: Genesis 1:1–2:2
KEY BIBLE VERSE: *God looked over all he had made, and he saw that it was excellent
in every way. This all happened on the sixth day.* (Genesis 1:31)

Pleasure was part of God's intention at creation. God saw that his work was
good. People sometimes feel guilty for having a good time or for feeling good
about an accomplishment. This need not be so. Just as God felt good about his
work, we can be pleased with ours. However, we should not feel good about our
work if God would not be pleased with it. What are you doing that pleases both
you and God?

BIBLE READING: Genesis 25:19-34
KEY BIBLE VERSE: *Jacob gave Esau some bread and lentil stew. Esau ate and drank
and went on about his business, indifferent to the fact that he had given up his
birthright.* (Genesis 25:34)

Pleasure should not be sought for its own sake. Esau traded the lasting benefits
of his birthright for the immediate pleasure of food. He acted on impulse, satisfying his immediate desires without pausing to consider the long-range consequences of what he was about to do. We can fall into the same trap. When we
see something we want, our first impulse is to get it. At first we feel intensely
satisfied and sometimes even powerful because we have obtained what we set
out to get. But in the immediacy of pleasure, we often lose sight of the future.
We can avoid making Esau's mistake by comparing the short-term satisfaction
with its long-range consequences before we act.

BIBLE READING: 1 Timothy 4:1-16
KEY BIBLE VERSE: *Since everything God created is good, we should not reject any
of it. We may receive it gladly, with thankful hearts. For we know it is made holy
by the word of God and prayer.* (1 Timothy 4:4-5)

Pleasure is one of God's wonderful gifts. In opposition to the false teachers, Paul affirmed that everything God created is good (see Genesis 1). We should ask for God's blessing on his created gifts that give us pleasure and thank him for them. This doesn't mean that we should abuse what God has made (for example, gluttony abuses God's gift of good food, lust abuses God's gift of love, and murder abuses God's gift of life). Instead of abusing them, we should enjoy these gifts by using them to serve and honor God. Have you thanked God for the good gifts he has given? Are you using the gifts in ways pleasing to you *and to God?*

Related Topics: FEELINGS, JOY, SEX

POLITICS (*see* GOVERNMENT)

POLLUTION (*see* EARTH)

POOR (*Impoverished, Lacking, Needy*)

How are we to respond to the poor?

BIBLE READING: Nehemiah 5:1-19

KEY BIBLE VERSE: *You must restore their fields, vineyards, olive groves, and homes to them this very day. Repay the interest you charged on their money, grain, wine, and olive oil.* (Nehemiah 5:11)

We are to help the poor. God's concern for the poor is revealed in almost every book of the Bible. Here, Nehemiah insisted that fairness to the poor and oppressed was central to following God. The books of Moses clearly spelled out the Israelites' responsibility to care for the poor (Exodus 22:22-27; Leviticus 25:35-37; Deuteronomy 14:28-29; 15:7-11). The way we help those in need ought to mirror God's love and concern.

We are not to profit from another's misfortune. Nehemiah told the rich Jews to stop their practice of charging interest on their loans to their needy brothers. God never intended people to profit from others' misfortunes. In contrast to the values of this world, God says that caring for one another is more important than personal gain. When a Christian brother or sister suffers, we all suffer (1 Corinthians 12:26). We should help needy believers, not exploit them. The Jerusalem church was praised for working together to eliminate poverty (Acts 4:34-35). Remember, "Whoever gives to the poor will lack nothing" (Proverbs 28:27). Make it a practice to help those in need around you.

BIBLE READING: Amos 5:18-27

KEY BIBLE VERSE: *I want to see a mighty flood of justice, a river of righteous living that will never run dry.* (Amos 5:24)

We are to act on behalf of the poor. Here are eight common excuses for not helping the poor: (1) They don't deserve help. They got themselves into poverty; let them get themselves out. (2) God's call to help the poor applies to another time. (3) We don't know any poor people. (4) I have my own needs. (5) Any money I give will be wasted, stolen, or spent on other things. The poor will never see it. (6) I may become a victim myself. (7) I don't know where to start, and I don't have time. (8) My little bit won't make any difference.

Instead of making lame excuses, ask what can be done to help the poor. Does your church have programs that help the needy? Could you volunteer to work with a community group that fights poverty? As one individual, you may not be able to accomplish much, but join up with similarly motivated people, and watch mountains begin to move.

BIBLE READING: 1 Timothy 5:1-25
KEY BIBLE VERSE: *If a Christian woman has relatives who are widows, she must take care of them and not put the responsibility on the church. Then the church can care for widows who are truly alone.* (1 Timothy 5:16)

We are to care for the poor in our families as well as in the church. Because there were no pensions, no social security, no life insurance, and few honorable jobs for women, widows were usually unable to support themselves. The responsibility for caring for the helpless naturally falls first on their families, the people whose lives are most closely linked with theirs. Paul stresses the importance of families caring for the needs of widows and not leaving it for the church to do, so the church can care for those widows who have no family. A widow who had no children or other family members to support her was doomed to poverty. From the beginning, the church took care of its widows, who in turn gave valuable service to the church.

We are to take the initiative in helping the poor. The church should support those who have no family and should also help the elderly, young, disabled, ill, or poverty-stricken with their emotional and spiritual needs. Often families who are caring for their own helpless members have heavy burdens. They may need extra money, a listening ear, a helping hand, or a word of encouragement. Interestingly, those who are helped often turn around and help others, turning the church into more of a caring community. Don't wait for people to ask. Take the initiative and look for ways to serve them.

Related Topics: GIVING, MONEY, WEALTH

POPULARITY (*Fame, Glory, Reputation*)

What are the hidden costs of popularity?

BIBLE READING: Matthew 9:9-13
KEY BIBLE VERSE: *When he heard this, Jesus replied, "Healthy people don't need a doctor—sick people do." Then he added, "Now go and learn the meaning of this Scripture: 'I want you to be merciful; I don't want your sacrifices.' For I have come to call sinners, not those who think they are already good enough."* (Matthew 9:12-13)

Popularity often comes at the expense of others. The Pharisees constantly tried to trap Jesus, and they thought his association with these "lowlifes" was the perfect opportunity. They were more concerned with their own appearance of holiness than with helping people, with criticism than encouragement, with outward respectability than practical help. But God is concerned for all people, including the sinful and hurting ones. The Christian life is not a popularity contest! Following Jesus' example, we should share the gospel with the poor, immoral, lonely, and outcast, not just the rich, moral, popular, and powerful.

BIBLE READING: Luke 6:17-26

KEY BIBLE VERSE: *What sorrows await you who are praised by the crowds; for their ancestors also praised false prophets.* (Luke 6:26)

Popularity often comes at the expense of truth. There were many false prophets in Old Testament times. They were praised by kings and crowds because their predictions—prosperity and victory in war—were exactly what the people wanted to hear. But popularity is no guarantee of truth, and human flattery does not bring God's approval. Sadness lies ahead for those who chase after the crowd's praise rather than God's truth.

BIBLE READING: John 2:12-25

KEY BIBLE VERSE: *Because of the miraculous signs he did in Jerusalem at the Passover celebration, many people were convinced that he was indeed the Messiah. But Jesus didn't trust them, because he knew what people were really like. No one needed to tell him about human nature.* (John 2:23-25)

Popularity often comes at the expense of faith. The Son of God knows all about human nature. Jesus was well aware of the truth of Jeremiah 17:9, which states, "The human heart is most deceitful and desperately wicked. Who really knows how bad it is?" Jesus was discerning, and he knew that the faith of some followers was superficial. Some of the same people claiming to believe in Jesus at this time would later yell "Crucify him!" It's easy to believe when it is exciting and everyone else believes the same way. But keep your faith firm even when it isn't popular to follow Christ.

BIBLE READING: 1 John 4:1-6

KEY BIBLE VERSE: *We belong to God; that is why those who know God listen to us. If they do not belong to God, they do not listen to us. That is how we know if someone has the Spirit of truth or the spirit of deception.* (1 John 4:6)

Popularity often comes at the expense of obedience. False teachers are popular with the world because, like the false prophets of the Old Testament, they tell people what they want to hear. John warns that Christians who faithfully teach God's Word will not win any popularity contests. People don't want to hear their sins denounced; they don't want to listen to demands that they change their behavior. A false teacher will be well received by non-Christians.

Related Topics: IMAGE, REPUTATION, TRUTH

POSITION (*Calling, Office, Vocation*)

How does God view our position in life?

BIBLE READING: 1 Samuel 3:1-21

KEY BIBLE VERSE: *The LORD came and called as before, "Samuel! Samuel!" And Samuel replied, "Yes, your servant is listening."* (1 Samuel 3:10)

Position is not a prerequisite for God's work. One would naturally expect an audible message from God to be given to the priest Eli and not to the child Samuel. Eli was older and more experienced, and he held the proper position. But God's chain of command is based on faith, not on age or position. In finding faithful followers, God may use unexpected channels. Be prepared for the Lord to work at any place, at any time, and through anyone he chooses.

BIBLE READING: Matthew 20:20-28

KEY BIBLE VERSE: *The mother of James and John, the sons of Zebedee, came to Jesus with her sons. She knelt respectfully to ask a favor. "What is your request?" he asked. She replied, "In your Kingdom, will you let my two sons sit in places of honor next to you, one at your right and the other at your left?"* (Matthew 20:20-21)

Position should not be sought in opposition to God's will. The mother of James and John asked Jesus to give her sons special positions in his kingdom. Parents naturally want to see their children promoted and honored, but this desire is dangerous if it causes them to lose sight of God's specific will for their children. God may have different work in mind—not as glamorous, but just as important. Thus parents' desires for their children's advancement must be held in check as they pray for God's will to be done in their children's lives.

BIBLE READING: Luke 20:41-47

KEY BIBLE VERSE: *Beware of these teachers of religious law! For they love to parade in flowing robes and to have everyone bow to them as they walk in the market-places. And how they love the seats of honor in the synagogues and at banquets.* (Luke 20:46)

Position is an opportunity for service, not selfish ambition. The teachers of the law loved the benefits associated with their position, and they sometimes cheated the poor in order to get even more benefits. Every job has its rewards, but gaining these rewards should never become more important than doing the job faithfully. God will punish people who use their position of responsibility to cheat others. Whatever resources you have been given, use them to help others and not just yourself.

Related Topics: INFLUENCE, POWER, SERVING

POSSESSIONS *(Goods, Property, Wealth)*

How are we to view possessions?

BIBLE READING: Leviticus 25:1-55

KEY BIBLE VERSE: *Remember, the land must never be sold on a permanent basis because it really belongs to me. You are only foreigners and tenants living with me.* (Leviticus 25:23)

Possessions are only temporary. The people would one day possess land in Canaan, but in God's plan, only God's ownership was absolute. He wanted his people to avoid greed and materialism. If you have the attitude that you are taking care of the Lord's property, you will make what you have more available to others. This is difficult to do if you have an attitude of ownership. Think of yourself as a manager of all that is under your care, not as an owner.

BIBLE READING: Matthew 6:19-34

KEY BIBLE VERSE: *No one can serve two masters. For you will hate one and love the other, or be devoted to one and despise the other. You cannot serve both God and money.* (Matthew 6:24)

Possessions can undermine our allegiance to God. Jesus says we can have only one master. We live in a materialistic society where many people serve money. They spend all their life collecting and storing it—only to die and leave it behind. Their desire for money and what it can buy far outweighs their commitment to God and spiritual matters. Whatever you store up, you will spend much of your time and energy thinking about. Don't fall into the materialistic trap, because "the love of money is at the root of all kinds of evil" (1 Timothy 6:10). Can you honestly say that God, not money, is your master? One test is to ask which one occupies more of your thoughts, time, and efforts.

Possessions must not be allowed to possess us. Jesus contrasted heavenly values with earthly values when he explained that our first loyalty should be to those things that do not fade, cannot be stolen or used up, and never wear out. We should not be fascinated with our possessions, lest *they possess us.* This means we may have to do some cutting back if our possessions are becoming too important to us. Jesus is calling for a decision that allows us to live contentedly with whatever we have, because we have chosen what is eternal and lasting.

BIBLE READING: Philippians 4:10-20

KEY BIBLE VERSE: *I know how to live on almost nothing or with everything. I have learned the secret of living in every situation, whether it is with a full stomach or empty, with plenty or little. For I can do everything with the help of Christ who gives me the strength I need.* (Philippians 4:12-13)

Possessions will not bring contentment. Are you content no matter what circumstances you face? Paul knew how to be content when he had plenty and when he was in need. The secret was drawing on Christ's power for strength. Do you have great needs, or are you discontented because you don't have what you want? Learn to rely on God's promises and Christ's power to help you be content. If you always want more, ask God to remove that desire and teach you contentment in every circumstance. He will supply all your needs, but in a way that he knows is best for you.

Possessions can never fill our emptiness. Paul was content because he could see life from God's point of view. He focused on what he was supposed to *do, not what he felt he should have.* Paul had his priorities straight, and he was grateful for everything God had given him. Paul had detached himself from the nonessentials so that he could concentrate on the eternal. Often the desire for more or better possessions is really a longing to fill an empty place in a person's life. To what are you drawn when you feel empty inside? How can you find true contentment? The answer lies in your perspective, your priorities, and your source of power.

Related Topics: GIVING, MONEY, WEALTH

POTENTIAL (*see* ABILITIES)

POVERTY (*see* POOR)

POWER (*Control, Influence, Strength*)

▶ **THE POWER OF GOD**

How do we experience the power of God?

BIBLE READING: Exodus 4:1-17

KEY BIBLE VERSE: *The LORD told him, "Take hold of its tail." So Moses reached out and grabbed it, and it became a shepherd's staff again. "Perform this sign, and they will believe you," the* LORD *told him. "Then they will realize that the* LORD, *the God of their ancestors—the God of Abraham, the God of Isaac, and the God of Jacob—really has appeared to you." (Exodus 4:4-5)*

We experience God's power in ordinary things. A shepherd's staff was commonly a three- to six-foot wooden rod with a curved hook at the top. The shepherd used it for walking, guiding his sheep, killing snakes, and many other tasks. Still, it was just a stick. But God used the simple shepherd's staff Moses carried as a sign to teach him an important lesson. God sometimes takes joy in using ordinary things for extraordinary purposes. What are the ordinary things in your life—your voice, a pen, a hammer, a broom, a musical instrument? While it is easy to assume God can use only special skills, you must not hinder his use of the everyday contributions you can make. Little did Moses imagine the power his simple staff would wield when it became the staff of God.

BIBLE READING: Mark 4:35-41
KEY BIBLE VERSE: *He asked them, "Why are you so afraid? Do you still not have faith in me?" And they were filled with awe and said among themselves, "Who is this man, that even the wind and waves obey him?" (Mark 4:40-41)*

We experience God's power as we trust him. The disciples panicked because the storm threatened to destroy them all, and Jesus seemed unaware and unconcerned. Theirs was a physical storm, but storms come in other forms. Think about the storms in your life—the situations that cause you great anxiety. Whatever your difficulty, you have two options: You can worry and assume that Jesus no longer cares, or you can resist fear, putting your trust in him. When you feel like panicking, confess your need for God and then trust him to care for you.

BIBLE READING: Mark 5:21-43
KEY BIBLE VERSE: *Holding her hand, he said to her, "Get up, little girl!" And the girl, who was twelve years old, immediately stood up and walked around! Her parents were absolutely overwhelmed. (Mark 5:41-42)*

We experience God's power through Christ. Jesus not only demonstrated great power; he also showed tremendous compassion. Jesus' power over nature, evil spirits, and death was motivated by compassion—for a demon-possessed man who lived among tombs, for a diseased woman, and for the family of a dead girl. The rabbis of the day considered such people unclean. Polite society avoided them. But Jesus reached out and helped anyone in need.

BIBLE READING: Acts 1:1-11
KEY BIBLE VERSE: *When the Holy Spirit has come upon you, you will receive power and will tell people about me everywhere—in Jerusalem, throughout Judea, in Samaria, and to the ends of the earth. (Acts 1:8)*

We experience God's power through the Holy Spirit. At Pentecost (2:1-4), the Holy Spirit was made available to all who believe in Jesus. When we receive Christ by faith, the Holy Spirit comes to reside within us. From that moment, the Holy Spirit begins a lifelong process of change, drawing us into a close personal relationship with God and making us more like Christ (Philippians 1:6).

▶ **THE POWER OF PERSONS**
How are we to view the use of power?

BIBLE READING: Esther 10:1-3

KEY BIBLE VERSE: *His great achievements and the full account of the greatness of Mordecai, whom the king had promoted, are recorded in* The Book of the History of the Kings of Media and Persia. (Esther 10:2)

Human power can be used to help the oppressed. Mordecai enjoyed a good reputation among the Jews because he was still their friend when he rose to a place of power. Corruption and abuse of authority often characterize those in power. But power used to lift the fallen and ease the burden of the oppressed is power used well. People placed by God in positions of power or political influence must not turn their back on those in need.

Human power is subject to the sovereignty of God. In the book of Esther, we clearly see God at work in the lives of individuals and in the affairs of a nation. Even when it looks as if the world is in the hands of evil people, God is still in control, protecting those who are his. Although we may not understand everything happening around us, we must trust in God's protection and retain our integrity by doing what we know is right. Esther, who risked her life appearing before the king, became a hero. Mordecai, who was effectively condemned to death, rose to become the second highest ranking official in the nation. No matter how hopeless our condition, or how much we would like to give up, we need not despair. God is in control of our world.

BIBLE READING: Nahum 3:1-19

KEY BIBLE VERSE: *O Assyrian king, your princes lie dead in the dust. Your people are scattered across the mountains. There is no longer a shepherd to gather them together.* (Nahum 3:18)

Human power is temporary. All the nations hated to be ruled by the merciless Assyrians, but the nations wanted to be like Assyria—powerful, wealthy, prestigious—and they courted Assyria's friendship. In the same way, we don't like the idea of being ruled harshly, so we do what we can to stay on good terms with a powerful leader. And deep down, we would like to have that kind of power. The thought of being on top can be captivating. But power is seductive, so we should not scheme to get it or hold on to it. Those who lust after power will be powerfully destroyed, as was the mighty Assyrian empire.

BIBLE READING: Matthew 4:1-11

KEY BIBLE VERSE: *Next the Devil took him to the peak of a very high mountain and showed him the nations of the world and all their glory. "I will give it all to you," he said, "if you will only kneel down and worship me."* (Matthew 4:8-9)

Worldly power can be Satan's trap. Did the devil have the power to give Jesus the kingdoms of the world? Didn't God, the Creator of the world, have control over these kingdoms? The devil may have been lying about his implied power, or he may have based his offer on his temporary control and free rein over the earth because of humanity's sinfulness. Satan was tempting Jesus to take the world as a political ruler right then, without carrying out God's plan to save the world from sin. Satan was trying to distort Jesus' perspective by making him focus on worldly power and not on God's plans.

Worldly power can turn us away from God. The devil offered the whole world to Jesus—if Jesus would only bow down and worship him. Today the devil offers us the world by trying to entice us with materialism and power. We can resist temptations the same way Jesus did. If you find yourself craving something that the world offers, quote Jesus' words to the devil: "You must worship the Lord your God; serve only him."

BIBLE READING: James 2:1-13

KEY BIBLE VERSE: *My dear brothers and sisters, how can you claim that you have faith in our glorious Lord Jesus Christ if you favor some people more than others?* (James 2:1)

Worldly power can violate kingdom values. James condemns acts of favoritism. Often we treat a well-dressed, impressive-looking person better than someone who looks shabby. We do this because we would rather identify with successful people than with apparent failures. The irony, as James reminds us, is that the supposed winners may have gained their impressive lifestyle at our expense. In addition, the rich find it difficult to identify with the Lord Jesus, who came as a humble servant. Are you easily impressed by status, wealth, or fame? Are you partial to the "haves" while ignoring the "have nots"? This attitude is sinful. God views all people as equals, and if he favors anyone, it is the poor and the powerless. We should follow his example.

Related Topics: GOD, INTEGRITY, OBEDIENCE

PRAISE (*Adoration, Appreciation, Worship*)

What is praise?

BIBLE READING: Psalm 9:1-20

KEY BIBLE VERSE: *I will thank you, LORD, with all my heart; I will tell of all the marvelous things you have done.* (Psalm 9:1)

Praise is giving thanks to God for who he is. Praise is saying thank you for each aspect of his divine nature. Our inward attitude becomes outward expression. When we praise God, we help ourself by expanding our awareness of who he is. In each psalm you read, look for an attribute or characteristic of God for which you can thank him.

BIBLE READING: Psalm 146:1-10

KEY BIBLE VERSE: *Praise the LORD! Praise the LORD, I tell myself. I will praise the LORD as long as I live. I will sing praises to my God even with my dying breath.* (Psalm 146:1-2)

Praise is focusing our heart on God. The last five psalms (146–150) are filled with praise. Each begins and ends with "Praise the Lord!" They show us where, why, and how to praise God. What does praise do? (1) Praise takes our minds off our problems and shortcomings and focuses them on God. (2) Praise leads us from individual meditation to corporate worship. (3) Praise causes us to consider and appreciate God's character. (4) Praise lifts our perspective from the earthly to the heavenly.

BIBLE READING: Psalm 103:1-22

KEY BIBLE VERSE: *Praise the LORD, I tell myself, and never forget the good things he does for me.* (Psalm 103:2)

Praise is thanking God for his many gracious gifts. David's praise focused on God's glorious deeds. It is easy to complain about life, but David's list gives us plenty for which to praise God—he forgives our sins, heals our diseases, redeems us from death, crowns us with love and compassion, satisfies our desires, and gives righteousness and justice. We receive all of these without deserving any of them. No matter how difficult your life's journey, you can always count your blessings—past, present, and future. When you feel as though you have nothing for which to praise God, read David's list.

BIBLE READING: Ephesians 2:1-10

KEY BIBLE VERSE: *God saved you by his special favor when you believed. And you can't take credit for this; it is a gift from God. Salvation is not a reward for the good things we have done, so none of us can boast about it.* (Ephesians 2:8-9)

Praise is thanking God for our salvation. When someone gives you a gift, do you say, "That's very nice—now how much do I owe you?" No, the appropriate response to a gift is "Thank you." Yet how often Christians, even after they have been given the gift of salvation, feel obligated to try to work their way to God. Because our salvation and even our faith are gifts, we should respond with gratitude, praise, and joy.

BIBLE READING: Hebrews 13:1-25

KEY BIBLE VERSE: *With Jesus' help, let us continually offer our sacrifice of praise to God by proclaiming the glory of his name.* (Hebrews 13:15)

Praise is a spiritual offering. These Jewish Christians, because of their witness that Jesus was the Messiah, no longer worshiped with other Jews. So praise and acts of service became their sacrifices—ones they could offer anywhere, anytime. This must have reminded them of the prophet Hosea's words, "Forgive all our sins and graciously receive us, so that we may offer you the sacrifice of praise" (Hosea 14:2). A "sacrifice of praise" today would include thanking Christ for his sacrifice on the cross and telling others about it. Acts of kindness and sharing are particularly pleasing to God, even when they go unnoticed by others.

Related Topics: PRAYER, THANKFULNESS, WORSHIP

PRAYER (*Asking, Communicating, Meditating*)

▶ **THE MYSTERY OF PRAYER**
What is prayer?

BIBLE READING: Genesis 18:16-33

KEY BIBLE VERSE: *The two other men went on toward Sodom, but the LORD remained with Abraham for a while. Abraham approached him and said, "Will you destroy both innocent and guilty alike? Suppose you find fifty innocent people there within the city—will you still destroy it, and not spare it for their sakes?"* (Genesis 18:22-24)

Prayer is an opportunity to bring our will into line with God's plan. Did Abraham change God's mind? Of course not. The more likely answer is that God changed Abraham's mind. Abraham knew that God is just and that he punishes sin, but he may have wondered about God's mercy. Abraham seemed to be probing God's mind to see how merciful he really was. He left his conversation with God convinced that God was both kind and fair. Our prayers won't change God's mind, but they may change ours just as Abraham's prayer changed his. Prayer helps us better understand the mind of God.

Prayer is an opportunity to demonstrate our trust in God. Why did God let Abraham question his justice and intercede for a wicked city? Abraham knew that God must punish sin, but he also knew from experience that God is merciful to sinners. God knew there were not ten righteous people in the city, but he was merciful enough to allow Abraham to intercede. He was also merciful enough to help Lot, Abraham's nephew, get out of Sodom before it was destroyed. God does not take pleasure in destroying the wicked, but he must punish sin. He is both just and merciful. We should be thankful that God's mercy extends to us.

BIBLE READING: Psalm 4:1-8

KEY BIBLE VERSE: *You can be sure of this: The LORD has set apart the godly for himself. The LORD will answer when I call to him.* (Psalm 4:3)

Prayer is speaking with God. The godly are those who are faithful and devoted to God. David knew that God would hear him when he called and would answer him. We too can be confident that God listens to our prayers and answers when we call on him. Sometimes we think that God will not hear us because we have fallen short of his high standards for holy living. But if we have trusted Christ for salvation, God has forgiven us, and he will listen to us. When you feel as though your prayers are bouncing off the ceiling, remember that as a believer, you have been set apart by God—and he loves you. He hears and answers, although his answers may not be what you expect. Look at your problems in the light of God's power instead of looking at God in the shadow of your problems.

BIBLE READING: Hebrews 4:14-16

KEY BIBLE VERSE: *So let us come boldly to the throne of our gracious God. There we will receive his mercy, and we will find grace to help us when we need it.* (Hebrews 4:16)

Prayer is an awesome privilege. Prayer is our approach to God, and we are to come boldly. Some Christians approach God meekly with heads hung low, afraid to ask him to meet their needs. Others pray flippantly, giving little thought to what they say. Come with reverence because he is your King. But also come with bold assurance because he is your Friend and Counselor.

▶ MOTIVES FOR PRAYER
Why should we pray?

BIBLE READING: Genesis 25:19-34

KEY BIBLE VERSE: *Isaac pleaded with the LORD to give Rebekah a child because she was childless. So the LORD answered Isaac's prayer, and his wife became pregnant with twins.* (Genesis 25:21)

Prayer reflects our dependence on God. As Isaac pleaded with God for children, so the Bible encourages us to ask—and even plead—for our most personal and important requests. God wants to grant our requests, but he wants us to ask him. Even then, as Isaac learned, God may decide to withhold his answer for a while in order to (1) deepen our insight into what we really need, (2) broaden our appreciation for his answers, or (3) allow us to mature so we can use his gifts more wisely.

BIBLE READING: Exodus 17:1-7

KEY BIBLE VERSE: *Tormented by thirst, they continued to complain, "Why did you ever take us out of Egypt? Why did you bring us here? We, our children, and our livestock will all die!"* (Exodus 17:3)

Prayer is far better than complaining to each other. Again the people of Israel complained about their problem instead of praying. They had followed God's leading into the desert, but now were doubting his ability to take care of them. Some problems can be solved by careful thought or by rearranging our priorities.

Some can be solved by discussion and good counsel. But some problems can be solved only by prayer. We should make a determined effort to pray when we feel like complaining, because complaining only raises our level of stress. Prayer quiets our thoughts and emotions and prepares us to listen.

BIBLE READING: Judges 16:23-31

KEY BIBLE VERSE: *Samson prayed to the LORD, "Sovereign LORD, remember me again. O God, please strengthen me one more time so that I may pay back the Philistines for the loss of my eyes."* (Judges 16:28)

Prayer can restore relationship with God. In spite of Samson's past, God still answered his prayer and destroyed the pagan temple and worshipers. God still loved him. He was willing to hear Samson's prayer of confession and repentance and use him this final time. One of the effects of sin in our life is to keep us from feeling like praying. But perfect moral behavior is not a condition for prayer. Don't let guilt feelings over sin keep you from your only means of restoration. No matter how long you have been away from God, he is ready to hear from you and restore you to a right relationship. Every situation can be salvaged if you are willing to turn again to him. If God could still work in Samson's situation, he can certainly make something worthwhile out of yours.

▶ **METHODS OF PRAYER**
How should we pray?

BIBLE READING: Ezra 8:1-36

KEY BIBLE VERSE: *There by the Ahava Canal, I gave orders for all of us to fast and humble ourselves before our God. We prayed that he would give us a safe journey and protect us, our children, and our goods as we traveled.* (Ezra 8:21)

We should pray with an attitude of deep respect for God. Ezra knew God's promises to protect his people, but he didn't take them for granted. He also knew that God's blessings are appropriated through prayer; so Ezra and the people humbled themselves by fasting and praying. And their prayers were answered. Fasting humbled them because going without food was a reminder of their complete dependence on God. Fasting also gave them more time to pray and meditate on God.

Too often we pray glibly and superficially. Serious prayer, by contrast, requires concentration. It puts us in touch with God's will and can really change us. Without serious prayer, we reduce God to a quick-service pharmacist with painkillers for our every ailment.

BIBLE READING: Nehemiah 2:1-10

KEY BIBLE VERSE: *The king asked, "Well, how can I help you?" With a prayer to the God of heaven, I replied, "If it please Your Majesty and if you are pleased with me, your servant, send me to Judah to rebuild the city where my ancestors are buried."* (Nehemiah 2:4-5)

We should pray with confidence in God's grace. With little time to think, Nehemiah immediately prayed. Eight times in this book we read that he prayed spontaneously (2:4; 4:4-5, 9; 5:19; 6:14; 13:14, 22, 29). Nehemiah prayed at any time, even while talking with others. He knew that God is always in charge, is always present, and hears and answers every prayer. Nehemiah could confidently pray throughout the day because he had established an intimate relationship with God during times of extended prayer (1:4-7). If we want to reach God with our emergency prayers, we need to take time to cultivate a strong relationship with God through times of in-depth prayer.

BIBLE READING: Matthew 6:5-15

KEY BIBLE VERSE: *When you pray, don't babble on and on as people of other religions do. They think their prayers are answered only by repeating their words again and again. Don't be like them, because your Father knows exactly what you need even before you ask him!* (Matthew 6:7-8)

We should pray with humility and sincerity. Some people, especially the religious leaders, wanted to be seen as "holy," and public prayer was one way to get attention. Jesus saw through their self-righteous acts, however, and taught that the essence of prayer is not public style, but private communication with God. There is a place for public prayer, but to pray only where others will notice you indicates that your real audience is not God.

BIBLE READING: Colossians 1:1-14

KEY BIBLE VERSE: *We always pray for you, and we give thanks to God the Father of our Lord Jesus Christ, for we have heard that you trust in Christ Jesus and that you love all of God's people.* (Colossians 1:3-4)

We should pray for others. Sometimes we wonder how to pray for missionaries and other leaders we have never met. Paul had never met the Colossians, but he faithfully prayed for them. His prayers teach us how to pray for others, whether we know them or not. We can request that they (1) understand God's will, (2) gain spiritual wisdom, (3) please and honor God, (4) bear good fruit, (5) grow in the knowledge of God, (6) be filled with God's strength, (7) have great endurance and patience, (8) stay full of Christ's joy, and (9) give thanks always. All believers have these same basic needs. When you don't know how to pray for someone, use Paul's prayer pattern for the Colossians.

▶ MODEL PRAYERS
What are the characteristics of prayers in the Bible?

BIBLE READING: Joshua 7:1-26

KEY BIBLE VERSE: *Joshua and the leaders of Israel tore their clothing in dismay, threw dust on their heads, and bowed down facing the Ark of the LORD until evening.* (Joshua 7:6)

Biblical prayers are marked by humility. Joshua and the elders tore their clothing and sprinkled dust on their heads as signs of deep mourning before God. They were confused by their defeat at the small city of Ai after the spectacular Jericho victory, so they went before God in deep humility and sorrow to receive his instructions. When our life falls apart, we also should turn to God for direction and help. Like Joshua and the elders, we should humble ourself so that we will be able to hear his words.

Biblical prayers are marked by honesty. Imagine praying this way to God. This is not a formal church prayer; it is the prayer of a man who is afraid and confused by what is happening around him. Joshua poured out his real thoughts to God. Hiding your needs from God is ignoring the only one who can really help. God welcomes your honest prayers and wants you to express your true feelings to him. Any believer can become more honest in prayer by remembering that God is all-knowing and all-powerful and that his love is everlasting.

BIBLE READING: 2 Chronicles 6:1-42

KEY BIBLE VERSE: *He prayed, "O LORD, God of Israel, there is no God like you in all of heaven and earth. You keep your promises and show unfailing love to all who obey you and are eager to do your will."* (2 Chronicles 6:14)

Biblical prayers are wide-ranging and specific. As Solomon led the people in prayer, he asked God to hear their prayers concerning a variety of situations: (1) crime (6:22-23); (2) enemy attacks (6:24-25); (3) drought (6:26-27); (4) famine (6:28-31); (5) the influx of foreigners (6:32-33); (6) war (6:34-35); (7) sin (6:36-39). God is concerned with whatever we face, even the difficult consequences we bring upon ourself. He wants us to turn to him in prayer. When you pray, remember that God hears you. Don't let the extremity of your situation cause you to doubt his care for you.

BIBLE READING: Matthew 6:5-15

KEY BIBLE VERSE: *Pray like this: Our Father in heaven, may your name be honored. May your Kingdom come soon. May your will be done here on earth, just as it is in heaven. Give us our food for today, and forgive us our sins, just as we have forgiven those who have sinned against us. And don't let us yield to temptation, but deliver us from the evil one.* (Matthew 6:9-13)

Biblical prayer is personal. The phrase "Our Father in heaven" indicates that God is not only majestic and holy, but also personal and loving. The first line of this model prayer is a statement of praise and a commitment to honor God's holy name. We can honor God's name by being careful to use it respectfully. If we use God's name lightly, we aren't remembering God's holiness.

Biblical prayer recognizes God's position. The phrase "May your Kingdom come soon" is a reference to God's spiritual reign, not Israel's freedom from Rome. God's kingdom was announced in the covenant with Abraham (8:11; Luke 13:28), is present as Christ reigns in the believer's heart (Luke 17:21), and will be complete when all evil is destroyed and God establishes the new heaven and earth (Revelation 21:1).

Biblical prayer recognizes our position. When we pray "May your will be done," we are not resigning ourself to fate, but praying that God's perfect purpose will be accomplished in this world as well as in the next.

Biblical prayer demonstrates complete dependence. When we pray, "Give us our food for today," we are acknowledging that God is our Sustainer and Provider. It is a misconception to think that we provide for our own needs. We must trust God *daily* to provide what he knows we need.

Biblical prayer asks God for guidance. God doesn't lead us into temptations, but sometimes he allows us to be tested by them. As disciples, we should pray to be delivered from these trying times and from Satan ("the evil one") and his deceit. All Christians struggle with temptation. Sometimes it is so subtle that we don't even realize what is happening to us. God has promised that he won't allow us to be tempted beyond what we can bear (1 Corinthians 10:13). Ask God to help you recognize temptation and to give you strength to overcome it and choose God's way instead.

BIBLE READING: John 17:1-26

KEY BIBLE VERSE: *I am praying not only for these disciples but also for all who will ever believe in me because of their testimony. My prayer for all of them is that they will be one, just as you and I are one, Father—that just as you are in me and I am in you, so they will be in us, and the world will believe you sent me.* (John 17:20-21)

Biblical prayer recognizes the spiritual warfare around us. This entire chapter is Jesus' prayer. From it, we learn that the world is a tremendous battleground where the forces under Satan's power and those under God's authority are at war. Satan and his forces are motivated by bitter hatred for Christ and his forces.

Jesus prayed for his disciples, including those of us who follow him today. He prayed that God would keep his chosen believers safe from Satan's power, setting them apart and making them pure and holy, uniting them through his truth.

Biblical prayer is not escape from the world. Jesus didn't ask God to take believers *out* of the world, but instead to use them *in* the world. Because Jesus sends us into the world, we should not try to escape from the world, nor should we avoid all relationships with non-Christians. We are called to be salt and light (Matthew 5:13-16), and we are to do the work that God sent us to do.

Biblical prayer binds us with other believers. Jesus prayed for all who would follow him, including you and others you know. He prayed for unity (17:11), protection from the evil one (17:15), and sanctity (holiness) (17:17). Knowing that Jesus prayed for us should give us confidence as we work for his kingdom.

Related Topics: CONFESSION, PRAISE, THANKFULNESS

PREACHING (*see* GOSPEL)

PREJUDICE (*Discrimination, Injustice, Intolerance*)

What is characteristic of prejudice?

BIBLE READING: Esther 3:1-15

KEY BIBLE VERSE: *When Haman saw that Mordecai would not bow down or show him respect, he was filled with rage. So he decided it was not enough to lay hands on Mordecai alone. Since he had learned that Mordecai was a Jew, he decided to destroy all the Jews throughout the entire empire of Xerxes.* (Esther 3:5-6)

Prejudice is marked by self-centered pride. Haman enjoyed the power and prestige of his position, and he was enraged when Mordecai did not respond with the expected reverential bow. Haman's anger was not directed just toward Mordecai, but toward what Mordecai stood for—the Jews' dedication to God as the only authority worthy of reverence. Haman's attitude was prejudiced: he hated a group of people because of a difference in belief or culture. Prejudice grows out of personal pride—considering oneself better than others. In the end, Haman was punished for his arrogant attitude (7:9-10). God will harshly judge those who are prejudiced or whose pride causes them to look down on others.

BIBLE READING: Mark 6:1-13

KEY BIBLE VERSE: *Then Jesus told them, "A prophet is honored everywhere except in his own hometown and among his relatives and his own family."* (Mark 6:4)

Prejudice is marked by blindness to the truth. Jesus was teaching effectively and wisely, but the people of his hometown saw him as only a common laborer. "He's no better than we are—he's just a carpenter," they said. They were offended that others could be impressed by Jesus and follow him. They rejected his authority because he was one of their peers. They thought they knew him, but their preconceived notions about who he was made it impossible for them to accept his message. Don't let prejudice blind you to truth. As you learn more about Jesus, try to see him as he really is.

BIBLE READING: Luke 10:25-37

KEY BIBLE VERSE: *"Now which of these three would you say was a neighbor to the man who was attacked by bandits?" Jesus asked. The man replied, "The one who showed him mercy." Then Jesus said, "Yes, now go and do the same."* (Luke 10:36-37)

Prejudice is marked by a lack of real love. There was deep hatred between Jews and Samaritans. The Jews saw themselves as pure descendants of Abraham, while the Samaritans were a mixed race produced when Jews from the northern kingdom intermarried with other peoples after Israel's exile. To this law expert, the person least likely to act correctly would be the Samaritan. In fact, he could not bear to say "Samaritan" in answer to Jesus' question. This "expert's" attitude betrayed his lack of the very thing that he had earlier said the law commanded—love.

Related Topics: FAIRNESS, LOVE, UNITY

PREMARITAL SEX (*see* MARRIAGE, SEX)

PREPARATION *(Anticipation, Design, Planning)*

In what ways is spiritual preparation important?

BIBLE READING: Exodus 12:1-30

KEY BIBLE VERSE: *Wear your traveling clothes as you eat this meal, as though prepared for a long journey. Wear your sandals, and carry your walking sticks in your hands. Eat the food quickly, for this is the LORD's Passover.* (Exodus 12:11)

Spiritual preparation is an act of faith. Eating the Passover Feast while dressed for travel was a sign of the Hebrews' faith. Although they were not yet free, they were to prepare themselves, for God had said he would lead them out of Egypt. Their preparation was an act of faith. Being prepared for the fulfillment of God's promises, however unlikely it may seem, demonstrates our faith.

BIBLE READING: Numbers 28:1-8

KEY BIBLE VERSE: *The LORD said to Moses, "Give these instructions to the people of Israel: The offerings you present to me by fire on the altar are my food, and they are very pleasing to me. See to it that they are brought at the appointed times and offered according to my instructions."* (Numbers 28:1-2)

Spiritual preparation is part of wholehearted obedience. Offerings had to be brought regularly and presented according to prescribed rituals under the priests' supervision. Following these rituals took time, and this gave the people the opportunity to prepare their heart for worship. Unless our heart is ready, worship is meaningless. In contrast, God is delighted, and we get more from it, when our heart is prepared to come before him in a spirit of thankfulness.

BIBLE READING: Ezra 8:15-36

KEY BIBLE VERSE: *There by the Ahava Canal, I gave orders for all of us to fast and humble ourselves before our God. We prayed that he would give us a safe journey and protect us, our children, and our goods as we traveled.* (Ezra 8:21)

Spiritual preparation reminds us of our dependence on God. Before making all the physical preparations for the journey, Ezra made spiritual preparations.

Their prayers and fasting prepared them spiritually by showing their dependence on God for protection, faith that God was in control, and affirmation that
they were not strong enough to make the trip without him. When we take time
to put God first in any endeavor, we are preparing well for whatever lies ahead.

BIBLE READING: Matthew 24:1-51
KEY BIBLE VERSE: *Be prepared, because you don't know what day your Lord is coming.* (Matthew 24:42)

Spiritual preparation is commanded by God. Jesus' purpose in telling about his
return is not to stimulate predictions and calculations about the date, but to
warn us to be prepared. Will you be ready? The only safe choice is to obey him
today (24:46).

Spiritual preparation is active. Jesus asks us to spend the time of waiting taking
care of his people and doing his work here on earth, both within the church
and outside it. This is the best way to prepare for Christ's return.

Spiritual preparation is focused on Christ's coming. Knowing that Christ's return
will be sudden and unexpected should motivate us always to be prepared. We are
not to live irresponsibly—sitting and waiting, doing nothing; seeking self-serving
pleasure; using his tarrying as an excuse not to do God's work of building his
kingdom; developing a false security based on precise calculations of events; or
letting our curiosity about the end times divert us from doing God's work.

BIBLE READING: 1 Peter 3:8-22
KEY BIBLE VERSE: *You must worship Christ as Lord of your life. And if you are asked
about your Christian hope, always be ready to explain it.* (1 Peter 3:15)

Spiritual preparation is necessary for sharing our faith. Some Christians believe
that faith is a personal matter that should be kept to oneself. It is true that we
shouldn't be boisterous or obnoxious in sharing our faith, but we should always
be ready to give an answer, gently and respectfully, when asked about our faith,
our lifestyle, or our Christian perspective. Can others see your hope in Christ?
Are you prepared to tell them what Christ has done in your life?

Related Topics: FAITH, PLANS, WAITING

PRESENCE *(Awareness, Being, Closeness)*

How can we know God's presence?

BIBLE READING: Psalm 27:1-14
KEY BIBLE VERSE: *The one thing I ask of the LORD—the thing I seek most—is to
live in the house of the LORD all the days of my life, delighting in the LORD's
perfections and meditating in his Temple.* (Psalm 27:4)

God's presence is experienced by those who truly desire it. By the "house of the
Lord" and "his Temple," David could be referring to the tabernacle in Gibeon—
the temporary sanctuary he had put up to house the ark of the covenant—or to
the temple that his son Solomon was to build. David probably had the temple
in mind because he made many of the plans for it (1 Chronicles 22). But David
may also have used the word *temple* to mean "the presence of the Lord." His
greatest desire was to live in God's presence each day of his life. Sadly, this is not
the greatest desire of many who claim to be believers. But those who desire to
live in God's presence each day will be able to enjoy that relationship forever.

BIBLE READING: Psalm 34:1-22
KEY BIBLE VERSE: *The LORD is close to the brokenhearted; he rescues those who are crushed in spirit. The righteous face many troubles, but the LORD rescues them from each and every one.* (Psalm 34:18-19)

God's presence is often experienced in difficult times. We often wish we could escape troubles—the pain of grief, loss, sorrow, and failure; or even the small daily frustrations that constantly wear us down. God promises to be "close to the brokenhearted," to be our source of power, courage, and wisdom, and to help us through our problems. Sometimes he chooses to deliver us from those problems. When trouble strikes, don't get frustrated with God. Instead, admit that you need God's help and thank him for being by your side.

BIBLE READING: Psalm 140:1-13
KEY BIBLE VERSE: *I know the LORD will surely help those they persecute; he will maintain the rights of the poor. Surely the godly are praising your name, for they will live in your presence.* (Psalm 140:12-13)

God's presence is known in times of persecution. To whom can the poor turn when they are persecuted? They lack the money to get professional help; they may be unable to defend themselves. But there is always someone on their side—the Lord will stand by them and ultimately bring about justice. This should be a comfort for us all. No matter what our situation may be, the Lord is with us. But this truth should also call us to responsibility. As God's people, we are required to defend the rights of the powerless.

Related Topics: FAITH, GOD, PROTECTION

PRESSURE *(Convince, Demand, Influence)*

How can we resist the pressure to do what is wrong?

BIBLE READING: Genesis 25:19-34
KEY BIBLE VERSE: *Jacob replied, "All right, but trade me your birthright for it." "Look, I'm dying of starvation!" said Esau. "What good is my birthright to me now?"* (Genesis 25:31-32)

Consider the long-term consequences of our behavior. Esau traded the lasting benefits of his birthright for the immediate pleasure of food. He acted on impulse, satisfying his immediate desires without pausing to consider the long-range consequences of what he was about to do. We can fall into the same trap. When we see something we want, our first impulse is to get it. At first we feel intensely satisfied and sometimes even powerful because we have obtained what we set out to get. But immediate pleasure often loses sight of the future. We can avoid making Esau's mistake by comparing the short-term satisfaction with its long-range consequences before we act.

BIBLE READING: Genesis 39:1-23
KEY BIBLE VERSE: *She kept putting pressure on him day after day, but he refused to sleep with her, and he kept out of her way as much as possible.* (Genesis 39:10)

Refuse to rationalize. Potiphar's wife failed to seduce Joseph, who resisted this temptation by saying it would be a sin against God. Joseph didn't say, "I'd be hurting you," or "I'd be sinning against Potiphar," or "I'd be sinning against myself." Under pressure, such excuses are easily rationalized away. Remember that sexual sin is not just between two consenting adults. It is an act of disobedience against God.

Run when necessary. Joseph avoided Potiphar's wife as much as possible. He refused her advances and finally *ran* from her. Sometimes merely trying to avoid temptation is not enough. We must turn and run, especially when the temptations seem very strong, as is often the case in sexual temptations.

BIBLE READING: Matthew 14:1-12
KEY BIBLE VERSE: *The king was sorry, but because of his oath and because he didn't want to back down in front of his guests, he issued the necessary orders.* (Matthew 14:9)

Be willing to experience embarrassment. Herod did not want to kill John the Baptist, but he gave the order so that he wouldn't be embarrassed in front of his guests. How easy it is to give in to the crowd and to let ourself be pressured into doing wrong. Don't get in a situation where it will be too embarrassing to do what is right. Determine to do what is right, no matter how embarrassing or painful it may be.

BIBLE READING: Mark 14:32-42
KEY BIBLE VERSE: *Keep alert and pray. Otherwise temptation will overpower you. For though the spirit is willing enough, the body is weak.* (Mark 14:38)

Seek God's help. In times of great stress, we are vulnerable to temptation, even if we have a willing spirit. Jesus gave us an example of what to do to resist: (1) pray to God (14:35); (2) seek support of friends and loved ones (14:33, 37, 40-41); (3) focus on the purpose God has given us (14:36).

Related Topics: GUIDANCE, PRAYER, TEMPTATION

PRIDE *(Arrogance, Conceit, Vanity)*

How can pride destroy our life?

BIBLE READING: Psalm 10:1-18
KEY BIBLE VERSE: *The wicked say to themselves, "God isn't watching! He will never notice!"* (Psalm 10:11)

Pride lures us into living independently of God. There is an incompatibility between blind arrogance and the presence of God in our heart. The proud person depends on himself or herself rather than on God. This causes God's guiding influences to leave his or her life. When God's presence is welcome, there is no room for pride, because he makes us aware of our true self.

BIBLE READING: Mark 6:1-13
KEY BIBLE VERSE: *Because of their unbelief, he couldn't do any mighty miracles among them except to place his hands on a few sick people and heal them.* (Mark 6:5)

Pride undermines our faith. Jesus could have done greater miracles in Nazareth, but he chose not to because of the people's pride and unbelief. The miracles he did had little effect on the people because they did not accept his message or believe that he was from God. Therefore, Jesus looked elsewhere, seeking those who would respond to his miracles and message.

BIBLE READING: Luke 18:9-14

KEY BIBLE VERSE: *I tell you, this sinner, not the Pharisee, returned home justified before God. For the proud will be humbled, but the humble will be honored.* (Luke 18:14)

Pride can cut us off from God and others. The Pharisee in Jesus' parable did not go to the temple to pray to God but to announce to all within earshot how good he was. The tax collector went recognizing his sin and begging for mercy. Self-righteousness is dangerous. It leads to pride, causes a person to despise others, and prevents him or her from learning anything from God. The tax collector's prayer should be our prayer because we all need God's mercy every day. Don't let pride in your achievements cut you off from God.

BIBLE READING: Ephesians 2:11-22

KEY BIBLE VERSE: *Christ himself has made peace between us Jews and you Gentiles by making us all one people. He has broken down the wall of hostility that used to separate us.* (Ephesians 2:14)

Pride distorts our view of ourself and others. Jews and Gentiles alike could be guilty of spiritual pride—Jews for thinking their faith and traditions elevated them above everyone else, Gentiles for trusting in their achievements, power, or position. Spiritual pride blinds us to our own faults and magnifies the faults of others. Be careful not to become proud of your salvation. Instead, humbly thank God for what he has done, and encourage others who might be struggling in their faith.

Related Topics: HUMILITY, SELF-RIGHTEOUSNESS, SIN

PRIORITIES *(Goals, Objectives, Purposes)*

How can we develop the right priorities?

BIBLE READING: Proverbs 3:1-35

KEY BIBLE VERSE: *Trust in the LORD with all your heart; do not depend on your own understanding. Seek his will in all you do, and he will direct your paths.* (Proverbs 3:5-6)

Right priorities begin with God. To receive God's guidance, said Solomon, we must acknowledge God in all our ways. This means turning every area of life over to him. About a thousand years later, Jesus emphasized this same truth (Matthew 6:33). Look at your values and priorities. What is important to you? In what areas have you not acknowledged him? What is his advice? In many areas of your life you may already acknowledge God, but it is the areas where you attempt to restrict or ignore his influence that will cause you grief. Make him a vital part of everything you do; then he will guide you because you will be working to accomplish his purposes.

BIBLE READING: Matthew 6:25-34

KEY BIBLE VERSE: *He will give you all you need from day to day if you live for him and make the Kingdom of God your primary concern.* (Matthew 6:33)

Right priorities grow out of consistent dependence on God. To "make the Kingdom of God your primary concern" means to turn to God first for help, to fill your thoughts with his desires, to take his character for your pattern, and to serve and obey him in everything. What is really important to you? People, objects, goals, and other desires all compete for priority. Any of these can quickly bump God out of first place if you don't actively choose to give him first place in *every* area of your life.

BIBLE READING: Matthew 8:18-22
KEY BIBLE VERSE: *Jesus told him, "Follow me now! Let those who are spiritually dead care for their own dead."* (Matthew 8:22)

Right priorities grow out of obedience to Christ. Jesus was always direct with those who wanted to follow him. He made sure they counted the cost and set aside any conditions they might have for following him. As God's Son, Jesus did not hesitate to demand complete loyalty. Even family loyalty was not to take priority over the demands of obedience. His direct challenge forces us to ask ourself about our own priorities in following him. The decision to follow Jesus should not be put off, even though other loyalties compete for our attention. Nothing should be placed above a total commitment to living for him.

Related Topics: CONSISTENCY, GOALS, OBEDIENCE

PRIVILEGE(S) *(Chances, Consideration, Opportunities)*

What privileges does God offer us?

BIBLE READING: Romans 1:1-7
KEY BIBLE VERSE: *Through Christ, God has given us the privilege and authority to tell Gentiles everywhere what God has done for them, so that they will believe and obey him, bringing glory to his name.* (Romans 1:5)

God offers us forgiveness. Christians have both privilege and great responsibility. Paul and the apostles received forgiveness as an undeserved privilege. But they also received the responsibility to share the message of God's forgiveness with others. God also graciously forgives our sins when we believe in him as Lord. In doing this, we are committing ourself to begin a new life. Paul's new life also involved a God-given responsibility—to witness about God's Good News to the world. God may or may not call you to be an overseas missionary, but he does call you (and all believers) to witness to and be an example of the changed life that Jesus Christ has begun in you.

BIBLE READING: Ephesians 3:1-13
KEY BIBLE VERSE: *Because of Christ and our faith in him, we can now come fearlessly into God's presence, assured of his glad welcome.* (Ephesians 3:12)

God offers us an intimate relationship with himself. It is an awesome privilege to be able to approach God with freedom and confidence. Most of us would be apprehensive in the presence of a powerful ruler. But thanks to Christ, by faith we can enter directly into God's presence through prayer. We know we'll be welcomed with open arms because we are God's children through our union with Christ. Don't be afraid of God. Talk with him about everything. He is waiting to hear from you.

BIBLE READING: Hebrews 10:19-39
KEY BIBLE VERSE: *Without wavering, let us hold tightly to the hope we say we have, for God can be trusted to keep his promise.* (Hebrews 10:23)

God offers us new life in Christ. We have significant privileges associated with our new life in Christ: (1) we have personal access to God through Christ and can draw near to him without an elaborate system (10:22); (2) we can grow in faith, overcome doubts and questions, and deepen our relationship with God (10:23); (3) we can pass on to others the news of what Christ has done; (4) we can enjoy encouragement from one another (10:24); (5) we can worship together (10:25).

Related Topics: GOD, GRACE, SALVATION

PROBLEMS *(Adversity, Difficulties, Obstacles)*

▶ **USEFUL PROBLEMS**
What good can come out of problems?

 BIBLE READING: Genesis 12:10-20
KEY BIBLE VERSE: *At that time there was a severe famine in the land, so Abram went down to Egypt to wait it out.* (Genesis 12:10)

Problems test our faith. When famine struck, Abram went to Egypt where there was food. Why would there be a famine in the land where God had just called Abram? This was a test of Abram's faith, and Abram passed. He didn't question God's leading when facing this difficulty. Many believers find that when they determine to follow God, they immediately encounter great obstacles. The next time you face such a test, don't try to second-guess what God is doing. Use the intelligence God gave you, as Abram did when he temporarily moved to Egypt, and wait for new opportunities.

BIBLE READING: Philippians 1:12-30
KEY BIBLE VERSE: *I want you to know, dear brothers and sisters, that everything that has happened to me here has helped to spread the Good News.* (Philippians 1:12)

Problems open up opportunities for service. Being imprisoned would cause many people to become bitter or to give up, but Paul saw it as one more opportunity to spread the Good News of Christ. Paul realized that his current circumstances weren't as important as what he did with them. Turning a bad situation into a good one, he reached out to the Roman soldiers who made up the palace guard and encouraged those Christians who were afraid of persecution. We may not be in prison, but we still have plenty of opportunities to be discouraged—times of indecision, financial burdens, family conflict, church conflict, or the loss of our jobs. How we act in such situations will reflect what we believe. Like Paul, look for ways to demonstrate your faith even in bad situations. Whether or not the situation improves, your faith will grow stronger.

BIBLE READING: 2 Thessalonians 1:1-12
KEY BIBLE VERSE: *God will use this persecution to show his justice. For he will make you worthy of his Kingdom, for which you are suffering.* (2 Thessalonians 1:5)

Problems may be confirmation that we are living for Christ. As we live for Christ, we will experience troubles because we are trying to be God's people in a perverse world. Some people say that troubles are the result of sin or lack of faith, but Paul teaches that they may be a part of God's plan for believers. Our problems can help us look upward and forward, instead of inward (Mark 13:35-36; Philippians 3:13-14); they can build strong character (Romans 5:3-4); and they can provide us with opportunities to comfort others who also are struggling (2 Corinthians 1:3-5). Your troubles may be an indication that you are taking a stand for Christ.

▶ **USELESS PROBLEMS**
What kinds of mistakes do we commonly make in handling problems?

BIBLE READING: Genesis 16:1-16
KEY BIBLE VERSE: *Sarai, Abram's wife, had no children. So Sarai took her servant, an Egyptian woman named Hagar, and gave her to Abram so she could bear his children. "The LORD has kept me from having any children," Sarai said to Abram. "Go and sleep with my servant. Perhaps I can have children through her." And Abram agreed. So Sarai, Abram's wife, took Hagar the Egyptian servant and gave her to Abram as a wife. (This happened ten years after Abram first arrived in the land of Canaan.)* (Genesis 16:1-3)

We fail to wait patiently for God's solution. Sarai took matters into her own hands by giving Hagar to Abram. Like Abram, she had trouble believing God's promise that was directed specifically toward Abram and Sarai. Out of this lack of faith came a series of problems. This invariably happens when we take over for God, trying to make his promise come true through efforts that are not in line with his specific directions. In this case, time was the greatest test of Abram and Sarai's willingness to let God work in their lives. Sometimes we too must simply wait. When we ask God for something and have to wait, it is a temptation to take matters into our own hands and interfere with God's plans.

We blame others when our solutions fail. Although Sarai arranged for Hagar to have a child by Abram, she later blamed Abram for the results. It is often easier to strike out in frustration and accuse someone else rather than admit an error and ask forgiveness. (Adam and Eve did the same thing in Genesis 3:12-13.)

We run from problems we should face. Hagar was running away from her mistress and her problem. The angel of the Lord gave her this advice: (1) to return and face Sarai, the cause of her problem, and (2) to submit to her. Hagar needed to work on her attitude toward Sarai, no matter how justified it may have been. Running away from our problems rarely solves them. It is wise to return to our problems, face them squarely, accept God's promise of help, correct our attitudes, and act as we should.

BIBLE READING: Job 2:1-10
KEY BIBLE VERSE: *Job replied, "You talk like a godless woman. Should we accept only good things from the hand of God and never anything bad?" So in all this, Job said nothing wrong.* (Job 2:10)

We question God's purposes in our life. Many people think that believing in God protects them from trouble, so when calamity comes, they question God's goodness and justice. But the message of Job is that you should not give up on God because he allows you to have bad experiences. Faith in God does not guarantee personal prosperity, and lack of faith does not guarantee troubles in this life. If this were so, people would believe in God simply to get rich. God is capable of rescuing us from suffering, but he may also allow suffering to come for reasons we cannot understand. It is Satan's strategy to get us to doubt God at exactly this moment. Here Job shows a perspective broader than seeking his own personal comfort. If we always knew why we were suffering, our faith would have no room to grow.

▶ **PROBLEM SOLVING**
How does God want us to respond to problems?

BIBLE READING: James 1:1-18

KEY BIBLE VERSE: *Dear brothers and sisters, whenever trouble comes your way, let it be an opportunity for joy. For when your faith is tested, your endurance has a chance to grow. So let it grow, for when your endurance is fully developed, you will be strong in character and ready for anything.* (James 1:2-4)

Realize that problems are inevitable. James doesn't say *if* you face trials, but *whenever* you face them. He assumes that we will have trials and that it is possible to profit from them. The point is not to pretend to be happy when we face pain, but to have a positive outlook ("let it be an opportunity for joy") because of what trials can produce in our life. James tells us to turn our hardships into times of learning. Tough times can teach us perseverance. For other passages dealing with perseverance (also called patience and steadfastness), see Romans 2:7; 5:3-5; 8:24-25; 2 Corinthians 6:3-7; and 2 Peter 1:3-9.

Expect to grow as a result of problems. We can't really know the depth of our character until we see how we react under pressure. It is easy to be kind to others when everything is going well, but can we still be kind when others are treating us unfairly? God wants to make us mature and complete, not to keep us from all pain. Instead of complaining about our struggles, we should see them as opportunities for growth. Thank God for promising to be with you in rough times. Ask him to help you solve your problems or to give you the strength to endure them. Then be patient. God will not leave you alone with your problems; he will stay close and help you grow.

BIBLE READING: John 6:1-15

KEY BIBLE VERSE: *Jesus soon saw a great crowd of people climbing the hill, looking for him. Turning to Philip, he asked, "Philip, where can we buy bread to feed all these people?"* (John 6:5)

Trust God for the means to solve the problem. When Jesus asked Philip where they could buy a great amount of bread, Philip started assessing the probable cost. Jesus wanted to teach him that financial resources are not the most important ones. We can limit what God does in us by assuming what is and is not possible. Is there some impossible task that you believe God wants you to do? Don't let your estimate of what can't be done keep you from taking on the task. God can do the miraculous; trust him to provide the resources.

BIBLE READING: Romans 8:28-39

KEY BIBLE VERSE: *We know that God causes everything to work together for the good of those who love God and are called according to his purpose for them.* (Romans 8:28)

Trust in God's sovereign purposes for our life. God works in "everything"—not just isolated incidents—for our good. This does not mean that all that happens to us is good. Evil is prevalent in our fallen world, but God is able to turn every circumstance around for our long-range good. Note that God is not working to make us happy, but to fulfill his purpose. Note also that this promise is not for everybody. It can be claimed only by "those who love God and are called according to his purpose." Those who are "called" are those the Holy Spirit convinces and enables to receive Christ. Such people have a new perspective, a new mind-set on life. They trust in God, not life's treasures; they look for their security in heaven, not on earth; they learn to accept, not resent, pain and persecution—because God is with them.

Related Topics: BURDENS, SPIRITUAL GROWTH, SUFFERING

PROCRASTINATION *(Avoidance, Delay, Laziness)*

What can we learn from our tendency to procrastinate?

BIBLE READING: Joshua 18:1-10

KEY BIBLE VERSE: *Joshua asked them, "How long are you going to wait before taking possession of the remaining land the LORD, the God of your ancestors, has given to you?"* (Joshua 18:3)

Procrastination reveals deeper problems. Joshua asked why some of the tribes were putting off the job of possessing the land. Often we delay doing jobs that seem large, difficult, boring, or disagreeable. But to continue putting them off shows lack of discipline, poor stewardship of time, and in some cases disobedience to God. Jobs we don't enjoy require concentration, teamwork, twice as much time, lots of encouragement, and accountability. Remember this when you are tempted to procrastinate.

BIBLE READING: Proverbs 10:1-32

KEY BIBLE VERSE: *Lazy people are soon poor; hard workers get rich. A wise youth works hard all summer; a youth who sleeps away the hour of opportunity brings shame.* (Proverbs 10:4-5)

Procrastination is the cause of many of our failures. Every day has twenty-four hours filled with opportunities to grow, serve, and be productive. Yet it is so easy to waste time, letting life slip from our grasp. Refuse to be a lazy person, sleeping or frittering away the hours meant for productive work. See time as God's gift, and seize your opportunities to live diligently for him.

BIBLE READING: Proverbs 26:1-28

KEY BIBLE VERSE: *The lazy person is full of excuses, saying, "I can't go outside because there might be a lion on the road! Yes, I'm sure there's a lion out there!" As a door turns back and forth on its hinges, so the lazy person turns over in bed. Some people are so lazy that they won't lift a finger to feed themselves. Lazy people consider themselves smarter than seven wise counselors.* (Proverbs 26:13-16)

Procrastination leads to an unproductive lifestyle. If a person is not willing to work, he or she can find endless excuses to avoid it. But laziness is more dangerous than a prowling lion. The less you do, the less you want to do, and the more useless you become. To overcome laziness, take a few small steps toward change. Set a concrete, realistic goal. Figure out the steps needed to reach it, and follow those steps. Pray for strength and persistence. To keep your excuses from making you useless, stop making useless excuses.

Related Topics: GOALS, LAZINESS, PLANS

PRODUCTIVITY *(Growth, Products, Results)*

What does it mean to be spiritually productive?

BIBLE READING: Matthew 3:1-12

KEY BIBLE VERSE: *Even now the ax of God's judgment is poised, ready to sever your roots. Yes, every tree that does not produce good fruit will be chopped down and thrown into the fire.* (Matthew 3:10)

We will exhibit spiritual fruit in our life. Just as a fruit tree is expected to bear fruit, God's people should produce a crop of good deeds. God has no use for people who call themselves Christians but do nothing about it. Like many people in John's day who were God's people in name only, we are of no value if we are Christians in name only. If others can't see our faith in the way we treat them, we may not be God's people at all.

We will obey God's commands. God's message hasn't changed since the Old Testament—people will be judged for their unproductive lives. God calls us to be *active* in our obedience. John compared people who claim they believe God but don't live for God to unproductive trees that will be cut down. To be productive for God, we must obey his teachings, resist temptation, actively serve and help others, and share our faith. How productive are you for God?

BIBLE READING: John 15:1-17

KEY BIBLE VERSE: *I am the true vine, and my Father is the gardener. He cuts off every branch that doesn't produce fruit, and he prunes the branches that do bear fruit so they will produce even more.* (John 15:1-2)

We will be growing in our relationship to Christ. Christ is the vine, and God is the gardener who cares for the branches to make them fruitful. The branches are all those who claim to be followers of Christ. The fruitful branches are true believers who by their living union with Christ produce much fruit. But those who become unproductive—those who turn back from following Christ after making a superficial commitment—will be separated from the vine. Unproductive followers are as good as dead and will be cut off and tossed aside.

Related Topics: ACHIEVEMENTS, PROGRESS, SPIRITUAL GROWTH

PROGRESS (*Achievement, Growth, Improvement*)

What do we need to understand about making spiritual progress?

BIBLE READING: Genesis 19:1-29

KEY BIBLE VERSE: *Lot's wife looked back as she was following along behind him, and she became a pillar of salt.* (Genesis 19:26)

Spiritual progress requires wholehearted commitment. Lot's wife turned back to look at the smoldering city of Sodom. Clinging to the past, she was unwilling to turn completely away. Are you looking back longingly at sin while trying to move forward with God? You can't make progress with God as long as you are holding on to pieces of your old life. Jesus said it this way in Matthew 6:24: "No one can serve two masters."

BIBLE READING: Numbers 33:1-4

KEY BIBLE VERSE: *At the LORD's direction, Moses kept a written record of their progress. These are the stages of their march, identified by the different places they stopped along the way.* (Numbers 33:2)

Spiritual progress is a process. Moses recorded the Israelites' journeys as God instructed him, providing a record of their spiritual as well as geographic progress. Have you made spiritual progress lately? Recording your thoughts about God and lessons you have learned over a period of time can be a valuable aid to spiritual growth. A record of your spiritual pilgrimage will let you check up on your progress and avoid repeating past mistakes.

BIBLE READING: Philippians 1:1-11
KEY BIBLE VERSE: *I am sure that God, who began the good work within you, will continue his work until it is finally finished on that day when Christ Jesus comes back again.* (Philippians 1:6)

Spiritual progress is dependent upon God. Do you sometimes feel as though you aren't making progress in your spiritual life? When God starts a project, he completes it! As with the Philippians, God will help you grow in grace until he has completed his work in your life. When you are discouraged, remember that God won't give up on you. He promises to finish the work he has begun. When you feel incomplete, unfinished, or distressed by your shortcomings, remember God's promise and provision. Don't let your present condition rob you of the joy of knowing Christ or keep you from growing closer to him.

Related Topics: ACCOMPLISHMENTS, FAITHFULNESS, SPIRITUAL GROWTH

PROMISE(S) *(Commitment, Covenant, Vow)*

▶ GOD'S PROMISES
What can we learn from God's promises?

BIBLE READING: Genesis 50:22-26
KEY BIBLE VERSE: *"Soon I will die,"* Joseph told his brothers, *"but God will surely come for you, to lead you out of this land of Egypt. He will bring you back to the land he vowed to give to the descendants of Abraham, Isaac, and Jacob."* (Genesis 50:24)

We can have confidence about the future. Joseph was ready to die. He had no doubts that God would keep his promise and one day bring the Israelites back to their homeland. What a tremendous example! The secret of that kind of faith is a lifetime of trusting God. Your faith is like a muscle—it grows with exercise, gaining strength over time. After a lifetime of exercising trust, your faith can be as strong as Joseph's. Then at your death, you can be confident that God will fulfill all his promises to you and to all those faithful to him who may live after you.

BIBLE READING: Exodus 2:11-25
KEY BIBLE VERSE: *God heard their cries and remembered his covenant promise to Abraham, Isaac, and Jacob. He looked down on the Israelites and felt deep concern for their welfare.* (Exodus 2:24-25)

We can know that God is faithful. God's rescue doesn't always come the moment we want it. God had promised to bring the Hebrew slaves out of Egypt (Genesis 15:16; 46:3-4). The people had waited a long time for that promise to be kept, but God rescued them when he knew the right time had come. God knows the best time to act. When you feel that God has forgotten you in your troubles, remember that God has a time schedule we can't see.

BIBLE READING: Mark 1:1-8
KEY BIBLE VERSE: *In the book of the prophet Isaiah, God said, "Look, I am sending my messenger before you, and he will prepare your way. He is a voice shouting in the wilderness: 'Prepare a pathway for the Lord's coming! Make a straight road for him!'"* (Mark 1:2-3)

We can know that God has a plan. Hundreds of years earlier, the prophet Isaiah had predicted that John the Baptist and Jesus would come. How did he know? God promised Isaiah that a Redeemer would come to Israel, and that a messenger calling in the desert would prepare the way for him. Isaiah's words comforted many people as they looked forward to the Messiah, and knowing that God keeps his promises can comfort you too.

BIBLE READING: Philippians 4:10-20

KEY BIBLE VERSE: *I know how to live on almost nothing or with everything. I have learned the secret of living in every situation, whether it is with a full stomach or empty, with plenty or little. For I can do everything with the help of Christ who gives me the strength I need.* (Philippians 4:12-13)

We can learn contentment. Are you content in any circumstances you face? Paul knew how to be content whether he had plenty or whether he was in need. The secret was drawing on Christ's power for strength. Do you have great needs, or are you discontented because you don't have what you want? Learn to rely on God's promises and Christ's power to help you be content. If you always want more, ask God to remove that desire and teach you contentment in every circumstance. He will supply all your needs, but in a way that he knows is best for you.

▶ **OUR PROMISES**
What should be characteristic of our promises?

BIBLE READING: Genesis 47:28-31

KEY BIBLE VERSE: *As the time of his death drew near, he called for his son Joseph and said to him, "If you are pleased with me, swear most solemnly that you will honor this, my last request: Do not bury me in Egypt. When I am dead, take me out of Egypt and bury me beside my ancestors." So Joseph promised that he would.* (Genesis 47:29-30)

Our promises ought to be dependable. Putting a hand under the thigh was a sign of making a promise, much like shaking hands today. Jacob had Joseph promise to bury him in his homeland. Few things were written in this culture, so a person's word then carried as much force as a written contract today. People today seem to find it easy to say, "I didn't mean that." God's people, however, are to speak the truth and live the truth. Let your words be as binding as a written contract.

BIBLE READING: 1 Samuel 1:21-28

KEY BIBLE VERSE: *"I asked the LORD to give me this child, and he has given me my request. Now I am giving him to the LORD, and he will belong to the LORD his whole life." And they worshiped the LORD there.* (1 Samuel 1:27-28)

Our promises should be kept even when they are costly. To do what she promised (1 Samuel 1:11), Hannah gave up what she wanted most—her son—and presented him to Eli to serve in the house of the Lord. In dedicating her only son to God, Hannah was dedicating her entire life and future to God. Because Samuel's life was from God, Hannah was not really giving him up. Rather, she was returning him to God who had given Samuel to Hannah in the first place. These verses illustrate the kind of gifts we should give to God. Do your gifts cost you little (Sunday mornings, a comfortable tithe), or are they gifts of sacrifice? Are you presenting God with tokens, or are you presenting him with your entire life?

BIBLE READING: John 13:31-38

KEY BIBLE VERSE: *"But why can't I come now, Lord?"* he asked. *"I am ready to die for you."* Jesus answered, *"Die for me? No, before the rooster crows tomorrow morning, you will deny three times that you even know me."* (John 13:37-38)

Our promises should be made with firm commitment. Peter proudly told Jesus that he was ready to die for him. But Jesus corrected him. He knew Peter would deny that he knew Jesus that very night to protect himself (John 18:25-27). In our enthusiasm, it is easy to make promises, but God knows the extent of our commitment. Paul tells us, "be honest in your estimate of yourselves" (Romans 12:3). Instead of bragging, demonstrate your commitment step by step as you grow in your knowledge of God's Word and in your faith.

Related Topics: FAITHFULNESS, INTEGRITY, TRUTH

PROPHECY (*Forecast, Prediction, Revelation*)

What was the purpose of biblical prophecy?

BIBLE READING: Deuteronomy 18:15-22

KEY BIBLE VERSE: *You may wonder, "How will we know whether the prophecy is from the LORD or not?" If the prophet predicts something in the LORD's name and it does not happen, the LORD did not give the message. That prophet has spoken on his own and need not be feared.* (Deuteronomy 18:21-22)

Prophecy was intended to reveal a message from the true God. As in the days of ancient Israel, some people today claim to have messages from God. God still speaks to his people, but we must be cautious before saying that someone is God's spokesperson. How can we tell when people are speaking for the Lord? (1) We can see whether or not their prophecies come true—the ancient test for judging prophets. (2) We can check their words against the Bible. God never contradicts himself, so if someone says something contrary to the Bible, we can know that he or she is not speaking for God.

BIBLE READING: Mark 13:1-37

KEY BIBLE VERSE: *Jesus replied, "Don't let anyone mislead you, because many will come in my name, claiming to be the Messiah. They will lead many astray. And wars will break out near and far, but don't panic. Yes, these things must come, but the end won't follow immediately."* (Mark 13:5-7)

Prophecy was intended to encourage obedience. Jesus warned his followers about the future so that they could learn how to live in the present. Many predictions Jesus made in this passage have not yet been fulfilled. He did not make them so that we would guess when they might be fulfilled, but to help us remain spiritually alert and prepared at all times as we wait for his return.

BIBLE READING: Revelation 1:1-8

KEY BIBLE VERSE: *God blesses the one who reads this prophecy to the church, and he blesses all who listen to it and obey what it says. For the time is near when these things will happen.* (Revelation 1:3)

Prophecy was intended to encourage trust in God. Revelation is a book of prophecy that is both *prediction* (foretelling future events) and *proclamation* (preaching about who God is and what he will do). Prophecy is more than telling the future. Behind the predictions are important principles about God's character and promises. As we read, we will get to know God better so that we can trust him completely.

Prophecy was intended to give hope. The typical news reports—filled with violence, scandal, and political haggling—are depressing, and we may wonder where the world is heading. God's plan for the future, however, provides inspiration and encouragement because we know he will intervene in history to conquer evil. John encourages churches to read this book aloud so everyone can hear it, apply it, and be assured of the fact that God will triumph.

Related Topics: BIBLE, PROMISE(S), TRUST

PROSPERITY (*see* POSSESSIONS)

PROTECTION (*Defense, Safety, Security*)

What kind of protection does God offer us?

BIBLE READING: Psalm 18:1-50
KEY BIBLE VERSE: *The LORD is my rock, my fortress, and my savior; my God is my rock, in whom I find protection. He is my shield, the strength of my salvation, and my stronghold.* (Psalm 18:2)

God's protection is unlimited. God's protection of his people is limitless and can take many forms. David characterized God's care with five military symbols. God is like (1) a *rock* that can't be moved by any who would harm us; (2) a *fortress* or place of safety where the enemy can't follow; (3) a *shield* that comes between us and harm; (4) the *strength* of our salvation; and (5) a *stronghold* high above our enemies. If you need protection, look to God.

BIBLE READING: Luke 21:5-24
KEY BIBLE VERSE: *Everyone will hate you because of your allegiance to me. But not a hair of your head will perish! By standing firm, you will win your souls.* (Luke 21:17-19)

God's protection is certain. Jesus warned that in the coming persecutions his followers would be betrayed by their family members and friends. Christians of every age have had to face this possibility. It is reassuring to know that even when we feel completely abandoned, the Holy Spirit will stay with us. He will comfort us, protect us, and give us the words we need. This assurance can give us the courage and hope to stand firm for Christ no matter how difficult the situation.

God's protection is for eternity. Jesus was *not* saying that believers would be exempt from physical harm or death during the persecutions. Remember that most of the disciples were martyred. Rather he was saying that none of his followers would suffer spiritual or eternal loss. On earth everyone will die, but believers in Jesus will be saved for eternal life.

Related Topics: POWER, PROBLEMS, SECURITY

PUNISHMENT *(Consequences, Discipline, Penalty)*

What does the Bible teach about punishment?

BIBLE READING: Genesis 3:1-24
KEY BIBLE VERSE: *"Who told you that you were naked?" the LORD God asked. "Have you eaten the fruit I commanded you not to eat?"* (Genesis 3:11)

Punishment is a consequence of sinful actions. Adam and Eve chose their course of action (disobedience), and then God chose his. As a holy God, he could respond only in a way consistent with his perfect moral nature. He could not allow sin to go unchecked; he had to punish it. If the consequences of Adam and Eve's sin seem extreme, remember that their sin set in motion the world's tendency toward disobeying God. That is why we sin today: Every human being ever born, with the exception of Jesus, has inherited the sinful nature of Adam and Eve (Romans 5:12-21). Adam and Eve's punishment reflects how seriously God views sin of any kind.

BIBLE READING: 2 Samuel 20:1-26
KEY BIBLE VERSE: *As they arrived at the great stone in Gibeon, Amasa met them, coming from the opposite direction. Joab was wearing his uniform with a dagger strapped to his belt. As he stepped forward to greet Amasa, he secretly slipped the dagger from its sheath. "How are you, my cousin?" Joab said and took him by the beard with his right hand as though to kiss him. Amasa didn't notice the dagger in his left hand, and Joab stabbed him in the stomach with it so that his insides gushed out onto the ground. Joab did not need to strike again, and Amasa soon died. Joab and his brother Abishai left him lying there and continued after Sheba.* (2 Samuel 20:8-10)

Punishment is inevitable. Joab's murderous act seemingly went unpunished, just as it did when he killed Abner (3:26-27). Eventually, however, justice caught up with him (1 Kings 2:28-35). It may seem that sin and treachery often go unpunished, but God's justice is not limited to this life. Even if Joab had died of old age, he would have to face the Day of Judgment.

BIBLE READING: Psalm 38:1-22
KEY BIBLE VERSE: *O LORD, don't rebuke me in your anger! Don't discipline me in your rage!* (Psalm 38:1)

Punishment refines our character. David saw his anguish as judgment from God for his sins. Although God does not always send physical illness to punish us for sin, this verse and others in Scripture (Acts 12:21-23; 1 Corinthians 11:30-32) indicate that he does in certain circumstances. Our sin can have physical or mental side effects that can cause great suffering. Sometimes God has to punish his children in order to bring them back to himself (Hebrews 12:5-11). When we repent of our sin, God promises to forgive us. He delivers us from sin's eternal consequences, although he does not promise to undo all of sin's earthly consequences.

Related Topics: CONSEQUENCES, JUDGMENT, JUSTICE

PURITY *(Goodness, Morality, Righteousness)*

How can our life become pure?

BIBLE READING: Joshua 6:1-27

KEY BIBLE VERSE: *They completely destroyed everything in it—men and women, young and old, cattle, sheep, donkeys—everything.* (Joshua 6:21)

True purity comes from radical commitment. Why did God demand that the Israelites destroy almost everyone and everything in Jericho? He was carrying out severe judgment against the wickedness of the Canaanites. This judgment, or *ban,* usually required that everything be destroyed (Deuteronomy 12:2-3; 13:12-18). Because of their evil practices and intense idolatry, the Canaanites were a stronghold of rebellion against God. This threat to the right kind of living that God required had to be removed. If not, it would affect all Israel like a cancerous growth (as it did in the sad story told in the book of Judges).

God wants us to be pure. He wants us to clean up our behavior when we begin a new life with him. We must not let the desire for personal gain distract us from our spiritual purpose. We must also reject any objects that are reminders of a life of rebellion against God.

BIBLE READING: Matthew 23:1-39

KEY BIBLE VERSE: *How terrible it will be for you teachers of religious law and you Pharisees. Hypocrites! You are so careful to clean the outside of the cup and the dish, but inside you are filthy—full of greed and self-indulgence!* (Matthew 23:25)

True purity comes from the heart. The Pharisees strained their water so they wouldn't accidentally swallow a gnat—an unclean insect according to the law. Meticulous about the details of ceremonial cleanliness, they nevertheless had lost their perspective on inner purity. Ceremonially clean on the outside, they had a corrupt heart. Jesus condemned the Pharisees and religious leaders for outwardly appearing saintly and holy but inwardly remaining full of corruption and greed. Living our Christianity merely as a show for others is like washing a cup on the outside only. When we are clean on the inside, our cleanliness on the outside won't be a sham.

BIBLE READING: John 17:1-26

KEY BIBLE VERSE: *Make them pure and holy by teaching them your words of truth.* (John 17:17)

True purity comes from God. A follower of Christ becomes sanctified (set apart for sacred use, cleansed and made holy) through believing and obeying the Word of God (Hebrews 4:12). He or she has already accepted forgiveness through Christ's sacrificial death (Hebrews 7:26-27). But daily application of God's Word has a purifying effect on our mind and heart. Scripture points out sin, motivates us to confess, renews our relationship with Christ, and guides us back to the right path.

Related Topics: HOLINESS, MATURITY, SALVATION

PURPOSE *(Goal, Objective, Plan)*

How can we find purpose in our life?

BIBLE READING: Numbers 9:15-23

KEY BIBLE VERSE: *They camped or traveled at the LORD's command, and they did whatever the LORD told them through Moses.* (Numbers 9:23)

We find purpose in obedience to God. The Israelites traveled and camped as God guided. When you follow God's guidance, you know you are where God wants you, whether you're moving or staying in one place. You are physically somewhere right now. Instead of praying, "God, what do you want me to do next?" ask, "God, what do you want me to do while I'm right here?" Direction from God is not just for your next big move. He has a purpose in placing you where you are right now. Begin to understand God's purpose for your life by discovering what he wants you to do now!

BIBLE READING: Proverbs 3:1-35

KEY BIBLE VERSE: *Then you will find favor with both God and people, and you will gain a good reputation. Trust in the LORD with all your heart; do not depend on your own understanding. Seek his will in all you do, and he will direct your paths.* (Proverbs 3:4-6)

We find purpose in trusting God. To receive God's guidance, said Solomon, we must acknowledge God in all our ways. This means turning every area of life over to him. About a thousand years later, Jesus emphasized this same truth (Matthew 6:33). Look at your values and priorities. What is important to you? In what areas have you not acknowledged him? What is his advice? In many areas of your life you may already acknowledge God, but it is in the areas where you attempt to restrict or ignore his influence that will cause you grief. Make him a vital part of everything you do; then he will guide you because you will be working to accomplish his purposes.

BIBLE READING: 2 Thessalonians 1:1-12

KEY BIBLE VERSE: *We keep on praying for you, that our God will make you worthy of the life to which he called you. And we pray that God, by his power, will fulfill all your good intentions and faithful deeds.* (2 Thessalonians 1:11)

We find purpose in becoming like Christ. Our "calling" from God, as Christians, is to become like Christ (Romans 8:29). This is a gradual, lifelong process that will be completed when we see Christ face to face (1 John 3:2). To be "worthy" of this calling means to *want* to do what is right and good (as Christ would). We aren't perfect yet, but we're moving in that direction as God works in us.

Related Topics: GOD'S WILL, GUIDANCE, PLANS

QUALIFICATION (*see* ABILITIES)

QUALITY (*Character, Value, Worth*)

Why is it important to strive for quality in our life?

BIBLE READING: Exodus 29:1-46
KEY BIBLE VERSE: *This is how you will ordain Aaron and his sons to their offices. The ordination ceremony will go on for seven days.* (Exodus 29:35)

The quality of our work can be an expression of obedience. Why were there such detailed rituals in connection with these sacrifices? Partly, it was for quality control. A centralized, standardized form of worship prevented problems of belief that could arise from individuals creating their own worship. Also, it differentiated the Hebrews from the pagan Canaanites they would meet in the Promised Land. By closely following God's instructions, the Hebrews could not possibly join the Canaanites in their immoral religious practices. Finally, it showed Israel that God was serious about his relationship with them.

BIBLE READING: Exodus 35:1-35
KEY BIBLE VERSE: *All the women who were skilled in sewing and spinning prepared blue, purple, and scarlet yarn, and fine linen cloth, and they brought them in.* (Exodus 35:25)

The quality of our work can be an expression of worship. Those who spun cloth made a beautiful contribution to the tabernacle. Good workers take pride in the quality and beauty of their work. God is concerned with the quality and beauty of what you do. Whether you are a corporate executive or a drugstore cashier, your work should reflect the creative abilities God has given you.

BIBLE READING: Luke 14:25-35
KEY BIBLE VERSE: *Salt is good for seasoning. But if it loses its flavor, how do you make it salty again? Flavorless salt is good neither for the soil nor for fertilizer. It is thrown away. Anyone who is willing to hear should listen and understand!* (Luke 14:34-35)

The quality of our life will have an effect on others. Salt can lose its flavor. When it gets wet and then dries, nothing is left but a tasteless residue. Many

Christians blend into the world and avoid the cost of standing up for Christ. But Jesus says if Christians lose their distinctive saltiness, they become worthless. Just as salt flavors and preserves food, we are to preserve the good in the world, help keep it from spoiling, and bring new flavor to life. This requires careful planning, willing sacrifice, and unswerving commitment to Christ's kingdom. Being "salty" is not easy, but if a Christian fails in this function, he or she fails to represent Christ in the world. How salty are you?

Related Topics: FAITHFULNESS, OBEDIENCE, VALUE

QUARRELS (*Arguments, Controversies, Fighting*)

What causes people to quarrel?

 BIBLE READING: Proverbs 13:1-25
KEY BIBLE VERSE: *Pride leads to arguments; those who take advice are wise.* (Proverbs 13:10)

Pride leads to quarrels. "I was wrong" or "I need advice" are difficult phrases to utter because they require humility. Pride is an ingredient in every quarrel. It stirs up conflict and divides people. Humility, in contrast, heals. Guard against pride. If you find yourself constantly arguing, examine your life for pride. Be open to the advice of others, ask for help when you need it, and be willing to admit your mistakes.

BIBLE READING: Titus 3:1-11
KEY BIBLE VERSE: *Do not get involved in foolish discussions about spiritual pedigrees or in quarrels and fights about obedience to Jewish laws. These kinds of things are useless and a waste of time.* (Titus 3:9)

Unprofitable discussion leads to quarrels. Paul warned Titus, as he warned Timothy, not to get involved in foolish and unprofitable arguments (2 Timothy 2:14). This does not mean we should refuse to study, discuss, and examine different interpretations of difficult Bible passages. Paul is warning against petty quarrels, not honest discussion that leads to wisdom. As foolish arguments develop, it is best to turn the discussion back to a helpful direction or politely excuse yourself.

Divisiveness leads to quarrels. A person must be warned when he or she is causing division that threatens the unity of the church. This warning should not be a heavy-handed action, but it is intended to correct the individual's divisive nature and restore him or her to fellowship. A person who refuses to be corrected should be put outside the fellowship. As Paul said, that person is sinning—and knows it. (See also Matthew 18:15-18 and 2 Thessalonians 3:14-15 for help in handling such problems in the church.)

BIBLE READING: James 4:1-12
KEY BIBLE VERSE: *What is causing the quarrels and fights among you? Isn't it the whole army of evil desires at war within you?* (James 4:1)

Sinful desires lead to quarrels. Conflicts and disputes among believers are always harmful. James explains that these quarrels result from evil desires battling within us—we want more possessions, more money, higher status, more recognition. When we want badly enough to fulfill these desires, we fight in order to do so. Instead of aggressively grabbing what we want, we

should submit ourself to God, ask God to help us get rid of our selfish
desires, and trust him to give us what we really need.

Related Topics: ARGUMENTS, DISAGREEMENTS, TRUTH

QUESTIONS *(Curiosity, Difficulty, Problems)*

How does God handle our questions?

BIBLE READING: Job 38:1-41
KEY BIBLE VERSE: *Then the LORD answered Job from the whirlwind: "Who is this
that questions my wisdom with such ignorant words? Brace yourself, because
I have some questions for you, and you must answer them." (Job 38:1-3)*

God sometimes answers our questions with questions. Out of a mighty storm,
God spoke. Surprisingly, he didn't answer any of Job's questions; Job's questions were not at the heart of the issue. Instead, God used Job's ignorance of
the earth's natural order to reveal his ignorance of God's moral order. If Job
did not understand the workings of God's physical creation, how could he
possibly understand God's mind and character? There is no standard or criterion higher than God himself by which to judge. God himself is the standard.
Our only option is to submit to his authority and rest in his care.

BIBLE READING: Job 42:1-17
KEY BIBLE VERSE: *You ask, "Who is this that questions my wisdom with such ignorance?" It is I. And I was talking about things I did not understand, things far
too wonderful for me. (Job 42:3)*

God sometimes leaves our questions unanswered. Throughout the book, Job's
friends had asked him to admit his sin and ask for forgiveness, and eventually
Job did indeed repent. Ironically, Job's repentance was not the kind called for
by his friends. He did not ask for forgiveness for committing secret sins, but
for questioning God's sovereignty and justice. Job repented of his attitude and
acknowledged God's great power and perfect justice. We sin when we angrily
ask, "If God is in control, how could he let this happen?" Because we are
locked into time, unable to see beyond today, we cannot know the reasons for
everything that happens. Thus we must often choose between doubt and trust.
Will you trust God with your unanswered questions?

BIBLE READING: Luke 7:18-35
KEY BIBLE VERSE: *John's two disciples found Jesus and said to him, "John the Baptist
sent us to ask, 'Are you the Messiah we've been expecting, or should we keep
looking for someone else?' " (Luke 7:20)*

God welcomes our questions. John was confused because the reports he
received about Jesus were unexpected and incomplete. John's doubts were
natural, and Jesus didn't rebuke him for them. Instead, Jesus responded in a
way that John would understand: Jesus explained that he had accomplished
what the Messiah was supposed to accomplish. God can handle our doubts,
and he welcomes our questions. Do you have questions about Jesus—about
who he is or what he expects of you? Admit them to yourself and to God, and
begin looking for answers. Only as you face your doubts honestly can you
begin to resolve them.

Related Topics: ANSWERS, DOUBT, TRUTH

QUIET *(Calm, Peace, Silence)*

What is the importance of quiet?

BIBLE READING: 1 Kings 19:1-18
KEY BIBLE VERSE: *"Go out and stand before me on the mountain,"* the LORD told him. *And as Elijah stood there, the LORD passed by, and a mighty windstorm hit the mountain. It was such a terrible blast that the rocks were torn loose, but the LORD was not in the wind. After the wind there was an earthquake, but the LORD was not in the earthquake. And after the earthquake there was a fire, but the LORD was not in the fire. And after the fire there was the sound of a gentle whisper. When Elijah heard it, he wrapped his face in his cloak and went out and stood at the entrance of the cave. And a voice said, "What are you doing here, Elijah?"* (1 Kings 19:11-13)

Sometimes we can only hear God speak when we are quiet. Elijah knew that the sound of the gentle whisper was God's voice. He realized that God doesn't reveal himself only in powerful, miraculous ways. To look for God only in something big (rallies, churches, conferences, highly visible leaders) may be to miss him, because he is often found gently whispering in the quietness of a humbled heart. Are you listening for God? Step back from the noise and activity of your busy life and listen humbly and quietly for his guidance. It may come when you least expect it.

BIBLE READING: Psalm 46:1-11
KEY BIBLE VERSE: *Be silent, and know that I am God! I will be honored by every nation. I will be honored throughout the world.* (Psalm 46:10)

Sometimes we can only recognize God's majesty when we are quiet. War and destruction are inevitable, but so is God's final victory. At that time, all will stand quietly before the Lord Almighty. How proper, then, for us to be still now, reverently honoring him and his power and majesty. Take time each day to be still and to exalt God.

Related Topics: AWE, MEDITATION, SILENCE

QUITTING *(see* GIVING UP)

R

RACISM (*see* PREJUDICE)

RATIONALIZING (*Excuse, Explain, Justify*)

What are some common patterns of rationalization?

BIBLE READING: Genesis 39:1-23

KEY BIBLE VERSE: *Joseph refused. "Look," he told her, "my master trusts me with everything in his entire household. No one here has more authority than I do! He has held back nothing from me except you, because you are his wife. How could I ever do such a wicked thing? It would be a great sin against God."* (Genesis 39:8-9)

We often rationalize when we are being tempted to sin. Potiphar's wife failed to seduce Joseph, who resisted this temptation by saying it would be a sin against God. Joseph didn't say, "I'd be hurting you," or "I'd be sinning against Potiphar," or "I'd be sinning against myself." Under pressure, such excuses are easily rationalized away. Remember that sexual sin is not just between two consenting adults. It is an act of disobedience against God.

BIBLE READING: Ezekiel 9:1-11

KEY BIBLE VERSE: *The sins of the people of Israel and Judah are very great. The entire land is full of murder; the city is filled with injustice. They are saying, "The LORD doesn't see it! The LORD has forsaken the land!"* (Ezekiel 9:9)

We often rationalize after we have sinned. The people said that the Lord had forsaken the land and wouldn't see their sin. People have many convenient explanations to make it easier to sin: "It doesn't matter," "Everybody's doing it," or "Nobody will ever know." Do you find yourself making excuses for sin? Rationalizing sin makes it easier to commit, but rationalization does not convince God or cancel the punishment.

BIBLE READING: Matthew 4:1-11

KEY BIBLE VERSE: *The Devil took him to Jerusalem, to the highest point of the Temple, and said, "If you are the Son of God, jump off! For the Scriptures say, 'He orders his angels to protect you. And they will hold you with their hands to keep you from striking your foot on a stone.'"* (Matthew 4:5-6)

We often rationalize from Scripture to cover our sin. The devil used Scripture to try to convince Jesus to sin! Sometimes friends or associates will present attractive and convincing reasons why you should try something you know is wrong. They may even find Bible verses that *seem* to support their viewpoint. Study the Bible carefully, especially the broader contexts of specific verses, so that you understand God's principles for living and what he wants for your life. Only if you really understand what the *whole* Bible says will you be able to recognize errors of interpretation when people take verses out of context and twist them to say what they want them to say.

Related Topics: DISOBEDIENCE, EXCUSES, OBEDIENCE

REACTION (*see* ATTITUDE)

READINESS (*see* PLANS)

READING (*Interpreting, Studying, Understanding*)

Why is Bible reading a basic spiritual discipline?

BIBLE READING: Deuteronomy 17:14-20

KEY BIBLE VERSE: *When he sits on the throne as king, he must copy these laws on a scroll for himself in the presence of the Levitical priests. He must always keep this copy of the law with him and read it daily as long as he lives. That way he will learn to fear the LORD his God by obeying all the terms of this law.* (Deuteronomy 17:18-19)

It is necessary to read God's Word in order to obey it. The king was to be a man of God's Word. He was to (1) have a copy of the law made for his personal use, (2) keep it with him all the time, (3) read from it every day, and (4) obey it completely. Through this process he would learn respect for God, keep himself from feeling more important than others, and avoid neglecting God in times of prosperity. We can't know what God wants except through his Word, and his Word won't affect our life unless we read and think about it regularly. With the easy availability of the Bible today, it is not difficult to gain access to the source of the king's wisdom. What is more of a challenge is following its directives.

BIBLE READING: Deuteronomy 31:9-13

KEY BIBLE VERSE: *Call them all together—men, women, children, and the foreigners living in your towns—so they may listen and learn to fear the LORD your God and carefully obey all the terms of this law.* (Deuteronomy 31:12)

It is necessary to read God's Word in order to teach it to others. The laws were to be read to the whole assembly so that everyone, including the children, could hear them. Every seven years the entire nation would gather together and listen as a priest read the law to them. There were no books, Bibles, or newsstands to spread God's Word, so the people had to rely on word of mouth and an accurate memory. Memorization was an important part of worship because if everyone knew the law, ignorance would be no excuse for breaking it. To fulfill God's purpose and will in our life, we need the content and substance of his Word in our heart and mind. For the Hebrews, this process began in childhood. Teaching our children and new believers should be one of our top priorities. Our finest teachers, best resources, and most careful thought should be directed toward showing young believers how to follow God in all life's situations.

BIBLE READING: John 20:24-31

KEY BIBLE VERSE: *Jesus' disciples saw him do many other miraculous signs besides the ones recorded in this book. But these are written so that you may believe that Jesus is the Messiah, the Son of God, and that by believing in him you will have life.* (John 20:30-31)

It is necessary to read God's Word in order to know the Lord. To understand the life and mission of Jesus more fully, all we need to do is study the Gospels. John tells us that his Gospel records only a few of the many events in Jesus' life on earth. But it includes everything we need to know to believe that Jesus is the Christ, the Son of God, through whom we receive eternal life.

Related Topics: BIBLE, MEDITATION, MEMORIZATION

REALITY (*see* TRUTH)

REASON (*see* THINKING)

REBELLION (*Disobedience, Resistance, Sin*)

What does the Bible say about rebellion?

BIBLE READING: Deuteronomy 31:1-29

KEY BIBLE VERSE: *I know how rebellious and stubborn you are. Even now, while I am still with you, you have rebelled against the LORD. How much more rebellious will you be after my death!* (Deuteronomy 31:27)

Rebellion is a basic part of our nature. Moses knew that the Israelites, in spite of all they had seen of God's work, were rebellious at heart. They deserved God's punishment, although they often received his mercy instead. We too are stubborn and rebellious by nature. Throughout our life we struggle with sin. Repentance once a month or once a week is not enough. We must constantly turn from our sins to God and let him, in his mercy, save us.

BIBLE READING: Joshua 24:1-33

KEY BIBLE VERSE: *If you are unwilling to serve the LORD, then choose today whom you will serve. Would you prefer the gods your ancestors served beyond the Euphrates? Or will it be the gods of the Amorites in whose land you now live? But as for me and my family, we will serve the LORD.* (Joshua 24:15)

Rebellion is a choice. The people had to decide whether they would obey the Lord, who had proven his trustworthiness, or obey the local gods, which were only man-made idols. It's easy to slip into a quiet rebellion—going about life in your own way. But the time comes when you have to choose who or what will control you. The choice is yours. Will it be God, your own limited personality, or another imperfect substitute? Once you have chosen to be controlled by God's Spirit, reaffirm your choice every day.

BIBLE READING: Jude 1:1-25

KEY BIBLE VERSE: *I must remind you—and you know it well—that even though the Lord rescued the whole nation of Israel from Egypt, he later destroyed every one of those who did not remain faithful.* (Jude 1:5)

Rebellion leads to judgment. Jude gave three examples of rebellion: (1) the children of Israel—who, although they were delivered from Egypt, refused to trust

God and enter the Promised Land (Numbers 14:26-39); (2) the angels—
although they were once pure, holy, and living in God's presence, some gave in
to pride and joined Satan to rebel against God (2 Peter 2:4); and (3) the cities
of Sodom and Gomorrah—the inhabitants were so full of sin that God wiped
them off the face of the earth (Genesis 19:1-29). If the chosen people, angels,
and sinful cities were punished, how much more would these false teachers be
severely judged?

Related Topics: DISOBEDIENCE, PRIDE, SIN

REBIRTH (*see* SPIRITUAL REBIRTH)

REBUKE (*see* CRITICISM)

RECOGNITION (*see* ACCOMPLISHMENTS)

RECONCILIATION (*Agreement, Forgiveness, Harmony*)

Why is reconciliation important?

BIBLE READING: Philemon 1:1-25
KEY BIBLE VERSE: *Perhaps you could think of it this way: Onesimus ran away for
a little while so you could have him back forever. He is no longer just a slave;
he is a beloved brother, especially to me. Now he will mean much more to you,
both as a slave and as a brother in the Lord.* (Philemon 1:15-16)

Reconciliation can transform hopeless relationships. Paul urged Philemon to
be reconciled to his slave and to receive him as a brother and fellow member
of God's family. *Reconciliation* means reestablishing relationship. Christ has
reconciled us to God and to others. Many barriers come between people—race,
social status, sex, personality differences—but Christ can break down these barriers. Jesus Christ changed Onesimus's relationship to Philemon from slave to
brother. Christ can transform our most hopeless relationships into deep and
loving friendships.

BIBLE READING: 2 Corinthians 5:11-21
KEY BIBLE VERSE: *All this newness of life is from God, who brought us back to himself through what Christ did. And God has given us the task of reconciling
people to him. For God was in Christ, reconciling the world to himself, no longer
counting people's sins against them. This is the wonderful message he has given
us to tell others.* (2 Corinthians 5:18-19)

Reconciliation is the central message of the gospel. God brings us back to himself (reconciles us) by blotting out our sins (see also Ephesians 2:13-18) and
making us righteous. We are no longer God's enemies, or strangers or foreigners
to him when we trust in Christ. Because we have been reconciled to God, we
have the privilege of encouraging others to do the same, and thus we are those
who have the "task of reconciling people to him."

BIBLE READING: Matthew 18:15-20
KEY BIBLE VERSE: *If another believer sins against you, go privately and point out the
fault. If the other person listens and confesses it, you have won that person back.*
(Matthew 18:15)

Reconciliation heals broken relationships. These are Jesus' guidelines for dealing with those who sin against us. They were meant for (1) Christians, not unbelievers, (2) sins committed against *you* and not others, and (3) conflict resolution in the context of the church, not the community at large. Jesus' words are not a license for a frontal attack on every person who hurts or slights us. They are not a license to start a destructive gossip campaign or to call for a church trial. They are designed to reconcile those who disagree so that all Christians can live in harmony.

Related Topics: Forgiveness, Grace, Salvation

REDEMPTION (*see* SALVATION)

REFUGE (*see* PROTECTION)

REGRET (*see* REPENTANCE)

REJECTION (*Denial, Disapproval, Loneliness*)

▶ **BEING REJECTED**
How should we respond when we feel rejected?

 BIBLE READING: Job 13:1-28
KEY BIBLE VERSE: *O God, there are two things I beg of you, and I will be able to face you. Remove your hand from me, and don't terrify me with your awesome presence.* (Job 13:20-21)

Remember that God's silence does not mean rejection. Job was especially upset because God was silent, giving no reasons for his suffering. Job misinterpreted God's silence as rejection, and once again he said that it was not his suffering that bothered him as much as this apparent rejection. If God had given reasons, however, Job's faith would probably not have been stretched and strengthened.

BIBLE READING: Mark 6:1-13
KEY BIBLE VERSE: *Then Jesus told them, "A prophet is honored everywhere except in his own hometown and among his relatives and his own family."* (Mark 6:4)

Remember that God's servants often experience rejection. Jesus said that a prophet (in other words, a worker for God) is never honored in his hometown. But that doesn't make his work any less important. A person doesn't need to be respected or honored to be useful to God. If friends, neighbors, or family don't respect your Christian work, don't let their rejection keep you from serving God.

Remember to encourage one another in times of rejection. The disciples were sent out in pairs. Individually they could have reached more areas of the country, but this was not Christ's plan. One advantage in going out by twos was that they could strengthen and encourage each other, especially when they faced rejection. Our strength comes from God, but he meets many of our needs through our teamwork with others. As you serve Christ, don't try to go it alone.

▶ **REJECTING GOD**
How do people reject God?

BIBLE READING: 1 Samuel 10:1-27

KEY BIBLE VERSE: *Samuel called all the people of Israel to meet before the* LORD *at Mizpah. And he gave them this message from the* LORD, *the God of Israel: "I brought you from Egypt and rescued you from the Egyptians and from all of the nations that were oppressing you. But though I have done so much for you, you have rejected me and said, 'We want a king instead!' Now, therefore, present yourselves before the* LORD *by tribes and clans."* (1 Samuel 10:17-19)

We sometimes trust human leaders more than we trust God. Israel's true king was God, but the nation demanded another king. Imagine wanting a human being instead of God as guide and leader! Throughout history, men and women have rejected God, and they continue to do it today. Are you rejecting God by pushing him aside and acknowledging someone or something else as your "king" or top priority? Learn from these stories of Israel's kings, and don't push God aside.

 BIBLE READING: Psalm 14:1-7

KEY BIBLE VERSE: *Only fools say in their hearts, "There is no God." They are corrupt, and their actions are evil; no one does good!* (Psalm 14:1)

We sometimes reject God by trusting our own judgment more than we trust him. The true atheist is either foolish or wicked—foolish because he ignores the evidence that God exists, or wicked because he refuses to live by God's truths. We become atheists in practice when we rely more on ourself than on God. The fool mentioned here is someone who is aggressively perverse in his actions. To speak in direct defiance of God is utterly foolish according to the Bible.

 BIBLE READING: Matthew 21:33-46

KEY BIBLE VERSE: *Then Jesus asked them, "Didn't you ever read this in the Scriptures?"* (Matthew 21:42)

We reject God when we reject his offer of salvation. In trying to reach us with his love, God finally sent his own Son. Jesus' perfect life, his words of truth, and his sacrifice of love are meant to cause us to listen to him and to follow him as Lord. If we ignore God's gracious gift of his Son, we reject God himself.

Related Topics: ABANDON, FELLOWSHIP, LONELINESS

REJOICING (*see* JOY)

RELATIONSHIP(S) (*Companions, Fellowship, Friendship*)

What general principles does the Bible give us about relationships?

 BIBLE READING: Exodus 33:7-11

KEY BIBLE VERSE: *Inside the Tent of Meeting, the* LORD *would speak to Moses face to face, as a man speaks to his friend. Afterward Moses would return to the camp, but the young man who assisted him, Joshua son of Nun, stayed behind in the Tent of Meeting.* (Exodus 33:11)

Our relationship to God is our most important relationship. God and Moses talked face to face in the Tent of Meeting, just as friends do. Why did Moses find such favor with God? It certainly was not because he was perfect, gifted, or powerful. Rather, it was because God chose Moses, and Moses in turn relied wholeheartedly on God's wisdom and direction. Friendship with God was a true privilege for Moses, out of reach for the other Hebrews. But it is not out of reach for us today. Jesus called his disciples—and, by extension, all of his followers— his friends (John 15:15). He has called you to be his friend. Will you trust him as Moses did?

BIBLE READING: John 16:16-33

KEY BIBLE VERSE: *At that time you won't need to ask me for anything. The truth is, you can go directly to the Father and ask him, and he will grant your request because you use my name. You haven't done this before. Ask, using my name, and you will receive, and you will have abundant joy.* (John 16:23-24)

Our relationship to God is made possible through Jesus. Jesus is talking about a new relationship between the believer and God. Previously, people approached God through priests. After Jesus' resurrection, any believer could approach God directly. A new day has dawned and now all believers are priests, talking with God personally and directly (see Hebrews 10:19-23). We approach God, not because of our own merit, but because Jesus, our great high priest, has made us acceptable to God.

BIBLE READING: 2 Corinthians 6:14-18

KEY BIBLE VERSE: *Don't team up with those who are unbelievers. How can goodness be a partner with wickedness? How can light live with darkness?* (2 Corinthians 6:14)

Our relationships with others should not compromise our faith. Paul urges believers not to form binding relationships with nonbelievers because this might weaken their Christian commitment, integrity, or standards. It would be a mismatch. Earlier, Paul had explained that this did not mean isolating oneself from nonbelievers (see 1 Corinthians 5:9-10). Paul even tells Christians to stay with their nonbelieving spouses (1 Corinthians 7:12-13). Paul wants believers to be active in their witness for Christ to nonbelievers, but they should not lock themselves into personal or business relationships that could cause them to compromise their faith. Believers should avoid situations that could force them to divide their loyalties.

BIBLE READING: Ephesians 2:11-22

KEY BIBLE VERSE: *We who believe are carefully joined together, becoming a holy temple for the Lord. Through him you Gentiles are also joined together as part of this dwelling where God lives by his Spirit.* (Ephesians 2:21-22)

Our relationships with others are made possible through Jesus. There are many barriers that can divide us from other Christians: age, appearance, intelligence, political persuasion, economic status, race, theological perspective. One of the best ways to stifle Christ's love is to be friendly with only those people that we like. Fortunately, Christ has knocked down the barriers and has unified all believers in one family. His cross should be the focus of our unity. The Holy Spirit helps us look beyond the barriers to the unity we are called to enjoy.

Related Topics: FAMILY, FRIENDSHIP, NEIGHBOR

RELIABILITY *(Consistency, Dependability, Integrity)*

What is reliability?

BIBLE READING: Ruth 3:1-18

KEY BIBLE VERSE: *Then Naomi said to her, "Just be patient, my daughter, until we hear what happens. The man won't rest until he has followed through on this. He will settle it today."* (Ruth 3:18)

Reliability is keeping your word. Naomi implied that Boaz would follow through with his promise at once. He obviously had a reputation for keeping his word and would not rest until his task was completed. Such reliable people stand out in any age and culture. Do others regard you as one who will do what you say? Keeping our word and following through on assignments should be high on our priority list. Building a reputation for integrity, however, must be done one brick, one act, at a time.

 BIBLE READING: 1 Chronicles 9:17-34

KEY BIBLE VERSE: *In all, there were 212 gatekeepers in those days, and they were listed by genealogies in their villages. David and Samuel the seer had appointed their ancestors because they were reliable men.* (1 Chronicles 9:22)

Reliability is faithfulness in every area of responsibility. Gatekeepers guarded the four main entrances to the temple and opened the gates each morning for those who wanted to worship. In addition, they did other day-to-day chores to keep the temple running smoothly—cleaning, preparing the offerings for sacrifice, and accounting for the gifts designated to the temple (9:22-32). Gatekeepers had to be reliable, honest, and trustworthy. The people in our churches who handle the offerings and care for the materials and functions of the building follow in a great tradition, and we should honor them for their reliability and service. The way we carry out our own responsibilities ought to always be marked by reliability.

 BIBLE READING: Psalm 33:1-22

KEY BIBLE VERSE: *The word of the LORD holds true, and everything he does is worthy of our trust.* (Psalm 33:4)

Reliability is a part of God's character. As in many of the Psalms, thoughts about the character of God begin with thoughts about the quality of his words. All God's words are right and true—they can be trusted. The Bible is reliable because, unlike people, God does not lie, forget, change his words, or leave his promises unfulfilled. We can trust the Bible because it contains the words of a holy, trustworthy, and unchangeable God.

Related Topics: BIBLE, INTEGRITY, RESPONSIBILITY

RELIGION *(Ceremonies, Faith, Rituals)*

What are the characteristics of true religion?

 BIBLE READING: Judges 9:1-20

KEY BIBLE VERSE: *They gave him seventy silver coins from the temple of Baal-berith, which he used to hire some soldiers who agreed to follow him.* (Judges 9:4)

True religion is never selfish. Politics played a major part in pagan religions such as the worship of Baal-berith. Governments often went so far as to hire temple prostitutes to bring in additional money. In many cases a religious system was set up and supported by the government so the offerings could fund community projects. Religion became a profit-making business. In Israel's religion, this was strictly forbidden. God's system of religion was designed to come from an attitude of the heart, not from calculated plans and business opportunities. It was also designed to serve people and help those in need, not to oppress the needy. Is your faith genuine and sincere, or is it based on convenience, comfort, and availability?

BIBLE READING: Isaiah 29:1-24

KEY BIBLE VERSE: *And so the Lord says, "These people say they are mine. They honor me with their lips, but their hearts are far away. And their worship of me amounts to nothing more than human laws learned by rote." (Isaiah 29:13)*

True religion comes from the heart. The people claimed to be close to God, but they were disobedient and merely went through the motions; therefore, God would bring judgment upon them. Religion had become routine instead of real. Jesus quoted Isaiah's condemnation of Israel's hypocrisy when he spoke to the Pharisees, the religious leaders of his day (Matthew 15:7-9; Mark 7:6-7). We are all capable of hypocrisy. Often we slip into routine patterns when we worship, and we neglect to give God our love and devotion. If we want to be called God's people, we must be obedient and worship him honestly and sincerely.

BIBLE READING: Matthew 21:18-22

KEY BIBLE VERSE: *In the morning, as Jesus was returning to Jerusalem, he was hungry, and he noticed a fig tree beside the road. He went over to see if there were any figs on it, but there were only leaves. Then he said to it, "May you never bear fruit again!" And immediately the fig tree withered up. (Matthew 21:18-19)*

True religion bears spiritual fruit. Why did Jesus curse the fig tree? This was not a thoughtless, angry act, but an acted-out parable. Jesus was showing his anger at religion without substance. Just as the fig tree looked good from a distance but was found fruitless on close examination, so the temple looked impressive at first glance, but its sacrifices and other activities were hollow because they were not done to worship God sincerely (see 21:43). If you only appear to have faith without putting it to work in your life, you are like the fig tree that withered and died because it bore no fruit. Genuine faith means bearing fruit for God's kingdom.

BIBLE READING: Colossians 2:1-23

KEY BIBLE VERSE: *Don't let anyone lead you astray with empty philosophy and high-sounding nonsense that come from human thinking and from the evil powers of this world, and not from Christ. (Colossians 2:8)*

True religion focuses on Christ. Paul writes against any philosophy of life based only on human ideas and experiences. Paul himself was a gifted philosopher, so he is not condemning philosophy. He is condemning teaching that credits humanity, not Christ, with being the answer to life's problems. That approach becomes a false religion. There are many man-made approaches to life's problems that totally disregard God. To resist heresy you must use your mind, keep your eyes on Christ, and study God's Word.

Related Topics: DOCTRINE, FAITH, TRUTH

RELUCTANCE (*see* OBEDIENCE)

REMEMBERING *(Look Back, Memorize, Recall)*

What are the most important things to remember?

BIBLE READING: Deuteronomy 8:1-20

KEY BIBLE VERSE: *Remember how the LORD your God led you through the wilderness for forty years, humbling you and testing you to prove your character, and to find out whether or not you would really obey his commands.* (Deuteronomy 8:2)

We should remember God's constant care for us. It's usually easy for us to take God's protection for granted. We seldom take notice or thank God when our car doesn't break down, our clothes don't rip, or our tools don't break. The people of Israel also failed to take notice, it seems, for they didn't even notice that in forty years of wandering in the desert, their clothes didn't wear out and their feet didn't swell. Thus, they did not remember to give thanks to God for these blessings. What has been working well for you? What has been giving you good service? What has been lasting for a long time without breaking down or apart? Remember to thank God for these quiet blessings.

BIBLE READING: Joshua 4:1-24

KEY BIBLE VERSE: *Joshua called together the twelve men and told them, "Go into the middle of the Jordan, in front of the Ark of the LORD your God. Each of you must pick up one stone and carry it out on your shoulder—twelve stones in all, one for each of the twelve tribes. We will use these stones to build a memorial. In the future, your children will ask, 'What do these stones mean to you?' Then you can tell them, 'They remind us that the Jordan River stopped flowing when the Ark of the LORD's covenant went across.' These stones will stand as a permanent memorial among the people of Israel."* (Joshua 4:4-7)

We should remember God's great blessings in the past. After the people safely crossed the river, what would be next? Conquering the land? Not yet. First, God directed them to build a memorial from twelve stones drawn from the river by twelve men, one from each tribe. This may seem like an insignificant step in their mission of conquering the land, but God did not want his people to plunge into their task unprepared. They were to focus on him and remember who was guiding them. As you are busy doing your God-given tasks, set aside quiet moments, times to build your own memorial to God's power. Too much activity may shift your focus away from God.

BIBLE READING: Ecclesiastes 12:1-14

KEY BIBLE VERSE: *Don't let the excitement of youth cause you to forget your Creator. Honor him in your youth before you grow old and no longer enjoy living.* (Ecclesiastes 12:1)

We should remember to seek God every day of our life. A life without God can produce a bitter, lonely, and hopeless old age. A life centered around God is fulfilling; it will make the days when disabilities, sickness, and handicaps cause barriers to enjoying life satisfying because of the hope of eternal life. Being young is exciting. But the excitement of youth can become a barrier to closeness with God if it makes young people focus on passing pleasures instead of eternal values. Make your strength available to God when it is still yours—during your youthful years. Don't waste it on evil or meaningless activities that become bad habits and make you callous. Seek God now.

Related Topics: DOUBT, MEDITATION, OBEDIENCE

RENEWAL *(Rebirth, Repair, Revival)*

How can we experience spiritual renewal in our life?

BIBLE READING: 2 Chronicles 30:1–31:21

KEY BIBLE VERSE: *King Hezekiah handled the distribution throughout all Judah, doing what was pleasing and good in the sight of the LORD his God. In all that he did in the service of the Temple of God and in his efforts to follow the law and the commands, Hezekiah sought his God wholeheartedly. As a result, he was very successful.* (2 Chronicles 31:20-21)

We are renewed by obeying God. Because Hezekiah did "what was pleasing and good in the sight of the LORD his God," he led the people of Judah in spiritual renewal. His actions serve as a model of renewal for us: (1) he remembered God's compassion (30:9); (2) he kept going despite ridicule (30:10); (3) he aggressively removed evil influences from his life (30:14; 31:1); (4) he interceded for the people, asking for the Lord's pardon (30:18-20); (5) he was open to spontaneity in worship (30:23); (6) he contributed generously to God's work (31:3). If any of these are lacking in your life, consider how you might apply them and renew your commitment to God.

BIBLE READING: Nehemiah 2:11-20

KEY BIBLE VERSE: *I said to them, "You know full well the tragedy of our city. It lies in ruins, and its gates are burned. Let us rebuild the wall of Jerusalem and rid ourselves of this disgrace!" Then I told them about how the gracious hand of God had been on me, and about my conversation with the king. They replied at once, "Good! Let's rebuild the wall!" So they began the good work.* (Nehemiah 2:17-18)

We are renewed by having a vision for God's work. Nehemiah had a vision, and he shared it with enthusiasm, inspiring Jerusalem's leaders to rebuild the walls. He took the time to make sure his vision was clear and compelling. The spark of his vision ignited the people he gathered around him.

We frequently underestimate people and don't challenge them with our dreams for God's work in the world. When God plants an idea in your mind to accomplish something for him, share it with others and trust the Holy Spirit to impress them with similar thoughts. Don't regard yourself as the only one through whom God is working. Often God uses one person to express the vision and others to turn it into reality. When you encourage and inspire others, you put teamwork into action to accomplish God's goals.

BIBLE READING: Luke 9:28-36

KEY BIBLE VERSE: *As Moses and Elijah were starting to leave, Peter, not even knowing what he was saying, blurted out, "Master, this is wonderful! We will make three shrines—one for you, one for Moses, and one for Elijah."* (Luke 9:33)

We are renewed through being active in ministry. Peter, James, and John experienced a wonderful moment on the mountain, and they didn't want to leave. Sometimes we too have such an inspiring experience that we want to stay where we are—away from the reality and problems of our daily life. Knowing that struggles await us in the valley encourages us to linger on the mountaintop. Yet staying on top of a mountain prohibits us from ministering to others. Instead of becoming spiritual giants, we would soon become dwarfed by our self-centeredness. We need times of retreat and renewal, but only so we can return to minister to the world. Our faith must make sense off the mountain as well as on it.

BIBLE READING: John 6:60-71

KEY BIBLE VERSE: *It is the Spirit who gives eternal life. Human effort accomplishes nothing. And the very words I have spoken to you are spirit and life.* (John 6:63)

We are renewed through being filled with the Holy Spirit. The Holy Spirit gives spiritual life; without the work of the Holy Spirit we cannot even see our need for new life (John 14:17). He reveals truth to us, lives within us, and then enables us to respond to that truth.

Related Topics: CHANGE, REPENTANCE, SALVATION

REPENTANCE *(Guilt, Regret, Sorrow)*

Why is repentance essential to a spiritual life?

BIBLE READING: Luke 3:1-18

KEY BIBLE VERSE: *Here is a sample of John's preaching to the crowds that came for baptism: "You brood of snakes! Who warned you to flee God's coming judgment? Prove by the way you live that you have really turned from your sins and turned to God. Don't just say, 'We're safe—we're the descendants of Abraham.' That proves nothing. God can change these stones here into children of Abraham."* (Luke 3:7-8)

Repentance opens the way for relationship with God. Repentance has two sides—turning away from sins and turning toward God. To be truly repentant, we must do both. We can't just say that we believe and then live any way we choose; neither can we simply live a morally correct life without a personal relationship with God, because that cannot bring forgiveness from sin. Determine to rid your life of any sins God points out, and put your trust in him alone to guide you.

Repentance demonstrates real faith. Confession of sins and a changed life are inseparable. Faith without deeds is dead (James 2:14-26). Jesus' harshest words were to the respectable religious leaders who lacked the desire for real change. They wanted to be known as religious authorities, but they didn't want to change their hearts and minds. Thus their lives were unproductive. Repentance must be tied to action, or it isn't real. Following Jesus means more than saying the right words; it means acting on what he says.

BIBLE READING: Matthew 3:1-12

KEY BIBLE VERSE: *In those days John the Baptist began preaching in the Judean wilderness. His message was, "Turn from your sins and turn to God, because the Kingdom of Heaven is near."* (Matthew 3:1-2)

Repentance makes inward change a visible reality. When you wash dirty hands, the results are immediately visible. But repentance happens inside with a cleansing that isn't seen right away. So John used a symbolic action that people could see: baptism. The Jews used baptism to initiate converts, so John's audience was familiar with the rite. Here, baptism was used as a sign of repentance and forgiveness. *Repent* means "to turn," implying a change in behavior. It is turning from sin toward God. Have you repented of sin in your life? Can others see the difference it makes in you? A changed life with new and different behavior makes your repentance real and visible.

BIBLE READING: John 12:1-11

KEY BIBLE VERSE: *The leading priests decided to kill Lazarus, too, for it was because of him that many of the people had deserted them and believed in Jesus.* (John 12:10-11)

Repentance breaks our bondage to sin. The chief priests' blindness and hardness of heart caused them to sink ever deeper into sin. They rejected the Messiah and planned to kill him, and then plotted to murder Lazarus as well. One sin leads to another. From the Jewish leaders' point of view, they could accuse Jesus of blasphemy because he claimed equality with God. But Lazarus had done nothing of the kind. They wanted Lazarus dead simply because he was a living witness to Jesus' power. This is a warning to us to avoid sin. Sin leads to more sin, and this downward spiral can be stopped only by repentance and the power of the Holy Spirit to change behavior.

Related Topics: FORGIVENESS, GOSPEL, SALVATION

REPRESENTATIVES (*Ambassadors, Messengers, Representatives*)

In what ways are Christians to be representatives of Christ?

BIBLE READING: 2 Corinthians 5:11-21
KEY BIBLE VERSE: *We are Christ's ambassadors, and God is using us to speak to you. We urge you, as though Christ himself were here pleading with you, "Be reconciled to God!"* (2 Corinthians 5:20)

Christians are to carry Christ's message to the world. An ambassador is an official representative on behalf of one country to another. As believers, we are Christ's ambassadors, sent with his message of reconciliation to the world. An ambassador of reconciliation has an important responsibility. We dare not take this responsibility lightly. How well are you fulfilling your commission as Christ's ambassador?

BIBLE READING: Ephesians 4:1-16
KEY BIBLE VERSE: *I, a prisoner for serving the Lord, beg you to lead a life worthy of your calling, for you have been called by God.* (Ephesians 4:1)

Christians are to live Christ's message in the world. God has chosen us to be Christ's representatives on earth. In light of this truth, Paul challenges us to live a life worthy of the calling we have received—the awesome privilege of being called Christ's very own. This includes being humble, gentle, patient, understanding, and peaceful. People are watching your life. Can they see Christ in you? How well are you doing as his representative?

Related Topics: AMBASSADORS, BELIEVERS, WITNESSING

REPUTATION (*Fame, History, Name*)

How can we achieve a good reputation?

BIBLE READING: Deuteronomy 4:1-14
KEY BIBLE VERSE: *If you obey them carefully, you will display your wisdom and intelligence to the surrounding nations. When they hear about these laws, they will exclaim, "What other nation is as wise and prudent as this!"* (Deuteronomy 4:6)

A good reputation comes from obeying God's Word. Some people work hard to make others think they are smart. The books they carry and the facts they quote are impressive. But Moses said that a reputation for wisdom comes by obeying

God's Word. This may not be the easiest or most glamorous way to earn a reputation, but it is the most authentic. Do you fall into the trap of trying to make
others think you are intelligent because of what you know or pretend to know?
Obeying God's Word will give you a far greater reputation, because it's not just
what you *know*, but what you *do* that really counts.

BIBLE READING: Ruth 2:1-23

KEY BIBLE VERSE: *Ruth fell at his feet and thanked him warmly. "Why are you being
so kind to me?" she asked. "I am only a foreigner." "Yes, I know," Boaz replied.
"But I also know about the love and kindness you have shown your mother-in-law
since the death of your husband. I have heard how you left your father and mother
and your own land to live here among complete strangers."* (Ruth 2:10-11)

A good reputation comes from consistent living. Ruth's life exhibited admirable
qualities: she was hardworking, loving, kind, faithful, and brave. These qualities
gained for her a good reputation, but only because she displayed them *consistently* in all areas of her life. Wherever Ruth went or whatever she did, her character remained the same.

Your reputation is formed by the people who watch you at work, in town, at
home, in church. A good reputation comes by consistently living out the qualities
you believe in—no matter what group of people or surroundings you are in.

Related Topics: IMAGE, POSITION, STATUS

REQUESTS (*see* PRAYER)

RESENTMENT (*Anger, Envy, Jealousy*)

What happens when resentment is allowed to remain in our life?

BIBLE READING: Exodus 20:1-26

KEY BIBLE VERSE: *Do not covet your neighbor's house. Do not covet your neighbor's
wife, male or female servant, ox or donkey, or anything else your neighbor owns.*
(Exodus 20:17)

Resentment can lead to sinful actions. To covet is to wish to have the possessions
of others. It goes beyond simply admiring someone else's possessions or thinking, "I'd like to have one of those." Coveting includes envy—resenting the fact
that others have what you don't. God knows, however, that possessions never
make anyone happy for long. Since only God can supply all our needs, true contentment is found only in him. When you begin to covet, try to determine if a
more basic need is leading you to envy. For example, you may covet someone's
success not because you want to take it away from him, but because you would
like to feel as appreciated by others as he is. If this is the case, pray that God will
help you deal with your resentment and meet your basic needs.

BIBLE READING: Judges 8:1-3

KEY BIBLE VERSE: *Then the people of Ephraim asked Gideon, "Why have you treated
us this way? Why didn't you send for us when you first went out to fight the
Midianites?" And they argued heatedly with Gideon.* (Judges 8:1)

Resentment can lead to wrongful accusations. Ephraim's leaders felt left out
because Gideon had not called them to join the battle, but had left them in

place to "clean up" the escaping Midianites—so they angrily confronted him. Gideon assured the leaders of Ephraim that their accomplishment was even greater than his own clan's (Abiezer). His diplomatic explanation pointed out that this rear guard had managed to capture the enemy's generals, thus cutting off the leaders from their army. Not every necessary job is a highly visible leadership role. Much of the necessary labor of any effective enterprise is considered by many to be dirty work. But such work is vital to getting any big task done. Engineers and millionaires may design and finance an elegant building, but it is the bricklayers who get the work done. Pride causes us to want recognition. Are you content to be God's bricklayer, or do you resent the work God has given you?

BIBLE READING: James 1:1-27

KEY BIBLE VERSE: *Dear brothers and sisters, whenever trouble comes your way, let it be an opportunity for joy. For when your faith is tested, your endurance has a chance to grow. So let it grow, for when your endurance is fully developed, you will be strong in character and ready for anything.* (James 1:2-4)

Resentment can prevent positive spiritual growth. We can't really know the depth of our character until we see how we react under pressure. It is easy to be kind to others when everything is going well, but can we still be kind when others are treating us unfairly? God wants to make us mature and complete, not to keep us from all pain. Instead of resenting our difficulties, we should see them as opportunities for growth. Thank God for promising to be with you in rough times. Ask him to help you solve your problems or to give you the strength to endure them. Then be patient. God will not leave you alone with your problems; he will stay close and help you grow.

Related Topics: ANGER, JEALOUSY, SPIRITUAL GROWTH

RESISTANCE (*see* TEMPTATION)

RESOURCES (*Assistance, Help, Power*)

How are we to think of the resources we have?

BIBLE READING: Exodus 3:1-22

KEY BIBLE VERSE: *"Now go, for I am sending you to Pharaoh. You will lead my people, the Israelites, out of Egypt." "But who am I to appear before Pharaoh?" Moses asked God. "How can you expect me to lead the Israelites out of Egypt?"* (Exodus 3:10-11)

Our resources are given to us by God. Moses made excuses because he felt inadequate for the job God asked him to do. It was natural for him to feel that way. He *was* inadequate all by himself. But God wasn't asking Moses to work alone. He offered other resources to help (God himself, Aaron, and the ability to do miracles). God often calls us to tasks that seem too difficult, but he doesn't ask us to do them alone. God offers us his resources, just as he did for Moses. We should not hide behind our inadequacies, as Moses did, but look beyond ourself to the great resources available. Then we can allow God to use our unique contributions.

BIBLE READING: Luke 12:35-48

KEY BIBLE VERSE: *People who are not aware that they are doing wrong will be punished only lightly. Much is required from those to whom much is given, and much more is required from those to whom much more is given.* (Luke 12:48)

Our resources are to be used responsibly. Jesus has told us how to live until he comes: we must watch for him, work diligently, and obey his commands. Such attitudes are especially necessary for leaders. Watchful and faithful leaders will be given increased opportunities and responsibilities. The more resources, talents, and understanding we have, the more we are responsible to use them effectively. God will not hold us responsible for gifts he has not given us, but all of us have enough gifts and duties to keep us busy until Jesus comes.

BIBLE READING: Luke 19:11-27

KEY BIBLE VERSE: *When he returned, the king called in the servants to whom he had given the money. He wanted to find out what they had done with the money and what their profits were.* (Luke 19:15)

God will call us to account for our use of his resources. This story showed Jesus' followers what they were to do during the time between Jesus' departure and his second coming. Because we live in that time period, it applies directly to us. We have been given excellent resources to build and expand God's kingdom. Jesus expects us to use these talents so that they multiply and the kingdom grows. He asks each of us to account for what we do with his gifts. While awaiting the coming of the kingdom of God in glory, we must do Christ's work.

Related Topics: GIFTS, MINISTRY, SERVING

RESPECT *(Appreciation, Honor, Obedience)*

Who is worthy of respect?

BIBLE READING: Exodus 3:1-22

KEY BIBLE VERSE: *"Do not come any closer,"* God told him. *"Take off your sandals, for you are standing on holy ground."* (Exodus 3:5)

God is worthy of great respect. At God's command, Moses removed his sandals and covered his face. Taking off his shoes was an act of reverence, conveying his own unworthiness before God. God is our friend, but he is also our sovereign Lord. To approach him frivolously shows a lack of respect and sincerity. When you come to God in worship, do you approach him casually, or do you come as though you were an invited guest before a king? If necessary, adjust your attitude so it is suitable for approaching a holy God.

BIBLE READING: 1 Samuel 24:1-22

KEY BIBLE VERSE: *But then David's conscience began bothering him because he had cut Saul's robe. "The LORD knows I shouldn't have done it,"* he said to his men. *"It is a serious thing to attack the LORD's anointed one, for the LORD himself has chosen him."* (1 Samuel 24:5-6)

Those in authority are worthy of respect. David had great respect for Saul, in spite of the fact that Saul was trying to kill him. Although Saul was sinning and rebelling against God, David still respected the position he held as God's anointed king. David knew he would one day be king, and he also knew it was not right to strike down the man God had placed on the throne. If he assassinated Saul, he would be setting a precedent for his own opponents to remove him some day.

Romans 13:1-7 teaches that God has placed the government and its leaders in power. We may not know why, but, like David, we are to respect the positions and roles of those to whom God has given authority. There is one exception, however. Because God is our highest authority, we should not allow a leader to pressure us to violate God's law.

BIBLE READING: Acts 5:12-42
KEY BIBLE VERSE: *The high priest and his friends, who were Sadducees, reacted with violent jealousy. They arrested the apostles and put them in the jail.* (Acts 5:17-18)

Those who are faithful to God are worthy of respect. The religious leaders were jealous—Peter and the apostles were already commanding more respect than they had ever received. The difference, however, was that the religious leaders demanded respect and reverence for themselves; the apostles' goal was to bring respect and reverence to God. The apostles were respected not because they demanded it, but because they deserved it.

Related Topics: HONOR, PRAISE, SUBMISSION

RESPONSIBILITY (*Integrity, Obedience, Trustworthiness*)

What are the qualities of a responsible person?

BIBLE READING: 1 Chronicles 21:1
KEY BIBLE VERSE: *Then David said to God, "I have sinned greatly and shouldn't have taken the census. Please forgive me for doing this foolish thing."* (1 Chronicles 21:8)

Responsible people admit their wrongs. When David realized his sin, he took full responsibility, admitted he was wrong, and asked God to forgive him. Many people want to add God and the benefits of Christianity to their life without acknowledging their personal sin and guilt. But confession and repentance must come before receiving forgiveness. Like David, we must take full responsibility for our actions and confess them to God before we can expect him to forgive us and continue his work in us.

BIBLE READING: Matthew 25:14-46
KEY BIBLE VERSE: *Again, the Kingdom of Heaven can be illustrated by the story of a man going on a trip. He called together his servants and gave them money to invest for him while he was gone.* (Matthew 25:14)

Responsible people are faithful with what they have been given. The master divided the money among his servants according to their abilities. No one received more or less than he could handle. If he failed in his assignment, his excuse could not be that he was overwhelmed. Failure could come only from laziness or hatred toward the master. The talents represent any kind of resource are given. God gives us time, gifts, and other resources according to our abilities, and he expects us to invest them wisely until he returns. We are responsible to use well what God has given us. The issue is not how much we have, but how well we use what we have.

Responsible people plan for the future. This parable describes the consequences of two attitudes to Christ's return. The person who diligently prepares for it by investing his or her time and talent to serve God will be rewarded. The person who has no heart for the work of the kingdom will be punished. God rewards faithfulness. Those who bear no fruit for God's kingdom cannot expect to be treated the same as those who are faithful.

BIBLE READING: Acts 6:1-7

KEY BIBLE VERSE: *Now look around among yourselves, brothers, and select seven men who are well respected and are full of the Holy Spirit and wisdom. We will put them in charge of this business. Then we can spend our time in prayer and preaching and teaching the word. (Acts 6:3-4)*

Responsible people know their abilities and their limitations. As the early church increased in size, so did its needs. One great need was to organize the distribution of food to the poor. The apostles needed to focus on preaching, so they chose others to administer the food program. Each person has a vital part to play in the life of the church (see 1 Corinthians 12). If you are in a position of leadership and find yourself overwhelmed by responsibilities, determine *your* God-given abilities and priorities and then find others to help. If you are not in leadership, you have gifts that can be used by God in various areas of the church's ministry. Offer these gifts in service to him.

Responsible people share the work load. The apostles' priorities were correct. The ministry of the Word should never be neglected because of administrative burdens. Pastors should not try—or be expected to try—to do everything. Instead, the work of the church should be spread out among its members.

Related Topics: ABILITIES, GIFTS, MINISTRY

REST *(Recuperation, Refreshment, Relaxation)*

What does the Bible say about rest?

BIBLE READING: Genesis 2:1-25

KEY BIBLE VERSE: *God blessed the seventh day and declared it holy, because it was the day when he rested from his work of creation. (Genesis 2:3)*

Rest is important to maintaining a balanced life. We live in an action-oriented world! There always seems to be something to do and no time to rest. Yet God demonstrated that rest is appropriate and right. If God himself rested from his work, then it should not amaze us that we also need rest. Jesus demonstrated this principle when he and his disciples left in a boat to get away from the crowds (see Mark 6:31-32). Our times of rest refresh us for times of service.

BIBLE READING: Exodus 20:1-26

KEY BIBLE VERSE: *Remember to observe the Sabbath day by keeping it holy. (Exodus 20:8)*

Rest is important for worship. The Sabbath was a day set aside for rest and worship. God commanded a Sabbath because human beings need to spend unhurried time in worship and rest each week. A God who is concerned enough to provide a day each week for us to rest is indeed wonderful. By observing a regular time of rest and worship in our fast-paced world, we demonstrate how important God is to us, and our spirit is refreshed. Don't neglect God's provision.

BIBLE READING: Hebrews 4:1-13

KEY BIBLE VERSE: *There is a special rest still waiting for the people of God. For all who enter into God's rest will find rest from their labors, just as God rested after creating the world. Let us do our best to enter that place of rest. For anyone who disobeys God, as the people of Israel did, will fall.* (Hebrews 4:9-11)

Rest is part of God's ultimate plan. God rested on the seventh day not because he was tired, but to indicate the completion of creation. The world was perfect, and God was well satisfied with it. This rest is a foretaste of our eternal joy when creation will be renewed and restored, every mark of sin will be removed, and the world will be made perfect again. Our full complete rest in Christ begins when we trust him to complete his good and perfect work in us.

Rest is a gift of God. God wants us to enter his rest. For the Israelites of Moses' time, this rest was the earthly rest to be found in the Promised Land. For Christians, it is peace with God now and eternal life in a new earth later. We do not need to wait for the next life to enjoy God's rest and peace; we may have it daily now! Our daily rest in the Lord will not end with death, but will become an eternal rest in the place that Christ is preparing for us (John 14:1-4).

Related Topics: GOSPEL, SALVATION, WORK

RESTITUTION *(Compensation, Payment, Settlement)*

What does the Bible teach about restitution?

BIBLE READING: Exodus 22:1-17

KEY BIBLE VERSE: *Suppose there is a dispute between two people as to who owns a particular ox, donkey, sheep, article of clothing, or anything else. Both parties must come before God for a decision, and the person whom God declares guilty must pay double to the other.* (Exodus 22:9)

Restitution is essential to justice. Throughout Exodus 22 we find examples of the principle of restitution—making wrongs right. For example, if a man stole an animal, he had to pay double the beast's market value. If you have done someone wrong, perhaps you should go beyond what is expected to make things right. This will (1) help ease any pain you've caused, (2) help the other person be more forgiving, and (3) make you more likely to think before you do it again.

BIBLE READING: Leviticus 6:1-7

KEY BIBLE VERSE: *Suppose some of the people sin against the LORD by falsely telling their neighbor that an item entrusted to their safekeeping has been lost or stolen. Or suppose they have been dishonest with regard to a security deposit, or they have taken something by theft or extortion. Or suppose they find a lost item and lie about it, or they deny something while under oath, or they commit any other similar sin. If they have sinned in any of these ways and are guilty, they must give back whatever they have taken by theft or extortion, whether a security deposit, or property entrusted to them, or a lost object that they claimed as their own, or anything gained by swearing falsely. When they realize their guilt, they must restore the principal amount plus a penalty of 20 percent to the person they have harmed.* (Leviticus 6:2-5)

Restitution is essential to righteousness. Here we discover that stealing involves more than just taking from someone. Finding something and not returning it or refusing to return something borrowed are other forms of stealing. These are sins against God and not just your neighbor, a stranger, or a large business. If you have gotten something deceitfully, then confess your sin to God, apologize to the owner, and return the stolen items—with interest.

BIBLE READING: Numbers 5:5-10

KEY BIBLE VERSE: *The LORD said to Moses, "Give these instructions to the people of Israel: If any of the people—men or women—betray the LORD by doing wrong to another person, they are guilty. They must confess their sin and make full restitution for what they have done, adding a penalty of 20 percent and returning it to the person who was wronged."* (Numbers 5:5-7)

Restitution is essential to forgiveness. God included restitution, a unique concept for that day, as part of his law for Israel. When someone was robbed, the guilty person was required to restore to the victim what had been taken and pay an additional interest penalty. When we have wronged others, we ought to do more than apologize. We should look for ways to set matters right and, if possible, leave the victim even better off than when we harmed him or her. When we have been wronged, we should still seek restoration rather than striking out in revenge.

Related Topics: FORGIVENESS, JUSTICE, PUNISHMENT

RESTORATION *(Healing, Renewal, Repair)*

How should we view restoration?

BIBLE READING: Psalm 126:1-6

KEY BIBLE VERSE: *Restore our fortunes, LORD, as streams renew the desert.* (Psalm 126:4)

Restoration is a gift from God. God's capacity for restoring life is beyond our understanding. Forests burn down and are able to grow back. Broken bones heal. Even grief is not a permanent condition. Our tears can be seeds that will grow into a harvest of joy, because God is able to bring good out of tragedy. When burdened by sorrow, know that your times of grief will end and that you will again find joy. We must be patient as we wait. God's great harvest of joy is coming!

BIBLE READING: Matthew 8:1-4

KEY BIBLE VERSE: *Jesus touched him. "I want to," he said. "Be healed!" And instantly the leprosy disappeared. Then Jesus said to him, "Go right over to the priest and let him examine you. Don't talk to anyone along the way. Take along the offering required in the law of Moses for those who have been healed of leprosy, so everyone will have proof of your healing."* (Matthew 8:3-4)

Restoration is part of the healing process. Leprosy, like AIDS today, was a terrifying disease because there was no known cure. In Jesus' day, the Greek word for *leprosy* was used for a variety of similar diseases, and some forms were contagious. If a person contracted the contagious type, a priest declared him a leper and banished him from his home and city. The leper was sent to live in a community with other lepers until he either got better or died. Yet when the leper begged Jesus to heal him, Jesus reached out and touched him, even though his skin was covered with the dread disease.

BIBLE READING: Ephesians 4:1-16

KEY BIBLE VERSE: *We will hold to the truth in love, becoming more and more in every way like Christ, who is the head of his body, the church. Under his direc-*

tion, the whole body is fitted together perfectly. As each part does its own special work, it helps the other parts grow, so that the whole body is healthy and growing and full of love. (Ephesians 4:15-16)

Restoration is the work of the body of Christ. Some Christians fear that any mistake will destroy their witness for the Lord. They see their own weaknesses, and they know that many non-Christians seem to have stronger character than they do. How can we grow up into Christ? The answer is that Christ forms us into a body—into a group of individuals who are united in their purpose and in their love for one another and for the Lord. If an individual stumbles, the rest of the group is there to pick that person up and help him or her walk with God again. If an individual sins, restoration can be found through the church (Galatians 6:1) even as the rest of the body continues to witness to God's truth. As part of Christ's body, do you reflect part of Christ's character and carry out your special role in his work?

Related Topics: FAILURE, HEALING, SALVATION

RESTRAINT (*see* AMBITION)

RESULTS (*Achievements, Conclusions, Goals*)

How should we view results in the Christian life?

BIBLE READING: Exodus 6:1-12
KEY BIBLE VERSE: *Moses told the people what the LORD had said, but they wouldn't listen anymore. They had become too discouraged by the increasing burden of their slavery.* (Exodus 6:9)

Faithful obedience does not always yield instant results. When Moses gave God's message to the people, they were too discouraged to listen. The Hebrews didn't want to hear any more about God and his promises because the last time they listened to Moses, all they got was more work and greater suffering. Sometimes a clear message from God is followed by a period when no change in the situation is apparent. During that time, apparent setbacks may turn people away from wanting to hear more about God. If you are a leader, don't give up. Keep bringing people God's message as Moses did. By focusing on God, who must be obeyed, rather than on the results to be achieved, good leaders see beyond temporary setbacks and reversals.

BIBLE READING: Judges 13:1-25
KEY BIBLE VERSE: *You will become pregnant and give birth to a son, and his hair must never be cut. For he will be dedicated to God as a Nazirite from birth. He will rescue Israel from the Philistines.* (Judges 13:5)

We cannot measure results by our timetable. Manoah's wife was told that her son would rescue Israel from Philistine oppression. It wasn't until David's day that the Philistine opposition was completely crushed (2 Samuel 8:1). Samson's part in subduing the Philistines was just the beginning, but it was important nonetheless. It was the task God had given Samson to do. Be faithful in following God, even if you don't see instant results, because you might be beginning an important job that others will finish.

BIBLE READING: Luke 10:17-24

KEY BIBLE VERSE: *"Yes," he told them, "I saw Satan falling from heaven as a flash of lightning! And I have given you authority over all the power of the enemy, and you can walk among snakes and scorpions and crush them. Nothing will injure you. But don't rejoice just because evil spirits obey you; rejoice because your names are registered as citizens of heaven."* (Luke 10:18-20)

Relationship with God is more important than the results of our work. The disciples had seen tremendous results as they ministered in Jesus' name and with his authority. They were elated by the victories they had witnessed, and Jesus shared their enthusiasm. He helped them get their priorities right, however, by reminding them of their most important victory—that their names were written in heaven. This honor was more important than any of their accomplishments. As we see God's wonders at work in and through us, we should not lose sight of the greatest wonder of all—our heavenly citizenship.

BIBLE READING: Luke 17:1-10

KEY BIBLE VERSE: *"Even if you had faith as small as a mustard seed,"* the Lord answered, *"you could say to this mulberry tree, 'May God uproot you and throw you into the sea,' and it would obey you!"* (Luke 17:6)

True faith will bring real results. A mustard seed is small, but it is alive and growing. Like a tiny seed, a small amount of genuine faith in God will take root and grow. Almost invisible at first, it will begin to spread, first under the ground and then visibly. Although each change will be gradual and imperceptible, soon this faith will have produced major results that will uproot and destroy competing loyalties. We don't need more faith; a tiny seed of faith is enough, if it is alive and growing.

Related Topics: ACCOMPLISHMENTS, ACHIEVEMENTS, GOALS

RESURRECTION (New Life, Return, Revival)

▶ THE RESURRECTION OF JESUS
What importance does the resurrection of Jesus have to the Christian faith?

BIBLE READING: Matthew 28:1-10

KEY BIBLE VERSE: *Then the angel spoke to the women. "Don't be afraid!" he said. "I know you are looking for Jesus, who was crucified. He isn't here! He has been raised from the dead, just as he said would happen. Come, see where his body was lying."* (Matthew 28:5-6)

The resurrection of Jesus is the foundation of the Christian faith. The resurrection of Jesus is the key to the Christian faith. Why? (1) Just as he promised, Jesus rose from the dead. We can be confident, therefore, that he will accomplish all he has promised. (2) Jesus' bodily resurrection shows us that the living Christ is ruler of God's eternal kingdom, not a false prophet or impostor. (3) We can be certain of our resurrection because he was resurrected. Death is not the end—there is future life. (4) The power that brought Jesus back to life is available to us to bring our spiritually dead self back to life. (5) The Resurrection is the basis for the church's witness to the world. Jesus is more than just a human leader; he is the Son of God.

BIBLE READING: 1 Corinthians 15:1-11

KEY BIBLE VERSE: *I passed on to you what was most important and what had also been passed on to me—that Christ died for our sins, just as the Scriptures said. He was buried, and he was raised from the dead on the third day, as the Scriptures said.* (1 Corinthians 15:3-4)

The Resurrection is the decisive point of the Christian faith. There will always be people who say that Jesus didn't rise from the dead. Paul assures us that many people saw Jesus after his resurrection: Peter, the disciples (the Twelve), more than five hundred Christian believers (most of whom were still alive when Paul wrote this, although some had died), James (Jesus' brother), all the apostles, and finally Paul himself. The Resurrection is a historical fact. Don't be discouraged by doubters who deny the Resurrection. Be filled with hope because of the knowledge that one day you and they will see the living proof when Christ returns.

▶ OUR RESURRECTION
What does the Bible teach about our resurrection?

BIBLE READING: 1 Corinthians 15:12-28

KEY BIBLE VERSE: *Tell me this—since we preach that Christ rose from the dead, why are some of you saying there will be no resurrection of the dead?* (1 Corinthians 15:12)

Our resurrection includes body and soul. Most Greeks did not believe that people's bodies would be resurrected after death. They saw the afterlife as something only for the soul. According to Greek philosophers, the soul was the real person, imprisoned in a physical body, and at death the soul was released. There was no immortality for the body, but the soul entered an eternal state. Christianity, in contrast, affirms that the body and soul will be united after resurrection. The church at Corinth was in the heart of Greek culture. Thus many believers had a difficult time believing in a bodily resurrection. Paul wrote this part of his letter to clear up this confusion about the resurrection.

Our resurrection is certain because of Christ's resurrection. The resurrection of Christ is the center of the Christian faith. Because Christ rose from the dead as he promised, we know that what he said is true—he is God. Because he rose, we have certainty that our sins are forgiven. Because he rose, he lives and represents us to God. Because he rose and defeated death, we know we will also be raised.

Our resurrection is our only hope for eternal life. Why does Paul say believers should be pitied if there were only earthly value to Christianity? In Paul's day, Christianity often brought a person persecution, ostracism from family, and, in many cases, poverty. There were few tangible benefits from being a Christian in that society. It was certainly not a step up the social or career ladder. Even more important, however, is the fact that if Christ had not been resurrected from death, Christians could not be forgiven for their sins and would have no hope of eternal life.

What will our resurrected body be like?

BIBLE READING: 1 Corinthians 15:35-58

KEY BIBLE VERSE: *Let me tell you a wonderful secret God has revealed to us. Not all of us will die, but we will all be transformed. It will happen in a moment, in the blinking of an eye, when the last trumpet is blown. For when the trumpet sounds,* the Christians who have died will be raised with transformed bodies. And then we who are living will be transformed so that we will never die. For our perishable earthly bodies must be transformed into heavenly bodies that will never die. (1 Corinthians 15:51-53)

Our resurrected body will be eternal. Paul launches into a discussion about what our resurrected body will be like. If you could select your own body, what kind would you choose—strong, athletic, beautiful? Paul explains that we will be recognized in our resurrected body, yet it will be better than we can imagine, for it will be made to live forever. We will still have our own personality and individuality, but these will be perfected through Christ's work. The Bible does not reveal everything that our resurrected body will be able to do, but we know it will be perfect, without sickness or disease (see Philippians 3:21).

Our resurrected body will be different than our present one. Paul compares the resurrection of our body with the growth in a garden. Seeds placed in the ground don't grow unless they "die" first. The plant that grows is very different looking from the seed because God gives it a new "body." There are different kinds of bodies—people, animals, fish, birds. Even the angels in heaven have bodies that are different in beauty and glory. Our resurrected body will be very different in some ways, but not all, from our earthly body.

Our resurrected body will not experience present limitations. Our present body is perishable and prone to decay. Our resurrection body will be transformed. Our spiritual body will not be limited by the laws of nature. This does not necessarily mean we'll be superpeople, but our body will be different from and more capable than our present earthly one. Our spiritual body will not be weak, will never get sick, and will never die.

Related Topics: ETERNAL LIFE, GOD, POWER

RETALIATION (*see* REVENGE)

REVELATION (*see* BIBLE)

REVENGE (*Get Even, Retaliate, Vengeance*)

What does the Bible teach concerning revenge?

BIBLE READING: 1 Kings 1:28-53
KEY BIBLE VERSE: *Solomon replied, "If he proves himself to be loyal, he will not be harmed. But if he does not, he will die." (1 Kings 1:52)*

Forgiveness is stronger than revenge. While Adonijah feared for his life and expected the severest punishment, Solomon simply dismissed his brother and sent him home. As a new king, Solomon had the power to kill his rivals, something Adonijah would have done had his conspiracy succeeded. But Solomon acted as if he had nothing to prove, thus demonstrating his authority and power. Sometimes forgiving a personal attack shows more strength than lashing out in revenge does. Trying to prove one's power and authority often proves only one's fear and self-doubt. Only after Adonijah made another attempt to secure royal power was Solomon forced to have him executed (1 Kings 2:13-25).

BIBLE READING: Matthew 5:38-48

KEY BIBLE VERSE: *You have heard that the law of Moses says, "If an eye is injured, injure the eye of the person who did it. If a tooth gets knocked out, knock out the tooth of the person who did it." But I say, don't resist an evil person! If you are slapped on the right cheek, turn the other, too.* (Matthew 5:38-39)

We should resist revenge in favor of love. When we are wronged, often our first reaction is to get even. But Jesus suggested a new, radical response to injustice: instead of demanding rights, give them up freely! According to Jesus, it is more important to be merciful than to demand justice. We are to do *good* to those who wrong us! Our desire should not be to keep score, but to love and forgive. This is not natural—it is supernatural. Only God can give us the strength to love as he does. Instead of planning vengeance, pray for those who hurt you.

BIBLE READING: Romans 12:9-21

KEY BIBLE VERSE: *Dear friends, never avenge yourselves. Leave that to God. For it is written, "I will take vengeance; I will repay those who deserve it," says the Lord.* (Romans 12:19)

Revenge should be left in God's hands. In this day of constant lawsuits and incessant demands for legal rights, Paul's command sounds almost impossible. When someone hurts us deeply, instead of giving him what he deserves, we are to befriend him. Why does Paul tell us to forgive our enemies? (1) Forgiveness may break a cycle of retaliation and lead to mutual reconciliation. (2) It may make the enemy feel ashamed and change his or her ways. (3) In contrast, repaying evil for evil hurts you just as much as it hurts your enemy. Even if your enemy never repents, forgiving him or her will free you of a heavy load of bitterness.

Related Topics: ANGER, FORGIVENESS, JUSTICE

REVERENCE (*see* HONOR)

REVIVAL (*see* RENEWAL)

REWARDS (*Consequences, Payments, Results*)

How does God reward us?

BIBLE READING: 2 Chronicles 15:1-19

KEY BIBLE VERSE: *And now, you men of Judah, be strong and courageous, for your work will be rewarded.* (2 Chronicles 15:7)

God rewards us with both temporal and eternal gifts. Azariah encouraged the men of Judah to keep up the good work, "for your work will be rewarded." This is an inspiration for us too. Recognition and reward are great motivators that have two dimensions: (1) *The temporal dimension.* Living by God's standards may result in acclaim here on earth. (2) *The eternal dimension.* Permanent recognition and reward will be given in the next life. Don't be discouraged if you feel your faith in God is going unrewarded here on earth. The best rewards are not in this life, but in the life to come.

BIBLE READING: Matthew 6:1-34

KEY BIBLE VERSE: *Take care! Don't do your good deeds publicly, to be admired, because then you will lose the reward from your Father in heaven.* (Matthew 6:1)

God rewards selfless acts done in secret. It's easier to do what's right when we gain recognition and praise. To be sure our motives are not selfish, we should do our good deeds quietly or in secret, with no thought of reward. Jesus says we should check our motives in three areas: generosity (6:2-4), prayer (6:5-6), and fasting (6:16-18). Those acts should not be self-centered, but God-centered, done not to make us look good, but to make God look good. The reward God promises is not material, and it is never given to those who seek it. Doing something only for yourself is not a loving sacrifice. With your next good deed, ask, "Would I still do this if no one would ever know I did it?"

BIBLE READING: Matthew 19:16-30
KEY BIBLE VERSE: *Everyone who has given up houses or brothers or sisters or father or mother or children or property, for my sake, will receive a hundred times as much in return and will have eternal life.* (Matthew 19:29)

God rewards us abundantly. Jesus assured the disciples that anyone who gives up something valuable for his sake will be repaid many times over in this life, although not necessarily in the same form. For example, a person may be rejected by his or her family for accepting Christ, but he or she will gain the larger family of believers.

God rewards us according to his standards. Jesus turned the world's values upside down. Consider the most powerful or well-known people in our world—how many got where they are by being humble, self-effacing, and gentle? Not many! But in the life to come, the last will be first—if they got in last place by choosing to follow Jesus. Don't forfeit eternal rewards for temporary benefits. Be willing to make sacrifices now for greater rewards later. Be willing to accept human disapproval, while knowing that you have God's approval.

Related Topics: ETERNAL LIFE, HEAVEN, JUSTICE

RICHES (*see* WEALTH)

RIDICULE (*see* PERSECUTION)

RIGHT (*Correct, Honest, Truthful*)

What does God expect of us?

BIBLE READING: Joshua 7:1-26
KEY BIBLE VERSE: *Israel was unfaithful concerning the things set apart for the LORD. A man named Achan had stolen some of these things, so the LORD was very angry with the Israelites. Achan was the son of Carmi, of the family of Zimri, of the clan of Zerah, and of the tribe of Judah.* (Joshua 7:1)

God wants us to do what is right all of the time. Why did Achan's sin bring judgment on the entire nation? Although it was one man's failure, God saw it as national disobedience to a national law. God needed the entire nation to be committed to the job they had agreed to do—conquer the land. Thus, when one person failed, everyone failed. If Achan's sin went unpunished, unlimited looting could break out. The nation as a whole had to take responsibility for preventing this undisciplined disobedience.

Achan's sin was not merely his keeping some of the plunder (God allowed it in some cases), but his disobeying God's explicit command to destroy everything connected with Jericho. His sin was indifference to the evil and idolatry of the city, not just a desire for money and clothes. God would not protect Israel's army again until the sin was removed and the army returned to obeying him without reservation. God is not content with our doing what is right some of the time. He wants us to do what is right all the time. We are under his orders to eliminate any thoughts, practices, or possessions that hinder our devotion to him.

BIBLE READING: Judges 17:1-13

KEY BIBLE VERSE: *In those days Israel had no king, so the people did whatever seemed right in their own eyes.* (Judges 17:6)

God wants us to do what he considers right. Micah and his mother seemed to be good and moral people and may have sincerely desired to worship God, but they disobeyed God by following their own desires instead of doing what God wanted. The attitude that prevailed in Micah's day was this: "Everyone did whatever he wanted to." This is remarkably similar to today's prevailing attitudes. But God has given us standards. He has not left our conduct up to us and our opinions. We can avoid conforming to society's low standards by taking God's commands seriously and applying them to life. Independence and self-reliance are positive traits, but only within the framework of God's standards.

How can we know what is right?

BIBLE READING: Isaiah 5:1-30

KEY BIBLE VERSE: *Destruction is certain for those who say that evil is good and good is evil; that dark is light and light is dark; that bitter is sweet and sweet is bitter.* (Isaiah 5:20)

God's Word reveals to us what is right. When people do not carefully observe the distinction between good and evil, destruction soon follows. It is easy for people to say, "No one can decide for anyone else what is really right or wrong." They may think getting drunk can't hurt them, extramarital sex isn't really wrong, or money doesn't control them. But when we make excuses for our actions, we break down the distinction between right and wrong. If we do not take God's Word, the Bible, as our standard, soon all moral choices will appear fuzzy. Without God, we are headed for a breakdown and much suffering.

BIBLE READING: Romans 2:1-16

KEY BIBLE VERSE: *God will punish the Gentiles when they sin, even though they never had God's written law. And he will punish the Jews when they sin, for they do have the law. For it is not merely knowing the law that brings God's approval. Those who obey the law will be declared right in God's sight. Even when Gentiles, who do not have God's written law, instinctively follow what the law says, they show that in their hearts they know right from wrong. They demonstrate that God's law is written within them, for their own consciences either accuse them or tell them they are doing what is right.* (Romans 2:12-15)

God has built an awareness of what is right into every society. If you traveled around the world, you would find evidence in every society and culture of God's moral law. For example, virtually all cultures prohibit murder, and yet in all societies that law has been broken. We belong to a stubborn race. We know what's right, but we insist on doing what's wrong. It is not enough to know what's right; we must also do it. Admit to yourself and to God that you fit the human pattern and frequently fail to live up to your own standards (much less to God's standards). That's the first step to forgiveness and healing.

Related Topics: GRACE, SIN, SALVATION

RIGHTEOUSNESS *(Goodness, Morality, Purity)*

How do we become righteousness?

 BIBLE READING: Psalm 51:1-19
KEY BIBLE VERSE: *Create in me a clean heart, O God. Renew a right spirit within me.* (Psalm 51:10)

We are not righteous by nature. Because we are born as sinners (51:5), our natural inclination is to please ourself rather than God. David followed that inclination when he took another man's wife. We also follow it when we sin in any way. Like David, we must ask God to cleanse us from within (51:7), making room for clean thoughts and right desires. Right conduct can come only from a clean heart and spirit. Ask God to create a pure heart in you.

 BIBLE READING: Isaiah 64:1-12
KEY BIBLE VERSE: *We are all infected and impure with sin. When we proudly display our righteous deeds, we find they are but filthy rags. Like autumn leaves, we wither and fall. And our sins, like the wind, sweep us away.* (Isaiah 64:6)

We do not become righteous by being good. This passage can easily be misunderstood. It does not mean that God will reject us if we come to him in faith, nor does it mean that he despises our efforts to please him. It means that if we come to him demanding acceptance on the basis of our "good" conduct, God will point out that our righteousness is nothing compared to his infinite righteousness. Sin makes us unclean so that we cannot approach God (Romans 3:23) any more than a beggar in rotten rags could dine at a king's table. Our best efforts are still infected with sin. Our only hope, therefore, is faith in Jesus Christ, who can cleanse us and bring us into God's presence.

 BIBLE READING: 2 Corinthians 5:11-21
KEY BIBLE VERSE: *God made Christ, who never sinned, to be the offering for our sin, so that we could be made right with God through Christ.* (2 Corinthians 5:21)

We become righteous through Christ. When we trust in Christ, we make an exchange—our sin for his righteousness. Our sin was poured into Christ at his crucifixion. His righteousness is poured into us at our conversion. This is what is meant by Christ's "atonement" for sin. In the world, bartering works only when two people exchange goods of relatively equal value. But God offers to trade his righteousness for our sin—something of immeasurable worth for something completely worthless. How grateful we should be for his kindness to us.

Related Topics: FORGIVENESS, GRACE, OBEDIENCE

RISK *(Adventure, Chance, Danger)*

Why do Christians need to take risks?

BIBLE READING: Acts 4:1-22

KEY BIBLE VERSE: *While Peter and John were speaking to the people, the leading priests, the captain of the Temple guard, and some of the Sadducees came over to them. They were very disturbed that Peter and John were claiming, on the authority of Jesus, that there is a resurrection of the dead. They arrested them and, since it was already evening, jailed them until morning.* (Acts 4:1-3)

Obeying Christ will involve risk. Not often will sharing the gospel send us to jail as it did Peter and John. Still, we run risks in trying to win others to Christ. We might be willing to face a night in jail if it would bring five thousand people to Christ, but shouldn't we also be willing to suffer for the sake of even one? What do you risk in witnessing—rejection, persecution? Whatever the risks, realize that nothing done for God is ever wasted.

BIBLE READING: Acts 26:1-32

KEY BIBLE VERSE: *I preached first to those in Damascus, then in Jerusalem and through-out all Judea, and also to the Gentiles, that all must turn from their sins and turn to God—and prove they have changed by the good things they do.* (Acts 26:20)

Sharing the gospel will involve risk. Paul was risking his life for a message that was offensive to the Jews and unbelievable to the Gentiles. Jesus received the same response to his message (Mark 3:21; John 10:20). To a worldly, materialis-tic mind, it seems insane to risk so much to gain what seems to be so little. But as you follow Christ, you soon discover that temporary possessions look very small next to even the smallest eternal reward.

BIBLE READING: 2 Corinthians 4:1-18

KEY BIBLE VERSE: *Yes, we live under constant danger of death because we serve Jesus, so that the life of Jesus will be obvious in our dying bodies. So we live in the face of death, but it has resulted in eternal life for you.* (2 Corinthians 4:11-12)

Living in the power of Christ will involve risk. Paul reminds us that though we may think we are at the end of our rope, we are never at the end of hope. Our body is subject to sin and suffering, but God never abandons us. Because Christ has won the victory over death, we have eternal life. All our risks, humiliations, and trials are opportunities for Christ to demonstrate his power and presence in and through us.

Related Topics: OBEDIENCE, SACRIFICE, SUFFERING

RITUAL (*see* RELIGION)

ROLES (*see* EXAMPLE)

ROMANCE (*see* LOVE)

RULES (*Commands, Guidelines, Standards*)

How are we to understand and respond to God's rules?

BIBLE READING: Matthew 5:17-20

KEY BIBLE VERSE: *Don't misunderstand why I have come. I did not come to abolish the law of Moses or the writings of the prophets. No, I came to fulfill them. I assure you, until heaven and earth disappear, even the smallest detail of God's law will remain until its purpose is achieved.* (Matthew 5:17-18)

Realize that God's rules are not ends in themselves. God's moral and ceremonial laws were given to help people love God with all their hearts and minds. Throughout Israel's history, however, these laws had been often misquoted and misapplied. By Jesus' time, religious leaders had turned the laws into a confusing mass of rules. When Jesus talked about a new way to understand God's law, he was actually trying to bring people back to its *original* purpose. Jesus did not speak against the law itself, but against the abuses and excesses to which it had been subjected. (See John 1:17.)

Realize that God's rules do not all carry the same force. If, by his own words, Jesus did not come to abolish the law, does that mean all the Old Testament laws still apply to us today? In the Old Testament, there were three categories of law: ceremonial, civil, and moral.

(1) The *ceremonial law* related specifically to Israel's worship (see Leviticus 1:2-3, for example). Its primary purpose was to point forward to Jesus Christ; these laws, therefore, were no longer necessary after Jesus' death and resurrection. While we are no longer bound by ceremonial laws, the principles behind them—to worship and love a holy God—still apply. Jesus was often accused by the Pharisees of violating ceremonial law.

(2) The *civil law* applied to daily living in Israel (see Deuteronomy 24:10-11, for example). Because modern society and culture are so radically different from that time and setting, all of these guidelines cannot be followed specifically. But the principles behind the commands are timeless and should guide our conduct. Jesus demonstrated these principles by example.

(3) The *moral law* (such as the Ten Commandments) is the direct command of God, and it requires strict obedience (see Exodus 20:13, for example). The moral law reveals the nature and will of God, and it still applies today. Jesus obeyed the moral law completely.

God's rules must be obeyed inwardly as well as outwardly. The Pharisees were exacting and scrupulous in their attempts to follow their laws. So how could Jesus reasonably call us to a greater righteousness than theirs? The Pharisees' weakness was that they were content to obey the laws outwardly without allowing God to change their hearts (or attitudes). Jesus was saying, therefore, that the quality of our goodness should be greater than that of the Pharisees. They looked pious, but they were far from the kingdom of God. God judges our heart as well as our deeds, for it is in the heart that our real allegiance lies. Be just as concerned about your attitudes that people don't see as about your actions that are seen by all.

BIBLE READING: Romans 7:1-6
KEY BIBLE VERSE: *Now we have been released from the law, for we died with Christ, and we are no longer captive to its power. Now we can really serve God, not in the old way by obeying the letter of the law, but in the new way, by the Spirit.* (Romans 7:6)

Realize that keeping God's rules does not save us. Some people try to earn their way to God by keeping a set of rules (obeying the Ten Commandments, attending church faithfully, or doing good deeds), but all they earn for their efforts is frustration and discouragement. However, because of Christ's sacrifice, the way to God is already open, and we can become his children simply by putting our faith in him. No longer trying to reach God by keeping rules, we can become more and more like Jesus as we live with him day by day. Let the Holy Spirit turn your eyes away from your own performance and toward Jesus. He will free you to serve him out of love and gratitude. This is living "in the new way."

Related Topics: LEGALISM, OBEDIENCE, RIGHTEOUSNESS

RUMORS (*see* GOSSIP)

RUNNING (*Avoiding, Escaping, Ignoring*)

When is running away appropriate?

 BIBLE READING: Genesis 16:1-16

KEY BIBLE VERSE: *The angel said to her, "Hagar, Sarai's servant, where have you come from, and where are you going?" "I am running away from my mistress,"* she replied. (Genesis 16:8)

Running away from our problems rarely solves them. Hagar was running away from her mistress and her problem. The angel of the Lord gave her this advice: (1) to return and face Sarai, the cause of her problem, and (2) to submit to her. Hagar needed to work on her attitude toward Sarai, no matter how justified it may have been. It is wise to face our problems squarely, accept God's promise of help, correct our attitudes, and act as we should.

 BIBLE READING: 2 Timothy 2:14-26

KEY BIBLE VERSE: *Run from anything that stimulates youthful lust. Follow anything that makes you want to do right. Pursue faith and love and peace, and enjoy the companionship of those who call on the Lord with pure hearts.* (2 Timothy 2:22)

Running away from temptation is often the best solution. Running away is sometimes considered cowardly. But wise people realize that removing themselves physically from temptation often can be the most courageous action to take. Timothy, a young man, was warned to flee anything that produced evil thoughts. Do you have a recurring temptation that is difficult to resist? Remove yourself physically from any situation that stimulates your desire to sin. Knowing when to run is as important in spiritual battle as knowing when and how to fight. (See also 1 Timothy 6:11.)

Related Topics: COMPROMISE, PROBLEMS, TEMPTATION

SACRIFICE (*Discipline, Gift, Offering*)

What types of sacrifice are pleasing to God?

BIBLE READING: 1 Chronicles 21:1-30
KEY BIBLE VERSE: *The king replied to Araunah, "No, I insist on paying what it is worth. I cannot take what is yours and give it to the LORD. I will not offer a burnt offering that has cost me nothing!"* (1 Chronicles 21:24)

God is pleased with a sacrifice that costs us something. When David wanted to buy Araunah's land to build an altar, Araunah generously offered it as a gift. But David refused, saying, "I will not . . . offer a burnt offering that has cost me nothing." David wanted to offer a sacrifice to God. The word *sacrifice* implies giving something that costs the giver in terms of self, time, or money. To give sacrificially requires more than a token effort or gift. God wants us to give voluntarily, but he wants it to mean something. Giving to God what costs you nothing does not demonstrate commitment.

BIBLE READING: Psalm 50:1-15
KEY BIBLE VERSE: *I don't need the bulls you sacrifice; I don't need the blood of goats. What I want instead is your true thanks to God; I want you to fulfill your vows to the Most High. Trust me in your times of trouble, and I will rescue you, and you will give me glory.* (Psalm 50:13-15)

God is pleased with a sacrifice that comes from true love and obedience. God's perfect moral nature demands that the penalty for sin be death. Under the old covenant, a person could offer an animal to God as a substitute for himself, symbolizing the person's faith in the merciful, forgiving God. But, the people were offering sacrifices as part of their worship ritual and forgetting their significance! The very act of sacrifice showed that they had once agreed to follow God wholeheartedly. But at this time their hearts were not in it, so their sacrifices were not pleasing to God, and thus were worthless. We may fall into the same pattern when we participate in religious activities, tithe, or attend church out of habit or conformity rather than out of heartfelt love and obedience. God wants righteousness, not empty ritual.

BIBLE READING: Matthew 8:18-22
KEY BIBLE VERSE: *One of the teachers of religious law said to him, "Teacher, I will follow you no matter where you go!" But Jesus said, "Foxes have dens to live in, and birds have nests, but I, the Son of Man, have no home of my own, not even a place to lay my head."* (Matthew 8:19-20)

God is pleased with the sacrifice of following his Son. Following Jesus is not always easy or comfortable. Often it means great cost and sacrifice, with no earthly rewards or security. Jesus didn't have a place to call home. You may find that following Christ costs you popularity, friendships, leisure time, or treasured habits. But while the cost of following Christ is high, the value of being Christ's disciple is even higher. Discipleship is an investment that lasts for eternity and yields incredible rewards.

BIBLE READING: Matthew 19:16-30
KEY BIBLE VERSE: *Jesus told him, "If you want to be perfect, go and sell all you have and give the money to the poor, and you will have treasure in heaven. Then come, follow me." * (Matthew 19:21)

God is pleased with a sacrificial attitude that puts everything we have at his disposal. Should all believers sell everything they own? No. We are responsible to care for our own needs and the needs of our families so that we will not be a burden on others. We should, however, be willing to give up anything if God asks us to do so. This kind of attitude allows nothing to come between us and God and keeps us from using our God-given wealth selfishly. If you are comforted by the fact that Christ did not tell all his followers to sell all their possessions, then you may be too attached to what you have.

BIBLE READING: Romans 9:1-5
KEY BIBLE VERSE: *In the presence of Christ, I speak with utter truthfulness—I do not lie—and my conscience and the Holy Spirit confirm that what I am saying is true. My heart is filled with bitter sorrow and unending grief for my people, my Jewish brothers and sisters. I would be willing to be forever cursed—cut off from Christ!—if that would save them.* (Romans 9:1-3)

God is pleased with a sacrificial attitude that shows real love for others. Paul expressed concern for his Jewish "brothers and sisters" by saying that he would willingly take their punishment if that would save them. While the only one who can save us is Christ, Paul showed a rare depth of love. Like Jesus, he was willing to sacrifice for others. How concerned are you for those who don't know Christ? Are you willing to sacrifice your time, money, energy, comfort, and safety to see them come to faith in Jesus?

BIBLE READING: Romans 12:1-8
KEY BIBLE VERSE: *Dear brothers and sisters, I plead with you to give your bodies to God. Let them be a living and holy sacrifice—the kind he will accept. When you think of what he has done for you, is this too much to ask?* (Romans 12:1)

God is pleased with sacrificial living, because it shows obedience and gratitude for his grace. When sacrificing an animal according to God's law, a priest would kill the animal, cut it in pieces, and place it on the altar. Sacrifice was important, but even in the Old Testament God made it clear that obedience from the heart was much more important (see 1 Samuel 15:22; Psalm 40:6; Amos 5:21-24). God wants us to offer ourself, not animals, as a *living* sacrifice— daily laying aside our own desires to follow him, putting all our energy and resources at his disposal and trusting him to guide us. We do this out of gratitude that our sins have been forgiven.

God has good, pleasing, and perfect plans for his children. He wants us to be transformed people with renewed minds, living to honor and obey him. Because he wants only what is best for us, and because he gave his Son to make our new life possible, we should joyfully give ourself as a living sacrifice for his service.

BIBLE READING: Hebrews 13:8-17

KEY BIBLE VERSE: *With Jesus' help, let us continually offer our sacrifice of praise to God by proclaiming the glory of his name. Don't forget to do good and to share what you have with those in need, for such sacrifices are very pleasing to God.* (Hebrews 13:15-16)

God is pleased with our genuine praise and receives it as a sacrifice. These Jewish Christians, because of their witness that Jesus was the Messiah, no longer worshiped with other Jews. So praise and acts of service became their sacrifices— ones they could offer anywhere, anytime. This must have reminded them of the prophet Hosea's words, "Forgive all our sins and graciously receive us, so that we may offer you the sacrifice of praise" (Hosea 14:2). A "sacrifice of praise" today would include thanking Christ for his sacrifice on the cross and telling others about it. Acts of kindness and sharing are particularly pleasing to God, even when they go unnoticed by others.

Related Topics: GIVING, DISCIPLINE, OBEDIENCE

SAFETY (*see* SECURITY)

SALVATION (*Conversion, Rescue, Spiritual Birth*)

▶ **GOD'S GIFT**
What is the salvation that God offers us?

BIBLE READING: Matthew 1:18-25

KEY BIBLE VERSE: *She will have a son, and you are to name him Jesus, for he will save his people from their sins.* (Matthew 1:21)

Salvation is something we can never accomplish on our own. *Jesus* means "Savior." Jesus came to earth to save us because we can't save ourselves from sin and its consequences. No matter how good we are, we can't eliminate the sinful nature present in all of us. Only Jesus can do that. Jesus didn't come to help people save themselves; he came to be their Savior from the power and penalty of sin. Thank Christ for his death on the cross for your sin, and then ask him to take control of your life. Your new life begins at that moment.

Salvation is the assurance of God's presence within us. Jesus was to be called *Immanuel* ("God is with us"), as predicted by Isaiah the prophet (Isaiah 7:14). Jesus was God in the flesh; thus God was literally among us, "with us." Through the Holy Spirit, Christ is present today in the life of every believer. Perhaps not even Isaiah understood how far-reaching the meaning of *Immanuel* would be.

BIBLE READING: Matthew 7:7-14

KEY BIBLE VERSE: *You can enter God's Kingdom only through the narrow gate. The highway to hell is broad, and its gate is wide for the many who choose the easy way. But the gateway to life is small, and the road is narrow, and only a few ever find it.* (Matthew 7:13-14)

Salvation is a single plan. The gate that leads to eternal life (John 10:7-9) is called "narrow." This does not mean that it is difficult to become a Christian, but that there is only *one* road that leads to eternal life with God, and only a few decide to take it. Believing in Jesus is the only way to heaven, because he alone died for our sins and made us right before God. Living his way may not be popular, but it is true and right. Thank God there is one way!

BIBLE READING: John 3:1-21

KEY BIBLE VERSE: *Just as you can hear the wind but can't tell where it comes from or where it is going, so you can't explain how people are born of the Spirit.* (John 3:8)

Salvation is a work done in our life by the Holy Spirit. Jesus explained that we cannot control the work of the Holy Spirit. He works in ways we cannot predict or understand. Just as you did not control your physical birth, so you cannot control your spiritual birth. It is a gift from God through the Holy Spirit (Ephesians 1:11-14; 2:8-9).

Salvation is much more than just knowing about Jesus. This Jewish teacher of the Bible knew the Old Testament thoroughly, but he didn't understand what it said about the Messiah. Knowledge is not salvation. You should know the Bible, but even more important, you should understand the God whom the Bible reveals and the salvation that God offers.

BIBLE READING: John 6:60-71

KEY BIBLE VERSE: *Simon Peter replied, "Lord, to whom would we go? You alone have the words that give eternal life. We believe them, and we know you are the Holy One of God."* (John 6:68-69)

Salvation is available only because of Christ. After many of Jesus' followers had deserted him, he asked the twelve disciples if they were also going to leave. Peter replied, "To whom would we go?" In his straightforward way, Peter answered for all of us—there is no other way. Though there are many philosophies and self-styled authorities, Jesus alone has the words of eternal life. People look everywhere for eternal life except to Christ, the only source. Stay with him, especially when you feel confused or alone.

Salvation is a matter of receiving or rejecting Christ. There is no middle ground with Jesus. When he asked the disciples if they would also leave, he was showing that they could either accept or reject him. Jesus was not trying to repel people with his teachings. He was simply telling the truth. The more the people heard Jesus' message, the more they divided into two camps: the honest seekers who wanted to understand more, and those who rejected Jesus because they didn't like what they heard.

BIBLE READING: Ephesians 2:1-10

KEY BIBLE VERSE: *God saved you by his special favor when you believed. And you can't take credit for this; it is a gift from God. Salvation is not a reward for the good things we have done, so none of us can boast about it.* (Ephesians 2:8-9)

Salvation is a gift to be profoundly appreciated. When someone gives you a gift, do you say, "That's very nice—now how much do I owe you?" No, the appropriate response to a gift is "Thank you." Yet how often Christians, even after they have been given the gift of salvation, feel obligated to try to work their way to God. Because our salvation and even our faith are gifts, we should respond with gratitude, praise, and joy.

Salvation cannot be earned. We become Christians through God's unmerited grace, not as the result of any effort, ability, intelligent choice, or act of service on our part. However, out of gratitude for this free gift, we will seek to help and serve others with kindness, love, and gentleness, and not merely to please ourselves. While no action or work we do can help us obtain salvation, God's intention is that our salvation will result in acts of service. We are not saved merely for our own benefit, but to serve Christ and build up the church (4:12).

▶ **RECEIVING THE GIFT**
How do we receive the salvation God offers us in Christ?

BIBLE READING: Luke 13:22-30

KEY BIBLE VERSE: *Someone asked him, "Lord, will only a few be saved?" He replied, "The door to heaven is narrow. Work hard to get in, because many will try to enter."* (Luke 13:23-24)

Salvation is not to be received lightly or casually. Receiving salvation requires more concentrated effort than most people are willing to put forth. Obviously we cannot save ourselves—there is no way we can work ourselves into God's favor. The effort we must put out to enter through the narrow door is earnestly desiring to know Jesus and diligently striving to follow him whatever the cost. We dare not put off making this decision because the door will not stay open forever.

Receiving salvation is a deep and total commitment. The people were eager to know who would be in God's kingdom. Jesus explained that although many people know something about God, only a few have acknowledged their sins and accepted his forgiveness. Just listening to Jesus' words or admiring his miracles is not enough—we must turn from sin and trust in God to save us.

BIBLE READING: Luke 14:15-24

KEY BIBLE VERSE: *Hearing this, a man sitting at the table with Jesus exclaimed, "What a privilege it would be to have a share in the Kingdom of God!"* (Luke 14:15)

Receiving salvation is not to be put off until later. The man sitting at the table with Jesus saw the glory of God's kingdom, but he did not yet understand how to get in. In Jesus' story, many people turned down the invitation to the banquet because the timing was inconvenient. We too can resist or delay responding to God's invitation, and our excuses may sound reasonable—work duties, family responsibilities, financial needs, or whatever they may be. Nevertheless, God's invitation is the most important event in our life, no matter how inconveniently it may be timed. Are you making excuses to avoid responding to God's call? Jesus reminds us that the time will come when God will pull his invitation and offer it to others—then it will be too late to get into the banquet.

Receiving salvation means also receiving the Savior. It was customary to send two invitations to a party—the first to announce the event, the second to tell the guests that everything was ready. The guests in Jesus' story insulted the host by making excuses when he issued the second invitation. In Israel's history, God's first invitation came from Moses and the prophets; the second came from his Son. The religious leaders accepted the first invitation. They believed that God had called them to be his people, but they insulted God by refusing to accept his Son. Thus, as the master in the story sent his servant into the streets to invite the needy to his banquet, so God sent his Son to the whole world of needy people to tell them that God's kingdom had arrived and was ready for them.

BIBLE READING: John 17:1-5

KEY BIBLE VERSE: *This is the way to have eternal life—to know you, the only true God, and Jesus Christ, the one you sent to earth.* (John 17:3)

Receiving salvation includes entering into a personal relationship with God. How do we get eternal life? Jesus tells us clearly here—by knowing God the Father himself through his Son, Jesus Christ. Eternal life requires entering into a personal relationship with God through his Son, Jesus Christ. When we admit our sin and turn away from it, Christ's love lives in us by the Holy Spirit.

BIBLE READING: Acts 2:14-41

KEY BIBLE VERSE: *Peter's words convicted them deeply, and they said to him and to the other apostles, "Brothers, what should we do?" Peter replied, "Each of you must turn from your sins and turn to God, and be baptized in the name of Jesus Christ for the forgiveness of your sins. Then you will receive the gift of the Holy Spirit."* (Acts 2:37-38)

Receiving salvation is a powerful, personal response to the gospel. After Peter's powerful, Spirit-filled message, the people were deeply moved and asked, "What should we do?" This is the basic question we must ask. It is not enough to be sorry for our sins—we must let God forgive them, and then we must live like forgiven people. Has God spoken to you through his Word or through the words of another believer? Like Peter's audience, ask God what you should do, and then obey.

Receiving salvation means we must repent of our sins. If you want to follow Christ, you must "turn from your sins . . . and be baptized." To "turn from sin" means changing the direction of your life from selfishness and rebellion against God's laws. At the same time, you must *turn to* Christ, depending on him for forgiveness, mercy, guidance, and purpose. We cannot save ourselves—only God can save us. Baptism identifies us with Christ and with the community of believers. It is a condition of discipleship and a sign of faith.

BIBLE READING: Romans 10:1-15

KEY BIBLE VERSE: *Salvation that comes from trusting Christ—which is the message we preach—is already within easy reach. In fact, the Scriptures say, "The message is close at hand; it is on your lips and in your heart." For if you confess with your mouth that Jesus is Lord and believe in your heart that God raised him from the dead, you will be saved. For it is by believing in your heart that you are made right with God, and it is by confessing with your mouth that you are saved.* (Romans 10:8-10)

Receiving salvation is simple, direct, personal, and public. Have you ever been asked, "How do I become a Christian?" These verses give you the beautiful answer—salvation is as close as your own mouth and heart. People think it must be a complicated process, but it is not. If we believe in our heart and say with our mouth that Christ is the risen Lord, we will be saved.

BIBLE READING: 1 Corinthians 1:18-31

KEY BIBLE VERSE: *To those called by God to salvation, both Jews and Gentiles, Christ is the mighty power of God and the wonderful wisdom of God. This "foolish" plan of God is far wiser than the wisest of human plans, and God's weakness is far stronger than the greatest of human strength.* (1 Corinthians 1:24-25)

Receiving salvation is simple, yet many still refuse. Paul continues to emphasize that the way to receive salvation is so simple that *any* person who wants to can understand it. Skill and wisdom do not get a person into God's kingdom—simple faith does—so no one can boast that his or her achievements helped secure eternal life. Salvation is totally from God through Jesus' death. There is *nothing* we can do to earn our salvation; we need only accept what Jesus has already done for us.

Related Topics: FAITH, GOSPEL, REPENTANCE

SARCASM (*see* CRITICISM)

SATAN (*Angel of Light, Devil, Evil One*)

What does the Bible teach us about Satan?

BIBLE READING: Genesis 3:1-24

KEY BIBLE VERSE: *The serpent was the shrewdest of all the creatures the LORD God had made. "Really?" he asked the woman. "Did God really say you must not eat any of the fruit in the garden?"* (Genesis 3:1)

Satan's goal is to keep us from knowing God. Disguised as a crafty serpent, Satan came to tempt Eve. Satan at one time was an angel who rebelled against God and was thrown out of heaven. As a created being, Satan has definite limitations. Although he is trying to tempt everyone away from God, he will not be the final victor. In Genesis 3:14-15, God promises that Satan will be crushed by one of the woman's offspring, the Messiah.

From the beginning of humanity, Satan has been the tempter. Why does Satan tempt us? Temptation is Satan's invitation to give in to his kind of life and give up on God's kind of life. Satan tempted Eve and succeeded in getting her to sin. Ever since then, he's been busy getting people to sin.

How could Eve have resisted temptation? By following the same guidelines we can follow. First, we must realize that *being tempted* is not a sin. We have not sinned until we *give in* to the temptation. Then, to resist temptation, we must (1) pray for strength to resist, (2) run, sometimes literally, and (3) say no when confronted with what we know is wrong. James 1:12 tells of the blessings and rewards for those who don't give in when tempted.

Satan attacks us through our weaknesses. The serpent, Satan, tempted Eve by getting her to doubt God's goodness. He implied that God was strict, stingy, and selfish for not wanting Eve to share his knowledge of good and evil. Satan made Eve forget all that God had given her and, instead, focus on the one thing she couldn't have. We fall into trouble, too, when we dwell on the few things we don't have rather than on the countless things God has given us. The next time you are feeling sorry for yourself and thinking about what you don't have, consider all you *do* have and thank God. Then your doubts won't lead you into sin.

Satan constantly tries to replace right with wrong. Satan tried to make Eve think that sin is good, pleasant, and desirable. A knowledge of both good and evil seemed harmless to her. People usually choose wrong things because they have become convinced that those things are good, at least for themselves. Our sins do not always appear ugly to us, and the pleasant sins are the hardest to avoid. So prepare yourself to resist the attractive temptations that may come your way. We cannot always prevent temptation, but there is always a way of escape (1 Corinthians 10:13). Use God's Word and God's people to help you stand against it.

Satan is our enemy. He will do anything he can to get us to follow his evil, deadly path. The phrase "you will strike his heel" refers to Satan's repeated attempts to defeat Christ during his life on earth. "He will crush your head" foreshadows Satan's defeat when Christ rose from the dead. A strike on the heel is not deadly, but a crushing blow to the head is. Already God was revealing his plan to defeat Satan and offer salvation to the world through his Son, Jesus Christ.

BIBLE READING: Matthew 4:1-11

KEY BIBLE VERSE: *Jesus was led out into the wilderness by the Holy Spirit to be tempted there by the Devil.* (Matthew 4:1)

Satan even tempted Christ himself. This temptation by the devil gave Jesus the opportunity to reaffirm God's plan for his ministry. It also gives us an example to follow when we are tempted. Jesus' temptation was an important demonstration of his humanness and sinlessness. He faced temptation, but he did not give in.

Christ set a pattern for resisting Satan's temptations. This time of testing showed that Jesus really was the Son of God, able to overcome the devil and his temptations. A person has not shown true obedience if he or she has never had an opportunity to disobey. We read in Deuteronomy 8:2 that God led Israel into the desert to humble and test them. God wanted to see whether or not his people would really obey him. We too will be tested. Because we know that testing will come, we should be alert and ready for it. Remember, your convictions are only strong if they hold up under pressure!

Satan has great, but temporary, powers in the world. Satan tempted Eve in the Garden of Eden, and here he tempted Jesus in the desert. Satan is a fallen angel. He is *real*, not symbolic, and he is constantly fighting against those who follow and obey God. Satan's temptations are also real. He is always trying to get us to live his way or our way rather than God's way. Jesus will one day reign over all creation, but Satan tried to force his hand and get him to declare his kingship prematurely. If Jesus had given in, his mission on earth—to die for our sins and give us the opportunity to have eternal life—would have been lost. When temptations seem especially strong, or when you think you can rationalize giving in, consider whether Satan may be trying to block God's purposes for your life or for someone else's life.

Satan's temptation of Jesus demonstrates ways in which we may be tempted. The devil's temptations focused on three crucial areas: (1) physical needs and desires, (2) possessions and power, and (3) pride (see 1 John 2:15-16 for a similar list). But Jesus did not give in. Hebrews 4:15 says that Jesus "faced all of the same temptations we do, yet he did not sin." He knows firsthand what we are experiencing, and he is willing and able to help us in our struggles. When you are tempted, turn to him for strength.

BIBLE READING: Ephesians 6:10-20
KEY BIBLE VERSE: *Put on all of God's armor so that you will be able to stand firm against all strategies and tricks of the Devil.* (Ephesians 6:11)

Satan is waging war against God's people. In the Christian life we battle against evil rulers and authorities of the unseen world (the powerful evil forces of fallen angels headed by Satan, who is a vicious fighter; see 1 Peter 5:8). To withstand their attacks, we must depend on God's strength and use every piece of his armor. Paul is not only giving this counsel to the church, the body of Christ, but to all individuals within the church. The whole body needs to be armed. As you do battle against "the evil rulers and authorities of the unseen world," fight as a body in the strength that comes from the Holy Spirit.

Satan's forces are supernatural. These who are not "flesh and blood" are demons over whom Satan has control. They are not mere fantasies—they are very real. We face a powerful army whose goal is to defeat Christ's church. When we believe in Christ, these beings become our enemies, and they try every device to turn us away from him and back to sin. Although we are assured of victory, we must engage in the struggle until Christ returns, because Satan is constantly battling against all who are on the Lord's side. We need supernatural power to defeat Satan, and God has provided this by giving us his Holy Spirit within us and his armor surrounding us. If you feel discouraged, remember Jesus' words to Peter: "Upon this rock I will build my church, and all the powers of hell will not conquer it" (Matthew 16:18).

BIBLE READING: James 4:1-10
KEY BIBLE VERSE: *Humble yourselves before God. Resist the Devil, and he will flee from you.* (James 4:7)

Satan is a defeated enemy. Although God and the devil are at war, we don't have to wait until the end to see who will win. God has *already* defeated Satan (Revelation 12:10-12), and when Christ returns, the devil and all he stands for will be eliminated forever (Revelation 20:10-15). Satan is here now, however, and he is trying to win us over to his evil cause. With the Holy Spirit's power, we can resist the devil, and he will flee from us.

Related Topics: DEMONS, EVIL, TEMPTATION

SATISFACTION (*Contentment, Enjoyment, Relaxation*)

What are the principles behind finding satisfaction in life?

BIBLE READING: Genesis 25:27-34

KEY BIBLE VERSE: *Jacob gave Esau some bread and lentil stew. Esau ate and drank and went on about his business, indifferent to the fact that he had given up his birthright.* (Genesis 25:34)

Beware of paying too high a price for temporary satisfaction. Esau traded the lasting benefits of his birthright for the immediate pleasure of food. He acted on impulse, satisfying his immediate desires without pausing to consider the long-range consequences of what he was about to do. We can fall into the same trap. When we see something we want, our first impulse is to get it. At first we feel intensely satisfied and sometimes even powerful because we have obtained what we set out to get. But immediate pleasure often loses sight of the future. We can avoid making Esau's mistake by comparing the short-term satisfaction with its long-range consequences before we act.

Beware of exaggerating needs in order to rationalize poor choices. Esau exaggerated his hunger. I am "dying of starvation," he said. This thought made his choice much easier because if he was starving, what good was an inheritance anyway? The pressure of the moment distorted his perspective and made his decision seem urgent. We often experience similar pressures. For example, when we feel sexual pressure, a marriage vow may seem momentarily unimportant. We might feel such great pressure in one area that nothing else seems to matter, and we lose our perspective. Getting through that short, pressure-filled moment is often the most difficult part of overcoming a temptation.

BIBLE READING: Psalm 63:1-11

KEY BIBLE VERSE: *O God, you are my God; I earnestly search for you. My soul thirsts for you; my whole body longs for you in this parched and weary land where there is no water.* (Psalm 63:1)

God alone can satisfy our deepest longings! Hiding from his enemies in the barren desert of Judah, David was intensely lonely. He longed for a friend he could trust to ease his loneliness. No wonder he cried out, "O God, . . . my soul thirsts for you, . . . in this parched and weary land." If you are lonely or thirsty for something lasting in your life, remember David's prayer.

BIBLE READING: Ecclesiastes 2:11-26

KEY BIBLE VERSE: *I decided there is nothing better than to enjoy food and drink and to find satisfaction in work. Then I realized that this pleasure is from the hand of God. For who can eat or enjoy anything apart from him? God gives wisdom, knowledge, and joy to those who please him. But if a sinner becomes wealthy,*

God takes the wealth away and gives it to those who please him. Even this, however, is meaningless, like chasing the wind. (Ecclesiastes 2:24-26)

Real, lasting satisfaction can only be found in God. Is Solomon recommending
we make life a big, irresponsible party? No, he is encouraging us to take pleasure in what we're doing now and to enjoy life because it comes from God's
hand. True enjoyment in life comes only as we follow God's guidelines for
living. Without him, satisfaction is a lost search. Those who really know how
to enjoy life are the ones who take life each day as a gift from God, thanking
him for it and serving him in it. Those without God will have no relief from
toil and no direction to guide them through life's complications.

BIBLE READING: John 6:22-40

KEY BIBLE VERSE: *They replied, "What does God want us to do?" Jesus told them,
"This is what God wants you to do: Believe in the one he has sent."* (John
6:28-29)

The desire to satisfy God's requirements ought to be our highest goal. Many
sincere seekers for God are puzzled about what he wants them to do. The religions of the world are mankind's attempts to answer this question. But Jesus'
reply is brief and simple: we must believe on him whom God has sent. Satisfying God does not come from the work we *do*, but from whom we *believe*. The
first step is accepting that Jesus is who he claims to be. All spiritual development is built on this affirmation. Declare in prayer to Jesus, "You are the Christ,
the Messiah, the Son of the living God" (see Matthew 16:16), and embark on
a life of belief that is satisfying to your Creator.

Christ's presence satisfies our deepest desires. People eat bread to satisfy physical hunger and to sustain physical life. We can satisfy spiritual hunger and
sustain spiritual life only by a right relationship with Jesus Christ. No wonder
he called himself the Bread of Life. But bread must be eaten to sustain life, and
Christ must be invited into our daily walk to sustain spiritual life.

Related Topics: ACCOMPLISHMENTS, CONTENTMENT, SPIRITUAL GROWTH

SAVIOR (*see* JESUS CHRIST)

SCHEDULE (*Expectations, Plans, Timetables*)

How does God fit into our schedule?

BIBLE READING: Joshua 3:1-11

KEY BIBLE VERSE: *Joshua told the Israelites, "Come and listen to what the LORD your
God says."* (Joshua 3:9)

In our schedule, giving attention to God ought to be our priority and center.
Just before crossing over into the Promised Land, Joshua gathered the people to
hear the words of the Lord. Their excitement was high. No doubt they wanted
to rush on, but Joshua made them stop and listen. We live in a fast-paced age
where everyone rushes just to keep up. It is easy to get caught up in our daily
tasks and become too busy for what God says is most important—listening to
his words. Before making your schedule, take time to focus on what God wants
from all your activities. Knowing what God has said before you rush into your
day may help you avoid foolish mistakes.

BIBLE READING: Psalm 31:1-24
KEY BIBLE VERSE: *My future is in your hands. Rescue me from those who hunt me down relentlessly.* (Psalm 31:15)

In our schedule, we should remember that every moment is a gift from God. In saying, "My future is in your hands," David was expressing his belief that all of life's circumstances are under God's control. Knowing that God loves and cares for us enables us to keep steady in our faith regardless of our circumstances. It keeps us from sinning foolishly by taking matters into our own hands or resenting God's timetable.

BIBLE READING: John 11:1-16
KEY BIBLE VERSE: *Although Jesus loved Martha, Mary, and Lazarus, he stayed where he was for the next two days and did not go to them.* (John 11:5-6)

In our schedule, we must recognize that God's plans take precedence. Jesus loved this family and often stayed with them. He knew their pain, but did not respond immediately. His delay had a specific purpose. God's timing, especially his delays, may make us think he is not answering, or at least not the way we want him to. But he will meet all our needs according to his perfect schedule and purpose (Philippians 4:19). Patiently await his timing.

Related Topics: PLANS, PRIORITIES, TIMING

SCRIPTURE (*see* BIBLE)

SECOND COMING OF JESUS (*Arrival, Return, Revelation*)

▶ **ANTICIPATING THE SECOND COMING OF JESUS**
How should we live while we await the second coming of Jesus?

BIBLE READING: Matthew 24:1-51
KEY BIBLE VERSE: *Later, Jesus sat on the slopes of the Mount of Olives. His disciples came to him privately and asked, "When will all this take place? And will there be any sign ahead of time to signal your return and the end of the world?"* (Matthew 24:3)

We must be preparing ourselves so we will be ready for the second coming of Jesus. Jesus was sitting on the Mount of Olives, the very place where the prophet Zechariah had predicted that the Messiah would stand when he came to establish his kingdom (Zechariah 14:4). It was a fitting place for the disciples to ask Jesus when he would come in power and what they could expect then. Jesus' reply emphasized the events that would take place before the end of the age. He pointed out that his disciples should be less concerned with knowing the exact date and more concerned with being prepared—living God's way consistently so that no matter when Jesus came in glory, he would claim them as his own.

We should be aware of the signs of the Second Coming, but realize that these signs are easily misread. The disciples asked Jesus for the sign of his coming and of the end of the age. Jesus' first response was "Don't let anyone mislead you." The fact is that whenever we look for signs, we become very susceptible to being deceived. There are many "false prophets" (24:11-24) around with counterfeit signs of spiritual power and authority. The only sure way to keep from being deceived is to focus on Christ and his words. Don't look for special signs, and don't spend time looking at other people. Look at Christ.

We are to continue to do the important work that needs to be completed before Jesus returns. Jesus said that before he returns, the gospel of the kingdom (the message of salvation) would be preached throughout the world. This was the disciples' mission—and it is ours today. Jesus talked about the end times and final judgment to show his followers the urgency of spreading the Good News of salvation to everyone.

We can be sure that Jesus' return will be universally unmistakable. In times of persecution even strong believers will find it difficult to be loyal. To keep from being deceived by false messiahs, we must understand that Jesus' return will be unmistakable (Mark 13:26); no one will doubt that it is he. If you have to be told that the Messiah has come, then he hasn't (24:27). Christ's coming will be obvious to everyone.

We keep working, realizing that we don't know exactly when Jesus will return. If we knew the precise date, we might be tempted to be lazy in our work for Christ. Worse yet, we might plan to keep sinning and then turn to God right at the end. Heaven is not our only goal; we have work to do here. And we must keep on doing it until death or until we see the unmistakable return of our Savior.

We remain prepared, realizing that each day is the possible day of Jesus' return. Knowing that Christ's return will be sudden and unexpected should motivate us always to be prepared. We are not to live irresponsibly—sitting and waiting, doing nothing; seeking self-serving pleasure; using his tarrying as an excuse not to do God's work of building his kingdom; developing a false security based on precise calculations of events; or letting our curiosity about the end times divert us from doing God's work.

BIBLE READING: 2 Thessalonians 3:6-15

KEY BIBLE VERSE: *Dear brothers and sisters, we give you this command with the authority of our Lord Jesus Christ: Stay away from any Christian who lives in idleness and doesn't follow the tradition of hard work we gave you.* (2 Thessalonians 3:6)

We are to keep busy because neither Jesus' delay nor his imminent arrival should be an excuse for idleness. Some people in the Thessalonian church were falsely teaching that because Christ would return any day, people should set aside their responsibilities, quit work, do no future planning, and just wait for the Lord. But their lack of activity only led them into sin. They became a burden to the church, which was supporting them, and they wasted time that could have been used for helping others. These church members may have thought that they were being more spiritual by not working, but Paul told them to be responsible and get back to work. Being ready for Christ means obeying him in every area of life. Because we know that Christ is coming, we must live in such a way that our faith and our daily practice will please him when he arrives.

▶ **EXPERIENCING THE SECOND COMING OF JESUS**
What will happen at the second coming of Jesus?

BIBLE READING: John 12:37-50

KEY BIBLE VERSE: *All who reject me and my message will be judged at the day of judgment by the truth I have spoken.* (John 12:48)

Jesus' second coming will have a different purpose than his first coming. The purpose of Jesus' first mission on earth was not to judge people, but to show them the way to find salvation and eternal life. When he comes again, one of his main purposes will be to judge people for how they lived on earth. Christ's words that we would *not* accept and obey will condemn us. On the Day of judgment, those who accepted Jesus and lived his way will be raised to eternal life (1 Corinthians 15:51-57; 1 Thessalonians 4:15-18; Revelation 21:1-8), and those who rejected Jesus and lived any way they pleased will face eternal punishment (Revelation 20:11-15). Decide now which side you'll be on, for the consequences of your decision will last forever.

BIBLE READING: John 14:1-7

KEY BIBLE VERSE: *There are many rooms in my Father's home, and I am going to prepare a place for you. If this were not so, I would tell you plainly. When everything is ready, I will come and get you, so that you will always be with me where I am.* (John 14:2-3)

At Jesus' second coming, we will be with him forever. There are few verses in Scripture that describe eternal life, but these few verses are rich with promises. Here Jesus says, "I am going to prepare a place for you," and "I will come and get you." We can look forward to eternal life because Jesus has promised it to all who believe in him. Although the details of eternity are unknown, we need not fear because Jesus is preparing for us to spend eternity with him.

BIBLE READING: 1 Corinthians 1:4-9

KEY BIBLE VERSE: *Now you have every spiritual gift you need as you eagerly wait for the return of our Lord Jesus Christ. He will keep you strong right up to the end, and he will keep you free from all blame on the great day when our Lord Jesus Christ returns.* (1 Corinthians 1:7-8)

At Jesus' second coming, we will fully experience the reality of our salvation. Paul guaranteed the Corinthian believers that God would consider them "free from all blame" when Christ returns (see Ephesians 1:7-10). This guarantee was not because of their great gifts or their shining performance, but because of what Jesus Christ accomplished for them through his death and resurrection. *All* who have faith in the Lord Jesus as their personal Savior will be saved and considered blameless when Jesus Christ returns (see also 1 Thessalonians 3:13; Hebrews 9:28). If you have faith in Christ, even if it is weak, you *are* and *will be* saved.

BIBLE READING: 1 Thessalonians 4:13-18

KEY BIBLE VERSE: *Brothers and sisters, I want you to know what will happen to the Christians who have died so you will not be full of sorrow like people who have no hope. For since we believe that Jesus died and was raised to life again, we also believe that when Jesus comes, God will bring back with Jesus all the Christians who have died.* (1 Thessalonians 4:13-14)

Jesus' second coming will include the resurrection of believers who have died. The Thessalonians were wondering why many of their fellow believers had died and what would happen to them when Christ returned. Paul wanted the Thessalonians to understand that death is not the end of the story. When Christ returns, all believers—dead and alive—will be reunited, never to suffer or die again.

Jesus' second coming will signal victory. Because Jesus Christ came back to life, so will all believers. All Christians, including those living when Christ returns, will live with Christ forever. Therefore, we need not despair when loved ones die or world events take a tragic turn. God will turn our tragedies to triumphs, our poverty to riches, our pain to glory, and our defeat to victory. All believers throughout history will stand reunited in God's presence, safe and secure. As Paul comforted the Thessalonians with the promise of the resurrection, so we should comfort and reassure each other with this great hope.

Related Topics: ETERNAL LIFE, JESUS CHRIST, SALVATION

SECURITY *(Comfort, Protection, Safety)*

What kind of security do we really need?

BIBLE READING: Exodus 3:1-15

KEY BIBLE VERSE: *Moses protested, "If I go to the people of Israel and tell them, 'The God of your ancestors has sent me to you,' they won't believe me. They will ask, 'Which god are you talking about? What is his name?' Then what should I tell them?" God replied, "I AM THE ONE WHO ALWAYS IS. Just tell them, 'I AM has sent me to you.' "* (Exodus 3:13-14)

We need the security only an unchanging God can provide. The Egyptians had many gods by many different names. Moses wanted to know God's name so the Hebrew people would know exactly who had sent him to them. God called himself *I Am*, a name describing his eternal power and unchangeable character. In a world where values, morals, and laws change constantly, we can find stability and security in our unchanging God. The God who appeared to Moses is the same God who can live in us today. Hebrews 13:8 says God is the same "yesterday, today, and forever." Because God's nature is stable and trustworthy, we are free to follow and enjoy him rather than spend our time trying to figure him out.

BIBLE READING: Obadiah 1:1-21

KEY BIBLE VERSE: *You are proud because you live in a rock fortress and make your home high in the mountains. "Who can ever reach us way up here?" you ask boastfully. Don't fool yourselves!* (Obadiah 1:3)

We need security that is based on God, not objects or people. The Edomites felt secure, and they were proud of their self-sufficiency. But they were fooling themselves because there is no lasting security apart from God. Is your security in objects or people? Ask yourself how much lasting security they really offer. Possessions and people can disappear in a moment, but God does not change. Only he can supply true security.

We need to be secure in humility rather than in pride. The Edomites were proud of their city carved right into the rock. Today Sela, or Petra, is considered one of the marvels of the ancient world, but only as a tourist attraction. The Bible warns that pride is the surest route to self-destruction (Proverbs 16:18). Just as Petra and Edom fell, so will proud people fall. A humble person is more truly secure than a proud person, because humility gives a more accurate perspective of oneself and the world.

BIBLE READING: John 6:35-40

KEY BIBLE VERSE: *This is the will of God, that I should not lose even one of all those he has given me, but that I should raise them to eternal life at the last day.* (John 6:39)

We need the security of being under Christ's protection. Jesus said he would not lose even one person whom the Father had given him. Thus anyone who makes a sincere commitment to believe in Jesus Christ as Savior is secure in God's promise of eternal life. Christ will not let his people be overcome by Satan and lose their salvation (see also John 17:12; Philippians 1:6).

 BIBLE READING: 1 John 5:1-15
KEY BIBLE VERSE: *This is what God has testified: He has given us eternal life, and this life is in his Son. So whoever has God's Son has life; whoever does not have his Son does not have life.* (1 John 5:11-12)

We need the security that comes from knowing we have eternal life. Whoever believes in God's Son has eternal life. He is all you need. You don't need to *wait* for eternal life, because it begins the moment you believe. You don't need to *work* for it, because it is already yours. You don't need to *worry* about it, because you have been given eternal life by God himself—and it is guaranteed.

Some people *hope* that they will receive eternal life. John says we can *know* we have it. Our certainty is based on God's promise that he has given us eternal life through his Son. This is true whether you feel close to God or far away from him. Eternal life is not based on feelings, but on facts. You can know that you have eternal life if you believe God's truth. If you aren't sure that you are a Christian, ask yourself, Have I honestly committed my life to Christ as my Savior and Lord? If so, you know by faith that you are indeed a child of God.

Related Topics: CONTENTMENT, HAPPINESS, SATISFACTION

SELF-CENTEREDNESS (*Egotism, Pride, Selfishness*)

Why is being self-centered dangerous?

 BIBLE READING: Psalm 100:1-5
KEY BIBLE VERSE: *Acknowledge that the LORD is God! He made us, and we are his. We are his people, the sheep of his pasture.* (Psalm 100:3)

Self-centeredness can easily lead to hopelessness. God is our Creator; we did not create ourselves. Many people live as though they are the creator and center of their own little world. This mind-set leads to greedy self-centeredness and, if everything should be taken away, a loss of hope itself. But when we realize that God created us and gives us all we have, we will want to give to others as God gave to us (2 Corinthians 9:8). Then if all is lost, we still have God and all he gives us.

 BIBLE READING: Matthew 3:1-12
KEY BIBLE VERSE: *In those days John the Baptist began preaching in the Judean wilderness.* (Matthew 3:1)

Self-centeredness is a sin that requires repentance. Almost thirty years had passed since the events of Matthew 2. Here John the Baptist burst onto the scene. His theme was "Repent!" Repentance means doing an about-face—a 180-degree turn—from the kind of self-centeredness that leads to wrong actions such as lying, cheating, stealing, gossiping, taking revenge, being abusive, and indulging in sexual immorality. A person who repents stops rebelling and begins following God's way of living, prescribed in his Word. The first step in turning to God is admitting your sin, as John urged. Then God will receive you and help you to live the way he wants you to. Remember that only God can get rid of sin. He doesn't expect us to clean up our life *before* we come to him.

BIBLE READING: Matthew 25:14-30

KEY BIBLE VERSE: *The servant with the one bag of gold came and said, "Sir, I know you are a hard man, harvesting crops you didn't plant and gathering crops you didn't cultivate. I was afraid I would lose your money, so I hid it in the earth and here it is."* (Matthew 25:24-25)

Self-centeredness is a characteristic of sinful human nature. This man was thinking only of himself. He hoped to play it safe and protect himself from his hard master, but he was judged for his self-centeredness. We must not make excuses to avoid doing what God calls us to do. If God truly is our Master, we must obey willingly. Our time, abilities, and money aren't ours in the first place—we are caretakers, not owners. When we ignore, squander, or abuse what we are given, we are rebellious and deserve to be punished.

BIBLE READING: Mark 8:31-38

KEY BIBLE VERSE: *If you try to keep your life for yourself, you will lose it. But if you give up your life for my sake and for the sake of the Good News, you will find true life.* (Mark 8:35)

Self-centeredness is not part of a Christlike character. We should be willing to lose our life for the sake of the gospel, not because our life is useless, but because nothing—not even life itself—can compare to what we gain with Christ. Jesus wants us to *choose* to follow him rather than to lead a life of sin and self-satisfaction. He wants us to stop trying to control our own destiny and to let him direct us. This makes good sense because, as the Creator, Christ knows better than we do what real life is about. He asks for submission, not self-hatred; he asks us only to lose our self-centered determination to be in charge.

BIBLE READING: 1 Peter 1:14-25

KEY BIBLE VERSE: *Now you can have sincere love for each other as brothers and sisters because you were cleansed from your sins when you accepted the truth of the Good News. So see to it that you really do love each other intensely with all your hearts.* (1 Peter 1:22)

A self-centered person cannot really love. Sincere love involves selfless giving; a self-centered person can't truly love. God's love and forgiveness free you to take your eyes off yourself and to meet others' needs. By sacrificing his life, Christ showed that he truly loves you. Now you can love others by following his example and giving of yourself sacrificially.

Related Topics: LOVE, PRIDE, SELFISHNESS

SELF-CONFIDENCE (*see* CONFIDENCE)

SELF-CONTROL (*see* DISCIPLINE)

SELF-ESTEEM (*Health, Maturity, Self-Love*)

How does God help us with our self-esteem?

BIBLE READING: Psalm 8:1-9

KEY BIBLE VERSE: *When I look at the night sky and see the work of your fingers—the moon and the stars you have set in place—what are mortals that you should think of us, mere humans that you should care for us?* (Psalm 8:3-4)

Our self-esteem is grounded in the value God places on our life. When we look at the vast expanse of creation, we wonder how God could be concerned for people who constantly disappoint him. Yet God created us only a little lower than himself or the angels! The next time you question your worth as a person, remember that God considers you highly valuable. We have great worth because we bear the stamp of the Creator. (See Genesis 1:26-27 for the extent of worth God places on all people.) Because God has already declared how valuable we are to him, we can be set free from feelings of worthlessness.

BIBLE READING: Luke 12:4-12
KEY BIBLE VERSE: *What is the price of five sparrows? A couple of pennies? Yet God does not forget a single one of them. And the very hairs on your head are all numbered. So don't be afraid; you are more valuable to him than a whole flock of sparrows.* (Luke 12:6-7)

We are valuable to God. Our true value is God's estimate of our worth, not our peers'. Other people evaluate and categorize us according to how we perform, what we achieve, and how we look. But God cares for us, as he cares for all of his creatures, because we belong to him. So we can face life without fear.

BIBLE READING: Romans 12:1-8
KEY BIBLE VERSE: *As God's messenger, I give each of you this warning: Be honest in your estimate of yourselves, measuring your value by how much faith God has given you.* (Romans 12:3)

Our self-esteem is affected by how closely we identify with Christ. Healthy self-esteem is important because some of us think too little of ourself; on the other hand, some of us overestimate ourself. The key to an honest and accurate evaluation is knowing the basis of our self-worth—our identity in Christ. Apart from him, we aren't capable of very much by eternal standards; in him, we are valuable and capable of worthy service. Evaluating yourself by the worldly standards of success and achievement can cause you to think too much about your worth in the eyes of others and thus miss your true value in God's eyes.

Related Topics: CONFIDENCE, GOOD, LOVE

SELFISHNESS *(Pride, Self-Centeredness, Sin)*

How does selfishness reflect our sinful nature?

BIBLE READING: Proverbs 28:1-13
KEY BIBLE VERSE: *When there is moral rot within a nation, its government topples easily. But with wise and knowledgeable leaders, there is stability.* (Proverbs 28:2)

Selfishness separates us from God and from others. For a government or a society to endure, it needs wise, informed leaders—and these are hard to find. Each person's selfishness quickly affects others. A selfish employee who steals from his company ruins its productivity. A selfish driver who drinks before taking the wheel makes the roads unsafe. A selfish spouse who has an adulterous affair often breaks up two families. When enough people live for themselves with little concern for how their actions affect others, the resulting moral rot contaminates the entire nation. Are you part of the problem . . . or the solution?

BIBLE READING: Malachi 3:7-18
KEY BIBLE VERSE: *"You have said terrible things about me," says the LORD. "But you say, 'What do you mean? How have we spoken against you?'" "You have said, 'What's the use of serving God? What have we gained by obeying his commands or by trying to show the LORD Almighty that we are sorry for our sins? From now on we will say, "Blessed are the arrogant." For those who do evil get rich, and those who dare God to punish them go free of harm.'"* (Malachi 3:13-15)

Selfishness is a rejection of God and all he represents. These verses describe the people's arrogant attitude toward God. When we ask, What good does it do to serve God? we are really asking, What good does it do for *me*? Our focus is selfish. Our real question should be, "What good does it do for God?" We must serve God just because he is God and deserves to be served.

BIBLE READING: Mark 8:31-38
KEY BIBLE VERSE: *How do you benefit if you gain the whole world but lose your own soul in the process? Is anything worth more than your soul?* (Mark 8:36-37)

Selfishness is ultimately self-destructive. Many people spend all their energy seeking pleasure. Jesus said, however, that a world of pleasure centered on possessions, position, or power is ultimately worthless. Whatever you have on earth is only temporary; it cannot be exchanged for your soul. If you work hard at getting what you want, you might eventually have a "pleasurable" life, but in the end you will find it hollow and empty. Are you willing to make the pursuit of God more important than the selfish pursuit of pleasure? Follow Jesus, and you will know what it means to live abundantly now and to have eternal life as well.

BIBLE READING: James 4:1-10
KEY BIBLE VERSE: *Even when you do ask, you don't get it because your whole motive is wrong—you want only what will give you pleasure.* (James 4:3)

Selfishness is at the heart of most problems between people. Conflicts and disputes among believers are always harmful. James explains that these quarrels result from evil desires battling within us—we want more possessions, more money, higher status, more recognition. When we want badly enough to fulfill these desires, we fight in order to do so. Instead of aggressively grabbing what we want, we should submit ourself to God, ask God to help us get rid of our selfish desires, and trust him to give us what we really need.

Related Topics: EVIL, SELF-CENTEREDNESS, SIN

SELF-PITY (*see* HOPELESSNESS)

SELF-RIGHTEOUSNESS (*Blame, Excuses, Rationalizing*)

Why does God judge self-righteousness?

BIBLE READING: Matthew 9:9-13
KEY BIBLE VERSE: *When he heard this, Jesus replied, "Healthy people don't need a doctor—sick people do." Then he added, "Now go and learn the meaning of this Scripture: 'I want you to be merciful; I don't want your sacrifices.' For I have come to call sinners, not those who think they are already good enough."* (Matthew 9:12-13)

Self-righteousness rejects the necessary admission of our sinfulness. Those who are sure that they are righteous can't be saved, because the first step in following Jesus is acknowledging our need and admitting that we don't have all the answers. As long as people insist on their own qualifications as good enough to stand before God, they are cut off from hope.

BIBLE READING: Luke 15:1-32

KEY BIBLE VERSE: *The older brother was angry and wouldn't go in. His father came out and begged him, but he replied, "All these years I've worked hard for you and never once refused to do a single thing you told me to. And in all that time you never gave me even one young goat for a feast with my friends. Yet when this son of yours comes back after squandering your money on prostitutes, you celebrate by killing the finest calf we have."* (Luke 15:28-30)

Self-righteousness presumes to judge the lives of others. In Jesus' story, the older brother represented the Pharisees, who were angry and resentful that sinners were being welcomed into God's kingdom. After all, the Pharisees must have thought, we have sacrificed and done *so much* for God. How easy it is to resent God's gracious forgiveness of others whom we consider to be far worse sinners than ourselves. But when our self-righteousness gets in the way of rejoicing when others come to Jesus, we are no better than the Pharisees.

BIBLE READING: Luke 18:9-14

KEY BIBLE VERSE: *I tell you, this sinner, not the Pharisee, returned home justified before God. For the proud will be humbled, but the humble will be honored.* (Luke 18:14)

Self-righteousness is evidence of pride. The Pharisee in this parable did not go to the temple to pray to God but to announce to all within earshot how good he was. The tax collector went recognizing his sin and begging for mercy. Self-righteousness is dangerous. It leads to pride, causes a person to despise others, and prevents him or her from learning anything from God. The tax collector's prayer should be our prayer because we all need God's mercy every day. Don't let pride in your achievements cut you off from God.

Related Topics: PRIDE, RIGHTEOUSNESS, SIN

SELF-WORTH (*see* SELF-ESTEEM)

SENSITIVITY (*Awareness, Softness, Tenderness*)

What kind of sensitivity should we be trying to develop?

BIBLE READING: Job 2:11-13

KEY BIBLE VERSE: *Three of Job's friends were Eliphaz the Temanite, Bildad the Shuhite, and Zophar the Naamathite. When they heard of the tragedy he had suffered, they got together and traveled from their homes to comfort and console him.* (Job 2:11)

We should develop sensitivity that responds with compassion to others' tragedy. Upon learning of Job's difficulties, three of his friends came to sympathize with him and comfort him. Later we learn that their words of comfort were not helpful—but at least they came. While God rebuked them for what they said (Job 42:7), he did not rebuke them for what they did—making the effort to come to someone who was in need. Unfortunately, when they came, they did a poor job of comforting Job because they were proud of their own advice and insensitive to Job's needs. When someone is in need, go to that person, but be sensitive about how you comfort him or her.

BIBLE READING: Jonah 4:1-11

KEY BIBLE VERSE: *The* LORD *said, "You feel sorry about the plant, though you did nothing to put it there. And a plant is only, at best, short lived. But Nineveh has more than 120,000 people living in spiritual darkness, not to mention all the animals. Shouldn't I feel sorry for such a great city?"* (Jonah 4:10-11)

We should develop sensitivity that focuses on the other person's needs. Jonah was angry at the withering of the vine, but not over what could have happened to Nineveh. Most of us have cried at the death of a pet or when an object with sentimental value is broken, but have we cried over the fact that a friend does not know God? How easy it is to be more sensitive to our own interests than to the spiritual needs of people around us.

BIBLE READING: 1 Thessalonians 5:12-28

KEY BIBLE VERSE: *Brothers and sisters, we urge you to warn those who are lazy. Encourage those who are timid. Take tender care of those who are weak. Be patient with everyone.* (1 Thessalonians 5:14)

We should develop sensitivity that fits the response to the need. Don't loaf around with the idle; warn them. Don't yell at the timid and weak; encourage and help them. At times it's difficult to distinguish between idleness and timidity. Two people may be doing nothing—one out of laziness and the other out of shyness or fear of doing something wrong. The key to ministry is sensitivity: sensing the condition of each person and offering the appropriate remedy for each situation. You can't effectively help until you know the problem. You can't apply the medicine until you know where the wound is.

Related Topics: COMPASSION, GIVING, SERVING

SEPARATION *(Difference, Distance, Uniqueness)*

What is the biblical meaning and use of the word separation?

BIBLE READING: Leviticus 18:1-5

KEY BIBLE VERSE: *The* LORD *said to Moses, "Say this to your people, the Israelites: I, the* LORD, *am your God. So do not act like the people in Egypt, where you used to live, or like the people of Canaan, where I am taking you. You must not imitate their way of life."* (Leviticus 18:1-3)

In the Bible, *separation* **usually means "difference" rather than "distance."** The Israelites moved from one idol-infested country to another. As God helped them form a new culture, he warned them to leave all aspects of their pagan background behind. He also warned them how easy it would be to slip into the pagan culture of Canaan, where they were going. Canaan's society and religions appealed to worldly desires, especially sexual immorality and drunkenness. The Israelites were to keep themselves pure and set apart for God. God did not want his people absorbed into the surrounding culture and environment.

Society may pressure us to conform to its way of life and thought, but yielding to that pressure will (1) create confusion as to which side we should be on and (2) eliminate our effectiveness in serving God. Follow God, and don't let the culture around you mold your thoughts and actions.

BIBLE READING: 2 Corinthians 6:14-18
KEY BIBLE VERSE: *Don't team up with those who are unbelievers. How can goodness be a partner with wickedness? How can light live with darkness?* (2 Corinthians 6:14)

Separation, for a Christian, means not being bound to unbelievers. Separation from the world involves more than keeping our distance from sinners; it means staying close to God (see 7:1-2). It involves more than avoiding entertainment that leads to sin; it extends to how we spend our time and money. There is no way to separate ourself totally from all sinful influences. Nevertheless, we are to resist the sin around us without either giving up or giving in.

BIBLE READING: 2 Chronicles 6:28-33
KEY BIBLE VERSE: *If your people offer a prayer concerning their troubles or sorrow, raising their hands toward this Temple, then hear from heaven where you live, and forgive. Give your people whatever they deserve, for you alone know the human heart.* (2 Chronicles 6:29-30)

Separation from God is real but need not be permanent. Have you ever felt far from God, separated by feelings of failure and personal problems? In his prayer, Solomon underscored the fact that God stands ready to hear his people, to forgive their sins, and to restore their relationship with him. God is waiting and listening for our confessions of guilt and our recommitment to obey him. He hears us when we pour out our needs and problems to him and is ready to forgive us and restore us to fellowship with him. Don't wait to experience his loving forgiveness.

BIBLE READING: Matthew 27:45-56
KEY BIBLE VERSE: *At about three o'clock, Jesus called out with a loud voice, "Eli, Eli, lema sabachthani?" which means, "My God, my God, why have you forsaken me?"* (Matthew 27:46)

Separation from God was Christ's experience in our behalf. Jesus was not questioning God; he was quoting the first line of Psalm 22—a deep expression of the anguish he felt when he took on the sins of the world, which caused him to be separated from his Father. *This* was what Jesus dreaded as he prayed to God in the garden to let the cup be taken away from him (Matthew 26:39). The physical agony was horrible, but even worse was the period of spiritual separation from God. Jesus suffered this double death so that we would never have to experience eternal separation from God.

BIBLE READING: 2 Thessalonians 1:3-12
KEY BIBLE VERSE: *They will be punished with everlasting destruction, forever separated from the Lord and from his glorious power.* (2 Thessalonians 1:9)

Separation from God is a biblical description of the reality of hell. The "everlasting destruction" that Paul describes is the lake of fire (see Revelation 20:14)—the place of eternal separation from God. Those people who are separated from God in eternity no longer have any hope for salvation.

Related Topics: HELL, PUNISHMENT, SALVATION

SERVING *(Assisting, Helping, Sacrificing)*

In what ways is serving others a key part of the Christian life?

BIBLE READING: 1 Samuel 2:1-11

KEY BIBLE VERSE: *Elkanah and Hannah returned home to Ramah without Samuel. And the boy became the LORD's helper, for he assisted Eli the priest.* (1 Samuel 2:11)

Serving others is one way of serving God. Samuel was Eli's helper, or assistant. In this role, Samuel's responsibilities would have included opening the tabernacle doors each morning (3:15), cleaning the furniture, and sweeping the floors. As he grew older, Samuel would have assisted Eli in offering sacrifices. The fact that he was wearing a linen ephod (a garment worn only by priests) shows that he was a priest-in-training (2:18). Because Samuel was Eli's helper, he was God's helper too. When you serve others—even in carrying out ordinary tasks—you are serving God. Every job has dignity because ultimately, the one we serve is God.

BIBLE READING: Matthew 5:1-12

KEY BIBLE VERSE: *One day as the crowds were gathering, Jesus went up the mountainside with his disciples and sat down to teach them. This is what he taught them: "God blesses those who realize their need for him, for the Kingdom of Heaven is given to them."* (Matthew 5:1-3)

Serving others is a distinguishing mark of Christians in the world. Jesus began his sermon with words that seem to contradict each other. But God's way of living usually contradicts the world's. If you want to live for God, you must be ready to say and do what seems strange to the world. You must be willing to give when others take, to love when others hate, to help where others have abused. By giving up your own rights in order to serve others, you will one day receive everything God has in store for you.

BIBLE READING: Matthew 20:20-34

KEY BIBLE VERSE: *Jesus called them together and said, "You know that in this world kings are tyrants, and officials lord it over the people beneath them. But among you it should be quite different. Whoever wants to be a leader among you must be your servant"* (Matthew 20:25-26)

By serving others, those in God's kingdom turn the world's values upside down. The other disciples were upset with James and John for trying to grab the top positions. *All* the disciples wanted to be the greatest (18:1), but Jesus taught them that the greatest person in God's kingdom is the servant of all. Authority is given not for self-importance, ambition, or respect, but for useful service to God and his creation.

Serving others is real leadership. Jesus described leadership from a new perspective. Instead of *using* people, we are to *serve* them. Jesus' mission was to serve others and to give his life away. A real leader has a servant's heart. Servant leaders appreciate others' worth and realize that they're not above any job. If you see something that needs to be done, don't wait to be asked. Take the initiative and do it like a faithful servant.

BIBLE READING: Romans 7:1-6

KEY BIBLE VERSE: *Now we have been released from the law, for we died with Christ, and we are no longer captive to its power. Now we can really serve God, not in the old way by obeying the letter of the law, but in the new way, by the Spirit.* (Romans 7:6)

Serving others is a Christian's best way to become more like Christ. Some people try to earn their way to God by keeping a set of rules (obeying the Ten Commandments, attending church faithfully, or doing good deeds), but all they earn for their efforts is frustration and discouragement. However, because of Christ's sacrifice, the way to God is already open, and we can become his children simply by putting our faith in him. No longer trying to reach God by keeping rules, we can become more and more like Jesus as we live with him day by day. Let the Holy Spirit turn your eyes away from your own performance and toward Jesus. He will free you to serve him out of love and gratitude. This is living "in the new way" of the Spirit.

Related Topics: DISCIPLINE, LEADERSHIP, OBEDIENCE

SEX *(Pleasure, Procreating, Sensuality)*

▶ INAPPROPRIATE SEX
Why does God put limits on our sexual expression?

BIBLE READING: Deuteronomy 22:13-30
KEY BIBLE VERSE: *If a man is discovered committing adultery, both he and the other man's wife must be killed. In this way, the evil will be cleansed from Israel.* (Deuteronomy 22:22)

Sexual sin is powerful and destructive. Why does God have so many laws about sexual sins? Instructions about sexual behavior would have been vital for 3 million people on a forty-year camping trip. But they would be equally important when they entered the Promised Land and settled down as a nation. Paul, in Colossians 3:5-8, recognizes the importance of strong rules about sex for believers, because sexual sins have the power to disrupt and destroy the church. Sins involving sex are not innocent dabblings in forbidden pleasures, as is so often portrayed, but powerful destroyers of relationships. They bring confusion and tear down the climate of respect, trust, and credibility so essential for solid marriages and secure children.

BIBLE READING: Proverbs 6:20-35
KEY BIBLE VERSE: *The man who commits adultery is an utter fool, for he destroys his own soul.* (Proverbs 6:32)

Sexual sin begins with desire and ends in tragedy. Regard lust as a warning sign of danger ahead. When you notice that you are attracted to a person of the opposite sex or preoccupied with thoughts of him or her, your desires may lead you to sin. Ask God to help you change your desires before you are drawn into sin.

Sex outside marriage always hurts somebody. Some people argue that it is all right to break God's law against sexual sin if nobody gets hurt. In truth, somebody always gets hurt. Spouses are devastated. Children are scarred. The partners themselves, even if they escape disease and unwanted pregnancy, lose their ability to fulfill commitments, to feel sexual desire, to trust, and to be entirely open with another person. God's laws are not arbitrary. They do not forbid good, clean fun; rather, they warn us against destroying ourself through unwise actions or running ahead of God's timetable.

📖 BIBLE READING: 1 Corinthians 6:12-20

KEY BIBLE VERSE: *Run away from sexual sin! No other sin so clearly affects the body as this one does. For sexual immorality is a sin against your own body.* (1 Corinthians 6:18)

The power of sexual sin must never be underestimated. Sexual immorality is a temptation that is always before us. In movies and on television, sex outside marriage is treated as a normal, even desirable, part of life, while marriage is often shown as confining and joyless. We can even be looked down on by others if we are suspected of being pure. But God does not forbid sexual sin just to be difficult. He knows its power to destroy us physically and spiritually. It has devastated countless lives and destroyed families, churches, communities, and even nations. God wants to protect us from damaging ourself and others, and so he offers to fill us—our loneliness, our desires—with himself.

Sexual sin is destructive, even when the effects are not immediately apparent. Christians are free to be all they can be for God, but they are not free *from* God. God created sex to be a beautiful and essential ingredient of marriage, but sexual sin—sex outside the marriage relationship—*always* hurts someone. It hurts God because it shows that we prefer following our own desires instead of the leading of the Holy Spirit. It hurts others because it violates the commitment so necessary to a relationship. It often brings disease to our body. And it deeply affects our personality, which responds in anguish when we harm ourself physically and spiritually.

Christians do not have the right to use their body as they wish. What did Paul mean when he said that our body belongs to God? Many people say they have the right to do whatever they want with their own body. Although they think that this is freedom, they are really enslaved to their own desires. When we become Christians, the Holy Spirit fills us and lives in us. Therefore, we no longer own our body. "For God bought you with a high price" refers to slaves purchased at auction. Christ's death freed us from sin, but also obligates us to his service. If you live in a building owned by someone else, you try not to violate the building's rules. Because your body belongs to God, you must not violate his standards for living.

How does sexual sin begin?

📖 BIBLE READING: Matthew 5:27-30

KEY BIBLE VERSE: *Anyone who even looks at a woman with lust in his eye has already committed adultery with her in his heart.* (Matthew 5:28)

Sexual sin begins in the mind—God considers mental adultery as serious as physical adultery. The Old Testament law said that it is wrong for a person to have sex with someone other than his or her spouse (Exodus 20:14). But Jesus said that the *desire* to have sex with someone other than your spouse is mental adultery and thus sin. Jesus emphasized that if the *act* is wrong, then so is the *intention.* To be faithful to your spouse with your body but not your mind is to break the trust so vital to a strong marriage. Jesus is not condemning natural interest in the opposite sex or even healthy sexual desire, but the deliberate and repeated filling of one's mind with fantasies that would be evil if acted out.

Lust must not be an excuse for sexual sin. Some think that if lustful thoughts are sin, why shouldn't a person go ahead with the lustful actions too? Acting out sinful desires is harmful in several ways: (1) it causes people to excuse sin rather than to stop sinning; (2) it destroys marriages; (3) it is deliberate rebellion against God's Word; and (4) it always hurts someone else in addition to the sinner. Sinful action is more dangerous than sinful desire, and that is why desires should not be acted out. Nevertheless, sinful desire is just as damaging to righteousness. Left unchecked, wrong desires will result in wrong actions and turn people away from God.

▶ APPROPRIATE SEX
Why should we follow God's laws about sex?

BIBLE READING: Proverbs 5:15-21
KEY BIBLE VERSE: *Let your wife be a fountain of blessing for you. Rejoice in the wife of your youth.* (Proverbs 5:18)

Sex is a gift God gives to married people for their mutual enjoyment. God does not intend faithfulness in marriage to be boring, lifeless, pleasureless, and dull. Real happiness comes when we decide to find pleasure in the relationship God has given or will give us and to commit ourself to making it pleasurable for our spouse. The real danger is in doubting that God knows and cares for us. We then may resent his timing and carelessly pursue sexual pleasure without his blessing.

BIBLE READING: 1 Corinthians 7:1-11
KEY BIBLE VERSE: *Do not deprive each other of sexual relations. The only exception to this rule would be the agreement of both husband and wife to refrain from sexual intimacy for a limited time, so they can give themselves more completely to prayer. Afterward they should come together again so that Satan won't be able to tempt them because of their lack of self-control.* (1 Corinthians 7:5)

God designed sex as part of the unique relationship of marriage. The Corinthian church was in turmoil because of the immorality of the culture around them. Some Greeks, in rejecting immorality, rejected sex and marriage altogether. The Corinthian Christians wondered if this was what they should do also, so they asked Paul several questions: Because sex is perverted, shouldn't we also abstain in marriage? If my spouse is unsaved, should I seek a divorce?
· Should single people and widows remain unmarried? Paul answered many of these questions by saying, For now, stay put. Be content in the situation where God has placed you. If you're married, don't seek to be single. If you're single, don't seek to be married. Live God's way, one day at a time, and he will show you what to do.

Sexuality is a natural, God-given desire. Sexual temptations are difficult to withstand because they appeal to the normal and natural desires that God has given us. Marriage provides God's way to satisfy these natural sexual desires and to strengthen the partners against temptation. Married couples have the responsibility to care for each other. Therefore, husbands and wives should not withhold themselves sexually from one another, but should fulfill each other's needs and desires.

God, as the creator of sex, ought to be our guide in the use of sexuality. Spiritually, our body belongs to God when we become a Christian, because Jesus Christ bought us by paying the price to release us from sin (see 6:19-20). Physically, our body belongs to our spouse because God designed marriage so that, through the union of husband and wife, the two become one (Genesis 2:24). Paul stressed complete equality in sexual relationships. Neither male nor female should seek dominance or autonomy.

BIBLE READING: 1 Thessalonians 4:1-8
KEY BIBLE VERSE: *God wants you to be holy, so you should keep clear of all sexual sin. Then each of you will control your body and live in holiness and honor—*

not in lustful passion as the pagans do, in their ignorance of God and his ways.
(1 Thessalonians 4:3-5)

**To keep from hurting ourself, sexual desires and activities must be placed
under Christ's control.** God created sex for procreation and pleasure, and as
an expression of love between a husband and wife. Sexual experience must be
limited to the marriage relationship to avoid hurting ourself, our relationship
to God, and our relationships with others.

Related Topics: HOMOSEXUALITY, LUST, MARRIAGE

SHAME *(Dishonor, Embarrassment, Humiliation)*

When should believers feel shame, and when shouldn't they?

 BIBLE READING: Genesis 2:8-25
KEY BIBLE VERSE: *Although Adam and his wife were both naked, neither of them
felt any shame.* (Genesis 2:25)

We should feel shame as a result of guilt over sin. Have you ever noticed how
little children can run naked through a room full of strangers without embarrassment? They are not aware of their nakedness, just as Adam and Eve were
not embarrassed in their innocence. But after Adam and Eve sinned, shame
and awkwardness followed, creating barriers between themselves and God. We
often experience these same barriers in marriage. Ideally a husband and wife
have no barriers, feeling no embarrassment in exposing themselves to each
other or to God. But, like Adam and Eve (3:7), we put on fig leaves (barriers)
because we have areas we don't want our spouse, or God, to know about.
Then we hide, just as Adam and Eve hid from God. In marriage, lack of spiritual, emotional, and intellectual intimacy usually precedes a breakdown of
physical intimacy. In the same way, when we fail to expose our secret thoughts
to God, we break our lines of communication with him.

BIBLE READING: Luke 9:18-27
KEY BIBLE VERSE: *If a person is ashamed of me and my message, I, the Son of Man,
will be ashamed of that person when I return in my glory and in the glory of the
Father and the holy angels.* (Luke 9:26)

We should never be ashamed of our allegiance to Jesus Christ. Luke's Greek
audience would have found it difficult to understand a God who could die, just
as Jesus' Jewish audience would have been perplexed by a Messiah who would
let himself be captured. Both would be ashamed of Jesus if they did not look
past his death to his glorious resurrection and second coming. Then they would
see Jesus not as a loser, but as the Lord of the universe, who through his death
brought salvation to all people.

BIBLE READING: Romans 1:8-17
KEY BIBLE VERSE: *I am not ashamed of this Good News about Christ. It is the power
of God at work, saving everyone who believes—Jews first and also Gentiles.*
(Romans 1:16)

We should never be ashamed of the gospel—it is a source of power. Paul was
not ashamed because his message was the gospel of Christ, the Good News. It
was a message of salvation, it had life-changing power, and it was for everyone.
When you are tempted to be ashamed, remember what the Good News is all

about. If you focus on God and on what God is doing in the world rather than on your own inadequacy, you won't be ashamed or embarrassed.

Related Topics: EMBARRASSMENT, GUILT, HUMILIATION

SHARING (*see* GIVING)

SICKNESS (*Disease, Suffering, Weakness*)

How does God want us to understand sickness?

BIBLE READING: Exodus 15:22-27

KEY BIBLE VERSE: *If you will listen carefully to the voice of the LORD your God and do what is right in his sight, obeying his commands and laws, then I will not make you suffer the diseases I sent on the Egyptians; for I am the LORD who heals you.* (Exodus 15:26)

Obedience to God is excellent preventive medicine. God promised that if the people obeyed him they would be free from the diseases that plagued the Egyptians. Little did they know that many of the moral laws he later gave them were designed to keep them free from sickness. For example, following God's law against prostitution would keep them free of venereal disease. God's laws for us are often designed to keep us from harm. Men and women are complex beings. Our physical, emotional, and spiritual lives are intertwined. Modern medicine is now acknowledging what these laws assumed. If we want God to protect us, we need to submit to his directions for living.

BIBLE READING: Matthew 4:23-25

KEY BIBLE VERSE: *Jesus traveled throughout Galilee teaching in the synagogues, preaching everywhere the Good News about the Kingdom. And he healed people who had every kind of sickness and disease. News about him spread far beyond the borders of Galilee so that the sick were soon coming to be healed from as far away as Syria. And whatever their illness and pain, or if they were possessed by demons, or were epileptics, or were paralyzed—he healed them all.* (Matthew 4:23-24)

The power to heal sickness is an area in which we can trust Christ. Jesus was teaching, preaching, and healing. These were the three main aspects of his ministry. *Teaching* shows Jesus' concern for understanding; *preaching* shows his concern for commitment; and *healing* shows his concern for wholeness. His miracles of healing authenticated his teaching and preaching, proving that he truly was from God.

Physical sickness can be a reminder of spiritual sickness. Jesus preached the gospel—the Good News—to everyone who wanted to hear it. The gospel is that the kingdom of heaven has come, that God is with us, and that he cares for us. Christ can heal us, not just of physical sickness, but of spiritual sickness as well. There's no sin or problem too great or too small for him to handle. Jesus' words were good news because they offered freedom, hope, peace of heart, and eternal life with God.

BIBLE READING: Matthew 8:5-17

KEY BIBLE VERSE: *Jesus said to the Roman officer, "Go on home. What you have believed has happened." And the young servant was healed that same hour.*

When Jesus arrived at Peter's house, Peter's mother-in-law was in bed with a high fever. But when Jesus touched her hand, the fever left her. Then she got up and prepared a meal for him. (Matthew 8:13-15)

Christ displays his power in healing sicknesses of all kinds. Through these events, Matthew continues to show Jesus' kingly nature. Through a single touch, Jesus healed (8:3-15); when he spoke a single word, evil spirits fled his presence (8:16). Jesus has authority over all evil powers and all earthly disease. He also has power and authority to conquer sin. Sickness and evil are consequences of living in a fallen world. But in the future, when God removes all sin, there will be no more sickness and death. Jesus' healing miracles were a taste of what the whole world will one day experience in God's kingdom.

Related Topics: HEALING, MIRACLES, SUFFERING

SIGNS (*see* MIRACLES)

SILENCE (*Quietness, Solitude, Stillness*)

What is the importance of silence in our life?

BIBLE READING: Job 2:11-13

KEY BIBLE VERSE: *They sat on the ground with him for seven days and nights. And no one said a word, for they saw that his suffering was too great for words.* (Job 2:13)

Often the best response to another person's suffering is silence. Why did the friends arrive and then just sit quietly? According to Jewish tradition, people who come to comfort someone in mourning should not speak until the mourner speaks. Job's friends realized that his pain was too deep to be healed with mere words, so they said nothing. (If only they had continued to sit quietly!) Often, we feel we must say something spiritual and insightful to a hurting friend. Perhaps what he or she needs most is just our presence, showing that we care. Pat answers and trite quotations say much less than empathetic silence and loving companionship.

BIBLE READING: Psalm 46:1-11

KEY BIBLE VERSE: *Be silent, and know that I am God! I will be honored by every nation. I will be honored throughout the world.* (Psalm 46:10)

Silence is one of the best expressions of respect for God. War and destruction are inevitable, but so is God's final victory. At that time, all will stand quietly before the Lord Almighty. How proper, then, for us to be still now, reverently honoring him and his power and majesty. Take time each day to be still and to exalt God.

BIBLE READING: Psalm 50:16-23

KEY BIBLE VERSE: *While you did all this, I remained silent, and you thought I didn't care. But now I will rebuke you, listing all my charges against you.* (Psalm 50:21)

God's silence may be an indication of his patience. At times God seems silent. By his silence he is not condoning sin, nor is he indifferent to it. Instead, he is withholding deserved punishment, giving time for people to repent (2 Peter 3:9). God takes no pleasure in the death of the wicked and wants them to turn from evil (Ezekiel 33:11). But his silence does not last forever—a time of punishment will surely come.

Related Topics: ABANDON, MEDITATION, SOLITUDE

SIMPLICITY (*Basic, Natural, Unworldly*)

Why should Christians value simplicity?

BIBLE READING: Matthew 11:25-30
KEY BIBLE VERSE: *Jesus prayed this prayer: "O Father, Lord of heaven and earth, thank you for hiding the truth from those who think themselves so wise and clever, and for revealing it to the childlike."* (Matthew 11:25)

Simplicity is a good foundation for faith. Jesus mentioned two kinds of people in his prayer: the "wise"—arrogant in their own knowledge—and the "child-like"—humbly open to receive the truth of God's Word. Are you wise in your own eyes, or do you seek the truth in childlike faith, realizing that only God holds all the answers?

BIBLE READING: 1 Corinthians 1:18-31
KEY BIBLE VERSE: *Since God in his wisdom saw to it that the world would never find him through human wisdom, he has used our foolish preaching to save all who believe.* (1 Corinthians 1:21)

Responding to the gospel is the greatest act of human simplicity. The message of Christ's death for sins sounds foolish to those who don't believe. Death seems to be the end of the road, the ultimate weakness. But Jesus did not stay dead. His resurrection demonstrated his power even over death. And he will save us from eternal death and give us everlasting life if we trust him as Savior and Lord. This sounds so simple that many people won't accept it. They try other ways to obtain eternal life (being good, being wise, etc.). But all their attempts will not work. The "foolish" people who simply accept Christ's offer are actually the wisest of all, because they alone will live eternally with God.

Christian simplicity is a thinking lifestyle. Is Christianity against rational thinking? Christians clearly do believe in using their minds to weigh the evidence and make wise choices. Paul is declaring that no amount of human knowledge can replace or bypass Christ's work on the cross. If it could, Christ would be accessible only to the intellectually gifted and well educated, and not to ordinary people or to children.

Simplicity reminds us of the futility of trying to earn salvation. Paul emphasizes that the way to receive salvation is so simple that *any* person who wants to can understand it. Skill and wisdom do not get a person into God's kingdom—simple faith does—so no one can boast that his or her achievements helped secure eternal life. Salvation is totally from God through Jesus' death. There is *nothing* we can do to earn our salvation; we need only accept what Jesus has already done for us.

Related Topics: FAITH, HUMILITY, PRIDE

SIN (*Disobedience, Evil, Rebellion*)

▶ DEFINITION OF SIN
What is sin?

BIBLE READING: Genesis 3:14-19
KEY BIBLE VERSE: *To Adam he said, "Because you listened to your wife and ate the fruit I told you not to eat, I have placed a curse on the ground. All your life you will struggle to scratch a living from it."* (Genesis 3:17)

Sin is disobeying God. Adam and Eve learned by painful experience that because God is holy and hates sin, he must punish sinners. The rest of the book of Genesis recounts painful stories of lives ruined as a result of the fall. Disobedience is sin, and it breaks our fellowship with God. But, fortunately, when we disobey, God is willing to forgive us and to restore our relationship with him.

BIBLE READING: Leviticus 4:1-12

KEY BIBLE VERSE: *The LORD said to Moses, "Give the Israelites the following instructions for dealing with those who sin unintentionally by doing anything forbidden by the LORD's commands."* (Leviticus 4:1-2)

Sin includes unintended wrongdoing. Have you ever done something wrong without realizing it until later? Although your sin was unintentional, it was still sin. One of the purposes of God's commands was to make the Israelites aware of their unintentional sins so they would not repeat them and so they could be forgiven for them. Leviticus 4 and 5 mention some of these unintentional sins and the way the Israelites could be forgiven for them. As you read more of God's laws, keep in mind that they were meant to teach and guide the people. Let them help you become more aware of sin in your life.

BIBLE READING: Matthew 8:1-4

KEY BIBLE VERSE: *Jesus touched him. "I want to," he said. "Be healed!" And instantly the leprosy disappeared.* (Matthew 8:3)

Sin is a disease beyond human cure. Leprosy, like AIDS today, was a terrifying disease because there was no known cure. In Jesus' day, the Greek word for *leprosy* was used for a variety of similar diseases, and some forms were contagious. If a person contracted the contagious type, a priest declared him a leper and banished him from his home and city. The leper was sent to live in a community with other lepers until he either got better or died. Yet when the leper begged Jesus to heal him, Jesus reached out and touched him, even though his skin was covered with the dread disease.

Sin is also an incurable disease—and we all have it. Only Christ's healing touch can miraculously take away our sins and restore us to real living. But first, just like the leper, we must realize our inability to cure ourself and ask for Christ's saving help.

BIBLE READING: Mark 7:1-23

KEY BIBLE VERSE: *Then he added, "It is the thought-life that defiles you. For from within, out of a person's heart, come evil thoughts, sexual immorality, theft, murder, adultery, greed, wickedness, deceit, eagerness for lustful pleasure, envy, slander, pride, and foolishness. All these vile things come from within; they are what defile you and make you unacceptable to God."* (Mark 7:20-23)

Sin has an inward as well as an outward aspect. Do we worry more about what is in our diet than what is in our heart and mind? As they interpreted the dietary laws (Leviticus 11), the Jews believed they could be clean before God because of what they refused to eat. But Jesus pointed out that sin actually begins in the attitudes and intentions of the inner person. Jesus did not degrade the law, but he paved the way for the change made clear in Acts 10:9-29 when God removed the cultural restrictions regarding food. We are not pure because of outward acts—we become pure on the inside as Christ renews our mind and transforms us into his image.

BIBLE READING: Romans 3:9-20

KEY BIBLE VERSE: *Are we Jews better than others? No, not at all, for we have already*

shown that all people, whether Jews or Gentiles, are under the power of sin.
(Romans 3:9-10)

Sin is the universal separation of people from God. Paul uses these Old Testament references to show that humanity in general, in its present sinful condition, is unacceptable before God. Have you ever thought to yourself, *Well, I'm
not too bad. I'm a pretty good person?* Look at these verses and see if any of them
apply to you. Have you ever lied? Have you ever hurt someone's feelings by your
words or tone of voice? Are you bitter toward anyone? Do you become angry
with those who strongly disagree with you? In thought, word, and deed, you,
like everyone else in the world, stand guilty before God. We must remember
who we are in his sight—alienated sinners. Don't deny that you are a sinner.
Instead, allow your desperate need to point you toward Christ.

Sin is in our nature and must be faced by every person. The last time someone
accused you of wrongdoing, what was your reaction? Denial, argument, and
defensiveness? The Bible tells us the world stands silent and accountable before
almighty God. No excuses or arguments are left. Have you reached the point
with God where you are ready to hang up your defenses and await his decision?
If you haven't, stop now and admit your sin to him.

▶ THE CHARACTERISTICS OF SIN
How can we recognize sinful behavior?

BIBLE READING: Genesis 3:1-24
KEY BIBLE VERSE: *At that moment, their eyes were opened, and they suddenly felt
shame at their nakedness. So they strung fig leaves together around their hips
to cover themselves.* (Genesis 3:7)

Sinful behavior often begins as a delightful and fun action. Satan tried to make
Eve think that sin is good, pleasant, and desirable. A knowledge of both good
and evil seemed harmless to her. People usually choose wrong things because
they have become convinced that those things are good, at least for themselves.
Our sins do not always appear ugly to us, and the pleasant sins are the hardest
to avoid. So prepare yourself for the attractive temptations that may come your
way. We cannot always prevent temptation, but there is always a way of escape
(1 Corinthians 10:13). God's Word and God's people can help you stand
against it.

Temptation to sinful behavior is rarely obvious at first. Notice what Eve did: She
looked, she took, she ate, and she gave. The battle is often lost at the first look.
Temptation often begins by simply seeing something you want. Are you struggling with temptation because you have not learned that looking is the first step
toward sin? You would win over temptation more often if you followed Paul's
advice to run from those things that produce evil thoughts (2 Timothy 2:22).

Sin's effects spread. After Eve sinned, she involved Adam in her wrongdoing. When
we do something wrong, we often try to relieve our guilt by involving someone
else. Like toxic waste spilled in a river, sin swiftly spreads. Recognize and confess
your sin to God before you are tempted to pollute those around you.

Sin usually causes guilt. After sinning, Adam and Eve felt guilt and embarrassment over their nakedness. Their guilty feelings made them try to hide from
God. A guilty conscience is a warning signal God placed inside you that goes
off when you've done wrong. The worst step you could take is to eliminate the
guilty feelings without eliminating the cause. That would be like using a painkiller but not treating the disease. Be glad those guilty feelings are there. They

make you aware of your sin so you can ask God's forgiveness and then correct your wrongdoing.

Sin creates a barrier between us and God. God desires to have fellowship with us, but we are afraid to have fellowship with him. Adam and Eve hid from God when they heard him approaching. God wanted to be with them, but because of their sin, they were afraid to show themselves. Sin had broken their close relationship with God, just as it has broken ours. But Jesus Christ, God's Son, opens the way for us to renew our fellowship with him. God longs to be with us. He actively offers us his unconditional love. Our natural response is fear, because we feel we can't live up to his standards. But understanding that he loves us, regardless of our faults, can help remove that dread.

Sinful behavior is almost always covered by excuses. When God asked Adam about his sin, Adam blamed Eve. Then Eve blamed the serpent. How easy it is to excuse our sins by blaming someone else or circumstances. But God knows the truth, and he holds each of us responsible for what we do (Genesis 3:14-19). Admit your wrong attitudes and actions and ask God for forgiveness. Don't try to get away with sin by blaming someone else.

BIBLE READING: 2 Samuel 11:1-27

KEY BIBLE VERSE: *When Bathsheba heard that her husband was dead, she mourned for him. When the period of mourning was over, David sent for her and brought her to the palace, and she became one of his wives. Then she gave birth to a son. But the LORD was very displeased with what David had done. (2 Samuel 11:26-27)*

Sin often leads to more sin. In the episode with Bathsheba, David allowed himself to fall deeper and deeper into sin. (1) David abandoned his purpose by staying home from war (11:1). (2) He focused on his own desires (11:3). (3) When temptation came, he looked into it instead of turning away from it (11:4). (4) He sinned deliberately (11:4). (5) He tried to cover up his sin by deceiving others (11:6-15). (6) He committed murder to continue the cover-up (11:15-17). Eventually David's sin was exposed (12:9) and punished (12:10-14). (7) The consequences of David's sin were far-reaching, affecting many others (11:17; 12:11, 14-15).

Sinful behavior can and should be stopped before it starts. David could have chosen to stop and turn from evil at any stage along the way. But once sin gets started, it is difficult to stop (James 1:14-15). The deeper the mess, the less we want to admit having caused it. It's much easier to stop sliding down a hill when you are near the top than when you are halfway down.

▶ **THE RESULTS OF SIN**
What are the results of sin?

BIBLE READING: Numbers 15:30-36

KEY BIBLE VERSE: *Those who brazenly violate the LORD's will, whether native Israelites or foreigners, blaspheme the LORD, and they must be cut off from the community. (Numbers 15:30)*

Sin deserves punishment. God was willing to forgive those who made unintentional errors if they realized their mistakes quickly and corrected them. However, those who defiantly and deliberately sinned received a harsher judgment. Intentional sin grows out of an improper attitude toward God. A child who knowingly disobeys his parents challenges their authority and dares them to respond. Both the act and the attitude have to be dealt with.

Sin is punished with death. Stoning a man for gathering wood on the Sabbath seems like a severe punishment, and it was. This act was a deliberate sin, defying God's law against working on the Sabbath. Perhaps the man was trying to get ahead of everyone else, in addition to breaking the Sabbath.

BIBLE READING: Genesis 20:1-18

KEY BIBLE VERSE: *Abraham moved south to the Negev and settled for a while between Kadesh and Shur at a place called Gerar. Abraham told people there that his wife, Sarah, was his sister. So King Abimelech sent for her and had her brought to him at his palace.* (Genesis 20:1-2)

Sinful actions can become sinful habits. Abraham had used this same trick before to protect himself (Genesis 12:11-13). Although Abraham is one of our heroes of faith, he did not learn his lesson well enough the first time. In fact, by giving in to the temptation again, he risked turning a sinful act into a sinful pattern of lying whenever he suspected his life was in danger.

No matter how much we love God, certain temptations are especially difficult to resist. These are the vulnerable spots in our spiritual armor. As we struggle with these weaknesses, we can be encouraged to know that God is watching out for us just as he did for Abraham.

BIBLE READING: Exodus 2:11-17

KEY BIBLE VERSE: *After looking around to make sure no one was watching, Moses killed the Egyptian and buried him in the sand.* (Exodus 2:12)

Hidden sins have a way of becoming public. Moses tried to make sure no one was watching before he killed the Egyptian. But as it turned out, someone did see, and Moses had to flee the country. Sometimes we mistakenly think we can get away with doing wrong if no one sees or catches us. Sooner or later, however, doing wrong will catch up with us as it did with Moses. Even if we are not caught in this life, one day we will have to face God and his evaluation of our actions.

BIBLE READING: Luke 12:1-12

KEY BIBLE VERSE: *Those who speak against the Son of Man may be forgiven, but anyone who speaks blasphemies against the Holy Spirit will never be forgiven.* (Luke 12:10)

Lifelong rebelliousness blasphemes the Holy Spirit. Jesus said that blasphemy against the Holy Spirit is unforgivable. This has worried many sincere Christians, but it does not need to. The unforgivable sin means attributing to Satan the work that the Holy Spirit accomplishes (see Matthew 12:24-32; Mark 3:22-29). Thus it is deliberate and ongoing rejection of the Holy Spirit's work and even of God himself. A person who has committed this sin has shut himself or herself off from God so thoroughly that he or she is unaware of any sin at all. A person who fears having committed it shows, by his or her very concern, that he or she has not sinned in this way.

BIBLE READING: Romans 6:15-23

KEY BIBLE VERSE: *The wages of sin is death, but the free gift of God is eternal life through Christ Jesus our Lord.* (Romans 6:23)

Without Christ, the results of sin are death. You are free to choose between two masters, but you are not free to manipulate the consequences of your choice. Each of the two masters pays with his own kind of currency. The currency of sin is death. That is all you can expect or hope for in life without God. Christ's currency is eternal life—new life with God that begins on earth and continues forever with God. What choice have you made?

With Christ, sins are forgiven and eternal life is given. Eternal life is a free gift from God. If it is a gift, then it is not something that we earn, nor something that must be paid back. Consider the foolishness of someone who receives a gift given out of love and then offers to pay for it. A gift cannot be purchased by the recipient. A more appropriate response to a loved one who offers a gift is graceful acceptance with gratitude. Our salvation is a gift from God, not something of our own doing (Ephesians 2:8-9). He saved us because of his kindness and pity, not because we were good enough to be saved (Titus 3:5). How much more we should accept with thanksgiving the gift that God has freely given to us.

▶ **COUNTERACTING SIN**

What should we do when we realize we are sinners?

BIBLE READING: Psalm 139:1-24

KEY BIBLE VERSE: *Search me, O God, and know my heart; test me and know my thoughts. Point out anything in me that offends you, and lead me along the path of everlasting life.* (Psalm 139:23-24)

Be open with God regarding our sins. David asked God to search for sin and point it out, even to the level of testing his thoughts. This is exploratory surgery for sin. How are we to recognize sin unless God points it out? Then, when God shows us, we can repent and be forgiven. Make this verse your prayer. If you ask the Lord to search your heart and your thoughts and to reveal your sin, you will be continuing on God's "path of everlasting life."

BIBLE READING: Matthew 5:43-48

KEY BIBLE VERSE: *You are to be perfect, even as your Father in heaven is perfect.* (Matthew 5:48)

Look to Jesus, who requires us to be perfect. How can we be perfect? (1) *In character.* In this life we cannot be flawless, but we can aspire to be as much like Christ as possible. (2) *In holiness.* Like the Pharisees, we are to separate ourself from the world's sinful values. But unlike the Pharisees, we are to be devoted to God's desires rather than our own and show his love and mercy to the world. (3) *In maturity.* We can't achieve Christlike character and holy living all at once, but we must grow toward maturity and wholeness. Just as we expect different behavior from a baby, a child, a teenager, and an adult, so God expects different behavior from us, depending on our stage of spiritual development. (4) *In love.* We can seek to love others as completely as God loves us.

We can be perfect if our behavior is appropriate for our maturity level—perfect, yet with much room to grow. Our tendency to sin must never deter us from striving to be more like Christ. Christ calls all of his disciples to excel, to rise above mediocrity, and to mature in every area, becoming like him. Those who strive to be like Jesus will one day be like him as a result of seeing him as he is (1 John 3:2-3).

BIBLE READING: Matthew 27:45-56

KEY BIBLE VERSE: *At about three o'clock, Jesus called out with a loud voice, "Eli, Eli, lema sabachthani?" which means, "My God, my God, why have you forsaken me?"* (Matthew 27:46)

Trust the truth that Jesus died for our sins. Jesus was not questioning God; he was quoting the first line of Psalm 22—a deep expression of the anguish he felt when he took on the sins of the world, which caused him to be separated from his Father. *This* was what Jesus dreaded as he prayed to God in the garden to take the cup from him (26:39). The physical agony was horrible, but even worse was the period of spiritual separation from God. Jesus suffered this double death so that we would never have to experience eternal separation from God.

Trust the truth that Jesus broke through the barrier separating people from God. The temple had three main parts—the courts, the Holy Place (where only the priests could enter), and the Most Holy Place (where only the high priest could enter, and only once a year, to atone for the sins of the nation—Leviticus 16:1-35). The curtain separating the Holy Place from the Most Holy Place was torn in two at Christ's death, symbolizing that the barrier between God and humanity was removed. Now all people are free to approach God because of Christ's sacrifice for our sins (see Hebrews 9:1-14; 10:19-22).

BIBLE READING: Luke 3:1-20

KEY BIBLE VERSE: *John went from place to place on both sides of the Jordan River, preaching that people should be baptized to show that they had turned from their sins and turned to God to be forgiven.* (Luke 3:3)

Repent in order to counteract sin. Repentance has two sides—turning away from sins and turning toward God. To be truly repentant, we must do both. We can't just say we believe and then live any way we choose (see 3:7-8); neither can we simply live a morally correct life without a personal relationship with God, because that cannot bring forgiveness from sin. Determine to rid your life of any sins God points out, and put your trust in him alone to guide you.

BIBLE READING: John 1:29-34

KEY BIBLE VERSE: *The next day John saw Jesus coming toward him and said, "Look! There is the Lamb of God who takes away the sin of the world!"* (John 1:29)

Remember that forgiveness is an ongoing process. Every morning and evening, a lamb was sacrificed in the temple for the sins of the people (Exodus 29:38-42). Isaiah 53:7 prophesied that the Messiah, God's servant, would be led to the slaughter like a lamb. To pay the penalty for sin, a life had to be given—and God chose to provide the sacrifice himself. The sins of the world were removed when Jesus died as the perfect sacrifice. This is the way our sins are forgiven (1 Corinthians 5:7). "The sin of the world" means everyone's sin, the sin of each individual. Jesus paid the price of *your* sin by his death. You can receive forgiveness by confessing your sin to him and asking for his forgiveness.

BIBLE READING: John 19:28-37

KEY BIBLE VERSE: *When Jesus had tasted it, he said, "It is finished!" Then he bowed his head and gave up his spirit.* (John 19:30)

Realize that Jesus' death and resurrection were God's final remedy for sin. Until this time, a complicated system of sacrifices had atoned for sins. Sin separates people from God, and only through the sacrifice of an animal, a substitute, could people be forgiven and become clean before God. But people sin continually, so frequent sacrifices were required. Jesus, however, became the final and ultimate sacrifice for sin. The word *finished* is the same as "paid in full." Jesus came to *finish* God's work of salvation (4:34; 17:4), to pay the full penalty for our sins. With his death, the complex sacrificial system ended because Jesus took all sin upon himself. Now we can freely approach God because of what Jesus did for us. Those who believe in Jesus' death and resurrection can live eternally with God and escape the penalty that comes from sin.

BIBLE READING: 1 John 1:5-10

KEY BIBLE VERSE: *If we confess our sins to him, he is faithful and just to forgive us and to cleanse us from every wrong.* (1 John 1:9)

Confess our sins to God. Confession is supposed to free us to enjoy fellowship with Christ. It should ease our consciences and lighten our cares. But some Christians do not understand how it works. They feel so guilty that they confess the same sins over and over; then they wonder if they might have forgotten something. Other Christians believe that God forgives them when they confess, but that if they died with unconfessed sins, they would be forever lost. These Christians do not understand that God *wants* to forgive us. He allowed his beloved Son to die just so he could offer us pardon. When we come to Christ, he forgives all the sins we have committed or will ever commit. We don't need to confess the sins of the past all over again, and we don't need to fear that God will reject us if we don't keep our slate perfectly clean. Of course we should continue to confess our sins, but not because failure to do so will make us lose our salvation. Our relationship with Christ is secure. Instead, we should confess so that we can enjoy maximum fellowship and joy with him.

Commit ourself not to continue in sin. We wouldn't be genuinely confessing our sins to God if we planned to commit them again and just wanted temporary forgiveness. We should also pray for strength to defeat temptation the next time we face it.

Be assured that God's forgiveness is guaranteed by Christ's death. If God has forgiven us for our sins because of Christ's death, why must we confess our sins? In admitting our sins and receiving Christ's cleansing, we are: (1) agreeing with God that our sin truly was sin and that we are willing to turn from it, (2) ensuring that we don't conceal our sins from him and consequently from ourself, and (3) recognizing our tendency to sin and relying on his power to overcome it.

Related Topics: FORGIVENESS, REPENTANCE, TEMPTATION

SINCERITY (*Diligence, Earnestness, Honesty*)

What are the benefits and limitations of sincerity?

BIBLE READING: Judges 17:1-13

KEY BIBLE VERSE: *"I know the LORD will bless me now,"* Micah said, *"because I have a Levite serving as my priest."* (Judges 17:13)

Sincerity must be based on the truth. Micah and his mother seemed to be good and moral people and may have sincerely desired to worship God, but they disobeyed God by following their own desires instead of doing what God wanted. The attitude that prevailed in Micah's day was this: "Everyone did whatever he wanted to." This is remarkably similar to today's prevailing attitudes. But God has given us standards. He has not left our conduct up to us and our opinions. We can avoid conforming to society's low standards by taking God's commands seriously and applying them to life. Independence and self-reliance are positive traits, but only within the framework of God's standards.

Sincere belief in a lie does not equal the truth. Today, as in Micah's day, everyone seems to put his or her own interests first. Time has not changed human nature. Most people still reject God's right way of living. The people in Micah's time replaced the true worship of God with a homemade version of worship. As a result, justice was soon replaced by revenge and chaos. Ignoring God's direction led to confusion and destruction. Anyone who has not submitted to God will end up doing whatever seems right to him or her at the time. This tendency is present in all of us. To know what is really right and to have the strength to do it, we need to draw closer to God and his Word.

BIBLE READING: Psalm 12:1-8
KEY BIBLE VERSE: *The LORD's promises are pure, like silver refined in a furnace, purified seven times over.* (Psalm 12:6)

The words of the Bible are sincerity based on truth. Sincerity and truth are extremely valuable because they are so rare. Many people are deceivers, liars, flatterers; they think they will get what they want by deception. As a king, David certainly faced his share of such people, who hoped to win his favor and gain advancement through flattery. When we feel as though sincerity and truth have nearly gone out of existence, we have one hope—the Word of God. God's words are as flawless as refined silver. So listen carefully when he speaks.

BIBLE READING: Zechariah 7:5-14
KEY BIBLE VERSE: *Say to all your people and your priests, "During those seventy years of exile, when you fasted and mourned in the summer and at the festival in early autumn, was it really for me that you were fasting? And even now in your holy festivals, you don't think about me but only of pleasing yourselves."* (Zechariah 7:5-6)

Even the right actions can be wasted without sincere motives. The Israelites had lost their sincere desire for a loving relationship with God. Zechariah told them that they had been fasting without a proper attitude of repentance or worship. They fasted and mourned during their exile with no thought of God or their sins that had caused the exile in the first place. When you go to church, pray, or have fellowship with other believers, are you doing these from habit or for what you get out of it? God says that an attitude of worship without a sincere desire to know and love him will lead to ruin.

BIBLE READING: Matthew 15:1-20
KEY BIBLE VERSE: *You hypocrites! Isaiah was prophesying about you when he said, "These people honor me with their lips, but their hearts are far away. Their worship is a farce, for they replace God's commands with their own man-made teachings."* (Matthew 15:7-9)

God expects sincerity in both our actions and attitudes. The prophet Isaiah also criticized hypocrites (Isaiah 29:13), and Jesus applied Isaiah's words to these religious leaders. When we claim to honor God while our hearts are far from him, our worship means nothing. It is not enough to act religious. Our actions and our attitudes must be sincere. If they are not, Isaiah's words also describe us.

Related Topics: ATTITUDE, HONESTY, TRUTH

SINGING (*see* PRAISE)

SINGLENESS (*Bachelor, Unmarried Woman, Widow*)

What does God say to those who do not marry?

BIBLE READING: Matthew 19:1-12
KEY BIBLE VERSE: *Some are born as eunuchs, some have been made that way by others, and some choose not to marry for the sake of the Kingdom of Heaven. Let anyone who can, accept this statement.* (Matthew 19:12)

Marriage is not automatically better than singleness. Although divorce was relatively easy in Old Testament times (Matthew 19:7), it is not what God originally intended. Couples should decide against divorce from the start and build their marriage on mutual commitment. There are also many good reasons for not marrying; one is to have more time to work for God's kingdom. Don't assume that God wants everyone to marry. For many it may be better if they don't. Be sure that you prayerfully seek God's will before you plunge into the lifelong commitment of marriage.

Some have physical limitations that prevent their marrying, while others choose not to marry because, in their particular situation, they can serve God better as single people. Jesus was not teaching us to avoid marriage because it is inconvenient or takes away our freedom. That would be selfishness. But singleness is sometimes a wise choice.

BIBLE READING: 1 Corinthians 7:1-11
KEY BIBLE VERSE: *This is only my suggestion. It's not meant to be an absolute rule. I wish everyone could get along without marrying, just as I do. But we are not all the same. God gives some the gift of marriage, and to others he gives the gift of singleness.* (1 Corinthians 7:6-7)

Both marriage and singleness are gifts from God. One is not morally better than the other, and both are valuable for accomplishing God's purposes. It is important for us, therefore, to accept our present situation. When Paul said he wished that all people were like him (i.e., unmarried), he was expressing his desire that more people would devote themselves *completely* to the ministry without the added concerns of spouse and family, as he had done. He was not criticizing marriage—after all, it is God's created way of providing companionship and populating the earth.

BIBLE READING: 1 Corinthians 7:25-40
KEY BIBLE VERSE: *Now let me say this, dear brothers and sisters: The time that remains is very short, so husbands should not let marriage be their major concern. Happiness or sadness or wealth should not keep anyone from doing God's work. Those in frequent contact with the things of the world should make good use of them without becoming attached to them, for this world and all it contains will pass away.* (1 Corinthians 7:29-31)

With Christ, it is possible to live a fulfilling single life. Some single people feel tremendous pressure to be married. They think their life can be complete only with a spouse. But Paul underlines one advantage of being single—the potential of a greater focus on Christ and his work. If you are unmarried, use your special opportunity to serve Christ wholeheartedly.

A good reason to remain single is to use the time and freedom to serve God. When Paul says the unmarried person does even better, he is talking about the potential time available for service to God. The single person does not have the responsibility of caring for a spouse and raising a family. Singleness, however, does not ensure service to God—involvement in service depends on the commitment of the individual.

Related Topics: FAITHFULNESS, MARRIAGE, RELATIONSHIP(S)

SKEPTICISM (*see* DOUBT)

SKILLS (*see* ABILITIES)

SLAVERY (*Bondage, Captivity, Servanthood*)

How does the Bible refer to the matter of slavery?

BIBLE READING: Romans 1:1-7
KEY BIBLE VERSE: *This letter is from Paul, Jesus Christ's slave, chosen by God to be an apostle and sent out to preach his Good News.* (Romans 1:1)

The Bible uses slavery to picture our relationship to Christ. Paul humbly calls himself a servant of Jesus Christ and an apostle ("one who is sent"). For a Roman citizen—which Paul was—to choose to be a servant was unthinkable. But Paul chose to be completely dependent on and obedient to his beloved Master. What is your attitude toward Christ, your Master? Our willingness to serve and obey Jesus Christ enables us to be useful and usable servants to do work for him—work that really matters.

BIBLE READING: Romans 6:1-23
KEY BIBLE VERSE: *Our old sinful selves were crucified with Christ so that sin might lose its power in our lives. We are no longer slaves to sin. For when we died with Christ we were set free from the power of sin.* (Romans 6:6-7)

The Bible uses slavery to picture our relationship to sin before Christ. The power and penalty of sin died with Christ on the cross. The part of us that "loves to sin" is our sinful nature, died once and for all, so we are freed from its power. The "sin-loving body" is not the human body, but our rebellious sin-loving nature inherited from Adam. Though our body willingly cooperates with our sinful nature, we must not regard the body as evil. It is the sin in us that is evil. And it is this power of sin at work in our body that is defeated. Paul has already stated that through faith in Christ we stand acquitted, "not guilty" before God. Here Paul emphasizes that we need no longer live under sin's power. God does not take us out of the world or make us robots—we will still feel like sinning, and sometimes we will sin. The difference is that before we were saved we were slaves to our sinful nature, but now we can choose to live for Christ (see Galatians 2:20).

BIBLE READING: 1 Corinthians 7:20-24
KEY BIBLE VERSE: *Are you a slave? Don't let that worry you—but if you get a chance to be free, take it. And remember, if you were a slave when the Lord called you, the Lord has now set you free from the awful power of sin. And if you were free when the Lord called you, you are now a slave of Christ.* (1 Corinthians 7:21-22)

The Bible portrays slavery as a shadow of all people's horrible slavery to sin. Slavery was common throughout the Roman empire. Some Christians in the Corinthian church were undoubtedly slaves. Paul said that although the Christian slaves were slaves to other human beings, they were free from the power of sin in their life. People today are slaves to sin until they commit their life to Christ, who alone can conquer sin's power. Sin, pride, and fear no longer have any claim over us, just as a slave owner no longer has power over the slaves he has sold. The Bible says we become Christ's slaves when we become Christians (Romans 6:18), but this actually means we gain our freedom, because sin no longer controls us.

BIBLE READING: Colossians 3:22–4:1
KEY BIBLE VERSE: *You slaves must obey your earthly masters in everything you do. Try to please them all the time, not just when they are watching you. Obey them willingly because of your reverent fear of the Lord.* (Colossians 3:22)

Human slavery was actually undermined by the freedom given through Christ.
Paul does not condemn or condone slavery, but explains that Christ transcends
all divisions between people. Slaves are told to work hard as though their master were Christ himself (Colossians 3:22-25); but masters should be just and
fair (Colossians 4:1). Perhaps Paul was thinking specifically of Onesimus and
Philemon—the slave and master whose conflict lay behind the letter to Philemon (see the book of Philemon). Philemon was a slave owner in the Colossian
church, and Onesimus had been his slave (Colossians 4:9).

Related Topics: FREEDOM, SERVING, WORK

SLEEP *(Rest, Repose, Slumber)*

How does God watch over our sleep?

 BIBLE READING: Psalm 3:1-8
KEY BIBLE VERSE: *I lay down and slept. I woke up in safety, for the* LORD *was watching over me.* (Psalm 3:5)

**Knowing God is watching over us can give us rest and peace even during times
of crisis.** Sleep does not come easily during a crisis. David could have had
sleepless nights when his son Absalom rebelled and gathered an army to kill
him. But he slept peacefully, even during the rebellion. What made the difference? David cried out to the Lord, and the Lord heard him. The assurance of
answered prayer brings peace. It is easier to sleep well when we have full assurance that God is in control of circumstances. If you are lying awake at night
worrying about circumstances you can't change, pour out your heart to God,
and thank him that he is in control. Then sleep will come.

BIBLE READING: Psalm 63:1-11
KEY BIBLE VERSE: *I lie awake thinking of you, meditating on you through the night.*
(Psalm 63:6)

When sleepless, we can reflect on God's watchfulness. The night was divided
into three watches. Someone aware of all three would be having a sleepless
night. A cure for sleepless nights is to turn our thoughts to God. There are
many reasons we can't sleep—illness, stress, worry—but sleepless nights can
be turned into quiet times of reflection and worship. Use them to review how
God has guided and helped you.

BIBLE READING: Psalm 121:1-8
KEY BIBLE VERSE: *My help comes from the* LORD, *who made the heavens and the
earth! He will not let you stumble and fall; the one who watches over you will
not sleep. Indeed, he who watches over Israel never tires and never sleeps.*
(Psalm 121:2-4)

We can be secure knowing that God never sleeps, but watches over us. This
song expresses assurance and hope in God's protection day and night. He not
only made the hills but heaven and earth as well. We should never trust a lesser
power than God himself. But not only is he all-powerful, he also watches over
us. Nothing diverts or deters him. We are safe. We never outgrow our need for
God's untiring watch over our life.

Related Topics: CONTENTMENT, REST, SECURITY

SOCIETY *(Civilization, Community, Culture)*

How does God want us, as Christians, to relate to our society?

BIBLE READING: Matthew 5:13-16

KEY BIBLE VERSE: *You are the salt of the earth. But what good is salt if it has lost its flavor? Can you make it useful again? It will be thrown out and trampled underfoot as worthless. You are the light of the world—like a city on a mountain, glowing in the night for all to see.* (Matthew 5:13-14)

Christians are to be the flavor of society. If a seasoning has no flavor, it has no value. If Christians make no effort to affect the world around them, they are of little value to God. If we are too much like the world, we are worthless. Christians should not blend in with everyone else. Instead, we should affect others positively, just as seasoning brings out the best flavor in food.

Christians are to shed the light of the gospel in society. Can you hide a city that is sitting on top of a hill? Its light at night can be seen for miles. If we live for Christ, we will glow like lights, showing others what Christ is like. We hide our light by (1) being quiet when we should speak, (2) going along with the crowd, (3) denying the light, (4) letting sin dim our light, (5) not explaining our light to others, or (6) ignoring the needs of others. Be a beacon of truth—don't shut your light off from the rest of the world.

BIBLE READING: Matthew 23:1-39

KEY BIBLE VERSE: *The greatest among you must be a servant. But those who exalt themselves will be humbled, and those who humble themselves will be exalted.* (Matthew 23:11-12)

Christians who follow Jesus will be in conflict with society's values. Jesus challenged society's norms. To him, greatness comes from serving—giving of yourself to help God and others. Service keeps us aware of others' needs, and it stops us from focusing only on ourself. Jesus came as a servant. What kind of greatness do you seek?

BIBLE READING: 1 Corinthians 11:2-16

KEY BIBLE VERSE: *Isn't it obvious that it's disgraceful for a man to have long hair? And isn't it obvious that long hair is a woman's pride and joy? For it has been given to her as a covering.* (1 Corinthians 11:14-15)

Christians are to fit in with their culture without being controlled by it. In talking about head coverings and length of hair, Paul is saying that believers should look and behave in ways that are honorable within their own culture. In many cultures long hair on men is considered appropriate and masculine. In Corinth, it was thought to be a sign of male prostitution in the pagan temples. And women with short hair were labeled prostitutes. Paul was saying that in the Corinthian culture, Christian women should keep their hair long. If short hair on women was a sign of prostitution, then a Christian woman with short hair would find it even more difficult to be a believable witness for Jesus Christ. Paul wasn't saying we should adopt all the practices of our culture, but that we should avoid appearances and behavior that detract from our ultimate goal of being believable witnesses for Jesus Christ who demonstrate our Christian faith.

Related Topics: CHURCH, CITIZENSHIP, GOVERNMENT

SOLITUDE (*Aloneness, Quietness, Silence*)

How may we benefit from solitude?

BIBLE READING: Matthew 14:1-14

KEY BIBLE VERSE: *As soon as Jesus heard the news, he went off by himself in a boat to a remote area to be alone. But the crowds heard where he was headed and followed by land from many villages.* (Matthew 14:13)

Solitude can be time to deal privately with pain. Jesus sought solitude after the news of John's death. Sometimes we may need to deal with our grief alone. Jesus did not dwell on his grief, but returned to the ministry he came to do.

BIBLE READING: Matthew 14:22-33

KEY BIBLE VERSE: *Afterward he went up into the hills by himself to pray. Night fell while he was there alone. Meanwhile, the disciples were in trouble far away from land, for a strong wind had risen, and they were fighting heavy waves.* (Matthew 14:23-24)

Solitude can be time spent with God. Seeking solitude was an important priority for Jesus. He made room in his busy schedule to be alone with the Father. Spending time with God in prayer nurtures a vital relationship and equips us to meet life's challenges and struggles. Develop the discipline of spending time alone with God—it will help you grow spiritually and become more and more like Christ.

BIBLE READING: Luke 4:38-44

KEY BIBLE VERSE: *Early the next morning Jesus went out into the wilderness. The crowds searched everywhere for him, and when they finally found him, they begged him not to leave them.* (Luke 4:42)

Solitude is important for prayer and refreshment, but will only be possible if we make it a priority. Jesus had to get up very early just to get some time alone. If Jesus needed solitude for prayer and refreshment, how much more is this true for us? Don't become so busy that life turns into a flurry of activity leaving no room for quiet fellowship alone with God. No matter how much you have to do, you should always have time for prayer.

Related Topics: MEDITATION, QUIET, SILENCE

SOLUTIONS (*see* PROBLEMS)

SORROW (*Grief, Repentance, Sadness*)

When might we expect to experience sorrow?

BIBLE READING: Judges 2:1-5

KEY BIBLE VERSE: *When the angel of the LORD finished speaking, the Israelites wept loudly. So they called the place "Weeping," and they offered sacrifices to the LORD.* (Judges 2:4-5)

Sometimes sorrow is a necessary part of repentance. The people of Israel knew they had sinned, and they wept aloud, responding with deep sorrow. Because we have a tendency to sin, repentance is the true measure of spiritual sensitivity. Repentance means asking God to forgive us, and then abandoning our sinful ways. But we cannot do this sincerely unless we are truly sorry for our sinful actions. When we are aware that we have done wrong, we should admit it plainly to God rather than try to cover it up or hope we can get away with it.

BIBLE READING: Luke 15:1-32
KEY BIBLE VERSE: *When he finally came to his senses, he said to himself, "At home even the hired men have food enough to spare, and here I am, dying of hunger!"* (Luke 15:17)

Sometimes sorrow is the clue that convinces us we have sinned. The younger son, like many who are rebellious and immature, wanted to be free to live as he pleased, and he had to hit bottom before he came to his senses. It often takes great sorrow and tragedy to cause people to look to the only one who can help them. Are you trying to live life your own way, selfishly pushing aside any responsibility or commitment that gets in your way? Stop and look before you hit bottom. You will save yourself and your family much grief.

BIBLE READING: Revelation 7:1-17
KEY BIBLE VERSE: *The Lamb who stands in front of the throne will be their Shepherd. He will lead them to the springs of life-giving water. And God will wipe away all their tears.* (Revelation 7:17)

We may experience sorrow while we are here on earth, but someday, sorrow will be no more. In verses 1-8 we see the believers receiving a seal to protect them through a time of great tribulation and suffering; in verses 9-17 we see the believers finally with God in heaven. All who have been faithful through the ages are singing before God's throne. Their tribulations and sorrows are over: no more tears for sin, for all sins are forgiven; no more tears for suffering, for all suffering is over; no more tears for death, for all believers have been resurrected to die no more.

Related Topics: PROBLEMS, REPENTANCE, SUFFERING

SOUL *(Being, Personality, Self)*

How can our soul be guarded and preserved?

BIBLE READING: Psalm 56:1-13
KEY BIBLE VERSE: *When I am afraid, I put my trust in you. O God, I praise your word. I trust in God, so why should I be afraid? What can mere mortals do to me?* (Psalm 56:3-4)

The human soul is out of reach of other people. David stated, "What can mere mortals do to me?" How much harm can people do to us? They can inflict pain, suffering, and death. But no person can rob us of our soul or our future beyond this life. How much harm can we do to ourself? The worst thing we can do is to reject God and lose our eternal future. Jesus said, "Don't be afraid of those who want to kill you. They can only kill your body; they cannot touch your soul" (Matthew 10:28). Instead, we should fear God, who controls this life and the next.

BIBLE READING: John 10:22-42
KEY BIBLE VERSE: *My sheep recognize my voice; I know them, and they follow me. I give them eternal life, and they will never perish. No one will snatch them away from me, for my Father has given them to me, and he is more powerful than anyone else. So no one can take them from me.* (John 10:27-29)

We can place our soul under the protection of Jesus Christ. Just as a shepherd protects his sheep, Jesus protects his people from eternal harm. While believers can expect to suffer on earth, Satan cannot harm their soul or take away their eternal life with God. There are many reasons to be afraid here on earth because this is the devil's domain (1 Peter 5:8). But if you choose to follow Jesus, he will give you everlasting safety.

BIBLE READING: Revelation 7:1-3

KEY BIBLE VERSE: *I saw another angel coming from the east, carrying the seal of the living God. And he shouted out to those four angels who had been given power to injure land and sea, "Wait! Don't hurt the land or the sea or the trees until we have placed the seal of God on the foreheads of his servants."* (Revelation 7:2-3)

Souls placed under God's protection are safe. A seal on a scroll or document identified and protected its contents. God places his own seal on his followers, identifying them as his own and guaranteeing his protection over their souls. This shows how valuable we are to him. Our physical body may be beaten, maimed, or even destroyed, but *nothing* can harm our soul when we have been sealed by God. (See Ephesians 1:13 for more on the seal of the Holy Spirit.)

Related Topics: PROTECTION, SALVATION, SECURITY

SOVEREIGNTY *(Authority, Control, Power)*

What does the Bible teach us about God's sovereignty?

BIBLE READING: Ezra 6:1-18

KEY BIBLE VERSE: *The Jewish leaders continued their work, and they were greatly encouraged by the preaching of the prophets Haggai and Zechariah son of Iddo. The Temple was finally finished, as had been commanded by the God of Israel and decreed by Cyrus, Darius, and Artaxerxes, the kings of Persia.* (Ezra 6:14)

Even the most powerful human rulers are controlled by God. Ezra carefully pointed out that rebuilding the temple was commanded first by God and then by the kings, who were his instruments. How ironic and wonderful that God's work was carried on by the discovery of a lost paragraph in a pagan library. All the opposition of powerful forces was stopped by a clause in a legal document. God's will is supreme over all rulers, all historical events, and all hostile forces. He can deliver us in ways we can't imagine. If we trust in his power and love, no opposition can stop us.

BIBLE READING: Job 36:22-33

KEY BIBLE VERSE: *Look, God is exalted beyond what we can understand. His years are without number.* (Job 36:26)

God is greater than we can understand. One theme in the poetic literature of the Bible is that God is incomprehensible; we cannot know him completely. We can have some knowledge about him, for the Bible is full of details about who God is, how we can know him, and how we can have an eternal relationship with him. But we can never know enough to answer all of life's questions (Ecclesiastes 3:11), to predict our own future, or to manipulate God for our own ends. Life always creates more questions than we have answers, and we must constantly go to God for fresh insights into life's dilemmas.

BIBLE READING: Job 37:1-24
KEY BIBLE VERSE: *We cannot imagine the power of the Almighty, yet he is so just and merciful that he does not oppress us.* (Job 37:23)

God's sovereignty is completely awe inspiring. Nothing can compare to God. His power and presence are awesome, and when he speaks, we must listen. Too often we presume to speak for God (as did Job's friends), to put words in his mouth, to take him for granted, or to interpret his silence to mean that he is absent or unconcerned. But God cares. He is in control, and he will speak. Be ready to hear his message—in the Bible, through the Holy Spirit, and through circumstances and relationships.

God's sovereignty is absolute. Elihu stressed God's sovereignty over all of nature as a reminder of his sovereignty over our life. God is in control—he directs, preserves, and maintains his created order. Although we can't see it, God is divinely governing the moral and political affairs of people as well. By spending time observing the majestic and intricate parts of God's creation, we can be reminded of his power in every aspect of our life.

BIBLE READING: Job 38:1-41
KEY BIBLE VERSE: *The LORD answered Job from the whirlwind.* (Job 38:1)

God is not required to explain anything to us. Out of a mighty storm, God spoke. Surprisingly, he didn't answer any of Job's questions; Job's questions were not at the heart of the issue. Instead, God used Job's ignorance of the earth's natural order to reveal his ignorance of God's moral order. If Job did not understand the workings of God's physical creation, how could he possibly understand God's mind and character? There is no standard or criterion higher than God himself by which to judge. God himself is the standard. Our only option is to submit to his authority and rest in his care.

BIBLE READING: Romans 8:28-39
KEY BIBLE VERSE: *I am convinced that nothing can ever separate us from his love. Death can't, and life can't. The angels can't, and the demons can't. Our fears for today, our worries about tomorrow, and even the powers of hell can't keep God's love away. Whether we are high above the sky or in the deepest ocean, nothing in all creation will ever be able to separate us from the love of God that is revealed in Christ Jesus our Lord.* (Romans 8:38-39)

God's sovereign love extends to every part of our life. Some believe these verses mean that before the beginning of the world, God chose certain people to receive his gift of salvation. They point to verses like Ephesians 1:11 that says God "chose us from the beginning, and all things happen just as he decided long ago." Others believe that God *foreknew* those who would respond to him and upon those he set his mark (predestined). What is clear is that God's *purpose* for people was not an afterthought; it was settled before the foundation of the world. People are to serve and honor God. If you have believed in Christ, you can rejoice in the fact that God has always known you. God's love is eternal. His wisdom and power are supreme. He will guide and protect you until you one day stand in his presence.

Related Topics: GOD, POWER, SALVATION

SPEAKING (*see* WORDS)

SPIRITUAL DISCIPLINES (*Control, Habits, Routines*)

What does spiritual discipline do for us?

BIBLE READING: 1 Corinthians 9:24-27

KEY BIBLE VERSE: *Remember that in a race everyone runs, but only one person gets the prize. You also must run in such a way that you will win.* (1 Corinthians 9:24)

Spiritual discipline helps us effectively "run the race." Winning a race requires purpose and discipline. Paul uses this illustration to explain that the Christian life takes hard work, self-denial, and grueling preparation. As Christians, we are running toward our heavenly reward. The essential disciplines of prayer, Bible study, and worship equip us to run with vigor and stamina. Don't merely observe from the grandstand; don't just turn out to jog a couple of laps each morning. Train diligently—your spiritual progress depends upon it.

Spiritual discipline focuses our spiritual goals. At times we must even give up something good in order to do what God wants. Each person's special duties determine the discipline and self-denial that he or she must accept. Without a goal, discipline is nothing but self-punishment. With the goal of pleasing God, our sacrifices seem like nothing compared to the eternal, imperishable reward that will be ours.

BIBLE READING: 1 Timothy 4:7-10

KEY BIBLE VERSE: *Do not waste time arguing over godless ideas and old wives' tales. Spend your time and energy in training yourself for spiritual fitness. Physical exercise has some value, but spiritual exercise is much more important, for it promises a reward in both this life and the next.* (1 Timothy 4:7-8)

Spiritual discipline makes us spiritually "fit." Are you in shape both physically and spiritually? In our society, much emphasis is placed on physical fitness, but spiritual health (godliness) is even more important. Our physical health is susceptible to disease and injury, but faith can sustain us through these tragedies. To be spiritually "fit," we must develop our faith by using our God-given abilities in the service of the church (1 Timothy 4:14-16). Are you developing your spiritual muscles?

BIBLE READING: Hebrews 12:1-4

KEY BIBLE VERSE: *Since we are surrounded by such a huge crowd of witnesses to the life of faith, let us strip off every weight that slows us down, especially the sin that so easily hinders our progress. And let us run with endurance the race that God has set before us.* (Hebrews 12:1)

Spiritual discipline strips away the nonessentials. The Christian life involves hard work. It requires us to give up whatever endangers our relationship with God, to run patiently, and to struggle against sin with the power of the Holy Spirit. To live effectively, we must keep our eyes on Jesus. We will stumble if we look away from him to stare at ourself or at the circumstances surrounding us. We should be running for Christ, not ourself, and we must always keep him in sight.

Related Topics: DISCIPLINE, GROWTH, MEDITATION

SPIRITUAL GIFTS (*Abilities, Talents, Tools*)

What is the nature and use of spiritual gifts?

BIBLE READING: Romans 12:1-8

KEY BIBLE VERSE: *Just as our bodies have many parts and each part has a special function, so it is with Christ's body. We are all parts of his one body, and each of us has different work to do. And since we are all one body in Christ, we belong to each other, and each of us needs all the others.* (Romans 12:4-5)

God gives us spiritual gifts so we can work together to serve him and each other. Paul uses the concept of the human body to teach how Christians should live and work together. Just as the parts of the body function under the direction of the brain, so Christians are to work together under the command and authority of Jesus Christ (see 1 Corinthians 12:12-31; Ephesians 4:1-16).

God gives us gifts so we can build up his church. To use them effectively, we must (1) realize that all gifts and abilities come from God; (2) understand that not everyone has the same gifts; (3) know who we are and what we do best; (4) dedicate our gifts to God's service and not to our personal success; and (5) be willing to utilize our gifts wholeheartedly, not holding back anything from God's service.

Our gifts, though different, are all useful. Our gifts differ in nature, power, and effectiveness according to God's wisdom and graciousness, not according to our faith. "Measuring your value by how much faith God has given you" (12:3) means that God will give the spiritual power necessary and appropriate to carry out each responsibility. We cannot, by our own effort or willpower, drum up more faith and thus be more effective teachers or servants. These are God's gifts to his church, and he gives faith and power as he wills. Our role is to be faithful and to seek ways to serve others with what Christ has given us.

Christians using their gifts to serve God and each other create an exciting fellowship. Look at the list of gifts in this passage and imagine the kinds of people who would have each gift. Prophets are often bold and articulate. Servers (those in ministry) are faithful and loyal. Teachers are clear thinkers. Preachers know how to motivate others. Givers are generous and trusting. Leaders are good organizers and managers. Those who comfort others are caring people who are happy to give their time to others. It would be difficult for one person to embody all these gifts. An assertive prophet would not usually make a good counselor, and a generous giver might fail as a leader. When you identify your own gifts (and this list is far from complete), ask how you can use them to build up God's family. At the same time, realize that your gifts can't do the work of the church all alone. Be thankful for people whose gifts are completely different from yours. Let your strengths balance their weaknesses, and be grateful that their abilities make up for your deficiencies. Together you can build Christ's church.

BIBLE READING: 1 Corinthians 12:1-31

KEY BIBLE VERSE: *Now there are different kinds of spiritual gifts, but it is the same Holy Spirit who is the source of them all. There are different kinds of service in the church, but it is the same Lord we are serving. There are different ways God works in our lives, but it is the same God who does the work through all of us.* (1 Corinthians 12:4-6)

Spiritual gifts have a single source and a special purpose. The spiritual gifts given to each person by the Holy Spirit are special abilities that are to be used to minister to the needs of the body of believers. This chapter is not an exhaustive list of spiritual gifts (see Romans 12; Ephesians 4; 1 Peter 4:10-11 for more examples). There are many gifts. Some people have more than one gift, and one gift is not superior to another. All spiritual gifts come from the Holy Spirit, and their purpose is to build up Christ's body, the church.

Spiritual gifts have at times been divisive because of pride and jealousy. Instead of building up and unifying the Corinthian church, the issue of spiritual gifts was splitting it. Spiritual gifts had become symbols of spiritual power, causing rivalries. Some people thought they were more "spiritual" than others because of their gifts. This was a terrible misuse of spiritual gifts because their purpose is always to help the church function more effectively, not to divide it. We can be divisive if we insist on using our gift our own way without being sensitive to others. We must never use gifts as a means of manipulating others or serving our own self-interest.

Spiritual gifts ought to be humbly used in service of others. The greater gifts are those that are more beneficial to the body of Christ. Paul has already made it clear that one gift is not superior to another, but he urges the believers to discover how they can serve Christ's body with the gifts God has given them. Your spiritual gifts are not for your own self-advancement. They were given to you for serving God and enhancing the spiritual growth of the body of believers.

BIBLE READING: 1 Thessalonians 5:12-28

KEY BIBLE VERSE: *Do not stifle the Holy Spirit. Do not scoff at prophecies, but test everything that is said. Hold on to what is good. Keep away from every kind of evil.* (1 Thessalonians 5:19-22)

Spiritual maturity neither denies nor overemphasizes spiritual gifts. By warning us not to "stifle the Holy Spirit," Paul means that we should not ignore or toss aside the gifts the Holy Spirit gives. Here, he mentions prophecy (5:20); in 1 Corinthians 14:39, he mentions tongues. Some spiritual gifts may be controversial, and they may cause division in a church. Rather than trying to solve the problems, some Christians just smother the gifts. This impoverishes the church. We should not stifle the Holy Spirit's work in anyone's life but encourage the full expression of these gifts to benefit the whole body of Christ.

Related Topics: CHURCH, GIVING, SERVING

SPIRITUAL GROWTH *(Development, Growth, Maturity)*

What promotes spiritual growth?

BIBLE READING: Deuteronomy 5:1-21

KEY BIBLE VERSE: *Moses called all the people of Israel together and said, "Listen carefully to all the laws and regulations I am giving you today. Learn them and be sure to obey them!"* (Deuteronomy 5:1)

Spiritual growth involves hearing, learning, and following. The people had entered into a covenant with God, and Moses commanded them to listen, learn, and obey his statutes. Christians also have entered into a covenant with God (through Jesus Christ) and should be responsive to what God expects. Moses' threefold command to the Israelites is excellent advice for all God's followers. *Hearing* is absorbing and accepting information about God. *Learning* is understanding its meaning and implications. *Following* is putting into action all we have learned and understood. All three parts are essential to a growing relationship with God.

BIBLE READING: Isaiah 27:2-13

KEY BIBLE VERSE: *The people are like the dead branches of a tree, broken off and used for kindling beneath the cooking pots. Israel is a foolish and stupid nation, for its people have turned away from God. Therefore, the one who made them will show them no pity or mercy.* (Isaiah 27:11)

Spiritual growth is always dependent on our vital connection to God. Isaiah compares the state of Israel's spiritual life with dead branches that are broken off and used to make fires. Trees in Scripture often represent spiritual life. The trunk is the source or channel of strength from God, giving life to the branches, which represent the people who serve him. Tree branches sometimes waver and blow in the wind. Like Israel, they may dry up from internal rottenness and become useless for anything except building a fire. What kind of branch are you? If you are withering spiritually, check to see if you are vitally connected to God.

BIBLE READING: Romans 14:1-9

KEY BIBLE VERSE: *Accept Christians who are weak in faith, and don't argue with them about what they think is right or wrong.* (Romans 14:1)

Encouraging other Christians is part of our own spiritual growth. Who is weak in faith and who is strong? We are all weak in some areas and strong in others. Our faith is strong if we can survive contact with sinners without falling into their patterns. It is weak if we must avoid certain activities, people, or places in order to protect our spiritual life. It is important to take a self-inventory in order to find out our strengths and weaknesses. Whenever in doubt, we should ask, Can I do that without sinning? Can I influence others for good, rather than being influenced by them?

In areas of strength, we should not fear being defiled by the world; rather we should go and serve God. In areas of weakness, we need to be cautious. If we have a strong faith but shelter it, we are not doing Christ's work in the world. If we have a weak faith but expose it, we are being extremely foolish.

BIBLE READING: Philippians 1:3-11

KEY BIBLE VERSE: *I am sure that God, who began the good work within you, will continue his work until it is finally finished on that day when Christ Jesus comes back again.* (Philippians 1:6)

God is intimately involved in our spiritual growth. The God who began a good work in us continues it throughout our lifetime and will finish it when we meet him face to face. God's work *for* us began when Christ died on the cross in our place. His work *in* us began when we first believed. Now the Holy Spirit lives in us, enabling us to be more like Christ every day. Paul is describing the process of Christian growth and maturity that began when we accepted Jesus and will continue until Christ returns.

God will keep working even when we are discouraged. Do you sometimes feel as though you aren't making progress in your spiritual life? When God starts a project, he completes it! As with the Philippians, God will help you grow in grace until he has completed his work in your life. When you are discouraged, remember that God won't give up on you. He promises to finish the work he has begun. When you feel incomplete, unfinished, or distressed by your shortcomings, remember God's promise and provision. Don't let your present condition rob you of the joy of knowing Christ or keep you from growing closer to him.

BIBLE READING: Colossians 2:1-15

KEY BIBLE VERSE: *Just as you accepted Christ Jesus as your Lord, you must continue to live in obedience to him. Let your roots grow down into him and draw up nourishment from him, so you will grow in faith, strong and vigorous in the truth you were taught. Let your lives overflow with thanksgiving for all he has done.* (Colossians 2:6-7)

Spiritual growth begins with Christ. Receiving Christ as Lord of your life is the beginning of life with Christ. But you must continue to follow his leadership by being rooted, built up, and strengthened in the faith. Christ wants to guide you and help you with your daily problems. You can live for Christ by (1) committing your life and submitting your will to him (Romans 12:1-2); (2) seeking to learn from him, his life, and his teachings (Colossians 3:16); and (3) recognizing the Holy Spirit's power in you (Acts 1:8; Galatians 5:22).

Spiritual growth continues in Christ. Paul uses the illustration of our being rooted in Christ. Just as plants draw nourishment from the soil through their roots, so we draw our life-giving strength from Christ. The more we draw our strength from him, the less we will be fooled by those who falsely claim to have life's answers. If Christ is our strength, we will be free from human regulations.

Related Topics: GROWTH, MATURITY, SPIRITUAL DISCIPLINES

SPIRITUAL REBIRTH *(Conversion, Salvation, Second Birth)*

What is spiritual rebirth?

BIBLE READING: John 3:1-21

KEY BIBLE VERSE: *Jesus replied, "I assure you, unless you are born again, you can never see the Kingdom of God."* (John 3:3)

Spiritual rebirth allows us to enter God's kingdom. "Of water and the Spirit" in John 3:5 could refer to (1) the contrast between physical birth (water) and spiritual birth (Spirit), or (2) being regenerated by the Spirit and signifying that rebirth by Christian baptism. The water may also represent the cleansing action of God's Holy Spirit (Titus 3:5). Nicodemus undoubtedly would have been familiar with God's promise in Ezekiel 36:25-26. Jesus was explaining the importance of a spiritual rebirth, saying that people don't enter the kingdom by living a better life, but by being spiritually reborn.

Spiritual rebirth is the Holy Spirit's work. Jesus explained that we cannot control the work of the Holy Spirit. He works in ways we cannot predict or understand. Just as you did not control your physical birth, so you cannot control your spiritual birth. It is a gift from God through the Holy Spirit (Romans 8:16; 1 Corinthians 2:10-12).

Spiritual rebirth involves accepting a priceless gift—eternal life. John's entire Gospel comes to a focus in 3:16. God's love is not static or self-centered; it reaches out and draws others in. Here God sets the pattern of true love, the basis for all love relationships—when you love someone dearly, you are willing to pay dearly for that person's responsive love. God paid dearly with the life of his Son, the highest price he could pay. Jesus accepted our punishment, paid the price for our sins, and then offered us the new life that he had bought for us. When we share the gospel with others, our love must be like Jesus'—we must be willing to give up our own comfort and security so that others might join us in receiving God's love.

📖 BIBLE READING: John 3:22-36

KEY BIBLE VERSE: *All who believe in God's Son have eternal life. Those who don't obey the Son will never experience eternal life, but the wrath of God remains upon them.* (John 3:36)

Spiritual rebirth begins a life that will never end; its alternative is worse than death. Jesus says that those who believe in him *have* (not *will* have) eternal life. To receive eternal life is to join in God's life, which by nature is eternal. Thus, eternal life begins at the moment of spiritual rebirth.

John, the author of this Gospel, has been demonstrating that Jesus is the true Son of God. Jesus sets before us the greatest choice in life. We are responsible to decide today whom we will obey (Joshua 24:15), and God wants us to choose him and life (Deuteronomy 30:15-20). The wrath of God is God's final judgment and rejection of the sinner. To put off the choice is to choose not to follow Christ. Indecision is a fatal decision.

📖 BIBLE READING: Romans 7:1-6

KEY BIBLE VERSE: *This is the point: The law no longer holds you in its power, because you died to its power when you died with Christ on the cross. And now you are united with the one who was raised from the dead. As a result, you can produce good fruit, that is, good deeds for God.* (Romans 7:4)

Spiritual rebirth means dying to the old life. When a person dies to the old life and belongs to Christ, a new life begins. An unbeliever's mind-set is centered on his or her own personal gratification. Those who don't follow Christ have only their own self-determination as their source of power. By contrast, God is at the center of a Christian's life. God supplies the power for the Christian's daily living. Believers find that their whole way of looking at the world changes when they come to Christ.

📖 BIBLE READING: 1 John 3:1-10

KEY BIBLE VERSE: *Those who have been born into God's family do not sin, because God's life is in them. So they can't keep on sinning, because they have been born of God.* (1 John 3:9)

Spiritual rebirth gives a new significance to sin. True believers do not make a practice of sinning, nor do they become indifferent to God's moral law. All believers still sin, but they are working to gain victory over sin. True believers do not make a practice of sinning, because God's new life has been born into them.

Spiritual rebirth presents us with a brand-new life. We are "born into God's family" when the Holy Spirit lives in us and gives us Jesus' new life. Being born again is more than a fresh start; it is a rebirth, receiving a new family name based on Christ's death for us. When this happens, God forgives us and totally accepts us; the Holy Spirit gives us a new mind and heart, lives in us, and begins helping us to become like Christ. Our perspective changes too because we have a mind that is renewed day by day by the Holy Spirit (see Romans 12:2; Ephesians 4:22-24). So we must begin to think and act differently.

Related Topics: BELIEF/BELIEVE, GOSPEL, SALVATION

STATUS *(Position, Power, Reputation)*

What part does status play in the life of a Christian?

BIBLE READING: Luke 14:7-14

KEY BIBLE VERSE: *Invite the poor, the crippled, the lame, and the blind. Then at the resurrection of the godly, God will reward you for inviting those who could not repay you.* (Luke 14:13-14)

Status should always get less honor than service. Jesus taught two lessons here. First, he spoke to the guests, telling them not to seek places of honor. Service is more important in God's kingdom than status. Second, he told the host not to be exclusive about whom he invites. God opens his kingdom to everyone.

A Christian leaves matters of status in God's hands. Jesus advised people not to rush for the best places at a feast. People today are just as eager to raise their social status, whether by being with the right people, dressing for success, or driving the right car. Whom do you try to impress? Rather than aiming for prestige, look for a place where you can serve. If God wants you to serve on a wider scale, he will invite you to take a higher place.

BIBLE READING: Galatians 2:1-10

KEY BIBLE VERSE: *The leaders of the church who were there had nothing to add to what I was preaching. (By the way, their reputation as great leaders made no difference to me, for God has no favorites.)* (Galatians 2:6)

There ought not to be status seeking within the body of Christ. It's easy to rate people on the basis of their official status and to be intimidated by powerful people. But Paul was not intimidated by the "great leaders" because all believers are equal in Christ. We should show respect for our spiritual leaders, but our ultimate allegiance must be to Christ. We are to serve him with our whole being. God doesn't rate us according to our status; he looks at our thoughts and intentions (1 Samuel 16:7).

BIBLE READING: James 2:1-13

KEY BIBLE VERSE: *Yes indeed, it is good when you truly obey our Lord's royal command found in the Scriptures: "Love your neighbor as yourself." But if you pay special attention to the rich, you are committing a sin, for you are guilty of breaking that law.* (James 2:8-9)

Power based on status is unacceptable among faithful believers. In this chapter James argues *against* favoritism and *for* the necessity of good deeds. He presents three principles of faith: (1) Commitment is an essential part of faith. You cannot be a Christian simply by affirming the right doctrines or agreeing with biblical facts (2:19). You must commit your mind and heart to Christ. (2) Right actions are the natural by-products of true faith. A genuine Christian will have a changed life (2:18). (3) Faith without good deeds doesn't do anybody any good—it is useless (2:14-17). James's teachings are consistent with Paul's teaching that we receive salvation by faith alone. Paul emphasizes the purpose of faith—to bring salvation. James emphasizes the results of faith—a changed life.

Christian love rejects favoritism based on status. James condemns acts of favoritism. Often we treat a well-dressed, impressive-looking person better than someone who looks shabby. We do this because we would rather identify with successful people than with apparent failures. The irony, as James reminds us, is that the supposed winners may have gained their impressive lifestyle at our expense. In addition, the rich find it difficult to identify with the Lord Jesus, who came as a humble servant. Are you easily impressed by status, wealth, or fame? Are you partial to the "haves" while ignoring the "have nots"? This attitude is sinful. God views all people as equals, and if he favors anyone, it is the poor and the powerless. We should follow his example.

Judgment by status is a poor substitute for Christian love. Why is it wrong to judge a person by his or her economic status? Wealth may indicate intelligence, wise decisions, and hard work. On the other hand, it may mean only that a person had the good fortune of being born into a wealthy family. Or it can even be the sign of greed, dishonesty, and selfishness. By honoring someone just because he or she dresses well, we are making appearance more important than character. Sometimes we do this because (1) poverty makes us uncomfortable; we don't want to face our responsibilities to those who have less than we do; (2) we want to be wealthy too, and we hope to use the rich person as a means to that end; or (3) we want the rich person to join our church and help support it financially. All these motives are selfish; they view neither the rich nor the poor person as a human being in need of fellowship. If we say that Christ is our Lord, then we must live as he requires, showing no favoritism and loving all people regardless of whether they are rich or poor.

Recognizing status can be the result of poor theology. We are often partial to the rich because we mistakenly assume that riches are a sign of God's blessing and approval. But God does not promise us earthly rewards or riches; in fact, Christ calls us to be ready to suffer for him and give up everything in order to hold on to eternal life (Matthew 6:19-21; 19:28-30; Luke 12:14-34; Romans 8:15-21; 1 Timothy 6:17-19). We will have untold riches in eternity if we are faithful in our present life (Luke 6:35; John 12:23-25; Galatians 6:7-10; Titus 3:4-8).

Related Topics: POWER, PRIDE, REPUTATION

STEWARDSHIP (*see* TITHING)

STRENGTH (*Ability, Energy, Power*)

Why must we take care in areas where we are strong?

BIBLE READING: Genesis 49:1-28
KEY BIBLE VERSE: *Dan will govern his people like any other tribe in Israel. He will be a snake beside the road, a poisonous viper along the path, that bites the horse's heels so the rider is thrown off. I trust in you for salvation, O LORD!* (Genesis 49:16-18)

Our strengths often get in the way of trusting God. In the middle of his prophecy to Dan, Jacob exclaimed, "I trust in you for salvation, O Lord." He was emphasizing to Dan that he would be a strong leader only if his trust was in God, not in his natural strength or ability. Those who are strong, attractive, or talented often find it easier to trust in themselves than in God who gave them their gifts. Remember to thank God for what you are and have so that your trust does not become misplaced.

BIBLE READING: Judges 7:1-25
KEY BIBLE VERSE: *The LORD said to Gideon, "You have too many warriors with you. If I let all of you fight the Midianites, the Israelites will boast to me that they saved themselves by their own strength."* (Judges 7:2)

God wants us to appreciate strength without becoming self-sufficient. Self-sufficiency is an enemy when it causes us to believe we can always do what needs to be done in our own strength. To prevent this attitude among Gideon's soldiers, God reduced their number from thirty-two thousand to three hundred.

With an army this small, there could be no doubt that victory was from God. The men could not take the credit. Like Gideon, we must recognize the danger of fighting in our own strength. We can be confident of victory only if we put our confidence in God and not ourself.

 BIBLE READING: Isaiah 40:25-31

KEY BIBLE VERSE: *He gives power to those who are tired and worn out; he offers strength to the weak. Even youths will become exhausted, and young men will give up. But those who wait on the LORD will find new strength. They will fly high on wings like eagles. They will run and not grow weary. They will walk and not faint.* (Isaiah 40:29-31)

We can depend on God as our source of strength. Even the strongest people get tired at times, but God's power and strength never diminish. He is never too tired or too busy to help and listen. When you feel all of life crushing you, and you cannot go another step, remember that you can call upon God to renew your strength.

Hoping in the Lord means expecting that his promise of strength will help us to rise above life's distractions and difficulties. It also means trusting God to fulfill this promise found in his Word.

BIBLE READING: Luke 4:1-13

KEY BIBLE VERSE: *The Devil said to him, "If you are the Son of God, change this stone into a loaf of bread."* (Luke 4:3)

Our strengths are actually a point of spiritual vulnerability. Often we are tempted not through our weaknesses, but through our strengths. The devil tempted Jesus where he was strong. Jesus had power over stones, the kingdoms of the world, and even angels, and Satan wanted him to use that power without regard to his mission. When we give in to the devil and wrongly use our strengths, we become proud and self-reliant. Trusting in our own powers, we feel little need of God. To avoid this trap, we must realize that all our strengths are God's gifts to us, and we must dedicate those strengths to his service.

Related Topics: ABILITIES, SPIRITUAL GIFTS, WEAKNESSES

STRESS *(Difficulty, Strain, Worry)*

What biblical principles deal directly with stress?

BIBLE READING: Exodus 16:1-12

KEY BIBLE VERSE: *The whole community of Israel spoke bitterly against Moses and Aaron.* (Exodus 16:2)

Stress may be an indication that our relationship with God is lacking. It happened again. As the Israelites encountered danger, shortages, and inconvenience, they complained bitterly and longed to be back in Egypt. But as always, God provided for their needs. Difficult circumstances often lead to stress, and complaining is a natural response. The Israelites didn't really want to be back in Egypt; they just wanted life to get a little easier. In the pressure of the moment, they could not focus on the cause of their stress (in this case, lack of trust in God); they could only think about the quickest way of escape. When pressure comes your way, resist the temptation to make a quick escape. Instead, focus on God's power and wisdom to help you deal with the cause of your stress.

BIBLE READING: Psalm 62:1-12

KEY BIBLE VERSE: *I wait quietly before God, for my salvation comes from him. He alone is my rock and my salvation, my fortress where I will never be shaken.* (Psalm 62:1-2)

In times of stress, prayer can release our tensions. David expressed his feelings to God and then reaffirmed his faith. Trusting God to be our rock, rescuer, defense, and fortress will change our entire outlook on life. No longer must we be held captive by resentment toward others when they hurt us. When we are resting in God's strength, nothing can shake us.

BIBLE READING: Romans 5:1-5

KEY BIBLE VERSE: *We can rejoice, too, when we run into problems and trials, for we know that they are good for us—they help us learn to endure. And endurance develops strength of character in us, and character strengthens our confident expectation of salvation.* (Romans 5:3-4)

Stress that cannot be avoided may help us grow in faith and character. For first-century Christians, suffering was the rule rather than the exception. Paul tells us that in the future we will *become,* but until then we must *overcome.* This means we will experience difficulties that help us grow. We rejoice in suffering not because we like pain or deny its tragedy, but because we know God is using life's difficulties and Satan's attacks to build our character. The problems that we run into will develop our patience—which in turn will strengthen our character, deepen our trust in God, and give us greater confidence about the future. You probably find your patience tested in some way every day. Thank God for those opportunities to grow, and deal with them in his strength (see also James 1:2-4; 1 Peter 1:6-7).

BIBLE READING: Philippians 4:4-9

KEY BIBLE VERSE: *Don't worry about anything; instead, pray about everything. Tell God what you need, and thank him for all he has done. If you do this, you will experience God's peace, which is far more wonderful than the human mind can understand. His peace will guard your hearts and minds as you live in Christ Jesus.* (Philippians 4:6-7)

Stress on the outside need not mean stress on the inside. It seems strange that a man in prison would be telling a church to rejoice. But Paul's attitude teaches us an important lesson: our inner attitudes do not have to reflect our outward circumstances. Paul was full of joy because he knew that no matter what happened to him, Jesus Christ was with him. Several times in this letter, Paul urged the Philippians to be joyful, probably because they needed to hear this. It's easy to get discouraged about unpleasant circumstances or to take unimportant events too seriously. If you haven't been joyful lately, you may not be looking at life from the right perspective.

Stress ought to remind us to pray. Imagine never worrying about anything! It seems like an impossibility—we all have worries on the job, in our homes, at school. But Paul's advice is to turn our worries into prayers. Do you want to worry less? Then pray more! Whenever you start to worry, stop and pray.

Let God's peace guard your heart against anxiety and stress. God's peace is different from the world's peace (see John 14:27). True peace is not found in positive thinking, in absence of conflict, or in good feelings. It comes from knowing that God is in control, that our citizenship in Christ's kingdom is sure, and that we can have victory over sin.

Stress is often self-inflicted by our choice of thought material. What we put into our mind determines what comes out in our words and actions. Paul tells us to program our mind with thoughts that are true, good, right, pure, lovely, admirable, excellent, and praiseworthy. Do you have problems with impure thoughts and daydreams? Examine what you are putting into your mind through television, books, conversations, movies, and magazines. Replace harmful input with wholesome material. Above all, read God's Word and pray. Ask God to help you focus your mind on what is good and pure. It takes practice, but it can be done.

Related Topics: DISCOURAGEMENT, PRESSURE, REST

STUBBORNNESS (*Arrogance, Pride, Uncooperativeness*)

Why should we make every effort to avoid stubbornness?

BIBLE READING: Exodus 8:1-19

KEY BIBLE VERSE: *"This is the finger of God!" the magicians exclaimed to Pharaoh. But Pharaoh's heart remained hard and stubborn. He wouldn't listen to them, just as the LORD had predicted.* (Exodus 8:19)

Stubbornness can lead to suffering. After repeated warnings, Pharaoh still refused to obey God. He hardened his heart every time there was a break in the plagues. His stubborn disobedience brought suffering upon himself and his entire country. While persistence is good, stubbornness is usually self-centered. Stubbornness toward God is always disobedience. Avoid disobedience, because the consequences may cause others also to suffer.

Stubbornness can make it difficult to believe. Some people think, *If only I could see a miracle, I could believe in God.* God gave Pharaoh just such an opportunity. When lice infested Egypt, even the magicians agreed that this was God's work ("the finger of God")—but still Pharaoh refused to believe. He was stubborn, and stubbornness can blind a person to the truth. When you rid yourself of stubbornness, you may be surprised to see how God will work in your life.

BIBLE READING: Psalm 81:1-16

KEY BIBLE VERSE: *My people wouldn't listen. Israel did not want me around. So I let them follow their blind and stubborn way, living according to their own desires.* (Psalm 81:11-12)

Stubbornness can become a permanent condition. God let the Israelites go on blindly, stubbornly, and selfishly, when they should have been obeying and pursuing God's desires. God sometimes lets us continue in our stubbornness to bring us to our senses. He does not keep us from rebelling because he wants us to learn the consequences of sin. He uses these experiences to turn people away from greater sin to faith in him.

BIBLE READING: Mark 2:18-22

KEY BIBLE VERSE: *And no one puts new wine into old wineskins. The wine would burst the wineskins, spilling the wine and ruining the skins. New wine needs new wineskins.* (Mark 2:22)

Stubbornness may prevent a change in us we desperately need. A wineskin was a goatskin sewed together at the edges to form a watertight bag. New wine, expanding as it aged, stretched the wineskin. New wine, therefore, could not be put into a wineskin that had already been stretched, or the taut skin would burst. The Pharisees had become rigid like old wineskins. They could not accept faith in Jesus that would not be contained or limited by man-made ideas or rules. Your heart, like a wineskin, can become rigid and prevent you from accepting the new life that Christ offers. Keep your heart pliable and open to accepting the life-changing truths of Christ.

BIBLE READING: John 20:24-31

KEY BIBLE VERSE: *They told him, "We have seen the Lord!" But he replied, "I won't believe it unless I see the nail wounds in his hands, put my fingers into them, and place my hand into the wound in his side." (John 20:25)*

Stubbornness can be the result of hardened doubts. Jesus wasn't hard on Thomas for his doubts. Despite his skepticism, Thomas was still loyal to the believers and to Jesus himself. Some people need to doubt before they believe. If doubt leads to questions, questions lead to answers, and the answers are then accepted, then doubt has done good work. It is when doubt becomes stubbornness and stubbornness becomes a lifestyle that doubt harms faith. When you doubt, don't stop there. Let your doubt deepen your faith as you continue to search for the answer.

Related Topics: GENTLENESS, HARD-HEARTEDNESS, SUBMISSION

STUMBLING BLOCKS (*see* EXAMPLE)

SUBMISSION (*Agreeableness, Cooperation, Obedience*)

What kind of submission does God expect from us?

BIBLE READING: Luke 14:25-35

KEY BIBLE VERSE: *You cannot be my disciple if you do not carry your own cross and follow me. (Luke 14:27)*

Submission to Christ's lordship is central in Christianity. Jesus' audience was well aware of what it meant to carry one's own cross. When the Romans led a criminal to his execution site, he was forced to carry the cross on which he would die. This showed his submission to Rome and warned observers that they had better submit too. Jesus spoke this teaching to get the crowds to think through their enthusiasm for him. He encouraged those who were superficial either to go deeper or to turn back. Following Christ means total submission to him—perhaps even to the point of death.

BIBLE READING: 1 Corinthians 11:2-16

KEY BIBLE VERSE: *There is one thing I want you to know: A man is responsible to Christ, a woman is responsible to her husband, and Christ is responsible to God. (1 Corinthians 11:3)*

Submission is a key to harmony in relationships. Submission is a key element in the smooth functioning of any business, government, or family. God ordained submission in certain relationships to prevent chaos. It is essential to understand that submission is not surrender, withdrawal, or apathy. It does not mean inferiority, because God created all people in his image, and all have equal value. Submission is mutual commitment and cooperation.

Biblical submission is based on valuing one another as equals. God calls for submission among *equals.* He did not make the man superior; he made a way for the man and woman to work together. Jesus Christ, although equal with God the Father, submitted to him to carry out the plan for salvation. Likewise, although equal to man under God, the wife should submit to her husband for the sake of their marriage and family. Submission between equals is submission by choice, not by force. We serve God in these relationships by willingly submitting to others in our church, to our spouses, and to our government leaders.

Biblical submission is choosing to obey and glorify God in relationships. God created lines of authority in order for his created world to function smoothly. Although there must be lines of authority, even in marriage, there should *not* be lines of superiority. God created men and women with unique and complementary characteristics. One sex is not better than the other. We must not let the issue of authority and submission become a wedge to destroy oneness in marriage. Instead, we should use our unique gifts to strengthen our marriages and to glorify God.

BIBLE READING: Ephesians 5:21-33

KEY BIBLE VERSE: *You will submit to one another out of reverence for Christ.* (Ephesians 5:21)

Biblical submission is a mark of equality rather than inequality. Submitting to another person is an often misunderstood concept. It does not mean becoming a doormat. Christ—at whose name "every knee will bow, in heaven and on earth and under the earth" (Philippians 2:10)—submitted his will to the Father, and we honor Christ by following his example. When we submit to God, we become more willing to obey his command to submit to others, that is, to subordinate our rights to theirs. In a marriage relationship, both husband and wife are called to submit to one another. For the wife, this means willingly following her husband's leadership in Christ. For the husband, it means putting aside his own interests in order to care for his wife. Submission is rarely a problem in homes where both partners have a strong relationship with Christ and where each is concerned for the happiness of the other.

Biblical submission is based on love. Why did Paul tell wives to submit and husbands to love? Perhaps Christian women, newly freed in Christ, found submission difficult; perhaps Christian men, used to the Roman custom of giving unlimited power to the head of the family, were not used to treating their wives with respect and love. Of course both husbands and wives should submit to each other (5:21), just as both should love each other.

Biblical submission attacked the root of slavery and inequality in the days of the New Testament. In Paul's day, women, children, and slaves were to submit to the head of the family—slaves would submit until they were freed, male children until they grew up, and women and girls their whole lives. Paul emphasized the equality of all believers in Christ (Galatians 3:28), but he did not suggest overthrowing Roman society to achieve it. Instead, he counseled all believers to submit to one another by choice—wives to husbands and also husbands to wives; slaves to masters and also masters to slaves; children to parents and also parents to children. This kind of mutual submission preserves order and harmony in the family while it increases love and respect among family members.

Biblical submission will not be understood by people who refuse to submit to God. Although some people have distorted Paul's teaching on submission by giving unlimited authority to husbands, we cannot get around it—Paul told wives to submit to their husbands. The fact that a teaching is not popular is no reason to discard it. According to the Bible, the man is the spiritual head of the family, and his wife should acknowledge his leadership. But real spiritual leadership involves service. Just as Christ served the disciples, even to the point of washing their feet, so the husband is to serve his wife. A wise and Christ-honoring husband will not take advantage of his leadership role, and a wise and Christ-honoring wife will not try to undermine her husband's leadership. Either approach causes disunity and friction in marriage.

Related Topics: HUMILITY, MARRIAGE, OBEDIENCE

SUCCESS *(Accomplishment, Affluence, Results)*

What is true success?

BIBLE READING: Joshua 1:1-9
KEY BIBLE VERSE: *Study this Book of the Law continually. Meditate on it day and night so you may be sure to obey all that is written in it. Only then will you succeed.* (Joshua 1:8)

Success is knowing and doing what God says. Many people think that prosperity and success come from having power, influential personal contacts, and a relentless desire to get ahead. But the strategy for gaining prosperity that God taught Joshua goes against such criteria. He said that to succeed, Joshua must (1) be strong and courageous because the task ahead would not be easy, (2) obey God's law, and (3) constantly read and study the Book of the Law—God's Word. To be successful, follow God's words to Joshua. You may not succeed by the world's standards, but you will be a success in God's eyes—and his opinion lasts forever.

BIBLE READING: Psalm 1:1-6
KEY BIBLE VERSE: *Oh, the joys of those who do not follow the advice of the wicked, or stand around with sinners, or join in with scoffers. . . . They are like trees planted along the riverbank, bearing fruit each season without fail. Their leaves never wither, and in all they do, they prosper.* (Psalm 1:1, 3)

Success by God's standards is not success by the world's standards. When Scripture says, "in all they do, they prosper," it does not mean immunity from failure or difficulties. Nor is it a guarantee of health, wealth, and happiness. What the Bible means by prosperity is this: when we apply God's wisdom, the fruit (results or by-products) we bear will be good and receive God's approval. Just as a tree soaks up water and bears luscious fruit, we also are to soak up God's Word, producing actions and attitudes that honor God. To achieve anything worthwhile, we must have God's Word in our heart.

BIBLE READING: Jeremiah 51:59-64
KEY BIBLE VERSE: *When you have finished reading the scroll, tie it to a stone, and throw it into the Euphrates River. Then say, "In this same way Babylon and her people will sink, never again to rise, because of the disasters I will bring upon her."* (Jeremiah 51:63-64)

Success is determined by our faithfulness to God. In the world's eyes, Jeremiah looked totally unsuccessful. He had no money, family, or friends. He prophesied the destruction of the nation, the capital city, and the temple, but the political and religious leaders would not accept or follow his advice. No group of people liked him or listened to him. Yet as we look back, we see that he successfully completed the work God gave him to do. Success must never be measured by popularity, fame, or fortune, for these are temporal measures. King Zedekiah, for example, lost everything by pursuing selfish goals. God measures our success with the yardsticks of obedience, faithfulness, and righteousness. If you are faithfully doing the work God gives you, you are successful in his eyes.

BIBLE READING: Mark 9:33-37

KEY BIBLE VERSE: *They didn't answer, because they had been arguing about which of them was the greatest.* (Mark 9:34)

Success by the world's standards ought not be a Christian's motivation in life. The disciples, caught up in their constant struggle for personal success, were embarrassed to answer Jesus' question. It is always painful to compare our motives with Christ's. It is not wrong for believers to be industrious or ambitious. But when ambition pushes obedience and service to one side, it becomes sin. Pride or insecurity can cause us to overvalue position and prestige. In God's kingdom, such motives are destructive. The only safe ambition is directed toward Christ's kingdom, not our own advancement.

Related Topics: ACHIEVEMENTS, POSITION, WEALTH

SUFFERING *(Affliction, Pain, Trouble)*

▶ **UNDERSTANDING SUFFERING**
What does the Bible teach us about suffering?

BIBLE READING: Matthew 16:21-28

KEY BIBLE VERSE: *From then on Jesus began to tell his disciples plainly that he had to go to Jerusalem, and he told them what would happen to him there. He would suffer at the hands of the leaders and the leading priests and the teachers of religious law. He would be killed, and he would be raised on the third day.* (Matthew 16:21)

The Bible clearly shows that God's plan included suffering. This passage corresponds to Daniel's prophecies: the Messiah would be cut off (Daniel 9:26); there would be a period of trouble (Daniel 9:27); and the king would come in glory (Daniel 7:13-14). The disciples would endure the same suffering as their King and, like him, would be rewarded in the end.

Suffering is not always avoidable. Peter, Jesus' friend and devoted follower who had just eloquently proclaimed Jesus' true identity, sought to protect him from the suffering he prophesied. But if Jesus hadn't suffered and died, Peter (and we) would have died in his sins. Be cautious of advice from a friend who says, "Surely God doesn't want you to face this." Often our most difficult temptations come from those who love us and seek to protect us from all harm and discomfort.

BIBLE READING: Mark 9:1-13

KEY BIBLE VERSE: *Jesus responded, "Elijah is indeed coming first to set everything in order. Why then is it written in the Scriptures that the Son of Man must suffer and be treated with utter contempt? But I tell you, Elijah has already come, and he was badly mistreated, just as the Scriptures predicted."* (Mark 9:12-13)

God is not immune to suffering. It was difficult for the disciples to grasp the idea that their Messiah would have to suffer. The Jews who studied the Old Testament prophecies expected the Messiah to be a great king like David, who would overthrow the enemy, Rome. Their vision was limited to their own time and experience.

They could not understand that the values of God's eternal kingdom were different from the values of the world. They wanted relief from their present problems. But deliverance from sin is far more important than deliverance from physical suffering or political oppression. Our understanding of and appreciation for Jesus must go beyond what he can do for us here and now.

BIBLE READING: John 9:1-41

KEY BIBLE VERSE: *"Teacher," his disciples asked him, "why was this man born blind? Was it a result of his own sins or those of his parents?" "It was not because of his sins or his parents' sins," Jesus answered. "He was born blind so the power of God could be seen in him."* (John 9:2-3)

Suffering is not always a result of sin. A common belief in Jewish culture was that calamity or suffering was the result of some great sin. But Christ used this man's suffering to teach about faith and to glorify God. We live in a fallen world where good behavior is not always rewarded and bad behavior not always punished. Therefore, innocent people sometimes suffer. If God took suffering away whenever we asked, we would follow him for comfort and convenience, not out of love and devotion. Regardless of the reasons for our suffering, Jesus has the power to help us deal with it. When you suffer from a disease, tragedy, or disability, try not to ask, "Why did this happen to me?" or "What did I do wrong?" Instead, ask God to give you strength for the trial and a clearer perspective on what is happening.

BIBLE READING: 1 Thessalonians 3:1-8

KEY BIBLE VERSE: *When we could stand it no longer, we decided that I should stay alone in Athens, and we sent Timothy to visit you. He is our co-worker for God and our brother in proclaiming the Good News of Christ. We sent him to strengthen you, to encourage you in your faith, and to keep you from becoming disturbed by the troubles you were going through. But, of course, you know that such troubles are going to happen to us Christians.* (1 Thessalonians 3:1-3)

God makes use of suffering in his plan for our life. Some think that troubles are always caused by sin or a lack of faith. Trials may be a part of God's plan for believers. Experiencing problems and persecutions can build character (James 1:2-4), patience (Romans 5:3-5), and sensitivity toward others who also face trouble (2 Corinthians 1:3-7). Problems are unavoidable for God's people. Your troubles may be a sign of effective Christian living.

▶ UNDERGOING SUFFERING
What should we remember when we suffer?

BIBLE READING: Luke 21:5-36

KEY BIBLE VERSE: *Everyone will hate you because of your allegiance to me. But not a hair of your head will perish! By standing firm, you will win your souls.* (Luke 21:17-19)

Jesus never promised that his followers would not suffer. Jesus was *not* saying that believers would be exempt from physical harm or death during the persecutions. Remember that most of the disciples were martyred. Rather he was saying that none of his followers would suffer spiritual or eternal loss. On earth, everyone will die, but believers in Jesus will be saved for eternal life.

For Christians, there is always hope and joy beyond the suffering. The picture of the coming persecutions and natural disasters is gloomy, but ultimately it is a cause not for worry but for great joy. When believers see these events happening, they will know that the return of their Messiah is near, and they can look forward to his reign of justice and peace. Rather than be terrified by what is happening in our world, we should confidently await Christ's return to bring justice and restoration to his people.

God does not expect us to enjoy suffering. Only days after telling the disciples to pray that they might escape persecution, Jesus himself asked God to spare him the agonies of the cross, if that was God's will (Luke 22:41-42). It is abnormal to *want* to suffer, but as Jesus' followers we should be *willing* to suffer if by doing so we can help build God's kingdom. We have two wonderful promises to help us as we suffer: God will always be with us (Matthew 28:20), and he will one day rescue us and give us eternal life (Revelation 21:1-4).

BIBLE READING: Hebrews 2:5-18
KEY BIBLE VERSE: *Since he himself has gone through suffering and temptation, he is able to help us when we are being tempted.* (Hebrews 2:18)

Through his suffering, Jesus fully identified with us. How was Jesus made perfect through suffering? Jesus' suffering made him a perfect leader, or pioneer, of our salvation. Jesus did not need to suffer for his own salvation, because he was God in human form. His perfect obedience (which led him down the road of suffering) demonstrates that he was the complete sacrifice for us. Through suffering, Jesus completed the work necessary for our own salvation. Our suffering can make us more sensitive servants of God. People who have known pain are able to reach out with compassion to others who hurt. If you have suffered, ask God how your experience can be used to help others.

We know that Jesus understands our suffering and will help us through. Knowing that Christ suffered pain and faced temptation helps us face our trials. Jesus understands our struggles because he faced them as a human being. We can trust Christ to help us survive suffering and overcome temptation. When you face trials, go to Jesus for strength and patience. He understands your needs and is able to help (see Hebrews 4:14-16).

BIBLE READING: Hebrews 5:1-10
KEY BIBLE VERSE: *Even though Jesus was God's Son, he learned obedience from the things he suffered.* (Hebrews 5:8)

Jesus was willing to obey, even beyond suffering when necessary. Jesus was in great agony as he prepared to face death (Luke 22:41-44). Although Jesus cried out to God asking to be delivered, he was prepared to suffer humiliation, separation from his Father, and death in order to do God's will. At times we will undergo trials, not because we want to suffer, but because we want to obey God. Let Jesus' obedience sustain and encourage you in times of trial. You will be able to face anything if you know that Jesus Christ is with you.

Suffering may be an opportunity to practice submission before God. Have you ever felt that God didn't hear your prayers? Be sure you are praying with reverent submission, willing to do what God wants. God responds to his obedient children.

Jesus did not avoid suffering because he had a higher purpose. Jesus' human life was not a script that he passively followed. It was a life that he chose freely (John 10:17-18). It was a continuous process of making the will of God the

Father his own. Jesus chose to obey, even though obedience led to suffering
and death. Because Jesus obeyed perfectly, even under great trial, he can help
us obey, no matter how difficult obedience seems to be.

BIBLE READING: James 1:2-8
KEY BIBLE VERSE: *Dear brothers and sisters, whenever trouble comes your way, let
it be an opportunity for joy. For when your faith is tested, your endurance has
a chance to grow.* (James 1:2-3)

Suffering is one of the unavoidable passages in life. James doesn't say *if* you face
trials, but *whenever* you face them. He assumes that we will have trials and that
it is possible to profit from them. The point is not to pretend to be happy when
we face pain, but to have a positive outlook ("be happy") because of what trials
can produce in our life. James tells us to turn our hardships into times of learning. Tough times can teach us patience. For other passages dealing with patience
(also called perseverance and steadfastness), see Romans 2:7; 5:3-5; 8:24-25;
2 Corinthians 6:3-7; 2 Peter 1:2-9.

What is true will remain true, even in suffering. We can't really know the depth
of our character until we see how we react under pressure. It is easy to be kind
to others when everything is going well, but can we still be kind when others are
treating us unfairly? God wants to make us mature and complete, not to keep us
from all pain. Instead of complaining about our struggles, we should see them
as opportunities for growth. Thank God for promising to be with you in rough
times. Ask him to help you solve your problems or to give you the strength to
endure them. Then be patient. God will not leave you alone with your problems; he will stay close and help you grow.

Related Topics: JOY, PAIN, PROBLEMS

SUPERIORITY (*see* STATUS)

SURPRISES (*Amazement, Astonishments, Awe*)

With God, what surprises can we expect along the way?

BIBLE READING: Exodus 3:1-6
KEY BIBLE VERSE: *Suddenly, the angel of the LORD appeared to him as a blazing fire
in a bush. Moses was amazed because the bush was engulfed in flames, but it
didn't burn up.* (Exodus 3:2)

God may choose to make himself known to us in unexpected ways. God spoke
to Moses from an unexpected source: a burning bush. When Moses saw it, he
went to investigate. God may use unexpected sources when communicating to
us too, whether people, thoughts, or experiences. Be willing to investigate, and
be open to God's surprises.

BIBLE READING: Jonah 4:1-11
KEY BIBLE VERSE: *He complained to the LORD about it: "Didn't I say before I left
home that you would do this, LORD? That is why I ran away to Tarshish! I knew
that you were a gracious and compassionate God, slow to get angry and filled
with unfailing love. I knew how easily you could cancel your plans for destroying
these people."* (Jonah 4:2)

We ought to be delighted when others surprise us with their response to God.
Jonah revealed the reason for his reluctance to go to Nineveh (Jonah 1:3). He

didn't want the Ninevites forgiven; he wanted them destroyed. Jonah did not understand that the God of Israel was also the God of the whole world. Are you surprised when some unlikely person turns to God? Is it possible that your view is as narrow as Jonah's? We must not forget that in reality, *we* do not deserve to be forgiven by God.

BIBLE READING: 1 Corinthians 2:6-16

KEY BIBLE VERSE: *That is what the Scriptures mean when they say, "No eye has seen, no ear has heard, and no mind has imagined what God has prepared for those who love him." But we know these things because God has revealed them to us by his Spirit, and his Spirit searches out everything and shows us even God's deep secrets.* (1 Corinthians 2:9-10)

We cannot imagine all that God has in store for us, both in this life and for eternity. He will create a new heaven and a new earth (Isaiah 65:17; Revelation 21:1), and we will live with him forever. Until then, his Holy Spirit comforts and guides us. Knowing the wonderful and eternal future that awaits us gives us hope and courage to press on in this life, to endure hardship, and to avoid giving in to temptation. This world is not all there is. There are many surprises ahead. The best is yet to come.

Related Topics: AWE, GRACE, SOVEREIGNTY

TALENTS (*see* ABILITIES)

TASKS (*Jobs, Vocation, Work*)

What principles can we bring to all our tasks in life?

BIBLE READING: Numbers 32:1-32
KEY BIBLE VERSE: *We will arm ourselves and lead our fellow Israelites into battle until we have brought them safely to their inheritance. Meanwhile, our families will stay in the fortified cities we build here, so they will be safe from any attacks by the local people.* (Numbers 32:17)

Cooperation will help get the task done. The land on the east side of the Jordan had been conquered. The hard work was done by all of the tribes together. But the tribes of Reuben and Gad and the half-tribe of Manasseh did not stop after their land was cleared. They promised to keep working with the others until everyone's land was conquered. After others have helped you, do you make excuses to escape helping them? Finish the whole job, even those parts that may not benefit you directly.

BIBLE READING: Numbers 34:1-29
KEY BIBLE VERSE: *The LORD said to Moses, "These are the men who are to divide the land among the people: Eleazar the priest and Joshua son of Nun. Also enlist one leader from each tribe to help them with the task."* (Numbers 34:16-18)

Determine the steps beforehand that will facilitate the completion of a task. In God's plan for settling the land, he (1) explained what to do, (2) communicated this clearly to Moses, and (3) assigned specific people to oversee the apportionment of the land. No plan is complete until each job is assigned and everyone understands his or her responsibilities. When you have a job to do, determine what must be done, give clear instructions, and put people in charge of each part.

BIBLE READING: Nehemiah 6:1-15
KEY BIBLE VERSE: *On October 2 the wall was finally finished—just fifty-two days after we had begun.* (Nehemiah 6:15)

God may give us tasks that seem impossible, but they *can* be done with his help. They said it couldn't be done. The job was too big, and the problems were too great. But God's men and women, joined together for special tasks, can solve huge problems and accomplish great goals. Don't let the size of a task or the length of time needed to accomplish it keep you from doing it. With God's help, it can be done.

Related Topics: JOBS, MINISTRY, WORK

___

TEACHING *(Guiding, Instructing, Training)*

What does the Bible say about effective teaching?

BIBLE READING: Deuteronomy 6:1-9
KEY BIBLE VERSE: *You must commit yourselves wholeheartedly to these commands I am giving you today. Repeat them again and again to your children. Talk about them when you are at home and when you are away on a journey, when you are lying down and when you are getting up again.* (Deuteronomy 6:6-7)

Effective teaching relates truth to life. The Hebrews were extremely successful at making religion an integral part of life. The reason for their success was that religious education was life-oriented, not information-oriented. They used the context of daily life to teach about God. The key to teaching your children to love God is stated simply and clearly in these verses. If you want your children to follow God, you must make God a part of your everyday experiences. You must teach your children diligently to see God in all aspects of life, not just those that are church related.

Effective teaching can occur in any place at any time. This verse not only instructs us to bring teaching into every facet of life, from morning until night, from meal to travel; it also assumes that all these events present opportunities for teaching.

BIBLE READING: Judges 2:6-17
KEY BIBLE VERSE: *After that generation died, another generation grew up who did not acknowledge the LORD or remember the mighty things he had done for Israel.* (Judges 2:10)

Teaching is vital because the truth is always one generation away from extinction. One generation died, and the next did not follow God. Judges 2:10–3:7 is a brief preview of the cycle of sin, judgment, and repentance that Israel experienced again and again. Each generation failed to teach the next generation to love and follow God. Yet this was at the very center of God's law (Deuteronomy 6:4-9).

Teaching truth to the next generation is the responsibility of every Christian. It is tempting to leave the job of teaching the Christian faith to the church or Christian schools. Yet God says that the responsibility for this task belongs primarily to the family. Because children learn so much by our example, faith must be a family matter.

BIBLE READING: Matthew 4:23-25
KEY BIBLE VERSE: *Jesus traveled throughout Galilee teaching in the synagogues, preaching everywhere the Good News about the Kingdom. And he healed people who had every kind of sickness and disease.* (Matthew 4:23)

Jesus consistently modeled effective teaching in his ministry. Jesus was teaching, preaching, and healing. These were the three main aspects of his ministry. *Teaching* shows Jesus' concern for understanding; *preaching* shows his concern for commitment; and *healing* shows his concern for wholeness. His miracles of healing authenticated his teaching and preaching, proving that he truly was from God.

BIBLE READING: Matthew 7:24-29

KEY BIBLE VERSE: *Anyone who listens to my teaching and obeys me is wise, like a person who builds a house on solid rock.* (Matthew 7:24)

Teaching has not been effective until obedience has begun. To build "on solid rock" means to be a hearing, responding disciple, not a phony, superficial one. Practicing obedience becomes the solid foundation to weather the storms of life. (See James 1:22-27 for more on putting into practice what we hear.)

Like a house of cards, the fool's life crumbles. Most people do not deliberately seek to build on a false or inferior foundation; instead, they just don't think about their life's purpose. Many people are headed for destruction, not out of stubbornness but out of thoughtlessness. Part of our responsibility as believers is to help others stop and think about where their life is headed and to point out the consequences of ignoring Christ's message.

BIBLE READING: 2 Timothy 2:14-26

KEY BIBLE VERSE: *The Lord's servants must not quarrel but must be kind to everyone. They must be able to teach effectively and be patient with difficult people. They should gently teach those who oppose the truth. Perhaps God will change those people's hearts, and they will believe the truth.* (2 Timothy 2:24-25)

The quality of the teacher often determines the quality of the teaching. As a teacher, Timothy helped those who were confused about the truth. Paul's advice to Timothy, and to all who teach God's truth, is to be kind and gentle, patiently and courteously explaining the truth. Good teaching never promotes quarrels or foolish arguments. Whether you are teaching church school, leading a Bible study, or preaching in church, remember to listen to people's questions and treat them respectfully, while avoiding foolish debates. If you do this, those who oppose you will be more willing to hear what you have to say and perhaps turn from their error.

Related Topics: DISCIPLINE, LEARNING, TRAINING

TEAMWORK (*Cooperation, Harmony, Unity*)

How is teamwork an important part of the Christian life?

BIBLE READING: 1 Corinthians 3:1-9

KEY BIBLE VERSE: *We work together as partners who belong to God. You are God's field, God's building—not ours.* (1 Corinthians 3:9)

Teamwork is a vital part of life in the body of Christ. God's work involves many different individuals with a variety of gifts and abilities. There are no superstars in this task, only team members performing their own special roles. We can become useful members of God's team by setting aside our desires to receive glory for what we do. Don't seek the praise that comes from people—it is comparatively worthless. Instead, seek approval from God.

BIBLE READING: Ephesians 4:1-16

KEY BIBLE VERSE: *He is the one who gave these gifts to the church: the apostles, the prophets, the evangelists, and the pastors and teachers. Their responsibility is to* equip God's people to do his work and build up the church, the body of Christ. (Ephesians 4:11-12)

Teamwork in the body of Christ requires everyone's contribution. God has given his church an enormous responsibility—to make disciples in every nation (Matthew 28:18-20). This involves preaching, teaching, healing, nurturing, giving, administering, building, and many other tasks. If we had to fulfill this command as individuals, we might as well give up without trying—it would be impossible. But God calls us as members of his body. Some of us can do one task; some can do another. Together we can serve God more fully than any of us could alone. It is a human tendency to overestimate what we can do individually and to underestimate what we can do as a group. But as the body of Christ, we can accomplish more together than we would dream possible working alone. Working together, the church can express the fullness of Christ.

BIBLE READING: Philippians 2:1-11
KEY BIBLE VERSE: *Don't be selfish; don't live to make a good impression on others. Be humble, thinking of others as better than yourself. Don't think only about your own affairs, but be interested in others, too, and what they are doing.* (Philippians 2:3-4)

Teamwork is the product of genuine love for one another. Many people—even Christians—live only to make a good impression on others or to please themselves. But selfishness brings discord. Paul therefore stressed spiritual unity, asking the Philippians to love one another and to be one in spirit and purpose. When we work together, caring for the problems of others as if they were our problems, we demonstrate Christ's example of putting others first, and we experience unity. Don't be so concerned about making a good impression or meeting your own needs that you strain relationships in God's family.

BIBLE READING: 1 Peter 2:4-10
KEY BIBLE VERSE: *Come to Christ, who is the living cornerstone of God's temple. He was rejected by the people, but he is precious to God who chose him. And now God is building you, as living stones, into his spiritual temple. What's more, you are God's holy priests, who offer the spiritual sacrifices that please him because of Jesus Christ.* (1 Peter 2:4-5)

Teamwork makes our individual effort go much farther. Peter portrays the church as a living, spiritual house, with Christ as the foundation and cornerstone and each believer as a stone. Paul portrays the church as a body, with Christ as the head and each believer as a member (see, for example, Ephesians 4:15-16). Both pictures emphasize *community.* One stone is not a temple or even a wall; one body part is useless without the others. In our individualistic society, it is easy to forget our interdependence with other Christians. When God calls you to a task, remember that he is also calling others to work with you. Together your individual efforts will be multiplied. Look for those people and join with them to build a beautiful house for God.

Related Topics: MINISTRY, TASKS, WORK

TEMPTATION *(Attraction, Seduction, Trap)*

▶ **EXPERIENCING TEMPTATION**

Why is it so easy to give in to temptation?

BIBLE READING: Genesis 3:1-7

KEY BIBLE VERSE: *Now the serpent was the shrewdest of all the creatures the LORD God had made. "Really?" he asked the woman. "Did God really say you must not eat any of the fruit in the garden?"* (Genesis 3:1)

Temptation is part of a crafty plan that appeals to our natural desires in attempt to separate us from God. Disguised as a crafty serpent, Satan came to tempt Eve. Satan at one time was an angel who rebelled against God and was thrown out of heaven. As a created being, Satan has definite limitations. Although he is trying to tempt everyone away from God, he will not be the final victor. In 3:14-15, God promises that Satan will be crushed by one of the woman's offspring, the Messiah.

Temptation is an invitation to live a self-serving life that leads to rebellion against God. Temptation is Satan's invitation to give in to his kind of life and give up on God's kind of life. Satan tempted Eve and succeeded in getting her to sin. Ever since then, he's been busy getting people to sin. He even tempted Jesus (Matthew 4:1). But Jesus did not sin!

Temptation feeds off our own tendency toward self-reliance. The serpent, Satan, tempted Eve by getting her to doubt God's goodness. He implied that God was strict, stingy, and selfish for not wanting Eve to share his knowledge of good and evil. Satan made Eve forget all that God had given her and instead focus on the one thing she couldn't have. We fall into trouble, too, when we dwell on the few things we don't have rather than on the countless things God has given us. The next time you are feeling sorry for yourself and thinking about what you don't have, consider all you *do* have and thank God. Then your doubts won't lead you into sin.

BIBLE READING: Deuteronomy 12:28-32

KEY BIBLE VERSE: *Do not be trapped into following their example in worshiping their gods. Do not say, "How do these nations worship their gods? I want to follow their example."* (Deuteronomy 12:30)

Temptation is subtle; what it offers may seem harmless at first glance. God did not want the Israelites even to ask about the pagan religions surrounding them. Idolatry completely permeated the land of Canaan. It was too easy to get drawn into the subtle temptations of seemingly harmless practices. Sometimes curiosity can cause us to stumble. Knowledge of evil is harmful if the evil becomes too tempting to resist. To resist curiosity about harmful practices shows discretion and obedience.

BIBLE READING: 1 Kings 11:1-13

KEY BIBLE VERSE: *Now King Solomon loved many foreign women. Besides Pharaoh's daughter, he married women from Moab, Ammon, Edom, Sidon, and from among the Hittites. The LORD had clearly instructed his people not to intermarry with those nations, because the women they married would lead them to worship their gods. Yet Solomon insisted on loving them anyway.* (1 Kings 11:1-2)

Temptation often hits hardest in our areas of weakness. For all his wisdom, Solomon had some weak spots. He could not say no to compromise or to lustful desires. Whether he married to strengthen political alliances or to gain personal pleasure, these foreign wives led him into idolatry. You may have strong faith, but you also have weak spots—and that is where temptation usually strikes. Strengthen and protect your weaker areas, because a chain is only as strong as its weakest link. If Solomon, the wisest man, could fall, so can you.

BIBLE READING: Matthew 4:1-11

KEY BIBLE VERSE: *Jesus was led out into the wilderness by the Holy Spirit to be tempted there by the Devil.* (Matthew 4:1)

Temptation can strike any area of life. The devil focused on three crucial areas when he tempted Jesus: (1) physical needs and desires, (2) possessions and power, and (3) pride (see 1 John 2:15-16 for a similar list). But Jesus did not give in. Hebrews 4:15 says that Jesus "faced all of the same temptations we do, yet he did not sin." He knows firsthand what we are experiencing, and he is willing and able to help us in our struggles. When you are tempted, turn to him for strength.

▶ RESISTING TEMPTATION

How can we resist temptation?

BIBLE READING: Genesis 3:1-7

KEY BIBLE VERSE: *The woman was convinced. The fruit looked so fresh and delicious, and it would make her so wise! So she ate some of the fruit. She also gave some to her husband, who was with her. Then he ate it, too.* (Genesis 3:6)

Resistance begins with being aware of temptation when it strikes. How could Eve have resisted temptation? By following the same guidelines we can follow. First, we must realize that temptation *in itself* is not a sin. We do not sin until we *give in* to the temptation. To resist temptation, we must (1) pray for strength to resist, (2) run, sometimes literally, and (3) say no when confronted with what we know is wrong. James 1:12 tells of the blessings and rewards for those who don't give in when tempted.

BIBLE READING: 2 Samuel 11:1-27

KEY BIBLE VERSE: *Late one afternoon David got out of bed after taking a nap and went for a stroll on the roof of the palace. As he looked out over the city, he noticed a woman of unusual beauty taking a bath.* (2 Samuel 11:2)

Resist immediately; any delay makes it more difficult. As David looked from the roof of the palace, he saw a beautiful woman bathing, and he was filled with lust. David should have left the roof and fled the temptation. Instead, he entertained the temptation by inquiring about Bathsheba. The results were devastating.

Have a plan for resisting temptation. To flee temptation, (1) ask God in earnest prayer to help you stay away from people, places, and situations that may tempt you. (2) Memorize and meditate on portions of Scripture that combat your specific weaknesses. At the root of most temptation is a real need or desire that God can fill, but we must trust in his timing. (3) Find another believer with whom you can openly share your struggles, and call this person for help when temptation strikes.

BIBLE READING: Matthew 4:1-11

KEY BIBLE VERSE: *For forty days and forty nights he ate nothing and became very hungry. Then the Devil came and said to him, "If you are the Son of God, change these stones into loaves of bread."* (Matthew 4:2-3)

Remember that temptation to seemingly harmless sins can lead to harmful consequences. The devil, also called the tempter, tempted Eve in the Garden of Eden, and here he tempted Jesus in the desert. Satan is a fallen angel. He is *real*, not symbolic, and is constantly fighting against those who follow and obey God. Satan's temptations are real, and he is always trying to get us to live his way or our way rather than God's way. Jesus will one day reign over all creation, but Satan tried to force his hand and get him to declare his kingship prematurely. If Jesus had given in, his mission on earth—to die for our sins so that we might have eternal life—would have failed. When temptations seem especially strong, or when you think you can rationalize giving in, consider whether Satan may be trying to block God's purposes for your life or for someone else's life.

Realize that temptation, in itself, is not a sin. Jesus was tempted by the devil, but he never sinned! Although we may feel dirty after being tempted, we should remember that temptation itself is not sin. We sin when we give in and disobey God. Remembering this will help us turn away from the temptation.

Do not be surprised by temptation at unlikely times and in unlikely places. Jesus wasn't tempted inside the temple, or at his baptism, but in the desert where he was tired, alone, and hungry, and thus most vulnerable. The devil often tempts us when we are most vulnerable—when we are under physical or emotional stress (for example, when we are lonely, tired, weighing big decisions, or faced with uncertainty). But he also likes to tempt us through our strengths, where we are most susceptible to pride. We must guard at all times against his attacks.

Related Topics: SIN, STRENGTH, WEAKNESSES

TEN COMMANDMENTS (*see* LAW OF GOD)

TESTIMONY (*see* WITNESS)

TESTING (*Demonstrating, Measuring, Proving*)

Why do we face testing in our life?

BIBLE READING: Genesis 12:10-20
KEY BIBLE VERSE: *At that time there was a severe famine in the land, so Abram went down to Egypt to wait it out.* (Genesis 12:10)

Tests throughout life can teach us to think clearly and to constantly trust in God. When famine struck, Abram went to Egypt where there was food. Why would there be a famine in the land to which God had just called Abram? This was a test of Abram's faith, and Abram passed. He didn't question God's leading when facing this difficulty. Many believers find that when they determine to follow God, they immediately encounter great obstacles. The next time you face such a test, don't try to second-guess what God is doing. Use the intelligence God gave you, as Abram did when he temporarily moved to Egypt, and wait for new opportunities.

Tests show us that making one good decision may not prevent another bad decision. Having trusted God and moved to Egypt for a while, Abram immediately made a bad choice. Acting out of fear, he asked Sarai to tell a half-truth and say that she was his sister. She *was* his half sister, but she was also his wife (see Genesis 20:11-12).

Abram's intent was to deceive the Egyptians. He feared that if they knew the truth, they would kill him to get Sarai. She would have been a desirable addition to Pharaoh's harem because of her wealth, beauty, and potential for political alliance. As Sarai's brother, Abram would have been given a place of honor.

As her husband, however, his life would be in danger, because Sarai could not enter Pharaoh's harem unless Abram was dead. So Abram lost faith in God's protection, even after all God had promised him, and told a half-truth. This shows how lying compounds the effects of sin. When he lied, Abram's problems multiplied. The tests became real trials.

BIBLE READING: Genesis 22:1-18

KEY BIBLE VERSE: *Later on God tested Abraham's faith and obedience. "Abraham!" God called. "Yes," he replied. "Here I am." "Take your son, your only son— yes, Isaac, whom you love so much—and go to the land of Moriah. Sacrifice him there as a burnt offering on one of the mountains, which I will point out to you."* (Genesis 22:1-2)

Tests are intended to make us, not break us. God tested Abraham, not to trip him and watch him fall, but to deepen his capacity to obey God and thus to develop his character. Just as fire refines ore to extract precious metals, God refines us through difficult circumstances. When we are tested, we can complain, or we can try to see how God is stretching us to develop our character.

Testing brings our real priorities out into the open. Why did God ask Abraham to perform human sacrifice? Pagan nations practiced human sacrifice, but God condemned this as a terrible sin (Leviticus 20:1-5). God did not want Isaac to die, but he wanted Abraham to "sacrifice" Isaac in his heart so it would be clear that Abraham loved God more than he loved his promised and long-awaited son. God was testing Abraham. The purpose of testing is to strengthen our character and deepen our commitment to God and his perfect timing. Through this difficult experience, Abraham strengthened his commitment to obey God. He also learned about God's ability to provide.

BIBLE READING: 2 Chronicles 32:24-33

KEY BIBLE VERSE: *When ambassadors arrived from Babylon to ask about the remarkable events that had taken place in the land, God withdrew from Hezekiah in order to test him and to see what was really in his heart.* (2 Chronicles 32:31)

Testing can bring out our true character. God tested Hezekiah to see what he was really like and to show him his own shortcomings and the attitude of his heart. God did not totally abandon Hezekiah, nor did he tempt him to sin, or trick him. The test was meant to strengthen Hezekiah, develop his character, and prepare him for the tasks ahead. In times of success, most of us can live a good life. But pressure, trouble, or pain will quickly remove our thin veneer of goodness unless our strength comes from God. What are you like under pressure or when everything is going wrong? Do you give in or turn to God? Those who are consistently in touch with God don't have to worry about what pressure may reveal about them.

BIBLE READING: Psalm 11:1-7

KEY BIBLE VERSE: *The LORD examines both the righteous and the wicked. He hates everyone who loves violence.* (Psalm 11:5)

Testing gives us a clear opportunity to grow, with God's help. God does not preserve believers from difficult circumstances, but he tests both the righteous and the wicked. For some, God's tests become a refining fire, while for others, they become an incinerator for destruction. Don't ignore or defy the tests and challenges that come your way. Use them as opportunities for you to grow.

Related Topics: PROBLEMS, SUFFERING, TEMPTATION

THANKFULNESS (*Appreciation, Gratitude, Praise*)

How important is it to express thankfulness?

BIBLE READING: 1 Chronicles 16:4-36

KEY BIBLE VERSE: *David appointed the following Levites to lead the people in worship before the Ark of the LORD by asking for his blessings and giving thanks and praise to the LORD, the God of Israel.* (1 Chronicles 16:4)

We should always be expressing thankfulness. Certain Levites were appointed to give continual praise and thanks to God. Praise and thanksgiving should be a regular part of our routine, not reserved only for celebrations. Praise God continually, and you will find that you won't take his blessings for granted.

There are four significant aspects of thankfulness. Four elements of true thanksgiving are found in this song (psalm): (1) *remembering* what God has done, (2) *telling* others about it, (3) *showing* God's glory to others, and (4) *offering* gifts of self, time, and resources. If you are truly thankful, your life will show it.

BIBLE READING: Psalm 92:1-15

KEY BIBLE VERSE: *It is good to give thanks to the LORD, to sing praises to the Most High. It is good to proclaim your unfailing love in the morning, your faithfulness in the evening,* (Psalm 92:1-2)

Thankfulness ought to be a major ingredient in all our relationships. During the Thanksgiving holiday, we focus on our blessings and express our gratitude to God for them. But thanks should be on our lips every day. We can never say thank you enough to parents, friends, leaders, and especially to God. When thanksgiving becomes an integral part of your life, you will find that your attitude toward life will change. You will become more positive, gracious, loving, and humble.

BIBLE READING: Romans 1:18-23

KEY BIBLE VERSE: *Yes, they knew God, but they wouldn't worship him as God or even give him thanks. And they began to think up foolish ideas of what God was like. The result was that their minds became dark and confused.* (Romans 1:21)

One of the first marks of rejecting God is forgetting to thank him. How could intelligent people turn to idolatry? Idolatry begins when people reject what they know about God. Instead of looking to him as the Creator and sustainer of life, they see themselves as the center of the universe. They soon invent "gods" that are convenient projections of their own selfish plans and decrees. These gods may be wooden figures, but they may also be goals or things we pursue such as money, power, or comfort. They may even be misrepresentations of God himself—making God in our image, instead of the reverse. The common denominator is this—idolators worship the things God or man made, rather than God himself. Is there anything you feel you can't live without? Is there any priority greater than God? Do you have a dream you would sacrifice everything to realize? Does God take first place? Do you worship God or idols of your own making?

BIBLE READING: Ephesians 2:1-10

KEY BIBLE VERSE: *God saved you by his special favor when you believed. And you can't take credit for this; it is a gift from God. Salvation is not a reward for the good things we have done, so none of us can boast about it.* (Ephesians 2:8-9)

Thankfulness ought to be the prime characteristic in a Christian's life. When someone gives you a gift, do you say, "That's very nice—now how much do I owe you?" No, the appropriate response to a gift is "Thank you." Yet how often Christians, even after they have been given the gift of salvation, feel obligated to try to work their way to God. Because our salvation and even our faith are gifts, we should respond with gratitude, praise, and joy.

Thankfulness can take on a variety of effective expressions. We become Christians through God's unmerited grace, not as the result of any effort, ability, intelligent choice, or act of service on our part. However, out of gratitude for this free gift, we will seek to help and serve others with kindness, love, and gentleness. While no action or work we do can help us obtain salvation, God's intention is that our salvation will result in acts of service. We are not saved merely for our own benefit, but to serve Christ and build up the church (Ephesians 4:12).

Related Topics: APPRECIATION, GRACE, SALVATION

THINKING (*Meditating, Problem Solving, Reasoning*)

What does the Bible say about our thoughts?

BIBLE READING: Proverbs 15:1-33
KEY BIBLE VERSE: *The godly think before speaking; the wicked spout evil words.* (Proverbs 15:28)

Thinking beforehand will help us to speak and act wisely. The righteous weigh their answers; the wicked don't wait to speak because they don't care about the effects of their words. It is important to have something to say, but it is equally important to weigh it first. Do you carefully plan your words, or do you pour out your thoughts without concern for their impact?

It is vital to think also before acting, to consider the effects of our choices. Think of your plans for today and consider what their long-range results will be. As we deal with others, we should keep these principles in mind. We should act responsibly and justly with all people—friends and enemies alike.

BIBLE READING: Mark 7:14-23
KEY BIBLE VERSE: *From within, out of a person's heart, come evil thoughts, sexual immorality, theft, murder, adultery, greed, wickedness, deceit, eagerness for lustful pleasure, envy, slander, pride, and foolishness.* (Mark 7:21-22)

We should discipline our thoughts to be pure—because actions begin with thoughts. An evil action begins with a single thought. Allowing your mind to dwell on lust, envy, hatred, or revenge will lead to sin. Don't defile yourself by focusing on evil. Instead, follow Paul's advice in Philippians 4:8 and think about what is true, good, right, pure, lovely, and fine.

BIBLE READING: Romans 12:1-8
KEY BIBLE VERSE: *Don't copy the behavior and customs of this world, but let God transform you into a new person by changing the way you think. Then you will know what God wants you to do, and you will know how good and pleasing and perfect his will really is.* (Romans 12:2)

After conversion, we must allow the Holy Spirit to change our thought patterns. God has plans for us that will really prove satisfying. He wants us to be new and different people with freshness in all we do and think as we live to honor and obey him. Because he wants only what is best for us, and because he gave his

Son to make our new life possible, we should joyfully give ourself as a living
sacrifice for his service.

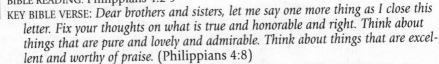

BIBLE READING: Philippians 4:2-9

KEY BIBLE VERSE: *Dear brothers and sisters, let me say one more thing as I close this
letter. Fix your thoughts on what is true and honorable and right. Think about
things that are pure and lovely and admirable. Think about things that are excellent and worthy of praise.* (Philippians 4:8)

**We should think about good things so our words and actions will be positive
and wise.** Paul tells us to program our mind with thoughts that are true, noble,
right, pure, lovely, admirable, excellent, and praiseworthy. Do you have problems with impure thoughts and daydreams? Examine what you are putting into
your mind through television, books, conversations, movies, and magazines.
Replace harmful input with wholesome material. Above all, read God's Word,
and pray. Ask God to help you focus your mind on what is pure. It takes practice, but it can be done.

Related Topics: ACTIONS, ATTITUDE, MEDITATION

TIME (*see* HISTORY)

TIMING (*Order, Plan, Sequence*)

What does the Bible teach us about God's timing?

BIBLE READING: Exodus 2:11-25

KEY BIBLE VERSE: *He looked down on the Israelites and felt deep concern for their
welfare.* (Exodus 2:25)

God's rescue comes in his timing, not ours. God had promised to bring the
Hebrew slaves out of Egypt (Genesis 15:16; 46:3-4). The people had waited a
long time for that promise to be kept, but God rescued them when he knew the
right time had come. God knows the best time to act. When you feel that God
has forgotten you in your troubles, remember that God has a time schedule
that we can't see.

BIBLE READING: Psalm 74:1-23

KEY BIBLE VERSE: *How long, O God, will you allow our enemies to mock you? Will
you let them dishonor your name forever?* (Psalm 74:10)

God's timing will not be affected by our impatience. From our perspective, God
sometimes seems slow to intervene on our behalf. But what might appear slow
to us is good timing from God's perspective. It's easy to become impatient while
waiting for God to act, but we must never give up on him. When God is silent
and you are in deep anguish, follow the method in this psalm. Review the great
acts of God throughout biblical history; then review what he has done for you.
This will remind you that God is at work, not only in history, but also in your
life today.

BIBLE READING: Luke 3:21-23

KEY BIBLE VERSE: *Jesus was about thirty years old when he began his public ministry.*
(Luke 3:23)

The nature of God's timing requires that we practice trust. Imagine the Savior
of the world working in a small-town carpenter's shop until he was thirty years

old! It seems incredible that Jesus would have been content to remain in Nazareth all that time, but he patiently trusted the Father's timing for his life and ministry. Thirty was the prescribed age for priests to begin their ministry (Numbers 4:3). Joseph was thirty years old when he began serving the king of Egypt (Genesis 41:46), and David was thirty when he began to reign over Judah (2 Samuel 5:4). Age thirty, then, was a good time to begin an important task in the Jewish culture. Like Jesus, we need to resist the temptation to jump ahead before receiving the Spirit's direction. Are you waiting and wondering what your next step should be? Don't jump ahead—trust God's timing.

BIBLE READING: Romans 5:1-11

KEY BIBLE VERSE: *When we were utterly helpless, Christ came at just the right time and died for us sinners.* (Romans 5:6)

God's timing is perfect. We were weak and helpless because we could do nothing on our own to save ourself. Someone had to come and rescue us. Not only did Christ come at a good time in history; he came at exactly the right time— according to God's own schedule. God controls all history, and he controlled the timing, methods, and results of Jesus' death.

BIBLE READING: 2 Peter 3:1-8

KEY BIBLE VERSE: *You must not forget, dear friends, that a day is like a thousand years to the Lord, and a thousand years is like a day. The Lord isn't really being slow about his promise to return, as some people think. No, he is being patient for your sake. He does not want anyone to perish, so he is giving more time for everyone to repent.* (2 Peter 3:8-9)

God's timing is controlled by his compassion. God may have seemed slow to these believers as they faced persecution every day and longed to be delivered. But God is not slow; he just is not on *our* timetable (Psalm 90:4). Jesus is waiting so that more sinners will repent and turn to him. We must not sit and wait for Christ to return, but we should live with the realization that time is short and that we have important work to do. Be ready to meet Christ any time, even today; yet plan your course of service as though he may not return for many years.

Related Topics: GOD'S WILL, PATIENCE, SOVEREIGNTY

TIRED (*see* REST)

TITHING (*Generosity, Giving, Returning*)

What are the biblical purposes and principles behind tithing?

BIBLE READING: Deuteronomy 14:22-29

KEY BIBLE VERSE: *You must set aside a tithe of your crops—one-tenth of all the crops you harvest each year. Bring this tithe to the place the LORD your God chooses for his name to be honored, and eat it there in his presence. This applies to your tithes of grain, new wine, olive oil, and the firstborn males of your flocks and herds. The purpose of tithing is to teach you always to fear the LORD your God.* (Deuteronomy 14:22-23)

Tithing is a clear way to demonstrate our priorities. The Bible makes the purpose of tithing very clear—to put God first in our life. We are to give God the first and best of what we earn. For example, what we do first with our money shows what we value most. Giving the first part of our paycheck to God immediately focuses our attention on him. It also reminds us that all we have belongs to him. A habit of regular tithing can keep God at the top of our priority list and give us a proper perspective on everything else we have.

BIBLE READING: Mark 12:41-44

KEY BIBLE VERSE: *He called his disciples to him and said, "I assure you, this poor widow has given more than all the others have given. For they gave a tiny part of their surplus, but she, poor as she is, has given everything she has."* (Mark 12:43-44)

Tithing should remind us of God's desire that we be generous. In the Lord's eyes, this poor widow gave more than all the others put together, though her gift was by far the smallest. The value of a gift is not determined by its amount, but by the spirit in which it is given. A gift given grudgingly or for recognition loses its value. When you give, remember—no matter how small or large your income, your tithe is pleasing to God when it is given out of gratitude and a spirit of generosity.

Related Topics: GIVING, MONEY, WEALTH

TOLERATION (*Acceptance, Patience, Understanding*)

When does toleration hurt the Christian faith, and when is it appropriate?

BIBLE READING: 2 Kings 10:16-36

KEY BIBLE VERSE: *They were all inside the temple to offer sacrifices and burnt offerings. Now Jehu had surrounded the building with eighty of his men and had warned them, "If you let anyone escape, you will pay for it with your own life."* (2 Kings 10:24)

Toleration of sin undermines our faith. Israel was supposed to be intolerant of any religion that did not worship the true God. The religions of surrounding nations were evil and corrupt. They were designed to destroy life, not uphold it. Israel was God's special nation, chosen to be an example of what was right. But Israel's kings, priests, and elders first tolerated, then incorporated surrounding pagan beliefs, and thus became apathetic to God's way.

We are to be completely intolerant of sin and remove it from our life. We should be tolerant of people who hold differing views, but we should not condone beliefs or practices that lead people away from God's standards of living.

BIBLE READING: Matthew 5:27-30

KEY BIBLE VERSE: *So if your eye—even if it is your good eye—causes you to lust, gouge it out and throw it away. It is better for you to lose one part of your body than for your whole body to be thrown into hell. And if your hand—even if it is your stronger hand—causes you to sin, cut it off and throw it away. It is better for you to lose one part of your body than for your whole body to be thrown into hell.* (Matthew 5:29-30)

We hurt ourself and others when we tolerate sinful behavior. When Jesus said to get rid of your hand or your eye, he was speaking figuratively. He didn't mean literally to gouge out your eye, because even a blind person can lust. But if that were the only choice, it would be better to go into heaven with one eye or hand than to go to hell with two. We sometimes tolerate sin in our life that, left unchecked, could eventually destroy us. It is better to experience the pain of removal (getting rid of a bad habit or something we treasure, for instance) than to allow the sin to bring judgment and condemnation. Examine your life for anything that causes you to sin, and take every necessary action to remove it.

BIBLE READING: Acts 5:12-42

KEY BIBLE VERSE: *My advice is, leave these men alone. If they are teaching and doing these things merely on their own, it will soon be overthrown. But if it is of God, you will not be able to stop them. You may even find yourselves fighting against God.* (Acts 5:38-39)

Careful toleration is sometimes a wise plan. Gamaliel presented some sound advice about reacting to religious movements. Unless disciples in these groups endorse obviously dangerous doctrines or practices, it is often wiser to be tolerant rather than repressive. Sometimes only time will tell if they are merely the work of humans or if God is trying to say something through them. The next time a group promotes differing religious ideas, consider Gamaliel's advice, just in case you "find yourselves fighting against God."

Related Topics: ACCEPTANCE, COMPASSION, COMPROMISE

TONGUE (*see* WORDS)

TRADITIONS (*Customs, Habits, Ways*)

How can Christians use traditions to nurture faith?

BIBLE READING: Exodus 12:1-8

KEY BIBLE VERSE: *Announce to the whole community that on the tenth day of this month each family must choose a lamb or a young goat for a sacrifice.* (Exodus 12:3)

Family traditions can promote spiritual values and lessons. Certain holidays were instituted by God himself. Passover was a holiday designed to celebrate Israel's deliverance from Egypt and to remind the people of what God had done. Holidays can be important today, too, as annual reminders of what God has done for us. Develop traditions in your family to highlight the religious significance of certain holidays. These serve as reminders to the older people and learning experiences for the younger ones.

BIBLE READING: Matthew 8:5-13

KEY BIBLE VERSE: *I tell you this, that many Gentiles will come from all over the world and sit down with Abraham, Isaac, and Jacob at the feast in the Kingdom of Heaven. But many Israelites—those for whom the Kingdom was prepared—will be cast into outer darkness, where there will be weeping and gnashing of teeth.* (Matthew 8:11-12)

Traditions can be effective expressions of faith, but only when there is real faith behind them. Jesus told the crowd that many religious Jews who should be in the kingdom would be excluded because of their lack of faith. Entrenched in their religious traditions, they could not accept Christ and his new message. We must be careful not to become so set in our religious habits that we expect God to work only in specified ways. Don't limit God by your mind-set and lack of faith.

BIBLE READING: Romans 4:1-12

KEY BIBLE VERSE: *Abraham is also the spiritual father of those who have been circumcised, but only if they have the same kind of faith Abraham had before he was circumcised.* (Romans 4:12)

Mindless performance of traditions has little to do with real faith. Rituals did not earn any reward for Abraham; he had been blessed long before the circumcision ceremony was introduced. Abraham found favor with God by faith alone, before he was circumcised. Genesis 12:1-4 tells of God's call to Abraham when he was seventy-five years old; the circumcision ceremony was introduced when he was ninety-nine (Genesis 17:1-14). Ceremonies and rituals serve as reminders of our faith, and they instruct new and younger believers. But we should not think that they give us any special merit before God. They are outward signs and seals that demonstrate inward belief and trust. The focus of our faith should be on Christ and his saving actions, not on our own actions.

Related Topics: FAITH, LAW OF GOD, WORSHIP

TRAINING (*Guidance, Preparation, Teaching*)

What is God's training plan?

BIBLE READING: Genesis 41:1-49

KEY BIBLE VERSE: *Turning to Joseph, Pharaoh said, "Since God has revealed the meaning of the dreams to you, you are the wisest man in the land! I hereby appoint you to direct this project. You will manage my household and organize all my people. Only I will have a rank higher than yours."* (Genesis 41:39-40)

Within God's plan, every experience may be training for the future. Joseph rose quickly to the top, from prison walls to Pharaoh's palace. His training for this important position involved being first a slave and then a prisoner. In each situation he learned the importance of serving God and others. Whatever your situation, no matter how undesirable, consider it part of your training program for serving God.

BIBLE READING: Psalm 78:70-72

KEY BIBLE VERSE: *He chose his servant David, calling him from the sheep pens. He took David from tending the ewes and lambs and made him the shepherd of Jacob's descendants—God's own people, Israel. He cared for them with a true heart and led them with skillful hands.* (Psalm 78:70-72)

Within God's plan, our past experiences may be put to unique and effective use. Although David had been on the throne when this psalm was written, he is called a shepherd, and not a king. Shepherding, a common profession in biblical times, was a highly responsible job. The flocks were completely dependent upon shepherds for guidance, provision, and protection. David had spent his early years as a shepherd (1 Samuel 16:10-11). This was a training ground for the future responsibilities God had in store for him. When he was ready, God took him from caring for sheep to caring for Israel, God's people. Don't treat your present situation lightly or irresponsibly; it may be God's training ground for your future.

BIBLE READING: 1 Timothy 4:6-16

KEY BIBLE VERSE: *Do not waste time arguing over godless ideas and old wives' tales. Spend your time and energy in training yourself for spiritual fitness.* (1 Timothy 4:7)

God's plan requires our willingness to be spiritually trained. Are you in shape both physically and spiritually? In our society, much emphasis is placed on physical fitness, but spiritual health (godliness) is even more important. Our physical health is susceptible to disease and injury, but faith can sustain us through these tragedies. To be spiritually "fit," we must develop our faith by using our God-given abilities in the service of the church (see 1 Timothy 4:14-16). Are you developing your spiritual muscles?

BIBLE READING: 2 Timothy 4:1-22

KEY BIBLE VERSE: *I solemnly urge you before God and before Christ Jesus—who will someday judge the living and the dead when he appears to set up his Kingdom: Preach the word of God. Be persistent, whether the time is favorable or not. Patiently correct, rebuke, and encourage your people with good teaching.* (2 Timothy 4:1-2)

God's training plan requires Christians to prepare the next generation. As Paul reached the end of his life, he could look back and know he had been faithful to God's call. Now it was time to pass the torch to the next generation, to prepare leaders to take his place so that the world would continue to hear the life-changing message of Jesus Christ. Timothy was Paul's living legacy, a product of Paul's faithful teaching, discipleship, and example. Because of Paul's work with many believers, including Timothy, the world is full of believers today who are also carrying on the work. What legacy will you leave behind? Whom are you training to carry on your work? It is our responsibility to do all we can to keep the gospel message alive for the next generation.

Related Topics: DISCIPLINE, SPIRITUAL DISCIPLINES, TEACHING

TRIALS (*see* TESTING)

TROUBLES (*see* PROBLEMS)

TRUST (*Confidence, Dependence, Faith*)

What are the characteristics of trust?

BIBLE READING: Genesis 30:1-24

KEY BIBLE VERSE: *Then God remembered Rachel's plight and answered her prayers by giving her a child. She became pregnant and gave birth to a son. "God has removed my shame," she said.* (Genesis 30:22-23)

Trust almost always involves patience. Eventually God answered Rachel's prayers and gave her a child of her own. In the meantime, however, she had given her maidservant to Jacob. Trusting God is difficult when nothing seems to happen. But it is harder still to live with the consequences of taking matters into our own hands. Resist the temptation to think God has forgotten you. Have patience and courage to wait for God to act.

BIBLE READING: Exodus 14:1-31

KEY BIBLE VERSE: *As Pharaoh and his army approached, the people of Israel could see them in the distance, marching toward them. The people began to panic, and they cried out to the LORD for help. Then they turned against Moses and complained, "Why did you bring us out here to die in the wilderness? Weren't there enough graves for us in Egypt? Why did you make us leave?"* (Exodus 14:10-11)

Trust often requires courage. Trapped against the sea, the Israelites faced the Egyptian army sweeping in for the kill. The Israelites thought they were doomed. After watching God's powerful hand deliver them from Egypt, their only response was fear, whining, and despair. Where was their trust in God? Israel had to learn from repeated experience that God was able to provide for them. God has preserved these examples in the Bible so that we can learn to trust him the first time. By focusing on God's faithfulness in the past, we can face crises with confidence rather than with fear and complaining.

BIBLE READING: Proverbs 3:1-8
KEY BIBLE VERSE: *Trust in the LORD with all your heart; do not depend on your own understanding. Seek his will in all you do, and he will direct your paths.* (Proverbs 3:5-6)

Trust involves heartfelt confidence in God. Leaning has the sense of putting your whole weight on something, resting on and trusting in that person or thing. When we have an important decision to make, we sometimes feel that we can't trust anyone—not even God. But God knows what is best for us. And he knows even better than we do what we really want. We must trust him completely in every choice we make. We should not omit careful thinking or belittle our God-given ability to reason; but we should not trust our own ideas to the exclusion of all others. We must not be wise in our own eyes. We should always be willing to listen to and be corrected by God's Word and wise counselors. Bring your decisions to God in prayer, use the Bible as your guide, and follow God's leading. He will make your paths straight by both guiding and protecting you.

Trust includes giving God our future plans. To receive God's guidance, said Solomon, we must acknowledge God in all our ways. This means turning every area of life over to him. About a thousand years later, Jesus emphasized this same truth (Matthew 6:33). Look at your values and priorities. What is important to you? In what areas have you not acknowledged him? What is his advice? In many areas of your life you may already acknowledge God, but it is the areas where you attempt to restrict or ignore his influence that will cause you grief. Make him a vital part of everything you do; then he will guide you because you will be working to accomplish his purposes.

BIBLE READING: Romans 3:21-28
KEY BIBLE VERSE: *Now God has shown us a different way of being right in his sight—not by obeying the law but by the way promised in the Scriptures long ago. We are made right in God's sight when we trust in Jesus Christ to take away our sins. And we all can be saved in this same way, no matter who we are or what we have done.* (Romans 3:21-22)

Trust is wholeheartedly believing in God's promises. After all this bad news about our sinfulness and God's condemnation, Paul gives the wonderful news. There is a way to be declared not guilty—by trusting Jesus Christ to take away our sins. Trusting means putting our confidence in Christ to forgive our sins, to make us right with God, and to empower us to live the way he taught us. God's solution is available to all of us regardless of our background or past behavior.

Related Topics: BELIEF/BELIEVE, CONFIDENCE, FAITH

TRUTH (*Correct, Factual, Real*)

What does the Bible say about truth?

BIBLE READING: Proverbs 12:1-28
KEY BIBLE VERSE: *Truth stands the test of time; lies are soon exposed.* (Proverbs 12:19)

Truth never changes. Truth is always timely; it applies today and in the future. Because it is connected with God's changeless character, it is also changeless. Think for a moment about the centuries that have passed since these proverbs were written. Consider the countless hours that have been spent in careful study of every sentence of Scripture. The Bible has withstood the test of time. Because God is truth, you can trust his Word to guide you.

BIBLE READING: Job 14:1-22
KEY BIBLE VERSE: *If mortals die, can they live again? This thought would give me hope, and through my struggle I would eagerly wait for release.* (Job 14:14)

Truth gains strength under pressure. Job's profound speech illustrates a great truth: to have a right set of doctrines is not enough. To know what to believe is not all that is required to please God. Truth untested by life's experiences may become static and stagnant. Suffering can bring a dynamic quality to life. Just as drought drives the roots of a tree deeper to find water, so suffering can drive us beyond superficial acceptance of truth to dependence on God for hope and life.

BIBLE READING: Mark 15:1-15
KEY BIBLE VERSE: *Pilate, anxious to please the crowd, released Barabbas to them. He ordered Jesus flogged with a lead-tipped whip, then turned him over to the Roman soldiers to crucify him.* (Mark 15:15)

Truth is not nullified by compromise or wrongdoing. Although Jesus was innocent according to Roman law, Pilate caved in to political pressure. He abandoned what he knew was right. Trying to second-guess the Jewish leaders, Pilate gave a decision that would please everyone while keeping himself safe. When we lay aside God's clear statements of right and wrong and make decisions based on the preferences of others, we fall into compromise and lawlessness. God promises to honor those who do right, not those who make everyone happy.

BIBLE READING: Luke 9:28-36
KEY BIBLE VERSE: *A voice from the cloud said, "This is my Son, my Chosen One. Listen to him."* (Luke 9:35)

Truth matches the teaching of Jesus Christ—the one who is truth. As God's Son, Jesus has God's power and authority; thus his words should be our final authority. If a person's teaching is true, it will agree with Jesus' teachings. Test everything you hear against Jesus' words, and you will not be led astray. Don't be hasty to seek advice and guidance from merely human sources and thereby neglect Christ's message.

BIBLE READING: John 8:31-47
KEY BIBLE VERSE: *Many who heard him say these things believed in him. Jesus said to the people who believed in him, "You are truly my disciples if you keep obeying my teachings. And you will know the truth, and the truth will set you free."* (John 8:30-32)

Truth sets us free. Jesus himself is the truth that sets us free (John 8:36). He is the source of truth, the perfect standard of what is right. He frees us from the consequences of sin, from self-deception, and from deception by Satan. He shows us clearly the way to eternal life with God. Thus Jesus does not give us freedom to do what we want, but to follow God. As we seek to serve God, Jesus' perfect truth frees us to be all that God meant us to be.

BIBLE READING: John 14:1-14

KEY BIBLE VERSE: *Jesus told him, "I am the way, the truth, and the life. No one can come to the Father except through me."* (John 14:6)

Truth challenges us to submit to its demands. Jesus says he is the *only* way to God the Father. Some people may argue that this way is too narrow. In reality, it is wide enough for the whole world, if the world chooses to accept it. Instead of worrying about how limited it sounds to have only one way, we should be saying, "Thank you, God, for providing a sure way to get to you!"

Truth is found in the person of Jesus. As the *way,* Jesus is our path to the Father. As the *truth,* he is the reality of all God's promises. As the *life,* he joins his divine life to ours, both now and eternally.

Related Topics: BELIEF/BELIEVE, BIBLE, FAITH

UNBELIEVERS (Agnostics, Non-Christians, Pagans)

How should Christians relate with unbelievers?

BIBLE READING: 1 Samuel 8:1-22

KEY BIBLE VERSE: *The people refused to listen to Samuel's warning. "Even so, we still want a king," they said.* (1 Samuel 8:19)

God does not want us to be imitators of those who don't believe. Israel was called to be a holy nation, separate from and unique among all others (Leviticus 20:26). The Israelites' motive in asking for a king was to be like the nations around them. This was in total opposition to God's original plan. It was not their desire for a king that was wrong, but their reasons for wanting a king.

There should be a significant difference between our life and that of an unbeliever. Often we let others' values and actions dictate our attitudes and behavior. Have you ever made a wrong choice because you wanted to be like everyone else? Be careful that the values of your friends or "heroes" don't pull you away from what God says is right. When God's people want to be like unbelievers, they are heading for spiritual disaster.

BIBLE READING: Psalm 26:1-12

KEY BIBLE VERSE: *I hate the gatherings of those who do evil, and I refuse to join in with the wicked.* (Psalm 26:5)

There should be significant, caring contact—but not imitation. Should we stay away from unbelievers? No. Although there are some places Christians should avoid, Jesus demonstrated that we must go among unbelievers to help them. But there is a difference between being *with* unbelievers and being *one of* them. Trying to be one of them harms our witness for God. Ask yourself this question about the people you enjoy: If I am with them often, will I become less obedient to God in outlook or action? If the answer is yes, carefully monitor how you spend your time with these people and what effect it has on you.

BIBLE READING: John 17:6-19

KEY BIBLE VERSE: *As you sent me into the world, I am sending them into the world.* (John 17:18)

We should remember that we have a mission among unbelievers. Jesus didn't ask God to take believers *out* of the world but instead to use them *in* the world. Because Jesus sends us into the world, we should not try to escape from the world, nor should we avoid all relationships with non-Christians. We are called to be salt and light (Matthew 5:13-16), and we are to do the work that God sent us to do.

BIBLE READING: 2 Corinthians 6:14-18

KEY BIBLE VERSE: *Don't team up with those who are unbelievers. How can goodness be a partner with wickedness? How can light live with darkness? (2 Corinthians 6:14)*

We should avoid situations that could force us to compromise. Paul urges believers not to form binding relationships with unbelievers, because this might weaken their Christian commitment, integrity, or standards. It would be a mismatch. Earlier, Paul had explained that this did not mean isolating oneself from unbelievers (see 1 Corinthians 5:9-10). Paul even tells Christians to stay with their unbelieving spouses (1 Corinthians 7:12-13). Paul wants believers to be active in their witness for Christ to unbelievers, but they should not lock themselves into personal or business relationships that could cause them to compromise their faith.

Paul does not forbid all contact with unbelievers. Jesus taught his followers to befriend sinners and lead them to him (Luke 5:30-32). He does, however, speak against condoning the lifestyle of people who make excuses for bad behavior and recommend its practice to others—whether they are in the church or outside of it (Ephesians 5:1-20). Such people can quickly pollute the church and endanger its unity and purpose. We must befriend unbelievers if we are to lead them to Christ, but we must be wary of those who are viciously evil, immoral, or opposed to all that Christianity stands for. Such people are more likely to influence us for evil than we are likely to influence them for good.

Related Topics: COMPASSION, GOSPEL, WITNESSING

UNDERSTANDING *(Comprehending, Discerning, Knowing)*

What should we know about understanding?

BIBLE READING: 1 Chronicles 15:1-15

KEY BIBLE VERSE: *Because you Levites did not carry the Ark the first time, the anger of the LORD our God burst out against us. We failed to ask God how to move it in the proper way. (1 Chronicles 15:13)*

Understanding is important, but obedience is more important. When David's first attempt to move the ark failed (13:8-14), he learned an important lesson: when God gives specific instructions, it is wise to follow them precisely. This time David saw to it that the Levites carried the ark (Numbers 4:5-15). We may not fully understand the reasons behind God's instructions, but we do know that his wisdom is complete and his judgment infallible. The way to know God's instructions is to know his Word. But just as children do not understand the reasons for all their parents' instructions until they are older, we may not understand all of God's reasons in this life. It is far better to obey God first, and then discover the reasons. We are never free to disobey God just because we don't understand.

BIBLE READING: Psalm 147:1-6

KEY BIBLE VERSE: *How great is our Lord! His power is absolute! His understanding is beyond comprehension! (Psalm 147:5)*

We can never understand all about ourself, but God understands us completely.
Sometimes we feel as if we don't understand ourself—what we want, how we
feel, what's wrong with us, or what we should do about it. But God's understanding has no limit, and therefore he understands us fully. If you feel troubled
and don't understand yourself, remember that God understands you perfectly.
Take your mind off yourself and focus it on God. Strive to become more and
more like him. The more you learn about God and his ways, the better you will
understand yourself.

BIBLE READING: Matthew 17:14-23
KEY BIBLE VERSE: *One day after they had returned to Galilee, Jesus told them,
"The Son of Man is going to be betrayed. He will be killed, but three days later
he will be raised from the dead." And the disciples' hearts were filled with grief.*
(Matthew 17:22-23)

Understanding is important, but sometimes trust comes first. Once again Jesus
predicted his death (see also 16:21); but more important, he told of his resurrection. Unfortunately, the disciples heard only the first part of Jesus' words and
became discouraged. They couldn't understand why Jesus wanted to go back
to Jerusalem, where he would walk right into trouble.

The disciples didn't fully comprehend the purpose of Jesus' death and
resurrection until Pentecost (Acts 2). We shouldn't get upset at ourself for
being slow to understand everything about Jesus. After all, the disciples were
with him, saw his miracles, heard his words, and still had difficulty understanding. Despite their questions and doubts, however, they believed. We
should do the same.

BIBLE READING: Mark 4:1-25
KEY BIBLE VERSE: *If you can't understand this story, how will you understand all the
others I am going to tell?* (Mark 4:13)

With Christ's help, our understanding will grow. We hear with our ears, but
there is a deeper kind of listening with the mind and heart that is necessary in
order to gain spiritual understanding from Jesus' words. Some people in the
crowd were looking for evidence to use against Jesus; others truly wanted to
learn and grow. Jesus' words were for the honest seekers.

**God reveals truth to people who will act on it, who will make it visible in their
life.** Some people do not understand God's truth because they are not ready
for it. When you talk with people about God, be aware that they will not understand if they are not yet ready. Be patient, taking every chance to tell them more
of the truth about God, and praying that the Holy Spirit will open their minds
and hearts to receive the truth and act on it.

The truth is clear, but our ability to understand is imperfect. The light of Jesus'
truth is revealed to us, not hidden. But we may not be able to see or to use all
of that truth right now. Only as we put God's teachings into practice will we
understand and see more of the truth. As we obey, we will sharpen our vision
and increase our understanding (see James 1:22-25).

Related Topics: LEARNING, OBEDIENCE, TEACHING

UNFAIRNESS *(Inequity, Injustice, Unbalanced)*

What should we do when confronted with unfairness?

BIBLE READING: Genesis 31:1-13

KEY BIBLE VERSE: *Jacob called Rachel and Leah out to the field where he was watching the flocks, so he could talk things over with them. "Your father has turned against me and is not treating me like he used to," he told them. "But the God of my father has been with me."* (Genesis 31:4-5)

We should never be unfair in return. Although Laban treated Jacob unfairly, God still increased Jacob's prosperity. God's power is not limited by lack of fair play. He has the ability to meet our needs and make us thrive even though others mistreat us. To give in and respond unfairly is to be no different from your enemies.

BIBLE READING: Judges 11:1-11

KEY BIBLE VERSE: *Jephthah said to them, "Aren't you the ones who hated me and drove me from my father's house? Why do you come to me now when you're in trouble?"* (Judges 11:7)

We should know that sometimes the unfairness in the world is made right. Jephthah, an illegitimate son of Gilead, was chased out of the country by his half brothers. He suffered as a result of another's decision and not for any wrong he had done. Yet in spite of his brothers' rejection, God used him. If you are suffering from unfair rejection, don't blame others and become discouraged. Remember how God used Jephthah despite his unjust circumstances, and realize that he is able to use you even if you feel rejected.

BIBLE READING: Job 14:1-22

KEY BIBLE VERSE: *How frail is humanity! How short is life, and how full of trouble!* (Job 14:1)

Remember that God offers an eternal answer to the unfairness in the world. Life is brief and full of trouble, Job laments in his closing remarks. Sickness, loneliness, disappointment, and death cause Job to say that life is not fair. Some understand verses 14 and 15 to mean that even in his gloom, Job hoped for the resurrection of the dead. If this is true, then Job understood the one truth that could put his suffering in perspective. God's solution to believers who live in an unfair world is to guarantee life with him forever. No matter how unfair your present world seems, God offers the hope of being in his presence eternally. Have you accepted this offer?

Related Topics: FAIRNESS, INJUSTICE, JUSTICE

UNITY *(Cooperation, Fellowship, Teamwork)*

How does the Bible describe the unity that should exist between Christians?

BIBLE READING: John 6:22-59

KEY BIBLE VERSE: *Yes, I am the bread of life! Your ancestors ate manna in the wilderness, but they all died. However, the bread from heaven gives eternal life to everyone who eats it. I am the living bread that came down out of heaven. Anyone who eats this bread will live forever; this bread is my flesh, offered so the world may live.* (John 6:48-51)

Christian unity is based on each person's connection with Christ. How can Jesus give us his flesh as bread to eat? To eat living bread means to accept Christ into our life and become united with him. We are united with Christ in two ways: (1) by believing in his death (the sacrifice of his flesh) and resurrection and (2) by devoting ourself to living as he requires, depending on his teaching for guidance and trusting in the Holy Spirit for power.

BIBLE READING: John 17:6-21
KEY BIBLE VERSE: *Now I am departing the world; I am leaving them behind and coming to you. Holy Father, keep them and care for them—all those you have given me—so that they will be united just as we are.* (John 17:11)

Jesus' great desire for his disciples was that they would become one. Jesus wanted his followers to be unified as a powerful witness to the reality of God's love. Are you helping to unify the body of Christ, the church? You can pray for other Christians, avoid gossip, build others up, work together in humility, give your time and money, exalt Christ, and refuse to get sidetracked arguing over divisive matters.

Christians are not intended to live out their faith in isolation. Jesus prayed for unity among the believers based on the believers' unity with him and the Father. Christians can know unity among themselves if they are living in union with God. For example, each branch living in union with the vine is united with all other branches doing the same (see John 15:1-15).

BIBLE READING: Romans 11:1-24
KEY BIBLE VERSE: *If the Gentiles were enriched because the Jews turned down God's offer of salvation, think how much greater a blessing the world will share when the Jews finally accept it.* (Romans 11:12)

In Christ, unity has been made possible, but it has not yet been fully achieved. Paul had a vision of a church where all Jews and Gentiles would be united in their love of God and in obedience to Christ. While respecting God's law, this ideal church would look to Christ alone for salvation. A person's ethnic background and social status would be irrelevant (see Galatians 3:28)—what mattered would be faith in Christ.

But Paul's vision has not yet been realized. Many Jewish people rejected the gospel. They depended on their heritage for salvation, and they did not have the heart of obedience that was so important to the Old Testament prophets and to Paul. Once Gentiles became dominant in many of the Christian churches, they began rejecting Jews and even persecuting them. Unfortunately, this practice has recurred through the centuries.

BIBLE READING: Philippians 1:3-11
KEY BIBLE VERSE: *I pray that your love for each other will overflow more and more, and that you will keep on growing in your knowledge and understanding.* (Philippians 1:9)

The love commanded by Christ should create deep unity among Christians. Have you ever longed to see a friend with whom you share fond memories? Paul had such a longing to see the Christians at Philippi. His love and affection for them was based not merely on past experiences, but also on the unity that comes when believers draw upon Christ's love. All Christians are part of God's family and thus share equally in the transforming power of his love. Do you feel a deep love for fellow Christians, friends and strangers alike? Let Christ's love motivate you to love other Christians and to express that love in your actions toward them.

BIBLE READING: Philippians 2:1-11
KEY BIBLE VERSE: *Is there any encouragement from belonging to Christ? Any comfort from his love? Any fellowship together in the Spirit? Are your hearts tender and*

sympathetic? Then make me truly happy by agreeing wholeheartedly with each other, loving one another, and working together with one heart and purpose. (Philippians 2:1-2)

Unity ought to be a distinctive mark among Christians. Many people—even Christians—live only to make a good impression on others or to please themselves. But selfishness brings discord. Paul therefore stressed spiritual unity, asking the Philippians to love one another and to be one in spirit and purpose. When we work together, caring for the problems of others as if they were our problems, we demonstrate Christ's example of putting others first, and we experience unity. Don't be so concerned about making a good impression or meeting your own needs that you strain relationships in God's family.

Related Topics: CHURCH, TASKS, TEAMWORK

USEFULNESS (*see* SERVICE)

VALUE (*Treasured, Usefulness, Worth*)

What does the Bible say about our value to God?

 BIBLE READING: Psalm 8:1-9
KEY BIBLE VERSE: *When I look at the night sky and see the work of your fingers—the moon and the stars you have set in place—what are mortals that you should think of us, mere humans that you should care for us? For you made us only a little lower than God, and you crowned us with glory and honor.* (Psalm 8:3-5)

God places high value on his human creations. When we look at the vast expanse of creation, we wonder how God could be concerned for people who constantly disappoint him. Yet God created us only a little lower than himself or the angels! The next time you question your worth as a person, remember that God considers you highly valuable. We have great worth because we bear the stamp of the Creator. (See Genesis 1:26-27 for the extent of worth God places on all people.) Because God has already declared how valuable we are to him, we can be set free from feelings of worthlessness.

BIBLE READING: Psalm 113:1-9
KEY BIBLE VERSE: *He lifts the poor from the dirt and the needy from the garbage dump. He sets them among princes, even the princes of his own people!* (Psalm 113:7-8)

God values us based on his own character, not ours. In God's eyes, a person's value has no relationship to his or her wealth or position on the social ladder. Many people who have excelled in God's work began in poverty or humble beginnings. God supersedes the social order of this world, often choosing his future leaders and ambassadors from among social outcasts. Do you treat the unwanted in society as though they have value? Demonstrate by your actions that all people are valuable and useful in God's eyes.

BIBLE READING: Psalm 139:1-24
KEY BIBLE VERSE: *How precious are your thoughts about me, O God! They are innumerable! I can't even count them; they outnumber the grains of sand! And when I wake up in the morning, you are still with me!* (Psalm 139:17-18)

God values us, and he knows us intimately. Sometimes we don't let people get to know us completely because we are afraid they will discover something about us that they won't like. But God already knows everything about us, even to the number of hairs on our head (Matthew 10:30), and still he accepts and loves us. God is with us through every situation, in every trial—protecting, loving, guiding. He knows and loves us completely.

What is the most valuable thing we can possess?

BIBLE READING: Matthew 13:44-46

KEY BIBLE VERSE: *The Kingdom of Heaven is like a treasure that a man discovered hidden in a field. In his excitement, he hid it again and sold everything he owned to get enough money to buy the field—and to get the treasure, too!* (Matthew 13:44)

The most valuable thing we can possess is our citizenship in God's kingdom. The kingdom of heaven is more valuable than anything else we can have, and a person must be willing to give up everything to obtain it. The man who discovered the treasure in the field stumbled upon it by accident but knew its value when he found it. The merchant was earnestly searching for the pearl of great value and when he found it, he sold everything he had to purchase it.

Related Topics: KINGDOM OF GOD/KINGDOM OF HEAVEN, PEOPLE, SELF-ESTEEM

VENGEANCE (*see* REVENGE)

VICTORY (*Accomplishment, Achievement, Success*)

How can we experience victory in our spiritual life?

BIBLE READING: 1 Samuel 4:1-22

KEY BIBLE VERSE: *"What's going on?" the Philistines asked. "What's all the shout - ing about in the Hebrew camp?" When they were told it was because the Ark of the LORD had arrived, they panicked. "The gods have come into their camp!" they cried. "This is a disaster! We have never had to face anything like this before!"* (1 Samuel 4:6-7)

Spiritual victories come only from alive and active faith. The Philistines were afraid because they remembered stories about God's intervention for Israel when they left Egypt. But Israel had turned away from God and was clinging to only a form of godliness, a symbol of former victories.

People (and churches) often try to live on the memories of God's blessings. The Israelites wrongly assumed that because God had given them victory in the past, he would do it again, even though they had strayed far from him. Today, as in Bible times, spiritual victories come through a continually renewed relationship with God. Don't live off the past. Keep your relationship with God new and fresh.

BIBLE READING: 1 Samuel 14:1-23

KEY BIBLE VERSE: *"All right then," Jonathan told him. "We will cross over and let them see us. If they say to us, 'Stay where you are or we'll kill you,' then we will stop and not go up to them. But if they say, 'Come on up and fight,' then we will go up. That will be the LORD's sign that he will help us defeat them."* (1 Samuel 14:8-10)

Spiritual victories often come from small steps taken for God. Jonathan did not have the authority to lead all the troops into battle, but he could start a small skirmish in one corner of the enemy camp. When he did, panic broke out among the Philistines, the Hebrews who had been drafted into the Philistine army revolted, and the men who were hiding in the hills regained their courage and returned to fight.

When you are facing a difficult situation that is beyond your control, ask yourself, What steps can I take now to work toward a solution? A few small steps may be just what is needed to begin the chain of events leading to eventual victory.

BIBLE READING: Hebrews 11:1-40

KEY BIBLE VERSE: *All of these people we have mentioned received God's approval because of their faith, yet none of them received all that God had promised. For God had far better things in mind for us that would also benefit them, for they can't receive the prize at the end of the race until we finish the race.* (Hebrews 11:39-40)

Our faith in Christ gives us present spiritual victory and assurance of final victory. The Old Testament records the lives of the various people who experienced great victories. Joshua and Deborah conquered kingdoms (the book of Joshua; Judges 4–5). Nehemiah administered justice (the book of Nehemiah). Daniel was saved from the mouths of lions (Daniel 6). Shadrach, Meshach, and Abednego were kept from harm in the furious flames of a fiery furnace (Daniel 3). Elijah escaped the swords of evil Queen Jezebel's henchmen (1 Kings 19:2ff.). Hezekiah regained strength after sickness (2 Kings 20). Gideon was powerful in battle (Judges 7). A widow's son was brought back to life by the prophet Elisha (2 Kings 4:8-37). All these achievements were examples of faith in action.

We, too, can experience victory through faith in Christ. Our victories over oppressors may be like those of the Old Testament saints, but more likely, our victories will be specific to the role God wants us to play. Even though our body will deteriorate and die, we will live forever because of Christ. In the promised resurrection, even death will be defeated, and Christ's victory will be made complete.

BIBLE READING: 1 John 3:1-10

KEY BIBLE VERSE: *Those who have been born into God's family do not sin, because God's life is in them. So they can't keep on sinning, because they have been born of God.* (1 John 3:9)

With Christ's help we can experience significant victory over sin. We all have areas in our life where temptation is strong and habits are hard to conquer. These weaknesses give the devil a foothold, so we must deal with our particular areas of vulnerability. If we are struggling with a particular sin, however, these verses are not directed at us, even if for the time we seem to keep on sinning. John is not talking about people whose victories are still incomplete; he is talking about people who make a practice of sinning and look for ways to justify it. Three steps are necessary to find victory over prevailing sin: (1) seek the power of the Holy Spirit and God's Word; (2) stay away from tempting situations; and (3) seek the help of the body of Christ—be open to their willingness to hold you accountable and to pray for you.

Related Topics: ACCOMPLISHMENTS, STRENGTH, SUCCESS

VIOLENCE (*see* ANGER)

VOLUNTEERS (*see* SERVING)

VOWS (*Commitments, Covenants, Promises*)

What does God say about our promises?

BIBLE READING: Leviticus 5:4-6

KEY BIBLE VERSE: *If they make a rash vow of any kind, whether its purpose is for good or bad, they will be considered guilty even if they were not fully aware of what they were doing at the time.* (Leviticus 5:4)

God expects us to take our promises very seriously. Have you ever sworn to do or not do something and then realized how foolish your promise was? God's people are called to keep their word, even if they make promises that are tough to keep. Jesus was warning against swearing (in the sense of making vows or oaths) when he said, "Just say a simple 'Yes, I will' or 'No, I won't' " (Matthew 5:37). Our word should be enough. If we feel we have to strengthen it with an oath, something is wrong. The only promises we ought not to keep are promises that lead to sin. A wise and self-controlled person avoids making rash promises.

BIBLE READING: Proverbs 20:25

KEY BIBLE VERSE: *It is dangerous to make a rash promise to God before counting the cost.* (Proverbs 20:25)

God takes our promises seriously and will hold us to them. This proverb points out the evil of making a vow rashly and then reconsidering it. God takes vows seriously and requires that they be carried out (Deuteronomy 23:21-23). We often have good intentions when making a vow—we want to show God that we are determined to please him. Jesus, however, says it is better not to make promises to God because he knows how difficult they are to keep (Matthew 5:33-37). If you still feel it is important to make a vow, make sure that you weigh the consequences of breaking that vow. (In Judges 11, Jephthah made a rash promise to sacrifice the first thing he saw on his return home. As it happened, he saw his daughter first.) It is better not to make promises than to make them and then later want to change them. It is better still to count the cost beforehand and then to fulfill them.

BIBLE READING: Matthew 5:33-37

KEY BIBLE VERSE: *Just say a simple, "Yes, I will," or "No, I won't." Your word is enough. To strengthen your promise with a vow shows that something is wrong.* (Matthew 5:37)

Jesus emphasized the importance of keeping our word. People were breaking promises and using sacred language casually and carelessly. Keeping oaths and promises is important; it builds trust and makes committed human relationships possible. The Bible condemns making vows or taking oaths casually, giving your word while knowing that you won't keep it, or swearing falsely in God's name (Exodus 20:7; Leviticus 19:12; Numbers 30:1-2; Deuteronomy 19:16-20). Oaths are needed in certain situations only because we live in a sinful society that breeds distrust.

God expects us to be known as people who keep our word. Oaths, or vows, were common, but Jesus told his followers not to use them—their word alone should be enough (see James 5:12). Are you known as a person of your word? Truthfulness seems so rare that we feel we must end our statements with "I promise." If we tell the truth all the time, we will have less pressure to back up our words with an oath or promise.

Related Topics: COMMITMENT, HONESTY, TRUTH

VULNERABILITY (*see* WEAKNESS)

WAITING *(Delay, Lull, Pause)*

What do we gain by learning to wait?

BIBLE READING: Psalm 27:1-14
KEY BIBLE VERSE: *Wait patiently for the LORD. Be brave and courageous. Yes, wait patiently for the LORD.* (Psalm 27:14)

Waiting creates time during which we can trust God. David knew from experience what it meant to wait for the Lord. He had been anointed king at age sixteen, but didn't become king until he was thirty. During the interim, he was chased through the wilderness by jealous King Saul. David had to wait on God for the fulfillment of his promise to reign. Later, after becoming king, he was chased by his rebellious son, Absalom.

Waiting for God is not easy. Often it seems that he isn't answering our prayers or doesn't understand the urgency of our situation. That kind of thinking implies that God is not in control or is not fair. But God is worth waiting for. Lamentations 3:24-26 calls us to hope in and wait on the Lord because often God uses waiting to refresh, renew, and teach us. Make good use of your waiting times by discovering what God may be trying to teach you in them.

BIBLE READING: Psalm 40:1-4
KEY BIBLE VERSE: *I waited patiently for the LORD to help me, and he turned to me and heard my cry.* (Psalm 40:1)

Waiting on God prepares us to have our real needs met. Waiting for God to help us is not easy, but David received four benefits from waiting: God (1) lifted him out of his despair; (2) set his feet on a hard, firm path; (3) steadied him as he walked; and (4) put a new song of praise in his mouth. Often blessings cannot be received unless we go through the trial of waiting.

BIBLE READING: Matthew 24:32-51
KEY BIBLE VERSE: *If the master returns and finds that the servant has done a good job, there will be a reward.* (Matthew 24:46)

Waiting encourages us to always be prepared for Christ's return. Knowing that Christ's return will be sudden and unexpected should motivate us always to be prepared. We are not to live irresponsibly—sitting and waiting, doing nothing; seeking self-serving pleasure; using his tarrying as an excuse not to do God's work of building his kingdom; developing a false security based on precise calculations of events; or letting our curiosity about the end times divert us from doing God's work.

Jesus asks us to spend the time of waiting taking care of his people and doing his work here on earth, both within the church and outside it. This is the best way to prepare for Christ's return.

BIBLE READING: 2 Thessalonians 3:6-15
KEY BIBLE VERSE: *Dear brothers and sisters, we give you this command with the authority of our Lord Jesus Christ: Stay away from any Christian who lives in idleness and doesn't follow the tradition of hard work we gave you.* (2 Thessalonians 3:6)

Waiting gives us opportunity to work out our faith. Some people in the Thessalonian church were falsely teaching that because Christ would return any day, people should set aside their responsibilities, quit work, do no future planning, and just wait for the Lord. But their lack of activity only led them into sin. They became a burden to the church, which was supporting them; they wasted time that could have been used for helping others; and they became busybodies. These church members may have thought that they were being more spiritual by not working, but Paul tells them to be responsible and get back to work. Being ready for Christ means obeying him in every area of life. Because we know that Christ is coming, we must live in such a way that our faith and our daily practice will please him when he arrives.

Related Topics: ENDURANCE, PATIENCE, ZEAL

WANTING (*see* DESIRE)

WARNINGS (*see* PROPHECY)

WEAKNESSES (*Failures, Limitations, Sins*)

How does God want us to handle weaknesses?

BIBLE READING: Romans 14:1-23
KEY BIBLE VERSE: *Accept Christians who are weak in faith, and don't argue with them about what they think is right or wrong.* (Romans 14:1)

We need to be aware of where our faith is strong and where it is weak. Who is weak in faith and who is strong? We are all weak in some areas and strong in others. Our faith is strong if we can survive contact with sinners without falling into their patterns. It is weak if we must avoid certain activities, people, or places in order to protect our spiritual life. It is important to take a self-inventory in order to find out our strengths and weaknesses. Whenever in doubt, we should ask ourselves, Can I do that without sinning? Can I influence others for good, rather than being influenced by them?

We can encourage others by our strengths and be encouraged by their strengths where we are weak. In areas of strength, we should not fear being defiled by the world; rather we should go and serve God. In areas of weakness, we need to be cautious. If we have a strong faith but shelter it, we are not doing Christ's work in the world. If we have a weak faith but expose it, we are being extremely foolish.

Weaknesses should be given special attention. What is weak faith? Paul is speaking about immature faith that has not yet developed the muscle it needs to stand against external pressures. For example, if a person who once worshiped idols were to become a Christian, he might understand perfectly well that Christ saved him through faith and that idols have no real power. Still, because of his past associations, he might be badly shaken if he knowingly ate meat that had been used in idol worship. If a person who once worshiped God on the required Jewish holy days were to become a Christian, he might well know that Christ saved him through faith, not through his keeping of the law. Still, when the feast days came, he might feel empty and unfaithful if he didn't dedicate those days to God.

We all need love in the midst of our weaknesses. Paul responds to both weak brothers in love. Both are acting according to their conscience, but their honest scruples do not need to be made into rules for the church. Certainly some issues are central to the faith and worth fighting for—but many are based on individual differences and should not be legislated. Our principle should be: In essentials, unity; in nonessentials, liberty; in everything, love.

BIBLE READING: 1 John 3:1-10
KEY BIBLE VERSE: *Those who have been born into God's family do not sin, because God's life is in them. So they can't keep on sinning, because they have been born of God.* (1 John 3:9)

The root weakness of our sinful nature can only be overcome by Christ's power. We all have areas where temptation is strong and habits are hard to conquer. These weaknesses give the devil a foothold, so we must deal with these areas of vulnerability. If we are struggling with a particular sin, however, these verses are not directed at us, even if for the time we seem to keep on sinning. John is not talking about people whose victories are still incomplete; he is talking about people who make a practice of sinning and look for ways to justify it.

The weaknesses of sins can be battled with Christ's help. Three steps are necessary to find victory over prevailing sin: (1) seek the power of the Holy Spirit and God's Word; (2) stay away from tempting situations; and (3) seek the help of the body of Christ—be open to their willingness to hold you accountable and to pray for you.

What are the benefits of weaknesses?

BIBLE READING: 2 Corinthians 12:1-10
KEY BIBLE VERSE: *Each time he said, "My gracious favor is all you need. My power works best in your weakness." So now I am glad to boast about my weaknesses, so that the power of Christ may work through me.* (2 Corinthians 12:9)

It is in our weaknesses that we most clearly experience God's strength. Although God did not remove Paul's physical affliction, he promised to demonstrate his power in Paul. The fact that God's power is displayed in weak people should give us courage. Though we recognize our limitations, we should not congratulate ourself and rest at that. Instead, we should turn to God to seek pathways for effectiveness. We must rely on God for our effectiveness rather than simply on our own energy, effort, or talent. Our weakness not only helps develop Christian character; it also deepens our worship, because in admitting our weakness, we affirm God's strength.

Weaknesses are reminders of our dependence on God. When we are strong in abilities or resources, we are tempted to do God's work on our own, and that can lead to pride. When we are weak, allowing God to fill us with *his* power, then we are stronger than we could ever be on our own. God does not intend for us to seek to be weak, passive, or ineffective—life provides enough hindrances and setbacks without us creating them. When those obstacles come, we must depend on God. Only his power will make us effective for him and help us do work that has lasting value.

Related Topics: GRACE, SIN, TEMPTATION

WEALTH *(Abundance, Money, Riches)*

▶ **DANGERS OF WEALTH**
How can wealth come between us and God?

 BIBLE READING: Jeremiah 9:23-24
KEY BIBLE VERSE: *This is what the LORD says: "Let not the wise man gloat in his wisdom, or the mighty man in his might, or the rich man in his riches. Let them boast in this alone: that they truly know me and understand that I am the LORD who is just and righteous, whose love is unfailing, and that I delight in these things. I, the LORD, have spoken!"* (Jeremiah 9:23-24)

Wealth can become the center of our life and take God's place. People tend to admire four qualities in others: human wisdom, power (strength), kindness, and riches. Each of these can be a source of great pride. But God puts a higher priority on knowing him personally and living a life that reflects his justice and righteousness. What do you want people to admire most about you?

BIBLE READING: Matthew 19:16-30
KEY BIBLE VERSE: *Jesus told him, "If you want to be perfect, go and sell all you have and give the money to the poor, and you will have treasure in heaven. Then come, follow me." But when the young man heard this, he went sadly away because he had many possessions.* (Matthew 19:21-22)

Wealth can easily become an idol. In response to the young man's question about how to have eternal life, Jesus told him to keep God's Ten Commandments. Jesus then listed six of them, all referring to relationships with others. When the young man replied that he had kept the commandments, Jesus told him that he must do something more—sell everything and give the money to the poor. Jesus' statement exposed the man's weakness. In reality, his wealth was his god, his idol, and he would not give it up. Thus he violated the first and greatest commandment (Exodus 20:3; Matthew 22:34-40).

BIBLE READING: Mark 10:17-27
KEY BIBLE VERSE: *Jesus said again, "Dear children, it is very hard to get into the Kingdom of God. It is easier for a camel to go through the eye of a needle than for a rich person to enter the Kingdom of God!"* (Mark 10:24-25)

Wealth can tempt us to deny our dependence on God. Jesus said it was very difficult for the rich to enter the kingdom of God. This is true because the rich, with most of their basic physical needs met, often become self-reliant. When they feel empty, they can buy something new to dull the pain that was meant to drive them toward God. Their abundance and self-sufficiency become their deficiency. The person who has everything on earth can still lack what is most important—eternal life.

▶ **TRUE WEALTH**
What is true wealth?

BIBLE READING: Matthew 19:23-30

KEY BIBLE VERSE: *Everyone who has given up houses or brothers or sisters or father or mother or children or property, for my sake, will receive a hundred times as much in return and will have eternal life.* (Matthew 19:29)

True wealth is far more than material rewards. In the Bible, God gives rewards to his people according to his justice. In the Old Testament, obedience often brought reward in this life (Deuteronomy 28), but obedience and immediate reward are not always linked. If they were, good people would always be rich, and suffering would always be a sign of sin. Our true reward is God's presence and power through the Holy Spirit. Later, in eternity, we will be rewarded for our faith and service. If material rewards in this life came to us for every faithful deed, we would be tempted to boast about our achievements and act out of wrong motivations.

True wealth is what we gain when we give up what we have to follow Christ. Jesus assured the disciples that anyone who gives up something valuable for his sake will be repaid many times over in this life, although not necessarily in the same form. For example, a person may be rejected by his or her family for accepting Christ, but he or she will gain the larger family of believers.

True wealth is eternal. Consider the most powerful or well-known people in our world—how many got where they are by being humble, self-effacing, and gentle? Not many! But in the life to come, the last will be first—if they got in last place by choosing to follow Jesus. Don't forfeit eternal rewards for temporary benefits. Be willing to make sacrifices now for greater rewards later. Be willing to accept human disapproval, while knowing that you have God's approval.

BIBLE READING: Luke 12:13-34

KEY BIBLE VERSE: *Sell what you have and give to those in need. This will store up treasure for you in heaven! And the purses of heaven have no holes in them. Your treasure will be safe—no thief can steal it and no moth can destroy it. Wherever your treasure is, there your heart and thoughts will also be.* (Luke 12:33-34)

True wealth is the opposite of the wealth that the world values. Jesus says that the good life has nothing to do with being wealthy, so be on guard against greed (desire for what we don't have). This is the exact opposite of what society usually says. Advertisers spend millions of dollars to entice us to think that if we buy more and more of their products, we will be happier, more fulfilled, more comfortable. How do you respond to the constant pressure to buy? Learn to tune out expensive enticements and concentrate instead on the truly good life—living in a relationship with God and doing his work.

True wealth is part of heaven—earthly wealth is not. The rich man in Jesus' story died before he could begin to use what was stored in his big barns. Planning for retirement—preparing for life *before* death—is wise, but neglecting life *after* death is disastrous. If you accumulate wealth only to enrich yourself, with no concern for helping others, you will enter eternity empty-handed.

True wealth is freely given for God's kingdom. Why do you save money? To retire? To buy more expensive cars or toys? To be secure? Jesus challenges us to think beyond earthbound goals and to use what we have been given for God's kingdom. Faith, service, and obedience are the way to become rich toward God.

True wealth cannot rust, be lost, or be stolen. Jesus commands us not to worry. But how can we avoid it? Only faith can free us from the anxiety caused by greed and covetousness. It is good to work and plan responsibly; it is bad to dwell on all the ways our planning could go wrong. Worry is pointless because it can't fill any of our needs; worry is foolish because the Creator of the universe loves us and knows what we need. He promises to meet all our real needs, but not necessarily all our desires.

True wealth is possessing a relationship with the King. Seeking the kingdom of God means making Jesus the Lord and King of your life. He must control every area—your work, play, plans, relationships. Is the kingdom only one of your many concerns, or is it central to all you do? Are you holding back any areas of your life from God's control? As Lord and Creator, he wants to help provide what you need as well as guide how you use what he provides.

True wealth is measured in part by how we use material wealth to benefit others. Money seen as an end in itself quickly traps us and cuts us off from both God and the needy. The key to using money wisely is to see how much we can use for God's purposes, not how much we can accumulate for ourself. Does God's love touch your wallet? Does your money free you to help others? If so, you are storing up lasting treasures in heaven. If your financial goals and possessions hinder you from giving generously, loving others, or serving God, sell what you must to bring your life into perspective.

Our concept of true wealth is defined by our focus. If you concentrate your money in your business, your thoughts will center on making the business profitable. If you direct it toward other people, you will become concerned with their welfare. Where do you put your time, money, and energy? What do you think about most? How should you change the way you use your resources in order to reflect kingdom values more accurately?

BIBLE READING: John 8:12-30

KEY BIBLE VERSE: *Jesus said to the people, "I am the light of the world. If you follow me, you won't be stumbling through the darkness, because you will have the light that leads to life."* (John 8:12)

True wealth is, above all else, having eternal life. People will die in their sins if they reject Christ, because they are rejecting the only way to be rescued from sin. Sadly, many are so taken up with the values of this world that they are blind to the priceless gift Christ offers. Where are you looking? Don't focus on this world's values and miss what is most valuable—eternal life with God.

Related Topics: MONEY, POOR, POSSESSIONS

WIFE (*see* MARRIAGE)

WILL OF GOD (*see* GOD'S WILL)

WILLINGNESS (*see* SERVICE)

WISDOM (*Application, Knowledge, Learning*)

What is wisdom, and how do we become wise?

BIBLE READING: 1 Kings 3:1-28

KEY BIBLE VERSE: *Give me an understanding mind so that I can govern your people well and know the difference between right and wrong. For who by himself is able to govern this great nation of yours?* (1 Kings 3:9)

Wisdom begins when we ask God to be our supply. When given a chance to have anything in the world, Solomon asked for wisdom—"an understanding mind"—in order to lead well and to make right decisions. We can ask God for this same wisdom (James 1:5). Notice that Solomon asked for discernment to carry out his job; he did not ask God to do the job for him. We should not ask God to do *for* us what he wants to do *through* us. Instead we should ask God to give us the wisdom to know what to do and the courage to follow through on it.

Wisdom is thinking and living as God designed us to live. Solomon asked for wisdom, not wealth, but God gave him riches and long life as well. While God does not promise riches to those who follow him, he gives us what we need if we put his kingdom, his interests, and his principles first (Matthew 6:31-33). Setting your heart on riches will only leave you dissatisfied because even if you get the riches you crave, you will still want something more. But if you put God and his work first, he will satisfy your deepest needs.

Wisdom is the ability to apply knowledge to everyday life. Solomon received wisdom from God, but it was up to Solomon to apply that wisdom to all areas of his life. Solomon was obviously wise in governing the nation, but he was foolish in running his household. Wisdom is both the ability to discern what is best and the strength of character to act upon that knowledge. While Solomon remained wise all his life, he did not always act upon his wisdom (11:6).

Solomon's settlement of the dispute described in 1 Kings 3:16-28 was a classic example of his wisdom. This wise ruling was verification that God had answered Solomon's prayer and given him a discerning heart. Discernment is the capacity to recognize truth and issues deeper than the surface appearance. We have God's wisdom available to us as we pray and request it. But, like Solomon, we must put it into action.

BIBLE READING: Psalm 119:97-112
KEY BIBLE VERSE: *Oh, how I love your law! I think about it all day long. Your commands make me wiser than my enemies, for your commands are my constant guide.* (Psalm 119:97-98)

We become wise by studying and applying God's Word. God's Word makes us wise—wiser than our enemies and wiser than any teachers who ignore it. True wisdom goes beyond amassing knowledge; it is *applying* knowledge in a life-changing way. Intelligent or experienced people are not necessarily wise. Wisdom comes from applying God's Word to our life.

The wisdom God offers in his Word is practical and must be applied to life. To walk safely in the woods at night, we need a light so we don't trip over tree roots or fall into holes. In this life, we walk through a dark forest of evil. But the Bible can be our light to show us the way ahead so we won't stumble as we walk. It reveals the entangling roots of false values and philosophies. Study the Bible, so you will be able to see your way clearly enough to stay on the right path.

BIBLE READING: Proverbs 1:1-7
KEY BIBLE VERSE: *Fear of the LORD is the beginning of knowledge. Only fools despise wisdom and discipline.* (Proverbs 1:7)

Trust in God—he will make you truly wise. In this age of information, knowledge is plentiful, but wisdom is scarce. Wisdom means far more than simply knowing a lot. It is a basic attitude that affects every aspect of life. The foundation of knowledge is to fear the Lord—to honor and respect God, to live in awe of his power, and to obey his Word. Faith in God should be the controlling principle for your understanding of the world, your attitudes, and your actions.

BIBLE READING: Ecclesiastes 8:1-8

KEY BIBLE VERSE: *How wonderful to be wise, to be able to analyze and interpret things. Wisdom lights up a person's face, softening its hardness.* (Ecclesiastes 8:1)

Wisdom is the ability to see life from God's perspective and then to know the best course of action to take. Most people would agree that wisdom is a valuable asset, but how can we acquire it? Proverbs 9:10 teaches that the reverence and fear of the Lord (respect and honor) are basic to all wisdom. Wisdom comes from knowing and trusting God; it is not merely the way to find God. Knowing God will lead to understanding and then to sharing this knowledge with others.

BIBLE READING: Luke 2:33-40

KEY BIBLE VERSE: *There the child grew up healthy and strong. He was filled with wisdom beyond his years, and God placed his special favor upon him.* (Luke 2:40)

We become wiser as we become more like Christ. Jesus was filled with wisdom, which is not surprising because he stayed in close contact with his heavenly Father. James 1:5 says God gives wisdom generously to all who ask. Even our children need to be encouraged to seek and develop wisdom. Like Jesus, we can grow in wisdom by walking with God.

BIBLE READING: James 1:2-8

KEY BIBLE VERSE: *If you need wisdom—if you want to know what God wants you to do—ask him, and he will gladly tell you. He will not resent your asking.* (James 1:5)

We can ask for God's wisdom to guide our choices. By *wisdom,* James is talking not only about knowledge, but about the ability to make wise decisions in difficult circumstances. Whenever we need wisdom, we can pray to God, and he will generously supply what we need. Christians don't have to grope around in the dark, hoping to stumble upon answers.

Wisdom means practical discernment. It begins with respect for God, leads to right living, and results in increased ability to tell right from wrong. God is willing to give us this wisdom, but we will be unable to receive it if our goals are self-centered instead of God-centered. To learn God's will, we need to read his Word and ask him to show us how to obey it. Then we must do what he tells us.

Related Topics: DISCERNMENT, EXPERIENCE, KNOWLEDGE

WITNESSING *(Sharing, Preaching, Telling)*

What are the key principles in witnessing?

BIBLE READING: 2 Kings 7:3-20

KEY BIBLE VERSE: *Finally, they said to each other, "This is not right. This is wonderful news, and we aren't sharing it with anyone! If we wait until morning, some terrible calamity will certainly fall upon us. Come on, let's go back and tell the people at the palace."* (2 Kings 7:9)

If we have experienced the gospel as real Good News, we will not be able to keep it to ourself. The lepers discovered the deserted camp and realized their lives had been spared. At first they kept the good news to themselves, forgetting their fellow citizens who were starving in the city. The Good News about Jesus

Christ must be shared too, for no news is more important. We must not forget those who are dying without it. We must not become so preoccupied with our own faith that we neglect sharing it with those around us. Our "wonderful news," like that of the lepers, will not "wait until morning."

BIBLE READING: Jonah 3:1-10

KEY BIBLE VERSE: *On the day Jonah entered the city, he shouted to the crowds: "Forty days from now Nineveh will be destroyed!" The people of Nineveh believed God's message, and from the greatest to the least, they decided to go without food and wear sackcloth to show their sorrow.* (Jonah 3:4-5)

Our responsibility is to witness; we can't determine who will respond. God's word is for everyone. Despite the wickedness of the Ninevite people, they were open to God's message and repented immediately. If we simply proclaim what we know about God, we may be surprised at how many people will listen. In Jonah's case, the witnessing was done grudgingly, but it was still effective. We cannot predict who will respond. We should never prevent someone from having the opportunity.

BIBLE READING: Matthew 28:16-20

KEY BIBLE VERSE: *Jesus came and told his disciples, "I have been given complete authority in heaven and on earth. Therefore, go and make disciples of all the nations, baptizing them in the name of the Father and the Son and the Holy Spirit. Teach these new disciples to obey all the commands I have given you. And be sure of this: I am with you always, even to the end of the age."* (Matthew 28:18-20)

Our witness is based on the authority of Jesus Christ. God gave Jesus authority over heaven and earth. On the basis of that authority, Jesus told his disciples to make more disciples as they preached, baptized, and taught. With this same authority, Jesus still commands us to tell others the Good News and make disciples for the kingdom.

Jesus' command compels us to witness. When someone is dying or leaving us, his or her last words are very important. Promising them that he would be with them always, Jesus left the disciples with these last words of instruction: by his authority to make more disciples, to baptize them, and to teach them to obey Christ. Whereas in previous missions Jesus had sent his disciples only to the Jews (10:5-6), their mission from now on would be worldwide. Jesus is Lord of the earth, and he died for the sins of people from all nations.

Therefore we are to go—whether it is next door or to another country—and make disciples. It is not an option, but a command to all who call Jesus "Lord." We are not all evangelists in the formal sense, but we have all received gifts that we can use to help fulfill the great commission. As we obey, we have comfort in the knowledge that Jesus is always with us.

BIBLE READING: Acts 1:1-11

KEY BIBLE VERSE: *When the Holy Spirit has come upon you, you will receive power and will tell people about me everywhere—in Jerusalem, throughout Judea, in Samaria, and to the ends of the earth.* (Acts 1:8)

Christians today may not be eyewitnesses, but we are faith witnesses to Christ's power in our life. Luke says that the disciples were eyewitnesses to all that had happened to Jesus Christ—his life before his crucifixion, and the forty days after his resurrection, when he taught them more about the kingdom of God. Today there are still people who doubt Jesus' resurrection. But Jesus appeared to the disciples on many occasions after his resurrection, proving that he was alive.

Look at the change the Resurrection made in the disciples' lives. At Jesus' death, they scattered—they were disillusioned, and they feared for their life. After seeing the resurrected Christ, they were fearless and risked everything to spread the Good News about him around the world. They faced imprisonment, beatings, rejection, and martyrdom, yet they never compromised their mission. These men would not have risked their life for something they knew was a fraud. They knew Jesus was raised from the dead, and the early church was fired with their enthusiasm to tell others. It is important to know this so we can have confidence in their testimony. Twenty centuries later we can still be confident that our faith is based on fact.

Related Topics: EVANGELISM, GOOD NEWS, GOSPEL

WOMAN (*see* IMAGE)

WORDS (*Communication, Expressions, Speech*)

Why should we be careful with the words we use?

BIBLE READING: Psalm 19:1-14
KEY BIBLE VERSE: *May the words of my mouth and the thoughts of my heart be pleasing to you, O LORD, my rock and my redeemer.* (Psalm 19:14)

Our words ought to please God. Would you change the way you live if you knew that every word and thought would be examined by God? David asked God to approve his words and thoughts as though they were offerings brought to the altar. He began this psalm noting that the whole creation manages to express God's glory. He ended his thoughts with a prayer that God might be pleased with his words. As you begin each day, determine to let God's love guide what you say and how you think.

BIBLE READING: Proverbs 13:1-6
KEY BIBLE VERSE: *Those who control their tongue will have a long life; a quick retort can ruin everything.* (Proverbs 13:3)

Words are so powerful that silence is sometimes the wisest action. You have not mastered self-control if you do not control what you say. Words can cut and destroy. James recognized this truth when he stated, "The tongue is a small thing, but what enormous damage it can do" (James 3:5). If you want to be self-controlled, begin with your tongue. Stop and think before you react or speak. If you can control this small but powerful member, you can control the rest of your body.

BIBLE READING: Matthew 12:33-37
KEY BIBLE VERSE: *You brood of snakes! How could evil men like you speak what is good and right? For whatever is in your heart determines what you say.* (Matthew 12:34)

Our words reveal what is in our heart. What kinds of words come from your mouth? That is an indication of what your heart is really like. You can't solve your heart problem, however, just by cleaning up your speech. You must allow the Holy Spirit to fill you with new attitudes and motives; then your speech will be cleansed at its source.

BIBLE READING: Colossians 4:2-6

KEY BIBLE VERSE: *Let your conversation be gracious and effective so that you will have the right answer for everyone.* (Colossians 4:6)

Our words are important because we are representatives of Christ. When we tell others about Christ, we should always be gracious in what we say. No matter how much sense the message makes, we lose our effectiveness if we are not courteous. Just as we like to be respected, we must respect others if we want them to listen to what we have to say.

Related Topics: COMMUNICATION, SILENCE, WITNESSING

WORK *(Efforts, Employment, Tasks)*

What principles does God give regarding our work?

BIBLE READING: Genesis 31:22-55

KEY BIBLE VERSE: *In fact, except for the grace of God—the God of my grandfather Abraham, the awe-inspiring God of my father, Isaac—you would have sent me off without a penny to my name. But God has seen your cruelty and my hard work. That is why he appeared to you last night and vindicated me.* (Genesis 31:42)

God wants Christians to be characterized by diligence in their work. Jacob made it a habit to do more than was expected of him. When his flocks were attacked, he took the losses rather than splitting them with Laban. He worked hard even after several pay cuts. His diligence eventually paid off: his flocks began to multiply. Making a habit of doing more than expected can pay off. It (1) pleases God, (2) earns recognition and advancement, (3) enhances our reputation, (4) builds others' confidence in us, (5) gives us more experience and knowledge, and (6) develops our spiritual maturity.

BIBLE READING: Exodus 16:13-36

KEY BIBLE VERSE: *[Moses] replied, "The LORD has appointed tomorrow as a day of rest, a holy Sabbath to the LORD. On this day we will rest from our normal daily tasks. So bake or boil as much as you want today, and set aside what is left for tomorrow."* (Exodus 16:23)

The same God who gives us abilities and work also tells us to rest. The Israelites were not to work on the Sabbath—not even to cook food. Why? God knew that the busy routine of daily living could distract people from worshiping him. It is so easy to let work, family responsibilities, and recreation crowd our schedules so tightly that we don't take time to worship. Carefully guard your time with God.

BIBLE READING: Exodus 35:4-35

KEY BIBLE VERSE: *Moses told them, "The LORD has chosen Bezalel son of Uri, grandson of Hur, of the tribe of Judah."* (Exodus 35:30)

God is the source of all our skills, and he wants us to use them to the best of our ability. This passage describes the blending of various artistic and construction skills in the building of the traveling sanctuary. Those who spun cloth made a beautiful contribution to the tabernacle. Good workers take pride in the quality and beauty of their work. God is concerned with the quality and beauty of what you do. Whether you are a corporate executive

or a drugstore cashier, your work should reflect the creative abilities God
has given you.

Our work, even if it isn't "spiritual," can still be done to God's glory. It is easy
to think that God would provide people with "spiritual" abilities like leadership, preaching, healing. And yet Bezalel was filled with God's Spirit in such a
way that all his artistic and design skills took on an added quality appropriate
to the work he was called to do. Whatever place God has designed you to fill in
life, ask him to make you skillful as you represent him in the workplace.

BIBLE READING: Ruth 2:1-13
KEY BIBLE VERSE: *She asked me this morning if she could gather grain behind the
harvesters. She has been hard at work ever since, except for a few minutes' rest
over there in the shelter.* (Ruth 2:7)

**God wants us to work hard and do our best, even with small and seemingly
insignificant responsibilities.** Ruth's task, though menial, tiring, and perhaps
degrading, was done faithfully. What is your attitude when the task you have
been given does not require your full potential? The task at hand may be all you
can do, or it may be the work God wants you to do. Or, as in Ruth's case, it may
be a test of your character that might open up new doors of opportunity.

BIBLE READING: 2 Kings 10:30-36
KEY BIBLE VERSE: *The LORD said to Jehu, "You have done well in following my
instructions to destroy the family of Ahab. Because of this I will cause your
descendants to be the kings of Israel down to the fourth generation." But Jehu
did not obey the law of the LORD, the God of Israel, with all his heart. He
refused to turn from the sins of idolatry that Jeroboam had led Israel to commit.*
(2 Kings 10:30-31)

Representing God is not always serving him. As with many of the kings of Israel,
Jehu did much of what the Lord told him to, but he did not obey him with all
his heart. He had become God's *instrument* for carrying out justice, but he had
not become God's *servant*. As a result, he gave only lip service to God while per-
mitting the worship of the golden calves. We need to check the condition of our
heart toward God. We can be very active in our work for God and still not give
the wholehearted obedience he desires.

BIBLE READING: Luke 19:11-27
KEY BIBLE VERSE: *The crowd was listening to everything Jesus said. And because he
was nearing Jerusalem, he told a story to correct the impression that the Kingdom of God would begin right away.* (Luke 19:11)

**Wherever we go and whatever we do, our work ought to leave behind an
impression that we are seeking to serve God rather than just people.** This
story showed Jesus' followers what they were to do during the time between Jesus'
departure and his second coming. Because we live in that time period, it applies
directly to us. We have been given excellent resources to build and expand God's
kingdom. Jesus expects us to use these talents so that they multiply and the kingdom grows. He asks each of us to account for what we do with his gifts. While
awaiting the coming of the kingdom of God in glory, we must do Christ's work.

BIBLE READING: John 3:22-36
KEY BIBLE VERSE: *John replied, "God in heaven appoints each person's work."* (John
3:27)

God gives each person a special job to do. John explained that because God had
given him his work, he had to continue it until God called him to do something

else. John's main purpose was to point people to Christ. Even with Jesus beginning his own ministry, John could still turn people to Jesus.

BIBLE READING: Ephesians 6:5-9
KEY BIBLE VERSE: *Work hard, but not just to please your masters when they are watching. As slaves of Christ, do the will of God with all your heart. Work with enthusiasm, as though you were working for the Lord rather than for people.* (Ephesians 6:6-7)

All our work ought to be done with Christ in mind. Paul's instructions encourage responsibility and integrity on the job. Christian employees should do their job as if Jesus Christ were their supervisor. And Christian employers should treat their employees fairly and with respect. Can you be trusted to do your best, even when the boss is not around? Do you work hard and with enthusiasm? Do you treat your employees as people, not machines? Remember that no matter whom you work for, and no matter who works for you, the one you ultimately should want to please is your Father in heaven.

Related Topics: MINISTRY, SERVING, WITNESSING

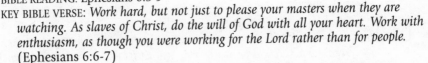

WORLD *(Creation, Environment, Humanity)*

What relationship does God want us to have with the world in which we live?

BIBLE READING: Matthew 5:13-16
KEY BIBLE VERSE: *You are the salt of the earth. But what good is salt if it has lost its flavor? Can you make it useful again? It will be thrown out and trampled underfoot as worthless. You are the light of the world—like a city on a mountain, glowing in the night for all to see.* (Matthew 5:13-14)

We are to have a positive influence on the world in which we live. If a seasoning has no flavor, it has no value. If Christians make no effort to affect the world around them, they are of little value to God. If we are too much like the world, we are worthless as "seasoning." We should not blend in with everyone else. Instead, we should affect others positively, just as seasoning brings out the best flavor in food.

God wants us to be a light to the world. Can you hide a city that is sitting on top of a hill? Its light at night can be seen for miles. If we live for Christ, we will glow like lights, showing others what Christ is like. We hide our light by (1) being quiet when we should speak, (2) going along with the crowd, (3) denying the light, (4) letting sin dim our light, (5) not explaining our light to others, or (6) ignoring the needs of others. Be a beacon of truth—don't shut your light off from the rest of the world.

BIBLE READING: John 17:6-19
KEY BIBLE VERSE: *I'm not asking you to take them out of the world, but to keep them safe from the evil one.* (John 17:15)

Christ wants Christians to make a difference in the world. The world hates Christians because their values are different from its own. Because Christ's followers don't cooperate with the world by joining into its sin, they are living accusations against the world's immorality. The world follows Satan's agenda, and Satan is the avowed enemy of Jesus and his people.

Jesus didn't ask God to take believers *out* of the world but instead to use them *in* the world. Because Jesus sends us into the world, we should not try to escape from the world, nor should we avoid all relationships with non-Christians. We are called to be salt and light (Matthew 5:13-16), and we are to do the work that God sent us to do.

BIBLE READING: Romans 8:18-28

KEY BIBLE VERSE: *All creation is waiting eagerly for that future day when God will reveal who his children really are. Against its will, everything on earth was subjected to God's curse. All creation anticipates the day when it will join God's children in glorious freedom from death and decay.* (Romans 8:19-21)

Our view of the world and our actions in it ought to be motivated by our awareness of God's plan. Sin has caused all creation to fall from the state in which God created it. So the world is subject to frustration and bondage to decay so that it cannot fulfill its intended purpose. One day all creation will be liberated and transformed. Until that time it waits in eager expectation for the resurrection of God's children.

God has much good for us to do in the world as we wait. Christians see the world as it is—physically decaying and spiritually infected with sin. But Christians do not need to be pessimistic, because they have hope for future glory. They look forward to the new heaven and new earth that God has promised, and they wait for God's new order that will free the world of sin, sickness, and evil. In the meantime, Christians go in Christ's name into the world to heal bodies and souls and to fight the evil effects of sin.

Related Topics: CREATION, GOD, HEAVEN

WORRY (*Anxiety, Concern, Fear*)

How can we keep from worrying?

BIBLE READING: Psalm 37:1-11

KEY BIBLE VERSE: *Stop your anger! Turn from your rage! Do not envy others—it only leads to harm.* (Psalm 37:8)

We must remember that worrying is choosing not to trust God. Anger and worry (fretting) are two very destructive emotions. They reveal a lack of faith that God loves us and is in control. We should not worry; instead, we should trust in God, giving ourself to him for his use and safekeeping. When you dwell on your problems, you will become anxious and angry. But if you concentrate on God and his goodness, you will find peace. Where do you focus your attention?

BIBLE READING: Matthew 6:25-34

KEY BIBLE VERSE: *Don't worry about having enough food or drink or clothing. Why be like the pagans who are so deeply concerned about these things? Your heavenly Father already knows all your needs, and he will give you all you need from day to day if you live for him and make the Kingdom of God your primary concern.* (Matthew 6:31-33)

We need to understand how harmful worry can become in our life. Because of the ill effects of worry, Jesus tells us not to worry about those needs that God promises to supply. Worry may (1) damage your health, (2) cause the object of your worry to consume your thoughts, (3) disrupt your productivity, (4) negatively affect the way you treat others, and (5) reduce your ability to trust in God. How many ill effects of worry are you experiencing? Here is the difference between worry and genuine concern—worry immobilizes, but concern moves you to action.

Instead of worrying about what we cannot do, we need to focus on what God can do. To "make the Kingdom of God your primary concern" means to turn to God first for help, to fill your thoughts with his desires, to take his character for your pattern, and to serve and obey him in everything. What is really important to you? People, objects, goals, and other desires all compete for priority. Any of these can quickly bump God out of first place if you don't actively choose to give him first place in *every* area of your life.

We need to keep things in proper perspective. Planning for tomorrow is time well spent; worrying about tomorrow is time wasted. Sometimes it's difficult to tell the difference. Careful planning is thinking ahead about goals, steps, and schedules, and trusting in God's guidance. When done well, planning can help alleviate worry. Worrying, in contrast, is being consumed by fear and finding it difficult to trust God. It is letting our plans interfere with our relationship with God. Don't let worries about tomorrow affect your relationship with God today.

BIBLE READING: Philippians 4:4-9
KEY BIBLE VERSE: *Don't worry about anything; instead, pray about everything. Tell God what you need, and thank him for all he has done.* (Philippians 4:6)

We cannot remove worry until we replace it with something better—prayer. Imagine never worrying about anything! It seems like an impossibility—we all have worries on the job, in our home, at school. But Paul's advice is to turn our worries into prayers. Do you want to worry less? Then pray more! Whenever you start to worry, stop and pray.

God's peace can replace worry. God's peace is different from the world's peace (see John 14:27). True peace is not found in positive thinking, in absence of conflict, or in good feelings. It comes from knowing that God is in control. Our citizenship in Christ's kingdom is sure, our destiny is set, and we can have victory over sin. Let God's peace guard your heart against anxiety.

Related Topics: PRAYER, SOVEREIGNTY, TRUST

WORSHIP *(Adoration, Awe, Praise)*

What does the Bible teach us about worship?

BIBLE READING: Exodus 3:1-6
KEY BIBLE VERSE: *"Do not come any closer," God told him. "Take off your sandals, for you are standing on holy ground."* (Exodus 3:5)

Worship is first and foremost an encounter with the living and holy God. At God's command, Moses removed his sandals and covered his face. Taking off his shoes was an act of reverence, conveying his own unworthiness before God. God is our friend, but he is also our sovereign Lord. To approach him frivolously shows a lack of respect and sincerity. When you come to God in worship, do you approach him casually, or do you come as though you were an invited guest before a king? If necessary, adjust your attitude so it is suitable for approaching a holy God.

BIBLE READING: Leviticus 7:28-38

KEY BIBLE VERSE: *These are the instructions for the whole burnt offering, the grain offering, the sin offering, the guilt offering, the ordination offering, and the peace offering. The* LORD *gave these instructions to Moses on Mount Sinai when he commanded the Israelites to bring their offerings to the* LORD *in the wilderness of Sinai.* (Leviticus 7:37-38)

Worship is only as real as the involvement of those participating. God gave his people many rituals and instructions to follow. All the rituals in Leviticus were meant to teach the people valuable lessons. But over time, the people became indifferent to the meanings of these rituals, and they began to lose touch with God. When your church appears to be conducting dry, meaningless rituals, try rediscovering the original meaning and purpose behind them. Your worship will be revitalized.

BIBLE READING: Numbers 28:1-8

KEY BIBLE VERSE: *The* LORD *said to Moses, "Give these instructions to the people of Israel: The offerings you present to me by fire on the altar are my food, and they are very pleasing to me. See to it that they are brought at the appointed times and offered according to my instructions."* (Numbers 28:1-2)

A true worship experience is often a direct result of preparation for worship. Offerings had to be brought regularly and presented according to prescribed rituals under the priests' supervision. Following these rituals took time, and this gave the people the opportunity to prepare their heart for worship. Unless our heart is ready, worship is meaningless. In contrast, God is delighted, and we get more from it, when our heart is prepared to come before him in a spirit of thankfulness.

BIBLE READING: Psalm 81:1-16

KEY BIBLE VERSE: *Sing praises to God, our strength. Sing to the God of Israel. Sing! Beat the tambourine. Play the sweet lyre and the harp. Sound the trumpet for a sacred feast when the moon is new, when the moon is full.* (Psalm 81:1-3)

Take advantage of every opportunity to worship and praise God. Israel's holidays reminded the nation of God's great miracles. They were times of rejoicing and times to renew one's strength for life's daily struggles. At Christmas, do your thoughts revolve mostly around presents? Is Easter only a warm anticipation of spring—and Thanksgiving only a good meal? Remember the spiritual origin of these special days, and use them as opportunities to worship God for his goodness to you, your family, and your nation.

Worship and music go hand in hand. David instituted music for the temple worship services (1 Chronicles 25). Worship should involve the whole person, and music helps lift a person's thoughts and emotions to God. Through music we can reflect upon our needs and shortcomings as well as celebrate God's greatness.

BIBLE READING: Matthew 2:1-12

KEY BIBLE VERSE: *They entered the house where the child and his mother, Mary, were, and they fell down before him and worshiped him. Then they opened their treasure chests and gave him gifts of gold, frankincense, and myrrh.* (Matthew 2:11)

Worship is bringing the best we have to Christ. The magi brought gifts and worshiped Jesus for who he was. This is the essence of true worship—honoring Christ for who he is and being willing to give him what is valuable to you.

Worship God because he is the perfect, just, and almighty Creator of the universe, worthy of the best you have to give.

BIBLE READING: Matthew 17:1-8
KEY BIBLE VERSE: *Even as he said it, a bright cloud came over them, and a voice from the cloud said, "This is my beloved Son, and I am fully pleased with him. Listen to him." (Matthew 17:5)*

Genuine worship results in submission and obedience to Jesus. Jesus is more than just a great leader, a good example, a good influence, or a great prophet. He is the Son of God. When you understand this profound truth, the only adequate response is worship. When you have a correct understanding of Christ, you will obey him.

BIBLE READING: 1 Corinthians 14:26-33
KEY BIBLE VERSE: *Well, my brothers and sisters, let's summarize what I am saying. When you meet, one will sing, another will teach, another will tell some special revelation God has given, one will speak in an unknown language, while another will interpret what is said. But everything that is done must be useful to all and build them up in the Lord. (1 Corinthians 14:26)*

Everything done in corporate worship must be beneficial to the worshipers. This principle touches every aspect—singing, preaching, and the exercise of spiritual gifts. Those contributing to a worship service (singers, speakers, readers) must have love as their chief motivation, speaking useful words or participating in a way that will strengthen the faith of other believers.

In worship, everything must be done in harmony and with order. Even when the gifts of the Holy Spirit are being exercised, there is no excuse for disorder. When there is chaos, the church is not allowing God to work among believers as he would like. Make sure that what you bring to worship is appropriate, but also make sure that you participate.

Related Topics: CHURCH, GOD, PRAISE

WORTH (*see* VALUE)

WRONG (*see* SIN)

YOUTH (*Adolescence, Child, Teen*)

What biblical principles apply specifically to youth?

BIBLE READING: 1 Samuel 2:18-26
KEY BIBLE VERSE: *Samuel, though only a boy, was the LORD's helper. He wore a linen tunic just like that of a priest.* (1 Samuel 2:18)

In choosing his servants, God is more interested in willingness than in age. Samuel was a young child, and yet he was called "the Lord's helper." Children can often serve God quite effectively. God will use anyone who is willing to learn from him and serve him. He has no age limits. Don't discount the faith of a child or let your age keep you from serving God.

BIBLE READING: Ecclesiastes 12:1-8
KEY BIBLE VERSE: *Don't let the excitement of youth cause you to forget your Creator. Honor him in your youth before you grow old and no longer enjoy living.* (Ecclesiastes 12:1)

Youth is a good time to begin and develop a relationship with God. A life without God can produce a bitter, lonely, and hopeless old age. A life centered around God is fulfilling; it will make growing old—when disabilities, sickness, and handicaps cause barriers to enjoying life—satisfying because of the hope of eternal life. Being young is exciting. But the excitement of youth can become a barrier to closeness with God if it makes young people focus on passing pleasures instead of eternal values. Make your strength available to God when it is still yours—during your youthful years. Don't waste it on evil or meaningless activities that become bad habits and make you callous. Seek God now.

BIBLE READING: Luke 2:41-52
KEY BIBLE VERSE: *He returned to Nazareth with them and was obedient to them; and his mother stored all these things in her heart. So Jesus grew both in height and in wisdom, and he was loved by God and by all who knew him.* (Luke 2:51-52)

Young people can trust in Jesus' ability to identify with their experiences. This is the first mention of Jesus' awareness that he was God's Son. But even though he knew his real Father, he did not reject his earthly parents. He went back to Nazareth with them and lived under their authority for another eighteen years. God's people do not despise human relationships or family responsibilities. If the Son of God obeyed his human parents, how much more should we honor our family members! Don't use commitment to God's work to justify neglecting your family.

Jesus is the perfect model of surviving the youthful years. The four items used to identify his teen years are general enough to use in any young person's life. What a great achievement to arrive at about twenty years of age and have your life summarized as growing "in height and in wisdom," and being "loved by God and by all who knew him"!

Related Topics: AGE, GIFTS, HUMILITY

ZEAL (*Commitment, Desire, Intensity*)

What is the value of zeal in a Christian's life?

 BIBLE READING: Romans 10:1-13
KEY BIBLE VERSE: *I know what enthusiasm they have for God, but it is misdirected zeal.* (Romans 10:2)

Zeal in practicing our faith is valuable as long as it is based on humble acceptance. Rather than living by faith in God, the Jews established customs and traditions (in addition to God's law) to try to make themselves acceptable in God's sight. But human effort, no matter how sincere, can never substitute for the righteousness God offers us by faith. The only way to *earn* salvation is to be perfect—and that is impossible. We can only hold out our empty hands and receive salvation as a gift.

BIBLE READING: Romans 12:9-21
KEY BIBLE VERSE: *Never be lazy in your work, but serve the Lord enthusiastically.* (Romans 12:11)

Zeal should be a characteristic of our life. Among the spiritual priorities that Paul lists in these verses is dedicated service. Love is to be sincere. Evil is to be hated; good clung to tightly. There is to be mutual, honoring devotion to one another. All these are noble purposes that become a reality as we practice them out of deep devotion to Christ.

Related Topics: CONSISTENCY, DEVOTION, FAITHFULNESS

Subject and Synonym Index

Each entry in the Handbook includes three synonyms. The following index will assist those locating entries by their primary words or their listed synonyms.

Index of Biblical Passages

OLD TESTAMENT

Leviticus

Numbers

Proverbs

Ecclesiastes

NEW TESTAMENT